Understanding People in Organizations

Understanding People in Organizations

Robert C. Dailey

Associate Professor of Organizational Behavior
A.B. Freeman School of Business
Tulane University
New Orleans, Louisiana

in collaboration with

Daniel S. Fogel

Director of Executive Education
A.B. Freeman School of Business
Tulane University
New Orleans, Louisiana

WEST PUBLISHING COMPANY
St. Paul New York Los Angeles San Francisco

Copyediting: Betsey Rhame
Design: Christy Butterfield
Artwork: Cartographics, Alice Thiede
Cover: Designteam, Paul Konsterlie
Photos: *2* Courtesy of Xerox Corporation;
22 Courtesy of Burlington Industries, Inc.;
60 Jeffrey Grosscup;
94 Chris Harris;
124 Jeffrey Grosscup;
158 Courtesy of Burlington Industries, Inc.;
188 Jeffrey Grosscup;
218 Courtesy of Hewlett-Packard Company;
256 Jeffrey Grosscup;
290 Courtesy of Bethlehem Steel Corporation;
309 Jeffrey Grosscup;
356 Courtesy of Hewlett-Packard Company;
392 Jeffrey Grosscup;
430 Courtesy of Hewlett-Packard Company;
468 Courtesy of Honeywell Inc.

Printed in the United States of America

Library of Congress Cataloging-in-Publication Data

Dailey, Robert C.
Understanding people in organizations.

Includes bibliographies and index.
1. Organizational behavior. 2. Organizational change. I. Title.
HD58.7.D34 1988 658.4 86–32460
ISBN 0–314–24254–6

About the Author

ROBERT C. DAILEY is Associate Professor of Organizational Behavior in the A. B. Freeman School of Business at Tulane University, New Orleans, Louisiana. He is area coordinator for the Department of Organizational Behavior. Dailey holds a D.B.A. in Organizational Behavior from the University of Colorado at Boulder. He has had extensive consulting experience in both large and small organizations. His current work is focused on improving productivity in hospitals through quantitative and behavioral means. He is professionally active in management training and continues to be a popular lecturer with students. He has received the Howard W. Wissner Award for excellence in teaching three times in the last eight years. Dailey publishes regularly in scholarly journals and is currently conducting research on the coping behaviors of professionals in high-stress jobs.

For Susan and my parents,
continuing gratitude and love.

Bob

Contents

Chapter 11

Power and Politics 329

Chapter 12

Effective Managers: One Key to Work Group Success 357

Chapter 13

The Details of Form and Function: Organizational Design 393

Preface

Most individuals spend nearly one third of their adult life working for one or more organizations. Because they will spend all of that time engaged in work activities, it makes sense to learn as much as possible about workers, managers, and their organizations. This book, UNDERSTANDING PEOPLE IN ORGANIZATIONS, is about people who must work for a living. The material presented details many of the events that shape behavior and attitudes on the job.

UNDERSTANDING PEOPLE IN ORGANIZATIONS develops a balanced view of the working world. The discussions of organizational life shift back and forth between the workers' viewpoint and the managerial viewpoint. Many students will make the successful transition in their career from worker to manager. A discussion of work events and patterns from both perspectives is therefore necessary, for the managerial and worker perspective do not always align. The stresses and strains of the manager-worker relationship are richly illustrated in this text. As readers progress through the chapters, they will gain an increasing appreciation of the dilemmas faced by both managers and workers. My goal, as I planned and wrote the book, was to create compelling and meaningful descriptions of work dilemmas, which would prepare students for the special challenges that confront the individual who embarks on a work career in an organization. The reader will learn how to motivate workers effectively and will soon see that workers have special needs, which can be satisfied by the rewards available in the workplace.

Studying this text will not make the reader become a manager. It can, however, channel and direct the reader's thinking about the ways in which we live and work in organizations. When study of the book is integrated with instructor-managed exercises and activities, students should possess a powerful learning package to prepare them for the challenges of the working world.

The Outlook of This Book

I wrote UNDERSTANDING PEOPLE IN ORGANIZATIONS with a particular outlook in mind. The text is based on two related ideas: (1) people can be workers and managers in all types of organizations, and (2) people learn best when the material presented involves their personal experiences. Let's consider these ideas.

First, the concepts discussed in UNDERSTANDING PEOPLE IN ORGANIZATIONS can be applied to any organization. The book features examples and concepts that involve businesses, hospitals, educational institutions, service organizations, family businesses, and government. Students who hope to become a worker, manager, or entrepreneur in any of these settings will find this text a valuable resource.

Second, as I planned each chapter, I was keenly aware of providing readers with examples and applications based on their experiences with organizations to this point. Reader experience as a student or employee is both valid and meaningful. My goal was to help readers use these experiences to make learning an active and absorbing process. The material presented soon convinces readers that they already have survived many "close encounters" wth organizational realities and that they do indeed have a meaningful experience base from which they can approach the working world. The dilemmas and problems presented have elements of immediacy and urgency that resemble real-life work and organizational experiences. If students read carefully, they will find solutions to many of the problems illustrated.

UNDERSTANDING PEOPLE IN ORGANIZATIONS is thus a "user friendly" book written in a conversational style to keep the reader actively involved in the task of understanding workers, managers, and organizations.

Structure

The text has five major parts. The first introduces the field of organizational behavior and addresses the issues of employee differences and motivation. Part two covers reward systems, job design, and employee reactions to stress. Part three develops the topics of group behavior and communication in organizations. Part four discusses the issues of leadership, entrepreneurship, and politics. The fifth presents the topics of organizational culture and climate, organizational development, social responsibility, and major trends of the future. The five sections are cumulative, so concepts introduced early in the book deepen the analyses in later chapters.

Key Features

I have indicated that UNDERSTANDING PEOPLE IN ORGANIZATIONS is a user friendly book that utilizes personal experience to facilitate learning about workers and managers. The text has a number of special features that sustain reader involvement and help readers merge personal experience with practical and theoretical concepts.

- Introductory Dilemma: Each chapter begins with a compelling description of a situation that spans the learning material featured in that chapter. Each dilemma involves the kinds of true-to-life decisions and problems that individuals actually face in real organizations. Solving the Dilemma questions are presented at the end of each dilemma and are answered at appropriate points in the chapter narrative.
- Knowledge Check: These self-test questions help students evaluate their understanding of each chapter section. A Knowledge Check can be done quickly and provides immediate feedback on the reader's retention and understanding of the material.
- Now It's Your Turn: These experiential activities deepen the student's personal understanding of the selected material in each chapter. Now It's Your Turn actively involves the reader in applying the chapter material. Each activity is a self-contained learning experience that anchors the text material to a facsimile organizational experience.
- Exploring: An Exploring feature appears at the end of each chapter and is based on actual circumstances in a real organization. Each Exploring mini-case illustrates the key ideas presented in the chapter. The questions that accompany the case can be used to generate interesting class discussions about urgent issues facing both workers and managers.
- Applying: An Applying feature also appears at each chapter conclusion. This feature is an experiential tool to help students learn how to use one or more of the major concepts developed in the chapter. Some exercises involve the student with real managers and employees of local organizations; others require teamwork to apply the chapter concepts to realistic work problems.

All of these tools add validity to the reader's experiences as student, worker, or manager in an organization. Whether students are returning to school after several years of work experience or are recent high school graduates, the tools in this book create the groundwork for learning.

In addition to validating the reader's organizational experiences and creating interesting class discussions, the intellectual aim of UNDERSTANDING PEOPLE IN ORGANIZATIONS is to clarify reader understanding of organizations and to help students build theories that explain organizations and their participants in behavioral terms.

When a behavioral understanding of organizations is coupled with an understanding of marketing, finance, accounting, and quantitative decision making, students will be on the road to developing a comprehensive management philosophy that will serve them well in their business career.

This text helps readers develop the "human" side of management philosophy. My task as author has been to explain and illuminate the fields of organizational behavior and human relations in organizations so readers can analyze any work situation, develop an informed response, and implement solutions systematically.

UNDERSTANDING PEOPLE IN ORGANIZATIONS contains these additional learning aids in each chapter to help students achieve their intellectual, analytical, and career objectives.

- Chapter outlines show the broad flow of information in each section.
- Chapter goals indicate the key analytical procedures the reader will be able to do after careful reading of the chapter.
- Summary points encapsulate the key concepts discussed.
- Questions assess reader comprehension of the material and help readers integrate their personal experiences with chapter content.
- Capstone cases challenge the reader to apply several major concepts introduced in the chapter to an actual situation at a well-known company.
- Suggested readings are noted to show the interested student where he or she can learn more about various chapter subjects. Many of the selections have been annotated.
- Glossary of key terms appears at the end of the text.

A full set of supporting materials accompanies the text. The INSTRUCTOR'S GUIDE contains a sample course syllabus, ideas for supplementing the course, a list of related films and other audiovisual materials for each chapter, teaching outlines, an analysis of each dilemma, comments and teaching tips for each chapter, answers to questions and discussion tips, analyses of the Exploring and Applying components, transparency masters, teaching aids for capstone cases, and a test bank (also available in computerized form). These materials match closely the organization of each chapter.

A NOTE FOR INSTRUCTORS

This book will make your teaching easier. The blending of the components discussed above should increase students' understanding of the material so that you will be able to accomplish more things in class. Students' frustrations with some of the ambiguities that exist in the field of organizational behavior should be lessened with this material because they are given opportunities to apply what they learn. This increases their self-confidence, and in turn, the quality of your classroom discussions should hold at a high level.

The capstone cases at the end of the text can be used to show students how to integrate organizational skills to address actual problems. These capstone cases are broader than any of the Exploring and Applying sections in any given chapter. The INSTRUCTOR'S GUIDE which accompanies the text clearly explains how to use them.

The INSTRUCTOR'S GUIDE anticipates a number of teaching issues that may arise as you cover the material in your course. The introduction to the INSTRUCTOR'S GUIDE clearly specifies goals and ways to make the course as effective as possible. It also identifies support materials which can be used to deepen students' understanding of the field. It is a comprehensive document that supports the book well.

Acknowledgements

I owe special thanks to Dan Fogel, Director of Management Education, A.B. Freeman School of Business, Tulane University. Dan was instrumental in the development and focus of key elements in Chapters 10, 11, 12, 13, and 15. These chapters would not possess the urgency and cutting-edge quality that they do without his contributions.

I also extend thanks to the many colleagues who carefully reviewed the manuscript drafts of this book and made suggestions that greatly improved the content: Hal Babson (Columbus Technical Institute), Steven Barr (Oklahoma State University), Robert Boozer (Memphis State University), Rick Camp (Eastern Michigan University), Phyllis Fowler (McComb Community College), Cynthia Fukami (University of Denver), Carol Giers (Orange Coast Community College), Ron Herrick (Mesa Community College), William Cobb (California State University, Sacramento), Robert Costi (Portland State Community College), Ralph Katerberg (University of Cincinnati), Barney Klecker (Normandale Community College), Elliot Kushell (California State University, Fullerton), Robert LeRosen (Northern Virginia Community College), Tom Mason (Brookdale Community College), Tim Matherly (Florida State University), Durward Hofler (Northeastern Illinois State University), Leo Kiesewetter (Illinois Central College), James A. McCambridge (Colorado State University), Randall Olson (University of Wisconsin, Whitewater), Floyd Patrick (Eastern Michigan University), Ken Sanford (Broome Community College), James Staszak (DePaul University), Stuart Sudduth (Santa Rosa Junior College), Darrell Millard (Kirkwood Community College), Robert Wagley (Wright State University).

West editors have provided exceptional support. Rich Wohl helped sustain the momentum for this project and has been the source of numerous improvements. Peggy Adams, production editor, has handled all production aspects of the project with grace and good humor. Stacey Lenzen, ancillary editor, provided valuable assistance in producing the instructor's manual. I also would like to thank Betsey Rhame, copy editor; Caroline Nielsen, promotion manager; and Alice Thiede, who did the artwork.

Finally, I thank my wife Susan, who chose wisely to ignore me as I struggled with this project. She reminded me of my obsessiveness, and from time to time she broke my glazed stare at the computer screen. She also insisted that I would need glasses before I finished, and she was right.

Robert C. Dailey
New Orleans, Louisiana

Understanding People in Organizations

MARCH

Understanding the Field of Organizational Behavior

Chapter 1

I. Dilemma: Angela Gets a Special Project
II. The Dynamic Field of Organizational Behavior
III. Organizational Behavior: The Supporting Disciplines
   A. The growing need to understand human behavior in organizations
   B. The importance of employee needs and organizational productivity
IV. The Role of Theory in Organizational Behavior
   A. Characteristics of a logical theory
   B. Why managers need to understand organizational behavior and its theories
   C. Distinguishing between organizational behavior theory and management
V. Summary Points
VI. Questions
VII. Exploring: The Maytag Corporation
VIII. Applying: Organizational Productivity and Employee Needs
IX. Suggested Readings
X. References

Chapter Goals

By the end of this chapter, you will be able to:

1. Distinguish organizational behavior and management as different yet related disciplines.
2. Define organizational behavior.
3. Describe issues related to organizational productivity and employee needs.
4. Describe different explanations for behavior in organizations.
5. Develop the steps to follow in scientific explanations for employee behavior in organizations.
6. Explain the types of systematic knowledge generated by practitioners in the field of organizational behavior.

Dilemma Angela Gets a Special Project

Angela has worked for Builders Inc. for eight years. She is a vice president. In the last two years, she has watched Builders grow from 30 employees and annual construction sales of $4.8 million to 65 employees and annual sales of $24 million. The major company problems were maintenance of new equipment and complaints about the behavior of construction crew supervisors.

Angela developed some figures on maintenance cost of new equipment. She also compiled figures on employee turnover for the last five years. From her analysis, she learned that the company was spending $58,000 per year on maintenance for graders, dump trucks, and end loaders. She discovered that the figure had increased an average of 24 percent per year for the last two years and that during the last three years the company had replaced all of its construction crews three times! This amounted to 100 percent turnover per year. As she dug deeper into the turnover figures, she realized that the company had taken on a full-time employee to keep up with all of the advertising, interviewing, and hiring work. The company had spent $22,000 to recruit construction superintendents for the same time period. At the present time, four months into 1987, six employees had already quit and among them were two of Builders six superintendents. At that rate, Angela estimated that turnover would cost the company $39,000 during 1986. When this figure was combined with the $58,000 for projected equipment maintenance in 1987, Angela decided it was time to have a talk with her boss.

Angela wondered how much Paul Randers, the owner of the business, had to do with the problem. She knew that Paul's attitudes toward the employees had something to do with the rising costs of maintenance and employee turnover. She decided to investigate the problem by talking to key company supervisors. Here are some excerpts from these conversations.

Phil Gleason, construction superintendent: "You should have seen the terrible mess we got into with the project engineer! Paul came to the job site and asked one of the supervisors why a laborer was moving a stack of pipe. The supervisor explained that the project engineer had requested that the pipe be moved for safety reasons. Well, Paul told the kid to move the stuff to its *former* spot. The engineer happened to see this, and he got on the supervisor. Paul, the engineer, and the supervisor went around and around for about 10 minutes. The only smart one was the kid who moved the pipe. He went to the sandwich truck and got a coke while they fought it out. The situation never did get resolved. Paul left in a huff—mumbling that 'stupid safety procedures' were going to bankrupt the company."

Andy Johnson, crew supervisor: "Paul issued another of his 'maintenance brainstorms.' For 18 months, he's been spot-checking the equipment at various job sites. This irritates the operators, who are trained to do their own routine maintenance. Here's the owner of the company, peering under hoods and pulling on fan belts half the time. They're afraid to say anything, because they might be putting their jobs on the line. Paul has fired several operators when he found some small equipment problem. People get very nervous when Paul shows up at the job site. The guys agree that maintenance is important, but some of them have given up. There's no way they can please Paul ..."

Greta Porsche, construction engineer. "I've been with Builders since I graduated from college. I've learned a lot in this job. My biggest problem is my boss, Charlie. Three of us are in the office: John, who's a construction engineer, Charlie, and myself. Charlie never went to college. He helped Paul start the business eight years ago. He's fond of pointing out that he's been with the company from the ground up. He never comes right out and says it, but Charlie resents the fact that John and I have degrees. He makes jokes about 'textbook solutions.' The message is clear to John and me. Charlie's afraid Paul will replace him with one of us ..."

Angela decided to talk to Paul about the increased turnover and maintenance expenses. As she was explaining the changes in cost over the past three years, Paul interrupted her:

"Angela, I appreciate your efforts to gather information on maintenance and turnover, but I don't consider these major problems. In light of the company's growth over the past two years, these expenses are really small potatoes. We need to concentrate on getting more business and on expanding our construction activity. Focus on the financial aspects of the business and leave motivation problems to me."

Paul's reaction did not surprise Angela. She decided not to tell Paul what she had learned in her employee interviews. She returned to her office wondering what the long-term outcome would be. Clearly the quality of construction would soon begin to suffer because of higher maintenance costs and the escalating problem of employee turnover.

Questions

1. What problems do you consider organizational behavior topics?
2. Why should Angela be concerned about equipment maintenance and employee turnover?
3. What role does organizational behavior play in solving problems like those at Builders Inc.?

The Dynamic Field of Organizational Behavior

The short case that you have just read illustrates the everyday nature of organizational behavior. As you begin your study of the interactions between people and organizations, you will be struck by the fact that you do not have to be working in a business to put what you learn to immediate use. Every subject discussed in this text can be applied directly to your school experiences.

The fact that you are taking a college course in organizational behavior indicates your intent to gain knowledge about employee needs in the workplace. Colleges and universities are validating the importance of employee needs by creating courses to explore the role of the workplace in our society. In today's world, an understanding of organizational behavior is as important as accounting, finance, or marketing. The problems that Angela faces represent major aspects of organizational behavior. Let's look closely at the nature of organizational behavior and how this field of study came into existence.

Organizational behavior is defined as the study of the behaviors, and attitudes of people in organizations. The focus is on human behavior and attitudes in work organizations because these two components, behavior and attitudes, are related to the effectiveness of any organization.

Managers are people who achieve results by supervising and motivating people in work organizations. A strong relationship exists between management and organizational behavior. Indeed, there are many theories of organizational behavior, but the true test of this body of knowledge is its usefulness in understanding organizational problems. Who has to solve these problems? Managers do. So the field of organizational behavior is never far away from management issues. Angela may be interested in organizational behavior theories, but she is even more interested in finding answers for the pressing problems that exist at Builders Inc.

In this book, we explore the important theories of organizational behavior. We go even further—we put the field on the line as each chapter challenges you to apply organizational behavior theory to your own experiences. In this way, you develop powerful tools to help you make sense of what is happening to you as an organization member. As your confidence in using the material grows, you build a useful perspective that will help in your transition from student to employee to manager.

Why do managers care about organizational behavior?

When we interview managers and ask them to describe the problems that they face at work, we get typical complaints:

- My employees won't give that extra 5 percent when a crisis occurs.
- My department's a revolving door: I have constant problems of employees quitting, not showing up for work, or coming to work late.
- I've got the most skilled employees in the business, yet I can't seem to increase their job satisfaction.
- My department heads don't spend much time rewarding excellent performance in their department. What can I do to correct this problem?
- Employees in the marketing department refuse to have anything more to do with the guys from the manufacturing department. It's a near-revolt! If I can't solve this problem, the competition will come out with a new product before we do.
- Why are employees in the production division resisting the new machinery arrangement? Management developed the arrangement after careful

study. Production workers should know that machine relocation is at the discretion of management.

The frustrations that people experience are not limited to the work setting. Opportunities to apply a knowledge of organizational behavior unfold whenever people are engaged in work behavior—in social clubs, church meetings, or meetings of volunteer organizations. If "people problems" are widespread and recurring, a fundamental misunderstanding of human behavior is at work. The individuals most often blamed for this lack of knowledge of human behavior are managers. Solving the Dilemma summarizes the kinds of problems addressed by the field of organizational behavior.

Solving the Dilemma

What problems are considered organizational behavior topics?

Angela's case involves several organizational behavior issues. Employees of Builders Inc. are unhappy with their supervisors and with company policy about replacing employees who quit. Employee turnover and maintenance costs are both increasing. Angela suspects that Paul's attitudes toward employees are contributing to the company problems. She knows that company employees are not working as hard as they could. Furthermore, many are unhappy enough with their jobs to quit and seek employment elsewhere. She also knows that company costs are rising. All of these problems fall within the field of organizational behavior.

What role does management play in organizational problem solving?

Supervisors and Managers are responsible for the work of the organization: they oversee the work of others who make products or perform services. A manager's job has three components: technical, conceptual, and human.

1. **Technical work** involves the use of equipment and technology to get results and improve productivity.
2. **Conceptual work** applies to the development of new ways for the company to operate, like designing a new way to handle customer complaints, or creating a new system to handle sales information about prices and quantities sold.
3. **Human work** consists of the actions that managers take to influence employee welfare, like setting up a program to screen day care services for employees who work evening and night shifts, and instituting a physical fitness program for employees interested in maintaining good health.

Management and Technical Problem Solving. Most organizations encourage managers to be technical problem solvers. Usually, managers are promoted in the organization on the basis of ability to resolve complex technical problems. The technical and conceptual aspects of management are the ones most often rewarded by employers. Until recently, the human component of managerial work was often neglected.

The problems caused by "poor people skills" are becoming increasingly clear to organization management and to the people who study such problems. This book is devoted to the explanation and understanding of "people problems" in organizations and to the steps that managers and employees can take to address those problems.

As you begin your study of organizational behavior, we will introduce you to numerous problems that occur in organizations. These problems will be similar to the ones you will confront when you work in an organization. The problems and topics presented are applicable also to your current experiences—to the organizational situations that you now face. The material presented uses examples that lend themselves to analysis. As you get more involved in the subject, you will find yourself looking at your own behavior and the behavior of others with more care and objectivity. This is an advantage of organizational behavior as a subject: it can be applied immediately. Everyone must deal with the realities of surviving within an organization. Knowing what causes our attitudes and behaviors at work can aid greatly in acquiring a realistic, flexible view of what makes organizations tick.

Organizational Behavior: The Supporting Disciplines

The study of organizational behavior emerged because of a growing need to understand human behavior in the work place. Before the Industrial Revolution, society had few large organizations. Religious, governmental, and military organizations were the only large organizations in existence.

By the 1920s, many large corporations had emerged under the system of capitalism. These corporations required large numbers of people to make them successful and profitable. In turn, the large corporations and organizations in U.S. society created the need to understand human behavior at work. Through the 1950s, much research was conducted on human behavior in large organizations. The managers of these organizations found the study information useful in improving their understanding of employee behavior.

A dual focus gradually emerged to further develop the field of organizational behavior. The first focus represented the managers' needs to understand employee behavior and attitudes. The second focus represented the growing need to understand how large organizations develop the systems and procedures that make them successful.

The Growing Need to Understand Human Behavior in Organizations

To understand human behavior in organizational settings, it is necessary to draw on a number of more established social science disciplines. The disciplines that have made the most important contributions to the field are (1) psychology, (2) social psychology, (3) sociology, (4) economics, and (5) political science. As more information about organizations was acquired, the new field of organizational behavior gradually developed. The existence of the field owes much to the sustained vitality of these supporting disciplines.

The techniques and methods used to answer questions in the field of organizational behavior never stray far from the field's supporting disciplines. Indeed, the field draws its unique characteristics from each of the disciplines noted. Knowledge in these areas provides the basis for study of individual behavior and attitudes in the work setting.

What issues does organizational behavior deal with?

The field of organizational behavior develops knowledge at three levels of analysis (Table 1.1). These levels conform to individual behavior, group behavior, and behavior of entire organizational systems. Table 1.1 shows the disciplines involved, that is, the areas of knowledge and the questions that concern each. All five knowledge areas make important contributions to the study of organizational behavior. Let's take a brief look at the impact of each on the field.

Psychology. Psychologists are concerned with the control, measurement, and prediction of animal and human behavior. An important branch of psychology is **industrial psychology.** Industrial psychologists examine the behavior of employees in the work organization. They address employee performance, training and skill development, promotion, hiring and selection systems, and career management. Important new developments in industrial psychology include stress management, design of work space, and analysis of how employees adjust to working conditions.

Sociology. Organizational sociologists focus on the entire organization as a unit of analysis rather than on individual behavior. For example, sociologists would be interested in how government regulations cause corporations to adjust their actions to avoid lawsuits and consumer complaints. Scholars who analyze these relationships are called **organizational theorists.** They seldom study individual behavior directly. They examine organizations and their components. Recent important advances in this field include analysis of how organizations form networks, such as trade associations. The current increase in merger activity and corporate takeovers are of interest to organizational theorists (1).

Social Psychology. This discipline blends the individual and group levels of analysis. Its practitioners study the effects of group norms on individual behavior. Social psychologists explore such issues as what factors cause group performance, and why individual members of a work group may conform to the group behavior. Social psychology bridges the gap between psychology and sociology.

Economics. Economists have made a sustained contribution to the field of organizational behavior. **Labor economics** helps define the meaning and measurement of labor productivity in our society and work organizations.

Table 1.1
Building Blocks of Organizational Behavior

Area of Knowledge	*Types of Questions Studied*	*Level of Analysis*
Psychology	How do people learn behavior? How does motivation occur? What is human personality? How do attitudes affect behavior? What causes job satisfaction? What are the components of leadership effectiveness? How can job performance be appraised on the job?	Individual employees
Sociology	How can organizational structures be described? How do organizations develop expectations about employee performance? How are new employees socialized in the organization? Does size of an organization influence its behavior? How do organizations handle conflict and change?	Organizational system
Social Psychology	How do groups become effective in the organization? What factors cause work groups to be cohesive? How do employees react to group leaders? Does a work group affect the behavior of its members? How does communication take place in organizations?	Groups
Economics	How do organizations determine the value of labor? How do organizations behave in different markets? What is the influence of government on organizations? How do resources flow through the organization? How can organizational efficiency be measured?	Organizational systems
Political Science	How do political processes develop in organizations? How is power allocated in organizations? Do organizations form networks to share power? Are there methods for resolving organizational conflicts?	Organizational systems

Economic history provides valuable insights into organizational adjustments to changing economic conditions. **Microeconomics** explains how managers make decisions such as investing in new equipment, hiring new workers, or expanding production. **Macroeconomics** focuses on larger issues such as the factors that determine interest rates in our commercial system, or the role played by government in influencing unemployment and business expansion. New contributions from the discipline of economics have, for example, improved our understanding of how competition with foreign companies influences business activity in the United States.

Political Science. By examining how organizations resolve confict and distribute power to groups and individuals, political science is adding to our understanding of organizational behavior. This discipline helps explain how organizations band together to gain greater control over their environment. New contributions by political scientists analyze the influence of political action committees (P.A.C.s) on legislation, which in turn influences the private sector of our economy. This discipline helps us to understand the political environment that generates the laws and public policies that influence business practices.

Table 1.1 does not show all of the interactions among the disciplines that support the study of organizational behavior. New linkages are being formed constantly between this field and other areas. For example, medicine and the field of organizational behavior are making combined contributions to define and identify the effects of job stress. Anthropology and organizational behavior are producing research that details the emergence, growth, and decline of organizations. Researchers in organizational behavior and the law are interacting to analyze employment practices and the legal obligations of employers to provide safe working conditions.

The Importance of Employee Needs and Organizational Productivity

As the organizations we live and work in become more complex, their growing complexity requires new knowledge about how organizations evolve and change. The two most pressing issues that govern organizational success or failure are the **needs of organizational members** and **organizational productivity.** Some major needs of organizational members are job satisfaction, adequate pay and fringe benefits, and safe working conditions. Recent opinion polls indicate that some disturbing social trends are redefining the meaning of "job satisfaction" (2). The polls found the following:

1. In 1960, 50 percent of Americans judged their work to be personally fulfilling. By the end of the 1970s, the percentage had dropped to 25 percent.
2. In the 1960s, 58 percent of employees believed that "hard work pays off." In the late 1970s, 43 percent of those polled believed this.
3. Perhaps most disturbing was the fact that only 13 percent of the work force thinks that work is more important than leisure.

These may seem at first to be random statistics that apply only to society in general but not to you or to the people you know. Consider, however, the following example:

> Sandy recently completed her degree in office administration. She found a job as a management trainee for a large manufacturer of security devices where she believed that within six months she could increase her work responsibilities so as to actually apply what she'd learned in school. Eighteen months passed, and she still had not been assigned to a permanent department. The company had moved her from one department to another so she could get a good feel for operations. Sandy's reaction was to dust off her resume. Lately she's been using her sick days to interview for a new job.

Sandy's reaction is an example of the higher expectations that younger employees have about the meaning of work in their lives. She expected her job to be fulfilling and challenging.

Organizational behavior investigators are generating knowledge to help organizations better meet employee needs. No organization wants new employees to have a work experience like Sandy's, so organizations are searching for ways to make work more meaningful. Consider the problems faced by the company described in the introductory dilemma.

Solving the Dilemma

Why must Angela be concerned about equipment maintenance and employee turnover?

These problems relate directly to the issues of organizational productivity and employee needs. The fact that Builders employees are quitting at a higher than average rate indicate problems with employee job satisfaction, motivation, and supervision. All of these areas contribute to employees' perceptions of their work environment. If their perceptions are negative (as they are at Builders), an increasing number of employees will quit their jobs. Angela noted that maintenance costs were rising. These costs in turn lower company productivity. High maintenance costs are caused in part by employees not taking an interest in correct operation of equipment. The low level of employee interest in their work was caused largely by Paul's meddling behavior. If these problems are not addressed soon, Builders could experience major problems with customers as well.

To become a well-rounded manager, you must develop an objective understanding of why employees are critical organizational resources. An effective management philosophy emphasizes the pivotal role that work plays in people's lives. In our study of organizational behavior, we draw from a variety of subjects and show how each affects employee needs and organizational productivity.

Organizational productivity represents the other area about which organizational behavior generates systematic knowledge. The field attempts to explain the connection between employee behavior, employee attitudes, and productivity. Consider the following example:

> Jose is a recently naturalized U.S. citizen. He emigrated from Puerto Rico nine years ago. For four years, he has worked for a trucking firm while he attended night school. He will graduate in May 1988 with a degree in business management. His boss has only praise for Jose's work. Indeed, Jose's management abilities are often singled out because he has found ways to save the firm money through more efficient work methods. His most recent innovation is a dispatching system that uses driver knowledge of trucking routes to save delivery time. The drivers are excited about the new plan because it allows them to be home on weekends on a regular basis. Company management is pleased because the plan saves money that used to be spent on overtime pay, fuel, and maintenance. The company hopes to keep Jose after he graduates, and several top managers have discussed promoting him.

This example demonstrates a company's concern both for employee needs (more satisfied drivers) and productivity (improved dispatching system).

The field of organizational behavior focuses on productivity from the standpoint of human resources. Within an organization, productivity can be increased two ways. A firm can acquire new technology and equipment to produce goods and services with less labor investment, or a firm can find ways to raise productivity by meeting employee needs more effectively. The study of organizational behavior facilitates the latter method. In this text, you will learn how numerous ideas about organizational behavior can be applied to improve organizational productivity through people. Not only will you learn about these organizational tools, but you will be able to create and analyze programs like the ones conceived by Jose. Your analyses will show how knowledge of organizational behavior can be used to address employee needs and organizational productivity at the same time. With a little practice, you will be prepared to use organizational behavior to solve work-related issues in your own life. Now, let's see what you have learned so far about organizational behavior. Try the following Knowledge Check.

Knowledge Check

1. The field of organizational behavior has developed because managers need to understand employee motivation and job satisfaction. T or F?
2. Organizational behavior is concerned only with employee behavior in industrial organizations. T or F?
3. Organizational behavior is more concerned with how individual employees behave than with how organizations set up chains of command. T or F?
4. Organizational behavior would not deal with the factors that cause students to be satisfied or dissatisfied with the courses they take in college. T or F?
5. The field of organizational behavior is best described as an applied discipline that focuses on the issues of employee welfare and organizational productivity. T or F?
6. Organizational behavior is not related to other areas of social science knowledge. T or F?

Answers:

1 T, 2 F, 3 F, 4 F, 5 T, 6 F

The Role of Theory in Organizational Behavior

When one has a **body of knowledge,** efficient ways to collect and analyze information must be devised. Organizational behavior is a social science that uses research tools from the disciplines noted in Table 1.1. A **research method** is an orderly way to collect and analyze information about a phenomenon under study. (3) A **theory** is a set of statements that describe relationships among certain events or facts. Important ingredients in any theory are hypotheses. **Hypothesis** is defined as a specified relationship between two components described in a theory. For example, a manager may believe that employee job satisfaction is related directly to pay raises. Another manager may believe that job applicants are more interested in the company's fringe benefit program. The opinions of these managers represent hypotheses because they specify a relationship between two events.

Are there different types of theories?

Many of your judgments about events that happen around you are based on personal experiential theories. An **experiential theory** relies solely on personal experiences and the inferences we draw from them. These theories are used often to explain personal behavior and the behavior of others. When a manager says, "My employees don't appreciate the meaning of work anymore," she is using a piece of one of her experiential theories to try to explain employee behavior. Experiential theories are thus based on intuition, biases, and accumulated personal experience.

Numerous problems occur when experiential theories are used. They are hard to verify because they are based on the accumulated experiences of only one person. They are *not* based on objective facts. Experiential theories are therefore idiosyncratic, and are seldom evaluated for objectivity or accuracy. Rather, they remain shrouded in personal bias and hunches. They are important, however, for, once understood, they can provide the basis for understanding the behavior of people around us.

Scientific theories are derived in a much different way from experiential models. A scientific theory is based on facts that are independent of personal opinion or preferences. The knowledge derived from scientific theories can be verified independently by researchers working separately from each other. In other words, scientific theories can be replicated. They represent knowledge that is independent of any one person. This definition distinguishes scientific from experiential theories. The key difference is that scientific theories are based on use of a consistent method to accumulate facts and form conclusions about how those facts are related. The steps in construction of a scientific theory are diagrammed in Figure 1.1.

The approach illustrated in Figure 1.1 is the general format for developing a scientific theory. Scientific theories substitute objectivity for subjectivity. The process starts with the observation of facts in a given situation. To show the importance of accumulating knowledge about organizations in a scientific manner, consider an example of a manager who does not follow the method in Figure 1.1. The problem faced by Jim was this:

Jim is the director of a small data processing unit at an insurance claims center. His boss, Hal, has asked him to find out why so many claims

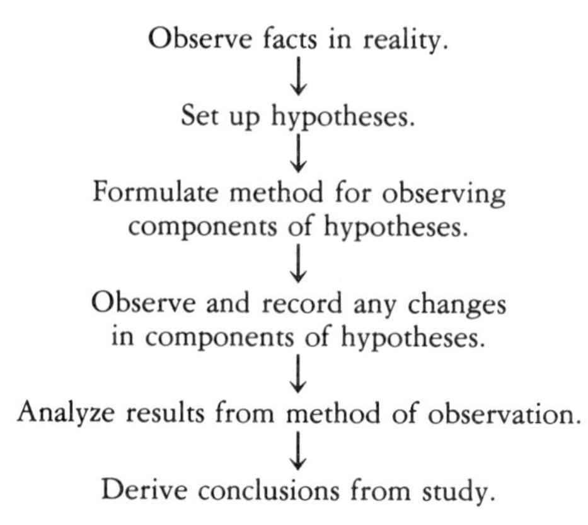

Figure 1.1
Steps in the process of accumulating objective information

simple steps yield dependable results, which would enable Jim to take concrete management action. For example, he might take his study results to his superior for review and action. Jim's boss may decide to increase pay levels, or he might help Jim design a system of flexible working hours. The point is that Jim and his boss can not be sure that they are taking the right problem-solving actions if they base their solutions on the scattered approach Jim first contemplated. They can be much surer that the steps they take are consistent with the trends in employee behavior over time (4).

Scientific theories are useful because they enable us to analyze behavior in a systematic manner. They do the following: (1) organize knowledge about a subject into discernable relationships, (2) summarize diverse findings to express a meaningful set of relationships, and (3) indicate direction for future research efforts. You can see the dynamic interaction among these three characteristics of scientific theory. All good theories undergo refinement constantly because investigators find new constructs that influence the theory components. For example, if Jim followed the steps noted above, he might apply his theory of job transfer to other groups of employees in the company. If he sticks with his experiential approach, he will not gain the systematic knowledge that will enable him to solve transfer problems in other parts of the firm.

Characteristics of a Logical Theory

In the previous section, we described the general characteristics of a scientific theory. Let's now become more analytical as we examine the qualities of a sound and logical theory (5, 6).

1. **Internal consistency:** Relationships in the theory are logical and free from contradictions.
2. **External consistency:** Relationships in the theory are consistent with the facts of the organizational situation.
3. **Scientific simplicity:** The theory clarifies a complex set of organizational facts and makes them more understandable.
4. **Generalizability:** The theory can explain an array of organizational situations.
5. **Verification:** The theory can be retested to reconfirm its organizational predictions.

When organizational researchers follow the steps outlined in Figure 1.1, they are more likely to produce theories that have these properties.

Why Managers Need to Understand Organizational Behavior and Its Theories

Managers make important decisions that influence organizational productivity and employee needs on a regular basis. Making high quality decisions in these two areas depends on a working knowledge of organizational behavior theories for the following reasons:

1. Behavioral theories help solve problems in the work setting. As a manager, you should use objective methods to attack problems related to employee needs and organizational productivity.

processors have asked for transfers to other departments. Hal tolc that the claims processing department is a revolving door and tha error rate on claims forms has jumped 22 percent. Hal indicated th wants a careful assessment of the situation and three possible solu within one month. Jim wondered how to address the problem. He his desk and wrote down the strategies he would like to try. Here aı ideas:

1. Talk to employees who have transferred.
2. Talk to employees currently working in data processing.
3. Interview supervisors of similar units at other companies.
4. Examine company policies and procedures.
5. Review performance of clerks and other department employees.
6. Measure employee level of job satisfaction.

All of these ideas are useful, but they may not help Jim develop solutions in a month's time. Jim's chance of achieving a successful solut low because he is not couching the transfer problem in terms of obser scientific theory of employee behavior. If he proceeds as he has starte efforts will be scattered, and he will generate a set of facts difficult to fi an overall pattern that directs him toward concrete managerial actic solve the problems. He will probably continue to take single isolated a that do not lead to a unified, coherent solution. In a word, his actions w scattered and ineffective. To be effective, Jim should follow a series of like the ones shown below.

1. **Obtain company records and document scope of problem.** (Pe age of errors on claims, number of employees who have quit, nu who asked for transfer, and rate of rising costs should all be docu ed.)
2. **Formulate hypotheses to explain underlying causes of prob** (Develop possible explanation for each problem such as: (a) empl who are quitting are dissatisfied with pay level and also have high rates or (b) employees who are transferring are unhappy with their schedule.)
3. **Formulate method to observe components of hypotheses.** might entail the following activities: interview employees who given notice that they intend to quit, interview employees wh transferring, and analyze work hours and error rates for all en ees.)
4. **Observe and record changes in hypotheses components.** (Cor information gathered in step 3 to see if correlations exist—for ins between the rate at which employees are quitting and their pay leve error rate, or the rate at which employees seek transfers and their ing hours.)
5. **Analyze results from method of observation.** (Generate specific tionships between error, pay, and employee quitting rates, and be working hours and transfer request rate.)
6. **Derive conclusions from study.** (Employees with high error rat quitting because they believe that their pay is too low and that wc hours are inflexible. Employees are transferring because of work s ule only.)

The steps noted above are consistent with the construction of an tive explanation for employee behavior in the data processing unit.

2. Knowledge of behavioral theories helps you understand and use new developments in the field of organizational behavior. You are an educated consumer of the new developments that might improve or refine your managerial abilities.
3. An understanding of behavioral theories helps you to evaluate effectively the proposed solutions to behavioral problems in organizations. Just as you need a knowledge of markets to evaluate new product potential, so you need also a knowledge of behavioral theories to evaluate proposals to change how employees and organizations act.

Distinguishing Between Organizational Behavior Theory and Management

The "appliers" of knowledge about organizational behavior are managers. Given the importance of systematically applying behavioral knowledge to solve organization problems, we must distinguish between organizational behavior and management. The two are highly complementary yet have different methods and goals.

The field of organizational behavior is concerned with how individuals, groups, and organizational components behave. Researchers in this field develop theories that describe behavior in these three areas. Management is concerned with attainment of organizational goals and objectives, that is, profitability, productivity, efficiency, meeting employee needs, and customer satisfaction. These goals are not attainable without employee input. The field of organizational behavior thus provides a knowledge base about human behavior at work; this base is indispensable to construction of effective management actions.

Organizational behavior as a body of knowledge tries to develop theories that describe and predict accurately how behavior occurs in organizations. Management that is action-oriented puts this knowledge to work by (1) planning employee activities, (2) controlling costs through budgets, (3) setting departmental and employee goals, (4) hiring new employees, (5) training employees in needed job skills, and (6) organizing employees to work in teams and departments.

The problems that Angela uncovered in her analysis of Builders Inc. represent a typical managerial orientation toward organizational behavior knowledge. She recognized that both employee turnover and equipment maintenance costs were closely related to company profitability and success. Like Jim in the preceding example, she wrestled with ways to correct organizational problems, yet without a thorough grounding in organizational behavior theory, she cannot generate solutions to Builders problems.

Managerial knowledge extends into technical areas that are also the focus of organizational behavior theory. Managers must have the technical knowledge to make determinations such as (1) how many units of a product or service to produce, (2) how many products or raw materials to keep on hand (i.e., inventory control), and (3) how to control costs (i.e., budgeting). These activities or determinations are a part of the technical work of managers, but they also affect the behavior and performance of employees. A knowledge of organizational behavior provides the basis for understanding these effects in both organizational and employee terms. Let's check your progress to this point.

Knowledge Check

1. A good theory does not suggest solutions to organizational problems. T or F?
2. Good managers can rely on their experiential theories to explain employee behavior accurately. T or F?
3. Experiential theories are based on objective information gathered in a systematic way. T or F?
4. A scientific theory of human behavior in organizations can be replicated and verified. T or F?
5. Managers have less need for organizational behavior theories because their work is action oriented. T or F?
6. The goals of managers and organizational behavior theory are always the same. T or F?

Answers:

1 F, 2 F, 3 F, 4 T, 5 F, 6 F

Summary Points

- The field of **organizational behavior** is a social science that develops knowledge about the behavior of people at work.
- Organizational behavior studies **organizational productivity** and **employee needs.** All aspects of organization performance relate to the former; work attitudes such as job satisfaction and organizational commitment relate to the latter.
- Management differs from organizational behavior in that it deals with **accomplishment of organizational goals** and involves the **technical, conceptual, and human side of organizational functioning.** The field of organizational behavior concentrates on the acquisition of knowledge about organizational productivity and employee needs.
- Organizational behavior focuses on three areas of analysis: (1) **the individual participant,** (2) **work groups,** and (3) **organizational units within the organization.** Specialized topics such as motivation, group performance, and organizational design emerge at each level.
- **Experiential theories** are based on personal biases, hunches, and intuition. They are hard to test because they are subjective. **Scientific theories** are independent of personal opinions and preferences.
- The characteristics of a good theory include **consistency** (both internal and external), **simplicity, generalizability,** and **verifiability.** These qualities make a theory effective, usable, and versatile.
- Organizational behavior theories are important to effective management because (1) they encourage the use of objective methods to solve problems, (2) they represent current developments in the field, and (3) they aid in evaluation of behavioral solutions to organizational problems.

Questions

1. You are a close friend of Angela's (from the introductory dilemma). She comes to you for advice on the problems she faces at Builders. How would you advise Angela to proceed to solve the employee turnover problem?
2. Organizational behavior has been described as one of the "most immediately applicable fields of study that you will encounter." Why is this true? On a sheet of paper, list three areas in which you can apply what you have learned from Chapter 1.
3. Using as an example the school where you are taking this course, list at least five examples of organizational productivity problems and areas of student need. Develop your answer from the standpoint of a manager who is viewing students as employees.
4. Pick up a copy of today's newspaper. Find an article about human behavior in an organization (i.e., sports team, religious group, government agency, political body, corporation). After you have read the article, identify examples of organizational productivity and employee welfare that were addressed. How relevant is behavior theory to the organization in the article?
5. Suppose that a close friend of yours works in a factory in your hometown. At a neighborhood party, he says, "Organizational behavior is a bunch of bunk. All this business about job satisfaction and meaningful work is lost on the morons who work in our plant. You're wasting your time studying that stuff. You'd be better off studying basketweaving!" How would you respond?
6. Go to the school library and find a recent management text book. Compare the table of contents in that book with the table of contents in **Understanding People in Organizations.** What are the differences between the two books? Are there any similarities?
7. Interview a friend or acquaintance who has a job. Ask him or her to identify three key goals relevant to organizational productivity and employee welfare. Next, ask this individual how a knowledge of employee behavior helps in handling a job. Ask your friend to explain the three most important skills that must be developed to be successful.

EXPLORING: *The Maytag Corporation*

Adapted from R. Levering, M. Moscovitz, and M. Katz, *The 100 Best Companies in America to Work For.* Reading, Mass.: Addison Wesley, 1984.

The Maytag Corporation of Newton, Iowa, has some motivated employees. Harvey Jackson works in this manufacturer's machine shop. While vacationing in the Bahamas, he met someone with a Maytag washer that didn't work. Harvey was concerned about his company's reputation, so he reported the incident to the management in Iowa. Within days, the malfunctioning washer was replaced. The defective machine was returned to Iowa and put in the "boneyard," where experts examined it to find out why it had not worked.

This example shows that Maytag strives to build quality into its products and that the company expects employees to share its concern for production excellence and customer service. The average Maytag washer lasts 14 years without problems. This fact is prominent in TV ads, which depict the lonely Maytag repairman who is never called. The company stands by its products and its employees.

Harvey should know. He says, "We're proud that we make the Cadillac of washing machines." He also happens to be president of the United Auto Workers Local 997, which represents production line workers at the Maytag plant. Maytag management has excellent relations with the union. There are several reasons for this harmony.

First, the company pays higher wages than its competitors and has one of the best employee benefits programs (pension plan and life, dental, and health insurance) in the appliance industry. The higher wages are based on a pay system that rewards higher employee productivity.

Second, the company further encourages productivity through an employee suggestion plan. In operation since 1947, the plan is recognized throughout the industry. Not only do employees make suggestions, but they have to summarize their suggestions in writing and present them to management. The program doesn't stop there. When an employee's idea is adopted by management, the employee receives one-half of the dollar savings that result from the suggestion for the first six months of implementation (up to a maximum of $5,000). During 1982, some 2,400 employee suggestions were implemented and the company paid out $141,000 to its innovative employees.

Supervisors also are encouraged to make improvement suggestions, but they are not paid for their specific contributions. In 1982, as a result of supervisor suggestions, Maytag saved over $4.5 million, or $26,600 per supervisor!

Discussion Questions

1. How does the Maytag Corporation obtain gains in organizational productivity?
2. How does the corporation address the issue of employee needs? Would you like to work for Maytag?
3. Do you think that Maytag has problems with employees wanting to quit their jobs? Why or why not?

APPLYING: *Organizational Productivity and Employee Needs*

1. Find and read a newspaper article about a company with productivity problems. Next, write a description of the problems from the standpoint of their effect on employees and on the company. HINT: Find an article about a company union that is on strike. From the employee standpoint, some possible problems could be reduced wages, loss of overtime pay, and loss of promotion opportunities. From the company view, problems might include declining employee performance and increased competition from other companies.
2. Develop a list of four possible consequences of the problem(s).
3. Did the company officials in the article seem to have a good understanding of employee needs?
4. What are three actions that you would take to increase the emphasis on productivity in the company discussed in the article?

Suggested Readings

Cummings, L. 1978. Toward Organizational Behavior. *Academy of Management Review* 3:90–98.

This article describes the field of organizational behavior as distinct from other social science fields.

The author identifies the basic themes and suggests future directions for work in the field.

Drucker, P. 1984. *Innovation and Entrepreneurship: Practice and Principles.* New York: Harper & Row.

Loeb, M. 1982. Some Happy Employees at Delta Want to Buy a Big Gift for the Boss. *Wall Street Journal* (28 September 1982), p. 29.

Mintzberg, H. 1973. *The Nature of Managerial Work.* Englewood Cliffs, N.J.: Prentice-Hall.

This book presents a coherent discussion of what managers really do. The presentation deviates from traditional views of managerial work in several significant ways, and emphasizes the importance of a knowledge of organizational behavior if one wants to become an effective manager.

Nadler, D., and Tushman, M. 1980. A Model for Diagnosing Organizational Behavior. *Organizational Dynamics* (Winter 1980) 35–51.

Toeffler, A. 1980. *The Third Wave.* New York: William Morrow.

This well-known author predicts the future of our society and how organizations will change. The "third wave" will move us beyond the industrial period (the second wave). The key features of the third wave are rapid change and information overload.

References

1. Jemison, D., and Sitkin, S. 1986. Corporate Acquisitions: A Process Perspective. *Academy of Management Review* 11:145–163.
2. Yankelovich, D. 1979. We Need New Motivational Tools. *Industry Week* (6 August 1979).
3. Wallace, M. 1983. Methodology, Research Practice, and Progress in Personnel and Industrial Relations. *Academy of Management Review* 8:6–13.
4. Steffy, B., and Grimes, A. 1986. A Critical Theory of Organizational Science. *Academy of Management Review* 11:322–336.
5. Schwab, D. 1980. Construct Validity in Organizational Behavior. In B. Staw and L. Cummings (Eds.). *Research in Organizational Behavior,* vol. 2, Greenwich, Conn.: JAI Press, 3–44.
6. Kaplan, A. 1964. *The Conduct of Inquiry.* San Francisco: Jossey Bass.

People at Work

Chapter 2

I. Dilemma: Trouble in the Company
II. Understanding Personality
    A. Attribution theory
    B. Individual characteristics in the workplace
III. Attitudes and How They Form
    A. The affective component of attitudes
    B. The cognitive component of attitudes
    C. The behavioral component of attitudes
    D. Attitude formation
IV. The Attitude-Behavior Relationship
V. The Crucial Role of Job Satisfaction
    A. The meaning of job satisfaction
    B. Determinants and consequences of job satisfaction
    C. Job satisfaction and performance
    D. How organizations measure job satisfaction
VI. Developments in the Study of Employee Work Attitudes
    A. Organizational commitment and its consequences
    B. Job involvement and its consequences
VII. Summary Points
VIII. Questions
IX. Exploring: Is Organizational Commitment on the Decline?
X. Applying: Measuring Job Involvement at Work
XI. Suggested Readings
XII. References

Chapter Goals

By the end of the chapter, you will be able to:

1. Describe the managerial importance of locus of control.
2. Explain the meaning of introversion and extroversion.
3. Discuss the impact of Machiavellianism on behavior in the workplace.
4. Predict the influence of emotionality on employee performance.
5. Break an attitude into its component parts.
6. Explain how attitudes are related to behavior.
7. Explain the nature of job satisfaction.
8. Recognize the determinants and consequences of job satisfaction.
9. Explain the important role of equity theory in the relationship between job satisfaction and performance.
10. Choose an appropriate method for measuring job satisfaction in the work setting.
11. Describe the importance of organizational commitment and job involvement.

Dilemma Trouble in the Company

Anderson Grading Company was started five years ago in Minneapolis by Tom and Marybeth Anderson. Tom got the firm started with two old dump trucks, a small bulldozer, and a backhoe. Initially, the company had four employees. Marybeth was the company president, Tom handled the estimates, while Phil and Ed (old high school chums) operated the equipment.

The Company Grows

As the company grew, Anderson Grading developed a reputation for excellent work completed on schedule. The three men prided themselves on meeting contractor specifications, especially in the area of site preparation for small shopping centers. Tom believed that the company could continue to grow by expanding services for shopping center construction work. Marybeth agreed and pointed out that the company should continue to do the type of work that had built its reputation. Tom obtained a line of credit to purchase new equipment (a grader and a heavy duty backhoe).

One evening Tom and Marybeth talked about hiring more employees. With the new equipment, Tom reasoned that they had to hire three more operators. He decided to turn the hiring job over to Phil, who would screen the applicants for their ability to run the equipment. Tom also wanted to be sure that employees would maintain the equipment to hold down repair costs. Phil eventually hired three men, and the company branched out to do larger shopping center work.

Tom Gets Back Into Operations

For the next four years the company succeeded beyond anyone's expectations. Contracts grew in size and number, and the firm added four new pieces of equipment. With 12 employees, Marybeth now had an assistant bookkeeper to oversee the growing load of paperwork at the office. The only problems were an increase in equipment breakdowns and consequent repair costs. Tom decided that he was too far removed from day-to-day operations. He began showing up at various construction sites at irregular intervals. While checking on the crews, he would issue orders about grading procedures and would show operators how to run and maintain the equipment. Phil became irritated by what he judged to be Tom's infringement on his job responsibilities.

The Proverbial Straw . . .

Tom hired Sally Johnson to do his estimation work. She was well qualified for the job; she had recently completed a degree in construction management. Her hiring freed Tom to spend even more time at the construction sites. As a result, the operators found themselves taking orders from both Tom and Phil, who often gave them conflicting instructions. Several operators quit in frustration and expressed their feeling that they were always in the middle between two bosses. Phil was spending less and less time at the construction sites. Tom had not noticed because he was so absorbed in inspection and maintenance work.

Phil was increasingly troubled by Tom's "meddling" in his job. Finally, one Monday morning, Phil walked into the construction trailer where Tom was going over some plans with Sally and told Tom that he had taken a job with Johnson Construction as a general foreman. Tom was floored. He was particularly upset that Phil had quit without explaining why. Tom tried to talk to Ed (his and Phil's mutual friend from their schooldays), but all Ed had to say was that Phil was happy with his job; he didn't need any management responsibility.

Six months passed and Tom had not found a replacement for Phil. He was doing Phil's work plus the coordination activities with Sally. Operator turnover was still a problem, and breakdowns were more common than ever. Although sales were still growing, Marybeth was concerned about a few customer complaints about missed deadlines and some low quality work. The latter had resulted in two complaints submitted to the Better Business Bureau.

One Sunday morning, when Tom and Marybeth were breakfasting at Zenia's Cafe, Tom noticed Phil and his wife seated across the dining room. Tom went over and asked how everything was going. Phil responded that the job was OK. They talked for 20 minutes and Tom then returned to his table. He commented to Marybeth that Phil did not seem too happy with his work. Marybeth stated that she had heard the same thing from Phil's wife. In fact, Phil had told his wife often that he would like to go back to work for Tom, if Tom would only *not* infringe on his authority.

That evening, Tom and Marybeth talked about getting Phil back in the company. The other employees would certainly be pleased, for they had all liked Phil's easy manner. Tom and Marybeth also reasoned that the new company profit sharing plan would be a real incentive for Phil. They worked out the preliminary figures, and decided that they could offer Phil a $3,500 annual raise if he would come back to Anderson Grading.

Tom called Phil the next morning. They had a long talk, and Tom explained both the profit sharing plan and the pay raise. Phil was flattered, but he pointed out that he had to have full control of operations and inspection. Tom agreed and promised that he would stay away from the job sites unless Phil called him. Phil said he would take the job.

Some weeks later, Phil pulled up to the construction site of the new medical clinic that Tom's company was building. Phil had managed this project very tightly and everything was on schedule. Operator maintenance work on equipment had improved significantly, and equipment repair costs were down 50 percent on this job. As Phil strolled to the excavation pit, he overheard Tom instructing an operator on running the backhoe. Phil thought to himself, "Here we go again . . ."

Questions

1. Why does Tom continue to interfere with Phil's job when he promised that he would stop?
2. What is the basis of the problem between Tom and Phil?

3. Do specific theories exist to help us understand Tom and Phil's behavior?
4. How can organizational commitment be used to analyze Phil's behavior?

Understanding Personality

Personality makes each of us unique. It distinguishes you from other people and is the basis of your nature. Most experts agree that personality is not a simple, unidimensional concept. **Personality** is defined as a relatively permanent psychological structure composed of stable traits and characteristics that interact with situational demands to shape personal preferences and behavior. Our discussion will focus on a number of important topics related to personality, especially those topics that are important in organizations. A knowledge of these topics will enhance your understanding of why people react the way they do in the work setting.

Attribution Theory

Attribution theory is a concept that makes the study of personality easier. The theory proposes that people observe the behaviors of others and then *attribute* causes for those behaviors. In other words, we try to attach causes to the behavior of others based on our own perceptions of reality. Figure 2.1 diagrams the attribution theory components (1).

We evaluate the behavior of ourselves and others in terms of consensus, consistency, and distinctiveness. **Consensus** refers to the degree to which other people would behave in the same way in the same situation. **Consistency** refers to the same person behaving in the same way in similar situations occurring at various times. **Distinctiveness** describes the same person behaving in the same way in other, varying situations (2). The outcome of

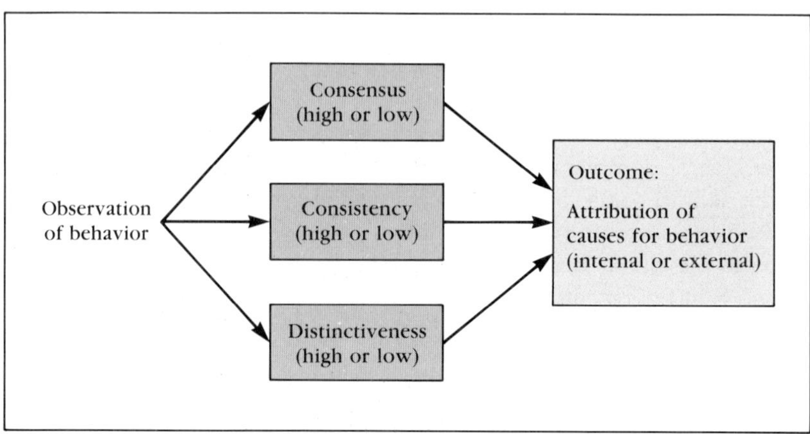

Figure 2.1
Attribution Theory

such a behavior analysis is a decision about whether the behavior originates inside the person or from the environment.

Let's consider an example of how to apply attribution theory. You might have a coworker who is irritable and short-tempered. If he is your only coworker who behaves in this way (low consensus), if he has not behaved in this way for several weeks (low consistency), and if you have not seen him be irritable in other situations (high distinctiveness), then you are likely to conclude that his behavior was caused by external factors. How we attribute causality has significant implications in terms of the judgments we make about employee behavior and personality (3).

Individual Characteristics in the Workplace

Individual differences are key determinants of employee behavior in the workplace. They are defined as basic aspects of personality from which we can predict (or explain) what people do at work. For instance, a tough, demanding boss is likely to have a certain effect on his employees as he pushes them to higher and higher levels of output. This "drill sergeant" supervisor creates certain attitudes and behaviors in his subordinates. His boss may admire his ability to make employees jump, but the employees probably do not share the admiration. They probably perceive their boss as a dictatorial person.

Our study of individual differences includes several that have been shown to explain important work-related behaviors (especially performance) and work attitudes (job satisfaction, job involvement, and organizational commitment). The individual differences that we focus on are locus of control, extraversion and introversion and Machiavellianism.

Locus of control is a well researched individual difference. Let's begin with an example before we define the term.

> Nancy has worked hard to finish a degree in office management. She has gone to school part-time in the evenings for four years. One semester remains, and she knows that her degree will help her move up to the assistant office manager position. In her company, formal training is viewed as an important basis for promotion. She has already received awards for outstanding employee performance, and her pay raises reflect her hard work. She believes that having the degree will put her in the right position for promotion. (Six months after she received the degree, Nancy was promoted.)
>
> Wanda works in Nancy's office and is skilled at her word processing job. She is one of the most efficient operators, yet she has not pursued outside educational opportunities to broaden her base of experience. She has told her friends often that "it doesn't matter how hard you work, management promotes people who happen to be in the right place at the right time." As a result of this philosophy, Wanda sees her job in narrow terms and takes a dim view of "doing all that extra schoolwork for a promotion that will never come."

Do Nancy and Tom (from the introductory dilemma) have anything in common?

They do. Both individuals believe that they can control their own fate at work. Psychologists would say that they possess an internal locus of control

(4). **Locus of control** is defined as an individual's belief that one's actions influence the outcomes one experiences in life (5). Notice that we do not specify positive or negative outcomes. Locus of control is neutral relative to type of outcome. The term simply refers to the strength of one's beliefs that personal action will or will not result in certain outcomes, be they positive or negative.

NOW IT'S YOUR TURN . . .

Instructions: Please circle one of the two statements for each item. Choose the statement that is closer to your opinion.

1. a. No matter how hard someone studies, they can still get poor grades in school.

   b. Doing well in school is a matter of studying hard.

2. a. Receiving a promotion is a matter of hard work, luck has nothing to do with it.

   b. Promotion is a matter of being in the right place at the right time.

3. a. There are some things that people should not attempt to change, because they're probably going to fail in the attempt.

   b. If a person is committed enough, he or she can accomplish anything.

4. a. Getting ahead in today's world is a matter of persistence and hard work.

   b. Whoever gets ahead in today's world must have connections.

5. a. When I believe that I'm right about something, I feel as if I can convince anyone.

   b. It is extremely difficult to change people's attitudes by talking with them.

6. a. Instructors often play favorites and give some students higher marks.

   b. Students generally earn the grades they get.

Scoring: Give yourself one point if you answered the six questions in the following manner: 1 a, 2 b, 3 a, 4 b, 5 b, 6 a. The closer your score is to five or six, the more *external* your locus of control. Low scores (one or two points) indicate an *internal* locus of control. Scores of three or four indicate that you may vary in your beliefs about internal and external control.

If you have an **internal locus of control,** you tend to see a strong connection between your behavior and what happens to you at work (and in your life). The individual with a strong internal orientation does not believe in luck or chance. She says, "I got here because I was willing to work hard and I stuck to the job." In the brief examples of Nancy and Wanda, Nancy possesses an internal locus of control. She believes that finishing her degree will result in improved career prospects at work. Indeed, after she finished her degree, her beliefs were confirmed. Tom, in the opening dilemma, shares this belief in personal control over life events. He and Marybeth started their business and continue to make it successful because they believe that they can meet the challenges of running their own firm.

Someone with an **external locus of control** does not believe that a dependable connection exists between his behavior and external events. The person with an external locus attributes outcomes in work and life to luck, chance, or fate (e.g., being in the right place at the right time). Wanda does not believe that going to school will improve her chances of promotion. She is resigned and holds the view that simply being in the right place at the right time determines who does or does not get promoted.

Table 2.1 shows some of the typical beliefs held by people with an internal and external locus of control. The locus of control pattern of belief about behavior consequences is a fundamental personality trait. If a person begins to doubt these beliefs, problems can arise as he struggles to understand the relationship between his behavior and its outcomes.

Locus of control is related to work behavior. Internals are more attracted to situations that offer opportunities for individual achievement. In school, internals often perform better than externals for reasons other than superior intelligence (i.e., internals are no smarter than externals). Internals are more motivated and are better performers if they perceive that performance is skill-based rather than luck-based. When work performance is presented as skill-based versus luck-based, internals usually outperform their externally oriented coworkers (6).

The managerial implication of this finding is that employees will work harder when they are told that rewards are based on superior skill and high performance. This message encourages development of an internal locus of control in employees. Furthermore, externally oriented employees will observe their coworkers being rewarded for acquiring new skills and achieving higher performance, and may become similarly motivated.

Locus of control affects how anxious and emotional employees behave following a traumatic event (7). Externals may be more likely to experience adverse emotional reactions to coworkers (especially supervisors) who put a lot of pressure on them. Internals are more trusting and tend to block out failure more completely. They prefer leaders who let them participate, and

Table 2.1
Characteristics of Internals and Externals

Internals tend to believe that:	*Externals tend to believe that:*
Pay raises are based on hard work, achievement, and initiative.	Pay raises are based on having the right job at the right time.
A high grade point average is a function of hard work and effective time management.	Teachers have favorites and give them higher marks.
Drug addiction indicates that some people are willing to give up control of their lives.	Anyone, given the right set of circumstances, can become addicted to drugs.
When a person believes he is right, he can often convince others.	People's attitudes cannot be changed easily by appealing to their logic.

they are more sensitive to organizational attempts to influence their behavior. These study results imply that internals must have input about work decisions that affect them.

Internals search more for relevant information before making decisions. Like Nancy, internals seek new knowledge that can lead to outcomes, which they believe to be within their personal control. Employees with an internal locus are more willing to take action when they are confused about job demands. When we study stress in the workplace (Chapter 7), you will see that this tendency may insulate these employees from some of the negative effects of stress.

Locus of control is related to entrepreneurial behavior and taking business risks (8, 9). The analysis is that internals are more comfortable with change than externals and are therefore more likely to launch a new business venture if they are dissatisfied with their current situation. Perhaps internals are quicker to act when they judge that their current work circumstances are limiting their options or suppressing their creativity (especially the acquisition of new skills that may lead to better performance).

Locus of control affects how employees behave when their jobs are unclear and ambiguous in terms of work demands. Internals seem better at determining how to structure their job and become productive. Internals are able to work more effectively than externals under loose or nonexistent supervision. Since internals prefer to structure their work themselves, they appreciate the opportunity to participate in making job decisions. When a job is well defined and supervision is close, externals turn out to be better performers.

Internals respond differently to rewards than externals do. If internals believe that good performance is rewarded fairly, they will believe that their efforts are more likely to result in success. A company's pay system should be designed to reinforce this employee belief. If the pay system is so structured, employees will become more internal in their work orientation. This is a highly desirable outcome for the company, because supervisors are then relieved of some of the burden of employee control.

Solving the Dilemma

Why does Tom insist on interfering in Phil's job, even when Tom promised that he would stop?

Tom's meddling behavior is a good example of one effect of an internal locus of control. Tom believes that he can control the situation by supervising the operators closely and by insisting that they do their work properly (especially preventive equipment maintenance). He believes that the negative outcomes of high repair costs and missed work deadlines can be influenced by his behavior. As a result, he encroaches gradually on Phil's job and removes more and more of Phil's responsibilities. Tom finds it difficult to change his behavior because he is certain that his actions can make a substantial difference in eliminating high repair costs and missed deadlines.

Extroversion and introversion. We have all met people who seem to be more sociable than others. These individuals who are outgoing and gregarious are described as **extroverts** (10). **Introverts,** on the other hand, are shyer and less willing to get involved in social activities (11). Eysenck explains **extroversion** as the need some people have to obtain as much social stimulation as possible from their environment. Those who crave social stimulation would probably have a very active social life, enjoy crowds, and be more attracted to adventures and exciting vacations (12). Extroverts also require variety in their experiences to maintain a constant level of stimulation. The individual who belongs to numerous social organizations, attends night classes, bowls on weekends, and coaches Little League baseball fits our description of an extrovert.

Introversion describes those who are less oriented to external stimulation. They need less socializing and may actively seek ways to "turn down the social noise" of their environment. Introverts tend to be more sensitive to their personal feelings and to what is going on inside. Note, however, that these individual differences exist on a continuum and that people experience both types of needs at different times and with varying intensity. In general, we all, whether introvert or extrovert, try to regulate the amount of social stimulation we receive (13).

Some organizations try to identify a job applicant's extroversion level before hiring. Companies hiring salespeople often use tests to assess this trait, and psychologists are sometimes used to interview potential salespeople. During the interview, the psychologist may present the applicant with a variety of hypothetical sales situations to assess the person's extroversion level. Sales managers clearly believe that extroversion is related to success in sales. Figure 2.2 contains questions that might appear on a test for extroversion. Note the emphasis on external stimulation and social interaction.

The implications of an employee's extroversion or introversion are not as clear as are the consequences of internal versus external locus of control. There are, however, some interesting findings. For instance, introverts generally have longer tenure and fewer unexcused absences than do extroverts (14). Introverts also perform better in work environments that have fewer external distractions. Too much external stimulation often

Figure 2.2
Sample items from a test to evaluate extroversion

1. I'd rather curl up with a good book than go to a party.
   T or F?
2. I prefer to be around people who are funny and clever.
   T or F?
3. If I had the choice, I would take a camping trip for my vacation versus a Caribbean cruise.
   T or F?
4. When I have to deal with a new situation involving other people, I usually jump in with both feet.
   T or F?
5. I greatly admire individuals who take bold public stands on controversial issues.
   T or F?
6. When I'm in an unfamiliar social setting, I generally feel self-confident and interested in meeting new people.
   T or F?

causes the introvert's performance to drop off quickly. When extroverts are confronted with boring work, they are more likely to engage in irrelevant behavior and goofing off. On the other hand, the extrovert begins to perform really well at a high level of external stimulation. Figure 2.3 summarizes these relationships.

The Machiavellian personality. "The end justifies the means" is an old expression. When translated into employee personality characteristics, it means "I'll do anything at work to meet my needs." This orientation tends toward manipulation of others and indicates that an individual will try any means to influence others to his particular way of thinking. An individual who prefers to captain the softball team or who believes that he is better at coaching than the coach may have a Machiavellian personality trait. The **Machiavellian personality** is defined as being cool interpersonally, amoral, pleased by manipulation of others, and highly rational (15).

(The) **Mach–V Scale** is a paper and pencil test that identifies Machiavellian tendencies. The Now It's Your Turn section shows some of the test items.

NOW IT'S YOUR TURN . . .

Circle the answer that most resembles your own opinion. An interpretation appears below the questions.

	Strongly Disagree	Disagree	Agree	Strongly Agree
1. You can get around people by telling them what they want to hear	1	2	3	4
2. A person should take action only when it is ethically right	1	2	3	4
3. In most cases, there is no excuse for lying	1	2	3	4
4. Most people would agree that all people have a mean streak, which comes out on a regular basis	1	2	3	4

Calculate your Mach–V score as follows:

Item 1 + (5 − Item 2) + (5 − Item 3) + Item 4

A personality with few Machiavellian tendencies is represented by scores under 10. The scores of the highly Machiavellian personality are closer to 20.

SOURCE: Adapted from Christie, R., and Geis, F., 1970. *Studies in Machiavellianism.* New York: Academic Press.

Can the Machiavellian individual have a negative influence on the organization?

When individuals get high scores on the full version of this questionnaire, some interesting conclusions can be drawn. People who have high Mach–V

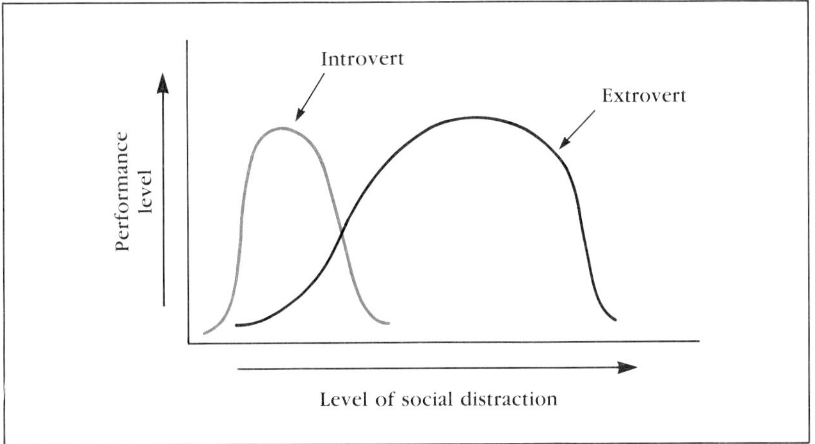

Figure 2.3 *Relationship of introvert and extrovert performance to social distraction level*

scores generally (1) attempt more interpersonal manipulations, (2) are more inventive in manipulating others, (3) conceive of more manipulations to choose from, and (4) experience more satisfaction from successful manipulations than do people with low Mach–V scores (16).

In 1974, President Richard Nixon was forced to resign because of mounting evidence that his administration had tried to cover up the Watergate break-in. Although he was eventually pardoned by President Gerald Ford, several of Nixon's aides were tried, found guilty, and sentenced to jail terms for their role in the cover-up. Many of these administrators and White House staff members believed at the time that they had to do whatever was necessary to protect the presidency and the powers of the executive branch of the government. Activities that were clearly illegal and unconstitutional were contemplated and implemented. One does not have to look very hard at the Watergate episode and its aftermath to find the behavioral patterns of Machiavellianism in the principal Watergate cover-up participants.

Emotionality. At one time or another, most of us have felt nervous or upset about an upcoming event. If a person experiences anxiety on a regular basis, even when an anxiety-producing event is *not* impending, he may be prone to emotionality. **Emotionality** encompasses a broad category of behaviors characterized by (1) emotional volatility, (2) broad mood swings, (3) tendencies toward self-reproach, (4) sensitivity to social stress (e.g., meeting new people), (5) experiencing tension at work, (6) excessive concern about physical health, and (7) hypersensitivity to criticism and negative feedback.

Most people fall somewhere between high and low emotionality. Anxiety is a normal aspect of life. Without it, we would have little impetus to prepare properly for upcoming events for which performance is crucial to personal success. For some individuals, however, the problem becomes how to handle chronic anxiety caused by a high level of emotionality. These issues are dealt with extensively in Chapter 7 on job stress. Identifying employees who experience high emotionality at work is useful. Table 2.2 [contrasts some of the behaviors of the emotional (anxious) employee with those of the calm employee.]

Table 2.2
Behaviors of Anxious Versus Calm Employees

Anxious employees tend to:	*Calm employees tend to:*
Worry excessively about failure.	Perceive failure as simply one more remotely possible outcome.
Blame themselves with accompanying loss of self-esteem when things go wrong at work.	Accept responsibility without excessive loss of self-esteem.
Need more supportive supervision.	Work well with or without supportive supervision.
Need tasks that are more structured and subject to supervisor approval.	Prefer tasks that are less structured.
Have difficulty making decisions under high pressure.	Make decisions equally well under low or high pressure.
Work feverishly both before trivial deadlines or deadlines well in the future.	Work at about the same pace throughout the time period allotted for a deadline.
Have difficulty setting work priorities (all work demands tend to be awarded high priority).	Willingly set work priorities and stick to them.
Dwell on negative feedback about job performance.	Do not dwell on negative feedback or necessarily accept it as valid.

Executive emotionality can have an impact on the behavior of the entire organization (17). Executives can have "neurotic styles" that influence all aspects of an organization. For example, executives with a suspicious style may cause the organization to become paranoid (e.g., the Nixon White House). Compulsive executives may cause the organization to become bureaucratic and impersonal. We examine the compulsive executive when we study job stress (Chapter 7).

Supervisors must recognize different levels of emotionality among their employees. Many supervisors make the mistake of thinking that the best supervisor is one who treats all employees the same way. Their motivational rule is: treat employees equally and they will perform equally well. Such managerial practices in fact lead to uneven employee performance. The more productive rule is: find ways to treat employees equitably so their inherent differences are recognized. In other words, the supervisor should put less pressure on the employee with high emotionality and more on the employee with low emotionality.

A manager needs to get to know her employees on a personal basis. No single management style is best for all employees. Recognizing individual employee differences is the first step in developing a management style that accommodates changing circumstances and job requirements. The effective manager knows her employees well enough to predict their behavior with reasonable accuracy, and this includes an understanding of individual differences. When we study the expectancy theory in Chapter 3, you will learn how to design effective motivational systems for all employees.

Knowledge Check

1. Individual differences are aspects of personality that partially explain employee behavior and attitudes. T or F?
2. An individual with an external locus of control is likely to believe that finding a good job is mostly a function of hard work and personal dedication. T or F?
3. In the introductory dilemma, Tom is more likely to have an ___________ locus of control.
4. Extroverted employees seek more stimulation from their social environment than do introverts. T or F?
5. A Machiavellian employee will go along with company goals regardless of whether she benefits from achieving those goals. T or F?
6. The highly emotional employee is likely to blame himself when things go wrong at work. T or F?
7. A good rule to follow when supervising employees is: treat all employees the same way. T or F?

Answers:
1 T, 2 F, 3 internal, 4 T, 5 F, 6 T, 7 F

Attitudes and How They Form

Now that you have an understanding of some major individual personality traits and differences, let's look at attitudes. An **attitude** is a learned predisposition to respond to people, objects, or institutions in a positive or negative way. The study of attitudes is critical to an understanding of organizational behavior because many attitudes are related to the productivity of the organization and to employee needs.

Return for a moment to the opening dilemma and examine Phil's thoughts about Tom. These thoughts represent Phil's attitudes toward Tom. Attitudes can be broken down into basic components. Let's examine the affective, cognitive, and behavioral components of attitudes from the standpoint of Phil's thoughts about Tom.

The Affective Component of Attitudes

The **affective component** consists of the feelings and emotions that a person has toward the focus of the attitude. This component develops as an emotional response, which is associated with punishing or rewarding circumstances. For example, an employee may have a strong dislike for a supervisor because the supervisor criticized one of the employee's ideas in front of his friends. Each time the employee sees these friends or the supervisor, he relives the embarrassing situation.

The following qualities represent the affective component of Phil's attitudes toward Tom:

- He feels comfortable socially with Tom.
- He feels frustrated with his own loss of control over operations.
- He is resentful that he cannot tell Tom directly (because of their long-standing friendship) that he is unhappy with his job.

Notice that the affective component can have both a negative and positive side. The intensity of the component may also vary. For this reason, some attitudes may be critical to an understanding of behavior (i.e., they predict behavior strongly), while other attitudes may be less important because the affective component lacks intensity. When an attitude lacks intensity, we are indifferent to the focus of the attitude (e.g., unconcern about the opinions of a supervisor from another department).

The Cognitive Component of Attitudes

The **cognitive component** of an attitude embodies the person's thoughts, beliefs, and ideas about the focus of the attitude. For example, your attitude toward nuclear reactors may be based on your understanding of the Three Mile Island incident in Pennsylvania, information from a public lecture you attended at college on the dangers of nuclear power plants, ideas from your brother who is a nuclear engineer, and so forth. The cognitive component is your belief about the characteristics of the attitude object. When pollsters sample people's opinions on a variety of subjects, they are tapping the cognitive component of attitude. What about the cognitive component of Phil's attitudes toward Tom? See if you agree with the following list:

- Tom has been my boss for almost nine years and my friend for a long time.
- Tom's company has grown steadily.
- Tom is a very hard worker who can't stand to remain uninvolved when problems arise in the firm.
- Tom has concentrated primarily on the sales and estimation aspects of the business.
- Tom values his friendships and tries to be equitable with his employees.
- Tom is a much better estimator and salesperson than he is an operations supervisor.

From Phil's point of view, all of this information is accurate. Tom might or might not agree with all of these statements, but that is irrelevant to our examination of Phil's perceptions of Tom. **Perceptions** are our sensations about the objects, people, and institutions in our environment. Regardless of their accuracy, Phil's perceptions have a powerful effect on him. This raises an important point. Reality is not what influences employee behavior, but rather the employee's perceptions of reality. The effective supervisor must become expert at managing employee perceptions. Remember, other employees in the company may not share Phil's perceptions of Tom.

The Behavioral Component of Attitudes

The **behavioral component** is one's tendency to behave toward or react to the focus of the attitude in certain ways. The behavioral component is that part of an attitude that is closest to one's actual behavior. The affective and cognitive components influence one's intentions toward the focus of attitude. Let's analyze the behavioral components of Phil's attitude toward Tom:

- I have to quit my job.
- I plan to find a job where my boss won't undermine my authority over subordinates.
- Once I find a new job, I may try to make amends with Tom.
- I won't return to Tom's company unless he agrees to behave differently.

Note the tendency to act in each expression. The behavioral component has a strong action orientation. If the behavioral component is not well developed, the attitude will not activate behavior.

When Tom indicated to Phil that he would behave differently and also that Phil would acquire an ownership interest in the business (i.e., the profit sharing plan), Phil's negative evaluation of the attitude object (Tom's meddling behavior) was substantially reduced. He was able to take his old job back without feeling awkward. Cognitive portions of his attitude began to reform, however, as soon as he saw Tom talking to one of the equipment operators on the medical clinic job.

Solving the Dilemma

What is the basis of the problem between Tom and Phil?

Phil formed an attitude toward Tom's behavior, which made it impossible for him to remain with the firm. He became frustrated with Tom's increased involvement with his operations responsibilities (affective component). Phil believed that an operations supervisory job requires constant monitoring by *one boss only* (cognitive component). When Phil decided to search for a new job, the affective and cognitive components had triggered the behavioral component of his attitude toward authority.

Attitude Formation

The process of attitude formation starts early in life. People acquire attitudes in three primary ways: (1) personal experience, (2) association, and (3) social learning. Let's look at each of these processes and develop some examples of how they operate.

Personal experience occurs through direct contact with people, objects, and entities (e.g., supervisors, coworkers, customers, company equipment and policies). Personal experience develops the cognitive component of attitudes. For example, Phil's direct experience with Tom's supervision of construction crews (regarding preventive maintenance) helped form the cognitive component of Phil's attitude about Tom's meddling behavior (and his authority). In another example, a college freshman might experience the following and then incorporate these experiences into an attitude about school:

- There are a lot of students on campus.
- Many of my courses are very difficult for me.

- My advisor doesn't seem to have time to help me select my courses.

The personal experiences of this student might result in an attitude that resembles the following: "I didn't expect college to be so difficult, and I expected my instructors to be more helpful." The attitude might also include: "This campus is too big for me, I'd be better off at a smaller school." Another student confronting the same set of circumstances might acquire an entirely different attitude toward the school.

Association occurs when an individual transfers part or all of an attitude toward a person or event to another person or event. Once an attitude is formed about a person or event, association has occurred. Let's consider an example. You make a good friend at school. You like this individual because you share similar interests. You see your friend in the school cafeteria with another person. You do not know this second individual, but you believe that she may have many of your friend's same qualities. You are therefore likely to **transfer** your positive attitude to your perceptions of this new individual. The process that causes you to connect two or more attitude objects creates the conditions for attitude association. Many of our attitudes "spread" in this way.

Social learning refers to the attitude formation and acquisition that occurs when you do not have direct experience with the person or event related to the attitude. For example, your close friend in the scene just described expresses his belief that the athletic department exploits athletes. Your formerly neutral opinion about the department may now turn into a negative attitude. Initially, this opinion change operates on the cognitive level. If you actually become acquainted with some of the athletes personally, social learning may develop affective and behavioral components of this particular attitude. (Your personal contact with the athletes may also convince you that your friend's opinion was wrong.)

Many of our attitudes are formed without direct experience of the people or events involved. Our attitudes about political activities, religious groups, and ethnic groups often are developed without personal contact with members of those groups. The attitudes that we form without direct contact can be either positive or negative, and the intensity of our judgments depends on the direction (positive or negative) of the affective component of our attitudes.

The Attitude-Behavior Relationship

Both managers and employees should be concerned with how attitudes affect behavior. This concern includes the relationship between attitudes such as job satisfaction, job involvement, and organizational commitment, and behaviors such as performance, absenteeism, job quitting, application for a job, and promotion seeking. In other words, employee work attitudes form the basis of many important work behaviors, yet attitudes are not the sole cause of work behaviors. They interact with characteristics of the work situation to influence behavior.

Do attitudes always predict behavior?

Attitudes do *not* always predict behavior for three reasons (18). First, the predicted behavior may be socially undesirable. Phil's attitude toward Tom does not result in his confronting Tom directly. Rather, Phil's attitude generated job search behavior, and Phil took another job before he told Tom about his dissatisfaction. Phil perceived confrontational behavior as socially undesirable. To personalize this idea, think of several attitudes that you have that you would *never act on* in a social setting. The reason that you do not act on these attitudes is that you judge the consequences of such behavior to be undesirable in some way. This reasoning is a powerful force that suppresses the connection between your attitude and your behavior.

A second reason why attitudes may not predict behavior is that attitudes relate to situations as well as to people and events (19). Attitudes toward a situation may override one's attitude toward the people or objects in the situation. A drill sergeant may believe that all new recruits are stupid and undisciplined. If, however, he encounters some new recruits in church, he does not order them to stand at attention while he points out their numerous shortcomings as soldiers. His attitude toward the situation (how to behave in church) overrides his attitude toward recruits. He would behave quite differently were he to encounter the same recruits lying around the barracks! In that situation, a strong linkage would occur between his immediate behavior and his attitude toward recruits.

The third reason why attitudes may not predict behavior is that many socially acquired attitudes have a strong cognitive component but have less developed affective and behavioral components. These are intellectualized attitudes, which do not easily produce behavior. Such attitudes have little to do with the individual's self-esteem. If one encounters behavior in others that violates these particular attitudes, the individual remains indifferent toward the behavior. Since these attitudes have no affective component, one does not have a strong emotional reaction to the behavior. Lets look at an example of this.

> You are a first line foreman in an assembly plant. You believe that labor unions have a negative impact on performance and productivity. You studied some of these effects in a night course in economics. You also have heard company managers condemn unions on similar grounds. You, however, have never had a negative encounter with union members. As you leave work, you see a group of employees placing union flyers on cars in the parking lot. You drive off and promptly forget the incident.

Although you have a negative cognitive component regarding labor unions, the affective and behavioral components of your attitude are either nonexistent or underdeveloped. You take no action with respect to the employees in the parking lot. You do not bother to report the incident to your superior. Your attitude toward labor unions has little to do with your self-image. In contrast, one can easily imagine a situation in which a foreman holds an attitude about labor unions that is based on direct experience. Strongly developed behavioral and affective components would then accompany the cognitive component. If these were all positive, the foreman might help the employees put flyers under windshield wipers!

Knowledge Check

1. The cognitive component of an attitude is that portion of the attitude that is closest to one's actual behavior. T or F?
2. Attitude association represents the process by which an attitude is generalized to other objects. T or F?
3. The link between an attitude and a behavior may be weak because of overdevelopment of the cognitive component and underdevelopment of the affective and behavioral components. T or F?

Answers:

1 F, 2 T, 3 T

The Crucial Role of Job Satisfaction

Job satisfaction is a key work attitude, which is determined by employee perceptions of events at work. In this section, we discuss (1) job satisfaction, its origins and consequences, and (2) the relationship between job satisfaction and performance.

The Meaning of Job Satisfaction

Job satisfaction is the most extensively studied job attitude in organizations. The components of job satisfaction are the same as those of other attitudes (i.e., affective, cognitive, and behavioral). Job satisfaction is composed of facets. These are: (1) satisfaction with the work itself, (2) satisfaction with the pay, (3) satisfaction with promotion, (4) satisfaction with the supervision, and (5) satisfaction with coworkers (20). A given employee may find some of these facets to be more relevant than others in a work situation. An employee might be very satisfied with his coworkers yet might find his work to be unfulfilling and meaningless (low satisfaction with the work itself).

How satisfied are U.S. workers as a whole?

Job satisfaction for certain types of employees is generally on the increase in the United States. Important trends may, however, be masked by the presentation of overall figures. Consider Figure 2.4. This graph indicates that, other than a plateau from 1971 to 1980, job satisfaction has increased over

Figure 2.4
Trends in Job Satisfaction

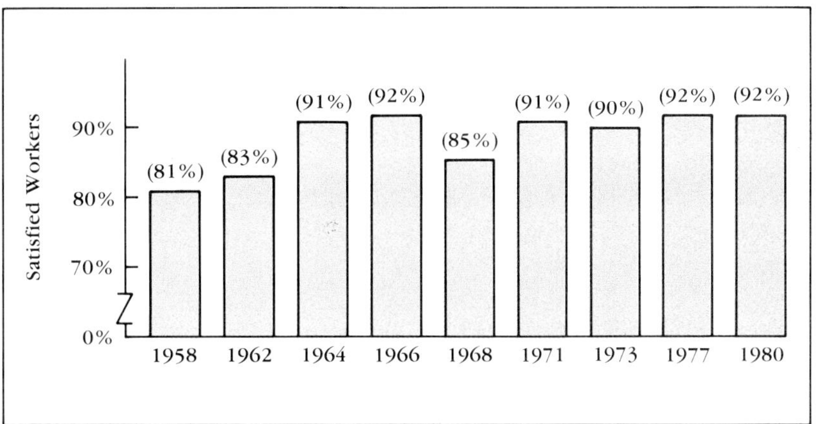

the last 22 years. Although this finding is encouraging from a national perspective, research indicates that job satisfaction decreases as one moves from analysis of higher level professionals to workers holding lower level positions. A major feature of these predictable declines in job satisfaction is related to the different ways in which jobs are designed for professionals versus laborers. Higher level positions have more challenges, variety, responsibility, and meaningfulness. These all contribute to greater job satisfaction.

Determinants and Consequences of Job Satisfaction

Personal traits influence levels of job satisfaction. Let's look at age and one's job expectations, two of the more important personal determinants of job satisfaction.

Age. As employees grow older, they experience more satisfaction at work. This trend continues until close to retirement, where a sharp decrease in job satisfaction usually occurs. Initially, a sharp decline in job satisfaction is evident after the first six months to two years on the job. The dip usually occurs because the employee learns that the job will not meet all of his or her personal needs. The long-term relationship between years on the job and job satisfaction is shown in Figure 2.5.

As retirement age lengthens and the work force ages, the individual's relationship with his job changes. People are in general healthier and live longer. Many individuals may be able to avoid the negative effects of retirement through innovative company programs (e.g., job sharing in which two people each work part-time at the same job) or serial careers (phasing out of formal work and into volunteer or service activities). Important changes will continue to occur because by the year 2010 there will be more people over 60 years of age than under 30 in the United States.

Expectations. Everyone develops expectations about future jobs. As students search for a job after graduation, their expectations about work are influenced heavily by the recruiting process. The expectations formed during these early encounters remain intact until individuals be-

Figure 2.5
Relationships between Years in the Job and Job Satisfaction

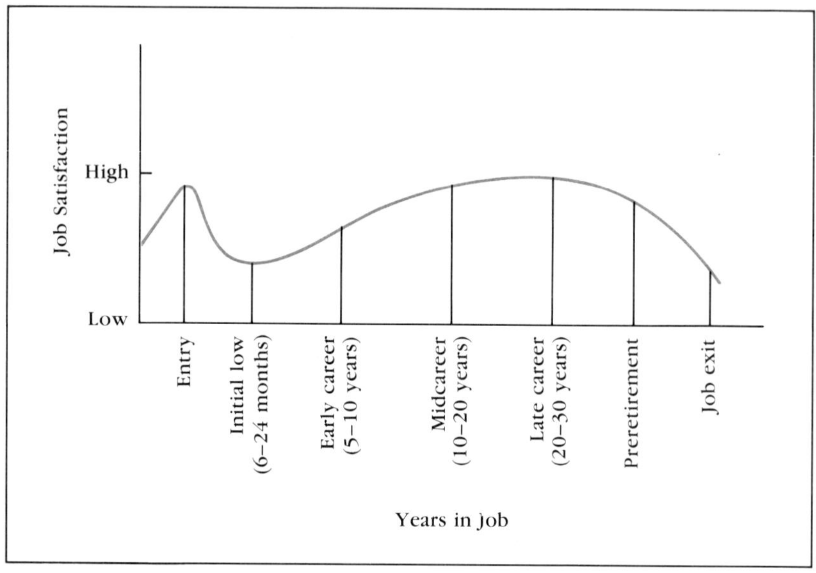

gin to participate in organizations. If prework expectations are met, satisfaction occurs. If they are not met, the individual experiences a decline in job satisfaction.

The initial job satisfaction low, which occurs 6 to 24 months into the job, is a subject of management concern (21). Large numbers of employees leaving their job at the same time can be a costly problem for an organization. Some companies try to lessen the decline in job satisfaction during the early career stage by using realistic job previews. The goal of these previews is to present both the desirable and undesirable features of the job and of the organization (22, 23). Potential employees whose expectations are not in line with the job then drop out during the recruiting process, which causes much less damage to the potential employee and to the organization. Here are some results of job preview programs.

1. Prudential Life agents: 71 percent of previewed employees stayed over six months, but only 57 percent of those without previews stayed over six months.
2. First year cadets at West Point: 91 percent of those previewed stayed more than a year, but only 86 percent of those not previewed stayed beyond a year.
3. Manhattan Industries: 89 percent of previewed sewing machine operators stayed over six weeks, but only 69 percent of those not previewed stayed beyond six weeks.

What are the organizational determinants of job satisfaction?

Several organizational determinants have a major effect on job satisfaction?

Supervision. In general, considerate supervision often leads to job satisfaction. If supervisors consult with subordinates on decisions or policies (i.e., allow some employee participation), employees are generally more satisfied. The employee participation has to be meaningful, however. Allowing employees to choose wall color or to select the site for the annual company picnic does not improve satisfaction. Participation has to occur on work matters of importance, that is, matters of product or service quality.

Job Challenge. When jobs require creativity, application of personal skills, and need to take risks, employees report higher levels of job satisfaction. Workers appear to be more satisfied when their job makes demands that require an expenditure of intellectual and physical effort. When employees are challenged, they become more committed to their work and more involved in what they are doing. Job challenge does not, however, ensure satisfaction, for all employees desire these qualities in their work.

Job Clarity. The extent to which employees understand what they are to do contributes to job satisfaction. When employees receive feedback on their performance, so they know where they stand, they experience more job satisfaction. Giving employees timely and accurate information about their performance increases their efforts on the job. If their efforts lead to better performance and subsequent rewards, job satisfaction increases.

Incentives. Extrinsic and intrinsic rewards are related to job satisfaction. **Extrinsic rewards** are those that the organization provides based on employee performance and effort. Examples of extrinsic rewards are pay raises, promotions, supervisor praise, job status symbols, and job security. **Intrinsic rewards** are those that the employee experiences internally. For example, feelings of competence, pride, and craftmanship are intrinsic rewards of a job well done. They occur as the employee's work unfolds. Since these rewards affect how the employee feels about himself, they can be very powerful for maintaining motivation and performance.

Employee job satisfaction levels are related to intrinsic rewards. Consider Phil in the opening dilemma. As Tom began to take over Phil's job (control of operations and supervision of the crews), Phil experienced a loss of intrinsic rewards. He had less responsibility and control over his job. He in turn experienced frustration as Tom meddled more and more in his work, and his job satisfaction decreased so much that he eventually quit. This example points out the connection between job dissatisfaction and turnover. Job satisfaction is also a predictor of unexcused absences. Let's consider some of the consequences of job satisfaction and dissatisfaction.

What are the key consequences of job satisfaction?

Increased physical and mental employee health. Both mental and physical health increase with job satisfaction. When employees are satisfied with their job, they report fewer ailments (heart disease, headache, sleep disturbance, stomach disorder). Less anxiety, tension, and stress occur among satisfied workers. Job satisfaction thus improves employee resistance to both mental and physical problems. In fact, some reports suggest that satisfied employees live longer; happier workers do indeed seem to be healthier workers.

Lower employee turnover and unexcused absences. Countless research studies have found dependable relationships between turnover and unexcused absences. Job previews were described as one technique to eliminate applicants who might quit or not come to work because of job dissatisfaction. When rates of turnover and absenteeism are high in an organization, indirect labor costs rise rapidly. High turnover causes more recruiting and subsequent hiring and training costs (all indirect costs), which go up since the organization is always processing new members. A high absenteeism rate also drives up indirect costs because the organization must keep more employees on reserve to fill in for those who do not show up for work. If an organization does not maintain a reserve, then more work must be distributed among fewer workers, which in turn creates more job dissatisfaction.

Job Satisfaction and Performance

Disagreement currently exists about the nature of the relationship between job satisfaction and performance. Three views are prevalent. (1) satisfaction causes performance, (2) performance causes satisfaction, (3) intrinsic and extrinsic rewards govern the performance-satisfaction relationship (24, 25).

Theories one and two have received weaker support. We can all recall employees who were satisfied with their work yet performed poorly. Likewise, someone may be extremely productive yet dissatisfied with all aspects of the job. On practical grounds, both theories could therefore be rejected. These two theories do not meet the criteria, advanced in Chapter 1, for useful theories.

The third theory is more realistic (and appealing) because it better explains the relationship between performance and job satisfaction. Figure 2.6 details the theory that currently has the most support (26).

The new concept in the model is **perceived equity,** which refers to the comparison an employee makes between rewards received and effort expended. This is called a "social comparison" because all people evaluate what happens to them relative to what is happening to other people around them. To make the comparison, an individual must select a comparison other. The **comparison other** may be an individual, all of the individuals in a group (or profession), or all of the individuals in similar organizations. If the individual is considering the fairness of his pay raise, the social comparison would look like this:

$$\frac{\text{My raise}}{\text{My efforts}} : \frac{\text{His raise}}{\text{His efforts}}$$

If results of the comparison seem fair, the individual is satisfied with the raise and experiences perceived equity. If, on the other hand, the individual judges the other person's reward to be greater than his own, a perceived inequity occurs. Perceived inequity represents a state of psychological imbalance. The only ways for the individual to restore psychological balance are to: (1) reduce level of effort, (2) change the comparison other (find

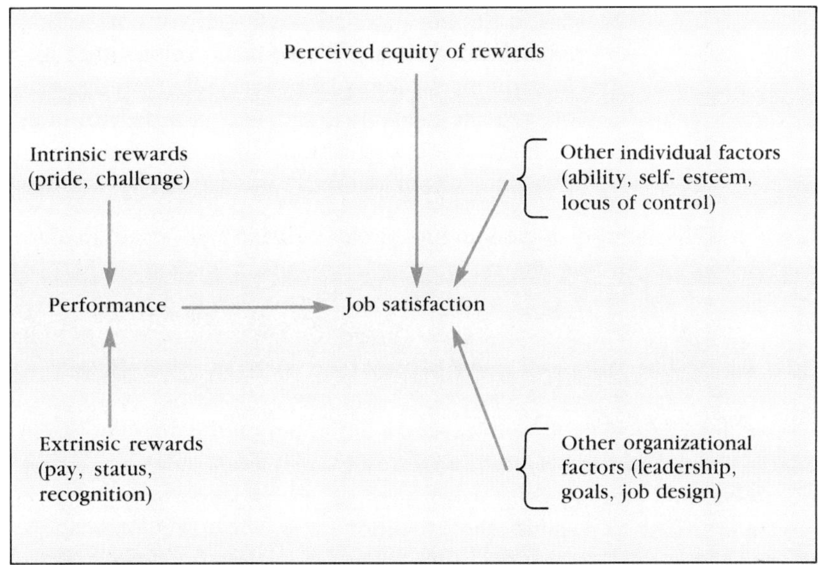

Figure 2.6 *The Job Satisfaction—Job Performance Relationship*

someone more suitable to compare with), (3) increase level of effort (to get more rewards), or (4) exit the situation entirely (quit the job).

Applying the reasoning of the model. Figure 2.6 indicates that satisfactory performance leads to rewards. Extrinsic rewards are available through the organization compensation system, while intrinsic rewards are based on the way in which the task is designed (e.g., level of challenge, variety of skills necessary, opportunity to use skills). If the pay system rewards the wrong employee, her colleague's perceptions of fairness will be adversely affected. To the extent that the equity comparisons are out of balance, employees will experience job dissatisfaction. Remember that *both* the compensation (reward) system and the job design system must function properly to ensure perceived equity.

A direct relationship does not exist between performance and job satisfaction. It is the equitable rewards that tie the two together. Consider the dilemma again. Phil decides to come back to work for Tom when he believes that he will get full job control plus a chance to share in company profits. In these new circumstances, he is convinced that his efforts will be more appropriately matched by his rewards. When Tom promises to stay out of operations, this reestablishes equity for Phil because his opportunities for intrinsic rewards are restored. All in all, he experiences more positive than negative feelings about his old job as he goes back to work for Tom. The chances that he can restore his job satisfaction pull Phil back to Anderson Grading. The perceived equity of rewards played a crucial role in his decision to return.

Individual differences influence job satisfaction. For example, the employee with a strong internal locus of control would experience more job dissatisfaction (through perceived inequity) if he believed the job offered little challenge and if his performance were not fairly compensated (ineffective reward system). The anxious employee would experience higher levels of job satisfaction if she perceived her supervisor to be considerate and sensitive to her inner feelings. (Supervision belongs in the "other organizational factors" box.) We could develop other examples of individual and organizational factors that determine job satisfaction levels. The point is this: Do not conclude that only performance and perceived equity influence the level of job satisfaction. Employee characteristics also interact with the work situation to influence job satisfaction level.

Solving the Dilemma

Do specific theories exist to help us understand Tom and Phil's behavior?

Our discussion sheds light on the relationship between performance and rewards. Tom and Phil have different attitudes about the increased repair costs and missed contract deadlines. The processes by which both men come to experience perceived inequity and lower job satisfaction are exactly the same. Tom perceives inequity and lower job satisfaction because his financial security as company owner is threatened by rising costs and missed deadlines. Phil perceives inequity and lower job satisfaction because Tom gradually reduces the scope of Phil's authority and responsibility for operations. Phil's job satisfaction drops rapidly and he quits because of an extreme perceived inequity. When Tom approaches Phil about returning to the company, Phil becomes convinced that perceived equity can be restored. He again believes that his levels of intrinsic and extrinsic rewards will match his levels of effort and performance on the job. Phil's perceived equity may not last too long, however, because Tom begins to meddle again!

How Organizations Measure Job Satisfaction

Job satisfaction is an important indicator of an organization's ability to meet the needs of its employees. For this reason, many methods have been developed to measure employee job satisfaction level. All of these methods are necessarily indirect, because job satisfaction can only be inferred; it is both intangible and personal. The methods include: (1) observation of employee behavior, (2) interviewing employees, and (3) paper and pencil tests of employee satisfaction. The least expensive and most dependable method is the paper and pencil test.

Figure 2.7 shows some sample items from the **Job Descriptive Index (JDI)**, which is the most widely used measure of job satisfaction (27). The employee responds to the questionnaire by indicating whether or not the adjectives apply to her job. The adjectives are organized into five categories. Each category covers one facet of job satisfaction noted earlier in the chapter. The JDI evaluates the cognitive component of job satisfaction. Its use of positive and negative adjectives provides balance and allows the user to avoid problems associated with other measures. The adjectives selected for the questionnaire enable the instrument to be used in any work situation and with any employee group.

Another tool that measures job satisfaction is the **Minnesota Satisfaction Questionnaire** (28). This questionnaire uses a different method to generate answers. Figure 2.8 shows some sample questions from this instrument. The format facilitates assessment of partial agreement with the various aspects of job satisfaction. Although this method takes longer than the JDI, it yields very dependable results.

Figure 2.7
Scale from the Job Descriptive Index

The instructions for each scale ask the subject to put "Y" beside an item if the item described the particular aspect of his/her job (e.g., work, pay, etc.), "N" if the item did not describe that aspect or "?" if he/she could not decide.

The response shown beside each item is the one scored in the "satisfied" direction for each scale.

Work	Work
Y Fascinating	Y Useful
N Routine	N Tiresome
Y Satisfying	Y Healthful
N Boring	Y Challenging
Y Good	N On your feet
Y Creative	N Frustrating
Y Respected	N Simple
N Hot	N Endless
Y Pleasant	Y Gives sense of accomplishment

SOURCE: Patricia Cain Smith, Lorne M. Kendall, and Charles L. Hulin. *The Measurement of Satisfaction in Work and Retirement.* (Chicago: Rand McNally and Company, 1969). Copyright © 1975. Bowling Green State University. Researchers wishing to use these scales in their own work are asked to purchase the scales from Bowling Green State University, Department of Psychology. Bowling Green, Ohio 43403.

Figure 2.8
Excerpt from the Minnesota Satisfaction Questionnaire

	Not Satisfied	Slightly Satisfied	Satisfied	Very Satisfied	Extremely Satisfied
My job security	1	2	3	4	5
The amount of pay for the work I do	1	2	3	4	5
The working conditions (heating, lighting, ventilation, etc.) on this job	1	2	3	4	5
The opportunities for advancement on this job	1	2	3	4	5
The technical "know-how" of my supervisor	1	2	3	4	5

SOURCE: D.J. Weiss, R.V. Davis, G.W. England, and L.H. Lofquist (1967). *Manual for the Minnesota Satisfaction Questionnaire* (Minnesota Studies in Vocational Rehabilitation No. 22). Minneapolis, MN: University of Minnesota Industrial Relations Center, Work Adjustment Project. Reproduced by permission. Copyright 1977 by Vocational Psychology Research, University of Minnesota.

Problems with using questionnaires. The use of questionnaires assumes that employees are both willing and capable of describing their feelings about work accurately, without distortion. We know that people often distort information for a variety of reasons. For example, a group of employees may decide to rate themselves as having low job satisfaction with supervision because they want to have their current boss replaced.

A second problem with such instruments is that the items do not have the same meaning for all employees. What is fascinating to you may seem dull and monotonous to someone else (see the JDI scale). Since these words can have different meanings to different people, the survey results can be biased in both systematic and unsystematic ways. These problems introduce systematic bias into the results of written surveys measuring job satisfaction.

Knowledge Check

1. Job satisfaction is composed of many facets. T or F?
2. Research indicates that all occupational groups are experiencing more job satisfaction. T or F?
3. One way to reduce potential job dissatisfaction for new employees is to use ____________ before the actual hiring.
4. Job satisfaction is less sensitive to intrinsic rewards than to extrinsic rewards. T or F?
5. Job satisfaction is important to organizations because it is a predictor of absenteeism and turnover. T or F?
6. Equity comparisons of rewards received in relation to efforts expended are important components of the job satisfaction-performance relationship. T or F?
7. Direct observation of employees is the most widely used method for assessing job satisfaction. T or F?
8. Paper and pencil tests to measure employee job satisfaction generally avoid the problem of employees' distorting their test answers. T or F?

Answers:

1 T, 2 F, 3 job previews, 4 F, 5 T, 6 T, 7 F, 8 F

Developments in the Study of Employee Work Attitudes

Job satisfaction is an important employee work attitude. We have shown that it relates to turnover, absenteeism, physical and emotional health, and job performance (through the moderating effects of rewards). During the past decade, other employee attitudes have been studied. In this section, we consider two of these: (1) organizational commitment, and (2) job involvement.

Organizational Commitment and Its Consequences

Organizational commitment is the strength of an employee's identification with the organization (29). Porter and his associates identify three components: (1) belief in and acceptance of the organization goals and values, (2) willingness to exert considerable effort on behalf of the organization, and (3) desire to maintain membership in the organization. (30).

Organizational commitment is more than loyalty to an employer (31). It means that the employee actively promotes the organization to colleagues, customers, or critics. The employee also shows willingness to give something of himself to the organization. When employees defend their employer and actively promote the organization goals, they are strengthening their organizational commitment. Fred Jensen, the employee described below, demonstrates organizational commitment. See if you can find examples of the components of organizational commitment in Fred's story.

> Fred Jensen is unusual in this age of job hopping and blue collar blues. Fred is 77 years old; he admits proudly that he's a company man and always will be one.
>
> When Fred—known as FJ to his friends—left his job as a machinist at Gibson Tools in 1986, he retired from the only employer he had ever known. He left behind a group of employees that he called a family.
>
> "I feel bad, I really do," said FJ as he punched the time clock for the last time. "I'm just not a spring chicken anymore."
>
> The former machinist, who has spent the better part of his life working at a jig-making machine—a device used to make patterns that are copied to manufacture machine tools—recalls his work life with fondness and nostalgia. Now his voice has a tinge of sadness as he comments that he entered the ranks of the retired.
>
> "I've loved my work, the company, and the people I've worked with over the years. I won't have any use for my machine tools now, so I guess I'll give them to the guys at work." FJ planned to return to work that same day to distribute his personal machinist tools among his work companions. He looked forward to visiting the tool shop, but contemplating the trip was also hard for him after 60 years of working at the same shop.
>
> "I just never wanted to take time off. Many's the time I'd show up at work with a fever or an upset stomach." FJ doesn't say it in so many words, but clearly he felt comfortable projecting the "company man" image. This company man would get out of bed at 4 A.M. to go to work and open up the tool shop. "Sometimes, just for the fun of it, I'd get up extra early to be the first one there. I guess that after a while I got the reputation around the shop of being an early bird." He opened the shop every day at 6 A.M., a full hour before most other employees reported to work.

> FJ lives about 2 miles from the machine shop. He has no plans for his future other than taking life as it comes, working in his garden, and visiting his two sons in Arizona.
>
> "I retired because I figured I didn't have that many more years left; I was getting to that age. I want to spend more time with my wife. We like to eat out and go places together."
>
> FJ admits that he's having trouble adjusting to a life of leisure. He's not too keen on sleeping late, and he misses the trip to work. "I guess I just got used to the sound of the time clock when I punched in and out," he muses. He confesses that he misses the weekday work schedule and that he's a little lonely after six decades at the same shop.
>
> "I just ate up my work and loved the people I worked with. My job was never a burden. I loved what I did, and always felt good about it. There's no question about it, I enjoyed going to work in the morning."
>
> FJ quickly notes that if he decides that retirement is not for him, the Gibson officials have said he can return to work at any time. "They said I could pick up where I left off—no problem. It makes a fella feel needed," FJ added.

Commitment to the organization is different from job satisfaction (32). First, commitment requires a wider perspective (toward the entire organization), while job satisfaction is organized around employee reactions to their job. Job satisfaction also fluctuates over the short term depending on the immediate conditions associated with the job (e.g., getting a new supervisor or learning about a pay raise). In contrast, commitment develops slowly and consistently over time, thus an employee may be satisfied with her job but may not be committed to the organization. This explains in part why employees change employers even when they may have been satisfied with the previous position. As employees progress within the organization, their organizational commitment increases. People who regularly change employers never acquire much organizational commitment.

What can organizations do to build employee commitment?

Organizations can act to raise levels of employee commitment. Let's look at an organizational innovation that raises commitment. Many organizations have established **quality circles** to help solve production quality problems (33). A quality circle is composed of a group of employees and their supervisor, who meet voluntarily to work on problems with product and service quality and efficiency. The circle operates on company time, and the quality circles present their ideas to management committees, who make implementation decisions.

Quality circles depend on voluntary employee participation. Without some initial organizational commitment, the circles would not work. The concept is expanding rapidly among corporations. Honeywell, for example, has 350 circles with 4,000 employees. Martin Marietta Corporation uses quality circles in construction of components for the space shuttle. The phenomenon is expanding because of a growing realization in the business community of the value of organizational commitment among employees.

What are the outcomes of organizational commitment?

Committed employees are less likely to quit their jobs. Organizational commitment correlates with employee turnover. Once employees identify with the goals and values of the organization, they are less likely to quit, even when they go through periods of lower job satisfaction. Organizational facilitation of employee commitment is sensible, for committed employees are more likely to accept pay cuts or transfers (both of which can lower job satisfaction) without quitting.

Employees with organizational commitment may be better performers. Since committed individuals generally expend more effort on the job, commitment results in greater productivity. Committed employees are often willing to set more ambitious goals when they participate in the goal setting. You can imagine that a group of highly committed salesmen would be willing to raise their sales goals even were they not going to realize bigger commissions.

Committed employees may experience more job involvement (34). As employees become more committed, they generally express it through their work. Note, however, that an employee may identify strongly with the goals of the employer, yet feel uninvolved with the job. Consider, Phil (in the dilemma), who might be very committed to the goals of his new employer, yet might perform his job with little zest because he misses Tom.

Solving the Dilemma

How can organizational commitment be used to understand Phil's behavior?

Phil's commitment to the Anderson Grading Company fits our definition of organizational commitment. He has a strong belief in and acceptance of the company goals. He accepts the company values as his own. If he failed at a company task, he would feel worse about himself, and he is willing to expend considerable effort on behalf of the company. He does this both for the company and for his friend Tom. As to the third aspect of commitment, however, we see that Phil does not fit the definition. He does not have a strong desire to maintain membership. He quits and then returns to the firm. After he returns, it is apparent that his level of organizational commitment is not what it used to be. He is quickly disillusioned by a single visit by Tom to the job site.

Job Involvement and Its Consequences

Job involvement is an important work attitude, and is defined as the degree to which employees identify with their job, participate actively in the job, and consider the job to be a key determinant of self-worth (35). Job involvement develops from the characteristics of the job.

Job involvement triggers different employee reactions from those triggered by organizational commitment. It activates beliefs that the job is a central component of one's life. Involved employees are likely to view work as a major source of life satisfaction. Active job participation refers to an employee's desire to be physically and psychologically involved in work.

For students, this component includes always being in class and finding numerous intrinsic rewards associated with doing homework for a given course. This component would probably activate classroom participation, assuming that the student is not too shy. The final component of job involvement is the job's contribution to one's self-worth. If an employee experiences increased self-worth through her work, numerous consequences can occur. For instance, if this were true for you, and if you were approached by someone who asked you what you're like, you would have a strong tendency to respond in work-related terms. Indeed, many of us who experience job involvement, describe ourselves in terms of what we do at work.

Job involvement may not be an accurate predictor of employee performance or job satisfaction (36). Certainly an employee can be uninvolved with work yet be a good performer. Likewise, an employee may be very involved with what he does for a living, yet be dissatisfied with his job. Since your own attitudes and behaviors are the best way for you to test these observations, see if you can generate your own examples of these two possibilities.

How can managers inspire organizational commitment and job involvement?

Remember that these two work attitudes form differently and refer to different entities (i.e., organizations versus jobs). There are, however, ways in which managers can encourage development of both. Let's examine briefly some of the actions that managers can take.

1. Managers should demonstrate that they honestly care about their employees' welfare. Often, managers are too busy to demonstrate much concern for employee welfare beyond creating safe working conditions. Many firms do go further to establish employee counseling programs, health and fitness programs, and career management programs. The expenditure of organization resources on such programs clearly puts "the company's money where its mouth is."
2. Create opportunities for employees to achieve their personal goals. If an employee has a desire to take on more responsibility, perhaps to increase her chance for promotion, the able supervisor does not feel threatened. Instead, he should work with the employee to identify how she can expand the job to take on more meaningful and challenging work.
3. Modify jobs so employees have more opportunity to achieve intrinsic rewards. Many employees feel the need to have more personal control over their jobs. An effective manager provides opportunities for employees to participate in decision making (e.g., quality circles) to help fill employees' needs for personal control over work.
4. Find ways to reward employees regularly. If supervisors are unavailable when employees encounter task problems, then organizational commitment and job involvement are less likely to form. If the supervisors only show up when something goes wrong, employees tend to associate their presence with punishment and criticism. The more effective alternative is to manage by walking around and reinforcing employees as they take the right actions.
5. Set goals with employees. This is a specific application of employee participation. Not only should managers explain why goals are impor-

tant, but employees should be involved in the goal-setting process. This does not mean that managers yield their control to employees. What it does mean is that, within intelligent guidelines, employees are given the opportunity to help define targets that they would like to pursue in their jobs.

Knowledge Check

1. Organizational commitment consists of three components. T or F?
2. Organizational commitment is generally the same thing as company loyalty. T or F?
3. Job satisfaction and organizational commitment form around the same attitude objects over similar periods of time. T or F?
4. Job involvement is always present when an employee is satisfied with his or her job. T or F?
5. A less important dimension of job involvement is the belief that the job contributes to one's self-worth. T or F?

Answers:

1 T, 2 F, 3 F, 4 F, 5 F

Summary Points

■ **Locus of control** refers to one's beliefs about what causes outcomes in life. **Internals** believe in the causality of personal behavior, while **externals** believe in the causality of environmental forces. Internals thus see themselves as the cause of outcomes, while externals assign the cause of outcomes to forces outside themselves.

■ **Extraversion** and **introversion** refer to the strength of one's need for external sensory stimulation. **Introverts** prefer less external "social noise" than **extraverts.** These qualities can influence performance markedly if a job is designed to be either high or low in social stimulation.

■ **Machiavellianism** is the need to influence others to achieve one's personal ends. It predisposes the individual to seek political solutions to organizational issues.

■ Three components make up attitudes: (1) **affective,** (2) **cognitive,** and (3) **behavioral.** These attitude components can be used to analyze employee work behaviors.

■ Attitude formation is governed by **personal experience, association,** and **social learning.** Association and social learning do not require direct experience with the attitude object. Attitudes can be formed by indirect means.

■ Attitudes do not always generate behavior. The reasons for this are that (1) the behavior may be socially inappropriate, (2) the importance of an attitude toward a situation may override an opposing attitude toward an object embedded in the situation, and (3) the attitude may have underdeveloped affective and behavioral components.

■ **Job satisfaction** is composed of **facets,** which can vary and change quickly. In general, job satisfaction has been on the rise for 30 years.

■ Organizational factors that influence job satisfaction are **supervision, job challenge, job clarity, and abundance and availability of incentives.**

■ Job satisfaction is not directly related to job performance. The connection is moderated by the availability of both intrinsic and extrinsic rewards, and by the perceived fairness of the way in which rewards are allocated (**perceived equity**).

■ **Organizational commitment** represents employee agreement with organizational goals, willingness to exert effort on behalf of the organization, and a strong desire to maintain organization membership. It takes longer to form than job satisfaction, but once formed, it is more resistant to change.

■ **Job involvement** develops through one's job and affects the employee self-worth and desire to participate. Employees can have job involvement without being committed to the organization.

■ **Management can take a number of specific actions to encourage employee commitment and involvement.** These actions include improving employee welfare by creating opportunities to achieve personal goals at work, improving employee job understanding, and facilitating participation in goal setting.

Questions

1. What kinds of problems would a supervisor confront if all of her subordinates had an external locus of control? Are there steps a supervisor can take to influence employee beliefs about the causality of work outcomes?
2. If the head of a department had a strong Machiavellian personality, what sort of work climate would you expect to develop? Be sure to comment on the following features: (a) nature of supervision, (b) nature of worker trust and support, (c) degree of emphasis on performance, (d) availability of rewards for performance, and (e) job clarity.
3. Think about your attitude toward accounting. Break this attitude into its three components. Compare your attitude components with those of a classmate. Discuss the reasons for the differences between your two attitudes. Be sure to note how your attitude toward accounting formed.
4. With the assistance of several classmates, design a questionnaire to measure job satisfaction. What aspects of job satisfaction would you include? How would you ensure that employees find the items meaningful, that is, applicable to their job?
5. Develop an account of the current thinking about the relationship between performance and job satisfaction. If a supervisor believes that "happy employees are productive employees," what kinds of problems might he encounter? Be sure to emphasize the role of rewards in your answer.
6. Describe a situation in which you felt as if you had no control over what was happening (try to think of a school-related example). List three actions that you might have taken to influence the situation.
7. Find an old friend who has graduated recently and taken a job. Ask that individual how realistic her or his expectations about the new job were. Did this person experience the job dissatisfaction that usually occurs about six months after taking a new job? Did the organization try to help their new employee form realistic job expectations?
8. You are an expert in the design of college courses and majors. A marketing instructor has approached you about his course. He tells you that the students in his class are uninvolved with the subject. What advice would you give him that might help raise the level of student involvement in the course?

EXPLORING: *Is Organizational Commitment on the Decline?*

Adapted from: Job Loyalty, Not the Virtue It Seems, *New York Times,* 3 March 1985.

Experts at Rohrer, Hibler & Replogle were called in to help a bank president choose a successor. The experts asked the president to select ten candidates who should be interviewed as possible successors. All ten had worked for the bank for at least ten years and were staunchly loyal to the organization. The president could not in good conscience promote any of them, so he retired in despair and his successor was selected from outside the bank. Within a year, the new boss had fired seven of the top ten executives. He was quoted as saying, "Sure, they had a lot of loyalty but none of the skills we need to compete."

This example shows how organizational commitment can be highly overrated. Increasingly, the loyal employee who follows orders blindly year after year is being labeled as dull, dependent, and a drag on organizational dynamism. Rosabeth Moss Kanter, professor of organizational management at the Yale Graduate School of Management, states that "The sleepy solid citizen who stays with the company for 30 years isn't loyal. He is simply viewed as having nowhere else to go."

John Teets, president of Greyhound Corporation, says, "I want spirited managers who will challenge the system. I don't want lukewarm employees. They breed mediocrity and a womb-to-tomb attitude."

Today's executives are very aware of increasing domestic and foreign competition. The last recession, the increasing number of takeovers, and the drive to cut costs have claimed 450,000 management jobs since 1979 (Bureau of Labor Statistics). As a result, companies have trimmed their staffs to such an extent that many employees no longer believe that their company will return employee loyalty in hard times. Experts warn that, just as loyalty begets loyalty, perceived betrayal begets cynicism and a focus on self-interest. A new breed of "disloyal employees" may be developing. Employees who feel betrayed by the company often acquire a once-burned-twice-shy attitude about their next employer. Corporate loyalty is being replaced by loyalty to family and friends.

Discussion Questions

1. Do you think that a company could have a "no layoff" policy and also have productive and creative employees?

2. Can employees be loyal to their superiors without being loyal to the employing organization?

APPLYING: *Measuring Job Involvement at Work*

This brief exercise is designed for a group of five students. The exercise goals are as follows:

1. Find five employees from the same organization who will fill out the job involvement survey (see Figure 2.9) contained in this exercise.
2. Record both the interview and questionnaire information.
3. Prepare a brief report on the results of the team project.

In this chapter we indicate that job involvement is an important work attitude. Involvement develops as employees gain more experience with their job. Your interviewing of employees from a local firm should make this concept more meaningful. Your instructor will then organize the class into teams of five and assist you in finding an organization that will cooperate with your team. You will then administer a questionnaire to assess employee job involvement.

Next, divide your team into two groups and interview five employees in your assigned firm. The interviews should last approximately 30 minutes each. Include the following interview questions.

1. What is your job title?

2. How long have you worked at this job?
3. What are the five key responsibilities that you have in your job?
4. What are the three aspects of your job that you like best?
5. What are two actions the company could take to make you more effective at your job?
6. If you could change your job in two ways, what would they be?

Your team will get the most information from the interview if you have the questions written out in advance. Use one sheet of paper for each employee.

The questionnaire that you should use is presented in Figure 2.9. Each employee circles an answer for each of the 12 items. Try to get ten employees to complete the questionnaire.

When your team has completed its interviews and has gathered the questionnaire data, your instructor will tell you how to analyze the results. Once your team has completed that activity, answer the following questions and prepare a brief written report. Be prepared to explain your results to the class.

Questions to Be Answered in the Team Report

1. What are the major job responsibilities of those employees interviewed?
2. How closely do the features that employees like about their jobs resemble their major job responsibilities?
3. Are the employee suggestions of ways to improve their personal effectiveness related to their job responsibilities?
4. Do the employees generally want to change their jobs relative to their major job responsibilities?
5. Do employees from the two levels surveyed perceive job involvement in the same way?
6. Do the job involvement scores for your company parallel the answers obtained in your interviews?

Figure 2.9 *Job involvement questionnaire*

INSTRUCTIONS: PLEASE CIRCLE THE CHOICE WHICH MOST CLOSELY MATCHES YOUR OPINION FOR EACH ITEM.

	STRONGLY AGREE	AGREE	DISAGREE	STRONGLY DISAGREE
1. Staying late to finish a job doesn't bother me.	1	2	3	4
2. You can tell a lot about a person by his work.	1	2	3	4
3. I get most of my satisfaction from my work.	1	2	3	4
4. My days at work really fly by.	1	2	3	4
5. I always arrive at work a little early to get things arranged.	1	2	3	4
6. The most important things that happen to me are related to work.	1	2	3	4
7. Sometimes I lie awake at night thinking ahead about work for tomorrow.	1	2	3	4

	STRONGLY AGREE	AGREE	DISAGREE	STRONGLY DISAGREE
8. I'm a work perfectionist.	1	2	3	4
9. I feel lousy when I fail at some part of my job.	1	2	3	4
10. I must admit that I am a real "workaholic."	1	2	3	4
11. I would keep on working even if I didn't need the money.	1	2	3	4
12. I get deeply involved in my work.	1	2	3	4
TOTALS	_____	_____	_____	_____
		GRAND TOTAL		_____

Suggested Readings

Bem D. J. 1982. Attitudes, Beliefs, and Human Affairs, 2nd ed. Belmont, Calif.: Brooks-Cole.

Block, J. 1981. Some Enduring and Consequential Structures of Personality. In *Further Explorations in Personality,* A. I. Rabin, et al., (eds.). New York: John Wiley and Sons.

This useful book covers many individual differences in much greater depth. The interested reader will find this volume to be informative about the work of psychologists and social psychologists in the areas of individual differences and personality.

Bowers, D. G. 1983. What Would Make 11,500 People Quit Their Jobs? *Organizational Dynamics.* Winter 1983:5–19.

Davis, S., and Gould, R. 1981. Three Vice Presidents in Mid-Life. *Harvard Business Review,* July-August 1981:118–130

Hatvany, N., and Pucik, V. 1981. Japanese Management Practices and Productivity. *Organizational Dynamics.* Spring 1981:5–21.

Herrman, N. 1981. The Creative Brain. *Training and Development Journal.* October 1935:10–16.

Rubin, A. 1981. Does Personality Really Change After 20? *Psychology Today.* 1981:18–27.

This lively article considers the current debate over whether or not aspects of personality can change as we grow older. The author takes a complex issue and makes it easy to follow.

Stumpf, S. 1981. Career Roles, Psychological Success and Job Attitudes. *Journal of Vocational Behavior.* 1981:98–112.

References

1. Kelley, H. 1971. *Attribution in Social Interaction.* Morristown, N.J.: General Learning Press.

2. Lorad, R., and Smith, J. 1983. Theoretical Information Processing and Situational Factors Affecting

Attribution Theory Models of Organizational Behavior. *Academy of Management Review* 8:50–60.
3. Foti, R., Fraser, J., and Lord, R. 1982. The Effects of Leadership Labels and Prototypes on Perceptions of Political Leaders. *Journal of Applied Psychology* 67:326–333.
4. Rotter, J. 1966. Generalized Expectancies for Internal vs. External Control of Reinforcement. *Psychological Monographs* 80:1–23.
5. Ibid.
6. Watson, D., and Baumol, E. 1967. Effects of Locus of Control and Expectation of Future Control Upon Present Performance. *Journal of Personality and Social Psychology* 6:212–215.
7. Organ, D., and Hammer, C. 1982. *Organizational Behavior,* 2nd ed. Plano, Tex.: Business Publications.
8. Gartner, W. 1985. A Conceptual Framework for Describing the Phenomenon of New Venture Creation. *Academy of Management Review* 10:696–706.
9. Brockhaus, P. 1982. The Psychology of the Entrepreneur. In C. A. Kent, D. L. Sexton, and K. H. Vespers (Eds.). *Encyclopedia of Entrepreneurship.* Englewood Cliffs, N.J.: Prentice Hall, pp. 39–56.
10. Eysenck, H. 1967. *The Biological Basis of Personality.* Springfield, Ill.: Charles C Thomas.
11. Ibid.
12. Ibid.
13. Ibid.
14. Cooper, R., and Payne, R. 1967. Extroversion and Some Aspects of Work Behavior. *Personnel Psychology* 20:45–67.
15. Christie, R., and Geis, F. 1970. *Studies in Machiavellianism.* New York: Academic Press.
16. Ibid.
17. Kets De Vries, M., and Miller, D. 1986. Personality, Culture and Organization. *Academy of Management Review* 11:266–279.
18. Mann, L. 1969. *Social Psychology.* New York: John Wiley & Sons.
19. Ibid.
20. Smith, D., Kendall, L., and Hulin, C. 1975. *The Measurement of Satisfaction in Work and Retirement.* Chicago: Rand McNally.
21. Sheridan, J. 1985. A Catastrophe Model of Employee Withdrawal Leading to Low Job Performance, High Absenteeism and Job Turnover During the First Year of Employment. *Academy of Management Journal* 28:88–109.
22. Wanous, J. 1977. Organizational Entry: The Individual's Viewpoint. In J. R. Hackman, E. E. Lawler, III, and L. W. Porter (Eds.). *Perspectives on Behavior in Organizations.* New York: McGraw-Hill, pp. 126–135.
23. Wanous, J. 1980. *Organizational Entry: Recruitment, Selection and Socialization of Newcomers.* Reading, Mass.: Addison-Wesley.
24. Petty, M., McGee, G., and Cavender, J. 1984. A Meta-Analysis of the Relationships Between Individual Job Satisfaction and Individual Performance. *Academy of Management Review* 9:712–721.
25. Porter, L., and Lawler, E., III. 1968. *Managerial Attitudes and Performance.* Homewood, Ill.: Richard D. Irwin Publishing Company.
26. Ibid.
27. Smith, D., et al., op. cit.
28. Loquist, L., and Davis, R. 1975. *Adjustment to Work: A Psychological View of Man's Problems in a Work-Oriented Society.* Chicago: Rand McNally.
29. Porter. L., Steers, R., Mowday, R., and Boulian, P. 1974. Organizational Commitment, Job Satisfaction and Turnover Among Psychiatric Technicians. *Journal of Applied Psychology* 59:603–609.
30. Ibid.
31. Steers, R. 1981. *Introduction to Organizational Behavior.* Glenview, Ill.: Scott-Foresman.
32. Ibid.
33. Yager, E. 1980. Quality Circles: A Tool for the 1980's. *Training and Development Journal* 34:60–62.
34. Steers, R., op. cit.
35. Rabinowitz, S., and Hall, D. 1977. Organizational Research on Job Involvement. *Psychological Bulletin* 31:265–288.
36. Reichers, A. 1985. A Review and Reconceptualization of Organizational Commitment. *Academy of Management Review* 10:465–476.

The Nature of Motivation: What Energizes People at Work

Chapter **3**

I. Dilemma: Jason Beats the Odds
II. A Question of Needs: Maslow's Hierarchy
  A. Implications of the need hierarchy
  B. Applying the need hierarchy
III. The Two Factor Theory of Motivation
  A. Comparing Maslow and Herzberg's models
IV. Acquired Need Theories of Motivation
  A. Need for achievement
  B. Need for affiliation
  C. Need for power
V. A Process Theory of Motivation: Expectancy Theory
  A. Understanding the basics of expectancy theory
  B. Applying expectancy theory
VI. Extending Expectancy Theory to the Individual and the Organization
  A. Individual differences have motivation effects
  B. Organizational factors and motivation
VII. Summary Points
VIII. Questions
IX. Exploring: The Quiet Hour at Contel
X. Applying: Your Mission and You Must Accept It
XI. Suggested Readings
XII. References

Chapter Goals

By the end of this chapter you will be able to:

1. Identify why employee levels of work motivation vary across situations at work.
2. Analyze work situations in terms of their potential for creating job satisfaction and motivation.
3. Understand why you sometimes feel excited about an upcoming task while at other times you'd prefer to skip the task and socialize instead with your friends.
4. Diagnose why organizational rewards may not be meaningful to employees.
5. Propose ways for management to motivate employees more effectively by clarifying work requirements.
6. Explain the major components of expectancy theory and how they relate to organizational processes.
7. Link individual differences to the expectancy theory model.
8. Use the expectancy theory to redesign organizational motivational systems.

Dilemma Jason Beats the Odds

Jason grew up poor in a black, southside neighborhood near the steel fabrication plant. His father worked in the plant until a back injury forced him to quit and seek worker's compensation. Jason and his younger brother took jobs in their after-school hours to help the family. Even though Jason was an above-average student and an excellent athlete, after graduating from high school he passed up an opportunity to attend a local college on a partial baseball scholarship. Instead, he took a job as a clerk in the supplies department of a small steel fabrication company. His father's health continued to deteriorate, and Jason responded to the problem of increased medical expenses by taking a second job as truck dispatcher for a local shipping company. In this way, Jason and his brother earned enough money so their mother could stay home and take care of their dad.

Jason's boss, Ernie, liked the way Jason had solved a supply problem at the fabrication plant. (Jason's solution would save the company $28,000 per year.) Ernie asked Jason if he would like to try his hand at learning how to keep the company books. The new accounting job would result in a 40 percent pay increase, so Jason could quit his second job and spend more time with his family and fiance. The new position would also make him eligible to participate in the company pension and insurance plans (the latter would give his dad slightly better medical coverage). Most important to Jason, however, was the opportunity to learn how the business worked from an accounting standpoint. He was interested in how companies justify and record expenses and maintain financial control. So, although he felt unprepared (he'd be the youngest in the department), he accepted the promotion.

Jason showed a flair for his work. His outgoing personality and easy manner made him popular with his new coworkers. Although he lacked formal training in ac-

counting, he was quick to grasp the basic company accounting policies. When his boss encountered a problem with supplies, he went straight to Jason because of his experience in that department.

Lately, sales had become a problem (they were slipping in most of the company territories). Ernie believed that the problem had to do with the way the company handled product pricing; he explained his reasoning to Jason. Jason said he'd consider the problem carefully and see if he could find a solution. As he thought about it, he remembered a conversation he'd had with one of the company salespeople. That person had complained about the company's lack of incentives for sales personnel who were trying to sell items that were less popular with customers. The individual complained about not knowing what the best price was on quantity sales to ensure a company profit.

Jason made a proposal to Ernie. Finished products would now be classified in categories established by how well the product sold. Each category would have a suggested price range within which the salesperson could set a price. Sales personnel would receive increasing bonuses for fast-moving items, and would get a one-time bonus for "bumping" an item into a higher category as a result of an order.

According to Jason's plan, salespeople would now be eligible for membership in the Ten Percent Club. A salesperson who averaged a 10 percent profit rate would also receive an annual bonus (usually about 25 percent of salary), and would thus qualify for club membership for the coming year. Jason presented his solution to Ernie and the company president. The program was adopted.

All this happened over 20 years ago. As Jason swung his chair away from his window overlooking the company's new steel assembly facility, he marvelled at the company's rapid growth: 2,500 employees, five plant sites, and a fleet of 300 trucks for hauling steel products nationwide. Time had flown since his promotion to Vice President of Finance three years ago. Until this moment, he hadn't thought much about what his father had said years ago when Jason gave up his chance to play baseball and go to college. Somewhat surprised by his recollection, he found himself repeating his dad's words: "If you do a good job today and work hard towards a goal, tomorrow will take care of itself."

He thought about those words and realized that he'd followed them over the years. His dad had always emphasized the importance of accomplishing what you set out to do. In the business world, Jason had been confronted with a number of challenges, and he'd met them all. He hadn't ever thought of them as obstacles or barriers. He believed that he had always done what he had to do under the circumstances.

His reflections shouldn't have surprised him. This was, after all, a day for remembering. June, his secretary, stepped in and said that the corporate board was ready to see him now. Jason stood up, put on his coat, adjusted his tie, and entered the boardroom, where he sat down at the large mahogany table. Philip Ralston, chairman of the board and company founder, announced that Jason would be named as the company's next chief executive officer . . .

Questions

1. Does Jason really "beat the odds," or is he headed for success from the beginning?
2. Why does Jason view problems as challenges rather than roadblocks?
3. What has sustained Jason's motivated behavior for so long?

A Question of Needs: Maslow's Hierarchy

To live is to be motivated. Virtually all human behavior is goal directed, that is, all human behavior has a goal, a focus. Indeed, some goals are pursued with terrific vigor. For example, Terry Fox attempted to jog across Canada to raise money for cancer research. Being a victim of the disease (he had lost a leg because of cancer), he wanted to show that those who have cancer can overcome the disease. Although he died while pursuing his goal, he became a national hero in the process, for people recognized his heoric level of motivation.

Motivation makes our behavior systematic. It sustains and directs our responses toward the goals we value. **Motivation** can be defined as the complex of factors that cause people to behave in certain ways (1).

What energizes human behavior?

The study of motivation is extremely complex, but it rests on the basic concepts of needs and motives (2). Figure 3.1 illustrates these concepts. A **need** is an experienced state of deficiency that pushes one's behavior. Examples of needs are hunger, thirst, and belongingness. A **motive** pulls one's behavior in a predictable direction. For example, you may need a pay raise to cover the cost of an addition to your house. You begin to work harder at your job, come to work on time, and avoid taking sick leave in the hope that you will secure a bigger raise. Your behavior is thus pulled in the direction of increased performance.

Abraham Maslow believed that motivation could be explained by organizing human needs into five levels (3). He did not formulate his theory with employees in mind, but his work was quickly applied to worker behavior within organizations. The five levels of Maslow's hierarchy are shown in Figure 3.2.

Physiological needs are the lowest level of needs in Maslow's hierarchy; they include food (hunger), water (thirst), shelter (warmth), and sex (reproduction). These basic needs are biological in nature and must be met for

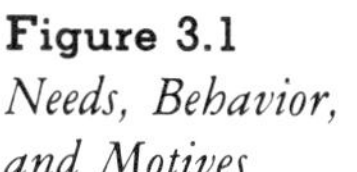

Figure 3.1
Needs, Behavior, and Motives

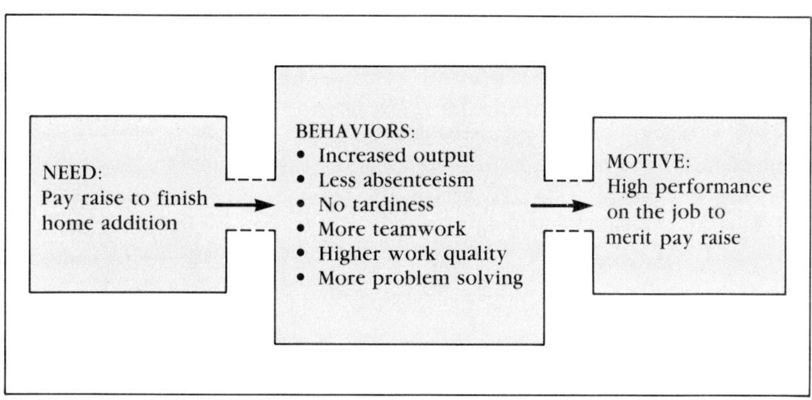

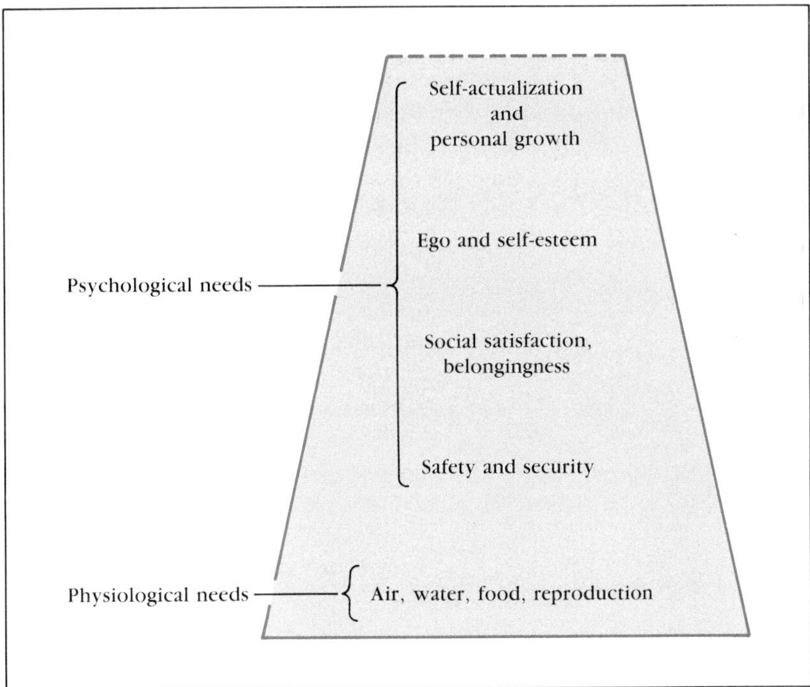

Figure 3.2
Maslow's Hierarchy of Human Needs

individual and species survival. We frequently overlook the importance of their influence on behavior because they are so basic. If, however, any of these needs is exaggerated (e.g., chronic starvation from famine and drought), we can observe their powerful grip on human behavior. For example, people in Ethiopia left their homes and possessions and walked hundreds of miles to relief areas to get food. As Maslow notes, physiological needs are basic to our biological survival and are therefore dominant over psychological needs. In other words, physiological needs must be satisfied first. For example, your concern about meeting a production goal will disappear rapidly if you arrive home to see your house ablaze. Your motivational base will shift dramatically to saving your family and possessions from fire.

Safety needs are activated next, after physiological needs are met. These are needs for protection against danger, threat, or deprivation. Once their physiological needs are satisfied, people want guarantees that their safety needs will be satisfied too. Economic and physical security are generally embodied in these needs. Safety needs are tied strongly to physiological needs because meeting safety needs ensures continuity and predictability for fulfillment of basic needs.

How do safety needs affect employee actions?

To answer this question, let's consider the behavior of two employees. One computer programmer provides for his continued employment (job security) by taking new programs home and perfecting them on his personal computer. A second programmer fulfills the same need by taking courses in computer applications at the local college. Because the company goal is to develop new software, she believes that she can be of most use to the company by learning how to solve new applications problems. Here are two employees behaving differently as a result of the same job demand. This example emphasizes the point that job security represents a goal that most people work for to ensure a continued flow of resources (money) to satisfy physiological needs.

Social needs constitute the third level of Maslow's hierarchy. These are represented by desire to give and receive love, affection, and friendship, and by desire to be accepted by a group, to belong. Social needs are higher order needs—needs that are considered personally infinite (i.e., you can never satisfy them completely). Higher order needs are learned and operate at psychological levels. These needs are developed through sustained contact with a social environment.

Ego needs represent the fourth hierarchy level. These needs have an **external component** identified as social status. Social status is defined as recognition, prestige, and appreciation. The **internal component** of ego needs is defined as achievement challenge, autonomy, and self-reliance. For employees, ego needs are closely related to personal feelings of adequacy and control at work. When their work does not adequately meet this need, employees describe their job as "not challenging" or "physically monotonous." Work that triggers these latter feelings leads to employee boredom and low performance.

Self-actualization is the fifth and final level at the top of the needs hierarchy. This need is defined as striving to grow personally and professionally, that is, to become all that a person can become. The carpenter, therefore, must build fine cabinets, the composer must compose satisfying music, and the doctor must cure illness. Self-actualization means attempting to achieve your full potential through the activities you pursue. When employees are self-actualizing, they do not view work as boring or monotonous. Instead, they describe their job as fulfilling and in many respects preferable to leisure activity. The self-actualizing person may be unaware of his or her state, because the individual is so absorbed in the activity or project.

Note that the pyramid in Figure 3.2 is cut off at the top by a dotted line. This symbolizes that people are constantly growing and striving at the fifth level. We never achieve self-actualization on a permanent basis. We achieve it for a time, then we slip down the need hierarchy. To achieve this high level of personal satisfaction at work, employees try to find outlets for their creative self-expression. When attainment of this need is frustrated, boredom and other forms of job withdrawal result. Organizations, in their preoccupation with efficiency, often design jobs in such a way that little opportunity exists to experience self-actualization. Managers in turn wonder what they must do to motivate lazy and indifferent employees!

Implications of the Need Hierarchy

Behavior is the result of needs and motives. Maslow's hierarchy implies that only one need level operates at a time. Behavior, however, often originates from several needs operating simultaneously. For example, an employee might organize a departmental softball team to feel more secure socially while also creating an opportunity for recognition (external ego needs).

The athletic competition might also provide a way to satisfy self-actualization needs.

Needs are not usually satisfied completely. Individuals usually satisfy more of their physiological needs than their psychological, or higher order needs. The U.S. work force can now take lower order needs more or less for granted because a number of mechanisms guarantee lower order need satisfaction. Federal and state governmental income support programs do this reasonably effectively.

In organizations, lower order needs are satisfied largely by external, monetary rewards. People learn at an early age that money is a reward that can be used to reduce virtually all physiological and safety needs. In contrast, higher order needs are satisfied by social interactions (to meet social and self-esteem needs) and by the creation of challenging and meaningful work through effective job design (to meet self-actualization needs).

Is the hierarchy of needs related to changing priorities of our economic system?

The answer is: *undoubtedly.* Early in our industrial history, the predominant concerns of workers were lower order needs. With the legalization of collective bargaining and the growth of labor unions, many workers felt more secure about their basic needs. Abundant educational opportunities combined with technological advances created more ways for workers to be economically secure. Higher order needs have now started to predominate as a motivational basis for the work force. In effect, the distribution of needs has been shifting upward, and experts believe it will continue to do so for the next 15 years. Figure 3.3 shows the pattern of need shifts over a 60–year span. The shift in need structure indicates some of the trends already noted. As workers become better educated, they expect more challenge and variety in their work. These expectations, when combined with more technologically and socially complex jobs, create more opportunities for satisfying higher order needs. As the graph shows, the distribution over time has shifted toward higher order needs. We are becoming a work force of self-actualizers! As a result, more and more companies are actively supporting employee efforts to gain professional training through a variety of educational programs.

Applying the Need Hierarchy

The need hierarchy parallels employee career development. Early career stages are characterized by security concerns, and fitting in with organizational values. After five years or so, concern shifts to professional identity (ego) and autonomy. This loosely parallels one's experience in college. You are concerned initially with adjusting to the school and coursework (i.e., meeting security needs and not flunking out). By senior year, your attention has shifted to getting a good job or an advanced degree (self-actualization).

Many employees seek to make organizational contributions that will endure after they leave. One way to achieve this is by becoming a mentor for a younger employee (a protege) who shows exceptional promise. Some individuals, who have strong entrepreneurial needs, choose to start their own business so they don't have to "take orders." Being a mentor or an

Figure 3.3
Profile of Worker Satisfaction for Different Levels of Maslow's Hierarchy

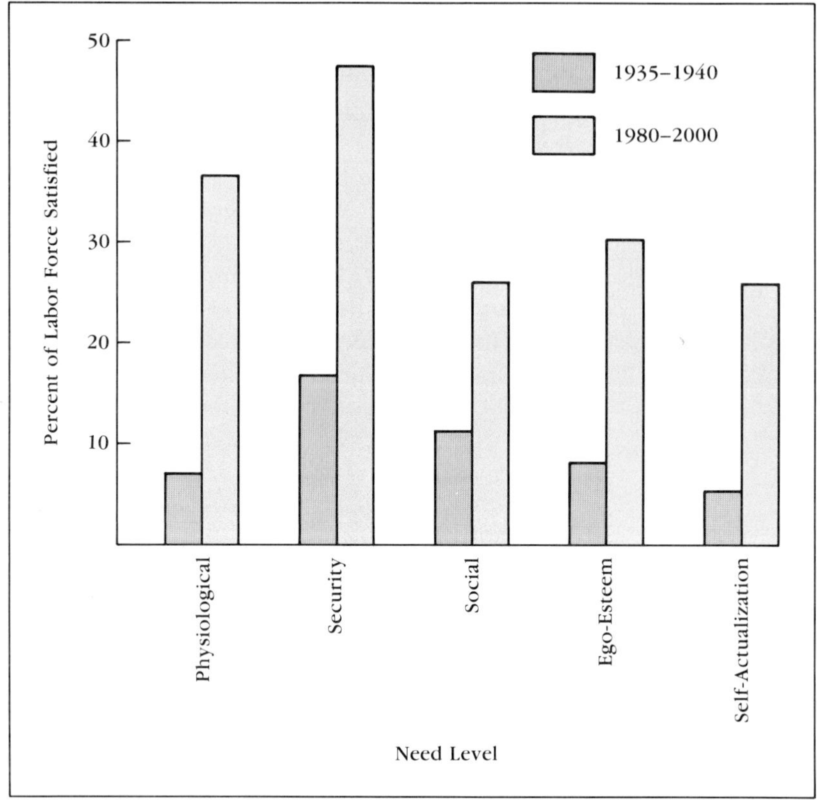

entrepreneur are specific work examples that meet Maslow's general categories of higher order needs.

Unmet needs are more motivating than needs that have been satisfied. It is where employees are going versus where they have been that motivates them. Satisfying future needs is thus a prime concern of management. The challenge for management is the productive guidance and direction of motivated behavior aimed at need satisfaction. The trick is to create employee work behavior that simultaneously satisfies personal employee needs while achieving organization performance objectives. The quality of the organization's managerial system determines in large part whether the path to employee need satisfaction is clear or hazy. We will have much more to say about how human needs are either satisfied or left unsatisfied by these important systems.

Criticisms of Maslow's hierarchy. Some of Maslow's critics believe that his needs hierarchy is really a philosophical value statement about human nature rather than a testable theory (4). Maslow's five-level formulation has little support from research. Empirical testing indicates that after lower order needs are satisfied, any of the higher order needs may be activated in random order. Maslow's hierarchical order of activation has been essentially ruled out (5). Researchers have also learned that while lower order needs become less important as they are satisfied, the response to satisfaction of higher order needs does not necessarily work in the same way (6). In other words, employees will continue to strive for recognition, challenge, and autonomy in their work even after experiencing considerable success. Too much of a good thing doesn't hurt when it comes to rewarding motivated performance!

Let's summarize. Strong evidence supports the view that unless lower order needs are satisfied, the higher order needs cannot come into play. As employees move through their career, their need pattern changes as they gain experience with an occupation and their organization. In early career stages, employees focus on job security and on developing an accepted position in the company (social and belonging needs). After five to ten years, the need emphasis shifts to achievement, recognition, and personal growth and competence. Without successive promotion, these needs may not be satisfied, and employee apathy can result.

Solving the Dilemma

Does Jason really "beat the odds," or was he headed for success from the beginning?

This question can be answered by using Maslow's hierarchy. As a teenager, Jason was highly motivated to help provide for his family's security and physiological needs. In high school, he was an outstanding athlete. He was able to obtain an athletic scholarship, which he turned down because of the basic physiological (lower order) needs of his family. He took a job with the steel company and immediately found ways to fulfill his higher order needs (social, self-esteem, and self-actualization) while continuing to help his family meet their basic needs. His work environment at the steel plant provided him with many opportunities to compete successfully and to satisfy his social and self-esteem needs. Early in his work career, Jason was motivated by the need to help the family. Once he was working, his job environment provided him with challenges, and responsibilities (internal component of self-esteem). These factors sustained his motivation to perform.

Knowledge Check

1. Employees are motivated by one need at a time. T or F?
2. Self-actualization is always a more important need than physiological or security needs. T or F?
3. Safety needs are not strongly related to physiological needs. T or F?
4. An employee who worries about being laid off is responding to ____________ needs.
5. Self-esteem needs have two components. T or F?

Answers:

1 F, 2 F, 3 F, 4 safety, 5 T

The Two Factor Theory of Motivation

A theory of work motivation that is closely related to Maslow's hierarchy is known as the motivator-hygiene theory developed by Frederick Herzberg (7). Herzberg studied engineers and accountants by asking them to describe situations that made them feel very good about their jobs and situations in which they felt very bad about their work. When employees in his study were asked to describe the job conditions that led to their feelings, Herzberg found that they named different factors when recounting their positive and negative reactions to work.

Herzberg concluded logically that separate factors influenced positive and negative feelings toward work. Figure 3.4 shows what these factors are. He noted that an absence of what he called "hygiene factors" leads to job dissatisfaction, but when present, hygiene factors do not necessarily provide job satisfaction or job motivation. In contrast, the presence of motivating factors does lead to job satisfaction and higher performance (8).

Figure 3.4
Herzberg's Two Factor Theory

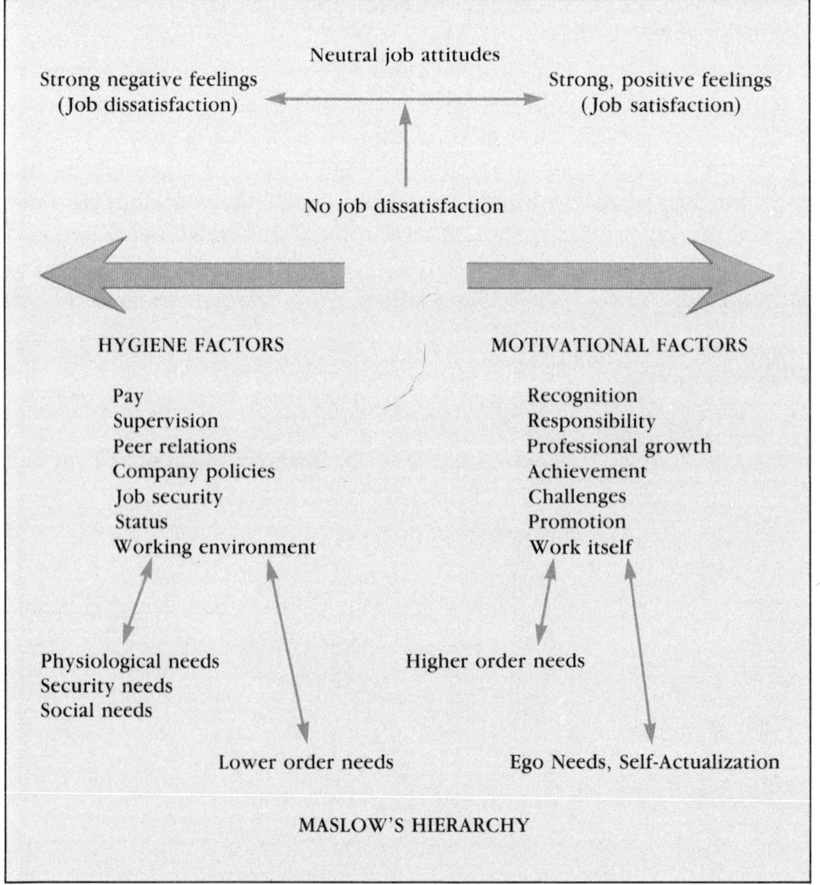

Why are the factors called hygienes and motivators?

The answer to this question lies in how employees perceive their job environment and how they react to the specific features of their job. The factors on the left side of the diagram in Figure 3.4 are part of the external work context. These are the **hygienes.** When they are *not* present, the employee's job is described as "being sick." The absence of hygienes leads to employee turnover, absenteeism, low performance, and apathy. Employees become disinterested in a job with poor hygienes. As these factors are improved, short-term positive feelings result, but the general improvement of hygiene factors does not lead to motivation in the long run. According to Herzberg, employees soon take good hygiene factors for granted, that is, they habituate them (9). If the hygiene factors are then taken away, job dissatisfaction results. (Hygiene factors are often referred to as "maintenance factors" for this reason.) As an example of these ideas, consider the following example:

> For years, employees of the Ajax Printing Company shared in a bonus plan through which 2 percent of profits were distributed as quarterly bonuses. The company had declared these bonuses for the last eight years. In some years, the bonuses had amounted to as much as 35 to 45 percent of an employee's salary. Because of poor sales in the second and third quarters of 1987, no bonuses were declared for production employees. Fifteen employees in sales and management did receive bonuses, although these were smaller than usual. Management had neglected to explain to production workers its policy change on bonuses and the company's financial position. Consequently, many employees were soon talking about a unionization drive.

Loss of the bonuses was perceived by production workers as a unilateral management move to reduce their status relative to sales and management personnel. (This perception threatened the security needs of the production workers.) Production employees tried to recover some of their lost security by encouraging installation of a union.

Hygiene factors do not raise job satisfaction or performance in the long run; motivational factors do this. These are factors such as recognition, responsibility, professional growth, achievement, challenge, promotion, and the work itself (see Figure 3.4). Motivational factors are related to the employee-job interaction, and are designated as job-centered characteristics. When these factors are present in one's work, employees are more likely to achieve satisfaction of Maslow's higher order needs. Absence of these motivators can lead in turn to strong job dissatisfaction because one's control over one's job has usually been taken away (10). This means that the employee's self-esteem needs are not satisfied. Consider the following example:

> Sandra was a highly successful office manager for over 15 years. During that time, her department grew in size to over 90 employees, all of whom are skilled computer operators. She has always been responsible for the training of new employees and for working with executives in other company departments to set up new work procedures. (All new procedures also had to have her final approval.) Last week, Sandra was told that a committee would now be responsible for devising new work systems which she would in-

stall with the help of the accounting department. Furthermore, accounting and personnel would now train new employees for Sandra's department.

The content motivators were removed from Sandra's job. Her autonomy and responsibility were curtailed by the committee's control of all new work systems. Her ability to meet challenges and obtain recognition through the training of new employees was lost also. Although all of her hygiene factors remain in place, one would not be surprised were she to begin to question these areas of her job as well. Her lowered level of job satisfaction may cause her to seek employment elsewhere. For Sandra, as for many people, there may be a strong connection between job dissatisfaction and desire to quit.

Motivators are personal rewards that occur when employees perform their job well. The availability of motivators encourages strong self-motivation, or what is called **intrinsic motivation** (11, 12). Intrinsic motivation is defined as the goal-directed behavior that originates from the desire to gain motivators. This type of motivation occurs as the employee's work unfolds. On the other hand, **extrinsic motivation** originates in the control systems of the organization (e.g., pay, supervision, and performance appraisal systems). Extrinsic motivators are much less subject to employee control than are intrinsic motivators.

Herzberg's work has influenced thinking in the field of organizational behavior (13). The most enduring benefit derived from his work has been the focusing of attention on the effect of company systems and the effect of job design (i.e., how work is organized and how much employees control their job) on employee motivation and performance.

Before Herzberg's two factor theory, employee motivation was thought of only in extrinsic terms (a full day's pay for a full day's work). Herzberg pointed out that motivation was more complex than that, although motivators are often subjective and harder to measure. We now know that concentration on hygiene factors only will not ensure that organizations have creative, involved, productive, and motivated employees (14).

Comparing Maslow and Herzberg's Models

Maslow and Herzberg's work is different yet related (see Figure 3.4). Herzberg is concerned with work motivation and performance; Maslow's theory is concerned with human needs that encompass a variety of situations, one of which is work. Maslow's lower order needs resemble hygiene factors because they maintain the individual so that psychological growth can occur. Maintenance or hygiene factors certainly do not guarantee this growth. They are necessary to the work environment but are not sufficient motivational conditions. Higher order needs and the opportunities to satisfy them relate to Herzberg's motivator factors. Herzberg's model is a specific example of Maslow's need hierarchy theory and applies many of Maslow's principles to the work setting.

Acquired Need Theories of Motivation

Have you ever known an individual who fit the following description?

> Alex insisted on seeing the supervisor's report himself. He had waited several weeks for this analysis of assembly line machine problems, and now he wanted to see the figures on work time lost. In fact, it was all he could do not to run the tests himself. Although he respected the production line people, he believed that they would not do the testing as carefully as he would. Alex insisted on such high performance standards that he often ended up performing the tests himself. In fact, he prided himself on being the most skilled at pinpointing machine problems on the line. He secretly enjoyed his colleagues' respect, even though he reacted by brushing off their compliments and commenting offhandedly, "It's all in a day's work."

What motivates Alex to be so responsible in his job?

Alex is so motivated to do excellent work that he has trouble delegating the testing responsibility to subordinates. He considers his coworkers and subordinates to be less concerned with high testing standards than he is. Alex's motivation is labeled "high need for achievement," which is one of three socially acquired needs. The other two socially acquired needs that we will study are need for affiliation and need for power.

A **socially acquired need** is defined as a need that is learned through personal contact with the social environment (15). Before we plunge into the study of socially acquired needs, however, do take a look at the Now It's Your Turn section and see how expressive you are when it comes to writing short stories.

NOW IT'S YOUR TURN...

Look at the drawing in Figure 3.5. Taking no more than eight minutes, write a narrative that presents your reactions to the following guideline questions:

1. What is this individual thinking?
2. Who are the people in the photograph?
3. What has led up to this situation?
4. What will happen in this situation?

Now, keep your narrative next to you as you read this section of Chapter 3.

Understanding the Thematic Apperception Test (TAT). The picture in Figure 3.5 is one of several that make up a test battery called the Thematic Apperception Test (TAT) (16). Since all of the pictures are ambiguous, people

Figure 3.5
Thematic Apperception Test *

* Reprinted with permission of the Tests and Scoring Division, McBer and Company, 137 Newbury Street, Boston, MA.

project their own needs, values, and motives into the content of their written narrative about the picture. Your story conveys information about your socially acquired needs. Generally a story is written for each of six different pictures and the narratives are then scored for socially acquired need imagery. Psychologists have developed ways to analyze and score the story content. Now let's consider the socially acquired needs.

Need for Achievement

In his book, McClelland cites the following narrative written by a businessman (17).

> The man is an engineer at a drafting board. The picture is of his family. He has a problem and is concentrating on it. It is merely an everyday occurrence—a problem which requires thought. How can he get that bridge to take the stress of possible high winds? He wants to arrive at a good solution to the problem by himself. He will discuss the problem with a few other engineers and make a decision which will be a correct one—he has the earmarks of competence. (p. 131)

Notice how this narrative is problem focused and clearly oriented to overcoming the problem. The man is described as channeling all of his energy and skill into the problem at hand. In other words, he has a high need for achievement. McClelland states that need for achievement is defined by the following qualities:

1. Taking moderate risks by pursuing goals that are difficult but not impossible.
2. Needing immediate feedback on performance and goal progress. (Go back to the example of Alex and see if you can identify this quality in him.)
3. Finding task activities and accomplishments to be intrinsically rewarding (regardless of the financial or economic rewards).
4. Defining work in terms of success approach versus failure avoidance.
5. Being totally task-absorbed (high job involvement) until the job is done (18).

These qualities are diagrammed in Figure 3.6.

Solving the Dilemma

Why does Jason view problems as challenges rather than roadblocks?

The introductory dilemma presents Jason as someone who is challenged by obstacles in his life and work. He does not wait idly for others to suggest solutions to his problems. Instead, he even seeks unsolved problems not yet recognized by others and initiates solutions to these problems himself. These are the characteristics of an individual with a high need for achievement. Because Jason is so active in defining problems in his own job area, he never perceives his work as dull or meaningless. Instead, he views his job as being full of challenges and opportunities for professional development. All of these factors underscore and reinforce his high need for achievement. In addition, his new position as chief executive officer will give him even more opportunities for self-actualization. His entire career with the company represents a series of successes that reinforced his need for achievement. He would probably point out these successes were he to become a mentor for a new, young, bright employee.

What have we learned so far about the importance of need for achievement?

Need for achievement explains human behavior in a variety of settings. Studies have shown that students at all academic levels who have high

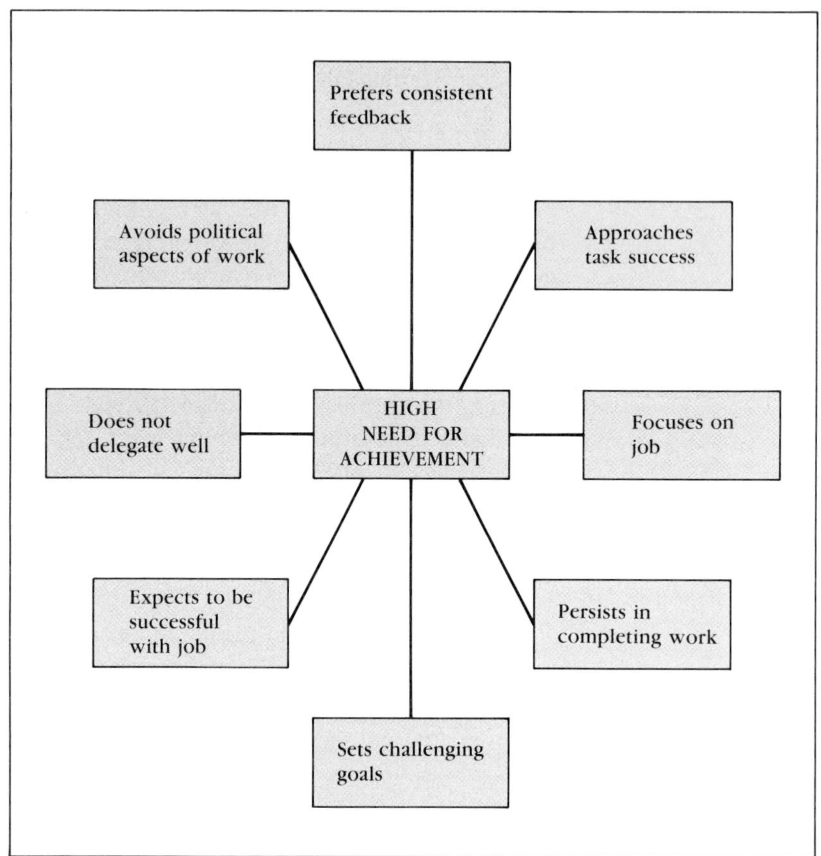

Figure 3.6
Characteristics of the Achieving Employee

need for achievement perform better than students with similar ability but lower levels of achievement need. Workers also tend to perform better when they have a higher need for achievement. If employees with a high need for achievement judge their work to be dull and boring, they will lower their performance accordingly. Similarly, if they do not receive feedback about performance, their performance will be lower. High need for achievement thus tends to matter most when: (1) ability level is good, (2) performance feedback is available, (3) the task is not too boring (19).

Need for achievement is related to the desire to be an entrepreneur. Individuals with a high need for achievement are more likely to start their own business, especially if they believe that their current employer is unresponsive to their efforts and ideas. Entrepreneurs are individuals who often become "product or idea champions" for trying out new products or processes in the organization. When the organization does not share their enthusiasm, they start their own business. The connection between need for achievement and entrepreneurship is well documented (20).

How can managers use this information about need for achievement?

Managers should apply the following motivational concepts, which are consistent with the current thinking on need for achievement:

1. Use need for achievement as one basis for screening job applicants.

2. Consider it an important factor in making promotion decisions.
3. Design jobs to be at least moderately challenging.
4. Design rewards and feedback that are closely tied to performance behaviors to create an achievement climate in the firm.

Need for Affiliation

People differ in their need to belong and interact with others. The desire to have and maintain a strong social support system, and to give and receive affection is defined as the **need for affiliation** (21). Consider the following narrative written for the TAT picture:

> The engineer is at work on Saturday when it is quiet and he has taken time to do a little daydreaming. He is the father of the two children in the picture—the husband of the woman shown. He has a happy home life and is dreaming about some pleasant outing they have had. He is looking forward to a repeat of the incident which is now giving him pleasure to think about. He plans on the following day, Sunday, to use the afternoon to take his family for a short trip. (p. 141)

This narrative is characterized by the desire to establish and maintain close, friendly relations with others. Individuals with these needs seek opportunities to give and to receive emotional support and warmth. This need is similar to Maslow's third level (social needs, or belongingness). A person with a high need for affiliation tends to (1) seek approval and reassurance from others, (2) be highly responsive to the expectations of others, and (3) be honestly concerned about the interests and welfare of coworkers, superiors, and subordinates.

Behavioral characteristics of the employee with a high need for affiliation. These individuals react positively to work experiences that enhance their feelings of belongingness, social involvement, and group morale. When these feelings are present, employees with high affiliation needs have excellent attendance records and seldom come to work late or call in sick. Affiliative employees can be excellent performers if supervisors realize that social support and inclusion in work group activities should be used to reinforce performance. When the employee with high need for affiliation performs well, the supervisor should make sure that abundant social rewards are immediately available. Qualities of the employee with a high affiliation need are shown in Figure 3.7.

Motivating the employee with a high need for affiliation. Managers must be prepared to work with employees who have a high need for affiliation. Some ways to ensure a high level of performance from these individuals are:

1. Let these employees be the mediators of work group disputes, for they are often skillful at solving conflicts.
2. Match need for affiliation tendencies with the social demands of the job. Make sure that sociable employees have socially active jobs.
3. Encourage these employees to be involved, in community affairs that parallel their job interests.
4. Use social incentives, such as praise, recognition, and increased social involvement at work, to reward employees with high affiliation needs. Be sure to make these rewards dependent on effective performance.

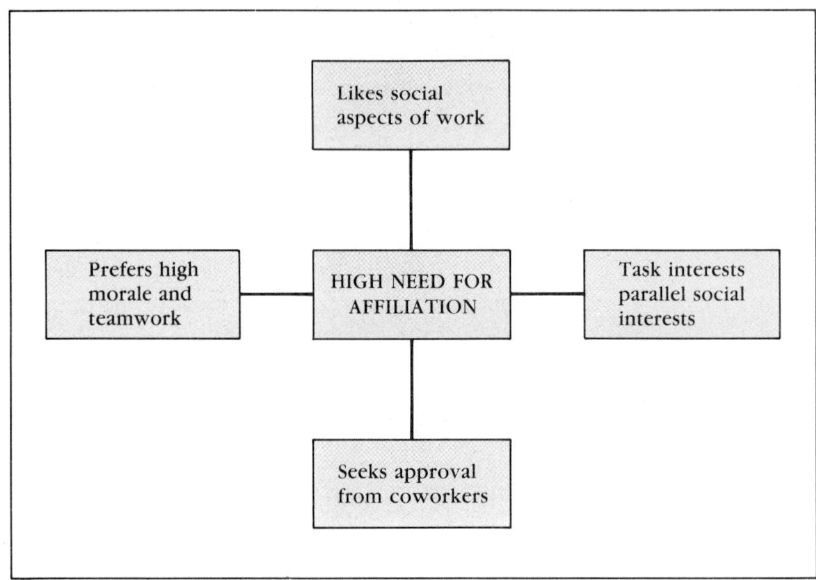

Figure 3.7
Characteristics of the Employee with a High Need for Affiliation

5. Recognize the inherent problem of the supervisor with high affiliation needs, for this individual may be more concerned with being well liked than with being productive.

Need for Power

Need for power refers to one's interest in influencing others and searching for opportunities to gain influence and control (22). We have all been around individuals who are attracted to the political aspects of a situation. You may have heard such a person comment, "I could do a better job than he's doing, if only I had the chance." This is an expression of a high need for power. Consider the following TAT narrative written about the picture in Figure 3.5.

> The man is an engineer. He is thinking of how he will present his plan at the design committee meeting. He wants to sell the idea and he knows he must persuade them to his view. He believes he will carry the day and refute any criticism. He wants badly to get the new project manager job which will be opening up. He thinks if he can win this coming battle he will be in a strong position to move up the ladder. Then he will be able to get people moving in the right direction at long last. (p. 163)

Notice how the theme of influencing others pervades this example. The choice of words is significant in this regard (e.g., sell the idea . . . persuade them . . . refute criticism). Note the concern for promotion coupled with more control over others. Power-oriented people look for more opportunities to exert influence.

In reality, the need for power has two faces (23). People with a **personalized need for power** are defined as those who try to dominate or rule simply because they enjoy intimidation of others. Encounters with such individuals (especially when one happens to be your boss) can make work unpleasant. Organizations often view these individuals as unproductive because they frequently exhibit the following behaviors.

1. Reject job responsibilities in favor of personal concerns.
2. Create poor group relations and negative group atmosphere by creating tension and anxiety in group members.
3. Are poorly adjusted to work (i.e., tend to be heavier users of drugs and alcohol).
4. Project their own inadequacies on coworkers and subordinates, which erodes work relations further.

Fortunately, the need for power also has a positive side. The **socialized need for power** is defined as behaviors that orient the individual toward the goals of the group or organization as a way to fulfill the power need (24). The individual with a socialized need for power raises the self-esteem of coworkers and subordinates by demonstrating her faith in them. This individual might say: "I know these goals are tough, but you're the best employees in the industry. I know you can meet the challenge! I've got good reason to be confident, because you've risen to the occasion so many times before." This manager is saying, "I feel good about you employees because I know you have confidence in yourselves." This is a powerful motivational message. It tells every employee that he is an expert at his job. The individual with a socialized need for power implies through her actions that the best kind of control in organizations is self-control.

Managing the employee with a socialized need for power. Those who supervise employees with a high social need for power should consider the following guidelines:

1. Employees who seek social power should be selected and promoted over employees who seek personal power.
2. Social power managers should be in visible positions because they help raise organizational commitment and job involvement.
3. Managers with a social power focus are best at restoring group performance and cohesiveness under new leadership conditions.
4. Social power managers are more likely to work through people than through tasks. They are effective delegators and develop the skills of subordinates quickly.
5. The job must provide opportunities for the manager with a socialized need for power to satisfy that need, or the individual may resort to satisfying power needs through less desirable personalized methods!

All factors considered, the socialized need for power is the most important determinant of managerial success. Individuals with this need move up the ladder because they instill confidence in subordinates as they accomplish organizational goals. The manager with a socialized need for power achieves his personal goals by fusing employee goals with the goals of the organization. This makes the manager more willing to delegate responsibility. (In contrast, the manager with a high achievement need is less capable of responsibility delegation.)

The characteristics of the two sides of the need for power are summarized in Figure 3.8.

Figure 3.8
Two Sides of the Need for Power

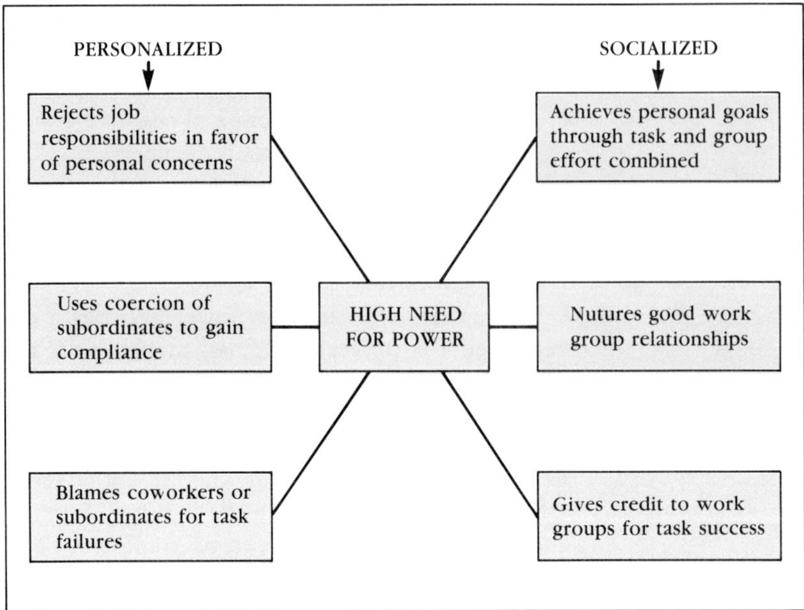

Knowledge Check

1. Motivator factors are easily habituated by employees, so these factors soon lose their motivational strength. T or F?
2. Motivator factors are those job characteristics in the external context of work. T or F?
3. High achievers are good delegators of responsibility to subordinates. T or F?
4. Individuals with a high need for affiliation would be good arbitrators of labor disputes. T or F?
5. An individual's need for power is more organizationally valuable if it is expressed as a personalized power need. T or F?

Answers:

1 F, 2 F, 3 F, 4 T, 5 F

A Process Theory of Motivation: Expectancy Theory

Thus far we have been concerned with theories of motivation that specify the causes of behavior. The theories we developed were Maslow's need hierarchy, Herzberg's two factor theory, and the theory of socially acquired needs. None of these tells us much about the mechanisms of motivation; instead, they identify what causes motivated behavior to occur. Such theories are called **content theories of motivation.** In contrast, a **process theory of motivation** not only tells us *what* causes motivation, but it also specifies *how* and *why* motivated behavior occurs. In this section, we discuss expectancy theory, which is a process theory of motivation. It will help us analyze why motivated behavior occurs at work and how that behavior can be channeled and directed. Let's start with an example.

> Joe was selected to assist Professor Able in a project that had interested the professor for some time. The project involved the study of those factors that cause individuals to want to become commodities brokers (i.e., the brokers who buy and sell wheat, corn, plywood, precious metals, and so forth). Joe realized that he was the logical choice as assistant on the project, yet he was not highly motivated about the problem, even though he worked well with Professor Able.
>
> Professor Able recognized that Joe was not highly motivated. On several occasions, he had tried to raise Joe's motivation level and enthusiasm for the project. He was not, however, successful until he sent Joe to meet Jeffery Newman, a commodities broker who bought and sold wheat at the Chicago Board of Trade. Newman pointed out to Joe that the project was important and that it could lead to a summer internship for Joe at the Board of Trade. Professor Able followed up on Newman's point. He indicated to Joe that an internship would look very good on Joe's resume and that it might even lead to full-time employment later on. Joe then became highly motivated. Suddenly his other courses seemed less interesting than the one he was taking from Professor Able, and he devoted more and more time to working on the professor's project.

Joe had a motivational problem. He had the ability to work on the project, but he was uninterested until Jeff Newman pointed out the connection between the project and an internship at the Board of Trade. Once Joe recognized a connection between the project and a goal he valued personally, his effort level on the project increased dramatically. The point to the example is this: motivated people view their activities as helping them to achieve personally important goals. The motivation process in the example can be reframed using the structure of expectancy theory.

Understanding the Basics of Expectancy Theory

The expectancy theory of motivation was developed by E.C. Tolman in 1930 (25). He realized that behavior is always purposeful and goal directed. He argued that the only way to understand behavior is in terms of the chances that a certain behavior will lead to certain outcomes valued by the individual. Professor Victor Vroom (1964) was the first scholar to apply Tolman's ideas to behavior within organizations (26). Following Vroom's work, expectancy theory has become one of the leading explanations for a variety of employee behaviors. It is used to explain such phenomena as why people join certain groups, why they choose certain careers and organizations, how performance levels can be determined, and why employees respond well to goal setting (27, 28). The list of expectancy theory applications to organizational behavior continues to grow.

Expectancy theory comes in several varieties, which use slightly different terminologies. For the sake of simplicity, we first describe expectancy theory components, give examples of those components, and then apply the model to Joe's situation.

Components of expectancy theory. **Valence** is defined as the personal attractiveness of different situational outcomes. If an outcome such as getting into a preferred course section has a positive valence, then the individual desires it. Negative valence is undesirable (e.g., getting a D from the excellent but hard professor who teaches the preferred section). The concept of valence is highly personalized and dependent on how we perceive our environment. Our teachers, friends, parents, and bosses all teach us how to value the outcomes that we receive in life. They teach us about valence, and these attitudes then become part of our personal experience.

Expectancy is the subjective belief that a given level of effort expended will lead to certain outcomes. Expectancy requires the individual to make a judgment about the outcomes that he would like to obtain and whether those outcomes are related to the level of effort he is willing to expend. When we look up at the sky and decide that there is a 50 percent chance of rain, we are forming an expectancy. If expectancy is zero, then we believe that there is no connection between effort and outcomes. For example, a student with a degree in zoology will not try very hard to get a job in a public accounting firm (even though he may be interested in the behavior of accountants). Based on his training, a positive outcome is unlikely despite a show of effort. If expectancy is high, then the individual believes that it is likely that a given level of effort will yield certain outcomes (think about your belief about the connection between studying hard and good grades). Expectancy is sensitive to our self-concept and environment. Would you expect a person with high self-esteem and a high need for achievement to set different expectancies from someone with a low self-esteem and a low need for achievement?

Outcomes in expectancy theory. Expectancy theory has two classes of outcome. **First level outcomes** are the result of expending effort in some directed way. Important first level outcomes at work would be performance, problem solving behavior, and working at home or on the weekends. These outcomes are valued highly by the organization, and they are valued by many employees. **Second level outcomes** occur after first level outcomes and are the direct result of achieving first level outcomes. They have personal meaning for the employee and span the continuum from extrinsic outcomes (i.e., pay, time off, company car, and expense account) to intrinsic outcomes (i.e., challenge, personal growth, promotion, greater responsibility).

Instrumentality is the belief that first level outcomes lead to second level outcomes. If instrumentality is negative, then the employee believes that a second level outcome will not necessarily occur when a given first level outcome occurs. For example, if a worker believes that he will not be accepted by his work group if he continues to out-produce them, then he may cut back on his output to ensure acceptance. Positive instrumentality means that the employee believes that if he performs at a given level, then the second level outcome (acceptance) is more likely to occur.

Instrumentality is the focus of management concern. When managers consider performance issues, they want employees to see a clear pathway from performance excellence to second level outcomes that are positively valent. If the performance appraisal and pay system are functioning optimally, then employees know that the organization values improved performance because they get rewarded fairly. This in turn strengthens positive employee instrumentalities for high performance by the secure connection employees perceive between performance and valued second level outcomes.

Let us now combine the concepts of expectancy theory to develop a theory of motivation. The model is diagrammed in Figure 3.9.

The individual exerts effort to achieve a first level outcome (performance on the job) for two reasons: (1) The first level outcome is valent in the sense that it generates feelings of self-fulfillment (many employees feel better about themselves when they put in a good day's work). (2) The employee believes that certain first level outcomes will generate valuable second level outcomes (instrumentality is positive and strong).

In contrast, no effort will be forthcoming if the employee believes that no connection exists between effort and performance (e.g., "No matter how hard I try, I'll never get an A in accounting."). Notice in Figure 3.9 that feedback about performance and rewards are necessary to sustain high levels of effort. In addition, ability also must be present for the individual to

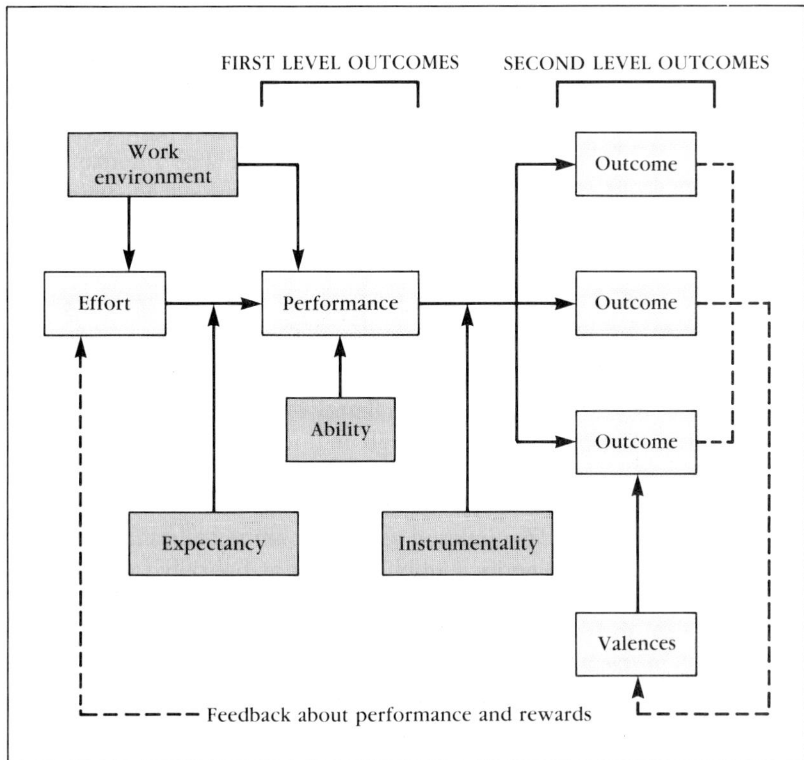

Figure 3.9
The Expectancy Theory of Employee Motivation

attain a given level of performance. If ability is low, no amount of effort will cause successful performance (first level outcome) to occur.

Applying Expectancy Theory

Many of the features in the episode of Joe and Professor Able conform to expectancy theory. Joe was extremely interested in the Board of Trade internship (it had a strong positive valence). He believed that he could be successful in the internship (high expectancy that effort would lead to performance). Joe also learned from Professor Able and Jeff Newman that high performance on the project could lead to an internship (high instrumentality that project performance would lead to a desirable second level outcome—getting the internship).

Once Joe perceived the connection between working with Professor Able on the project and an improved opportunity to get the internship, his level of effort (motivation) improved. Valence for both project and internship became positive and strong. Assuming that Joe is a helpful assistant, his performance on the project should be excellent. (He has the necessary ability to achieve high performance.) This last observation emphasizes the importance of ability in expectancy theory. If ability is inadequate, then no performance occurs regardless of motivation level.

Note the role of Professor Able and Mr. Newman in this analysis. These individuals represent part of the "work environment" in Figure 3.9. As Joe's superior, Professor Able materially improved Joe's expectancy and instrumentality (for obtaining the internship) because he put Joe in contact with Mr. Newman. Mr. Newman in turn pointed out the connection between the project and the internship. Joe was previously unaware of this connection, so his instrumentalities for the school project had been low. Joe has excellent abilities, so Professor Able knew he could be a high performer. Through Mr. Newman, the professor cleared a pathway for Joe from performance to reward. He raised Joe's instrumentalities for a highly valent second level outcome (the internship). This example emphasizes the critical role of leadership as a component of the work environment.

Solving the Dilemma

What has sustained Jason's motivated behavior for so long?

Expectancy theory provides an answer to this question. Jason has been very successful in his work because a close connection existed between his excellent performance on the job and outcomes received (i.e., providing for his family, and promotion and recognition for work achievements). Jason has always perceived a strong connection between his job behavior and his desired outcomes. In the terminology of expectancy theory, you might say that instrumentality and his excellent personal qualifications (ability) have gotten him where he is today!

Extending Expectancy Theory to the Individual and the Organization

Expectancy theory is useful as a motivational tool for organizations and their managers. We have already learned that a number of important factors affect the way the model works to explain motivation. We cannot deal here with all of these factors, but we can address some that fall in two major categories: (1) individual differences, and (2) organizational factors (Figure 3.10).

Individual Differences Have Motivational Effects

Need for achievement is an individual difference that systematically influences level of effort, instrumentality, and expectancy. The achieving employee believes that her performance can and should be very high, and she is willing to expend large amounts of effort on the job. Furthermore, if she believes that the organization rewards high performance fairly, then her instrumentalities will be high. (Remember, individuals with high achievement needs are more likely to be entrepreneurs.)

Locus of control can influence the expectancy model. It represents an individual's beliefs about whether personal behavior influences outcomes. If an employee has a strong external locus of control, he may see no connection between first and second level outcomes, that is, instrumentality is zero. The employee is saying to himself that "the rewards I receive from work are due to luck or chance, and have little to do with my on-the-job performance." On the other hand, the individual with an internal locus of control believes that a strong connection exists between behavior and valued outcomes. Under conditions that enable this employee to exert control over her job, the internal worker will be more motivated than her external coworker.

Locus of control raises the important issue of providing employees with opportunities to control significant aspects of their work (29). Organizations tend to create complicated reward systems that distribute extrinsic rewards only. These systems are often viewed by employees as excessive layers of management control which makes the employees conclude that managers do not trust them to control their own behavior on the job. Such reward systems may have been designed to raise motivation, but the actual effect may be to cause employees to believe that they should not seek control over their work. Managers must think hard about intrinsic rewards in the workplace if they want to encourage employees to be "masters of their own fate."

Self-esteem influences the expectancy theory model. If an employee has a positive self-image, then he is likely to believe that ability leads to success at a task. He believes that his effort will lead to satisfactory performance, which will lead in turn to valued rewards. The employee with low self-esteem is more likely to believe that a weak connection exists between performance and reward. This individual is not a good judge of her own

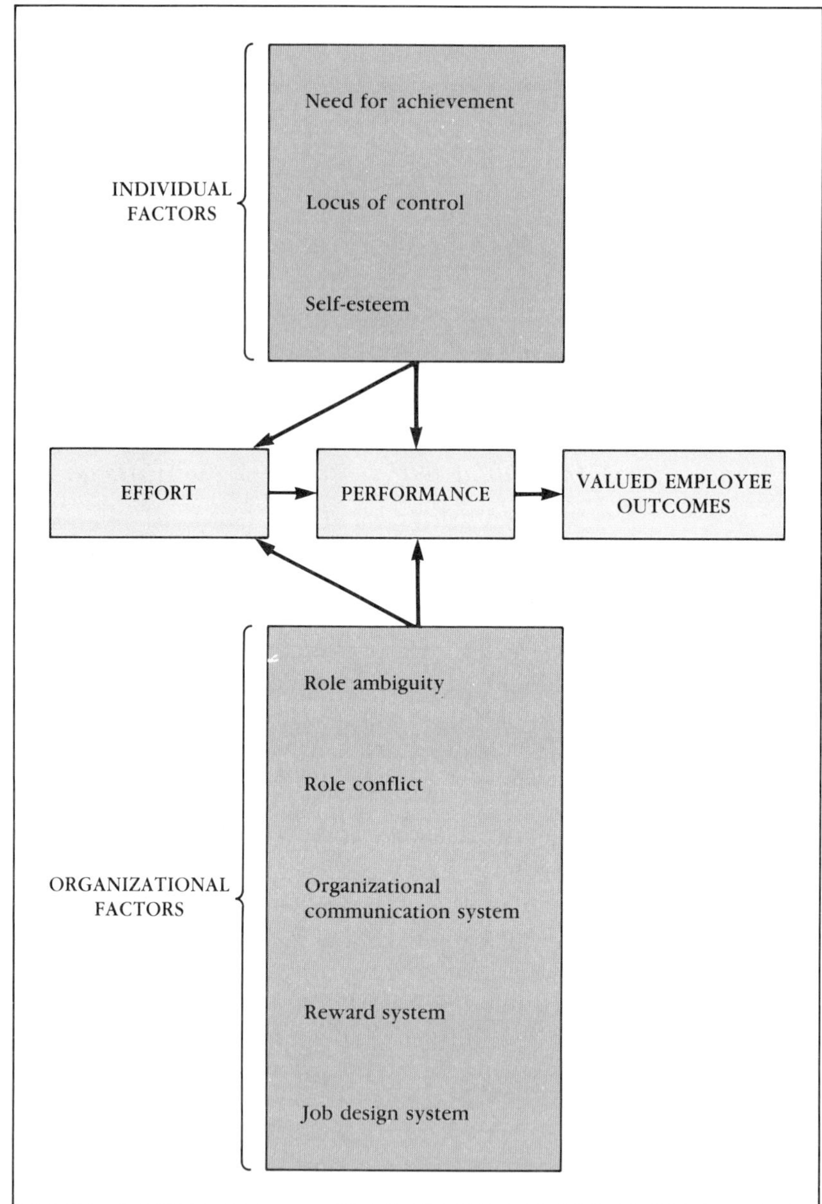

Figure 3.10 *Individual and Organizational Factors in Motivation*

ability to succeed. The self-assured employee poses less of a motivational problem for supervisors.

Organizational Factors and Motivation

Numerous organizational factors influence employee motivation. Here we discuss the most prominent organizational features that influence the expectancy model of motivation.

Role ambiguity is one of the most important motivational influencers. It is defined as lack of clarity or lack of understanding of job or work demands. When supervisors explain or give feedback about their expectations, employee performance, or goal setting, then role ambiguity is removed and employees are able to see the connection between effort, performance, and second level outcomes. If supervisors do not take the time to explain their performance expectations or if they do not give feedback on employee performance, subordinates will have lower expectancies and instrumentalities about performance and its connection with rewards.

Role conflict is inconsistent work expectations. The essence of role conflict is having two bosses or two job goals that conflict. If the two bosses cannot agree about what the employee is supposed to do at work, the employee is in a "damned if you do and damned if you don't" situation. Nothing creates motivational paralysis faster—especially if the employee cannot get clarification about supervisory expectations. Recall a situation in which you experienced role conflict relative to two of your instructors regarding course work. How confident were you that you could do well in both courses?

When role conflict and role ambiguity are both high, the accuracy of employee perceptions about expectancy and instrumentality deteriorates. Employees experience wide fluctuations in instrumentalities under these conditions. One day they may feel good about their chances for promotion and a pay raise, but the next day they may be depressed about their chances because of what the boss hasn't said!

The organizational communication system plays a large role in the expectancy theory model. An important dimension of communication in organizations is in the area of performance appraisal and meeting established performance goals. All organizations must attempt to assess whether or not goals are being achieved efficiently. Performance appraisal is the process by which this information is cycled back to employees from management. If workers do not receive such evaluative information on a regular basis, their need for achievement is lowered. Their expectancies regarding the belief that personal effort leads to improved performance then erode and their effort drops.

Supervisors must keep employees informed of their progress toward meeting organization goals. The best way to do this is by having both a formal and an informal communication process. (We consider the formal assessment process in Chapter 5 on performance appraisal.) The informal process is quite simply, "management by walking around" (30). Employees will demonstrate much higher motivation if their supervisors "catch them doing things right versus doing things wrong (31). For the effective manager, there is no substitute for mingling with the employees and recognizing them for a job well done. Informal employee contact provides abundant opportunities to administer praise and recognition and to give cogent feedback on performance.

The reward system plays a key role in the expectancy model. No one may be confused about how to be a successful performer (expectancies are high), because supervision keeps everyone abreast of company expectations. If, however, the poorer performers consistently get larger rewards than the more competent performers, then the instrumentalities for the higher performers disintegrate. They no longer perceive a positive connection between high performance and pay, so their level of motivation drops, because they recognize the reward system as unfair. The poorer performers may think that the reward system is terrific. Meanwhile, the star performers are working on their resumes and are looking for new jobs. (The valence of alternative jobs has increased for them!) An organization in this dismal situation is stuck with the duds; it has inadvertently thinned its ranks of the high performers. Some of you may have returned to school for precisely this reason. Your valence for going back to school suddenly became stronger than the attraction of keeping a job that did not reward you adequately for your performance.

The organization's job design system is the last major factor that influences the expectancy model. Employees prefer more control rather than less control, over their work. One way of gaining control over one's job is to go out and start one's own business (particularly if the existing job seems stifling and the employee has a high need for achievement) (32). Most employees instead try to satisfy their control and autonomy needs by getting promotions. Promotions are not, however, available to all employees, so the organization must act to make existing jobs more interesting and motivating. One way to do this is to reward employees for acquiring new job skills. The more skills they learn, the more control those employees are given over their work assignments. When an organization strives to make jobs more challenging to provide more opportunity for personal growth, and to give more meaningful performance feedback, then employees see stronger connections between their performance and second level outcomes (rewards).

The best way to make jobs more motivating is to get employees involved in designing their own jobs. Participation in the job design process is the essence of personal control over one's work. When employees help change their job within management guidelines, they have a greater stake in their work. Although such participation may not be effective for all jobs or for all employees, for many workers it can be a powerful force, which raises expectancy and improves instrumentalities.

Knowledge Check

1. Content theories of motivation address the how's and why's of motivated behavior. T or F?
2. In the expectancy theory example, Joe initially had high expectancies but low instrumentalities. T or F?
3. Instrumentality is the belief that effort will lead to performance. T or F?
4. Locus of control is an individual difference that systematically affects components of the expectancy model. T or F?
5. The organizational reward system has minimal influence on the high performer's perception of the relationship between performance and reward. T or F?

Answers:

1 F, 2 F, 3 F, 4 T, 5 F

Summary Points

- **Motives** initiate, sustain, and channel behavior. **Motivation** moves through a sequence of need, behavior, and goal attainment.
- Behavior can be activated by **needs** (push) or **motives** (pull). The degree of personal attractiveness of goals or outcomes is called **valence.**
- **Maslow's hierarchy** consists of two general levels: **physiological needs** and **psychological needs.** These levels are also called **extrinsic needs** and **intrinsic needs.** Individuals can progress up the hierarchy as their careers advance or as they grow older or both. Ideally, one becomes increasingly concerned with higher order needs, such as autonomy and control over life events.
- **Herzberg's two factor theory** states that motivation is the result of factors that are different from those that result in lack of motivation. Motivation is created by **motivators** such as promotion, challenge, and recognition. Lack of motivation is avoided by providing satisfactory **hygienes** (i.e., pay, supervision, pleasant coworkers, and decent work conditions).
- The socially acquired needs of **achievement, affiliation,** and **power** are important factors in understanding employee behavior. Achievement motivation is a primary cause of entrepreneurial behavior. Affiliation needs energize supportive and collaborative behavior in work groups. Need for power has two forms of expression: personalized and socialized power. The socialized need for power is an important managerial quality that is associated with organizational effectiveness.
- **Expectancy theory** is a process theory of motivation that explains how motivation occurs and what direction it will take. In contrast, content theories of motivation answer the question: What causes motivation?

Questions

1. As a person gains more experience, seniority, and income from a job, would you expect pay to become a more or less important motivating factor? Cite some theories to support your answer.
2. If you were a supervisor with three skilled employees, all of whom had ten years of experience as word processors, how would you try to improve their levels of achievement motivation? See if you can outline three steps.
3. Which of the socially acquired needs do you consider to be the most powerful? Why? Is the one you selected also one that organizations value highly in employees?
4. The personalized need for power has been described as being generally *not* useful in organizational settings. Can you think of some circumstances in which it could serve organizational needs? Could these circumstances persist indefinitely?
5. Explain Maslow's hierarchy to a friend who has been working for some time. See if your friend is motivated primarily by higher order needs. Think about the needs that motivated you when you first started college. Are the same needs as important to you now?
6. Recall the best teacher you have had for a class. Why was this teacher so effective in his or her work? Use the Herzberg theory to do your analysis.

EXPLORING: *The Quiet Hour at Contel*

Adapted from the *Times Picayune/States Item* (14, July 1985).

The boss schedules more meetings, the phones are ringing off the hook, other employees are asking procedural questions. It gets hard to concentrate, and employees at

Continental Telephone Company believe that their productivity suffers as a result. At the western regional office, accounting workers now have a "quiet hour" that lasts from 8:00 A.M. to 9:00 A.M. when they work on long-term projects, research reports, or other creative work that requires few disturbances and lots of concentration. The hour has a company label: Achieving Maximum Potential (AMP). It was started in the fall of 1984, because accounting employees were working in a large open area, which made concentration almost impossible.

"It's like an invisible force field we can create to allow us one hour of quiet time. The rest of us don't have offices and don't have doors we can close," says Ted Carrier, Contel's staff manager for general accounting.

Employees throughout Contel's ten-state western region are getting used to the fact that they can't telephone accounting between 8:00 A.M. and 9:00 A.M. During AMP hour, employees aren't involved in meetings, errands, running printers, or any other distracting activity. Carrier maintains that so far employees are in unanimous agreement: AMP works. Carrier notes that "Most people outside the department run hot or cold on AMP hour. Some felt it was an inconvenience, but most thought it was favorable. The staff is flexible. If there is an emergency during the hour, we will respond."

Donna Miller, who processes the regional payroll, said she had received just one emergency call during AMP the first month the program was in operation. "We just informed personnel that this hour is not a time to contact us. And most people think this is a good idea and wish they could have a similar program."

Discussion Questions

1. What kind of employee needs is Contel trying to satisfy among personnel in its accounting department?
2. How might the AMP program influence the motivation of employees in other departments? (HINT: Think in terms of instrumentality and second level outcomes for high and low performers in other departments.)
3. How could a program like this one backfire for Contel?

APPLYING: *Your Mission and You Must Accept It!*

You're an expert in employee motivation. You've been called by the president of the Goodenough Company to interview a group of employees who work in a poorly performing department. Goodenough manufactures a wide array of products from aircraft braking systems to radiation detection equipment. The work involves sophisticated product design and requires that employees have and maintain a high level of manufacturing skills. Employees at all levels are expected to coordinate with customers regarding product performance problems. The president tells you that several first-rate design experts and some key supervisors have recently left the firm and have gone to work for competitors. Although he views this as a problem, his request is that you focus on the production employees.

To help you analyze the nature of the motivational problems in the production division, the president has asked you to interview some of the division's employees. You decide to interview three production workers: Phyllis, Wendell, and Lyle. The next day, you talk with them during a morning session. In the afternoon, you decide to interview Susan, a manager in the division. Excerpts from both interview sessions follow.

Morning Interview With Production Employees

Lyle: I've been with this company over 25 years, so I have to be pretty satisfied with my job. The retirement benefits are great, and I expect to retire soon. We plan to move to a small place in the country where I can raise a few vegetables during the summer. I'll be able to sell them to the local supermarkets at a good price.

Wendell: Lyle's always talking about his country place. Some of us aren't as close to retirement as he is, and we can't think that far ahead. As for me, I'd like to see a few changes around here now. For example, supervisors spend most of the day in their offices. They only come around when there's a problem, and then it's usually to find fault and to criticize.

Consultant: Is anything else bothering you, Wendell, about the way things are done in production?

Wendell: Well, lately we've been putting in a lot of overtime, and management seems to think that we should always appreciate the opportunity to come to work and make more money. After a while, though, our families begin to suffer, not to mention our backs! The extra money's OK, but weekend and night work is making it real tough for me to keep up with night school. I've been working on an associate degree at the junior college, and the courses demand more study time. I'm falling farther and farther behind, and my instructors don't want to hear any more excuses.

Consultant: Phyllis, how about you, what do you think about your job?

Phyllis: My job's OK, I guess. I took this job because I've got two boys who are getting ready to go to college, and we need the money for their tuition. My job helps out. My biggest problem is finding the right parts to make quota on my circuit tester. You see, I need several types of nylon inserts to hold the units in place as I test them, and they're never available.

Lyle: You know, I've had a problem like that myself. Since we went to the new parts control system, I can never seem to keep enough circuit boards at my work station. I'd like to go back to the old system where you fill out the inventory control cards and the supply guys deliver. Some of the others have started going back to the old system on their own. If Susie finds out, there will be trouble!

Consultant: Tell me more about supervision in your department. (They look at each other, to see who will start. There is an awkward silence.)

Lyle: Since I've been here the longest and have seen lots of supervisors come and go, I'll start. Susan came up through the ranks; she's been a supervisor for about 18 months. She's loyal to the company and she really goes by the book. She expects everyone to follow regulations, even if a better method is obvious. She doesn't have to be such a stickler, but she hasn't learned that yet. Most of the other supervisors use their people more effectively. Maybe she feels she has something to prove.

Phyllis: What Lyle says is right. Since Susie is a new supervisor, she feels she has to go by the book. It's a shame that she doesn't rely on us more. We'd be glad to show her some better ways of doing things. After all, we want good relations in the department.

Wendell: I used to want to do good work on the circuits assembly. Before the system changes and the new (and unfair) zero-defects program, we all got together to iron out production problems. Sometimes we even held meetings on our own right after work. These stupid management systems cause more problems than they solve.

Afternoon Interview With Susan

Susan: As you probably know already, I've been with the company for 15 years. Before I was a supervisor, I worked at one time or another on all of the assembly lines in this division. I've also been an instructor in our training program, and I've gotten excellent reviews in all of my positions. The last 18 months in this job, though, have had their ups and downs.

Consultant: Could you be more specific?

Susan: Well, we've installed a new inventory control system designed to tie up less money in unfinished inventory and parts. The company has had some cash flow problems, and management opted to try to lower costs versus laying people off. Management has tried to keep this quiet so no one would have to worry about layoffs.

Consultant: Could you tell me a little about the zero-defects program?

Susan: Sure. That was the brain child of the people from engineering. They tried a pilot program in another department and liked the results. From there, it was installed over here. We got a two-hour training program on new machine procedures and they handed us department goals for the next six months. We're four months into the program and no one has come close to the goals. Rumor has it that the engineers are coming back to raise the standards! That's one of the problems around here. We learn more from rumors than we do from management.

Consultant: If you could pick one thing in your area that you could change, what would it be?

Susan: That's easy. I'd like my people to appreciate the pressure I'm under to get production out the door and to guarantee quality. Every month the quotas get tougher to meet. I know the employees think I'm too hard on them. What choice do I have? Management is on my back, so it all rolls downhill. I'd like to be friends with the employees, but they'd only try to take advantage of me. I'd rather be respected than loved.

Consultant: Do you think there may be some ways that you could use your employees differently?

Susan: I've tried all that stuff. I've got so much paperwork to do that I can't be running around holding hands. You give an inch and they'll take a mile. Besides, if I let up on them, my boss will think I'm getting soft. No, I leave them alone unless they start making mistakes. Besides, you're the expert, you tell me!

Questions

1. List all of the hygienes and motivators that you can find in this case.
2. What are some of the rewards that employees value and are *not* now receiving?
3. From the viewpoint of expectancy theory, why are the three production employees not very motivated, although they seem to like their jobs? What specific features are missing?
4. Develop a plan to correct the motivation problems that you have identified. Justify each step of the plan.

Suggested Readings

McClelland, D. 1961. *The Achieving Society.* New York: Van Nostrand.

This book explains clearly the thinking behind the socially acquired needs of achievement, power, and affiliation. Emphasis is on the achievement motive and its relationship to entrepreneurship. This has recently become a popular topic of new management "how to do it" books.

McGregor, D. 1960. *The Human Side of Enterprise.* New York: McGraw Hill.

This book is a classic in the field of organizational behavior. It represents the author's considerable managerial experience, which he distills into a humanistic, sensitive management philosophy. He also details the importance and impact of managerial assumptions about human behavior.

Quick, T. 1976. *Understanding People at Work.* New York: Executive Enterprise Publications.

This short book is read easily at one sitting. Many excellent ideas are advanced about how to deal with employee motivation problems. The book's philosophy generally parallels the philosophy developed in this chapter.

Roller, R. 1975. *Theory of Motivation.* 2nd ed. New York: Harper & Row. "30 Ways to Motivate Employees to Perform Better," Training/HRD, March 1980.

Time Magazine. Why We Do What We Do: Sociobiology—A New Theory of Behavior. (1 August 1977).

References

1. Steers, R., and Porter, L. 1983. *Motivation and Work Behavior,* 3rd ed. New York: McGraw Hill.
2. Pinder, C. 1984. *Work Motivation.* Glenview, Ill.: Scott Foresman.
3. Maslow, A. 1954. *Motivation and Personality.* New York: Harper & Row.
4. Wahba, M., and Bridwell, L. 1976. Maslow Reconsidered: A Review of Research on the Need Hierarchy Theory. *Organizational Behavior and Human Performance* 15:212–240.
5. Lawler, E.E., III, and Suttle, J. 1972. A Causal-Correlational Test of the Need Hierarchy Concept. *Organizational Behavior and Human Performance* 7:265–287.
6. Ibid.
7. Herzberg, F., Mausner, B., and Snyderman, B. 1959. *The Motivation to Work,* 2nd ed. New York: Wiley.
8. Herzberg, F. 1966. *Work and the Nature of Man.* Cleveland: World.
9. Ibid.
10. Ibid.
11. Staw, B. 1976. *Intrinsic and Extrinsic Motivation.* Morristown, N.J.: General Learning Press.
12. Deci, E. 1971. The Effects of Externally Mediated Rewards on Intrinsic Motivation. *Journal of Personality and Social Psychology* 18:105–115.
13. Herzberg, F., (1966) op. cit.
14. Ibid.
15. McClelland, D. 1961. *The Achieving Society.* Princeton, N.J.: Van Nostrand.
16. Ibid.
17. Ibid.
18. Ibid.
19. Ibid.
20. McClelland, D. 1962. Business Drive and National Achievement. *Harvard Business Review* 40:99–112.
21. McClelland, D., (1961), op. cit.
22. Ibid.
23. Ibid.
24. McClelland, D., (1962), op. cit.
25. Tolman, E., and Honzik, C. 1930. Introduction and Removal of Reward and Maze Performance of Rats. *University of California Publications in Psychology* 4:257–275.
26. Vroom, V. 1964. *Work and Motivation.* New York: Wiley.
27. Stahl, M., and Harrell, A. 1983. Using Decision Modeling to Measure Second Level Valences in Expectancy Theory. *Organizational Behavior and Human Performance* 22:23–34.
28. Wanous, J., Keon, T., and Latack, J. 1983. Expectancy Theory and Occupational/Organizational Choices: A Review and Test. *Organizational Behavior and Human Performance* 22:66–86.
29. Stahl, M. 1983. Achievement, Power, and Managerial Motivation: Selecting Managerial Talent With the Job Choice Exercise. *Personnel Psychology* 36:775–790.
30. Peters, T., and Waterman, R. 1982. *In Search of Excellence.* New York: Harper & Row.
31. Blanchard, K., and Lorber, R. 1984. *Putting the One Minute Manager to Work.* New York: Morrow.
32. McClelland, D., 1962, op. cit.

Organizational Behavior Modification

Chapter 4

Chapter Goals

By the end of the chapter, you will be able to:

1. Clearly distinguish between cognitive and environmental theories of motivation.
2. Explain the principle of classical conditioning and how it determines the affective component of attitudes.
3. Describe how employees can be vicariously conditioned at work.
4. Differentiate classical conditioning from organizational behavior modification.
5. Use examples from your own experience to explain contingencies of reinforcement.
6. Identify different forms of partial reinforcement schedules used in organizations.
7. Explain why managers should practice the rule of "stretching the ratio" in providing rewards.
8. Detail company programs that are based on behavior modification principles.
9. Develop the pros and cons of using punishment in the workplace.

Dilemma Sandy Changes the Department

Sandy had been the manager of the shipping department for a catalogue company for three years. The work of her 25 employees and four supervisors consisted of filling prioritized customer orders. The orders are filled according to the customer's geographic location, the shipping charges incurred by the company, order date, and value of ordered goods. After Sandy had been on the job for 15 months, she noticed that problems were developing with shipping. Some of the problems she noted were these:

1. In about 35 percent of shipments, mistakes were being made about which order to fill first.
2. Shipping clerks frequently put incorrect merchandise in order shipments. When questioned about this, they responded that no one had ever checked or complained.
3. Orders of small value were often filled before larger, more expensive orders. Employees were filling orders *before* the orders had been prioritized.
4. Employees expressed dissatisfaction with work procedures. They felt there was not enough control over work schedules, no way to trace mistakes to particular clerks, and it was hard to correct recurring errors.

Sandy recalled a shipping system that she had studied in a management seminar. It was a method used by Emery Air Freight to improve the packing of air freight containers. The company had problems similar to Sandy's in its shipping division. She concluded that the two situations were similar enough to make it feasible for her to try the procedures described in the seminar. Here are the steps she put in place:

1. She first investigated the adequacy of employee training. Sandy concluded that the clerks could perform the tasks, but they had a poor understanding of acceptable work standards. She also determined that they were not getting adequate feedback about how well they were doing their jobs. She observed, however, that the employees were

indeed motivated to do the job correctly.

2. Next, she studied the shipping behaviors that were incorrect. She isolated these behaviors as (1) mistakes in filling orders, (2) improper shipping priority and (3) no follow-up on errors. She also identified the rate of correct shipping behaviors in each of these three areas and determined that they were 56, 48, and 35 percent, respectively. She knew she had a long way to go to reach perfection.
3. Sandy conferred with her supervisors, and they established performance goals of 99, 95, and 100 percent for the three behavior areas noted in step 2. These were called "Goals of Excellence," and all of the clerks were informed of the new standards.
4. Sandy devised a feedback system, which she trained the supervisors to use. The clerks helped design the feedback forms and were instructed in how to keep their own performance records. Supervisors reviewed the forms with the clerks on a daily basis. If a clerk was having a performance problem, the supervisor did not criticize. Instead, supervisor and clerk worked together to devise a system to correct the problem.
5. Supervisors were taught to use praise and recognition as positive motivators. Praise was used liberally as the clerks achieved performance gains above the starting percentages cited in step 2. Supervisors were authorized to distribute merit points, which the clerks accumulated for excellent performance. The individual point totals were displayed prominently on the department walls. When a clerk accumulated 500 points, he was eligible to win a bonus ranging from $25 to $150. For any given bonus drawing (12 per year were scheduled), six awards were given. Sandy estimated that the merit program cost the company about $5,000 annually. She totaled the costs of training supervisors and printing performance feedback forms. These combined expenses equaled $3,500. The total program cost came to $8,500.
6. Sandy put the program into action. She let it run for three months (through two bonus drawings). Initially she hoped that a few clerks would be able to get close to the Goals for Excellence in a month-long period. If they were able to do that, she reasoned that at least six employees could accumulate enough merit points to be eligible for the bonus drawing. It was with some concern that she put the plan into action.

Program Effects

Two weeks into the program, 21 of 25 clerks were above 85 percent for all three goal areas. The four clerks who did not make the 85th percentile were new and had not yet worked in all phases of shipping. After six months, all clerks were consistently within 2 percent of the Goals for Excellence. By year-end, all 25 employees had been able to earn the 500 merit points at least eight times, and all had earned at least five money awards (three employees had received over $600 each).

During the first six months of the program, the savings to the company totaled $50,000. Several other department heads have learned about Sandy's program, and the company is considering trying some of Sandy's ideas in other locations.

Questions

1. What are the different ways in which employees can learn new behaviors?
2. What roles do positive and negative reinforcement play in motivation?
3. What roles do praise and monetary reward play in learning new performance behaviors on the job?
4. What are the key aspects of the system that Sandy installed in the shipping department?

Modifying Employee Behavior Using Reinforcement Theory

All of the motivation models discussed in Chapter 3 were cognitive motivation theories. These models emphasize that people are motivated by thoughts, feelings, sentiment, and mental processes. In cognitive theories, the individual is perceived as the energizer, or processor, of motivated behavior. These theories view the person as the center of the motivational puzzle. In this chapter, we shift the emphasis from the individual to the environment surrounding the individual. An "environmental" explanation is thus developed for human behavior. This explanation is called **behavior modification.**

Contrasting behavior modification and cognitive motivation theories. Behavior modification is an environmental theory of motivation. This means that behavior modification de-emphasizes the role of the individual in the motivation process and emphasizes instead the role of the environment. Concepts such as those developed by Maslow's hierarchy and Herzberg's two factor theory are *not* emphasized. Where as Maslow's hierarchy predicts that a person is highly motivated by self-esteem, behavior modification predicts that motivated behavior occurs because of past reinforcement of successful project completion. According to behavior modification theory, self-esteem has little to do with motivation. The person simply values the rewards that her superior, who is part of the environment, gives to her.

Behavior modification has become a widely accepted explanation for motivated behavior, and has had a major impact on our understanding of how people learn new behaviors. It is in fact frequently referred to as a "learning theory." You will find that behavior modification has broad organizational applications in a variety of settings. We also discuss some applications in specific company settings. Finally, we develop guidelines for the use of behavior modification to increase and improve employee performance.

Applying Classical Conditioning to Human Behavior

Before we explain classical conditioning in detail, consider the following case history:

> Joe is hopeful that he will be promoted to assistant manager. Phil is also a candidate for the position, but Joe believes that he will get the promotion because of his superior work record and greater seniority. Phil and Joe are friends; they regularly eat lunch together in the cafeteria. One day their boss, Andy, approaches and asks if he can join them. He begins to talk about the upcoming promotion. He explains that Phil is going to get the job. Andy says that the store manager thinks that Joe should be transferred to another store because of the high levels of theft in Joe's department. No one is accusing Joe, of course, but "the boss feels it would be good to start again with a clean slate."

Joe is devastated. His head is spinning, and he excuses himself abruptly from the table. He wonders how he can finish out his last month at the store while he waits for the transfer. Why was he indirectly accused of stealing? As time passes, Joe finds himself trying to avoid Phil, although he knows that Phil had nothing to do with his problems. In fact, whenever he sees Phil, he experiences again many of the same painful feelings that he had that day in the lunchroom.

Behavioral psychologists would say that Joe has been classically conditioned to experience negative emotions at the sight of Phil. **Classical conditioning** is the association of positive or negative feelings with an object or person in the environment. It is based on human behaviors called **reflexes,** those reactions over which we have little or no control. Pupil dilation, salivation, and emotional responses such as elation or anger are all human reflexes. The emotions that Joe now experiences when he sees Phil were learned through classical conditioning.

Classical conditioning takes place at an emotional level. Professor Pavlov's experiments with dog salivation clarified the mechanism of classical conditioning. In his efforts to understand the effects of the digestive process of salivation, he fed bits of food to dogs and then studied their digestion. He noticed that the dogs began to drool in anticipation of being given small bits of meat. Later, the dogs were drooling at the mere sight of Professor Pavlov. The professor decided to be more systematic in his study of the salivation reflex. In his next experiment, he rang a bell immediately before meat was placed on the dog's tongue. The piece of meat first caused the salivation reflex. He repeated this sequence many times. Soon, the ringing of the bell alone caused salivation.

Figure 4.1 applies classical conditioning to Joe's experience. Before the event, Joe has positive emotional reactions to Phil and Andy. He associates both men with positive feelings and high liking. During the conditioning episode, he learns of his imminent transfer, the store manager's suspicions, and that Phil will receive the promotion. He now associates embarrassment with both men and resentment with Phil. In the wake of this episode, Joe re-experiences these negative emotions whenever he encounters Phil or Joe. He has been classically conditioned at the reflexive (emotional) level.

Operant Conditioning and Behavior Modification

Behavior modification is rooted in the work of B.F. Skinner. Skinner has labeled his ideas "operant conditioning." **Operant conditioning** states that behavior is a function of its consequences. Remember, cognitive motivation theories state that behavior is determined by *internal* needs and motives. Operant conditioning argues that *external* consequences determine behavior. Table 4.1 defines the key terms used in operant conditioning, or behavior modification.

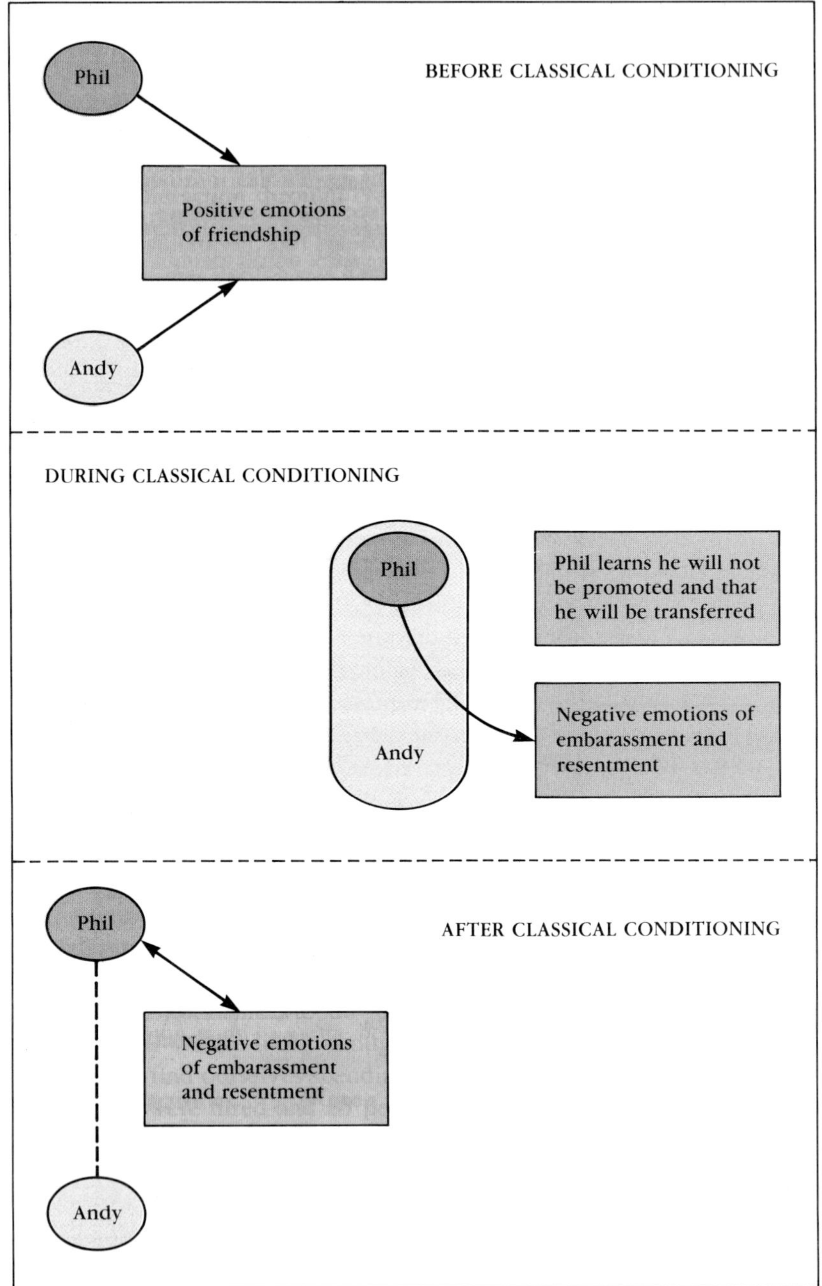

Figure 4.1 *Classical Conditioning and How People Acquire Emotions*

Principles of Behavior Modification

The main principles of behavior modification (and of operant conditioning) are the four methods of reinforcement defined in Table 4.1. Figure 4.2 will help you to distinguish between these principles. Both positive and negative reinforcement strengthen behavior. In the case of positive reinforcement, a pleasant outcome is obtained. In the case of negative reinforcement, an

Table 4.1
Key Concepts in Operant Conditioning, or Behavior Modification

Key Concept	*Definition*
Operant conditioning	Reinforcement that modifies behavior through its consequences
Law of effect	Tendency to repeat behaviors that result in favorable consequences, and not to repeat behaviors that result in unfavorable (negative) consequences
Positive reinforcers	Favorable or pleasant consequences
Negative reinforcers	Unfavorable or unpleasant consequences
Neutral reinforcers	Consequences that are neither favorable nor unfavorable
Positive reinforcement	Strengthening of a behavior by occurrence of a pleasant consequence
Negative reinforcement	Strengthening of a behavior by removing an unfavorable consequence
Punishment	Weakening a behavior by occurrence of an unfavorable consequence
Extinction	Weakening a behavior with occurrence of a neutral consequence or removal of a positive consequence
Behavioral shaping	Successively closer and closer approximation of desired behavior
Schedule of reinforcement	Frequency with which reinforcement accompanies behavior
Stretching the ratio of reinforcement	Shifting the reinforcement schedule from one rate of reinforcement to another

unpleasant consequence is avoided. Individual needs are satisfied in both cases, so behavior is in both instances strengthened.

In extinction, a pleasant consequence is removed or a neutral consequence occurs. This has the effect of weakening a behavior. Consider what happens when you repeatedly raise your hand in class and the instructor never calls on you. How does this influence your urge to participate in class discussions? In the lower left box in Figure 4.2, note that punishment occurs when an unpleasant consequence is presented. These two strategies, punishment and extinction, lessen the strength of a particular behavior. We now

Figure 4.2
Contingencies of Reinforcement

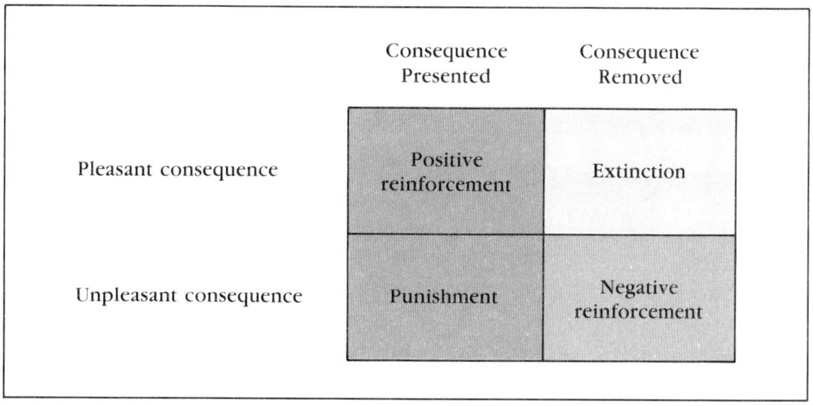

	Consequence Presented	Consequence Removed
Pleasant consequence	Positive reinforcement	Extinction
Unpleasant consequence	Punishment	Negative reinforcement

see that behavior can be linked with its consequences in four ways. Each of these linkages is called a **contingency of reinforcement.** Let's develop an example of each of these contingencies.

Positive reinforcement. A behavior is strengthened by the occurrence of positive outcomes. An instructor gives a student a difficult homework assignment. The student exerts great effort and completes the homework on time with accuracy (his response). The instructor reviews the work and not only gives the student a high mark, but also asks the student to assist other students who had difficulty with the assignment (consequences). (You may not agree that the second outcome is a positive reinforcer!)

Negative reinforcement. A behavior is strengthened by removal of an unpleasant consequence. This is called *avoidance learning.* Students come to class on time to avoid finding themselves locked out of the classroom, or they may come on time to avoid interrupting the instructor's discussion and being asked in consequence if they have a severe case of sleeping sickness.

Extinction. A behavior is weakened if a positive consequence does not follow. For example, the traveling salesman goes to the farmhouse to sell encyclopedias. He knocks on the door and no one answers. He comes back the next day, again ready to make a sale. Still no answer when he knocks. Eventually he gives up and never returns.

Punishment. A behavior is weakened if an unpleasant consequence occurs after the behavior. A student has been talking during class and helping the person next to him finish the crossword puzzle in the campus newspaper. The disgusted instructor pulls out a drop slip for the course and writes the student's name on it.

Solving the Dilemma

What are the different ways in which employees can learn new behaviors?

Employees learn new behaviors through positive reinforcement, negative reinforcement, punishment, and extinction. These are contingencies of reinforcement that specify the relationship between employee behavior and its consequences. They all occur frequently in the work setting.

Behavioral shaping is an important extension of contingencies of reinforcement. Skinner has successfully taught pigeons to play ping-pong and to dance. He did this by using behavioral shaping, that is, requiring closer and closer approximations of the desired behavior. In his work with pigeons, Skinner initially would reinforce any behavior that remotely resembled the desired behavior. Soon, the pigeon would be moving in the desired direction. Further reinforcement would occur only as the movements came closer and closer to the desired pattern. Eventually the pigeons were dancing like feathered Fred Astaires. With successively closer approximations and continued reinforcement, the birds acquired the dancing or ping-pong behaviors. How do you suppose trainers at Sea World are able to get dolphins to jump over wires 10 feet in the air? They use the same training method. They start with wires well below the water surface, and the dolphins are reinforced whenever they swim over them. Presto! The dolphins are soon jumping high in the air as a result of behavioral shaping.

Behavioral shaping and employees. Sandy trained her supervisors to give positive reinforcement in the forms of praise, recognition, and merit points. She stressed that positive reinforcement should occur regularly, and especially in the following circumstances: (1) when employees exceeded earlier excellence goals, (2) when they reported accurately their self-monitored performance level, and (3) when they came up with new money-saving ideas. Initially, Sandy and her supervisors could not expect employees to jump from their low performance level to the high standards set as the Goals of Excellence. Through positive reinforcement, they had to shape successive approximations of employee behavior to achieve the final, desired behaviors. Eventually the employees were routinely meeting or exceeding the established shipping standards. The concept of behavioral shaping supports the old saying: "You have to learn to walk before you can run."

Solving the Dilemma

What roles do positive and negative reinforcement play in motivation?

Positive and negative reinforcement increase the strength of a behavior. In Sandy's department, for example, positive reinforcement strengthens correct packing of shipping containers because employees know that this behavior leads to desired consequences (i.e., praise, recognition, and merit points). Negative reinforcement also strengthens behavior, but for different reasons. In negative reinforcement, employees learn that certain behaviors prevent unpleasant consequences from occurring. A shipping clerk may complete a mail order form correctly because she wants to avoid her boss's criticism. An employee who is negatively reinforced on a regular basis soon becomes expert at avoiding the supervisor's punishers! Overuse of negative reinforcement at work creates distrust and tension between supervisors and employees.

The Interesting Case of Partial Reinforcement

In our discussions thus far we have described rewards that occur predictably after each relevant behavior. This is called **continuous reinforcement** and represents only one of an infinite number of possible reinforcement schedules. **Partial reinforcement schedules** refer to the number of behaviors occurring before reinforcement or to amount of elapsed time between reinforcers. These reinforcement schedules and an organizational example of each are shown in Table 4.2.

What are the effects of schedules of reinforcement?

Each of the schedules noted in Table 4.2 has a unique effect on behavior response rate. Behavior learned under partial reinforcement is extremely resistant to change or to extinction.

Two distinctions are evident in Table 4.2. When rewards occur after a given elapsed time, the reinforcement is called an **interval schedule** (fixed or variable). When rewards occur after a certain number of behaviors, the reinforcement is called a **ratio schedule** (again, fixed or variable). As the table indicates, four types of partial reinforcement schedule are used in organizations.

Characteristics of Partial Reinforcement Schedules

Let's examine the partial schedule types of reinforcement and see if we can develop another organizational example of each.

Table 4.2
Schedules of Reinforcement

Schedule	*Description*	*Example*
CONTINUOUS	Consequence follows each response.	Supervisor praises employee each time she finishes checking a set of customer accounts.
PARTIAL SCHEDULES	Consequence does not follow every response.	
	Types of Partial Schedule Reinforcement	
Schedule	*Description*	*Example*
1. Fixed ratio (FR)	A fixed number of behaviors must occur before reinforcement occurs.	After selling 25 product units, a salesman becomes eligible for a 10 percent commission on each new sale.
2. Variable ratio (VR)	A variable number of behaviors (around some average number) must occur before reinforcement.	A store clerk might be rewarded in one instance after correctly handling five customer complaints, then she might be rewarded again after correctly handling seven complaints.
3. Fixed interval (FI)	After a given amount of time has elapsed, reinforcement occurs.	Coworkers get together for a congenial break at 10:00 A.M. and 2:00 P.M.
4. Variable interval (VI)	After a variable amount of time (varying around an average time) has elapsed, reinforcement occurs.	In one instance, a supervisor rewards employee performance after two days; in the next instance, he lets four days elapse before reinforcement occurs.

The **fixed ratio schedule** welds the reward to a given number of responses. This schedule produces an extremely high response rate. For example, firms often use **piece rate pay systems** to generate high output. These systems require a certain number of items to be produced before the worker can obtain an incentive reward. Under piece rate pay systems, employees will work very hard to achieve the incentive condition. The concept also is used for sales commission systems. If a commission of 10 percent is earned for each pair of shoes sold beyond a fixed number (say 25 pairs), the salesperson will work hard to sell those first 25 pairs. At this point, she then works hard to sell additional pairs because of the incentive effect.

The **variable ratio schedule** provides rewards based on an average number of responses. A variable ratio schedule means that an uncertain (but around some average) number of behaviors must occur before the reward is given. One time an employee might be rewarded after 16 behaviors, while at another time the reward might come after 4 behaviors. The pattern would average out to 10 behaviors to generate a reward. The Las Vegas one-armed bandit is an example of a variable ratio schedule. If you have ever been to Las Vegas or to other legalized gambling settings, you will agree that gambling behaviors are very resistant to extinction!

A **fixed interval schedule** requires that a constant amount of time pass before the reward is given. This schedule produces response rates punctuated by bursts of high and low activity. Consider an example. Imagine your work behavior if your supervisor came into your work area each day at exactly 10:00 A.M. and 2:00 P.M. Your work activity level would rise and fall around those time periods. Similar patterns are noticeable in student behavior as their work intensity rises and falls near midterms and finals.

The **variable interval schedule** means that a reward is given for the first behavior after a variable amount of time has passed. The interval between responses always averages out to a pre-established time. An example of this schedule is the company policy of trying to promote entry level accountants to senior accountant level within one year. Some make it in 8 months, others take 10 months, and still others require 14 months. The average promotion time is 12 months.

NOW IT'S YOUR TURN . . .

Correctly Identifying Reinforcement Schedules

Instructions: After the description of each work example, indicate the type of reinforcement schedule in operation.

1. Two hours of time off if bank tellers are error-free in calculation of total daily deposits. ____________
2. Giving a $50 bonus to hourly workers if insurance premiums can be reduced by 5 percent. ____________
3. Dividing all profits above 6 percent among salespeople. ____________
4. Giving an extra four hours of wages to employees who are not absent from or late for work over a month-long period. ____________
5. The time clock on the wall where employees punch in and out of work. ____________

6. Employees are paid every Friday. ___________

7. If employees are not late for work for a period of one month, they become eligible for a drawing in which they can win from $25 to $50. ___________

Answers:

1 Fixed interval, 2 Fixed ratio, 3 Fixed ratio, 4 Fixed interval, 5 Fixed interval, 6 Fixed interval, 7 Variable ratio

Stretching the Ratio of Reinforcement

Maintaining the appropriate response rate to reinforce the desired employee behaviors is important. Let's return to Sandy's department for a moment. She forgot to teach her supervisors how to **stretch the ratio of reinforcement.** Remember from Table 4.1 that this term is defined as shifting a reinforcement schedule from one rate to another. Sandy wanted her employees to improve their performance, so she taught her supervisors to slowly shape employee behavior toward the Goals of Excellence. Initially the supervisors should have rewarded each behavior that was an improvement by using a continuous reinforcement schedule. This they did. After the employees began to demonstrate sustained progress, the supervisors should have switched their praise and recognition to a fixed ratio schedule. As the clerks moved closer to the excellence goals, the supervisors could, for example, have readjusted to a variable ratio schedule. Once the clerks were achieving the desired standards continuously, the ratio of reward to behavior should be increased (i.e., stretched) to sustain the desired order-processing behavior at the correct performance level.

Stretching the ratio is not designed to provide fewer rewards. Instead, the procedure is used to keep employees from taking rewards for granted. This can be a problem when reinforcers such as praise and recognition are used on a continuous basis. At first, the rewards are appreciated, but if they continue to occur too often, they can lose their meaningfulness. Incidentally, what kind of reinforcement schedule was the merit point system that Sandy established in her department?

Solving the Dilemma

What roles do praise and monetary reward play in learning new performance behaviors on the job?

These are extrinsic rewards, which management all too often does *not* use effectively to motivate employees. When employees are being taught desirable new behaviors, praise and monetary reward are most useful if administered on a fixed ratio basis. After the behaviors are well learned, the supervisor can shift the rewards to a variable ratio schedule. Well-learned performance behaviors can then be maintained quite adequately when the ratio is stretched. Care must be taken, however, not to stretch the ratio too far, or employees will perceive the system as exploitative.

Behavior Modification in Perspective

The major benefit of behavior modification is that it provides an objective basis for analyzing behavior to improve motivation and performance. Because it focuses on tangible, observable behavior, advocates of behavior modification argue that it is more objective and equitable than other systems. Some experts however, criticize behavior modification on philosophical grounds (1, 2). Critics state that behavior modification methods are undemocratic and that the methods undermine important individual rights such as free choice. Opponents call these the manipulative aspects of behavior modification (Table 4.3). To assume that organizations could be managed free of manipulation, persuasion, or influence is unrealistic. These are natural aspects of organizational life. The relevant issue is whether the employees are active participants in the design and administration of behavior modification programs.

Behavior modification systems can be designed to help workers. Proponents of the theory argue that management of contingencies of reinforcement for performance and reward can come under employee control (3). Note that the employees designed their own feedback form in the dilemma. The feedback process is more meaningful when employees can be trusted to generate their own performance information, which is then checked regularly by both employees and their supervisor. The consistent interaction of employees with supervisors on the issue of performance can have the effect of eventually reacquainting employees with intrinsic work outcomes (higher order need satisfaction). Participation in the design and administration of such programs raises the chances that these desirable outcomes will occur (4).

Employees are more motivated when they believe that rewards are contingent on performance (5, 6). Conversely, employees react negatively when rewards are *not* performance contingent. When workers are not rewarded for excellent performance, their motivation and job satisfaction decline, and positive work attitudes are extinguished.

Table 4.3
Pros and Cons of Behavior Modification

Supporters Say:	*Opponents Say:*
▪ It focuses on observable employee behavior instead of on less tangible personality traits.	▪ It undermines employee respect and dignity.
▪ No manipulation occurs when employee participation in the behavior modification is voluntary.	▪ It makes organizations more manipulative and exploitative.
▪ It improves employee instrumentalities.	▪ It makes employees dull and dehumanized—extensions of the machines they operate.
▪ Feedback to employees about their performance is improved.	▪ It is undemocratic.
	▪ It oversimplifies work behavior.

Behavior modification has developed critics (7). On the surface, behavior modification violates some of our most closely held assumptions about importance of individuality in the workplace. Critics believe that behavior modification methods ignore the complexity and spontaneity of human beings. They charge that such programs reduce the differences between employees and have a tendency to dehumanize. The critics also claim that behavior modification is rigid and oversimplifies work behavior.

These programs have been criticized because they apply only to highly routine behavior, that is, tasks that can be learned in a short period of time. As job tasks become more complex, as a variety of behaviors may be appropriate, and as tasks require more creativity, behavior modification becomes less appropriate. Behavior modification programs also become less applicable if the work is machine paced (versus employee determined). This last criticism is perhaps the most accurate, because in some procedures machines can have more control over behavior than the employee has. This is the ultimate form of behavior control at work. All that remains to be done is to design machines that provide positive reinforcement!

Critics also accuse behavior modification of being based more on animal than on human behavior. Animal studies conducted in laboratories are far removed from the realities of organizational life and the complexities of human behavior. Under laboratory conditions, great control can be exercised, even when the experimental subjects are people. These conditions do not exist in organizations. Behavior modification programs often succeed in organizations because employees participate in the design process. External control (by management) is less important to program success. When management believes that employees are capable of self-control (e.g., they can be trusted to help design the system and to keep their own performance records), then concern for employee needs has been incorporated in the program.

The most important behavior modification lesson is that all rewards must always be contingent on performance (8). For example, when organizations reward employees for seniority, this has little to do with performance. The best control systems administer rewards based on performance excellence only. To do otherwise sends the wrong message to high performers. Behavior modification offers useful criteria for cementing the relationship between performance and reward in the employee's mind.

Knowledge Check

1. Before a behavior modification program can be put into effect, the manager must determine the current level of employee performance. T or F?
2. In the long run, praise and recognition are most effective when administered under a continuous reinforcement schedule. T or F?
3. Behavior modification is a cognitive process theory of motivation. T or F?
4. Attitudes toward smoking are acquired primarily by classical conditioning. T or F?

5. The connection between a behavior and its consequence is called a *contingency of reinforcement.* T or F?
6. Negative reinforcement weakens a behavior. T or F?
7. If you want employees to learn a new work behavior, you should start them on a continuous reinforcement schedule. T or F?
8. The year-end bonus is an example of a variable interval reinforcement schedule. T or F?
9. Behavior modification programs tend to be most effective when management designs the program and then trains supervisors and employees to use it. T or F?

Answers:
1 T, 2 F, 3 F, 4 T, 5 T, 6 F, 7 T, 8 F, 9 F

The Social Learning Theory

Trying to understand human behavior from the standpoint of individual differences has been criticized as being too dependent on individual states of mind and elusive personality traits. Social learning theory was developed to bridge the gap between personality-based theories of human behavior and behavior modification (9). This approach emphasizes the interaction of the person, his environment, and his behavior (Figure 4.3). In social learning, the appropriate unit of analysis is still the individual's behavior. The assumption behind social learning theory is that behavior is simultaneously dependent on personal traits and environmental determinants. The person and the environment do not function as independent units. They determine behavior in combination. All of the relationships in the theory model (Figure 4.3) are reciprocal. This means that people's behavior influences their environment while it shapes their personality traits. Similarly, the environ-

Figure 4.3
Social Learning Theory

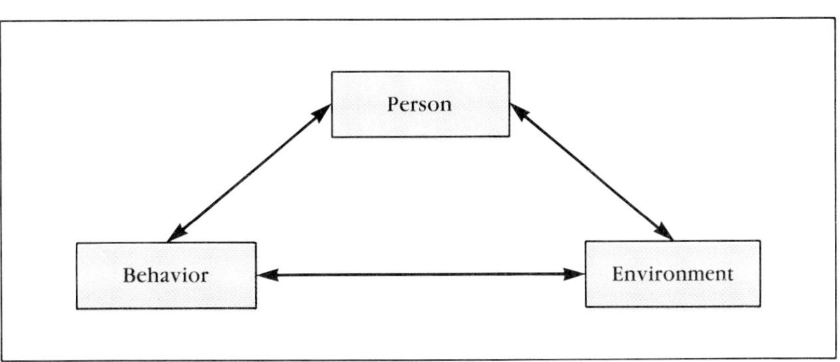

ment plays a role in determining behavior. The model suggests that people's actions can influence their environment significantly.

Applying social learning theory to employee behavior. The behavior of leaders and managers becomes more understandable if we realize that their behavior is both a function of individual personality and the environment in which they lead. The behavior of the shipping clerks in the opening dilemma makes sense when we consider both personality components of the situation and the work environment. Before Sandy's program, the work environment did not provide meaningful feedback on employee performance. The clerks rightly concluded that the orders could be packed and shipped in various ways (versus a "correct" way). Had Sandy believed in cognitive behavior theories only, she would have concluded that the clerks had little ability, or that they needed an extensive training program to correct their work deficiencies. Had she subscribed simply to the behavior modification view, she would have perceived the performance problems as being merely a function of reinforcement schedules and stretching the ratio of reinforcement. This latter approach minimizes the importance of the clerks' personal characteristics. For this reason, behavior modification is often labeled as "mechanistic" or "dehumanizing."

Sandy applied social learning theory to achieve an understanding of the clerks' behavior. She recognized that the personalities of the clerks and supervisors influenced the work environment in the shipping department. She believed that their work behavior could be corrected by considering their needs and aspirations, and by isolating and correcting feedback deficiencies. Her approach used the simple relationships diagrammed in Figure 4.3.

In summary, social learning is readily applicable to work settings. When used correctly, it results in construction of motivation and reward systems that allow for employee personality differences and the demands of the work environment. Approaches grounded in social learning theory also counter many of the criticisms leveled at behavior modification (e.g., approach to motivation and control of employee behavior).

Punishment: Sorting Out the Controversy

Thus far we have emphasized mainly the role of positive reinforcement in influencing employee behavior. Organizations also must eliminate undesirable employee behaviors as well as encourage positive behaviors. This section addresses the problem by considering the uses and abuses of punishment in the workplace.

Punishment is defined as unpleasant consequences following a behavior (see Table 4.1). In organizations, no one likes to talk about punishment, because this implies that someone must play the role of controller or punisher of employees (11), yet punishment is common in the day-to-day affairs of organizations.

If punishment is so common, why does it receive so little attention in management circles? The connotations of punishment make people uncomfortable. Webster's dictionary defines punishment as: "to impose a penalty on a criminal or wrongdoer for an offense." What manager wants to view employees as criminals or himself as their warden? The definition does not create a positive view of human behavior.

In our social organizations, we try to make punishment less visible. Because we do not want to view human beings as criminals, we discourage the use of punishment as a behavior control device. Teachers and parents are told about the extensive dangers inherent in use of punishment as part of the learning process (i.e., it damages self-esteem and lowers interest in learning). Managers are advised to use only positive reinforcement or extinction to change employee behavior. These two examples illustrate the complexity of the social values surrounding the implications of punishment and the role it plays in our organizations. Punishment is more complex than positive reinforcement, and predicting whether it will be helpful or not is more difficult than analyzing straightforward positive reinforcement. Consider the following example.

> Andy has worked in the nuclear fuel assembly department for 25 years. He is respected by his coworkers and by his manager. He has consistently set production records and is a model of efficiency in what is described as a complicated assembly process (the fuel components are radioactive and must be handled by remote control equipment).
>
> Andy is a big kidder and talker at work. His coworkers like him for this reason, because his humor helps the time pass quickly. Andy finds the protective mask that he has to wear cumbersome when he's trying to tell a joke. The company safety regulations absolutely must be observed, however, and his department had a good safety record. From time to time, Andy removes his mask to tell a story.
>
> Three days ago, a serious incident occurred. Andy was telling a joke, and as usual, his mask was giving him trouble. Out of frustration, he pulled it off and tossed it across the room. At the same moment, a technician who was carrying cannisters of nuclear fuel entered the room. The mask hit the technician, who dropped the cannisters, one of which came apart and released fine radioactive material into the work area. The company considered this to be a serious violation of safety procedures. All of the employees in that work area had to be decontaminated, and the work area was sealed off for 15 days. Andy had to go through extensive testing for the next six months as part of the company's radiation control program.

As Andy's supervisor, what would you do about his behavior?

Any supervisor would be aware of Andy's tendency to entertain his coworkers. His earlier infractions should have been corrected through discipline (punishment). The inability of Andy's supervisor to take strong action invited disaster. Both men should have been the focus of disciplinary action. Job termination would be too strong, but both individuals should be required to reattend the entire company safety program. In addition, letters of censure should be included in each individual's work record. The infraction was dangerous and costly, the punishment should fit the infraction!

Punishment occurs when unpleasant consequences follow a behavior. These unpleasant consequences have a heavy emotional impact on the individual being punished. The outcomes of punishment are unpredictable, especially with adults (12). Distinguishing between the terms **punisher** and **punishment** is necessary to an understanding of the dynamics that take place. A **punisher** is a subjective consequence in the mind of the person being punished. **Punishment** is a contingency of reinforcement that governs the relationship between behavior and its consequences. An example will clarify the distinction:

> Emilo is manager of a credit department. One of his analysts, Rene, has been goofing off on the job, and her number of processed forms is consistently below quota. Rene has a history of being a problem employee and has recently accused a coworker of sexual harassment on unsubstantiated grounds.
>
> Emilo approached Rene and politely inquired about her lowered productivity. Rene exploded and in a loud tone of voice (all 25 of her coworkers could hear her) she accused Emilo of sexual harassment. He was taken aback, but he retained his composure and asked Rene to step into his office.

From Emilo's point of view, he has been punished, and he received a punisher. He will be much less likely to approach Rene in the future, and he will behave very tentatively around her. On the other hand, Rene has been negatively reinforced! Because the consequence of her behavior was positive (i.e., getting Emilo's attention off her dismal performance record), she may be more inclined to use such behavior again. The exchange between Emilo and Rene points out that the occurrence of punishers is no guarantee that punishment has taken place in the perception of the people involved!

To understand punishment, we must focus on behavior and its consequences. Remember, punishment should always weaken behavior. Since punishers are so subjective (and emotion laden), what one person perceives as punishment may turn out to be positive or negative reinforcement from another person's point of view. In the next section, we consider the pros and cons of punishment in the workplace.

Why Is Punishment so Common?

As we noted (and you may have experienced), control through punishment is common practice in organizations. Indeed, many circumstances in organizations can be viewed as being potential punishers. For example, budgets, production quotas, deadlines, and so forth all occur naturally in the course of work (and school). Successful performance relieves the explicit pressure generated by these requirements. Many times employees define success as escaping from the punishing consequences of not meeting such requirements. Because of the exploitative nature of punishment, opponents raise the following objections to its use in organizations (13):

1. For punishment to be effective, supervisors must monitor employee behavior constantly. This is wasteful use of high-priced managerial time.

2. Punishment never eliminates undesirable behavior. It only suppresses it temporarily. When the threat of punishment is removed, the undesirable behavior returns.
3. Punishment has undesirable side effects. Employees become anxious, lose their initiative, fear reprisal, and may refuse to accept delegated responsibility.

Alternatives to Punishment

Opponents of punishment point out that managers often are not very creative in their behavior control strategies and frequently fall back on punishment out of laziness. Punishment is overused. Because we have had it done to us, we are impressed by its immediate effects, so we use it! Experts who believe that punishment is inhumane suggest the alternatives listed in Table 4.4.

The Positive Side of Punishment

On the other side, some view punishment as having its uses in organizations (14). Much behavior is learned in the presence of naturally occurring punishers. Mother Nature punishes us quickly if we stay too long in the sun or try to swim after a big meal. Our environment thus punishes us quite effectively and we learn without sustaining permanent emotional damage.

There is often no reasonable alternative to punishment. Because many activities provide their own reinforcement, that is, they alter moods or enhance pleasure, they may be difficult to eliminate. Employee drug or alcohol abuse on the job are examples (16), for these behaviors provide their own positive consequences. Suggestions made earlier (see Table 4.4)

Table 4.4
Alternatives to the Use of Punishment

Alternative	*Description*
Extinction	Much unruly employee behavior is designed to gain attention of coworkers; the show-off endangers himself and others because he finds it positively reinforcing. When supervisor and coworkers ignore obnoxious behavior, they remove its positive consequences. The show-off is then no longer the center of attention and unruly behavior ceases.
Reengineer work environment so undesirable behavior cannot occur	Change the work environment so behavior is not possible. For example, if employees goof off by the water cooler, which is in a remote office area, reposition the cooler by the door to the boss's office!
Reward behavior that is physically incompatible with undesirable behavior	Rather than punish employees for dirty and unsafe work areas, reward them for cleaning up.
Be patient and allow time for undesirable behavior to disappear	Allow employees to make mistakes without threatening punishment. When a manager says, "It's O.K. to make mistakes around here, we learn from them," you are encountering this amiable philosophy.

to use extinction or reengineer the work environment will not work for the drug-taking employee, and ignoring these employees sends the wrong message to other employees. The supervisor is boxed in a corner, and punishment may be the only way out.

How can punishment be used effectively?

Punishment can be an effective tool for removing undesirable behavior if these rules are observed (16):

1. **Do not allow undesirable behaviors to become bad employee habits.** The best managerial course is to take corrective action *before* employees become accustomed to working incorrectly. Little is gained by not acting and hoping that employees will correct their own behavior. Managers should do the correcting as soon as they observe the problem occurring (17). Losing patience after observing several infractions creates unintended emotional consequences for both supervisor and employee. The manager must strike while the iron is hot!
2. **Punishment is most effective when it is intense and immediate.** There can be no mistake about the offending behavior, and the punisher should be of sufficient intensity to weaken the undesirable behavior. Incremental disciplinary programs that provide progressively more severe punishers are not as effective as swift, intense punishment, because in the former case, employees can build up resistance to the punishers. The punisher also should occur close in time to the offense. A manager must not put off administering discipline, because employees can then become confused about the meaning of the punisher.
3. **Punishment should be equitable across people and infractions.** Match the punisher to the infraction. Do not fall back on discharge as the only recourse (18). Infractions should not go unnoticed simply because other procedures are going well, nor should senior employees or more productive employees be immune from discipline (remember the example of Andy). Hard-to-replace employees should not be able to avoid discipline. In short, punishment must be nondiscriminatory.
4. **Punishment must have information value.** After a punisher has been given, the employee should (a) receive an explanation as to why the behavior was undesirable, (b) be told how to correct the behavior, and (c) be told the consequences of further infractions.
5. **After corrective action has been taken, the supervisor should reaffirm the employee's value to the work group and to the organization.** Punishment should leave the self-esteem of the employee intact. If an employee sincerely believes that only his behavior is being criticized, then strong emotional reactions are less likely.
6. **Punishment should not be followed by noncontingent rewards.** For example, the supervisor who punishes a worker for tardiness should not turn around and immediately invite the employee to lunch because he feels guilty. The supervisor's action could have the effect of reinforcing the undesirable behavior because punishment is combined with a noncontingent reward (going to lunch with the boss at his expense).

These six rules for successful use of punishment are called the "Hot Stove Rules." Figure 4.4 shows what these ideas look like in supervisory practice.

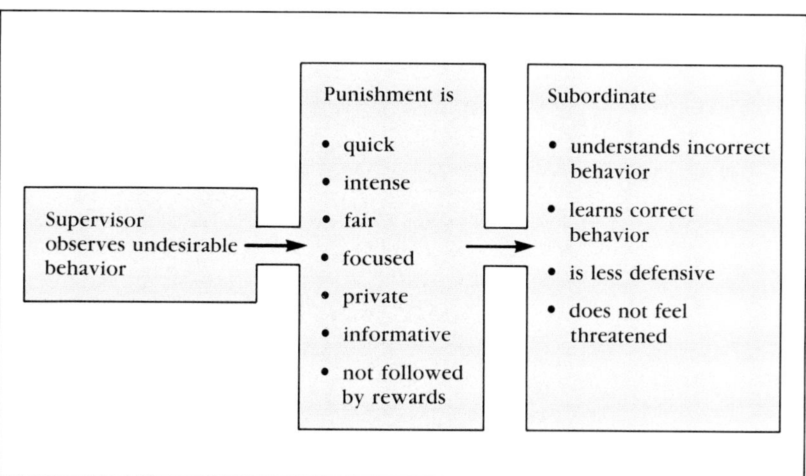

Figure 4.4
The Hot Stove Rules for Using Punishment

Solving the Dilemma

What are the key aspects of the system Sandy installed in the shipping department?

Sandy's system was not complicated. She realized that any new work system had to be based on the work activities of the clerks, so she used employee expertise and supervisor input to set up the system and establish performance goals. Sandy capitalized on the principle of employee participation. She realized that the clerks would be more likely to accept the new system if they had a hand in designing it. After starting the program, she had the employees operating at the targeted levels in short order! Her only omissions were behavioral shaping and stretching of the ratio of reinforcement after employees had successfully learned the new performance behaviors.

Knowledge Check

1. It is safe to say that people are usually damaged emotionally when they are affected by naturally occurring punishers. T or F?
2. In the example of Andy's infraction, the best course of action for his supervisor to take is to overlook Andy's mistake because Andy is a valued employee. T or F?
3. Punishment can be used effectively even if it is not applied equally to all offending employees. T or F?
4. Behavior modification programs can be criticized because they always manipulate employees toward managerially self-serving ends. T or F?

Answers:

1 F, 2 F, 3 F, 4 F

Setting Up a Behavior Modification Program

Many firms have used behavior modification successfully in their organizations (20–22). Such efforts share many common characteristics. The purpose of this section is to develop a general model for behavior modification programs and to point out how Sandy's successful program parallels behavior modification guidelines. Figure 4.5 shows the typical characteristics of a program for a business organization.

Let's discuss briefly the nine steps involved in implementing a behavior modification program.

1. **Conduct a job analysis** to define the responsibilities of jobs that will be included in the program. A job analysis results in updating of employee job descriptions (the principal responsibilities and duties of a particular work position). This step generates employee understanding of the basic requirements of the job. Supervisors, in turn, understand better the jobs of their subordinates. Sandy conducted a job analysis to learn if employee ability was the cause of the shipping problems.
2. **Define performance behaviors and set performance goals.** Management must define the precise meaning of "performance" so employees can understand what they have to do to be successful at their job. Employees must understand their job in behavioral terms that can be learned easily. Likewise, management working with employees should set performance goals that are reasonable and attainable. Such goals might involve accuracy rates, number of workhours used, rate of customer calls handled, and so forth. These goals should, whenever possible, be specified in numerical terms. Some employee participation at this stage can be very important to ensure employee commitment to the program. Sandy identified clearly the correct shipping clerk behaviors that had to be improved, and she had the clerks work with their supervisors to produce a feedback form that employees could use to chart their own performance.
3. **Conduct a baseline audit** to identify the existing rate of employee behavior. For example, accuracy rates may be 55 percent at the beginning of the program. A reasonable target might be 94 percent (established in step 2) as an accuracy rate goal. A deficiency of 39 percent would thus be identified through the baseline audit. Sandy conducted a baseline audit to determine the magnitude of the performance deficiency in three key behavior areas of the clerk job.
4. **Select powerful and abundant reinforcers** to motivate and reward excellent performance. As employees move toward the performance goals, they should be reinforced with rewards that they value. Supervisors also should be sure of the punishers that they will use to eliminate undesirable behavior. This means that supervisors must be prepared to use both positive reinforcement and punishment. Sandy's program used praise, recognition, and merit points to reinforce the correct behavior in handling customer orders.

Figure 4.5
Designing a behavior modification program

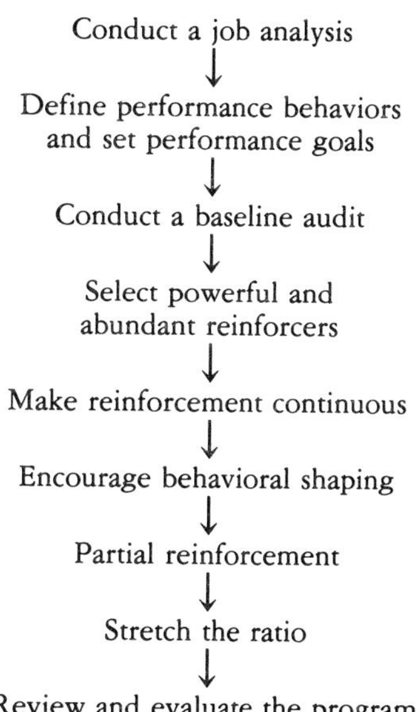

5. **Make reinforcement continuous** to encourage new behaviors from employees. The best rewards to use in this step are praise and recognition. As the new employee behaviors become more dependable, go to step 6. Sandy trained her supervisors in the use of reinforcement. She also taught them how to use praise and recognition.
6. **Encourage behavioral shaping** so closer and closer approximations of the desired behavior occur. As employees get closer to the performance goals, their performance increases should be explicitly reinforced. Slippage in performance would not be reinforced. Instead, it would be a problem that the supervisor and the employee solved together. Sandy's program did this in the following way: When employees had a performance problem, they were not criticized by their supervisor. Instead, the supervisor helped the clerk solve the performance problem, so teamwork was stressed as the best problem-solving method to use.
7. **"Stamp in" desired behaviors.** At this stage, new positive reinforcers that employees value can also be added. In the introductory dilemma, Sandy installed the merit point system for excellent performance at about this point in her program. This was a fixed ratio reinforcement schedule, and it was very effective in maintaining a high level of employee performance.
8. **Stretch the ratio** to move employees from continuous reinforcement to a partial reinforcement schedule. As employees get better at meeting the performance goals, the supervisor should no longer rely exclusively on continuous reinforcement, because praise and recognition may begin to lose their meaning for the employees. Instead, the supervisor should switch these rewards to a variable ratio or variable interval schedule. New reinforcers also should be introduced at this point in the program. Sandy did this in the opening dilemma when she initiated her merit points program.
9. **Review and evaluate the program** to identify and measure target goals such as cost reduction, improved employee attendance, improved pro-

ductivity, and so forth. After the program has been operating for a certain period, the designer should remeasure these criteria to see if the program has been effective.

Some reminders about starting a behavior modification program. These nine steps are neither complicated nor excessively expensive. They do take time to develop and implement, however. Before a behavior modification program is installed, management should do a preliminary check of certain organizational features. The following conditions must be present to help ensure the success of a behavior modification program.

1. At least a minimal level of trust must exist between employees who will be affected by the program and their supervisors.
2. Employees must perceive good workplace hygiene. In other words, they must believe that (a) their pay is fair, (b) their coworkers are likable, (c) their working conditions are safe and comfortable, and (d) company policies are generally fair.
3. Employees must have some control over the work they do. Behavior modification does not work well when employee work activities must conform to the speed at which machinery operates.
4. Employee ability cannot be a feature of the performance problems to be corrected.
5. Employees must have proper understanding of their work requirements, and they should be accustomed to getting good performance feedback from supervisors.
6. Supervisors must be committed to the program and willing to work closely with subordinates to improve performance.

Summary Points

- **Behavior modification** is the same as **operant conditioning.** It is a theory of motivation that stresses the role of environment.
- **Classical conditioning** is a process that explains how strong emotional reactions are learned. It is a passive form of learning, which does not require the person to actively manipulate or change her environment.
- **Positive and negative reinforcement** increase the strength of a behavior. **Punishment and extinction** reduce behavior strength.
- The relationship between a behavior and its consequence is called a **contingency of reinforcement.** A contingency of reinforcement can be patterned according to various **reinforcement schedules.**
- **Behavioral shaping** is a process that induces closer and closer approximations of a desired behavior. Behaviors that deviate too much from the standard are not reinforced.
- **Social learning theory** emphasizes the interaction of personality, environment, and human behavior.
- **Behavior modification** cannot be applied as effectively when tasks are not well defined or are too complex. The programs work best when jobs can be reduced easily to specific behavior components.
- **Behavior modification principles** can also help correct random and inconsistent supervisory behavior. Supervisors who administer performance-based positive and negative consequences become more effective leaders. Employees are in turn clearer about which behaviors lead to positive and negative consequences. Under these conditions, both supervisor and subordinate can agree about performance expectations.

- **Punishment is common in organizations,** because many punishers occur naturally in the work environment.
- When punishment is used according to the "**Hot Stove Rules,**" it can be an effective tool for behavioral change. These rules minimize the damaging emotional consequences of punishment.

Questions

1. How similar are behavior modification and the expectancy theory? Identify at least three similarities between these two theories.
2. Does the concept of expectancy in expectancy theory have any applicability in behavior modification? How about instrumentality?
3. Imagine that you have to correct an employee attendance problem (employees are coming to work an average of 15 minutes late). If you choose to solve this problem by using behavior modification, will your solution differ from an expectancy theory solution? Please discuss what you believe would be some of the differences between the two solutions.
4. In your opinion, does the weekly paycheck that employees receive each Friday motivate excellent on-the-job performance? Why or why not?
5. Using the principles of classical conditioning, explain how teenagers acquire favorable emotional responses to smoking. (Hint: Why is the Marlboro man an appealing figure?)
6. How would you answer a friend who says that attempts to control employee behavior smack of manipulation?
7. Why is punishment so common in organizations?

EXPLORING: *Quality Control at Tennant Company*

Adapted from *The Wall Street Journal* (10 April 1985).

The Tennant Company is a manufacturer of maintenance equipment for industrial floors. In 1979, the company decided to develop a program to increase employee productivity and product quality. The company was concerned because too many of its machines were coming off the production line with major defects. The first step that the organization took was to assign dollar values to the additional production time and service calls caused by the defects. The company then asked groups of employees and managers to identify specific manufacturing activities that were contributing to the problems.

One employee group found that leaking hydraulic lines were a consistent repair problem. Another group found that management had not trained assembly workers adequately to install hydraulic joints. Further analysis indicated that the company engineers had not kept up with the latest designs in joint technology, and that suppliers were sometimes providing incorrect parts because of inadequate part specifications received from Tennant.

In 1980, the cost of correcting errors had been 17 percent of total sales. By the end of 1984, manufacturing defects had decreased by 52 percent, and the cost of correcting errors was cut to 6.9 percent of total sales. For 1988, the company has set a goal of 2.8 percent of total sales as the cost of correcting errors.

All of the company's 1200 employees received 40 or more hours of instruction in how to improve product quality and control costs. Employees eventually realized that management was giving quality control a high priority. Tennant executives are convinced that their program has succeeded because everyone, from the president to the hourly employee, is involved. Tennant's employee-based quality control program has been so successful that the company organized a two-day seminar to handle all of the inquiries about the program characteristics. Last year, the seminar attracted 170 executives. This year, the company expects over 600!

Discussion Questions

1. What effect did attaching a dollar value to additional production time and additional service calls have on employee behavior?
2. Would you make rewards contingent on achieving goals in areas of production time and reduced cost of service calls?
3. What two factors made the Tennant program so successful?

APPLYING: *Behavior Modification and You*

Behavior modification can be applied to your college situation. Consider yourself an expert in taking college courses and evaluating what makes a course successful or unsuccessful. Let's suppose that you are on a committee with faculty and other students, and that the committee is responsible for improving course quality. Your committee has been presented with the following problems that are occurring in a management course.

1. Low attendance for problem-solving and tutorial sessions
2. Low completion and submission of homework assignments

None of the committee members is very familiar with behavior modification principles. Interest is, however, widespread among the group members to solve the problems noted. In fact, the department head has expressed grave concern about the situation. She believes that these problems, if left unchecked, will affect adversely student opinion about the entire management department. Everyone is therefore willing to work hard to correct the problems.

Given your knowledge of behavior modification, you volunteer to develop a plan to address the problems. You are to prepare an analysis of the problem so the committee can adopt a solution. You must do the following:

1. Recommend a plan to determine reasons for the problems.
2. Develop a series of steps to follow to correct the problems.
3. Suggest ways to measure and assess program effectiveness.
4. Suggest ways to actively involve students in your solutions.

Now that your responsibilities are clear, your instructor will divide the class into teams. Each team will prepare solutions, and the instructor will appoint a team spokesperson to summarize the team suggestions.

Suggested Readings

Connellan, T. 1978. *How to Improve Human Performance.* New York: Harper & Row.

Hammer, E., and Hammer, E. 1976. Behavior Modification and the Bottom Line. *Organizational Dynamics* (Spring 1976):3–21.

This article cuts through the dense terminology that accompanies many discussions of behavior modification. It is readable, and the authors discuss the cost effectiveness of behavior modification programs in industry.

Kerr, S. 1975. On the Folly of Rewarding A While Hoping for B. *Academy of Management Review* 18:769–783.

This often-cited article points up the supervisory tendency to reinforce certain behaviors in the hope that other performance behaviors will follow. The author points out the ineffectiveness of this supervisory fantasy and suggests practical ways to avoid it at work.

Krietner, R. 1975. PM—A New Method of Behavior Change. *Business Horizons* (December 1975):82.

Lockwood, D., and Luthans, F. 1984. Contingent Time Off: A Nonfinancial Incentive for Improved Productivity. *Management Review* (July 1984):48–52.

Luthans, R., and Davis, T. 1979. Behavior Self-Management: The Missing Link in Managerial Effectiveness. *Organizational Dynamics* (Summer 1979):42–60.

Luthans, F., and Krietner, R. 1985. *Organizational Behavior Modification,* 2nd ed., Glenview, Ill.: Scott Foresman.

This award-winning book clarifies the principles of behavior modification. The authors detail many successful organization programs, so the reader can easily apply guidelines from the book.

Manz, C. 1983. *The Art of Self-Management.* Englewood Cliffs, N.J.: Prentice Hall.

Snyder, C., and Luthans, F. 1983. Using OB Mod to Increase Hospital Productivity. *Personnel Administrator* (August 1983):67–73.

References

1. Locke, E. 1977. The Myths of Behavior Mod in Organizations. *Academy of Management Review* 2:533–553.
2. Gray, J. 1977. The Myths of Behavior Modification in Organizations. *Academy of Management Review* 2:121–129.
3. Luthans, F., and Krietner, R. 1985. *Organizational Behavior Modification and Beyond,* 2nd ed. Glenview, Ill.: Scott Foresman.
4. Luthans, F., Maciag, W., and Rosenkrantz, S. 1983. OB Mod: Meeting the Productivity Challenge With Human Resource Management. *Personnel* 28–36.
5. Cherrington, D., Reitz, H., and Scott, E. 1971. Effects of Contingent and Noncontingent Rewards on the Relationship Between Performance and Job Satisfaction. *Journal of Applied Psychology* 51:531–536.
6. Hayes, R., Pines, R., and Fitch, H. 1982. Reducing Accident Rates With Organizational Behavior Modification. *Academy of Management Journal* 25:407–416.
7. Hammer, M. 1971. The Application of Behavior Conditioning Procedures to the Problems of Quality Control: Comment. *Academy of Management Journal* 14:529–532.
8. Davis, T., and Luthans, F. 1979. Leadership Reexamined: A Behavioral Approach. *Academy of Management Review* 4:237–248.
9. Bandura, A. 1969. *Principles of Behavior Modification.* New York: Holt, Rinehart & Winston.
10. Ibid.
11. Luthans, F., and Krietner, R. 1985, op. cit.
12. Ibid.

13. Organ, D., and Bateman, T. 1986. *Organizational Behavior,* 3rd ed. Plano, Tex.: Business Publications Incorporated.
14. Bandura, A. 1969, op. cit.
15. *Time.* 1986. Drugs on the Job. (17 March 1986):52–61.
16. Solomon, R., 1964. Punishment. *American Psychologist* 19:239–253.
17. Ibid.
18. Ibid.
19. Beyer, J., and Trice, H. 1984. A Field Study of the Use and Perceived Effects of Discipline in Controlling Work Performance. *Academy of Management Journal* 27:743–764.
20. 239–253.
21. Lockwood, E., and Luthans, F. 1984. Contingent Time Off: A Nonfinancial Incentive for Improving Productivity. *Management Review* (July 1984):48–52.
22. Luthans, F., and Davis, T. 1979. Behavior Self Management: The Missing Link in Managerial Effectiveness. *Organizational Dynamics* (Summer 1979):42–60.

Assessing and Rewarding Excellence in Organizations

Chapter 5

I. Dilemma: Fair or Unfair Layoff?
II. Why Organizations Need to Assess Performance
III. Performance Appraisal Issues and Practices
  A. Common errors in performance appraisal
  B. Performance appraisal methods
IV. Rewards and Reward Systems
  A. Classifying organizational rewards
  B. Distributing rewards in organizations
  C. Employee beliefs about reasons for pay raises
  D. Comparing company pay practices
  E. Comparable worth: The pay issue of the 80s
V. Individual and Group-Based Rewards
  A. Cost savings plans
  B. Profit sharing plans
VI. Summary Points
VII. Questions
VIII. Exploring: The Louisiana Superdome
IX. Applying: Deciding Employee Pay Raises
X. Suggested Readings
XI. References

Chapter Goals

By the end of the chapter, you will be able to:

1. Explain why organizations must evaluate employee performance.
2. Describe the outcomes of the performance appraisal process.
3. Recognize the common problems that occur in using performance appraisal systems.
4. Describe appraisal methods and discuss their comparative characteristics.
5. Classify the rewards that organizations use to sustain employee motivation and performance.
6. Discuss some of the more successful company programs for rewarding excellent performance.
7. Explain the common bases for distributing rewards.
8. Outline the different types of company benefits and pay practices.
9. Describe the value of designing and implementing group-based reward systems.

Dilemma Fair or Unfair Layoff?

Alice Clemons and Bob Reed were both employed as technicians in the metal testing department of Bayou Steel and Fabrication, a medium-sized steel reprocessing plant located in a southern state. Both have an associate of arts degree in metal technology, and each has held a position at Bayou for the past eight years.

Three weeks ago, George Jefferson, their department head, was told to cut costs by 22 percent because of poor sales performance. George's department has employed five people for the past four years. Since the department just purchased expensive new testing equipment, George could find no other solution to the cost-cutting problem than to lay off one of the technicians.

Both Alice and Bob earned the same salary ($29,500 per year). Because they had equal seniority, George had to make a tough decision. He pulled their latest performance evaluations. George made these evaluations about eight months ago, but he had not communicated the results to the respective employees. In fact, each employee had received a 5 percent raise. (Employees at Bayou typically learn about a raise either by receiving a letter from the personnel department or simply by noticing an increase in their paycheck.)

Alice was elated about her raise because she could finally purchase a new condominium. She was pleased about this decision, and was going to tell Bob and George. Bob was indifferent about his raise. He believed that the company automatically gave 5 percent raises, so what was the big deal?

George intended to communicate the results of his performance evaluations to the two employees, but he just didn't seem to find the time. He was kept busy installing and calibrating the new testing devices in the lab. He prided himself on his ability to calibrate equipment. Why shouldn't he get to perform some of the tasks he liked to do best? In evaluating his technicians, he had focused on each employee's behavior during the week before the appraisals were due. In that period, George had been particularly pleased with Alice's work (he admired her skillful calibration and use of the metal stress machine).

On the basis of the performance evaluations, George made his decision to lay off

Bob Reed. George informed Bob, who was most upset by the decision. He naturally demanded an explanation. George countered by saying that he was department head and that his performance evaluations were totally up-to-date and objective. Besides, Bob had known of the impending layoff, and it should have come as no surprise to him or anyone else. George also explained that several employees besides Bob would have to go. Bob was unmoved by George's reasoning and demanded to have access to the information that George had used to arrive at his decision (Figure 5.1). George resisted.

When Bob Reed walked in the front door of his home and slumped in his favorite easy chair, his wife Blanche knew what had happened; they had talked about the possibility of a layoff when the company had first announced cost control measures. The Reeds spent the next four hours going over their family finances, and Bob became more and more upset as he thought about the way his layoff had been handled.

The next morning he went to the company personnel department. He spoke to Willard Masters, the company's Affirmative Action officer. Masters went over the layoff decision with Reed. Based on the available information, Willard decided to hold a hearing with Reed, Jefferson, and John Bears, a representative of the local Employment Opportunity office. As George read over the memo informing him of the meeting, he wondered if he had been thorough enough in his employee assessments.

Questions

1. What are the mistakes that Jefferson made in his performance appraisal?
2. How could Jefferson have handled this problem more effectively?
3. Does Bob Reed have a legitimate complaint about Jefferson's handling of the incident?
4. What lessons can be learned from Bayou Steel's performance appraisal system?

Why Organizations Need to Assess Performance

An organization's **performance appraisal system** is defined as a process that generates information about employee effectiveness at work for the purpose of making informed human resource decisions. Organizations must evaluate employee performance for a number of reasons.

1. Employees must behave in the desired way on the job.
2. Employee work must be evaluated for its contributions to organizational goals.
3. Information about employee performance levels is used to make decisions about rewards (e.g., salary increases, promotion, bonuses).
4. The performance appraisal system should increase and channel employee motivation.
5. The system identifies employees who need additional training.
6. The system is a communication device that should help employees better understand the organizational expectations of their work.

Figure 5.1
Reviews for Alice Clemons and Bob Reed

Employee: Alice Clemons Supervisor: G. Jefferson
Unit: Metal Testing Date: January 11, 1987

	Quantity of Output	Quality of Output	Work Attitude
Extremely Poor			
Poor			
Average			
Above Average			
Excellent	✓	✓	✓

Employee: Bob Reed Supervisor: G. Jefferson
Unit: Metal Testing Date: January 11, 1987

	Quantity of Output	Quality of Output	Work Attitude
Extremely Poor			
Poor			
Average			
Above Average			
Excellent	✓	✓	✓

To have effective managers, organizations must have good appraisal systems. Supervisors use performance feedback as a motivational tool. Providing employees with feedback about their performance represents one of the most important activities of supervision. The absence of a formal, objective performance appraisal system contributes to the employee perceptions that an organization is unfair and uninterested in treating them fairly. Table 5.1 summarizes some of the more important effects of performance appraisal from the organizational viewpoint and from the employee viewpoint.

Table 5.1
Effects of Performance Appraisal

For the Organization	*For the Employee*
▪ Performance improvement ▪ Validation of selection system ▪ Employee counseling ▪ Identifying promotable employees ▪ Identifying employees who need training ▪ Validation of training and development program ▪ Clarify job expectations ▪ Perform goal setting ▪ Administer praise and recognition ▪ Determine pay raises ▪ Make transfer decisions ▪ Make termination decisions ▪ Communicate company and departmental goals ▪ Develop employee potential ▪ Manpower planning ▪ Documentation of personnel decisions ▪ Research of performance standards ▪ Assessment of existing performance	▪ Need fulfillment (security, social, self-esteem) ▪ Equity comparisons of personal effort with rewards ▪ Job satisfaction ▪ Organizational commitment ▪ Job involvement ▪ Satisfaction with supervision ▪ Satisfaction with pay ▪ Satisfaction with promotion ▪ Satisfaction of higher order intrinsic needs (i.e., personal growth, competence, craftsmanship) ▪ Greater responsibility ▪ Improved understanding of job requirements ▪ Opportunity to participate in goal setting ▪ Knowledge of strengths and weaknesses

Performance Appraisal Issues and Practices

Few would question an organization's need to judge the performance behavior of its employees. While such judgments may not always be pleasant ones, they are necessary to assess organization progress toward goals. Given the numerous important performance appraisal outcomes, it is crucial that the process maximize accuracy and fairness. Organizations exist for many reasons, and all have a need to conduct appraisals, yet the evaluation method selected often does not match the organization needs. When the mismatch is serious, a number of problems can result from poor performance appraisal. They are detailed in the following section.

Common Errors in Performance Appraisal

Most of the performance appraisal problems that occur are of the type that threaten the validity and reliability of the performance measure (1). **Validity** is defined as a performance measure that actually measures what it is supposed to measure. **Reliability** is defined as the consistency of results obtained each time the measure is used. A good appraisal system should have both properties: validity and reliability. Let's consider an example that clarifies these concepts.

If one of the principal requirements of a job is to ensure that all customer complaints are processed in 15 minutes or less, but if employees are evaluated instead on total customer sales handled, then the measurement lacks validity. The appraisal is not measuring the most important performance aspect: speed of handling each customer complaint. If employees handle customer complaints exactly the same way each time, yet their performance evaluations vary, then the measurement lacks reliability. When performance appraisals lack these two properties, employees soon conclude that the system is worthless.

A number of issues are related to the validity and reliability of performance appraisal systems (2). A discussion of some of these follows.

Personal biases. Supervisors often allow their personal feelings to influence appraisals. Like all of us, supervisors develop biases for many reasons. Indeed, biases are nothing more than attitudes. A particular supervisor's attitude, or bias, for or against certain subordinates may have no logical basis. Indeed, when a supervisor is biased, the employee's behavior may be of little consequence, for the supervisor's perceptions are determining the evaluation. Do you think that George Jefferson was biased toward Alice in the introductory dilemma?

Halo effect. This problem is related to the problem of personal bias. If a supervisor draws a general conclusion about an employee based on a single characteristic (e.g., pleasantness, appearance, intelligence) and if the supervisor then allows that impression to govern his rating of specific employee traits, then the halo effect is operating (3). Students often make this type of error when rating the effectiveness of their instructors. If a student focuses on a trait such as likability and allows that trait to influence all aspects of the course evaluation, then the halo effect has emerged. Recruiting, hiring, and promotion decisions can all be distorted by this process. When the halo effect is operating, the evaluator allows a personal characteristic to override other performance dimensions.

Recency error. Supervisors are busy individuals who are responsible for much more than performance appraisal. When appraisals are due, they often emphasize more recent examples of employee performance in arriving at their final evaluation. In effect, the boss ignores employee performance issues until about two weeks before appraisals have to be submitted. The problem is that these two weeks may not be representative of an employee's overall performance. Appraisal results can thus be artificially raised or lowered. George Jefferson's evaluations were unreliable for this reason. If appraisals are done in proximity to important organizational events, performance results also can be distorted. Supervisors with a pattern of recency error invite erratic subordinate performance.

Central tendency error. Supervisors may rate their subordinates within too narrow a performance range, so little variation exists from one employee appraisal to another. This appraisal pattern suppresses performance differences among employees, and very good or very poor performances may go unrecognized. This is great for the low performers, but star performers begin to dust off their resumes!

Central tendency error lowers the expectancies of high performing employees. When these individuals realize that mediocre performers are getting the same performance evaluation that they are getting, they ask themselves the logical question: "Why am I killing myself when these other guys get the same rating I do?" High performers cut back on their effort (and motivation) to re-establish perceived equity.

Strictness or leniency error. Leniency is defined as the supervisor conviction that all subordinates measure up to the standards. **Strictness** is defined as the supervisor belief that none of the subordinates measure up to performance appraisal standards. In either case, the equity of excellent performers can be upset.

Central tendency, strictness, and leniency are all supervisor errors that suppress individual employee differences in performance. When this occurs, employees soon realize that their efforts are not commensurate with their rewards (especially in the case of high performers). Employee needs are best served and employees perform best when they believe that a dependable connection exists between performance and reward. The supervisor is responsible for minimizing the errors noted. If supervisors do not attempt to minimize these errors, then employees soon develop negative attitudes about the organization's performance appraisal system.

Similarity error. Supervisors sometimes give undue emphasis to their own personal qualities as a basis for making judgments about employee performance. For example, if a supervisor values her personal decisiveness, she may give employees who possess this quality appraisals that are favorably biased. Many supervisors would deny this personal tendency, yet when one observes the frequent similarity between bosses and their subordinates, one is given pause for thought!

Forcing the rating to match other criteria. Supervisors sometimes decide on an overall rating, and then go back and adjust individual performance ratings to justify the overall rating they have given. This is more likely to occur in organizations that have unusually complex appraisal systems. Managers place a low priority on doing these complicated appraisals, so they manipulate the system to produce the numbers they want. This type of appraisal problem usually indicates a poor organizational climate in which low trust exists between employees at successive levels. The problem will not be fixed until supervisors are rewarded for good appraisal work and trust becomes a prominent organizational feature.

Training supervisors to recognize appraisal errors is important. It is generally agreed that supervisors can be trained to be better judges of employee performance behavior (4, 5, 6). Management studies indicate that rater effectiveness is improved the most (and errors are most reduced) when the raters are involved actively in performance appraisal training. Smith (1986) recommends that organizations use exercises and simulations of the performance appraisal process as key aspects of supervisory training (7). Some experts argue that training should go even further and match the appraisal process selected with the type of task performed by the employees being evaluated (8). The results of this matching process are improved accuracy of performance observation, better recording of performance observations by supervisors, and minimization of the errors already noted.

The following dilemma question addresses many of the problems associated with employee performance appraisal.

Solving the Dilemma

What are the mistakes that Jefferson made in his performance appraisal?

If you return to the dilemma, you will see that Jefferson commits a number of serious errors in his appraisal. He has a bias toward certain tasks (e.g., he dislikes giving employees performance feedback and he puts off conducting appraisals because he prefers to do equipment testing and calibrating). These biases cause him to make the following errors: (1) recency error (he gets involved in employee evaluation one week before the appraisals are due), (2) similarity error (he takes pride in his ability to calibrate equipment and admires this same skill in Alice), (3) halo effect (Jefferson allows his judgments about Alice's calibrating work to influence his appraisal of all aspects of her work), and (4) leniency error (Jefferson rates both employees high on all three aspects of performance). All of Jefferson's errors influence his decision to keep Alice and to lay off Reed.

Knowledge Check

1. Performance appraisal helps control employee behavior and communicate work expectations. T or F?
2. Employee needs that are met by appraisal are in general lower order needs. T or F?
3. The halo effect sometimes influences student ratings of instructors. T or F?
4. Which of the following is *not* a systematic rater error? (a) central tendency, (b) strictness, (c) recency error.
5. Similarity error occurs when a rater uses personal qualities to judge and rate subordinates. T or F?

Answers:

1 T, 2 F, 3 T, 4 c, 5 T

Performance Appraisal Methods

No performance appraisal system can eliminate all of the errors discussed, although managers like to believe that if a system is well designed, the errors will go away. A good appraisal system is dependent on other factors besides the method used to gather performance data. If no trust exists between employees and supervisors (poor work climate), then the best appraisal system will not ensure valid ratings.

The most prominent features of any system are the types of forms and data-gathering instruments used. Perhaps these features of appraisal are most prominent because they are the part of the system that is most tangible, that is, the supervisor records his or her observations on these devices. When subordinates receive negative evaluations, they are most often written. In reality, the forms are a procedural component only, but from the standpoint of those affected by the system, they may loom large!

Absolute Standards This method judges each employee against a fixed and inflexible performance criterion. Each subordinate is compared with one or more performance standards. When you take a course in which the instructor adheres to the old 90, 80, 70, 60, 55 percentage breakdown as a grading system, you are being evaluated against an absolute standard. These systems result in upwardly biased ratings (leniency effect), which probably occurs because supervisors prefer to give positive rather than negative feedback (nobody likes to play judge, jury, and executioner). Figure 5.2 shows an example of an absolute standards rating instrument, which requires the rater to respond with a "yes" or "no" answer for each performance trait.

The performance dimensions on the rating form in Figure 5.2 have an "all or nothing" quality. The dimensions are personality-based and do not assess actual job behaviors. The rater must make judgments about the employee traits. This evaluation method can easily lack validity. How would you react if your boss checked the NO box for intelligence in rating your work?

Graphic rating scales. These are the most popular appraisal systems in use today (9). Indeed, surveys indicate that 57 percent of organizations with appraisal systems employ this method (10). A typical graphic rating scale form lists performance criteria that are meaningful both to the supervisor and employee. Using a specified rating scale, the supervisor assigns a number to each criterion. An example of the graphic rating scale method appears in Figure 5.3.

This employee rating method highlights the differences among employees (in contrast, the absolute standards system does not do this). Graphic rating scales create a tendency to spread employees out along each scale. Because degrees of performance success or failure are possible for each dimension, supervisors can better assess the strengths and weaknesses of each employee when a graphic rating scale is used. This improves the quality of information given to the employee during a performance counseling session.

The graphic rating scale method does not, however, eliminate the systematic errors discussed previously. Supervisors may have a tendency to use only part of each rating scale because of individual supervisor strictness, central tendency, or leniency. Some companies get around this problem by requiring raters to generate a distribution of performance levels (10 percent of employees must be rated either excellent or poor, with the remaining 80 percent rated between the two extremes). These forced distributions can create employee problems relative to perceived equity.

Figure 5.2
Example of an Absolute Standards Rating Method

Name ____________________ Supervisor ____________________

Date of Hiring ____________ Time in Position ______________

Work Qualification ____________

Please check the YES or NO box beside each employee trait with respect to how well the job of salesperson is performed.

	YES	NO
Good manners (is polite, tactful)	☐	☐
Intelligence (possesses good judgment and problem-solving ability)	☐	☐
Stamina (maintains good health habits)	☐	☐
Company commitment (is loyal to the firm)	☐	☐
Self-confidence (believes in himself/herself)	☐	☐
Leadership (gets things done through people)	☐	☐
Enthusiasm (has and keeps can-do attitude)	☐	☐
Cooperative (works well with others)	☐	☐
Initiative (starts jobs on his/her own)	☐	☐
Tenacity (sticks with the job until done)	☐	☐

Critical incidents. This appraisal method requires supervisors to maintain a record of each subordinate's work behavior that leads to success or failure on the job. The supervisor must record success and failure episodes in predetermined categories such as planning, accepting responsibility, application of knowledge, and other skill areas. The format specifies either a daily or weekly recording pattern for these critical incidents. Before the formal appraisal period ends, the supervisor constructs a final appraisal, which is a written narrative summarizing the employee's successes and failures. An example is shown in Figure 5.4.

The critical incidents method requires heavy supervisor involvement. The system can be effective under certain conditions. When the work cycle

Figure 5.3
Sample Form Featuring Graphic Rating Scale Evaluation Method

Employee name: ________________ Employee dept: ____________

Job classification: ______________ Performance period: ________

Supervisor name: ______________

Instructions: Please judge the employee according to each performance dimension by circling a number on the rating scale. The higher the number, the better the rating is.

1. The employee's dependability is:

5	4	3	2	1
Excellent	Good	Average	Below average	Poor

2. The employee's ability to work with others is:

5	4	3	2	1
Excellent	Good	Average	Below average	Poor

3. The employee's courtesy to customers is:

5	4	3	2	1
Excellent	Good	Average	Below average	Poor

4. The employee's ability to accept responsibility is:

5	4	3	2	1
Excellent	Good	Average	Below average	Poor

Figure 5.4
Sample Component from a Critical Incidents Method Narrative Summary

Employee: Jane Doe
Performance area: Personnel supervision
Performance level: Excellent

Once a year, Jane conducts the performance evaluations of six bank tellers. Her decisions are used to aid in making promotion, salary, and bonus decisions for all tellers. She uses the performance evaluations to provide feedback to the tellers in a timely manner. She keeps her tellers abreast of their performance by giving them informal feedback on customer satisfaction at least once a week. She tries to give employees only recent examples of performance behaviors in these informal sessions. Once each month, she holds a group meeting with the tellers and they discuss work problems and new methods to improve customer service.

is particularly long and when sustained time and effort are thus required to accomplish a particular goal, then the method can be useful. If employee behavior outcomes have a major impact on organization success or failure (typically, when upper management positions are involved), this method of appraisal can fit organizational needs. Success of the method requires that supervisors be convinced that a major part of their job is providing feedback on employee behavior. The approach generates qualitative data on performance. Both superior and subordinate are provided with the opportunity to analyze performance situations in depth. Without the generation of "hard performance data," this system probably should not be used as a basis for promotion and pay raise decisions. Firms that find the critical incidents method useful for appraisal often combine the method with graphic rating scales to generate quantitative data as well.

Behavior anchored rating scales (BARS). These scales provide concrete examples of behaviors for different levels of performance. Employees often complain that they do not know what is expected of them. Furthermore, they resent being evaluated on personality factors, which they perceive as having nothing to do with the quality of their work. If we return to the dilemma and review the method used by Jefferson, we see that the third performance dimension, *work attitude,* fits the criticism of personality-based appraisal. Many employees would say that little relationship exists between what they do on the job and how their work is evaluated. Instead of traits (i.e., friendliness, good work attitude, agreeability), BARS systems emphasize work *behavior* and focus appraisal on *how* the work gets done; less emphasis is placed on the results of work.

The design and implementation of a BARS system requires considerable work. Employees are consulted during the design process to identify critical behaviors that lead to success or failure on the job. The evaluation system can be completed only after workers have identified critical performance dimensions. The example in Figure 5.5 shows a BARS for assessing judgment and knowledge of grocery clerks.

In Figure 5.5, note that each level of performance is defined in behavioral terms. These are the **behavioral anchors.** Anchors provide meaningful examples of possible behaviors related to the particular performance dimension. These behaviors are the ones that employees can learn easily. They should be highly relevant to employees, since employees have participated in the BARS design process. Furthermore, employees typically select the relevant anchors to be used in the BARS. There are five to eight BARS in any system.

In making an assessment, supervisors select the behavioral description that best fits the employee's typical performance. This rating should have high meaning to the employee, because it indicates what he has to do to become a better performer. Under a BARS system, the employee is presented with more meaningful feedback about job behavior.

How BARS differ from other performance appraisal systems. First, BARS systems emphasize how the work is performed (through behavioral examples) versus a listing of employee personality traits. Because the focus is job behavior, BARS systems perhaps place more importance on performance than other evaluation systems do. Second, the BARS emphasis on perform-

Figure 5.5
Bars for Assessing Knowledge and Judgement of Grocery Store Clerks

Performance level	Scale	Behavioral anchor
Extremely good performance	7-	
		By knowing the price of items, this checker would be expected to look for mismarked and unmarked items.
Good performance	6-	
		This checker would be aware of items that constantly fluctuate in price.
Slightly good performance	5-	
		When in doubt, this checker would ask the other clerk if the item is taxable. This checker can be expected to verify with another checker a discrepancy between shelf and marked price before ringing up the item.
Neither poor nor good performance	4-	
		When operating the quick check line (12 items or less), this checker can be expected to check out a customer with 15 items.
Slightly poor performance	3-	
		This checker will ask the customer to supply the price of an item that he does not know. In the course of daily personal relationships, this clerk may be expected to linger in long conversations with a customer or another checker.
Poor performance	2-	
		To take a break, this checker can be expected to block off the checkstand with customers in line.
Extremely poor performance	1-	
		This checker delays opening up the line.

ance dimensions lessens the chance that extraneous employee traits or peripheral job requirements will find their way into the evaluation. Third, BARS apply to a closely grouped, specific set of tasks, for the behavioral anchors are unique. This may in fact be a disadvantage, because an organization may have many job groupings, which requires the development of multiple BARS systems.

NOW IT'S YOUR TURN ...

Your job is to evaluate George Jefferson's appraisal system relative to the features of a BARS system. Read the statements on the left, then place a check in the space under the appraisal system that you think the statement best describes. Note that a third possibility exists; the statement may not apply to either system. Correct answers are at the end.

	Jefferson's System	BARS Appraisal System	Neither System
1. The appraisal system has performance dimensions with better validity.	________	____________	______
2. The system defines highly meaningful employee job behaviors.	________	____________	______
3. Employees would be consulted about design of the appraisal system.	________	____________	______
4. Feedback data generated is job-relevant.	________	____________	______
5. The system focuses in part on employee personality traits.	________	____________	______
6. The system can be generalized to jobs that are not related to those under immediate appraisal.	________	____________	______

Answers:

Statements 1, 2, 3, and 4 apply to a BARS system. Statements 5 and 6 apply to Jefferson's system.

Pros and cons of BARS systems. The quality of feedback in a BARS system may be better than that of other assessment procedures, because the emphasis is placed on behavior and *not* on whether the individual is a "good or bad" employee. This can cause the employee to react positively to the BARS feedback, because less emphasis is placed on personality and more on behavior and this reduces employee defensiveness. On the negative side, BARS systems take a long time to design and are expensive. They also cannot be generalized to a variety of job classifications. Each classification must have its own BARS system, because the behavioral anchors are job-specific. Finally, BARS systems work best when job behavior is always observable. Designing a BARS system for jobs that require creativity, intellectual curiosity, and complex problem-solving skills is more difficult. Jobs such as lawyer, physician, professor, scientist, and engineer do not meet BARS requirements.

Solving the Dilemma

How could Jefferson have handled this problem more effectively?

Based on our discussion, Jefferson could have taken a number of steps to handle the situation more effectively. First, he does not view his appraisal work as an important aspect of his supervisory activity. He fails to follow-up his appraisals with formal feedback sessions with subordinates, and he also fails to communicate their salary increase to them personally. These two failures can lower employee motivation dramatically over the long run. Failure to communicate performance feedback and failure to link rewards to good performance both violate important rules in the application of expectancy theory to motivation. Performance appraisal systems should stimulate employees to attain excellence on the job. Jefferson's approach is likely instead to produce employee snickers!

Knowledge Check

1. Graphic rating scales generate numerical evaluations of employees on a number of performance dimensions. T or F?
2. Graphic rating scales lessen the chances of systematic errors. T or F?
3. The critical incident method is useful for appraisals involving jobs that require creativity, intelligence, and curiosity. T or F?
4. Behavior anchored rating scales (BARS) emphasize employee personality traits. T or F?

Answers:

1 T, 2 F, 3 T, 4 F

Rewards and Reward Systems

Employees work to obtain important outcomes that satisfy their needs. Before most workers will demonstrate performance, they look for a payoff that has personal meaning. Since work organizations depend on employee participation, they are obliged to provide abundant and readily available rewards. Not all organizations are effective in this regard, and they reap the problems that can develop as a result. Before we examine some of these problems, let's examine the effects that rewards have on employee behavior.

How are rewards related to motivation?

Companies view money as the major motivator of employee performance. Money can be used to meet or reduce many of the basic needs in

Maslow's hierarchy. It is a convenience mechanism that has considerable value as a medium of exchange. All employees do *not* respond to money in the same way. Consider the situation in the dilemma. George gave both employees exactly the same raise, yet Alice and Bob had entirely different reactions to their pay increases. Alice sees hers as a boost to her self-esteem (for a job well done). In contrast, Bob feels that the company does not know how to reward performance, so his raise does not contribute to his self-esteem nor are we told that it improves his standard of living. The same raise thus produces entirely different reactions.

Rewards influence employee effort and performance level. Employees at all levels compare their efforts with those of other employees. Comparisons of effort level (and performance achieved) lead to comparisons of rewards received. The **perceived equity** of effort and commensurate reward is critical to job satisfaction, and ultimately, to performance. How the rewards are perceived can outweigh the actual rewards in terms of employee satisfaction. Expectancy theory makes it clear that if employees see no connection between performance and reward, then the rewards no longer function as motivators. Perceived inequity causes satisfaction with pay to plummet. The high-achieving employees who have experienced the most perceived inequity head for the door.

Classifying Organizational Rewards

Rewards fall into two general categories: extrinsic rewards and intrinsic rewards. **Intrinsic rewards** are defined as those rewards that employees are able to give to themselves as their work unfolds. These rewards create opportunities for employees to satisfy higher order needs such as self-esteem and self-actualization. **Extrinsic rewards** are defined as those administered by the organization through the formal reward system. These rewards are external to the job itself.

Extrinsic rewards can be broken down further into direct and indirect compensation. Those rewards that are given directly as money or near-money equivalents (i.e., stock options, expense account, use of company car) are **direct compensation. Indirect compensation** can also be an important part of the extrinsic reward system. These are rewards that are given regardless of the employee's level of work performance. For example, if only upper management is entitled to country club membership or to an American Express Gold Card, these perquisites are a function of job level and not a function of performance. If, however, indirect rewards are given only for meritorious performance, then these rewards can have a strong motivational property (11). The types and relationships of the different organizational rewards are shown in Figure 5.6.

Extrinsic rewards can be in the form of nonfinancial compensations. Peters and Waterman, in their provocative book *In Search of Excellence,* describe many company programs that emphasize the importance of "hoopla." **Hoopla** (defined by Webster's as "gaudy, pretentious show") is a form of nonfinancial reward that many employees find desirable. The different forms of hoopla are endless. Expectancy theory helps us understand the importance of hoopla. Some employees may

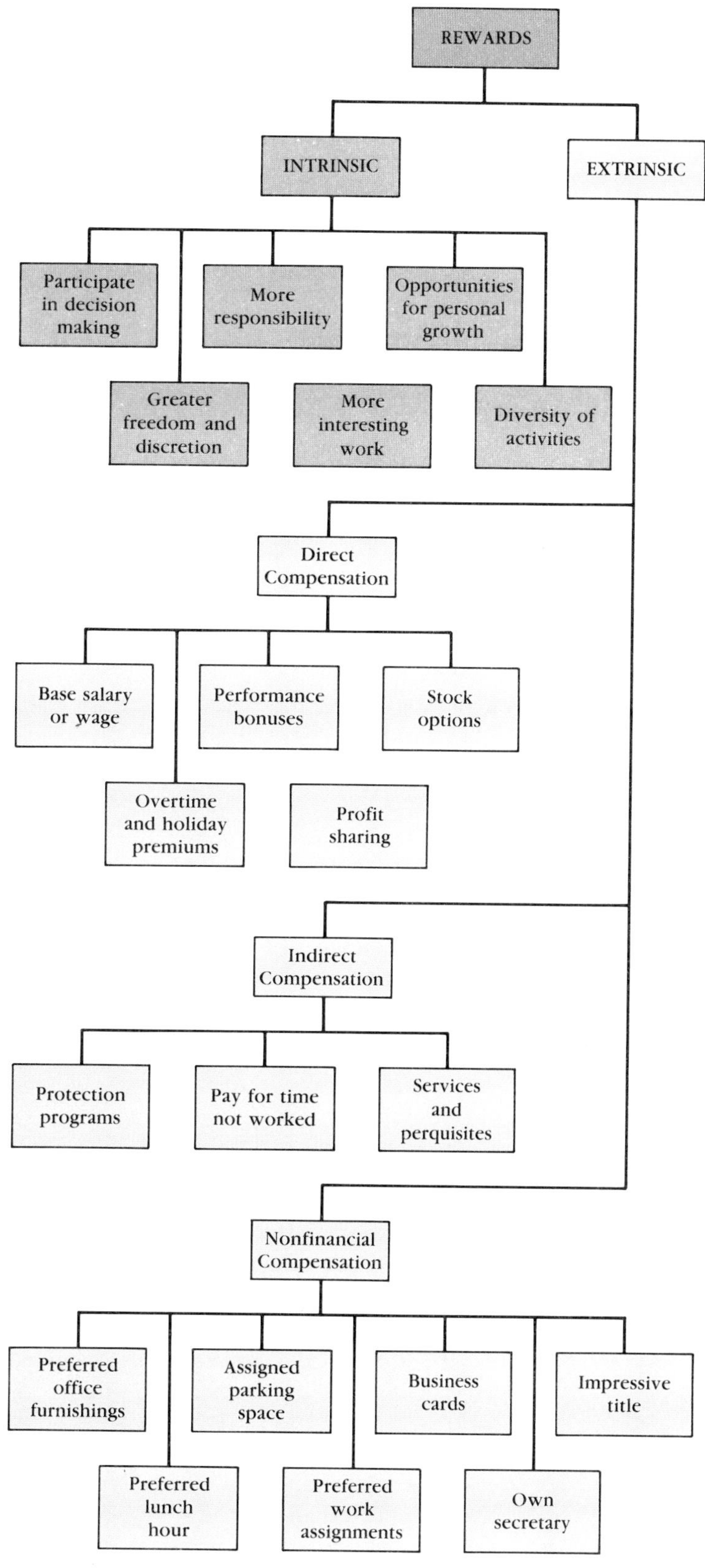

Figure 5.6
Types of Organizational Rewards

view a preferred parking space as a key reward. Others may view company jackets or tee shirts as equally desirable. The point is that a manager can tie any of these rewards to performance. Hoopla should be abundant and readily available to employees (12). The astute manager rewards excellent performance in as many ways as possible (i.e., catching employees doing things right versus doing things wrong). Returning for a moment to the dilemma, note that Jefferson does a poor job in this regard. He's so interested in his work that he fails to use any hoopla to motivate Bob or Alice.

A good example of powerful hoopla is exemplified by the Tupperware Company (13). Every Monday night, "At Rally" is held across the nation for the company's 80,000 salespeople. At a distributor's "At Rally" meeting, everyone marches up on stage in reverse order of last week's sales (known as the process of "Count Up"). Almost everyone receives a pin or badge to recognize achievement. During the "At Rally," everyone's performance becomes public knowledge, so the competitive power of the event is significant. Because an "At Rally" is conducted in an atmosphere of hoopla and positive expectations, everyone is perceived as a winner, and perceptions of the rewards tend to match sales results achieved.

Tupperware does not stop with the "At Rally" concept. Each week the company sponsors a huge array of contests. For 30 days each year, "Jubilee" is held. This event usually involves approximately 15,000 company employees, and all sorts of awards and prizes are given out during various employee-focused ceremonies (14). The company remains the most successful in its industry.

The Tupperware program emphasizes the importance of positive reinforcement. The company uses no formal performance review system. The "At Rally" alone is a powerful enough motivational tool to maximize sales behavior. It uses positive reinforcement, administered in a public setting, and combined with performance appraisal to achieve organizational goals.

Distributing Rewards in Organizations

All organizations are interested in rewards and the most effective ways to use them. Indeed, considerable confusion exists about the best way to administer rewards. Managers generally agree that merit is a good basis for dispensing rewards. Seniority, effort, and potential are also cited as reasons for giving rewards. Let's take a look at some of these different reasons and how their use might affect the organization.

Performance. Assessing the presence or absence of performance occupies numerous people in any organization. When rewards are allocated based on performance level, then performance becomes a motivator. Our discussion of performance appraisal systems centered on how to ensure that the relevant job behavior is featured in the appraisal system.

Effort. In the interest of keeping their employees, many organizations reward expenditure of effort. Effort does not necessarily produce performance. For example, a new employee who has not yet learned all performance behaviors may receive a reward simply because her boss wants to acknowledge potential. The manager reasons that the reward will keep the new employee from becoming discouraged, and hopes that effort and potential will soon be replaced by actual performance. We all sympathize with the employee who tries hard: "It's not whether you win or lose, but how you play the game." As a result, rewards often are distributed on this nonperformance-contingent basis. If, however, the distribution of such rewards becomes widespread, high performers may conclude that "it's not what I accomplish but how busy I look that counts." Expectancy theory then predicts that performance will decline among high performers.

Seniority. "Last in, first out." Seniority is understandably a major concern of labor unions, which function to protect the seniority of workers. Length of service is used to rank employees to determine who gets laid off first. Seniority also can become the basis for administering rewards. The government civil service system does not reward performance. Instead, endurance (i.e., sticking with a job so you progress through various pay grades) is rewarded. Even the various pay grades have little to do with performance. The original civil service pay system was designed to prevent political exploitation of government workers when newly elected officials were installed. The system removed (for a time) the threat of losing one's job because of one's political party affiliation. All too frequently, however, seniority can become a substitute for performance—in the civil service or in any organization. Note how readily observable seniority is, and consider all the ways in which employees express it.

Compensable factors. Many companies set up job classification systems that rate jobs against each other based on a number of dimensions. These dimensions are called **compensable factors** and are in turn the basis for a variety of salary decisions. For example, compensable factors determine the starting wages for various job classifications and define the relationships between pay grades. The compensable factors of interest to business organizations are defined as follows:

1. **Skill requirements** are the types of training and educational background that the employee needs to be technically qualified for the position. A refrigeration engineer needs a special certification indicating that he or she finished so many hours of technical training.
2. **Mental requirements** are the intellectual and emotional demands of the job. These may be problem-solving skills, decision-making aptitude, or ability to respond rationally under extreme pressure (e.g., hospital emergency room technician).
3. **Physical requirements** include health, strength, height, and weight. Although some of these requirements have been altered in recent years, many job descriptions still contain physical specifications.
4. **Responsibility** refers to impact of the job on the organization. Expressions of job responsibility include number of people supervised, dollar value of budgets overseen, and value of equipment managed.
5. **Working conditions** are those environmental factors that affect work performance. Temperature, noise level, lighting, and humidity are some of the factors that determine the working conditions.

Solving the Dilemma

Does Bob Reed have a legitimate complaint about Jefferson's handling of the incident?

Based on our discussion of performance appraisal, the answer is definitely *yes*. The system that Jefferson used is too personality-based, and was not designed in terms of compensable factors. There is also a weak link between the performance appraisal system and the reward system. Jefferson has no idea whether Bob or Alice's salaries reflect the compensable factors! His failure to document their performance (after eight months, it's still not done) represents a serious oversight. If Bob were to press a discrimination suit, a judge would view this fact unfavorably. Jefferson also has not explained the appraisal system to his subordinates. Bob and Alice have no idea how the system operates or what the data from the system mean. These facts also would go against Jefferson in a lawsuit. In short, Jefferson and his employer have a serious problem indeed!

Employee Beliefs About Reasons for Pay Raises

Let's look for a moment at the other side of the pay issue. We have discussed the reasons why organizations allocate rewards, but what do employees think about those rewards? Table 5.2 sheds some light on this issue. In the left-hand column are enumerated the reasons why employees think pay raises are given by their employers (15). Notice how employee perceptions change as you move across the employee categories.

The table shows that worker productivity was not perceived by any group as a major determinant of pay increases. Officers and executives viewed their pay as dependent on overall company financial results and prospects. The two categories of salaried workers have comparable perceptions. They believe that market forces determine pay increases, and believe further that their employers do industry salary surveys to find out what competitors are paying for comparable jobs. To a great extent, they are right. Compensation surveys are a useful organizational tool for ensuring that salary offers to new employees are close to the average market salaries across particular occupational classifications. When salary offers are too high or too low, the motivational impact of the company's pay system is damaged.

The greatest variance in perception about pay increases occurs between groups at the organizational extremes, that is, organization executives rank the items in nearly opposite order from the rankings assigned by hourly union workers. Top executives focus on the external dimensions of company performance, while hourly employees emphasize union demands and contract settlements. Note in both cases that individual worker productivity fails again to be number one!

Salaries of top executives are in fact seldom related to company performance (16). Although employees believe that executive pay is tied closely to company performance measures (e.g., profits, market share, cost containment), research on the linkage proves otherwise. How, then, can we justify our strong arguments for the need to link rewards to performance? And

Table 5.2 *Employee Beliefs About Reasons for Pay Raises*

Factors Determining Pay Increases	*Officers and Executives*	*Employee Category* * *Exempt Salaried*	** *Nonexempt Salaried*	*Nonunion Hourly*	*Union Hourly*
Worker productivity	4	7	5	3	9
Company's financial results	1	2	3	5	7
Company's financial prospects	2	3	4	4	5
Internal equity among groups	6	5	6	6	8
Pay increases by industry leaders	5	6	8	7	4
Area surveys	3	1	1	1	6
Ability to hire	7	8	7	10	10
National bargaining settlements	9	10	10	8	2
Union demands	10	9	9	9	1
Cost-of-living index	8	4	2	2	3

* Not paid for overtime.
** Paid for overtime.
NOTE: Importance rating determined by frequency of mentions in first, second, or third place in a ranking from 1 to 10. Employee sample composed of manufacturing (44%), banking and insurance (38%), utility (15%), and retail (3%) firms.
SOURCE: Adapted from D.A. Weeks, *Compensating Employees: Lessons of the 1970's*. Report no. 707 (New York: The Conference Board, 1976), pp. 12–14.

how does this linkage get broken for executives? Some possible reasons for the weak linkage are these: (17).

1. Although corporate officers are associated with overall company performance, they may be able to do little in the short run to influence it.
2. Emphasis on profitability has caused companies to de-emphasize the longer strategic viewpoint, and overall corporate performance across industries is declining. (Foreign competition is seen by many as the enemy.)
3. The roles of corporate officers are too complex to be reduced to simple performance-reward relationships.
4. Profitability is a good predictor of executive compensation only when the executive owns the business.
5. The political aspects of organizations break the linkage between performance and reward for executives. In other words, executives who play the political game best often get the rewards!

Comparing Company Pay Practices

The systems we discuss rest on the assumption that motivational linkage between performance and reward is highly desirable. Given this view, a pay system should be merit based. Obstacles, however, are lurking in organizations—just waiting to break the link between performance and reward. Several "new approaches to pay" are being discussed in business and academic circles (18). We turn now to these.

Cafeteria-style fringe benefits. Employees select a package of fringe benefits designed to fit their individual needs. Also called "flexible benefits packages," these programs match the fringe benefits to the organization's work force. The U.S. work force has changed dramatically in the last 20 years. Fifty percent of today's labor force is female. The work force is generally older, with more members who are likely to be single heads of households. More minority group members are now working. These demographic changes have put pressure on organizations to design more flexible benefits packages. Today's businesses seek to provide the special benefits required by a more diverse work force. For example, older employees may want to take more of their benefits as retirement income. Younger, married employees with children may prefer instead to have a better dental plan for the entire family.

Lump-sum pay systems. These plans allow employees to decide how their pay will be received during the coming year. Possible plans range from weekly pay checks to one large check at the beginning of the year. The lump sum is usually treated as an advance, which the employee then pays back throughout the work year. If an employee quits before year end (and has received a lump-sum payment), the unearned portion must be paid back to the employer.

You can imagine the difficulty of administering such lump-sum salary systems, particularly in an industry with high labor turnover. Indeed, these systems probably are not usable under such conditions. Lump-sum pay systems can also create short-term cash flow problems for companies.

Skill-based evaluation. This practice is based on a procedure called **job evaluation,** which is defined as the comparison of all jobs to each other based on the compensable factors listed on page 143. Jobs are awarded points for each compensable factor involved. This produces a ranking of jobs by skill level, and these rankings then are used as a basis for creating pay grades. An external compensation survey is performed to establish the pay range for each pay grade, and the pay grades are adjusted periodically for cost-of-living increases. Skill-based evaluation encourages the organization to be systematic in its use of pay increases as motivators. Such systems have the added benefit of being balanced in terms of salaries paid by competitors. Finally, the system encourages employees to seek additional training to qualify for jobs that are ranked higher on compensable factors. Employees realize the value of attaining better paying jobs that are more challenging.

Open-salary information. Pay secrecy can obscure the actual relationships between performance and rewards. If pay raise practices are poorly understood, employees are more likely to perceive a pay inequity. Employees often underestimate their own pay relative to coworkers and superiors, but they tend to overestimate their effort levels relative to these two groups. These tendencies are exaggerated under conditions of pay secrecy, and everyone is misinformed. You can see the negative impact on motivation. Management may not want to make individual pay decisions public, but publicizing the following features of a pay system has motivational value: (1) ranges for pay increases, (2) number of pay grades, (3) company guidelines on meaning of excellent performance, and (4) policies on bonuses and fringe benefits. Open pay practices can reduce significantly the adverse motivational effects of the old grapevine.

Participative pay plans. In the past, participatively determined pay systems were confined to collective bargaining agreements between labor and management. In recent years, however, some inventive firms have linked these pay systems to participative performance appraisal systems. An example of an organization that makes this work is the Woodward Governor Company in Rockford, Illinois. If the proper organizational climate is established, mistrust between management and labor can be virtually eliminated, and if these conditions are accompanied by work systems that create clear job expectations and reward excellent performance, then employees often become very concerned about good performance.

Employee participation in design of the pay system is a powerful incentive. Participative pay programs are more common in companies that are owned by the employees and in organizations that function as cooperatives (e.g., farmers cooperatives, artists cooperatives). Table 5.3 lists the newer pay practices and some of the factors that must be considered before adopting a given practice.

Comparable Worth: The Pay Issue of the 80s

Should a registered nurse in Milwaukee earn more than a garbage collector in San Francisco? If you believe in the law of supply and demand, the "going wage" for each job should be determined by the "fair market value" of that job. On the other hand, if you believe in "distributive

Table 5.3 *Summary of New Pay Practices*

Pay Practice	*Major Employee Advantages*	*Organizational Costs*	*Organizational Advantages*
Cafeteria-style fringe benefits	Increased satisfaction with pay and benefits	Cost of administration	Well-educated, heterogeneous work force
Lump-sum salary increases	Increased satisfaction with pay, greater visibility of pay increases	Cost of administration	Fair pay rates
Skill-based evaluation	More flexible and skilled work force, increased satisfaction	Cost of training and higher salaries	Employees who want to improve their skills, jobs that are interdependent
Open-salary information	Increased satisfaction with pay, greater trust and motivation, better salary administration	Pressure to pay all employees the same, complaints about pay rates	Open climate, fair pay rates, pay based on performance
Participative decisions	Better pay decisions, increased satisfaction, motivation, and trust	Time consumed	Democratic pay management climate, work force that wants to participate and is concerned about organizational goals

SOURCE: Reprinted by permission of the publisher from "New Approaches to Pay: Innovations that Work." E.E. Lawler. *Personnel,* September-October 1976.

justice" as a basis for determining pay, then a mechanism should be created to "correct the social injustice" of the market mechanism for making salary determinations. This is, in a nutshell, the issue of comparable worth in pay (19).

The issue of comparable worth is prominent because of social concern for the welfare of different groups of wage earners, especially women and minorities. Experts believe that an "earnings gap" exists between male and female employees (women consistently average 60 percent of male earnings) (20). The earnings gap is building the pressure to change the way in which salaries are determined. Comparable worth advocates insist that jobs be compared relative to (1) skill requirements, (2) level of responsibility, and (3) physical and mental demands (21). These comparisons are then used to determine the job's fair salary level. This mechanism is supposed to remove the biases and discrimination that inflate salaries for men when the supply and demand approach is used.

Comparable worth may upset traditional mechanisms for determining pay levels. Free market advocates believe that the comparable worth approach would raise prices, hurt lower-skilled employees, and ultimately harm the entire economy (22). In other words, raising women's salaries would not increase economic output; it would only raise prices (23). Which point of view do you take?

Individual and Group-Based Rewards

Our focus thus far has been on the properties of individual-based reward systems. There are many instances, however, when the goals of the organization depend on teamwork and joint employee effort. Group-based performance behavior also needs to be guided by management, and to the extent that teamwork is necessary to accomplish organization goals, group-based reward systems should encourage teamwork and collaboration.

What are group-based reward systems?

Group-based reward systems are tied to an individual-based reward system. The group-based portion has specific group performance behaviors that are linked with rewards received by groups. These systems are organization-wide incentive plans that use profits or cost savings as a basis for reward allocation to various employee groups.

Cost Savings Plans

The first systematic cost savings, group-based reward system was the **Scanlon plan,** developed in 1937. This plan tries to reduce labor costs below an historic base level. Groups are motivated by bonuses, which are contingent on reducing costs below the base rate. Let's consider an example:

Historically, labor costs at Omega Inc. have been 50 percent of output. Last month, the value of total output was $2 million, and labor costs were $900,000, or 10 percent below the 50 percent base rate. Under the Scanlon plan, the $100,000 savings would be put in an incentive fund, some of which (perhaps 30 percent) would be retained as a reserve (to cover those future months when labor costs go above 50 percent). Another 25 percent of the savings might be set aside for management, and the remaining 45 percent ($45,000) would be earmarked as a bonus for labor.

Scanlon plans focus on more than bonuses to motivate employees. These systems typically have a series of committees, interlocked across company levels, which generate and evaluate suggestions to achieve cost savings. Scanlon plans are powerful communication systems that encourage employee participation in cost reduction decisions. They can create strong bonds between labor and management, and the net effect can be widespread concern about productivity and cost control. Some companies have been very successful with the Scanlon plan, and report higher job satisfaction (and lower turnover) among both management and labor (24, 25). The Scanlon plan currently is used by about 100 U.S. companies.

Profit Sharing Plans

There are many examples of profit sharing plans; at least 175,000 U.S. companies use such systems. The rationale for these systems is that all employees contribute to success of the organization, so all should share in increased profits. The popularity of profit sharing plans varies in direct proportion to the health of the economy. The sense of partnership created by profit sharing has prompted numerous organizations to adopt such plans, and many companies boast of their success. Little research has, however, been done to validate these claims. One program, that of the Lincoln Electric Company, has a well-documented pattern of success. Let's examine that company's plan.

The Lincoln Electric Company was founded in 1896, and is the largest manufacturer of electrodes and arc welding equipment in the United States. The 2,000 company employees share approximately 80 percent of the company profits each year. The formal profit sharing plan was introduced in 1934 and has operated continuously ever since. Bonuses are determined by the following factors: (1) overall company profits, (2) supervisor merit ratings, and (3) cost savings suggestions.

Management stresses the importance of recognition in the reward system. Mr. Lincoln has written:

> The worker must feel that he is recognized in accordance with his contribution to success. If he does not have that feeling of self-respect and the respect of others because of his skill, he will think he is being played for a sucker if he increases his output so the owners can have more profit. . . . It is not necessary that this reward be solely in money. As a matter of fact, the amateur athlete gets no money, yet he tries harder than the professional who is paid. [Mr. Lincoln wrote this in 1951, before big-time college athletics were on the scene.] This athlete, however, does get the respect and position resulting from his achievement. That is his reward.

Mr. Lincoln's words highlight the importance of competition to the Lincoln Electric plan. The company places special emphasis on hiring employees who are intelligent and have competed in athletics in school. Management encourages competition for higher positions. Through a companywide network, employees sit on committees designed to solve production problems and to control costs. A "Suggestion System Board" reviews suggestions once a week.

How can a company decide which system, cost savings or profit sharing, to use?

Five guidelines can help management make decisions about adoption of cost savings versus profit sharing plans.

1. Any plan should be tied as closely as possible to employee performance. In our discussions of behavior modification and expectancy theory, we emphasize the importance of managing performance contingencies and instrumentalities. The plan should ensure that any group-based rewards are tied to performance. The shorter the time period between performance and reward, the higher the level of motivation.
2. The program should, as much as possible, allow for individual differences. Individuals want different rewards from work. Both the Lincoln Electric program and the Scanlon plan include abundant and various intrinsic and extrinsic rewards.
3. The plan should reflect the structure and goals of the organization. Performance appraisal systems channel and direct behavior toward goals. If unclear or inappropriate goals emerge from the organizational system, both systems will falter. If a company is unionized, for example, it would be inappropriate to try to install a program like Lincoln Electric's, but the Scanlon plan might be quite appropriate.
4. The plan must reinforce the work climate of the organization. For example, if trust between various company levels is minimal, forget group-based reward systems. If the company does not have a strong achievement-oriented climate, then group-based systems will probably fail. Indeed, before any system can be installed, deficiencies in the organization climate must be addressed.
5. The plan must be monitored over time to ensure that rewards are being distributed equitably, and that the design of the reward system parallels the way work gets done. For instance, if a firm decided to use computer controlled robots, the reward system for employees should be reevaluated. If product characteristics change, the sales department reward system should probably be analyzed, and so forth.

These five guidelines indicate that management is largely responsible for preserving the relevance and integrity of the reward system. If the system's effectiveness begins to deteriorate, then deterioration of the performance appraisal system will soon follow. Assuming that a good reward system need only be designed, installed, and then forgotten is a classic motivational mistake of management. Productivity declines in numerous sectors of our economy (with accompanying surges in productivity of foreign competitors) can be laid at the doorstep of management. On inspection of these productivity problems, the performance appraisal and reward systems often emerge as the major culprits that are undermining the organization. Managers must recognize that changing business conditions and competition necessitate creative changes in performance appraisal and reward system design. A company should always be looking for new ways to evaluate and reward employee performance.

Solving the Dilemma

What lessons can be learned from Bayou Steel's performance appraisal system?

Answers to the other dilemma questions all lead to one conclusion: Bayou Steel's performance appraisal system should be scrapped; the company should design a new system from the ground up. Employees from all departments should be consulted about design of the new system (a BARS system might be most appropriate). Employee objections to the present system should be analyzed thoroughly, and the goals and objectives of the firm should be translated into meaningful performance dimensions (compensable factors would be useful here). Once the basic system is designed, it should be pilot-tested with current employees. This step would help establish the validity of the BARS. Finally, supervisors should be trained in how to evaluate performance and how to give productive feedback. All employees should be educated as to how the system operates and what their rights of review are under the new approach. If these basic steps had been followed, Bayou Steel might not be facing the problem created by Jefferson.

Knowledge Check

1. Rewards influence motivation and performance through equity comparisons. T or F?
2. Which of the following is *not* one of the bases for which rewards are usually given? (a) performance, (b) seniority, (c) compensable factors, (d) effort, or (e) level of job satisfaction.
3. Generally speaking, top management and hourly union employees rank the reasons for pay raises in the same order. T or F?
4. Changes in composition of the work force have caused companies to use more flexible benefits programs. T or F?
5. When pay systems are based on secrecy, employees tend to be more satisfied with their pay levels. T or F?
6. The __________ is an example of a group-based, cost savings incentive system.
7. The Lincoln Electric plan has elements of both cost savings and profit sharing. T or F?
8. If the organization work climate encourages trust between labor and management, a profit sharing plan has a good chance for success. T or F?

Answers:

1 T, 2 e, 3 F, 4 T, 5 F, 6 Scanlon plan, 7 T, 8 T

Summary Points

■ **Performance appraisal systems** track progress toward meeting company goals, communicate performance expectations to employees, and create informed data for making personnel decisions.

■ **Validity** and **reliability** are the two single most important properties of a performance appraisal system.

■ **Central tendency, leniency,** and **strictness** are systematic errors made in performance appraisal. Other forms of rating bias can result from **personal bias, halo effect, recency error, similarity error,** and **forcing the rating to match other criteria.**

■ **Graphic rating scales** are the most popular assessment tool. This method overcomes some of the limitations of absolute standards.

■ **BARS systems** are designed with the help of employees, and can generate useful behavioral data that employees perceive as relevant to successful job performance. BARS systems are more expensive to design, but they can be extremely useful when jobs have very specific behavioral requirements.

■ Management often overlooks the motivational impact of **nonfinancial rewards,** or **"hoopla."** Many companies report increased motivation and performance when these features are added to the extrinsic rewards package.

■ Pay systems should be built on **job evaluation,** and ranking of jobs should be based on **compensable factors. Salary surveys** are useful for establishing salary ranges for different job categories. A pay system based on compensable factors encourages employees to seek further training to improve their skill level and pay grade.

■ **Cafeteria-style fringe benefits** are becoming more popular as the composition of the labor force becomes more diverse.

■ **Group-based incentive programs** can improve productivity when labor and management view themselves as being in a performance partnership. The **Scanlon plan** and the profit sharing program at **Lincoln Electric Company** are the two best known programs.

Questions

1. What are the basic purposes of using a performance appraisal system in the organization? What are some of the ways that management can ensure that both company and employee needs are being satisfied by the performance appraisal process?
2. Working in a small group, see if you can develop a BARS for two performance dimensions associated with giving a class presentation. Ask several other students outside the group to evaluate the meaningfulness of your group's behavioral anchors. Does the second group agree with the importance of the two dimensions developed by your team?
3. Develop three reasons why BARS may not be the best method for evaluating performance of employees who have jobs with uncertain or ambiguous requirements.
4. Recalling the discussion of compensable factors, what are the compensable factors associated with the job of "student"? Be sure to describe the academic version of these compensable factors.
5. Why does pay secrecy often lead to widespread job dissatisfaction, even though most company employees may be getting pay raises?
6. How do incentive systems like the Scanlon plan and the Lincoln Electric program influence the work climate of an organization? Do these programs really do more than "just hang more carrots in front of the employees"? Give some examples to justify your reasoning.
7. What types of hoopla could be used by college instructors to motivate students? Do you think that the use of hoopla is appropriate in the classroom?
8. Think back to when you were dissatisfied with a course grade. Were there errors made in the appraisal of your performance? Describe these errors and how to correct them.
9. Ask a working friend about his or her firm's performance appraisal system. What are its good and bad features? Does your friend think that the system motivates performance?

EXPLORING: *Performance Appraisal at the Louisiana Superdome*

The Louisiana Superdome is the largest indoor sports and assembly facility in the world. It is home to the New Orleans Saints and an often-used site for rock concerts and huge conventions. The facility is run by a division of the Hyatt Corporation. The corporation had a performance appraisal system that was trait based. Both employees and management believed that the system should be dropped in favor of one that was based on more objective criteria.

Redesign of the performance appraisal system was started by organizing a steering committee of employees who were interested in changing the system. With the assistance of consultants, the steering committee revised all of the employee job descriptions. As a part of this task, employees were interviewed in small groups to gather their opinions about work dimensions that could be directly observed and assessed across all relevant jobs involving the Superdome. In this way, the following dimensions were developed:

Acceptance of responsibility
Productivity orientation
Working with others
Following safety procedures
Applying job knowledge
Planning time and work

With the help of supervisors, the steering committee next developed at least six behaviors to support each of the performance dimensions. A numerical rating scale was approved by the employees, and the entire performance appraisal system was pilot-tested for validity and reliability. The steering committee and the consultants then coauthored a training manual to teach all supervisors how to use the new performance appraisal system. In one-day training sessions, supervisors were taught: (1) how to recognize appraisal errors, (2) how to conduct feedback sessions properly, (3) how to set objectives in the context of performance appraisal, and (4) how to handle employee disagreements about performance ratings.

The new system was put in place in 1984 and has been well received by Superdome employees. Several employees have been promoted to higher level positions, and two employees are managing other sport facilities run by the Hyatt Corporation. The Superdome employees believe that the new appraisal system represents their job activities much more accurately. They also believe that the information provided to them during the feedback sessions is more meaningful and job related than the information they received before the system was revised.

Supervisors also are pleased with the updated system. Most find that the new behavioral approach makes performance appraisals more accurate. Furthermore, they state that they are more willing to keep accurate records in their employee appraisal work because subordinates are now more willing to act on the feedback they receive.

Discussion Questions

1. Why is it important that employees have a hand in designing a new performance appraisal system?
2. What additional functions did the steering committee perform besides helping to design the new performance appraisal system?
3. Why do the Superdome employees believe that the new system is more valid and reliable than the old trait-based system?

APPLYING: *Determining Employee Pay Raises*

Read the following supervisory narratives written about five employees, then use all or only part of the information to determine independently how large each employee's raise should be. (Assume that you have $15,000 that could be distributed among the five employees. You are not required to use the entire $15,000, nor do all employees have to receive a raise. If you choose, termination is an option for any employee. Make your decisions and record the size of your raise in the space next to each employee's name. When you have finished this part of the assignment, your instructor may want you to gather in small groups to compare and discuss your conclusions.)

_____ Willard Jones has been with the insurance agency for six months. His coworkers describe him as friendly, and several customers have sent letters to his supervisor indicating their satisfaction with his work. Willard has a habit of keeping his own work hours, and he frequently cuts his office time short. He says, "I can get more work done away from the office." A company policy requires all sales personnel to be in the office from 8 to 9 A.M. and 4 to 5 P.M. His sales are about average, and he has met his sales quota for three of the past six months.

_____ Wanda Waymer has also been with the agency for six months. She has exceeded her sales quota four times (the last four months in a row). Some customers have called to complain about her "hard sell, high-pressure techniques." She is a single parent and is raising two youngsters who are both in day care. She observes all company rules carefully, her paperwork is always flawless.

_____ Reggie Axelrod has been with the agency for three months and has not yet made the sales quota. He has a history of absenteeism and frequently misses the required morning and afternoon office hours. His coworkers describe him as "aloof" and "standoffish." He is currently going to night school and will graduate with a degree in insurance management sometime next year. He is working at the agency to support his mother and sister, who live together.

_____ Beth Rosemont is highly regarded by her coworkers, even though she has been with the agency for only eight months. She is responsible for several innovations that have saved the agency several thousand dollars. She has met her sales quota for three of the eight months. Beth has indicated that she would like eventually to manage an agency for the company. The other salespeople agree that she has excellent management skills.

_____ Jerry Beaumont has been with the agency for six months. His performance has been quite good; he has met the sales quota for each month. He had significant experience with another agency before taking this job. Several competitors have tried to hire him, but he seems content with his current situation here. His skill in all aspects of insurance work occasionally make him the object of employee envy. Customers call him frequently, and he's always on top of all of the details of their accounts. He willingly observes all company rules and procedures in his work.

Suggested Readings

Cascio, W., and Bernardin, H. 1981. Implications of Performance Appraisal Litigation for Personnel Decisions. *Personnel Psychology* (Summer 1981): 211–26.

Dalton, G., Thompson, P., and Rice, L. 1977. A New Look at Performance Appraisal by Professionals. *Organizational Dynamics* (Summer 1977): 19–42.

Henderson, R. 1982. *Compensation Management.* Reston, Va.: Reston Publishing.

This text provides an excellent discussion of employee rewards and methods for classifying them. It explains the important relationship between performance appraisal and reward systems. You will be amazed at all of the rewards that can exist in organizations.

Landy, F., and Farr, J. 1980. Performance Rating. *Psychological Bulletin* (February 1980): 72–107.

Latham, G., and Wexley K. 1981. *Increasing Productivity Through Performance Appraisal.* Reading, Mass.: Addison-Wesley.

The authors make a strong case for the important role played by performance appraisal in making both employees and organizations effective. You have enough knowledge from this chapter to make reading this book extremely useful.

Patten, T. 1977. *Employee Compensation and Incentive Plans.* Riverside, N.J.: The Free Press.

Peters, T., and Waterman, R. 1982. *In Search of Excellence.* New York: Harper & Row.

While not the last word on reward systems and how to design them, this book will get you excited about the potential power of reward systems. The authors present their analyses of many corporations—organizations that believe in the importance of catching employees "doing things right"!

Schliemann, W. 1983. *Managing Human Resources/1983 and Beyond.* Chestnut Hill, Mass.: Opinion Research Corporation.

The author does a credible job of discussing some of the important developments in the area of performance appraisal. With an eye to the future, he describes some organizational trends that may change the performance appraisal process radically.

Schnier, D. 1978. The Impact of EEO Legislation on Performance Appraisals. *Personnel* (July-August 1978): 24–34.

References

1. Hall, D., and Goodale, J. 1986. *Human Resource Management: Strategy, Design and Implementation.* Glenview, Ill.: Scott Foresman.
2. Smith, D. 1983. *Increasing Rater Accuracy Through Rater Training: A Look at the Performance Appraisal Process.* Unpublished doctoral dissertation, Colorado State University, Fort Collins, Colo.
3. Jacobs, R., and Kozlowski, S. 1985. A Closer Look at Halo Error in Performance Ratings. *Academy of Management Journal* 29:201–212.
4. Smith, D. 1986. Training Programs for Performance Appraisal: A Review. *Academy of Management Review* 11:22–40.
5. Pulakos, E. 1984. A Comparison of Training Programs: Error Training and Accuracy Training. *Journal of Applied Psychology* 69:581–583.
6. Smith, D., op. cit., 1986.
7. Ibid.
8. Lee, C. 1985. Increasing Performance Appraisal Effectiveness: Matching Task Types, Appraisal Process and Rater Training. *Academy of Management Review* 10:322–336.

9. Locher, A., and Teel, K. 1977. Performance Appraisal: A Survey of Current Practices. *Personnel Journal* (May 1977):245–247.
10. Ibid.
Hampton, D., Summer, C., and Webber, R. 1982. *Organizational Behavior and the Practice of Management,* 4th ed. Glenview, Ill. Scott Foresman.
Singular, J. 1975. Has MBO Failed? *MBA* (October 1975):47–50.
Hampton, D., et al., op. cit., 1982.
Erez, M., and Kanfer, F. 1983. The Role of Goal Acceptance in Goal Setting and Task Performance. *Academy of Management Review* 8:454–463.
Erez, M., Earley, P., and Hulin, C. 1985. The Impact of Participation on Goal Acceptance and Performance: A Two-Step Model. *Academy of Management Journal* 28:50–66.
11. Robbins, S. 1983. *Organizational Behavior Concepts, Controversies, and Applications.* Englewood Cliffs, N.J.: Prentice Hall.
12. Peters, T., and Waterman, R., Jr. 1982. *In Search of Excellence.* New York: Harper & Row.
13. Ibid.
14. Ibid.
15. Weeks, D. 1976. Compensating Employees: Lessons of the 1970's. New York: The Conference Board (Report No. 707):12–14.
16. Ungson, G., and Steers, R. 1984. Motivation and Politics in Executive Compensation. *Academy of Management Review* 9:313–323.
17. Ibid.
18. Lawler, E., III. 1981. *Pay and Organizational Development.* Reading, Mass.: Addison-Wesley.
19. Mahoney, T. 1983. Approaches to the Definition of Comparable Worth. *Academy of Management Review* 8:14–22.
20. Grune, J. 1980. *A Manual on Pay Equity: Raising Wages for Women's Work.* Washington, D.C.: Conference on Alternative State and Local Policies.
21. Ibid.
22. Samuelson, R. 1985. The Myths of Comparable Worth. *Newsweek* (22 April 1985):71–72.
23. Ibid.
24. Geare, A. 1976. Productivity from Scanlon Type Plans. *Academy of Management Review* 3:99–108.
25. White, J. 1979. The Scanlon Plan: Causes and Correlates of Success. *Academy of Management Journal* 22:192–212.

2-20-85
Chris Angell
10-17-84
Machines
Manpower
Rough Rollers 3
Roller not turning
Temperature Not Adequate 4
Size Improperly Mixed 1
Size Build-Up
Ends
Fuzzy Yarn
Dirty Size 1
Poor Quality PVA 3
Hot Size 6
Weak Yarn 4
Yarn Picking up Too Much Size
Foil
Cut Away View

Job Design

Chapter 6

Chapter Goals

By the end of the chapter, you will be able to:

1. Explain why job redesign has become an important way of counteracting the effects of excessive job specialization.
2. Describe the difference between enriched jobs and jobs that are in need of redesign.
3. Explain the major approaches to job redesign at the employee level.
4. Develop reasons for management's interest in the effects of job redesign.
5. Understand the important role of growth need strength in job redesign.
6. Apply the principles of job redesign.
7. Develop the reasoning behind job redesign at the group level.
8. Explain the pros and cons of employee participation in the workplace.
9. Describe the characteristics of a participative organizational design.
10. Discuss new developments in the design of employee participation systems that are for work groups.

Dilemma Computech's Experiment With Job Redesign

Computech installs and services computer equipment in retail firms. Computech actually owns the equipment, and through a leasing arrangement, maintains the equipment for its customers. The company has 1,500 field "tech reps" who are graduates of the company's training program. The reps are highly trained and specialize in repair of certain types of equipment. Lately, the tech reps have been complaining about many features of their job. The director of field services is concerned because the reps' average number of service calls per month has slipped. Absenteeism and turnover have also increased, and the director was then informed that several key customers had cancelled their leases.

A job redesign expert was contacted to analyze the work problems. In discussing the problems with the director of field services, the expert was told that "our reps are the best in the business. Each one goes through 40 hours of training on maintenance procedures each year." The director noted the following features of a tech rep's job and also pointed out some problems.

1. The reps did not seem motivated to "go the extra 10 percent." Few would do weekend service calls, even though each rep was assigned weekend duty only once every two months.
2. The reps' salary levels, fringe benefits, and vacation benefits were consistent with the industry.
3. The reps got along well together, although they mostly worked alone. Computech management set the work schedules, and occasionally a team of reps was organized to work on a large job.
4. Instructors in the training program had noted that the reps were less satisfied with their job. They reported also that the reps talked about their job in negative terms.
5. The company has documented a decline in applications to their technical training school.

The job design expert decided to interview some tech reps. He talked with over 100 reps from all of the field territories. A summary of their comments follows.

1. We can't order parts. Management does the ordering, and it's often too little and too late.
2. We aren't allowed to carry nonroutine parts. Management is worried about the cost of parts and these have to be special-ordered.
3. To get technical assistance from engineering, we have to go through management first.
4. Management gives us fixed work schedules and sets our customer routing schedules.
5. All customer complaints must be referred to the divisional sales manager. We're not authorized to take any on-site action on complaints.
6. Management determines the maintenance schedule for our vans, and management must approve all repairs first.

The reps had other important reactions to their job. They enjoyed the training seminars because they got to learn new repair methods. Most said that they found their work challenging, yet they were frustrated because they could not act directly on customer complaints. As a result, they felt that they couldn't deliver quality service. This problem reflected badly on them personally, they believed, for they were the Computech employees who had the most sustained contact with customers. The reps indicated that they were basically satisfied with company benefits and with the pay system. They did not have problems working together either. Several reps admitted candidly that they were considering job opportunities with other firms despite the fair pay and generally good working conditions at Computech.

The expert organized a series of meetings attended in each instance by two supervisors and four reps. These "job expert groups" were challenged to come up with as many changes for the tech rep position as possible. After they generated a list, the group screened the suggestions for feasibility. Ten of these meetings were conducted in the Chicago-Milwaukee area. Below is a partial list of the suggestions created by the groups:

1. Reps should have full authority to order routine and nonroutine parts.
2. Reps should go directly to engineering for technical assistance.
3. Reps should handle their own vehicle maintenance up to $500 in annual repair costs.
4. Reps should design their own territory coverage and be able to operate from their homes. Each rep could have a beeper to stay in contact with the office.
5. Reps should process customer complaints up to $1,000 in repair work.
6. Reps should maintain their own quality control reports.
7. Reps should help select new job applicants, and should take turns instructing at the company's technical school.

Based on these suggestions, the job expert implemented his plan for job redesign. Fifty reps and their supervisors were selected to participate in a small pilot program. In this program, work attitudes (i.e., job satisfaction and job involvement), performance, and motivation were measured. In addition, customer satisfaction was assessed before the above changes were implemented. The pilot program was instituted in the Chicago-Milwaukee area. (Similar measurements were made for tech reps in the St. Louis area, but for the time being, none of the job changes were implemented there.)

After eight months, the attitude, motivation, performance, and customer satisfaction measures were taken again. The director of field services had good reason to be very pleased. Little change was noted for the St. Louis reps, but a much changed picture emerged for the Chicago-Milwaukee reps. In the latter geographic area, the following results were obtained:

1. Tech rep turnover had dropped 10 percent, and performance was up 16 percent.
2. Job satisfaction, job involvement, and motivation all measured higher for the reps in the pilot program.
3. Vehicle maintenance costs had not risen during the period, and reps reported less vehicle down time.

4. Reps reported better customer relations, and customers reported greater satisfaction with their leases. Customer complaints were down 37 percent.

Questions

1. Why were the tech reps so dissatisfied with their job?
2. What were the effects of the changes made in the tech rep job?
3. Why did the tech reps respond so favorably to the job changes?
4. Did employee participation play an important role in the success of the Computech job redesign program?

Understanding Job Redesign

Job redesign is an application of motivational theory. It also is a component of the broader subject of **quality of work life,** and is defined as the meaningfulness of work in the lives of employees (1). The basic task in a quality of work life program is to design jobs that are both meaningful for employees and excellent for production. The program is specifically concerned with humanizing work so jobs provide more opportunities for employees to satisfy their higher order needs while improving performance. Quality of work life programs try to integrate employee needs with the organizational goals.

How were jobs designed before quality of work life programs?

Traditionally, job design focused on the principles of **scientific management.** Scientific management is a systematic process, developed by Frederick Taylor, whereby work is broken down into basic task units that are assigned to specific workers. It was an outgrowth of the Industrial Revolution, and its purpose was to find efficient ways to produce products (2). Here are the basic principles of scientific management:

1. **Machine pacing:** Production is determined by equipment speed and not by workers
2. **Repetitiveness:** Tasks are performed over and over during a work shift. On an assembly line, the operator may perform a task every four minutes, for a total of 120 tasks per day. Many jobs require performance of a given operation up to as many as 500 times per day.
3. **Low skill requirements:** With specialized jobs, training costs are low because the tasks can be learned quickly.
4. **Task specialization:** Each job has only a few operations as the product is passed from one step to another down the assembly line.
5. **Limited social interaction:** Because of the speed requirements, noise, and physical space limitations, workers find it hard to talk or interact during work.

6. **Tools and techniques are specified:** Company experts determine the best way to do the work so efficiency and production are maximized (3).

Scientific management can lead to problems. Scientific management led to the development of the modern-day assembly line. Praised around the world for its efficiency, it became the industrial model followed by manufacturers. As companies rushed to get on the productivity bandwagon, they forgot about the needs and goals of the people who performed these "scientifically designed jobs." Overdependence on rules and work procedures took job control away from employees. The physical work arrangements often caused employees to feel isolated, and many lost their sense of pride and craftsmanship in their work. After all, they never saw the finished product. All they did was perform a small task over and over and over.

Employee job dissatisfaction led to organizational problems. Firms with scientifically designed work systems began to experience high labor turnover, absenteeism, and lower productivity. Job satisfaction and job involvement declined, and labor grievance rates rose as employees tried to improve their work conditions through union activity. In general, management's response to these problems was to tighten controls (after all, employees are simply lazy and avoid responsibility) and to increase the number of supervisors on the shop floor. The work environment was tightly organized according to Taylor's six principles listed. A downward spiral was set in motion by these practices and trends. Workers became bored and more alienated from their work, and management reacted more "scientifically" to restore order and efficiency.[1]

Is job redesign becoming more popular?

With time, management finally realized that work design based on Taylor's principles had major drawbacks for both organizations and their employees. Better educated employees expect more from their work (see Maslow's hierarchy, Chapter 3). The work force also has changed dramatically in the last 25 years. More employees are college graduates, and more women are now in the work force. These demographic shifts have created additional pressure to change work designs. The scientific management system simply does not focus adequate attention on employee needs and work aspirations. Indeed, widespread application of Taylor's principles has led instead to labor problems and dissatisfaction among workers (commonly called the "blue collar blues" and the "white collar woes") (4, 5).

Herzberg's Contributions to Job Design

Recall from Chapter 3 that Herzberg developed the two factor theory of job motivation (6). His theory proposes that job dissatisfaction has a different origin (i.e., absence of hygiene factors) from motivation, which Herzberg says is caused by motivators. (The theory is detailed in Figure 3.4 on page 70.) In his studies, Herzberg found that employees are motivated by work when the motivating factors are present (challenge, responsibility, pride in work, personal growth, and so forth). When employees are dissatisfied,

1. See J. O'Toole, Lordstown: Three Years Later. *Business and Society Review* (Spring 1975): 69.

then the hygiene factors are probably absent (salary, coworkers, supervision, work policies, and so forth).

Herzberg argues that changing hygiene factors is nonproductive when the goal is increased motivation and performance (7). Hygiene must be maintained at an appropriate level and efforts should be made to improve the motivating aspects of the job (8). Herzberg summarizes the principles of job design as follows:

1. Employees should have maximum control over the mechanisms of task completion.
2. Employees should be held accountable for their performance.
3. Supervisors have a responsibility to provide direct, clear, and frequent feedback to employees.
4. Within limits, employees should be able to set their own work pace.
5. Jobs should allow employees to experience accomplishment.
6. Employees should learn new and different procedures on the job and be able to experience some degree of personal growth (9).

With these principles in mind, let's see how you would apply them. Now Its Your Turn presents some information from the Computech dilemma. See if you can identify correctly which of Herzberg's rules applies to the various job changes made for tech reps.

NOW IT'S YOUR TURN . . .

Instructions: In column 1 are Herzberg's job redesign rules. Column 2 indicates Computech's job changes for reps. In column 3, write the number(s) of the Herzberg rule or rules that apply to the job changes in column 2. Any given rule may apply to more than one job change, and a job change may represent the use of multiple rules.

1 *Herzberg's Rules*	2 *Computech's Job Changes*	3 *Appropriate Herzberg Rule(s)*
1. Control over resources	A. Reps have authority to order parts.	A. ______
2. Accountability	B. Reps go directly to engineering for technical assistance.	B. ______
3. Feedback	C. Reps set up own maintenance schedules.	C. ______
4. Work pace	D. Vehicle repairs up to $500 done by reps.	D. ______
5. Achievement opportunities	E. Reps work from home.	E. ______
6. Personal growth and development	F. Reps process client complaints up to $1000.	F. ______
	G. Reps complete quality control reports.	G. ______
	H. Reps screen job applicants.	H. ______
	I. Reps are trainers at company school.	I. ______

Answers:

A 1 and 4, B 1, C 2 and 4, D 1 and 4, E 2 and 4, F 4, G 1, 5 and 6, H 2 and 3, I 2, 5 and 6

Herzberg's rules and scientific management compared. Herzberg's principles represent a radical departure from the scientific management approach to job design. His philosophy assumes that employees want to work hard and that they have work-based aspirations that are not satisfied by money alone. In contrast, scientific management assumes that organization executives know what is best for all employees, and that job specialization leads to efficiency and easily controlled employee needs.

Solving the Dilemma

Why were the tech reps so dissatisfied with their job?

Herzberg's job design principles provide an easy answer to this question. The original tech rep job configuration indicates that the reps have little opportunity to satisfy their higher order needs. The only time that they are able to do this is when they have their annual training on new equipment maintenance procedures. Their levels of job motivation and satisfaction go up during training. Job frustration can be removed by (1) giving reps more control over work resources, (2) making reps accountable for client relationships, (3) providing better performance feedback, (4) allowing reps to control their own scheduling (work pace), and (5) providing real opportunities for achievement and personal development.

Knowledge Check

1. The problem faced by Computech is best described as a problem of job design. T or F?
2. Job redesign represents the methods that are applied to improve quality of work life. T or F?
3. Designing jobs that have low skill requirements is a basic component of job redesign. T or F?
4. Scientific management should be replaced as a way of designing work because it takes an over-simplified view of human nature in the workplace. T or F?
5. Herzberg's two factor theory is a cornerstone of job design. T or F?
6. Herzberg's approach to job design accounts for not all people wanting a redesigned job. T or F?

Answers:

1 T, 2 T, 3 F, 4 T, 5 T, 6 F

The Job Characteristics Model

In proposing his two factor theory, Herzberg made the first systematic effort to understand the relationships between employees and their job. Another approach to work redesign has been developed (10). This approach, called the **job characteristics model** (Figure 6.1), integrates the results of many earlier job design studies (11, 12).

Let's look carefully at the components of the model.

Core job dimensions. These are the specific task characteristics that lead to the critical psychological states. They are the features of a job that can be controlled and changed to influence employee behavior. Each one is defined as follows.

1. **Skill variety** is the degree to which a job requires a number of different skills, talents, and abilities to accomplish task activities. Jobs that require both technical and interpersonal skills typically possess high skill variety (e.g., lawyer or physician).

Figure 6.1
The Job Characteristics Model

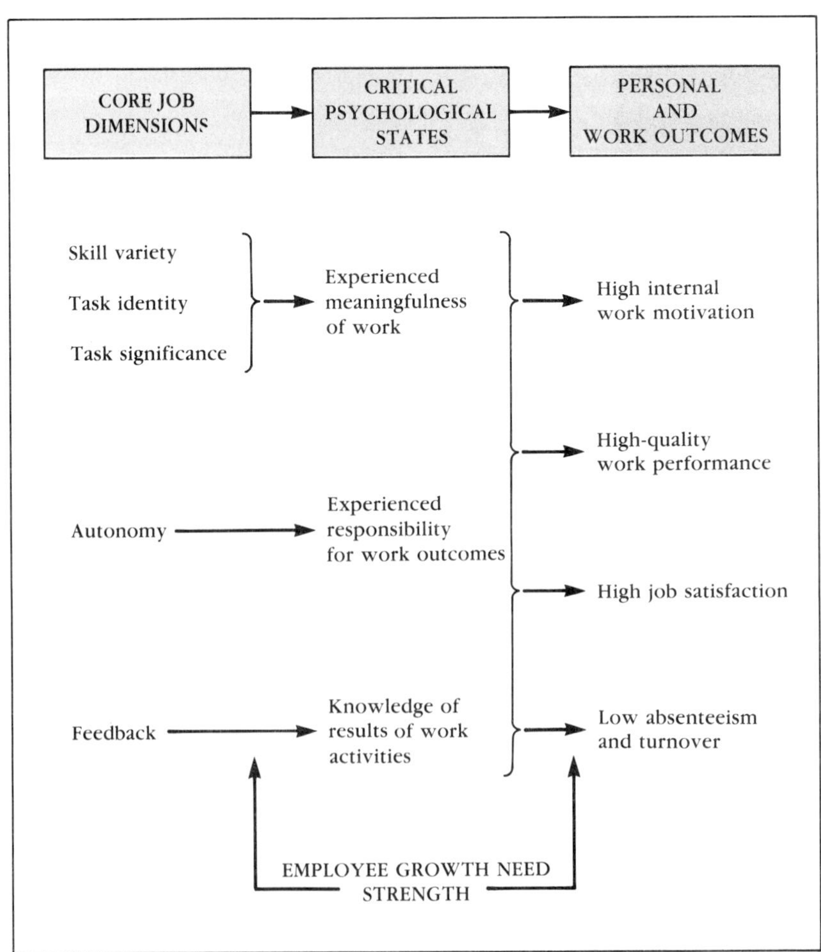

SOURCE: J. Richard Hackman, "Work Design," in J.R. Hackman and J.L. Suttle, (eds.), *Improving Life at Work,* Santa Monica, CA: Scott, Foresman, and Company, 1977, p. 129.

2. **Task identity** is the degree to which the job requires doing a complete task from beginning to end and experiencing a visible and identifiable outcome (e.g., building kitchen cabinets from scratch).
3. **Task significance** is the degree to which the job has a substantial and lasting influence on the lives of employees and other people, both in the immediate organization and in society in general. As examples of jobs with high task significance, think of a surgeon or judge.
4. **Autonomy** is the degree to which a job gives the employee personal freedom and discretion to control work activities and schedules. Autonomy is high for entrepreneurs and other self-employed individuals.
5. **Feedback** is the degree to which the task itself provides direct and complete information on the effectiveness of employee work behavior. Being a waiter is a good example (13).

Now that you have an understanding of these core job dimensions, let's test your understanding of the tech rep job at Computech before and after the company job redesign program. The Now It's Your Turn section lists core job dimensions in the left column. The middle column represents the "before job redesign" condition. Use the scale to assess the tech rep job on each core job dimension *before* and *after* job redesign. When you have completed your assessment, total the points in the "before" and "after" columns. You should have a difference of at least 15 to 20 points, and the new job design should be rated a significant improvement for each job dimension. If your score totals did not reflect these improvements, go back and reread the dilemma and the definitions of the core job dimensions.

NOW IT'S YOUR TURN . . .

Use the following rating scale to assess the core job dimensions of the tech rep job *before* and *after* the job redesign program at Computech.

1	2	3	4
VERY POOR	POOR	GOOD	EXCELLENT

CORE JOB DIMENSIONS	BEFORE JOB REDESIGN	AFTER JOB REDESIGN
Skill variety	________	________
Task identity	________	________
Task significance	________	________
Autonomy	________	________
Feedback	________	________
TOTAL	________	________

Critical psychological states. The first three core job dimensions influence the **meaningfulness of work,** which is defined as having a job that has significant impact on both the individual and the employer. Autonomy determines **experienced responsibility,** or the extent to which employees believe they are accountable for their work.

Feedback influences **knowledge of results,** which is defined as receiving information about the quality of one's work as the task unfolds. This type of feedback referred to in the model is called "feedback from the work itself." In contrast, feedback from supervisors or coworkers is external feedback from the work environment. The feedback in the job characteristics model is intrinsic to the task.

The **critical psychological states** are basic employee reactions to core job dimensions. In many ways, these states represent the employee readiness to become physically and mentally involved in the work. When the critical psychological states are operating fully, supervisors do not have to tell employees what to do next; the employees know. Under these conditions, employees are guided by their own standards, which coincide closely with those of the organization. The full operation of the critical psychological states means that employees are fully involved with their job.

The **motivational potential score** for a given job represents that job's ability to activate full employee involvement. For a job to have a high score, both autonomy and feedback must be available. These core dimensions are more important than the other three. If autonomy or feedback is low, high levels of skill variety, task significance, and task identity will not increase the motivating potential of the job to any appreciable extent. Managers must work first on autonomy and feedback of jobs in need of redesign.

Employee growth need strength is also a model component (see Figure 6.1). This phrase refers to a cluster of higher order needs that includes (1) achievement, (2) affiliation, (3) socialized need for power, (4) independence, and (5) control. This component influences the relationships between core job dimensions, critical psychological states, and personal and work outcomes. More specifically, it influences the model at two points: (1) directly after core job dimensions and (2) directly after critical psychological states.

How does growth need strength work for employees?

Consider an employee with high growth need strength (someone who is highly motivated by achievement, control, and affiliation) who works at a job with low growth potential. She will be frustrated and bored with work. Her critical psychological states will be low, and her personal and work outcomes will be unpleasant. Her job is a candidate for job redesign, because she is oriented to high performance and motivation, but the job does not create these outcomes. Employees with high growth need strength prefer improved core job dimensions (14, 15).

Individual differences must be recognized in job redesign. Employees with low growth need strengths do not desire jobs with high core job dimensions. Indeed, if their jobs are redesigned to raise those dimensions, they react with anxiety and dissatisfaction. Their response is: "Leave me and my job alone! All I want is my paycheck at the end of the week." Job redesign does not work for all people. It works best for employees with high growth need strength who are working at jobs with low motivating potential.

The dilemma indicates that tech reps in general have high growth need strength. Their current job design does not take this into account. The tech reps viewed their job as a bundle of obstacles that kept them from enjoying the intrinsic satisfactions of fixing complicated and expensive computer equipment. They were just fine, their jobs were not healthy! In the Computech case, job redesign should be very beneficial, as was proven by the company's pilot program.

Personal and work outcomes. A number of important organizational and individual outcomes occur in the interaction of growth need strength, core job dimensions, and critical psychological states. When employees with high growth need strength experience the psychological states noted in the model, they demonstrate high levels of motivation, performance, and job satisfaction, and absenteeism and employee turnover diminish.

Applying Job Redesign Concepts

When jobs are redesigned using the job characteristics model, the jobs provide more opportunities for employees to satisfy higher order needs. For employees with high growth need strength, this is extremely important, for these individuals are strongly motivated by higher order needs.

The job characteristics model has advantages over other methods of job redesign. First, it is a valid way to describe how employees interact with their job psychologically. Second, it pinpoints areas in which jobs can be changed (i.e., core job dimensions) to improve their motivating potential. Third, the model shows how redesign can lead to improvements in performance and worker attitudes. A byproduct of the model can also be improved quality of goods or services. Recall from the Computech case that customers became more satisfied with the work of those reps in the pilot program. Such outcomes affect organization performance significantly.

Job redesign improves work attitudes in successful programs. Employees report a higher quality of work life. More job satisfaction leads in turn to lowered costs for the organization because both turnover and absenteeism are reduced. Firms report lowered grievance rates in successful programs. (As you will learn in the next chapter, job redesign can lower job stress levels as well.)

Principles of Job Redesign

In the Computech case, note the many suggestions of ways to change the tech rep job. These changes were all based on the following principles of job redesign (16).

Form client relationships. A powerful way to change any job is to connect employees with the user of the product or service. Clients are full of both good and bad feedback, which can influence employee work orientations. Employees also develop new interpersonal skills when they have increased customer contact. (When employees deal only with supervisors and coworkers, opportunities for improvement are fewer.)

Schedule own work. Employees often are denied control over their work procedures and deadlines. Giving some of this control back to employees is a simple process. Highly motivated employees do better when they set their own work pace. Such changes increase experienced autonomy and they are called **vertical job loading.**

The growing practice of **flexitime** lets employees decide, within general management guidelines, when they come to work and when they leave (17). Flexitime allows employees to vary arrival and departure around "core hours of work." For example, all employees may have to be at work between 10:00 A.M. and 2:00 P.M., but they can set their own arrival and departure times. If employees work independently, flexitime is a useful innovation in work hours. It is a job modification that improves autonomy, and it can have a positive effect on employee organizational commitment (18).

Create a whole job. If employees do the entire job from beginning to end, they are more likely to identify with the product or service. The more specialized a task is, the less opportunity employees have for product and service identification. The net effect of specialization is reduction of task significance and loss of task identity (see Figure 6.1).

Open feedback channels. As noted, most feedback on the job comes from the supervisor. While external feedback is important as the cornerstone of the performance appraisal system, it is not a substitute for feedback from the job itself. The most common way to improve feedback from one's work is to put employees in charge of their own feedback. For example, internal feedback channels are opened when employees are allowed to communicate directly with each other versus going through their respective supervisors.

Now It's Your Turn checks your job redesign knowledge in terms of the Computech case. In the left column are the principles of job redesign that we have discussed. In the center column are the changes that were made in the tech rep job. The right column is where you note the job redesign principle that apply to each job change made by the company. Note that any given job change may represent one or more redesign principles.

NOW IT'S YOUR TURN ...

Job Redesign Principles	*Job Changes*	*Relevant Principles*
1. Form client relationships by linking employees and customers.	A. Authority to order parts	A. ______
2. Schedule own work by giving employees control over time goals and work methods.	B. Contact engineering directly	B. ______
3. Create an entire job by allowing employees to do the task from beginning to end.	C. Set own vehicle maintenance schedules	C. ______
4. Open feedback channels by giving employees responsibility for quality control. Put employees in direct contact with one another.	D. Handle vehicle repairs up to $500	D. ______
	E. Set own territory coverage	E. ______
	F. Work from home	F. ______
	G. Process client complaints up to $1000	G. ______
	H. Screen school applicants	H. ______
	I. Act as trainers at the school	I. ______

Answers:

A 3, B 4, C 2, D 3, E 2, F 2, G 3, H 4, I 3

Are there other approaches to job change besides the ones described so far?

Yes, and these approaches invoke the same principles of job redesign. Indeed, they overlap with job redesign and are becoming more and more common in organizations.

Job rotation and horizontal job loading. If a company has a set of jobs that cannot be redesigned, one alternative is **job rotation,** that is, cycling employees through the different jobs on a planned basis. Employee rotation lowers boredom and expands skill variety. Experience with a number of jobs also makes employees more interchangeable and creates flexible employees for the firm.

Horizontal job loading gives employees more tasks to do without increasing their control over work. As an example, an employee who works in a grocery store might learn to stock shelves, unload trucks, and occasionally run a check-out line. These are horizontal loadings. When this technique is used, companies frequently grant pay increases based on number of new skills learned.

Four day work week. Estimates indicate that over one million employees work less than the 4/40 (four days/forty hours) system in over 2000 firms (19). The trade-off is higher productivity in exchange for more leisure time. These programs also enable some employees to add part-time jobs to their existing job schedule or to attend school. While productivity gains can occur in these programs, accident rates and fatigue levels have also increased. Such programs do not always fit employee needs. For example, the working mother, who prefers, to be home when her children return from school, would not want the 4/40 system.

Job sharing. In job sharing, two people fill one job. The concept allows mothers to work as they raise a family. In general, shared jobs mean less boredom and fatigue, and higher productivity. The organization benefits not only from higher productivity, but fringe benefit costs either remain the same or decline.

Home employment. Because of recent advances in home-oriented computer technology, a variety of professional employees can now work without leaving home. For example, commodities brokers can do their trading with a computer, and insurance claims can be processed by employees working at home. Computer technology has allowed many people to return to a high-tech version of cottage industry (20).

Why Should Managers Be Interested in Job Redesign?

As we noted in Chapter 1, organizations focus on two kinds of outcomes: (1) organizational productivity, and (2) employee needs. Job redesign programs focus on both areas, and because management often perceives beneficial outcomes from job redesign in both areas, redesign concepts continue to be refined. Improvement in redesign methods, better understanding of the process itself, and greater confidence in results are all taking place. Professor Richard Hackman offers four reasons why the outlook has improved for job redesign programs:

1. Work redesign alters the relationship between people and their jobs. The vertical loading quality of job redesign expands the scope of available intrinsic rewards. Jobs become better pathways to improved employee self-image.
2. Work redesign directly changes behavior. Since job redesign focuses on what employees do versus what they feel (attitudes and emotions), behavior changes tend to last with job redesign. Behavior modification supports this point because it states that it is easier to change behavior than it is to change attitudes. Once behavior changes, attitude change follows.
3. Work redesign opens opportunities for initiating other changes. A successful job redesign effort unfreezes attitudes about change in the organization. People become willing to try innovations in other aspects of the firm.
4. Work redesign can ultimately result in organizations that can better satisfy employee needs. Scientific management job designs eliminate higher order need satisfaction. In job redesign employees are rewarded for creativity and innovation in their work. Improved feedback on performance and acceptance of responsibility raises employees' need for achievement (21).

The bottom line on job redesign is that it can benefit the organization as it improves the relationship between employees and their job.

Aren't there ever any problems with these job redesign programs?

Job redesign can be hampered by many different types of problems:

1. **Technological contraints.** The job simply cannot be redesigned because of the way the work is done or because of the types of machinery used.
2. **Cost of starting and sustaining the program.** Key cost items include tools for training and expensive consultants. If a program is started and the economic environment then deteriorates, the job redesign program will be the first organization feature to go.
3. **Failure to recognize employee preferences.** Remember, not everyone wants a redesigned job.
4. **Mickey Mouse changes.** Some programs have failed because the organization tried to treat minor job changes as significant alterations in core job dimensions. Moving the water fountain closer to the employees is *not* job redesign.
5. **Managerial and union resistance.** Managers can feel threatened by job redesign if they believe that their autonomy is being sacrificed. Unions also are often lukewarm about such programs because they believe that job redesign can undermine union solidarity (22).

In summary, job redesign alters employee behavior first. New behaviors then lead to rewards that were not available to employees under a scientifically designed work system. If employees begin to value these new outcomes, their work behaviors will be strengthened and attitude changes eventually occur. Careful job redesign can lead to improved quality of work life. As employees become better educated and as their lower order needs are largely satisfied, they will expect their job to have higher motivational potential.

Solving the Dilemma

What were the effects of the changes made in the tech rep job?

The job redesign principles used by the expert had the effect of raising the motivational potential score of the tech rep job. Since the reps' growth need strength was already quite high, application of the redesign principles created an excellent fit between the reps and their job. All of the critical psychological states shifted from negative to positive. The change in the reps' perceptions of the job led to the desired individual and organizational outcomes specified in the job characteristics model. The success of the pilot program will probably lead to companywide incorporation of the redesign changes into the tech rep job.

Knowledge Check

1. It is generally true that increasing skill variety is the same as horizontal job loading. T or F?
2. Job redesign is important because it focuses only on improving the employees quality of work life. T or F?
3. Successful job redesign programs can make the organization more flexible and better able to deal with change. T or F?

4. Autonomy leads to knowledge of work results. T or F?
5. Employee growth need strength resembles need for achievement. T or F?
6. Flexitime is an example of the redesign principle that employees can schedule their own work. T or F?

Answers:

1 T, 2 F, 3 T, 4 F, 5 T, 6 T

Semiautonomous Work Groups: The Team Approach to Job Design

Semiautonomous work groups represent a group-based approach to job redesign. A **semiautonomous work group** is defined as a self-contained work unit that makes many of its own work decisions (23). Using participative methods, the team ensures that the work gets done. These self-managed work teams can be responsible for accomplishments as diverse as attaining production goals, establishing work procedures, distributing tasks to group members, setting the work pace, and making human resource decisions (e.g., hiring, firing, training, and rewarding team members).

European Use of Semiautonomous Work Groups: Volvo's Kalmar Facility

Several companies have pioneered in the use of semiautonomous work groups. The most visible experiment is Volvo's production facility in Kalmar, Sweden. This auto assembly facility was designed to accommodate semiautonomous work groups. The program has been characterized as follows:

> The basic idea of Kalmar is flexibility—how people can choose the way in which they assemble a car. The facility has fewer supervisors than does a normal auto plant. Whereas assembly-line workers would be rooted in position doing a single specialized chore all day, Kalmar's workers are grouped in about 25 teams of 15–25 persons each. Each team handles a general area, such as door assembly, electric wiring, or fitting upholstery. Members of teams can exchange jobs or change teams when they wish. They can also vary the pace of work, keeping up with the general flow of production but speeding up or pausing as they wish—because the car-carrying trolleys can be delayed for a while both before entering and after leaving each team's work areas. While conventional assembly-line workers must perform operations on the undercarriage by the tiring method of working from beneath, the Kalmar worker presses a button and the trolley rolls an auto 90 degrees on its side so the work can be

done from a comfortable position. The Kalmar facility differs markedly from conventional plants. While they tend to look like large rectangles, Kalmar consists of four six-sided structures—three of them two stories tall and the other single-story—that fit together forming the general shape of a cross. The windows are big, and the workshop is compartmented so the workers, located along the outer walls, have natural light and the sensation of being in a comfortably small workshop (24).

The semiautonomous work group approach improves the social climate of work. Employees at Kalmar have considerable face-to-face contact with each other. Each team organizes itself and sets responsibilities for all work procedures not defined by higher management. The teams satisfy individual needs by using combinations of job rotation, smaller team assembly work, and assignment of specific work tasks to group members (25).

The teams at Kalmar have considerable control over their work. They do their own quality control (inspection), and they contract with management on the number of units to be produced. They also determine their own break schedules.

Volvo program benefits. The Volvo experiment at Kalmar is the most ambitious to date. Program results indicate that productivity is about the same as that of conventional assembly lines in other Volvo facilities. Turnover and absenteeism, however, are 5 percent lower, and the Kalmar employees think that using semiautonomous work teams is an excellent way to build cars.

An American Experiment With Semiautonomous Work Teams

General Foods built a new pet food plant in Topeka, Kansas. Because of serious labor problems in other company facilities (e.g., sabotage, high waste, low morale, and absenteeism), management decided to design the new plant differently and to set up a work system that would operate on the basis of teamwork and cooperation among employees. These are the major features of the General Foods program:

1. Autonomous work groups, consisting of 7 to 14 employees, have the following responsibilities: (a) processing, (b) packaging and shipping, and (c) office duties. No team member has fixed duties, and each team is responsible for hiring, firing, and assigning work.
2. Teams are self-governing. They are responsible for setting their policies and procedures. Teams made fewer rules and there were fewer restrictions on team members.
3. Each member's job is designed to maximize variety, autonomy, significance, and feedback.
4. A single job classification system was developed and pay raises are given based on employee ability to learn new skills and handle new jobs. Pay increases thus became a function of capability versus what was actually done.
5. All work teams have equal access to the following plant data: production output, quality control information, and economic forecasts.
6. All status symbols were eliminated, so the differentiation between management and labor is minimal. There is a common dining area, no reserved parking spaces, and so forth.

7. Production output and worker attitudes are monitored continuously. Changes based on attitude surveys are implemented only after the effects of attitude on performance are determined (26).

After initial problems were ironed out, the program was set in motion, and the company realized the following effects:

1. Twenty to 40 percent cost savings were achieved. This savings translated to over $2 million per year.
2. Quality control improved, and rejection rates dropped over 80 percent.
3. No sabotage or worker-induced shutdowns occurred.
4. Absenteeism dropped to 1.5 percent, and turnover fell to 10 percent.
5. Job attitudes and organizational commitment were more positive and stronger than in other plants (27).

These results make a work redesign based on semiautonomous work teams seem appealing. Background provided by Mitchell Fein sheds more light on the Topeka experiment:

> General Foods-Topeka is a controlled experiment; a small plant with conditions set up to achieve desired results. The employees are not a cross section of the larger employee population; or even of Topeka. The plant and its operations are not typical of those in industry today. The results obtained are valid only for this one plant. What are other managers to do? Should they screen out nine of ten possible candidates and hire only from the select group that remains (like Topeka). . . . If the investigators had shown how they converted a plant bursting with labor problems into one where management and employees told glowingly of their accomplishments the study would truly merit the praise it has received. Instead, they turned their backs on the company's parent plant in Kankakee, which has many of the problems of big city plants. Even worse, they tantalize management with the prospect that, in building a new plant with new equipment, carefully selected employees, and no union, productivity will be higher (28).

Fein is saying, in effect, that you can get the results you want if you control all aspects of a situation. In the 1970's, the situation in the Topeka plant had deteriorated (29). The failure was not in the work design; rather, the political climate for the work system had changed. A *Business Week* article reported the following:

> The problem has been not so much that the workers could not manage their own affairs as that some management and staff personnel saw their own positions threatened because the workers performed almost too well. One former employee says the system built around a team concept came squarely up against the company's bureaucracy. Lawyers, fearing reaction from the National Labor Relations Board, opposed the idea of allowing team members to vote on pay raises. Personnel managers objected because team members made hiring decisions. Engineers resented workers doing engineering work. Creating a system is different from maintaining it. There were pressures almost from the inception, and not because the system didn't work. The basic reason was power. We flew in the face of corporate policy. People like stable states. This system has to be changing or it will die (30).

The struggle caused conflict in the company because managers believed in more control imposed through job classifications, increased supervision, and less employee participation. Many employees quit. General Foods, however, describes the Topeka experience as a success, and the firm has installed smaller versions of the Topeka experiment in other facilities.

The Growing Importance of Employee Participation

Job redesign is one example of how participation can be used by organizations. **Participation** is the active involvement of employees in making decisions about issues that will affect them on the job. Participation has three important features.

1. **Psychological involvement.** When employees are participating, they usually are absorbed in what they are doing. This is more than mere physical involvement with work. Jobs do get accomplished through physical involvement, but this does not mean that employees are interested in what they are doing. There is a difference between psychological involvement and "looking busy." Meaningful participation helps employees satisfy higher order needs (i.e., self-esteem and self-actualization). Physical work involvement does not create higher order need satisfaction.
2. **Motivation to contribute.** Participation encourages employees to make a contribution. The social and work systems should create an abundance of rewards that employees value. Employees do not have to be forced to participate when they are rewarded for participation. Rewards internalize the motivation to contribute.

   When employees are pushed to participate, management gets unmotivated and uninspired compliance. Employees only approve of and go along with management decisions; they do not actively back them up. Compliance is a one-way, passive process. Participation is an active, two-way process that spans levels of the management hierarchy. When participation occurs, subordinates create ideas and follow through on them.

   Expectancy theory adds weight to this reasoning. Participation may be a reward in itself for some employees, especially for those with high growth need strength. These employees learn that participation helps them gain control over work activities and that control is rewarding.
3. **Acceptance of responsibility.** Employees experience more control over their work when they have authority to make work-related decisions (tech reps were given more control over work procedures in the dilemma). Greater authority is, however, accompanied by greater responsibility. When workers can decide how to get things done, they experience more ownership of their jobs. Effort is contributed to teamwork. Employees come to depend on their team, and see great value in contributing to a winning effort. (Nobody likes to be on a losing team.) Acceptance of responsibility contributes to teamwork.

Solving the Dilemma

Why did the tech reps respond so favorably to the job changes?

The reps responded well to the pilot program because it provided opportunities to satisfy their higher order needs. Before job redesign, a way to meet higher order needs did not exist (i.e., reps had no authority, could not schedule work, and could not order parts). The job changes modified their instrumentalities and created better linkages between performance and intrinsic rewards. The dilemma shows how job redesign is related to expectancy theory.

Taking Participation Organization-Wide (The Likert System)

We have noted three features of participation from the employee perspective. An organizational side exists as well, and this view is captured by the work of Rensis Likert (31). His work led him to conclude that effective organizations differ from ineffective ones. He maintains that effective organizations encourage and reward managers to build work groups with challenging goals. In contrast, he points out that ineffective organizations do the following:

1. Introduce job specialization
2. Hire people to do repetitive tasks that require few job skills
3. Train employees to do their jobs in the most efficient manner (scientific management)
4. Control the behavior of employees
5. Use only money as a motivator (32).

These characteristics do not encourage participation. Likert decided that a more people-oriented system that encouraged employees to work in teams would be more effective. He described a people-oriented system with eight dimensions, and called it the **system 4 organization.** The scientific management model he named the **system 1 organization,** because it is less effective and does not adapt well to change. Think about this for a moment. If employees do not participate in their work, how can constructive change come about? The essence of participation is change. It attacks the status quo in the organization.

Table 6.1 shows the dimensions of Likert's systems. The system 4 organization contains the elements to make participation work for the organization and its employees. The "4" organization creates the conditions for individual participation.

Can participation be used to make all firms become system 4 organizations?

The truth of the matter is that many companies operate quite successfully as system 1 organizations, and there is still great economic sense in much system 1 thinking. It is worthwhile to examine the prerequisites for participation:

1. Employees must have time to practice participation before action is required. It will not be useful or effective under emergency conditions.

2. The potential benefits of participation should be greater than its costs. It makes sense when the goal is development of employee decision-making skills.
3. Employees must view participation as relevant to their work. If it is bothersome, it will deteriorate to the level of busy work or compliance.
4. Employees must have the ability to participate in decisions that involve their work.
5. Employees must speak the same work language to make participation work. Participation that crosses departmental boundaries can be expensive and hard to install.
6. Employees and managers must believe that their positions are not threatened by participation. If either group feels threatened, need satisfaction will be removed and they will not participate (33).

Participative Alternatives to the System 4 Organization

Several participation innovations can be installed that do *not* require an organization to adopt system 4 completely.

The **Scanlon plan** is a system that sets up a series of interlocking employee committees to do the following: (1) review work procedures, (2) evaluate suggestions for improving productivity and cutting costs, and (3) involve employees in production decision making. The most important are the **production committees** composed of supervisor and representatives elected by employees or appointed by the union. These committees screen improvement suggestions made by employees and management. If the suggestions are adopted and save the firm money, then a portion of the savings

Table 6.1
Contrasting Likert's System 1 and System 4 Organizations

System 1 Organization	*System 4 Organization*
1. Leadership does not instill confidence and trust. Superiors and subordinates do not solicit each other's opinions.	1. Leadership instills confidence and trust. Superiors and subordinates feel free to discuss problems.
2. Motivational processes operate only for lower order needs. Motivation is external and based on fear and threats.	2. Motivational processes tap the full hierarchy of needs. Employees show high organizational commitment.
3. Communication flows downward and is often distorted and inaccurate.	3. Communication flows in all directions with clarity and accuracy.
4. Subordinates have little involvement in goal setting and work design.	4. Subordinates have high involvement with goal setting and work design.
5. Decision making is concentrated at the top.	5. Decision making occurs at all levels.
6. Goal setting occurs only at the top, and participation is discouraged at lower levels.	6. Goal setting encourages participation at all levels and more ambitious goals are set.
7. Control processes are centralized, and emphasize catching people "doing things wrong" (punitive systems).	7. Control processes are dispersed and emphasize self-control.
8. Performance goals are low and are pursued passively.	8. Performance goals are high and mutually pursued by employees at all levels.

is passed on to employees as bonus checks. The individual bonuses are in proportion to employee wage rate, seniority, and level of responsibility.

Benefits of Scanlon plans include greater participation, readier acceptance of changes in work procedure, increased efficiency, and better labor-management relations. If the Scanlon plan is to work, however, the plan must meet the prerequisites for participation already noted.

The Lincoln Electric program depends on an advisory board composed of 30 employees and several executives. The board reviews and makes suggestions for improvements. Fifty percent of the savings from a successful suggestion are then distributed to employees during the first year. When work groups are able to beat production standards, they also are given bonuses. The company maintains that bonuses are *not* substitutes for wage increases.

Quality circles, a recent innovation, are small groups of 5 to 12 employees who meet weekly with their supervisor to try to solve work-related problems on company time. The circles focus on problems such as quality of output, production bottlenecks, and increasing production costs. They do not deal with employee grievances or control systems such as performance appraisal. A typical meeting schedule is one hour per week.

Employee benefits of quality circles include increased employee job involvement, satisfaction of meeting social needs, and more job challenge and opportunities for personal growth (34). Circles can be instituted at any organizational level and can be implemented with any set of jobs. The quality circle concept is based on several factors: (1) time for participation, and (2) trust between management and workers. Circles can spread as the company finds other ways to involve employees in decisions.

The circles are included here in our discussion of job redesign because of the tools used in quality circle work. Circle members have to develop team presentations for management. Members are trained to do financial analyses, management assessment, and computational work. These skills represent vertical job loading and are applied by the circle much as they would be by a semiautonomous work team.

Quality circles benefit the organization because they provide another structure for making decisions (35, 36). The circles add to both the flexibility and responsiveness of the formal decision-making system (chain of command).

Are there any problems with quality circles?

Quality circles were started in Japan. Through trial and error, U.S. firms are now wiser and have learned that what works in Japan does not necessarily work in the United States (37). Japanese workers are not motivated in the same ways as their U.S. counterparts. Cultural differences are an important factor that can lead to failure when organizations try to transfer a successful feature from one culture to the other. This must be considered in the installation of quality circles. Other reasons why quality circles may or may not work are as follows:

1. Quality circles work better in industries with a history of labor-management cooperation. The aerospace industry fits this criterion. The Martin Marietta Corporation has had success with quality circles. The company is a defense contractor that builds components for the space shuttle. The firm currently has 350 quality circles functioning in the New Orleans plant.

2. Management may not support the quality circle concept. Some managers are threatened by employee participation because they believe that their personal power will be undermined (recall the difference between personalized and socialized need for power). Many managers do not want employees involved in production quality decisions. If this attitude is widespread, quality circles will not survive.
3. Leadership of the quality circle can be an obstacle. The circle leader role should not be a formal leadership position, yet a supervisor or foreman often assumes the role. The position requires good organizational, facilitative, and problem-solving skills. A supervisor who is a circle leader and who does not have these skills will have a less effective quality circle.

Solving the Dilemma

The sequence of redesign steps followed by Computech indicates that participation was an important component of the program. Recall that the expert used meetings and interviews to find ways to improve the tech rep job. Teams of supervisors and reps screened the suggestions and assessed their feasibility. A pilot study was done in a region serviced by the firm. Indeed, the entire process of job redesign was highly participative. Interlocking participation (by reps, supervisors, and customers) created a successful program!

Limits of Participation in Organizations

Organizational arrangements and systems can make participation both expensive and time consuming. Some organizations have good reasons for avoiding participation. Let's examine a few of these reasons.

1. Work methods and equipment have made some organizations so complex and jobs so specialized that employees cannot participate beyond their narrow specialties. Operational terminology can overwhelm outsiders who could not fathom departmental communications.
2. When employees try to solve problems, they are not always competent to attack. Their solutions are then rejected or ignored, and the employees can become alienated from their jobs. The urge to participate diminishes accordingly.
3. Employees have a right not to participate. Not all employees want a redesigned job that requires them to be involved in decision making. Many people prefer to remain uninvolved in their work. Should organizations make employees participate? We think not.
4. As with quality circles, supervisors who are threatened by employee participation can undermine cooperative attempts. Many managers equate participation with "sitting on the fence" or "management by committee." They say to themselves, "If I get started with participation, pretty soon I'll work myself out of a job." These attitudes erode the philosophy of participation. Most managers, however, take little comfort in philosophy, and will not view participation as a valuable way to improve how the organization functions.

5. Organizations can lose their way and be deflected from the goals of participation. This occurs, for example, when too much attention is given to methods of participation and not enough to the original goals. Closely related to this is the situation that arises when an organization becomes very mechanical in its use of participation. Management looks for the surface indicators of participation (e.g., people having meetings and being nice to one another). This is time wasting more than participative problem solving.

In summary, participation is woven through a variety of organizational systems and procedures. It plays a fundamental role in job redesign, and can be used also to design effective appraisal systems (see Chapter 5). While there are many obstacles in the path of the organization that wishes to use participation, these can be overcome, and organizations that are interested in finding more humanistic ways to operate will do so.

Knowledge Check

1. Likert's system 1 organization is based on principles of participation and teamwork. T or F?
2. The system 4 organization is based on scientific management. T or F?
3. Sufficient time and trust are prerequisites of effective participation. T or F?
4. All employees prefer participation in their job. T or F?
5. Computech (dilemma) is ready for a more participative management system. T or F?
6. Management can sit back and reap the benefits of employee involvement once a participative system is installed. T or F?

Answers:

1 F, 2 F, 3 T, 4 F, 5 T, 6 F

Summary Points

■ **Job redesign** and **employee participation** are key components of the **quality of work life.** Both humanize the workplace.

■ **Scientific management** finds the one best way to do any given job. This is accomplished by breaking down the task into specialized parts and controlling employee social interaction. Under scientific management, motivation is a function of pay.

■ Job redesign alters employee behavior because it changes the way employees interact with their job. Effective job redesign can improve both attitudes and performance.

■ The **job characteristics model** takes individual differences into account as well as **growth need strength.** The model is very useful as a predictor of whether employees will respond favorably to job redesign.

■ **Forming client relationships, employee work scheduling, opening feedback channels, and creating whole jobs** are all core principles of job redesign.

■ Job redesign programs can fail for a number of reasons. These include technological constraints, cost, failure to recognize employee needs, substituting superficial changes for major changes, and organizational resistance from either management or unions.

■ **Semiautonomous work teams** assume responsibility for work control. Both Volvo and General Foods have used work teams and report performance improvements.

■ **Participation** in the organization consists of (1) mental and physical involvement, (2) motivation to contribute, and (3) acceptance of responsibility. Without participation, job redesign programs can easily fail.

■ **Likert's system 4 organization** is an organization-wide approach to participation. The **system 1 organization** is characterized as scientific management. The Scanlon plan, the Lincoln Electric program, and quality circles represent participative alternatives that are between the two extremes of system 4 and system 1 organizations.

Questions

1. What are the reasons that job redesign programs fail? Can you outline a process that would minimize failure?
2. Why is it important to consider individual differences in job redesign programs?
3. Do you think that all businesses should strive to be system 4 organizations? Can you suggest any programs that could be installed without going all the way to system 4?
4. Across the top of a sheet of paper, write a description of your most recent job. Next, list the core job dimensions down the left side of the paper. Now, on the right, indicate the strengths and weaknesses of your job with respect to each dimension. What recommendations would you make to your employer about redesigning that job?
5. Do you think that scheduling courses to attain your degree is analogous to a principle of job redesign?
6. Do you think that semiautonomous work teams could be used to redesign college courses? How might you go about redesigning a college course based on "principles of semiautonomous work teams"?

EXPLORING: *The Steelcase Corporation*

Adapted from Levering, R., Moskowitz, M., and Katz, M. 1985. *The 100 Best Companies to Work for in America,* 2nd ed. Reading, Mass.: Addison-Wesley.

Factory work is often viewed as monotonous, difficult, and boring. The Steelcase Company, a Michigan manufacturer of office furniture, turned away 30,000 job applicants last year. With less than a 3 percent turnover rate, nobody seems to be leaving. At the company's assembly plant, employees turn out office furniture without using an assembly line. They say that the work is difficult, but express pride in the high production levels they're expected to maintain. All employees participate in a generous bonus and profit sharing plan. James Soule, vice president for human resources, believes that these programs are responsible for a level of productivity that is 37 percent higher than the industry average.

Soule notes that the company has never had a union nor has it ever experienced a work stoppage in its 58 year history. Work force stability is a key feature of the company. Ninety percent of the local workers employed by the firm ten years ago are still with Steelcase. Seventy one percent of those hired after 1970 are still there. Steelcase workers are among the highest paid hourly and salaried employees in the nation. When base wages, bonuses, and incentive pay are added up, they earn about 20 percent above the competitive market rate.

Employees are frequently asked to participate on teams that assess working conditions and company benefits. These teams have proposed counseling programs for teenage children of employees, a company fitness program, and a program that subsidizes low cost employee vacations at Camp Swampy, the firm's 1,178 acre recreational facility. Employee suggestions do not stop at benefits, however. During 1985, 123 ideas for productivity improvement were evaluated by employee task forces and 60 were implemented.

Steelcase has a nationally recognized program that screens child care services, lends the services needed equipment at no charge, and spot-checks their operations. This program helps employees who work night shifts and cannot easily screen child care facilities. Employees know that the company is taking a serious interest in their families.

Steelcase's interest in families does not stop with the children of employees. The company employs over 300 husband-wife combinations, and many workers have several relatives as coworkers. One family has 23 members who are company employees. The firm believes this family orientation is part of its team spirit, which supports a close-knit work force.

Mr. Soule states: "These programs are not us being Santa Claus, they're the right thing to do as we define ourselves. Our business is oriented toward bettering the life of our customers' employees, so it would kind of fly in the face of that if we didn't do the same for our employees."

Discussion Questions

1. What motivators and hygienes are used by Steelcase?
2. What are two examples of vertical job loading at Steelcase?
3. Why don't more firms follow the lead of Steelcase?

APPLYING: *The Shop Right Store*

Jim Burton, manager of the Shop Right store, had been studying new methods of work design for retail stores and had discussed some of his ideas with Steve Helms, the regional manager. Jim believed that job redesign ideas could be applied to his store. Steve agreed, and Jim began a program for his 50 employees.

Jim set up employee groups after he had assessed thoroughly current working conditions, performance levels, and employee attitudes. He asked one group to evaluate his information, and he also asked the group to select those areas in which employees believed that changes could be made. One such area was the building materials department.

The building materials department sells about $2.2 million worth of supplies each year. Retail sales represent 65 percent of the department's total sales. The remaining 35 percent are sales to small contractors. A list of the job redesign changes developed by employees from that department follows:

1. Give employees responsibility for establishing a job rotation system to improve cross-training of all departmental employees.
2. Establish an employee group that develops and manages a flexible working hours system.

3. Warehouse employees should be allowed to inspect trucks once they are loaded. Current policy requires the department manager to inspect each truck.
4. A group of four employees should evaluate customer complaints and suggest ways to address them. Store management would have to approve the group's recommendations before any action is taken.
5. An employee of the month program should be established to recognize outstanding performance and customer service.
6. Employees should be given authority to complete work orders and sign off on all orders up to $1,000. An employee would have to work in the department for one year before being given this responsibility.
7. Employees would be responsible for training new workers in the area of product knowledge. This is an important aspect of job training since the department has 1,100 different product classifications.
8. After six months, employees would be eligible for a job bid system that allows them to move to another department. Getting a job transfer would depend on the needs of both departments and the seniority of the applicant.
9. Warehouse employees would be responsible for setting up a new system of lumber storage. They would have full responsibility for inspecting all lumber and insulation products received from suppliers.
10. Warehouse workers and lumberyard employees will rotate jobs every four weeks. Employees who load trucks and stock bins would rotate to operating yard forklifts and so forth.

Your job is to evaluate each of these job changes in terms of horizontal and vertical job loading. Your instructor will assign you to a group with two other students. Every group should write one paragraph on each job change listed. Evaluate each suggested change according to the following criteria:
1. Is the job change one that will influence the planning and control portion of the job?
2. Will the job change persist over time, or is it short-lived?
3. Is the job change sufficiently specific and clear?
4. Does the change influence the employee's job as well as departmental activities?

If your team answers *yes* to the four questions about each job change, then you must agree that the change represents a vertical job loading. Try to confine your analyses to one paragraph per job change. Construct a table to summarize the analyses of your group and be prepared to defend your analyses! Your instructor will explain how each team should present its findings to the class. Good luck!

Suggested Readings

Davis, L., and Cherns, A. (eds.) 1975. *The Quality of Working Life.* New York: Free Press.

This book, written by experts, presents a readable discussion of many aspects of job redesign. The selections detail the procedures of job redesign and how organizations should use the concept.

Davis, L., and Taylor, J. (eds.) 1979. *Design of Jobs.* Santa Monica, Calif.: Goodyear.

This book presents some common-sense ideas about how to make job redesign effective. Anyone who is considering a job redesign project should read it.

Ford, R. 1972. *Motivation Through the Work Itself.* New York: American Management Association.

Gibson, C. 1973. Volvo Increases Productivity Through Job Enrichment. *California Management Review* (Summer 1973):64–66.

Griffin, R. 1982. *Task Design.* Glenview, Ill.: Scott Foresman.

Gyllenhammar, P. 1977. *People at Work.* Reading, Mass.: Addison-Wesley.

This book describes the Volvo job redesign program. The author was the principal program architect, so his book provides a valuable look at the reasoning and philosophy of job redesign in Europe.

Latham, G., Cummings, L., and Mitchell, T. 1981. Behavioral Strategies to Improve Productivity. *Organizational Dynamics* (Winter 1981):4–23.

Monczka, R., and Reif, W. 1973. A Contingency Approach to Job Enrichment Design. *Human Resource Management* (Winter 1973):9–17.

Passmore, W. 1982. Overcoming the Roadblocks to Work Restructuring Efforts. *Organizational Dynamics* (Spring 1982):54–67.

Rendall, E. 1981. Quality Circles—A "Third Wave" Intervention. *Training and Development Journal* (March 1981):28–31.

Walter, R. 1975. *Job Enrichment for Results: Strategies for Successful Implementation.* Reading, Mass.: Addison-Wesley.

References

1. Rice, R., McFarlin, D., Hunt, R., and Near, J. 1985. Organizational Work and the Perceived Quality of Life: Toward a Conceptual Model. *Academy of Management Review* 10:296–310.
2. Walker, C., and Guest, R. 1952. *The Man on the Assembly Line.* Cambridge, Mass.: Harvard University Press.
3. Ibid.
4. Dowling, W. 1973. Job Redesign in the Assembly Line: Farewell to the Blue Collar Blues? *Organizational Dynamics* (Spring 1973) .51–67.
5. Scobel, D. 1975. Doing Away With the Factory Blues. *Harvard Business Review* (December 1975) .132–142.
6. Herzberg, F., Mauser, B., and Snyderman, B. 1959. *The Motivation to Work,* 2nd ed. New York: Wiley.
7. Herzberg, F. 1977. Orthodox Job Enrichment. *Defense Management Journal* 13 .21–27.
8. Ibid.
9. Herzberg, F. 1968. One More Time: How Do You Motivate Employees? *Harvard Business Review* (January 1968) .102–114.
10. Hackman, R., and Lawler, E. III. 1971. Employee Reactions to Job Characteristics. *Journal of Applied Psychology* 55.259–286.
11. Ibid.
12. Tunner, A., and Lawrence, P. 1965. *Industrial Jobs and the Worker.* Cambridge, Mass.: Harvard University Press.
13. Hackman, R., and Lawler, E. III., op. cit., 1971.
14. Hackman, R., and Oldham, G. 1976. Motivation Through the Design of Work: A Test of a Theory. *Organizational Behavior and Human Performance* 16 .250–279.
15. Brosseau, K. 1983. Toward a Dynamic Model of Job-Person Relationships: Findings, Research Questions, and Implications for Work System Design. *Academy of Management Review* 8 .33–45.
16. Hackman, R., Work Design. In Hackman, J.R. and J.L. Suttle, J.L. (eds.) *Improving Life at Work.* Santa Monica, Calif.: Goodyear.
17. Pierce, J., and Newstrom, J. 1982. Employee Responses to Flexible Work Schedules: An Inter-organizational, Inter-system Comparison. *Journal of Management* 8 .9–25.
18. Ibid.
19. Dickson, P. 1975. *The Future of the Work Place.* New York: Wybright and Talley.
20. Shamir, B., and Salomon, I. 1985. Work-At-Home and the Quality of Life. *Academy of Management Review* 10 .455–464.
21. Hackman, R., op. cit., 1976.
22. Ivancevich, J., and Glueck, W. 1983. *Foundations of Personnel,* 3rd ed. Plano, Tex. :BPI.
23. Cummings, T. 1978. Self-Regulating Work Groups: A Sociotechnical Synthesis. *Academy of Management Review* 3.625–634.
24. Bowen, N. 1977. Auto Plant in Sweden Scores Some Success With Work Teams. *The Wall Street Journal* (19 March 1977).
25. Cummings, T., op. cit., 1978.
26. Steers, R. 1984. *Introduction to Organizational Behavior,* 2nd ed. Glenview, Ill.: Scott Foresman.
27. Dulworth, E. The Changing World of Work. (In Glazer, E.M. 1976. *Productivity Gains Through Worklife Improvements.* New York: Harcourt Brace Jovanovich).
28. Fein, M. 1974. Job Enrichment: A Reevaluation. *Sloan Management Review* (Winter 1974) .69–88.

29. Ibid.
30. *Business Week* 1978. Productivity Gains for a Pat on the Back. (23 January 1978) .56–62.
31. Likert, R. 1967. *New Patterns of Management,* 2nd ed. New York: McGraw-Hill.
32. Ibid.
33. Tannenbaum, R., and Schmidt, W. 1973. How to Choose a Leadership Style. *Harvard Business Review* (May-June 1973) .54–65.
34. Bank, J., and Wilpert, B. 1983. What's So Special About Quality Circles? *Journal of General Management* 9 .21–37.
35. Goldstein, S. 1985. Organizational Dualism and Quality Circles. *Academy of Management Review* 10 .504–517.
36. Chase, L. 1983. Quality Circles in Education. *Educational Leadership* 40 .19–26.
37. Munchus, G., III. 1983. Employer-Employee Based Quality Circles in Japan: Human Resource Policy Implications for American Firms. *Academy of Management Review* 8 .255–261.

Work Stress: Employee Reactions and Company Programs

Chapter **7**

Chapter Goals By the end of the chapter, you will be able to:

1. Describe the stages of the general adaptation syndrome as a reaction to job stress.
2. Explain the bodily changes that accompany stress response.
3. Spot employee reactions to stress.
4. Understand how personality may contribute to employee stress reactions.
5. Take concrete action to reduce your reactions to job frustration.
6. Explain the relationship between chronic job stress and diseases of adaptation.
7. Describe stressors in the work setting.
8. Summarize the major features of company stress management programs.

Dilemma: The Distress of Life

Norma is a suburban housewife who has three children. She is 42 years old. Her husband, Fred, is a foreman in a plant that makes farm machinery. They live in a midwestern town where agriculture is the mainstay of the economy. Crop prices and farmland prices have been dropping over the past two years. Thirty percent of the plant's work force has been laid off, and the company is running on two work shifts. More layoffs are expected as demand for the company's equipment continues to decrease.

Norma and Fred's home mortgage is partially paid. They recently purchased a camper to use on summer vacations and for weekend fishing trips. Norma has been dipping into the family savings regularly to make ends meet since Fred had to accept a 10 percent pay cut. Fred continues to insist that "the economic picture will turn around," but Norma believes that she eventually will have to take a job outside the home. Fred resists this idea, stating, "None of the other guys' wives work, and you should be home with the kids."

Because Norma handles the family finances, she knows that they soon will have to sell the camper if she does not go to work. She doesn't mind going to work, but she feels uneasy about not being at home for her children (all of whom are in school). A few of her friends have jobs, and they have all confided to her that it's hard for them to accept their children coming home to an empty house after school.

Fred resisted the idea of Norma's working. She tried to cut financial corners. The extras, like piano lessons and baseball camp for the children, were too expensive and had to be stopped. When the time came for Norma to pay the monthly bills, she found herself dreading the chore. She put it off, made excuses, did anything to avoid it.

Lately she was experiencing shortness of breath and intermittent chest pain. She attributes the discomfort to the coldness of the fall weather and tries not to think about it. She has started a free aerobics exercise program and tells herself that the aches and pains are her body's way of adjusting to the exercise.

One late afternoon Norma was working at the kitchen sink. Fred came in and slumped at the table. She noticed that he did not describe "Charlie's latest screw-up at the plant." In fact, he didn't say anything as he sat and stared at his glass of orange juice. Finally he looked up at Norma and admitted sadly—"My assembly crew was laid off today, and the company has put me on six weeks notice pending a possible layoff. The situation is so bad at the plant that layoffs are beginning to cut into management ranks."

Norma thought hard as she looked at Fred's downcast face. She noticed the familiar pain returning in her chest. She told Fred that she had accepted a job as bookkeeper at the local drugstore.

Questions

1. What are Norma's physical and psychological reactions to stress?
2. Are some people more prone to stress than others?
3. Is stress related to health and disease?
4. What can be done to lessen and manage stress?

The Meaning of Stress in Life and Work

Stress is an everyday term that we all interpret in highly individual ways. Some people choose to describe stress in mostly external terms. In the dilemma, Fred or Norma might point to the sagging local economy, high unemployment rate, and rising layoffs in local plants as examples of the external qualities of stress. At the same time, Norma might acknowledge that her emotional reactions to the family's deteriorating financial situation are stressful. She feels guilty about her decision to go back to work while her children are still in school. Part of her stress is related to the emotions aroused by her husband's job insecurity and by possible changes in her role as a mother. She might also have realized that her physical symptoms of shortness of breath and chest pain could be related to the increasing uncertainty confronting her family. For the moment, she feels more secure if she can blame the symptoms on her new exercise class.

External events, internal emotional reactions, and physical symptoms are the human ingredients of stress. **Stress** is defined as the body's reactions to any demand placed on it (1). In the dilemma, Norma associates stress with **distress,** which are stressful events that have unpleasant physical and psychological effects (2). This is, however, only half of the stress picture. Stress is in fact any demand that requires adjustment or adaptation. Pleasant and unpleasant occurrences are both stressful. A stressful event that is positively interpreted is **eustress** (3). In the dilemma, we see that loss of control over family events, frustration, and conflict cause stress for both Norma and Fred. Stress is a normal part of life. (To experience no stress is to be either dead or comatose!) Stress is damaging only when it is too severe or when it continues indefinitely. We all need to learn how to cope with stress. These issues are the substance of this chapter.

Professor Hans Selye has studied the effects of stress on people and has developed the concept of the **general adaptation syndrome,** a term he applies to the body's adjustment process to stress. (4). He concludes that humans react in the same way to any stressor—severe cold, an award for high performance, a speeding ticket, a reprimand from the boss, or a financial setback.

What is the pattern of the general adaptation syndrome?

The general adaptation syndrome consists of three stages: (1) alarm reaction, (2) adaptation stage, and (3) exhaustion stage (5). The **alarm reaction** activates the process as we first become aware of the stressor (be it an unexpected letter from the IRS or a policeman's car in the rearview mirror right after we've run a red light). At this stage, a chemical alarm is sounded by the body, and hormones cause important bodily changes. Respiration rate increases, blood pressure rises, more cholesterol is circulated in the bloodstream, pupils dilate, and all senses are heightened. These changes occur in less than one tenth of a second and represent the activation of the body's defense mechanism. This instant response is called the **fight or flight response,** or the alarm reaction. If it is short-lived, the general adaptation syndrome will not proceed beyond this stage (e.g., the IRS letter is your tax refund, or the policeman speeds on by). Symptoms of physical and emotional discomfort then disappear, because the stressor has dissipated. If the stressor does not abate, however, the adaptation stage is entered.

The **adaptation stage** is defined as the body's attempts to identify the coping systems best suited to dealing with the long-term effects of a given stressor (6). The strong bodily changes associated with the alarm reaction stage disappear as we begin to adjust to the level of the stressor. To understand this fully, think about your body's initial reactions as you try to get yourself in better physical shape by starting a running program. Initially you experience extreme shortness of breath, rubber legs, upset stomach, sore muscles, and lack of energy. As you "toughen up" (the adaptation stage), your muscles strengthen, your heart pumps more blood to your lungs and legs, and you find that you can run farther and faster with less discomfort. Your body has adjusted and identified those systems that will help it deal with these new physical demands.

Now, suppose that your running program bolsters your self-confidence (a useful byproduct of exercise programs), and you enter a marathon even though you have never run more than five miles. Halfway through the event, you begin to notice that your knees ache, your legs are rubbery, and your chest aches. You are experiencing the **exhaustion stage** of the general adaptation syndrome. This stage is defined as depletion of the body's adaptive energy as a result of prolonged exposure to a chronic and persistent stressor (7). Note that many of the symptoms associated with the alarm reaction stage have returned! Returning to the marathon example, you are getting a clear message from your body to go find a park bench or curb (perhaps a hammock and a fan would be even better). (The general adaptation syndrome is represented in Figure 7.1.)

The more often the general adaptation syndrome is triggered and the longer it lasts, the more wear and tear the stress creates in the individual, for persistent adaptation to distress is a costly human reaction. Experts note: "Like any other machine, the body has limits beyond which it cannot continue to function (8);" other experts point out that "the more frequently [it] is in the fight or flight mode, the more susceptible the individual is to fatigue, disease, disability, aging and death . . ." (9)

Figure 7.1
The General Adaptation Syndrome

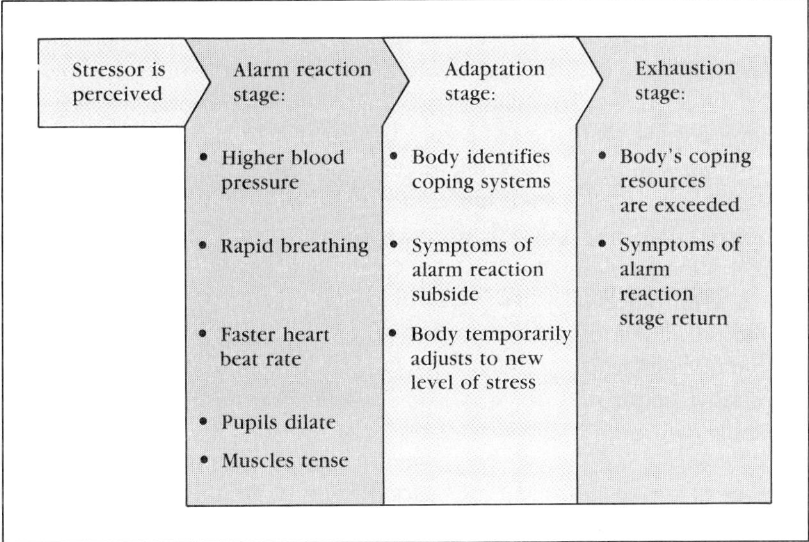

The Employee and Stress

The quotations at the conclusion of the previous section make an important point. If too much stress occurs, an individual's abilities to handle stress can be depleted. No where is depletion of ability to handle stress more apparent than at work. Too much job stress can cause employee performance to deteriorate. Understanding the meaning of job stress and employee reactions to stress is thus important both in terms of the well being of the individual and of the organization.

What is job stress?

Job stress is defined as a work demand that causes the employee to deviate from normal functioning at work. It is a demand that upsets the employee's work equilibrium. The employee then detects the disequilibrium and tries to restore balance by behaving differently. The different behaviors that employees exhibit are attempts to restore balance by adjusting to the demands of the workplace. Sometimes these adjustments are effective; other times they are not.

Each employee has a different **stress response threshold,** defined as the point at which performance begins to deteriorate from the effects of too much job stress. The employee with a low threshold demonstrates performance deterioration when any stressor out of the ordinary occurs. The low-threshold employee is extremely susceptible to any kind of external stressor (time pressures, deadlines, insensitive supervisors, and so forth). For example:

> Jack is a slightly nervous person who takes his work very seriously. He anticipates his boss's needs and starts projects on his own without being told. Phil, on the other hand, is a "laid back" employee who takes things as they come. Even repeated warnings from the boss do not always get him moving.

In the example, Phil has a high stress response threshold. Much more stress must occur before he begins to perform and before his performance begins to deteriorate. These relationships are graphed in Figure 7.2.

Figure 7.2 illustrates the idea that Jack is a self-starter on the job because he has a very low stress response threshold. In contrast, Phil's threshold is much higher. Phil, therefore, must have more external pressure applied to keep him at a productive performance level. Two new concepts are introduced in Figure 7.2: (1) job burnout, and (2) job rustout. **Job burnout** means that the employee is overextended and chronically overstressed by work. This is true for Jack when external pressure is only at moderate levels. **Job rustout** is defined as being consistently understimulated by work. This is generally true for Phil unless the level of external pressure is high.

Managerial implications of stress response thresholds. Managers should know their employees well enough to predict their stress response thresholds. Jack and Phil's supervisor must treat these two employees quite differently in terms of external pressure to produce on the job. Jack is a self-starter who needs personal support from the boss when external pressure to produce becomes high. His supervisor should give Jack personal feedback on his value to the organization. Jack also should be kept informed regarding duration of the pressure to perform. Phil, on the other hand, should be supervised more closely and the boss should be clear about the consequences of low performance and poor initiative. In short, the rule is: Treat employees differently according to their different stress response thresholds.

Spotting the Signs of Employee Stress

Anyone has only so much capacity to resist the effects of stress. Knowing that work is itself a stressor, what are the reactions that you should look for in yourself and in others to indicate that too much stress is causing lowered performance and lessened job satisfaction? Table 7.1 provides the clues.

Aside from the specific symptoms of excessive job stress noted in Table 7.1, physicians have identified a number of general warning signs that indicate high likelihood of job stress overload.

Figure 7.2
Job Stress and Stress Response Thresholds for Jack and Phil

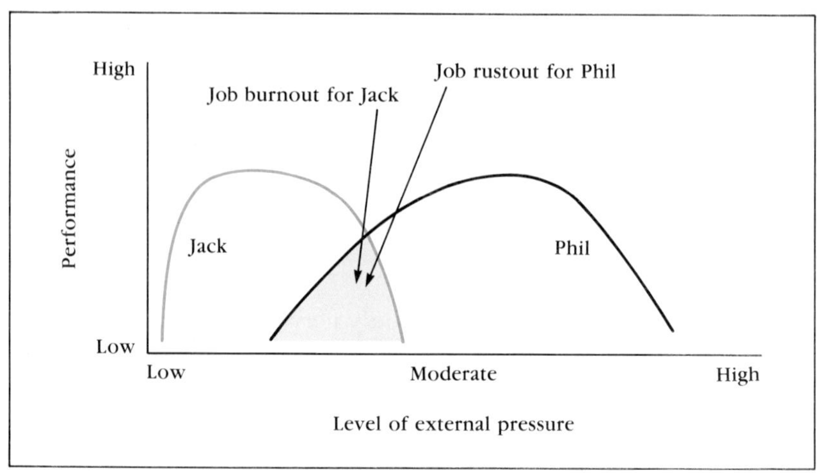

Table 7.1
Warning Signals of Too Much Job Stress

In Yourself	*In Your Coworkers*
Pounding heart	Sensitivity to criticism
Dryness of mouth	Poor work relationships
Poor concentration	Absenteeism and lateness
Excessive anxiety	Accident proneness
Insomnia	Drug use
Changes in appetite	Excessive drinking and/or smoking
Chest pains (no known cause)	Emotional outbursts
Rapid and shallow breathing	Frequent complaints
Stomach pain	Excessive guilt
Nervousness or loneliness	Nervous laughter
Impulsiveness	Poor time management
Forgetfulness	

1. **Diseases of adaptation** are symptomatic of the end of the adaptation stage of general adaptation syndrome. They include coronary artery disease, intestinal problems (ulcers and colitis), chronic headaches and backaches, diabetes, kidney disease, skin disorders, and forms of arthritis. As stressors become chronic over long periods of time, these problems appear.
2. **Depression** is loss of self-esteem and the feeling that one can control one's destiny. It is the most prevalent stress-related ailment. A prolonged feeling of having no control over one's job can precipitate onset of depression. The depressed employee typically has trouble making decisions and meeting deadlines while worrying excessively about both of these areas of job responsibility.
3. **Chronic anxiety** with no apparent external cause can be a response to excessive job stress. The employee may, for example, fear looking stupid in front of coworkers and will thus avoid situations that challenge her job skills.
4. **Abrupt mood swings** with accompanying erratic and unpredictable behavior can result from job stress. The ordinarily calm employee becomes hostile and temperamental or perhaps insensitive and cynical. These behaviors can have their origin in poorly defined jobs or work situations in which the employee's skills do not match job demands.

The Role of Gender in Stress at Work

Experts on job stress are realizing that gender may play a part in employee reactions to stress at work (10, 11). How employees view gender differences seems to be the key to these effects, rather than the actual physical differences between men and women. This finding reinforces strongly the importance of the psychological aspects of work stress.

The effects of job stress on professional women are an important application of these ideas (12, 13). Consistent with the biases as to why men and women behave the way they do, professional women may face work demands that are quite different from those faced by men. Because organizations are male dominated, working women must confront male-generated work expectations. Often these expectations are based on stereotypes (women are less effective under pressure, they are more emotional, they are only looking for a husband, and so forth). Professional women face other stressors as well. They receive less pay than their male counterparts and are subjected to more career and promotion discrimination (14). Women earn 57 to 86 percent of comparable males' salaries depending on occupation. Lack of advancement opportunities compound the problem. Employers must become aware of these effects and create equal opportunities for female employees. This in turn will equalize work expectations for men and women and help both to manage their work stress better.

Solving the Dilemma

What are Norma's physical and psychological reactions to stress?

Although Norma is not experiencing job stress directly, her reactions are exactly the same as those of an employee experiencing work-related stress. She is noticing inability to concentrate, excessive anxiety, chest pains for no apparent reason, and forgetfulness. Norma may not yet understand fully the origins of these stress symptoms, but she knows that her family's situation is now less certain. If the uncertainty continues, she will begin to experience more symptoms such as nervousness, insomnia, or stomach problems. In time, Norma will come to associate these unpleasant reactions with the financial uncertainty that her family faces.

Knowledge Check

1. Greater control over a source of stress usually results in less experienced stress. T or F?
2. Stress is composed of external factors, emotional reactions, and physical symptoms. T or F?
3. Reactivation is part of the general adaptation syndrome. T or F?
4. Outward symptoms of stress disappear during the alarm reaction stage of the general adaptation syndrome. T or F?
5. Job stress is a state of imbalance between a person and her job. T or F?
6. The point at which employee performance begins to deteriorate is job burnout. T or F?

Answers:

1 T, 2 T, 3 F, 4 F, 5 T, 6 F

Emotional Reactions to Job Stress

As we learned in Chapter 2, emotions are a basic component of our attitudes; they help us gauge (sometimes inaccurately) our reactions to situations around us. Like the physical reactions of the flight or fight response, emotions are accompanied by physical changes that include increased heart beat rate, higher blood pressure, and pupil dilation. These changes are governed by our nervous system, over which we have little control. Indeed, strong emotions such as fear, anger, joy, and jealousy trigger pronounced physical reactions.

What triggers strong emotional responses on the job?

Frustration is a major source of strong, negative emotional responses on the job. It is defined as the reaction that occurs when an obstruction comes between a behavior and its goal. Table 7.2 shows some selected types of job frustration and gives an example of each. Such frustrations can occur in any situation, one of which happens to be work.

Frustration can have desirable effects at work. If job stress is temporary and does not push the individual beyond the stress response threshold on a continuous basis, and if alternative behaviors are available, then frustra-

Table 7.2
Selected Types of Frustration at Work

Type of Frustration	*Example*
Receiving no reward after a pattern of reward has been established	Under one boss, an employee was given bonuses for filling out so many orders correctly. The new boss does not give bonuses for processing a certain number of orders correctly.
Delay in receiving rewards	Students who are used to getting test feedback the next day must wait two weeks to learn their grade.
Reward value change	Students are told that the midterm will be worth 80 points versus the original 50 points.
Failure	A real estate agent does all of the work necessary to make a sale but does not sell a single piece of property for the next six months.
Blockage of a strong behavior	A manager is told that he must work all weekend after he promised to coach his son's Saturday baseball game.
Punishment	A student is reprimanded by an instructor when she tries to ask a question during a lecture.
Conflict between two strong, but incompatible, responses.	A supervisor who must evaluate employee performance, yet he dislikes intensely giving any negative feedback.

tion can create new behaviors and innovations. Indeed, frustration can be challenging and can lead the employee to constructive change, especially when the supervisor helps the employee channel behavior around the obstacle.

Frustration can develop employee hardiness, which is defined as being capable of deliberate, rational action in the face of emotionally disturbing work stress. Consider the salesperson who encounters an irate customer during the Christmas shopping season. The hardy employee continues to measure his responses to the customer and refuses to engage in a shouting match. His inner resources are not exceeded by the situational demands, and he continues to demonstrate rational behavior during the interaction. If the employee were to give in consistently in such situations (and perhaps argue with customers), job disinterest and boredom would soon set in. Ineffective behaviors are soon noticed by supervisors and job loss can also result.

Executives and employee hardiness. AT & T executives with employee hardiness have been determined better able to cope with stress. Because they believe that they have control over their lives, they are less troubled by work or life changes (15). These researchers point out that "Accepting stress as a part of life and seeking to alter stressful situations and benefit from them or at least learn from them is a more healthy and realistic approach." (16).

Frustration and Aggression

Aggression is a common response to frustration on the job. Consider this account:

> Police said the 46–year old accountant was frustrated with her job and went on a 30–minute rampage in her car that did $50,000 damage to plate glass windows, cars, buildings, a gas pump and an ice machine. Before taking the wild drive, Nancy Appling Proctor set fire to her office causing $1,000 in damage.
>
> She said: "I went out and got rid of my frustration." She made good sense when she talked. "She thought it was funny," said the police sergeant who arrested her. She said it wasn't an accident, she did it on purpose. An office clerk said "She was laughing as she left the smoky office."
>
> The police sergeant said that Ms Appling-Proctor appeared calm and lucid when she was arrested and she told officers she was "Just having fun." (Pensacola Times, July 17, 1983)

This example demonstrates the problems with direct aggression, which is a dangerous course to take because it usually leads to socially unacceptable consequences in the organization.

Is aggression always direct?

No, a range of responses can occur, for direct aggression is usually inappropriate in organizations. One alternative is **displaced aggression.** This is defined as aggressive behavior that is directed at a "safe" target, one that is less powerful or threatening. Displaced aggression frequently "cascades." The executive who is frustrated by slack sales cannot go and confront or bully customers. Instead, he goes home and yells at his wife, and she in turn yells at the kids to clean their rooms. They do this chore reluctantly, and in the process tease the family cat, who runs out an open door. Only the cat is left with no displacement options!

Displaced aggression need not be externally directed. It may take the form of self-reproach or guilt. These types of displaced aggression are designated **intropunitive aggression.** The individual directs the aggression inward, toward herself. If an employee is locked in an abusive work relationship with a boss who is arbitrary and unfair, intropunitive aggression can occur. Here's an example:

> Shirley felt that her situation with the boss was hopeless. He continued to run her down in front of her coworkers for the smallest work-related error. He expected her to be informed of every detail regarding office matters. She could not quit the job because she soon would need money to pay for her daughter's braces. Her work began to deteriorate more and more, and her former enthusiasm for her job faded. After a while, she began to feel guilty about her low performance, because she believed she was making more work for her coworkers.

Shirley's withdrawal from this work situation is blocked for financial reasons, so she has resigned herself to taking abuse from her boss. Many of her emotional responses to her job resemble intropunitive aggression. In addition, she could begin to experience depression. If these work stressors persist, she may start to accept passively her boss's abuse and blame herself. The misfortune of such situations is that they can spread to other aspects of one's life. Eventually Shirley may begin to feel as if she cannot control any of the events in her life. At the same time, she would experience self-blame for the way things turned out. Depressed employees often blame themselves for both their behavior and character. They come to believe that no hope for constructive change exists in either area.

Knowledge Check

1. Frustration is the first, most likely response to being prevented from achieving a school-related goal. T or F?
2. Frustration does not occur when an employee is faced with two equally attractive offers from competing firms. T or F?
3. Employee hardiness refers to an individual's capacity to tolerate frustration at work. T or F?
4. The behavioral reactions to intropunitive aggression and depression are very similar. T or F?

Answers:

1 T, 2 F, 3 T, 4 T

Personality and Job Stress: You Are What You Feel

Consider this example:

> The executive sits at his desk and tries to finish two reports that he has taken over from a coworker. Both reports deal with a problem that could affect the company for the next five years. As he works, he accepts a call from a major client, and they plan an early business dinner for that evening. His secretary reminds him that his evening schedule allows him only 45 minutes for dinner, but he makes the commitment anyway! He then learns that tomorrow he must give presentations on both reports, so he makes a note to cancel his 6:30 A.M. racketball match. He now realizes that tomorrow he must get up at 4 A.M. to prepare for the presentations.

How Personality Influences Reactions to Stress

The executive in the example is creating his own stress at work. Individuals who impose excessive work demands on themselves and who prefer to work close to their physical and mental limits are defined as **Type A personalities** (17). A more rigorous definition is:

> an action-emotion complex that can be observed in any person who is aggressively involved in a chronic, incessant struggle to achieve more and more in less and less time (18).

Type A individuals are locked in a constant struggle with their work and social environments to maintain their self-esteem (19). They believe that hard work will overcome any obstacle, and they push themselves to keep proving this (to themselves). To be efficient, the Type A frequently performs many activities at the same time because of "**hurry sickness**" (20). This is defined as extreme impatience with the existing pace of life. The features of hurry sickness are these:

1. **Impatience with waiting or idleness** of any sort, especially waiting in lines, being stuck in traffic, or encountering unexpected delays.
2. **Experiencing time pressure** and frequently finishing or taking on the work of others.
3. **Becoming impatient with others who work at a slower pace** or who talk at a slower pace (Type A's often finish the sentences of slower speakers!).
4. **Self-centeredness in terms of goals and work activities.** If conversations drift to "less relevant" topics, the Type A will interrupt and steer the conversation back to his area of interest.

Type A's thrive on tight deadlines and multiple goals. When they are well matched with the job demands, they can turn out terrific quantities of work. They excel in middle management and sales work, yet they seldom make it to the top of the organization. The reason for this is simple. They are so compulsive about work that they do not take the time (because of hurry sickness) to weigh critical options in making major decisions. Furthermore, they can be so impatient that they make others nervous (they transmit stress). Type A's therefore often "work hard" instead of "working smart." Table 7.3 shows characteristics of Type A's and of their more relaxed, Type B counterparts.

Solving the Dilemma

Are some people more prone to stress than others?

The Type A person tends to have the following characteristics: (1) hurry sickness, (2) competitiveness, (3) doing many things at the same time, (4) denial of stress, and (5) compulsiveness. Such a person activates the flight or fight response many more times per day than a Type B person. This chronic excitation of the alarm reaction over time can lead to: (1) higher blood pressure, (2) higher cholesterol, and (3) more compulsive behaviors such as drinking, smoking, and overeating. These tendencies eventually lead to greater susceptibility to illness and stress-related disease.

Further comparisons of Type A and Type B. The Type A individual is always striving to perfect her work skills by setting challenging goals. The Type B demonstrates much broader interests in life. The Type A accepts external standards as valid and tries to set personal records at work. Any obstacle in the path to these goals is confronted with barely suppressed hostility. The Type B accepts work standards by adjusting effort to meet variable work demands. The Type A is indeed a driven person who takes great pride in his capacity to work and meet job pressures head on. Type B person paces herself and "works smart and hard" as necessary.

Table 7.3
Comparing Type A and Type B Personality and State of Health

Type A Personality Characteristics	*Type B Personality Characteristics*
1. Very competitive and irritable	1. More relaxed and easy going
2. Highly task oriented	2. Able to match effort to task demands
3. Very satisfied with work	3. Balances work and life interests
4. Impatient and hostile when frustrated or delayed	4. Can do jobs one at a time
5. Transmits stress to subordinates and peers	5. Finds outlets besides work for competitive energy
6. Less able to recognize stress	6. Recognizes stress more readily
Long-Term Effects of Stress for Type A	*Long-Term Effects of Stress for Type B*
1. More diseases of adaptation (e.g., high blood pressure, heart disease)	1. Fewer diseases of adaptation
2. Elevated cholesterol level	2. Lower cholesterol level
3. Poor physical condition	3. Better physical condition
	4. Greater chance of promotion

Type A individuals are unfortunately often deniers of stress build-up in their lives. This form of Type A stress denial is defined as the dismissal of negative personal and work-stress reactions. For instance, the Type A's response to increased work loads is to keep all other activities going while adding another hour to the workday plus working all day Sunday. The Type B will not do this because he values balance in work and leisure activities. Because the Type A is so likely to see the path to happiness as work related, he usually denies that work is a source of dissatisfaction.

The Type A Personality and Health

Type A denial tendencies do not stop with work-generated job dissatisfaction. Their hard-charging style causes blood pressure and cholesterol levels to elevate several times each workday. Over time, they become predisposed to higher risk of coronary artery disease (21, 22). Type B individuals are thought to be less susceptible to coronary artery diseases because they do not trigger their flight or fight responses as often as Type A's. In effect, the Type A's physical resources begin to break down, and they are susceptible to diseases of adaptation by their late thirties through fifties. Their denial tendency can cause them to ignore early warning signals (e.g., chest pain and undue fatigue). Type A's seem to rationalize and conclude: "I'm not working hard enough." Huge capacity for work, denial of physical symptoms, and early onset of diseases of adaptation thus cause the Type A to be a less likely candidate for the executive suite. In many ways, Type A's lack the durability (employee hardiness) of the Type B's (23).

A clear link exists between Type A behavior and coronary artery disease (24). In large-scale studies, researchers have found that over a nine-year period, Type A's (between 39 and 59 years) who were originally free of coronary diseases were six times more likely to experience heart disease than their Type B counterparts (25). Additional results indicate that Type A's have higher cholestrol level and higher blood pressure. Type A behavior can be dangerous to your health! Use the NOW IT'S YOUR TURN to assess your own Type A tendencies.

NOW IT'S YOUR TURN . . .

A Type A Test

Circle the appropriate number on each scale that best represents your behavior for each trait.

1. Casual about appointments	1 2 3 4 5 6 7 8	Never late
2. Not competitive	1 2 3 4 5 6 7 8	Very competitive
3. Never feel rushed even under pressure	1 2 3 4 5 6 7 8	Always rushed
4. Take things one at a time	1 2 3 4 5 6 7 8	Try to do many things at once
5. Deliberate in doing work	1 2 3 4 5 6 7 8	Fast at work and leisure

6. Willingly express feelings	1 2 3 4 5 6 7 8	Bottle up feelings
7. Have many interests	1 2 3 4 5 6 7 8	Few interests besides work

Total score:______ × 3 = ______

Interpretation:

Number of points	Personality type
Less than 90	B
90–99	B+
100–105	A–
106–119	A
over 120	A+

Source: Adapted from R. Bortner, A Short Rating Scale: A Measure of Pattern A Behavior. *Journal of Chronic Diseases,* 1966, 22.87–91.

A final comparison of Type A's and Type B's. Most medical experts equate stress with the Type A personality (26, 27). Type B's are described as relaxed and more easy going. In fact, if you're a Type A, you may have concluded that Type B's are lazy! This is incorrect for two reasons (28). First, Type B's can be extremely goal-oriented and interested in work achievement. They simply work toward success in ways that do not extract the same stress price. Type B's can therefore rise more easily to the demands of a tough job. They have no trouble dropping back, however, to an unhurried pace when they believe the pressure is off.

Improving the Type A's Health Odds

Remember that one's risk of having coronary disease is influenced heavily by the incidence of cardiac disease present in your family history. Second, weight and diet can be potent risk factors if allowed to get out of control. The first constructive step toward reducing or managing Type A reactions is to improve one's self-awareness and one's ability to recognize stress symptoms (Table 7.4).

In summary, personality is related to the stress response. Over long periods of time, Type A's can become susceptible to diseases of adaptation as their stress defenses erode through countless alarm reaction episodes triggered by work. Denial of stress symptoms is a key aspect of the Type A response pattern. Type B's are more aware of the effects of stress. They pace themselves at work accordingly and develop numerous leisure interests. Organizations reward Type A behavior, and this may contribute to employee stress level. Type A behavior can be changed through improved self-awareness and rechanneling behavior.

Table 7.4
The Basics of Self-Awareness and Managing Type A Tendencies

Key Questions for Improved Self-Awareness

1. Do you know your resting pulse rate?
2. Do you know what your blood pressure is and how it varies with different activities and time of day?
3. Do you know your energy peaks during the day?
4. Do you notice how you waste time each day?
5. Do you know what situations trigger the stress response?

Key Indicators of an Ongoing Stress Response

1. Rapid or pounding heart (without physical exertion).
2. Increased sweating, especially forehead and arms, when room temperature is not high.
3. Muscle tension in neck, forehead, jaw, and back.
4. Inability to sit quietly—restlessness.

Tips for Reducing Hurry Sickness

1. Eat lunch away from your job or school (find a nearby park).
2. Don't be afraid to say *no* to another project.
3. Take time to enjoy contemplative activities (reading in the public library).
4. Work on catching people doing things right rather than doing things wrong. (Giving recognition to others helps you feel better about yourself.)
5. Practice number 4 all of the time.
6. Analyze your daily schedule for conflicting demands, and reduce unnecessary work load.
7. Develop multiple interests outside of work or school.
   (If you choose sports, don't keep score all the time.)
8. Practice speaking more slowly, especially when you're in a hurry.
9. Monitor your breathing rate while at work or school. Practice regular, slow breathing.
10. Make "time out periods," when you can get away from your routine for five or ten minutes.
11. Develop some Type B friends, especially at work or school.

Solving the Dilemma

Is stress related to health and disease?

Stress is an inevitable aspect of life. In many cases, however, we have a choice about whether we allow stressful events to upset us or not. We know that the Type A individual is more likely to become upset in the presence of chronic stress. Type B individuals also experience stress, but they are more likely to adjust their reactions to it. When there is no pressure, they relax. Type A's do not know how to relax. They "burn the candle at both ends," and over time, they have less resistance to various types of physical and emotional illness. This slow erosion of "stress immunity" extracts a toll from Type A's. If the Type A has a family history of heart disease, his personality may hasten disease onset.

Knowledge Check

1. Type A's try to do only a few things at any given time. T or F?
2. Type A's are more likely than Type B's to achieve high company positions. T or F?
3. Type B's regularly deny that they are experiencing stress. T or F?
4. No clear connection exists between personality and risk of coronary disease. T or F?

Answers:

1 F, 2 F, 3 F, 4 F

Sources of Job Stress in Organizations: Welcome to the Treadmill

In this section we deal with two categories of work stressors: (1) individual level stressors, and (2) physical environment stressors. (Figure 7.3) The essence of stress management is recognizing stressors and devising a plan to handle them. The final section of this chapter discusses company programs designed to help employees deal with stress.

Figure 7.3
Sources of Job Stress

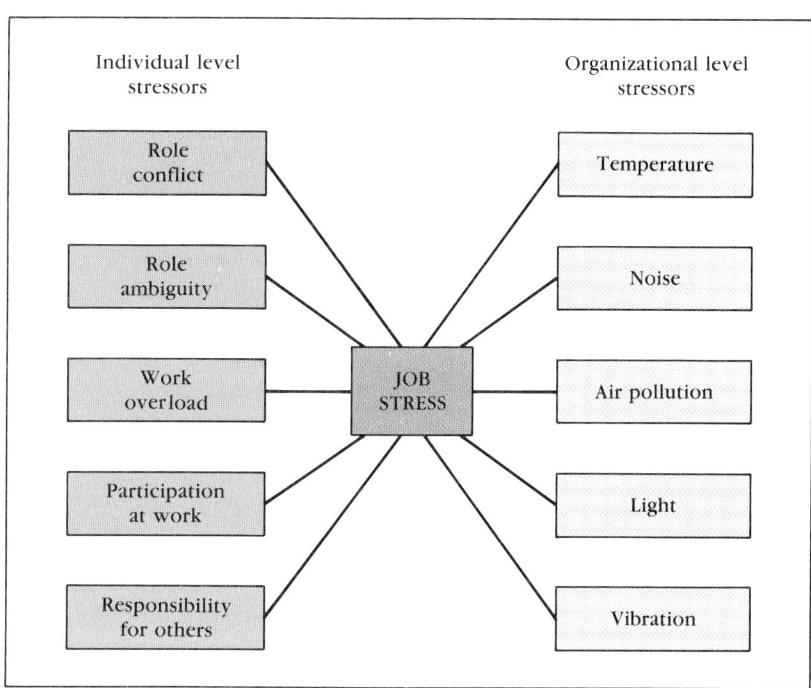

Individual Level Stressors

Role conflict. Have you ever been in a situation in which, if you go along with one person's wishes, you automatically upset someone else? That is **role conflict,** which is defined as mutually incompatible expectations. In other words, compliance with one demand makes it difficult or impossible to comply with another. This situation can be a relatively permanent feature of some jobs and contributes greatly to the employee's experienced level of job stress.

Role ambiguity. A lack of clarity about job expectations and job goals is called **role ambiguity.** Role ambiguity makes it hard to set goals, to decide on work activities, and to determine how to allocate one's time (29). It has many sources in the organization. A new job, new supervisor, change in work procedure, new work group members, a promotion, or a job transfer can all cause role ambiguity.

Role conflict and role ambiguity are related to job dissatisfaction, lower level of self-confidence, and elevated blood pressure (30, 31). Under these conditions, employees show decreased motivation, more anxiety, poorer family relations, and more depression (32, 33). Recalling the expectancy theory model, we see that role conflict and role ambiguity influence people in predictable ways. Their beliefs that effort will lead to performance (expectancy) and that performance will lead to desirable rewards (instrumentality) are undermined. This uncertainty generates stress and performance decline.

These problems cannot be erased completely from the organization. A certain amount of role ambiguity and conflict are necessary to energize innovative solutions as employees search for ways to overcome obstacles. In other words, these stressors can precipitate constructive change when they are held to manageable levels. A certain amount of stress adds spice to life!

Work overload comes in two forms. **Quantitative overload** is defined as having too many things to do and not enough time in which to do them. **Qualitative overload** represents a poor match between employee work experience and job demands. As a result, the employee simply cannot meet the job demands. When these conditions are chronic, they can lead to maladaptive responses such as alcoholism, drug abuse, personal problems at home, persistent anxiety and tension, and higher accident rates.

Both forms of work overload are linked with coronary disease (34). When employees feel as if they are working two jobs at the same time and have no "personal" time, they experience elevated cholesterol, blood pressure, and pulse rate. These employees eventually can become susceptible to diseases of adaptation.

Participation at work. Being involved in the decision-making process reduces the effects of stress for employees (35). Employee participation in work unit decision making can satisfy the needs for responsibility, autonomy, and control. Employees experience more stress when they have quantitative work overload and low autonomy. (36). The principles of job design discussed in Chapter 6 are excellent management tools for increasing employee participation and reducing the effects of stress.

Responsibility for others. When people have great personal responsibility for the safety and welfare of others, they are more susceptible to the effects of stress. In police work, for example, these responsibilities can occur in the extreme, which explains the high rate of job burnout for this profession. Similarly, air traffic controllers experience chronic stress symptoms because of their responsibility for (and little control over) people aboard aircraft (37). The problem in both professions is tremendous responsibility (the consequences of errors are massive) combined with little or no direct control over many aspects of the situation. In similar fashion, managers often have great responsibility for the life-style of employees (e.g., pay raises, promotion, transfer, and firing may all depend on the manager). Managers agree that one of the toughest aspects of their job is dismissing employees, especially those near the same job level as the manager. These job responsibilities all add up to increased stress. . . .

Physical Work Environment Stressors

Physical work environment stressors originate in the external aspects of the work environment versus the psychological or social dimensions of work. These stressors are numerous. We focus here on temperature, noise, air pollution, vibration, and light.

Note that physical work stressors are not confined to blue collar jobs. These stressors affect people who use computers, work under fluorescent lights, work in tightly sealed high rise office buildings, and so forth.

Temperature. Human beings, with protection, are capable of working in a huge temperature range (− 250 to + 500 degrees Fahrenheit). Most jobs do not require employees to work under such extremes, however. Temperature can have an effect on worker performance, especially when employees must work outdoors in either very hot or very cold climates. As workers get closer to their tolerance limit for heat or cold, the quality of their decision making begins to erode, and they become more prone to accidents because their reactions are impaired. For these reasons, companies that require employees to work in extreme temperature ranges should take special precautions in terms of protective clothing and machine modifications.

Noise. Employees are affected quickly by noise level and by noise level changes. Hearing loss is one of the most pervasive medical problems in the United States. Modern existence means prolonged exposure to noise, and indeed, people can adapt to noise quite well. Individuals who have trouble falling asleep because of noise can be aided by "white noise," that is, noise with a regular, nonvarying quality like the sound of rolling waves or a bubbling brook. The white noise can mask unpredictable noise from sources such as airplanes, trains, or telephones and can aid in getting to sleep. White noise machines sooth the troubled soul and contribute to a good night's rest!

Industry and government are aware of the effects of noise. Industry regularly monitors noise level in work areas. The Occupational Safety and Health Administration sets guidelines for acceptable noise levels in various industries and occupations. These regulations frequently require employees to wear ear protection and in some cases require employers to install noise level monitors.

Air pollution. If employees must work with hazardous materials, air pollution can be a stressor. Simply getting to and from work can be a source of air pollution stress in some areas. The pollution created by automobile exhaust fumes can trigger respiratory illness when these compounds are mixed with ozone in the air. In Mexico City, this problem has become so acute that patients line up to get into the hospital to receive oxygen while they wait for their examination! We do not as yet have problems of this magnitude in the United States. Current concerns about acid rain in the eastern United States are, however, causing widespread calls for research and joint US-Canadian prevention activities.

Another air pollution concern is that tightly sealed office buildings may expose workers to higher concentrations of formaldehyde, a poisonous compound that is a byproduct of the deterioration of building materials. Current environmental research is being conducted to determine if this is a long-term health risk for workers.

Light. The type of light that we are exposed to in office buildings may be a work stressor. The light from computer displays has been associated with eye strain and headaches. Fluorescent lighting is related to hyperactivity in children; when the fluorescent lights in classrooms are filtered, hyperactivity decreases. Inappropriate lighting can influence employee performance significantly. Inadequate lighting raises worker frustration level because more time is required to complete tasks. The simple eye strain associated with poor lighting is a stressor.

Some tasks require special lighting. For example, surgery, microchip processing, and laboratory work can require up to six times more light than the amount we need to read comfortably. Eye strain can be increased under these conditions, because if lighting is inadequate, employees may have to view objects under magnifiers or scanners. The long-term effects of this work on vision have not been determined. In some industries, technological advances have been so rapid that study of the lighting requirements has fallen behind the technology. As we learn more about lighting requirements and the new technology, better safety guidelines will be established.

Vibration. If vibration is intense and chronic, it can seriously affect employees. Heavy equipment such as bulldozers and earth moving equipment generate intense vibration and noise. Operators must be rotated off of these machines after a certain time period to avoid kidney or hearing damage. Manufacturers have invested heavily in product designs that protect operators from vibration and noise created by heavy equipment.

Solving the Dilemma

What can be done to lessen and manage stress?

Many popular books have been written to help us adjust to stress. The various approaches advocated for stress management fall into several categories: (1) physical exercise, (2) psychological adjustment, (3) behavior modification (i.e., eliminating bad habits such as drinking or smoking), and

(4) diet and nutrition. In many respects, the common theme in all categories is improvement of self-image and self-esteem. Most stress management systems start with improving the person's abilities to recognize stress in himself. Self-awareness begins the process. Next comes the work of learning how and when stress affects you most (identifying when your symptoms of physical and emotional discomfort are greatest). Last comes the ambitious job of learning how to control your stress response, for we all have choices in deciding how upset to get in a stressful situation. Learning how to manage the "level of upsetness" is the key to controlling stress.

Company Stress Management Programs

Information about stress has spread quickly from medical laboratories to corporations. With this knowledge has come an increased orientation in organizations toward preventative maintenance in the form of stress reduction programs for employees. A **preventative maintenance** approach means that potential stress problems are identified and managed before the symptoms of stress (i.e., diseases of adaptation) begin to appear in employees. Such programs can be cost effective in concrete terms such as (1) fewer health insurance claims filed, (2) reduced accident rates, (3) less absenteeism, (4) less smoking and better nutritional control, (5) reduced length and number of hospital stays, and (6) increased employee need satisfaction. A program that deals with stress-related problems before they become chronic can be a major contributor to the quality of work life for employees. The second part of a stress management program is the systematic lowering of stressors to optimal or manageable levels.

What kinds of programs do companies set up?

Wellness programs can be extremely comprehensive and may be designed to provide employees with information regarding a number of subjects: stress management, health risk assessment, nutrition, exercise, smoking, weight loss, and alcohol use. Most company wellness programs are voluntary. Until recently, these programs were viewed as executive "perks," and were generally available only to individuals in high organizational positions. The recent popularization of physical fitness and routine exercise has caused many firms to broaden their commitment to the employee health. The Kimberly-Clark Corporation has invested $3 million in a comprehensive health management program. Company officials report that the program has lowered insurance costs and absenteeism. They also state that it has raised employee morale, for employees are happy to report weight loss, less smoking, and an improved level of cardiovascular fitness (38).

Atco Properties Management Company of New York had a program that paid employees $100 for each pound lost between January and July 1985. Employees received an extra $50 per pound for weight taken off from July through December 1985. The program was so successful that one senior executive lost 47 pounds and earned $5,200! Atco employees also earn $500 if they quit smoking for one year, and another $500 if they exercise each day (39).

At the University of Wisconsin at Stevens Point, the establishment and development of wellness programs has become a college major. All entering students have their health risks assessed. Furthermore, the surrounding community participates in the university programs. Students report that the wellness program is a great stress reducer around examination time, and many believe that they are laying the groundwork for good health habits in future. The university runs a summer conference on wellness programs. In 1985, the conference covered 35 topics, and nearly 1,000 individuals attended from all over the country.

Wellness programs are being established by more and more organizations. Companies believe that these programs save costs and increase employee productivity. Consulting organizations and hospitals now have specialists who design and administer these programs for corporate clients. In some instances, the programs are operated in the hospital facilities.

Drug and alcohol abuse programs. Companies are responding also to the problems of employee drug dependence. Illegal drugs are used by workers in virtually all industries (40). Many firms are setting up employee assistance programs (EAPs) to deal with drug dependent employees. These confidential programs are designed to assist the troubled employee before she has to face dismissal for absenteeism or for poor performance caused by substance abuse. To set up such a program, the corporation generally contracts with a local medical organization that has the expertise to assist employees who are having problems with drugs or alcohol. Supervisors are trained to identify the behaviors of troubled employees. If an employee has a chemical dependence problem, the supervisor counsels the employee and explains that he must participate in the program or face dismissal. Program participation becomes in effect a condition of employment. After the initial supervisor contact, the process is confidential, between the employee and his EAP contact. Supervisors are trained also to look for gains in employee performance and dependability.

EAPs have spread as companies have realized increasingly that job stress often leads to substance abuse. Recent reports about drug abuse in a variety of organizations and occupations have prompted decisive action (41). Furthermore, several prominent citizens have described publicly their efforts to cope with drug problems. The organizations that regulate professional sports also are making a sincere effort to eradicate drug use among professional athletes. These efforts help create a positive public awareness of the dangers of drug and alcohol abuse.

EAPs can be cost effective. For example, the Norfolk and Western Railway established a program for drug and alcohol abuse after the company realized that $8 million was being lost annually as a result of accidents, absenteeism, and on-the-job injuries—many of which were drug and alcohol related. The armed forces has experimented with EAPs, and both the army and navy have reported excellent results (42). Enlisted personnel and officers report improved performance and job satisfaction as participants learned to re-establish control over their lives and to shed their dependence on "chemical self-confidence."

Mental relaxation. We can *unlearn* our reactions to stress in the same way that we learn negative behavioral and emotional stress responses. Specific behavioral techniques for mental relaxation include (1) deep muscle relaxation, (2) biofeedback, (3) deep breathing, and (4) visualization techniques. All of these methods are based on the concept that the central nervous system cannot tell the difference between a real and a vividly imagined experience. If a person breathes deeply and regularly while imagining a peaceful scene, the body will orient itself in useful ways to this imagined experience. Blood pressure will drop, pulse rate slow, and muscles relax (43, 44). The stress response can be unlearned through these visualization or concentration techniques.

Too many companies have stress management programs to mention them all, but several company programs stand out as good examples (45). Kaiser Permanente's stress prevention program uses a variety of techniques already mentioned. Its program lasts four days and uses both educational and experiential components to teach employees how to manage stress. Employees learn about the physiology of stress, how stress can affect them personally, and what to do about it. Principles of nutrition and exercise are discussed as aspects of illness prevention. Employees are taught various forms of stress management, such as deep breathing, so they can raise their stress response thresholds. They learn to become more assertive in their work relationships, and they study their own stress profiles. For four weeks after the seminar, employees are instructed to keep stress diaries so they can better learn how to recognize their stress reactions. At the end of this period, a follow-up session is held and participants review what they have learned. They complete the program by developing their own action plan for coping with stress (46). Equitable Life Insurance Company, B. F. Goodrich Company, Caterpillar Company, and Converse Shoe Corporation have similar programs (47).

Many firms decide to focus their resources on providing physical fitness centers for employees. Xerox, Pepsico., and Weyerhauser have facilities that are staffed by physical fitness professionals. These facilities have state-of-the-art fitness equipment including hydraulic exercise machines, treadmills, ergometers (a special stationary bicycle), and padded jogging tracks. The most impressive of these facilities has been built by Kimberly-Clark Corporation at a cost of $2.5 million. This includes a 7,000 square foot health testing facility and a 32,000 square foot fitness center (48).

Knowledge Check

1. Role conflict and role ambiguity are examples of individual level stressors. T or F?

2. An example of role ambiguity is having two bosses who tell you to do opposite things. T or F?

3. Most managers would agree that all forms of individual stress should be removed from the organization. T or F?

4. Qualitative role overload occurs when employee skills and training do not match the job demands. T or F?

5. Air traffic controllers experience stress because of responsibility for others. T or F?
6. A rock concert represents white noise. T or F?
7. A corporate wellness program is not an example of a preventative maintenance approach to job stress. T or F?

Answers:

1 T, 2 F, 3 F, 4 T, 5 T, 6 F, 7 F

Summary Points

- **Stress** refers to any demand made on the body that requires psychological or physical adjustment. Some stressors are evaluated in **external terms,** while others are described in terms of the emotional reactions and physical symptoms they cause in individuals. When people describe their **personal reactions** to stress, they often do it in **physical terms.** In fact, stress itself is neutral. Human judgments of stress cause it to be interpreted in positive (**eustress**) or negative (**distress**) terms.
- **The general adaptation syndrome (GAS)** describes how the stressed individual first reacts (**alarm reaction**), compensates (**adaptation**), and eventually gives in (**exhaustion**) to stress.
- **The fight or flight response** (alarm) causes major changes in our physical reactions. Blood pressure, pulse rate, breathing rate, and cholesterol level are all elevated.
- **The stress response threshold** is the point at which a stressor shifts from being a **motivator** (positively related to performance) to being a **distressor** (negatively related to performance).
- **Frustration** is a major cause of stress response, but it also can be a motivator and lead to **employee hardiness.**
- **Aggression** is a common response to stress. Aggression can be directed outward or inward (**intropunitively**) by the individual. If the latter condition persists, depression may result.
- **Type A behavior** is characterized by **hurry sickness, competitiveness, denial of stress, and doing many things at once.** It can lead to coronary artery disease. Changing Type A behavior begins with improved self-awareness of personal stress symptoms.
- **Role ambiguity and role conflict** represent individual stressors that can trigger the stress response. Both conditions undermine the individual's sense of autonomy and job predictability, thus lowering performance and job satisfaction.
- **Company stress management programs** are usually preventative in nature. These programs help employees to identify and manage stress before symptoms appear. Program examples include wellness programs, employee assistance programs (EAPs), company exercise centers, and training in mental relaxation.

Questions

1. What are some of the indicators that you would look for in yourself if you believed that you were chronically in the adaptation stage of the general adaptation syndrome.

2. You are a supervisor with two subordinates, Jane and Dick. Dick has a low stress response threshold at work, while Jane's is much higher. Both employees can perform at the same level of

excellence. Based on your knowledge of individual differences and job stress, how would you manage these two employees?

3. Describe the behavior of the Type A supervisor. Explain how he or she might transmit stress to co-workers at the same job level. How does the behavior of this individual compare with your behavior at school?

4. Explain why air traffic controllers experience stress on the job. What are other stressful occupations? Are these jobs stressful for the same reasons as the air traffic controller job?

5. Describe a process that you would follow to effectively manage role conflict and role ambiguity for first-line supervisors. Be sure to emphasize recognition of stress and ways to deal with it.

6. On a sheet of paper, list three of your most powerful stressors in school. Next, write down your emotional and physical reactions to each. Ask a close friend to do the same, then compare your stressors and discuss the differences between your reactions.

7. Students sometimes experience work overload in school, especially during exams. From an administrative point of view, what do you think your school could do to help students manage their stress levels better? Should colleges and universities be concerned with test-generated stress?

8. Call a local hospital and set up an appointment to visit their wellness program or stress management clinic. How does the hospital's program compare with the programs described in this chapter?

EXPLORING: *The Hardy Executive*

Adopted from Oliver Niehouse, Stress and the Hardy Executive. *Industry Week* (November 12, 1984). 96–98.

We can all point to someone who, without any stress-management training, shoulders an incredible amount of work and balances it skillfully with other activities. Peter Stam (not his real name) is just such a person. He is the creative director of a small New York advertising agency. He is actively involved in raising his sons, restoring a Manhattan brownstone, coordinating civic activities, and writing his version of the great American novel. When possible, he squeezes in travel to such exotic places as Samaraland and Sri Lanka.

Peter's friends don't know how he does it. A close friend remarked, "I get tired just thinking about all the things he does. I know that someday it's all going to catch up with him. It has to!"

Last August, his close friends thought that "someday" had arrived when Peter's mother had a fatal heart attack in Florida. She had been operating a nursing home for 20 elderly women.

Peter suddenly inherited a new business that he didn't have the foggiest idea how to operate. He recalls his first reaction: "I remember wondering—what am I going to do? Who's going to serve the meal to the ladies in the home this very night? I now owned a business! I landed quickly on solid ground thanks to the support of my wife, my kids, and the agency, then I began to do what I thought had to be done."

Peter established priorities, formulated a master plan based on his thoughts and discussions with his family, then mustered all of his energies and skills in juggling his life and a business located 1,200 miles away.

"Every Monday through Thursday I dealt with eccentrically creative people, demanding clients, life in New York, and teaching my eldest son how to use our home computer," he remembers. "Then, from Friday through Sunday, I dealt with ordinary, small-town people, food purchasing and inventory, and arranging outings for elderly ladies. They were two very different worlds, very different."

Peter planned to sell the retirement home within a year and use the money to establish his own advertising agency. He exceeded his goal by four months. He had managed, too, to overcome the grief of losing his mother, and he had held the retirement home together so that he could insure the continued care of its residents once it was sold.

Discussion Questions

1. Does Peter demonstrate employee hardiness? Why or why not?
2. What are the differences between the approach to life of the Type A person versus the stress-hardy individual?
3. Is Peter simply a Type A person?

APPLYING: *Am I Overstressed?*

Drs. Thomas Holms and Richard Rahe believe that major life changes cause increased stress. They hypothesize that stressful events reduce the body's natural defenses against illness and disease. Their research shows that grief and mourning often precede a major illness. They have identified 43 life events that can raise a person's chances of experiencing a debilitating illness after the events occur. They call their diagonistic tool the Social Readjustment Rating Scale (SRRS) (Figure 7.4).

Illness is perhaps a narrow interpretation of the accumulating effects of stress as measured by the SRRS. A stress-induced crisis could be an accident caused by inattentiveness, that is, the magnitude of stress-caused change in a person's life may be so great that he is preoccupied while driving to work and is therefore involved in a serious automobile accident.

While many problems are identified by the SRRS, only one quarter of the items are job-related, and only ten are decidedly negative in wording. Experts have found, however, that the scale is a dependable way to measure overall stress level in adults.

Using the scale in Figure 7.4, place a check beside those events that apply to you for the last year. When you have done this, total the life crisis units that apply to the life events you checked. Compare your total with the following standards:

0–180—No significant problems
155–199—Mild life crisis (33 percent chance of experiencing illness within the next year)
200–299—Moderate life crisis (50 percent chance of experiencing illness within the next year)
over 300—Major life crisis (80 percent chance of experiencing illness within the next year).

A high SRRS score means that additional stress should be avoided and that you should increase your capacity to tolerate stress (i.e., lengthen your adaptation stage). A part of handling stress is learning stress management skills and how you personally react to stress (self-awareness). Serious stress problems are best handled with the help of professionals, but many forms of stress can be overcome by using one's common sense. Let's discuss two stress reduction methods that you can put into practice now: (1) exercise, and (2) building a social support system.

Exercise is the easiest way to create stress hardiness in yourself and to bring about positive changes in your life-style and self-image. Cardiovascular endurance is often considered to be the most important indicator of physical health. Experts agree that 30 minutes of sustained aerobic exercise performed four times per week will keep an individual in excellent shape. Aerobic exercise is the type of physical exersion that builds endurance. During exercise periods, you must maintain a training heart rate. This is the level at which your heart beats during aerobic exercise to maintain your physical capacity and enable you to use large quantities of oxygen without becoming unduly fatigued. To determine your training heart rate, simply subtract your age from 220, and multiply the difference by .80. Americans

Figure 7.4 *The Social Readjustment Rating Scale*

Check	Rank	Life Event	Life Crisis Units
___	1	Death of spouse	100
___	2	Divorce	73
___	3	Marital separation	65
___	4	Jail term	63
___	5	Death of a close family member	63
___	6	Personal injury or illness	53
___	7	Marriage	50
___	8	Fired at work	47
___	9	Marital reconciliation	45
___	10	Retirement	45
___	11	Change in health of family member	44
___	12	Pregnancy	40
___	13	Sex difficulties	39
___	14	Gain of new family member	39
___	15	Business readjustment	39
___	16	Change in financial state	38
___	17	Death of close friend	37
___	18	Change to different line of work	36
___	19	Change in number of arguments w/ spouse	35
___	20	Mortgage over $10,000	31
___	21	Foreclosure of mortgage or loan	30
___	22	Change in responsibilities at work	29
___	23	Son or daughter leaving home	29
___	24	Trouble with in-laws	29
___	25	Outstanding personal achievement	28
___	26	Wife begins or stops work	26
___	27	Begin or end school	26
___	28	Change in living conditions	25
___	29	Revision of personal habits	24
___	30	Trouble with boss	23
___	31	Change in work hours or conditions	20
___	32	Change in residence	20
___	33	Change in school	20
___	34	Change in recreation	19
___	35	Change in church activities	19
___	36	Change in social activities	18
___	37	Mortgage or loan less than $10,000	17
___	38	Change in sleeping habits	16
___	39	Change in number of family get-togethers	15
___	40	Change in eating habits	15
___	41	Vacation	13
___	42	Christmas	12
___	43	Minor violations of the law	11

Adapted with permission from T.H. Holmes and R.H. Rahe, 1957. Social Readjustment Rating Scale. *Journal of Psychosomatic Research* (Reprinted with permission from Pergamon Press, Ltd.)

generally prefer the following forms of aerobic exercise: (1) swimming, (2) bicycling, (3) jogging, or (4) racket sports (e.g., tennis, racketball, squash).

While you are engaged in these activities, take your pulse occasionally by counting your heart beat rate for six seconds (begin counting at zero) and then multiplying that value by 10. This is easy to do, and won't disrupt your activity, but it will tell you if you are sustaining your training heart rate during the workout. When you are able to perform aerobic activities comfortably for at least thirty minutes, begin to check your recovery time. This is the amount of time that it takes your heart to return to its normal number of beats per minute characteristic of periods when you are not exercising. When you are able to recover to that rate in three to four minutes, you know you're in excellent shape!

Several words of advice: If you are over 40, you should check with your physician before starting an exercise program. If you carry excess weight (more than 20 pounds) or have had a serious illness, you should also consult a doctor before starting an exercise program, even if you are less than 40 years of age.

Building social support systems is the other important key to handling the kinds of accumulating stressors measured by the SRRS. Individuals with strong family and social ties recover from serious illness more quickly than individuals with weak or nonexistent social support systems. Some physicians estimate that a social support system reduces hospital stays by as much as three days for people recovering from serious illness. These findings point to the importance of building social networks (49). These support systems cushion and buffer the effects of stressful events because the individual experiencing illness has many who are willing to lend a helping hand.

A good social support system spans work and nonwork roles, but family and friends are the cornerstones of the system. Development and maintenance of a support system is crucial, especially for individuals who must move or confront change in their jobs and lives. Being independent and capable of making major life decisions is indeed important, but these decisions often generate uncertainty and stress. Family and friends can greatly cushion the stressful effects and keep you from accumulating the effects of too much stress!

Suggested Readings

Applebaum, S. 1982. A Human Resources Counseling Model: The Alcoholic Employee. *Personnel Administrator* (August 1982):35.

Bensinger, P. 1982. Drugs in the Workplace. *Harvard Business Review* (November-December 1982):48–60.

Cherey, L. 1977. The Man Who First Named Stress. *Psychology Today* (March 1977).

This article details the work and discoveries of Hans Selye, "the father of stress research." Selye's work has influenced medical research on the effects of stress on people.

Follman, J. 1976. *Alcoholics and Business.* New York: American Management Association.

Frew, D. 1977. *Management of Stress: Using TM at Work.* Chicago: Nelson-Hall.

This readable book looks at the use of transcendental meditation (TM) in the workplace. The author discusses evidence that supports the benefits of TM, and explains how TM can be used by organizations to increase employee performance and job satisfaction.

Kahn, R. 1981. *Work and Health.* New York: Wiley.

Peters, R., and Benson, H. 1978. Time Out From Tension. *Harvard Business Review* (January-February 1978):120–124.

Schreier, J. 1983. A Survey of Drug Abuse in Organizations. *Personnel Journal* (June 1983):478–484.

Wrich, J. 1982. *Guidelines for Developing an Employee Assistance Program.* New York: American Management Association.

References

1. Selye, H. 1976. *Stress in Health and Disease.* Boston: Butterworths.
2. Ibid.
3. Ibid.
4. Ibid.
5. Ibid.
6. Ibid.
7. Ibid.
8. Ibid.

9. Ivancevich, J., and Matteson, M. 1980. *Stress and Work: A Managerial Perspective.* Glenview, Ill.: Scott-Foresman.
10. Jick, T., and Mitz, L. 1985. Sex Differences in Work Stress. *Academy of Management Review* 10:408–420.
11. Deaux, K. 1984. From Individual Differences to Social Categories: Analysis of a Decades' Research on Gender. *American Psychologist* 39:105–116.
12. Nelson, D., and Quick, J. 1985. Professional Women: Are Distress and Disease Inevitable? *Academy of Management Review* 10:206–218.
13. Cooper, C., and Davidson, M. 1982. The High Cost of Stress on Women Managers. *Organizational Dynamics* 10:44–53.
14. Rubin, D. 1984. Fifth Annual Salary Survey: Who Makes What, Where? *Working Woman* 9:59–63.
15. Kobasa, J., Hilker, R., and Maddi, S. 1979. Who Stays Healthy Under Stress? *Journal of Occupational Medicine* 21:595–598.
16. Ibid.
17. Friedman, M., and Rosenman, R. 1974. *Type A Behavior and Your Heart.* New York: Knopf.
18. Ibid.
19. Matthews, K. 1982. Psychological Perspectives on the Type A Behavior Pattern. *Psychological Bulletin* 91:293–323.
20. Friedman, M., and Rosenman, R., op. cit., 1974.
21. Ibid.
22. Rosenman, R., Friedman, M., Strauss, R., Worm, M., Jenkins, C., and Messinger, H. 1976. Coronary Heart Disease in the Western Collaborative Group Study: A Follow-up Experience of Two Years. *Journal of the American Medical Association* 195:130–136.
23. Parasuraman, S., and Alutto, J. 1984. Sources and Outcomes of Stress in Organizational Settings: Toward the Development of a Structural Model. *Academy of Management Journal* 24:330–350.
24. Rosenman, R., et al., op. cit., 1976.
25. Ibid.
26. Matthews, K., op. cit. 1982.
27. Friedman, M., and Rosenman, R., op. cit., 1974.
28. Ivancevich, J., and Matteson, M., op. cit., 1980.
29. Saleh, S., and Desai, K. 1986. Occupational Stressors for Engineers. *IEEE Transactions on Engineering Management* 33:6–11.
30. Caplin, R., and Jones, L. 1975. Effects of Work Load, Role Ambiguity and Type A Personality on Anxiety, Depression and Heart Rate. *Journal of Applied Psychology* 60:713–719.
31. French, J., and Caplin, R. Organizational Stress and Individual Stress. (In Morrow, A. (Ed.) 1973. *The Failure of Success.* New York: AMACOM.)
32. Jackson, S. 1983. Participation in Decision Making as a Strategy for Reducing Job-Related Strain. *Journal of Applied Psychology* 68:3–19.
33. Jackson, S., and Maslach, C. 1982. After-Effects of Job-Related Stress: Families as Victims. *Journal of Occupational Behavior* 3:63–77.
34. Ivancevich, J., and Matteson, M., op. cit. 1980.
35. Schuler, R. 1980. A Role and Expectancy Perceptions Model for Participation in Decision Making. *Academy of Management Journal* 22:331–340.
36. Karasek, R. 1979. Job Demands, Job Decision Latitude and Mental Strain: Implications for Job Redesign. *Administrative Science Quarterly* 29:285–307.
37. Rose, R., Jenkins, C., and Hurst, J. 1978. Air Traffic Controller Health Change Study. FAA Department of Transportation, Washington, D.C.
38. Ivancevich, J., and Matteson, M., op. cit., 1980.
39. *Times Picayune/States* Item (30 April 1985).
40. *Time Magazine.* Drugs on the Job. (17 March 1986).
41. Ibid.
42. Ivancevich, J., Matteson, M., op. cit. 1980.
43. Fuller, G. 1978. Current State of Biofeedback in Clinical Practice. *American Psychologist* 33:39–48.
44. Benson, H. 1975. *The Relaxation Response.* New York: Morrow.
45. Goldberg, P. 1978. *Executive Health.* New York: McGraw-Hill.
46. Ibid.
47. Ibid.
48. Ivancevich, J., and Matteson, M., op. cit., 1980.
49. Bhagart, R. 1983. Effects of Stressful Life Events on Individual Performance Effectiveness and Work Adjustment Processes Within Organizational Settings: A Research Model. Academy of Management Review 8:660–671.

Getting the Job Done: Key Management Features of Groups

Chapter 8

Chapter Goals

By the end of the chapter, you will be able to:

1. Differentiate clearly the different types of groups that exist in work organizations.
2. Describe how to use project groups successfully to accomplish organizational goals.
3. Describe the factors that cause people to join groups.
4. Explain the managerial importance of group cohesiveness.
5. Discuss the relationship between cohesiveness and group performance.
6. Recognize group norms and describe their effects on the behavior of group members.
7. Recognize the symptoms of groupthink and describe methods used to correct the problem.

Dilemma The Positive Power of Groups

Johnson Heating and Air Conditioning is a medium-sized commercial installer of heating and air conditioning equipment. Bert Johnson started the business after the Korean war, and now his two sons have assumed control since Bert retired 3 years ago.

At the present time, 14 crews operate from three separate locations in the metropolitan area. Most teams have three employees (usually an electrician, an installer, and a sheet metal fabricator to do duct work). The crew members are fairly interchangeable, for installation involves a variety of jobs. On a rotating basis, two teams are always on call over weekends to ensure that emergency service is available for equipment installed by the firm.

One of the unique features of Johnson Heating is the general employee attitude toward equipment installation and repair. Members from one of the firm's most productive teams made a number of interesting points.

Sally Rand (licensed electrician with eight years work experience): Working with Phil Gleason is like working with my dad in the garage. He's very patient and approaches each new job as a challenge. Phil welcomed me to the team when I was hired, and right away I felt included. Don, my other team member, is good to work with too. He's dynamite on sheet metal work. He's so good at installing ducting that everybody calls him "Donald Duct"! Don has introduced my husband and me to several of his friends, and our families have begun to spend time together outside of work, especially since we both have little boys about the same age.

Don Preston (sheet metal worker and duct work installer): We've got a good group all right. Nobody wears their feelings on their sleeve. Even when we're on-call for the weekend, nobody gets up-tight or pulls any stunts. We always know a month in advance anyway, so it's easy to plan for. Besides, the double-time pay is hard to turn down. You may not know it, but our team holds the company record for most service calls in a week with no customer complaints. A lot of our success is due to Sally. She can just look at a unit and tell you what's wrong.

Philip Gleason is perhaps the most active team advocate. This is in part the result of his team's having received several large company bonuses for new maintenance procedures they suggested. These procedures saved the company $110,000 the first year they were used. Management was so pleased that Phil received a $5,000 bonus plus another $8,000 to distribute between Sally and Don. Phil maintains, however, that the team would be effective anyway, even without the bonuses. It's clear that all of the team members are willing to expend that extra "10 percent" in a pinch. Phil had this to say about his team:

> It's the people I work with that make this job worthwhile. We really enjoy the time we spend together, and since we all like each other, the time passes pretty quickly. Another thing about these guys is that they'll all do whatever's necessary to get the job done. Heck, any of them could handle my job—lots of times they do—without blinking an eye!
>
> Johnson has been in business for a long time. They've build up a real good reputation in the commercial heating and cooling business. One of the reasons I like working for them is that they leave their teams alone. We take our own calls, and we plan our own routes and service calls. Its sort of like running your own little business. Don't think though that they forget about us, no way! We all have to do 40 hours of training per year, and the old man himself (Bert Johnson, the founder) shows up and goes through the training with us! Let's face it, he doesn't have to work, but it sure says something to the rest of us when we see him crawling around a furnace or an AC unit. Maybe he's old fashioned, but one thing's for sure: he's got the best repair teams in the business.

Bert Johnson, company founder:

> I've never believed that you have to prod employees to get them to work. If you make sure that they're qualified and understand the meaning of customer service, then you'll make money. Once people get the hang of their job, all you have to do is pay them fairly and let them decide how to do the work. I've never seen a manager yet who knew more about wiring than an electrician. The idea is to let people practice their trade. The more you sit on them, the more they resist. Oh yeah, there's one other thing. Just like in police work, you have to know how to create a successful team to make it in this industry. You have to understand how people will mix before you start them working together. That may be the biggest trick in the business, and I'm not giving away any of my secrets!

The Johnson team members demonstrate a number of important ideas in the area of group behavior. Although the team is left alone to do its own work, at its own pace, with its own equipment, team members never consider *not* working hard. In an arrangement in which the team could take things pretty easy on a regular basis, members describe their team's high performance record in glowing terms.

Questions

1. Why do members of Sally's team like working together so much?
2. Why does the high cohesiveness in the repair team cause it to be so effective in its work?
3. What are the key norms operating in Sally's repair team?
4. What has happened at the company level to cause the repair teams to be so effective in their work?

Understanding the Territory of Group Dynamics

The introductory dilemma illustrates the success that work teams can encounter as they attempt to achieve the goals of the group. Groups and teams are responsible for most of the work that gets done in organizations. As you learned in Chapter 6, jobs can be redesigned around the work team. You have learned also that quality circles and other forms of employee participation can increase greatly the effectiveness of the organization while providing opportunities for employee need fulfillment. To understand fully why employee participation and worker involvement influence organizational effectiveness requires a knowledge of group dynamics. As work tasks become more complex, employees must cooperate more in their work. The need for cooperation creates in turn the need for skillful managing of interpersonal relationships. Managers simply cannot be effective if they are unable to manage work teams.

What do we mean by a "group" within the organization?

A **group** is defined as a collection of two or more people who (1) interact with each other, (2) perceive themselves as sharing some common interests or goals, (3) come together or are brought together to accomplish some work activity (1). In this definition, note the restrictions, which eliminate social gatherings and friendship groups. Certainly the latter are groups in the general sense, but they do not meet our definition because they are not brought formally together to accomplish work activity.

In the Johnson Company, employees are assigned formally to a work team, or group, that services heating and cooling equipment. These groups are supposed to accomplish the work of the company. The service teams are in some ways like any other work group established by management, they represent formal groups. A **formal group** is defined as one to which members are assigned specifically by the organization. Whether the organization uses committees, departments, task forces, or project teams, it is operating through formal groups. A formal group usually has four specific characteristics: (1) two or more members, (2) defined interaction patterns, (3) stated purpose(s) for the group's existence, and (4) members who are aware of the group's existence and of their involvement in it (2).

Consider this example of a formal group:

> Sandy's quality circle meets on Friday afternoons for the purpose of discussing production problems encountered by her 12 assemblers during the past week. Sandy does not always lead these meetings; her subordinates frequently describe problems that have escaped her attention. This does not trouble her very much because she trusts her employees to be attentive and involved in their work. Several of the employees have helped recently to prepare a formal presentation to management, and the entire team participated in the presentation. Members of Sandy's quality circle frequently eat lunch together, and there's talk of organizing a softball team to compete in the summer adult softball league.

This example clarifies the fact that Sandy's quality circle is a formal group. It has more than two members who interact according to defined interaction patterns (i.e., several members were responsible for working with Sandy to prepare the management presentation, and all of the circle members had a part in the presentation). The quality circle has the stated purpose of generating ideas to improve production methods and product quality. Lastly, members are very aware of the circle's existence. They eagerly attend meetings, and their involvement has generated the secondary byproducts of strong friendship and social interaction beyond the workplace (a softball team). Note, however, that even though a group may have all of the characteristics of a formal group, no guarantee exists that members will work effectively and productively together.

Are all organizational groups formal groups?

Informal groups are also created constantly within organizations. An informal group is defined as a collection of people who come together voluntarily for a common purpose, which may or may not be work related. Informal groups develop naturally out of volunteerism. Within Sandy's quality circle, we see two examples of informal groups. The members of her formal assembly team get together for lunch on a regular basis (the common purposes are to socialize and discuss production problems). In addition, circle members are organizing a softball team, a second informal group. This example represents an informal group that is contained totally within a formal group. Clearly membership in informal groups can span departmental or even organizational boundaries.

Management does not always encourage formation of informal groups within the organization. Many managers believe that informal groups develop goals that are not consistent with organizational goals. For example, an informal group of employees may agitate actively for more employee benefits. They may even threaten management with a unionization drive. In similar fashion, employees may actively restrict output among members of the informal work group to discourage management from setting higher production standards. Problems also can occur when a formal work group fails to accept new members or attempts to sabotage the efforts of a new supervisor. Such examples of subversion are typically attributed to informal groups of employees who have banned together to resist various forms of management action or organizational goals. Because of negative experiences with informal groups, managers can become opposed to their existence. As one might surmise, when management resistance increases, informal groups with goals counter to organizational goals pop up all over the organization. When widespread job dissatisfaction exists among employees, numerous informal groups develop and usually have goals that are inconsistent with those of the organization. To the extent that an organizational system allows for the regular satisfaction of individual needs, informal goals will often parallel and reinforce the goals of formal groups in the organization. For this to happen, employees must perceive equity in the performance appraisal, reward, and job design systems. If they do perceive equity, formal groups will be effective, and formal group members will tend to be satisfied, especially if group-based rewards are readily available.

Organizations use a variety of formal groups to accomplish work (3). Two prominent forms of formal groups are functional groups and project teams. A **functional group** is defined as a formal group responsible for handling a set of ongoing organizational activities that are closely related. For example, the marketing department is responsible for all organization activities that involve sales forecasting and product promotion. The department is a functional group that has responsibility for product promotion and market coverage, both of which are related and ongoing work activities. A **project team** is defined as a formal group with a specific purpose that must be accomplished within a given period of time. Ad hoc committees and task forces are examples of project teams. In organizations, project teams usually are assembled for the specific purpose of developing a new product or process. Once this goal is accomplished, the team is disbanded and its members often return to their functional group (i.e., to engineering, production, marketing, or purchasing).

Many very successful organizations use project teams effectively to come up with solutions to important organizational problems (4). In fact, some companies develop an entire culture of excellence around project teams. The method for creating effective project teams is described below.

1. The life of the typical task force is short. For instance, Texas Instruments sets up teams with life-spans of less than four months.
2. Membership is voluntary. Because individuals also keep their functional group affiliation, the problems to be solved by the task force must be perceived as highly interesting and motivating. If they are viewed as dull and meaningless, employees will avoid participation.
3. The task force is pulled together quickly; formation is not accomplished by a formal chartering selection process. Thus, employees who have an intrinsic interest in a problem area are drawn to the task force. This quality provides great flexibility for quickly establishing a task force to deal with a problem that is fresh and important.
4. Follow-up is swift. Once the task force is created, immediate links with higher management are forged. As the task force begins to obtain results, management is therefore activated to search for business applications and opportunities.
5. Support staff is not assigned to the task force. This prevents the task force from becoming "bureaucratized" and paralyzed by rigid operating procedures. As Peters and Waterman describe the process, task force members become experts at gaining support as the project progresses.
6. Communication and documentation are informal. This quality prevents any shifting of task force attention from the problem at hand to organizational procedures. The task force is not required to generate a deep and wide paper trail (5).

Not all organizations see the value of task forces, but evidence continues to accumulate as to how extremely large and successful companies use groups as building blocks to obtain breakthroughs in product and service developments. Nor is use of the task force concept limited to multiproduct firms with major functional divisions that employ hundreds of people.

Any small business starts off as a task force, because its employees must be willing to attack any problem that arises. If the new small business overlooks such "brush fires" (as often happens), it can easily spell disaster.

A rule of thumb for any entrepreneur should therefore be to operate the business as much like a task force as possible. It is interesting to note that as organizations grow and become more successful, the lessons that initially created the success are frequently forgotten. Large, successful firms, by using the temporary task force concept, have learned to recreate some of the urgency of the small business.

Why People Join Groups

Since membership in any work organization is a voluntary decision on the part of the employee, management must consider the reasons why people join organizations and why they join certain groups within the organization. The key point in the joining process is the idea that the person perceives group membership as a pathway to the satisfaction of individual needs. It then follows that the more individual needs a group fulfills for its members, the more important the group will be.

Four reasons for joining groups are: (1) attraction to members of the group (i.e., interpersonal attraction), (2) attraction to activities of the group, (3) attraction to goals of the group (i.e., the member values group's goals), and (4) group membership per se (6). These factors are described in Table 8.1 with an example of each. Let's examine them in order.

Interpersonal attraction. This is an extremely important determinant of people's desire to join groups. It is defined as the desirability of group membership, and has a number of facets that are often interrelated. Proximity

Table 8.1
Factors Causing Group Formation

Factor	*Example in the Workplace*
1. Interpersonal Attraction	
a. Proximity	Secretaries in a typing pool form an informal friendship clique because their work stations are close together.
b. Physical attraction	Young professionals join an expensive health club in the hope of meeting attractive sweaty people of the opposite sex.
c. Attitude similarity	Employees who believe that management is exploiting them ban together to form a union.
d. Economic and social similarity	Chief executive officers of major corporations are asked to serve on the boards of major firms.
e. Race and gender similarity	Black female employees form an informal discussion group to study career problems of minorities.
f. Perceived ability of others	A formal project group is created to study a new computer application. Members are selected based on their expertise.
2. Activities of the group	Employees organize a softball team to compete in a summer league.
3. Goals of the group	Employees organize a relief effort to collect money for Ethiopian famine victims.
4. Group membership	Middle managers seek promotion to obtain executive rewards and status recognition associated with being a member of top management.

frequently energizes people to join groups. For instance, regardless of personal background or college major, students form friendship groups based on their physical living arrangements in dormitories. Likewise, employees who are required to work in proximity to each other are likely to form an informal group. As we will see later in the chapter, physical arrangements can have a strong influence on job satisfaction and on group productivity.

A major feature of interpersonal attraction is **physical attraction.** "When a person exemplifies the physical characteristics which contribute to the perception of beauty or handsomeness in a given culture, others are prone to be attracted to, and want to associate with him or her" (7). Research continues to attest to the importance of physical attractiveness, and many studies confirm that this factor explains much of the behavior of college students.

Similarity is another component of interpersonal attraction. It is defined as sharing characteristics with others, especially values and attitudes. People are much more likely to be attracted to a group if they think that its members have attitudes similar to their own. The individual who contemplates group membership believes that his beliefs and attitudes are much more likely to be confirmed in a group with members who have similar attitudes. Expectancy theory provides a partial explanation of this process. The person's efforts to join a group will increase if she believes that membership will lead to more opportunities to reaffirm personal beliefs. Membership in political parties and religious groups operates on this principle.

Similarity of economic status, social status, and gender. Similarity of economic and social status can be a powerful form of attraction. Country clubs and social organizations try to project an image of exclusivity to appeal to individuals who see such groups as having highly desirable characteristics (these groups are called **reference groups**). The individual typically believes that his self-image will be enhanced by obtaining membership in such groups.

Race and gender similarity. When organizations base some of their attraction on race or gender similarity, another powerful form of attraction is in operation. As women make vertical career progress in large organizations, they sometimes form career interest groups and discussion groups that examine informally those work issues of particular interest to members. Minority trade associations and other business groups also demonstrate this property.

Using race and gender similarity in organizations. Military organizations utilize these effects. For example, military recruiters use the "buddy system" in which two or more friends are guaranteed the same geographic assignment if they enlist together. A number of famous army units were composed of ethnically similar soldiers. During World War II, Navajo Indians were responsible for construction of a military code that the Japanese were unable to crack. Such examples of unusual effectiveness undoubtedly resulted in large part from ethnic similarities in these units.

Perceived ability of others also provides a basis for group affiliation. Business-oriented research indicates that individuals prefer to work with other people who have successfully solved problems in the areas of current group activity (8). In other words, people prefer to associate with others of similar ability. In work situations, ability often supersedes other forms of attraction, thus multi-racial, male-female work groups may be formed around the quality of expertise. Quite simply, members judge their group to have a greater chance for task success when problem-solving abilities of group members are proven.

Interpersonal attraction is thus a major reason why people join groups. Such attraction is based on the degree to which individuals perceive similarity among group members regarding race, gender, economic and social background, and ability. In many cases, management controls some of these factors when formal task groups are formed.

These factors become harder to manage when the character of the group is informal.

Group activities. People are attracted to a variety of organizations because of the activities carried out by them. Membership in the Better Business Bureau or the Jaycees is often dependent on the attraction of the group's activities to business people. These activities can range from the purely social to business-based and community-based work. Group activities generally function as a basis for joining groups because members find the group's activities to be intrinsically motivating. In many respects, simply participating in the activities may be enough to sustain group membership as well as to attract new members.

Group goals. Distinguishing the activities of the group from its goals is sometimes very difficult (9). For example, an employee may volunteer to work for the company United Fund Drive because he enjoys fund-raising volunteer work. The goals of a group are powerful tools used to recruit individuals into organizations such as the Peace Corps and Vista. All organizations that rely on volunteers to deliver part of their services rely also on the intrinsic value of their group goals. Altruism and a sense of social responsibility are powerful magnets for creating highly motivated and involved teams of volunteers.

Group membership. Involvement per se may stimulate the individual's desire to join a particular group. Need for affiliation and belonging energize the group-joining behavior. Some researchers have proposed that groups perform the important function of reducing the anxiety level among their members (11, 12). To the extent that a group can dissipate or buffer personal stress levels, membership is perceived as being more valuable to those who would like to join. As the group perceives more external threat, the members band together to try to present a united front. This works fairly well until the threat level becomes excessive. When this happens, individuals begin to view the costs of continued membership as exceeding the benefits. "We're all in this together" changes to "Every man for himself!"

Solving the Dilemma

Why do members of Sally's team like working together so much?

Sally's team is a good example of the power of interpersonal attraction. All of the members are very satisfied with the team membership. The factors operating in her group are: (1) proximity, (2) attitude similarity, (3) economic and social similarity, (4) high perceived ability of members, (5) similarity of work activities, (6) same performance goals of team (and company), and (7) group membership itself (besides satisfying numerous personal goals, members are attracted by group membership per se). In sum, team members have high similarity of personal traits, task skills, and attitudes.

Knowledge Check

1. A college football team is an example of a __________ group.
2. A group of accounting students who organize a study group represents an __________ group.
3. Formal task groups seldom provide a basis for formation of friendship groups or cliques. T or F?
4. Temporary project teams usually outlast their specific goals. T or F?
5. An effective task force has all of these characteristics *except:* (a) voluntary membership, (b) informal communication and documentation, (c) swift follow-up, (d) formal support staff.
6. Large, successful companies are trying to regenerate the "can do" attitude of small businesses by organizing temporary task forces. T or F?
7. A college's homecoming court is an informal group with membership based on __________.
8. Interpersonal attraction is the most researched area related to why people join groups. T or F?
9. The intrinsic value of group goals will not motivate people to join a particular group. T or F?
10. Groups can function to reduce the anxiety level of members if the external threat is not too great. T or F?

Answers

1 formal, 2 informal, 3 F, 4 F, 5 d, 6 T, 7 physical attractiveness, 8 T, 9 F, 10 T

Group Composition and Cohesiveness

How do you feel about the groups to which you belong? Are you involved and interested in one group because it seems warm and friendly? Perhaps another group makes you feel alienated and unmotivated. Your reactions to these two different groups may be based on the specific similarities and differences among group members. This phenomenon refers to **group composition,** which is defined as the degree of similarity or differences among members of a group. The composition of groups can vary in several ways. These variations not only influence the reactions of members, as already noted, but also influence the interactions among group members and the effectiveness of the group's decision making.

A group is composed of the personal characteristics of its members. The composition of the group may be **homogeneous** or **heterogeneous** with respect to particular member traits. If a group is homogeneous, all of its members possess a specific trait (e.g., internal locus of control, high need for achievement, or Type A behavior). If, however, group members vary from low to high on a particular trait, then the group is defined as being heterogeneous with regard to that member trait.

The influence of homogeneity and heterogeneity on group performance has been investigated, and results are contradictory. Most managers believe that a better job can be done when people work with others who are like themselves. Studies, however, conclude the opposite and support the value of heterogeneity as a key factor in maintaining high decision quality (13).

Heterogeneity has two effects. First, it creates more interpersonal conflict in the group. Groups composed of members with very different personalities tend to experience more conflict and less satisfaction and to have poorer morale. Heterogeneity, however, does increase a group's potential problem-solving ability (14). Group members who are different from each other can offer more alternatives, are less susceptible to constant member biases, and can provide a wider base for criticism of alternatives.

Heterogeneity and the group's task. Heterogeneous groups are more effective if the task is difficult and member traits vary according to task demands. For example, a group composed of young and old members would be able to perform better than a uniformly young or old group when the task requires a knowledge of the needs of the young and old.

Heterogeneity and problem solving. Heterogeneity may create more potential for solving problems, but it does not always work to a group's advantage. For example, differences in attitudes toward the group goal can have detrimental effects. Suppose that you are on a jury that has some members who believe that capital punishment is a good way to deter homicide, while other members think that capital punishment is socially and morally wrong. Lawyers have known for a long time that such jury conditions lead to strong attitudinal conflicts which lead in turn to ineffective decision making. Such a heterogeneous jury will deliberate longer, take up more of the court's time, and be more likely to wind up as a "hung jury" (unable to reach any decision). As a result, attorneys for the prosecution and defense question potential jurors carefully about attitudinal areas related to the case at hand. They try to control for effects of group composition on jury decision making.

Heterogeneity can interfere with group decision making. Imagine a task force composed of some individuals with high need for achievement while others have a high need for power. The members with high achievement need may be willing to take considerable risk but at the same time may not be willing to delegate much responsibility to others. The individuals with a high need for power may become quickly disillusioned with the task force leadership, especially if its leaders are achievement oriented. The high need for power individuals can easily undermine the goals of the leaders and attempt to install their own leaders. Major power struggles in companies are often based on this sort of group difference. Corporate boards may possess the composition noted above, and as a result, some members may work very hard to oust the chief executive officer who does not share their personal characteristics. Would J. R. Ewing ever let this happen?

What are the effects of group composition?

Perhaps the most important outcome of group composition is cohesiveness. (14). **Cohesiveness** is defined as having three components: (1) attraction to the group, including resistance to leaving it, (2) morale, or level of motivation shown by group members, and (3) coordination of member efforts. (15). Group cohesiveness is usually associated with the level of motivation maintained by the membership (16). Table 8.2 compares the qualities of

Table 8.2
Characteristics of Work Groups With High and Low Cohesiveness

Groups With High Cohesiveness Tend to:	*Groups With Low Cohesiveness Tend to:*
Exhibit high performance if group goals conform to organizational goals.	Demonstrate low performance regardless of organizational goals.
Have members who are more energetic and motivated to achieve group goals.	Have members who are indifferent to strong effort put forth on behalf of the group.
Have members who are less likely to be absent or late for team tasks.	Suffer from high absenteeism and member turnover.
Have members who are personally very pleased when the group succeeds and sad when it fails.	Have members who are indifferent to group success and failure.
Have members who believe in the value and importance of the group's goals.	Have members who are unconcerned with group goals and unwilling to suggest alternatives.
Have members who are unwilling to give up their membership (i.e., members resist transfer).	Have members who willingly seek transfer from the group.
Have members who view the group as an important vehicle for achieving personal goals.	Have members who satisfy their personal needs outside the group.
Have members who become more similar to each other over time.	Show no tendency toward greater member similarity or difference.

highly cohesive groups with the qualities of groups lacking cohesiveness. First, let's look at the main determinants of cohesiveness, then let's consider the relationship between group cohesiveness and performance.

Cohesiveness: The Super Glue of Groups

Cohesiveness is a complex group quality. We have already discussed those factors that cause individuals to join a group. If the person finds, after joining, that the factors, which first attracted her, are indeed present in the group, then many of the determinants for cohesiveness may be in place. For example, groups composed of individuals who have similar attitudes tend to be more cohesive than groups composed of people with less similar attitudes (17). Attitude similarity may not show up in work groups right away. As work group members get to know each other (primarily through task-generated interactions), the teams become much more cohesive if attitude similarity is present from the start. These results also indicate that as time passes, group members gain knowledge about each other's attitudes. If key attitudes are similar, cohesiveness begins to form (18).

Success or failure of the group influences cohesiveness. When watching a successful sports team that has just won a playoff competition, one cannot help but be struck by the power of the cohesiveness in the winner's locker room. In similar manner, successful work groups also can be extremely cohesive as the reputation of their successes spreads through the company. Everyone likes to be on a winning team.

When groups are unsuccessful, less basis for cohesiveness is present. For professional sport teams, a losing season can create division between the players and coaching staff. The New York Yankees are a good example of a team that has lost its cohesiveness for a variety of reasons, George Steinbrenner being a major one. George constantly shuffles coaches and condemns players to the press. His undermining of the manager's authority sometimes leads to disagreements in the dugout and locker room. As a result, although he has bought the best baseball players money can buy, they tend to play more as individuals than as a team. The missing ingredient is cohesiveness.

Clarity of group goals can influence cohesiveness. When procedures to be followed are clear to all members, cohesiveness is great, and when all group members agree on work procedures (consensus), uniformity of opinion inspires a group-based self-confidence. The members thus, find their group to be more attractive because they perceive greater task certainty. In essence, the team believes that it's likely to be successful in accomplishing the task. The situation is analogous to expectancy theory applied at group level. The group believes that a strong likelihood exists that effort will lead to successful task performance. One of the second level outcomes associated with successful task performance may be high cohesiveness among group members.

Managers can use group goals to raise group cohesiveness. By setting clear work procedures that lead to understandable goals, group managers capitalize on the group tendency to develop higher cohesion if attitude similarity is present. If a manager can design a group based on attitude similarity and at the same time make task requirements clear and unambiguous, the group will be more cohesive, all other things being equal.

The nature of group conflict can influence cohesiveness. If the conflict among group members occurs because of personal principles, then cohesiveness is affected negatively. If the group leader asks a member to do something that violates that member's sense of personal ethics, group cohesiveness will be damaged. As an example, suppose that a department head tells one of his employees to disregard a safety rule to ensure greater departmental productivity. If, in the process, a department employee is injured on the job, cohesiveness will surely be damaged.

If conflict is generated by perceptions of a common enemy, cohesiveness may be enhanced. The group may become more cohesive as it contemplates ways to deal with external threats created by the enemy. In many respects, companies capitalize on this idea by informing employees about what is going on in competing firms and what must be done to "meet the competition." As long as the external threat is manageable and group members believe that numerous ways exist to best the competition, then internal group conflict tends to raise levels of cohesiveness. If the external threat becomes too great, however, cohesiveness may break down and the attitude of "Every man for himself" may prevail.

The nature and timing of group feedback influences cohesiveness. Positive feedback activates higher levels of cohesion. If positive feedback is also timed to occur before negative feedback, cohesion levels are not as adversely affected as they would be if negative feedback came first. Like individuals, groups have a quality that resembles self-esteem. This quality is dependent on the amount of cohesiveness in the group. If negative feedback always occurs before positive feedback, the group's collective self-esteem is affected more adversely. (There's a managerial rule to remember in there somewhere!)

Putting Cohesiveness to Use in the Organization

Much research has been done in this area, and a number of important outcomes identified. Cohesiveness affects the following: (1) extent of communication within the group, (2) degree to which members adhere to group norms and resist changes in the group, (3) levels of member satisfaction with the group, and (4) performance of the group (19).

Communication tends to be enhanced by cohesiveness. Group members spend more time talking and exchanging facts in cohesive groups. If the group believes strongly in the value of performance, then information regarding task activities is likely to dominate team discussions. For example, highly cohesive quality circles with a history of successful production innovations will often be found holding discussions about more ways to increase production effectiveness and product and service quality.

Group rules and resistance to change affect cohesiveness. When groups are highly cohesive, they often have rules that are backed strongly by group members. In other words, when a group member violates the rules, the group will police itself and insist that the member alter behavior to fit the rules. These rules are often extremely important to group cohesiveness because they provide the main basis for the group's sense of identity. Any change in the group that requires change in its rules is therefore, often resisted. Consider the following example:

> Middle management in the Essex Company had always prided itself on the ability to respond to customer needs within a 24–hour period. The company maintains customer records with a manual cardex system that is accessed at a centralized point. Managers in the cardex department were very proud of their system and were frequently recognized by the company for outstanding performance.
>
> Because of increased work loads, the company decided to computerize customer records so a record could be accessed in a random fashion from any department in the firm. Managers from the cardex department were supposed to assist in the conversion to the new customer information system. They frequently objected to various aspects of the planned change and pointed out that the conversion would allow individuals with minimal knowledge of customer records to have access to the entire system.
>
> The Essex company management eventually abandoned their plan to computerize customer records. The firm decided to stay with its manual system even though all competitors in the industry had automated customer record-keeping functions.

Management rules in the cardex department were so strong and widely accepted that the automated system was successfully resisted. Company management finally caved in and abandoned the innovation. The manual system was preserved (i.e., the status quo was maintained), and the company placed itself in jeopardy relative to the competition. The speed of handling customer complaints will no doubt decrease as the manual system becomes more and more strained, and the cost per customer inquiry will escalate as a result of the inefficient, centralized manual system. These trends do not create optimism about the future of Essex in the industry.

Cohesiveness is related to the job satisfaction of group members. Cohesive groups tend to have a history of satisfying the individual needs of members. After a while, members begin to associate positive qualities with their group because their individual needs are more likely to be met through group membership. The group itself becomes attractive as a result of its high potential for meeting member needs. Sally Rand's service team, described in the chapter's opening dilemma, clearly fits the characteristics of a group that provides ample opportunities for members to satisfy their individual needs. For this reason, the three team members are very positive about their group involvement. They would each work hard to preserve their group membership. In other words, Sally would be very upset if Phil or Don decided to quit.

Management believes that cohesive groups are usually more productive. This reasoning is similar to the belief that satisfied workers tend to be productive workers. The latter belief was found to be over-simplified and inadequate when we studied the relationship between performance, rewards, and job satisfaction. Similarly, studies have shown that group cohesiveness can be related either positively or negatively to performance.

What determines if cohesiveness will be positively related to performance?

Three factors influence this determination: (1) cohesiveness of the group, (2) performance goals set by the group, and (3) degree of agreement between group performance goals and organizational performance goals. When these three factors are all high and coaligned, then cohesiveness definitely contributes to group performance (Figure 8.1). Three possible situations are illustrated in the figure. If the group is not cohesive and if little agreement exists between the group and the organizational performance goals (situation no. 1), then group performance will be low or at best moderate. Highly cohesive groups with goals that do not agree with organizational goals will exhibit low performance (situation 2). Finally, if a cohesive group has a high degree of identification with organizational goals, then the group will perform strongly (situation 3).

Solving the Dilemma

Why does the high cohesiveness in the repair team cause it to be so effective in its work?

The answer to this question organizes around two features of the repair team. First, the team exhibits high member agreement about the importance of achieving performance goals set by the group. Second, the performance goals valued by the repair team conform closely to the performance goals of the company. A high congruence thus exists between team expectations and company expectations about excellent performance. These are precisely the conditions that maximize the beneficial effects of cohesiveness.

Group Norms: Yardsticks for Judging Behavior

We have already begun our study of group norms in an informal way. **Group norms** are defined as the group's standards for behavior. Norms are a prominent feature of cohesive groups, but they do not apply to all situations encountered by the group (20). In general, norms are to groups what personal standards are to the individual. In other words, they say, "This is how we view our work as a team, and this is what we expect of you as a member of this team."

What are the characteristics of group norms?

There are five properties of group norms. These are noted below.

1. **Norms streamline and summarize the influence process in the group.** They function in a highly efficient manner as a basis for policing the member behavior. If strong norms exist, the leader does not have to spend much time supervising member behavior and member efforts will be more performance directed.

Figure 8.1
Cohesiveness, Goals, and Group Performance

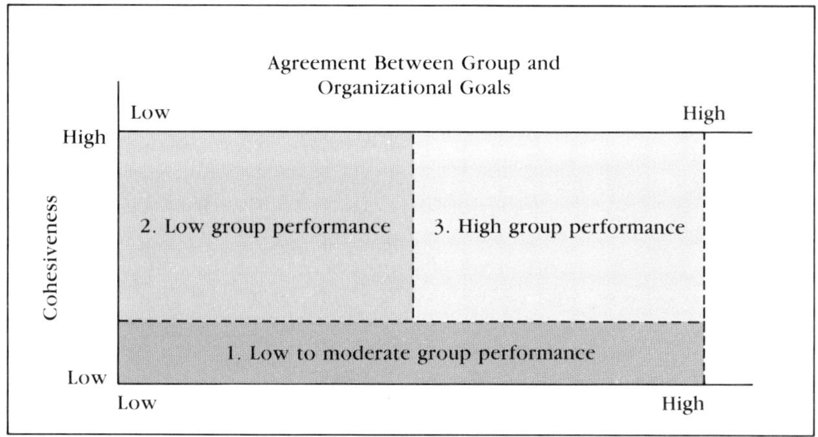

2. **Norms apply only to member behavior and not to member thoughts.** A person is thus perceived as a good team member even if she privately disagrees with some aspect of group activity. As long as she keeps her opinion to herself, no harm is done as far as the group is concerned. What counts is behavior, not thoughts.
3. **Norms develop only for those behaviors that the group considers to be important regarding level of member effort and group goals.** In other words, norms are enforced if they express the central beliefs of the group and if they clarify the distinctive nature of the group.
4. **Norms develop slowly over time, and as a result, are resistant to change.** Norms can remain intact even if group membership changes. In effect, norms can be passed to successive generations of group members in the form of traditions and rituals. If you have ever been a member of a sorority or fraternity, you know what we mean. Norms teach new members of the group how to behave.
5. **Some members have more right to deviate from group norms than other members do.** Usually, the higher up you are in a group, the more rights you have. Even those at the top, however, can be replaced if they agitate for too much change in group norms too quickly (21, 22).

Management Concern for Group Norms

Like most other aspects of the workplace, group norms are factors that management often overlooks until decline in performance is detected. As usual, we advocate a preventative approach. From this point of view, management must watch for ways to put group norms to work to benefit both the group and the organization. This means that management must *actively manage* group norms. Consider the following comment:

> Standards are necessary if a group is to be a viable unit. Most members support and follow these standards. Persons who deviate from the standards are pressed by colleagues to keep in line and, in the extreme case, removed from the group if they will not do so. Standards stating how group members should behave are created to ensure that valued qualities will be achieved in those units. Responsible members exert social pressures to support these standards and do a number of things to increase the influence of their pressures. Yet not all members need to conform;

they can, if they are able, resist their group's pressures or even change group standards in ways the members come to see as desirable (23).

NOW IT'S YOUR TURN ...

Consider what action managers must take to effectively direct conformity to group norms. The rules are listed on the left. On the right, indicate by writing *yes* or *no* in the space provided whether the rule applies to Sally's work team at Johnson Heating and Cooling. (Correct answers are at the end of the next Knowledge Check.)

Management Rules

1. Create a desire to remain in the group. ______
2. Show members how team standards of achievement create ability to obtain team goals as well as provide a basis for unity. ______
3. Ask each team member to give up individual gains in favor of team success. ______
4. Demonstrate whenever possible the small difference between what members might prefer personally and what the team asks of members. ______
5. Spend time showing members how their contributions help the team achieve its goals. ______
6. Give team members a say in creating work standards. ______
7. Develop a basis for monitoring team member adherence to team performance standards. ______
8. Develop abundant and important rewards to acknowledge members who conform to team performance standards. Make the rewards public knowledge. ______
9. Insist that members try to achieve team goals, and explain how this contributes to pride and personal accomplishment. ______
10. When creativity is necessary to insure team success in the long run, encourage members to come up with new ideas (even if norms may be violated in the short run). ______
11. Make it understood that individuals who do not conform to norms of performance will be expelled from the team. ______
12. Do not expel members who deviate from norms if (1) they have a history of helping the team, (2) they are high-status team members, and (3) the team has a history of helping versus isolating deviants. ______
13. If a deviant is expelled from the team, help him or her deal with loss of self-esteem or guilt. ______

Adapted from A. Zander, 1982, *Making Groups Effective.* San Francisco: Jossey-Bass, pp. 55–56.

Solving the Dilemma

What are the key norms operating in Sally's repair team?

Many norms can be inferred from the information given in the dilemma, but let's focus on those that specify level of effort of team members and those that specify ways to accomplish work. For the effort norms, members are expected to comply willingly with the weekend on-call policy. They also are expected to help each other with tough jobs. The company recognizes effort that leads to setting company records for unblemished service. The company also has several norms that deal with ways to accomplish work within the team. For example, members are expected to come up with cost saving measures that can be evaluated by higher management. There is even a norm about accomplishing work and gender. Group members believe that gender has nothing to do with job success. Finally, a norm exists concerning "professionalism." Every team member is expected to be a craftsman and not to let personal issues stand in the way of excellent performance.

Groupthink: When Cohesiveness and Conformity Go Awry

When cohesiveness and conformity are extremely high, conditions for undermining the quality of group decisions may be present. When the group's critical thinking process is suspended because of conditions of high cohesiveness and conformity, **groupthink** is operating. Professor Irving Janis has studied many "historic fiascos" of government policy. For example, his study of the Bay of Pigs invasion undertaken by the Kennedy administration concludes that critical thinking did not occur in President Kennedy's cabinet of advisors. Similarly, he explains how the Johnson administration failed to understand U.S. involvement in Vietnam and continued to act as if the light at the end of the tunnel were visible. All of these disastrous situations were, he concludes, the result of groupthink (24).

Symptoms of Groupthink

When groupthink is operating, group members are often more concerned about maintaining friendly relationships than about arriving at good solutions. Symptoms of groupthink that relate to this idea are as follows:

1. **Illusion of invulnerability.** A group with too much member conformity has a tendency to assume that it can succeed against high odds by taking extreme risks.
2. **Collective rationalization.** Group members do not perceive any problems because of tunnel vision and blind spots. In effect, the team believes that it cannot fail.

3. **Mindguards.** Just as bodyguards protect the individual, so mindguards protect the group from considering contradictory information that might threaten unanimity. Groups that suffer from groupthink are therefore likely to admit only the outside information that conforms to the group position.
4. **Belief in the inherent morality of the group.** When members demand excessive conformity from each other, the group begins to assume that its position is the only morally and ethically justifiable one. As a result, the group's moral judgment is dulled.
5. **Applying negative stereotypes to the opposition.** A group that suffers from groupthink often characterizes the opposition as dull or stupid. Competitors are viewed as inept and ineffective.
6. **Direct pressure is applied to dissenters.** If a group member disagrees with group position, considerable pressure is applied to bring him back in line. Mindguards often exert this pressure on behalf of the group.
7. **Self-censorship.** This occurs when members consciously limit their contributions because they do not want to upset agreement and good feelings within the group. Doubt about the group's direction is therefore not expressed.
8. **Illusion of unanimity.** As a result of many of the factors noted, group members assume that all other members are in favor of the group's course of action. Each member mistakes the silence of other members for agreement with the group position (25).

Remedies for Groupthink

Professor Janis has some specific recommendations for correcting the problem of groupthink (26). His suggested methods for handling groupthink are as follows.

1. The group leader should assign the role of critical evaluator to each group member. The group also should give a high priority to members airing their objections and doubts. The leader must set an example by allowing his or her position on key issues to be criticized.
2. In the beginning, when a group is created, expectations and policies should not be framed. Instead, an impartial position should be adopted. In other words, do not prespecify a solution. This will encourage exploration of more options.
3. Management might consider having several groups deal with the same issue to prevent the target group from becoming too insulated. Organize the groups under different leaders.
4. At successive intervals and before a decision is adopted, the leader should have group members discuss the general direction of the target group with departmental colleagues not in the group (assuming preservation of security and confidentiality).
5. On a staggered basis, outside experts should be invited to attend and to challenge the views of group decision makers.
6. At each meeting where policy is formulated, one member should be required, on a rotating basis, to play the role of devil's advocate. Members should be reminded that the role of devil's advocate is one of "loyal disagreement."

7. When competitive organizations are the focus of group decision making, sessions should be devoted to exploration of warning signals from the opposition and to consideration of possible forms of retaliation.
8. From time to time, the group should form subgroups to determine policy. Results of these deliberations should be discussed with all members present.
9. A "second-chance" meeting should be held after the group has adopted an official position or has made a major decision. The purpose of the second-chance meeting is to provide a forum for expressing any residual doubts.

In summary, groupthink is a serious problem that emerges when groups are very cohesive and when pressure to conform to group norms is excessive. Groupthink has specific symptoms, and is powerful, but it can be corrected. The biggest obstacle to change is usually the individual who runs the group. Leadership is often the weak link that breaks and allows groupthink to influence adversely the quality of group decision making. The recommendations noted by Janis can improve the quality of group decisions (27).

Solving the Dilemma

What has happened at the company level to cause the repair teams to be so effective in their work?

The Johnson Company represents an excellent example of the relationship between company culture and group norms. The top management emphasis on learning and excellence comes through strongly. The 40 hours of annual training for team members underscores the learning norm, and the company founder still goes through training with team members! In effect, the founder is an outstanding role model. In addition, a strong company norm exists as to the value of operating a team like a small business. Entrepreneurship is thus valued highly at all company levels. Furthermore, the company backs up this norm tangibly. Last year, Sally's team split $13,000 in bonus money. Such powerful incentives reinforce key norms at both team and company levels.

Knowledge Check

1. Current research indicates that homogeneity of member characteristics is much more likely to create the basis for high levels of cohesiveness in a group. T or F?
2. Group attractiveness, high levels of group morale, and coordinated member effort are all dimensions of cohesiveness. T or F?
3. Managers should always strive to develop cohesive work groups. T or F?
4. Which of the following is *not* a basis for cohesion in a work team?

   (a) past record of group successes, (b) clarity about group goals, (c) attitude similarity among members, or (d) high levels of external threat.

5. Cohesiveness can influence positively the levels of employee turnover and absenteeism. T or F?
6. When cohesiveness is high and group goals are consistent with organizational goals, the group probably will be productive, all other things being equal. T or F?
7. Norms function as behavioral control mechanisms in groups. T or F?
8. Most managers overlook group norms. T or F?
9. When a group believes that its course of action is moral and that its opposition is weak and disorganized, the group is likely to be suffering from __________.
10. Group members who prevent negative information from reaching other group members are functioning as __________.
11. Do you think that Sally Rand's work team at Johnson Heating and Cooling is suffering from groupthink?

Answers:

1 T, 2 T, 3 T, 4 d, 5 T, 6 T, 7 T, 8 T, 9 groupthink, 10 mindguards, 11 no

Answers:

1–13, all yes

A Question of Anatomy: Significant Aspects of Group Structure

Just as organizations have form and shape (i.e., different management levels and a chain of command), so groups have structural properties. When these properties are well understood, managers can expect to design groups that are more cohesive, better performing, more stable, and perhaps more flexible and capable of dealing with external threat. Our purpose here is threefold: (1) to describe the important structural aspects of groups, (2) to discuss how management can control these structural aspects, and (3) to show how structural characteristics of groups are related to performance, communication, and cohesiveness.

Group structure is the arrangement of roles or positions within the group. For our purposes, "roles" and "positions" are interchangeable concepts. Consider the group shown in Figure 8.2, which depicts the configuration of a surgical team.

Each position or role in Figure 8.2 is evaluated in terms of status, prestige, and recognition received from other group members (Steiner, 1981). Clearly the chief surgeon position has the most status, recognition, and

Figure 8.2
Structure of a Surgical Team

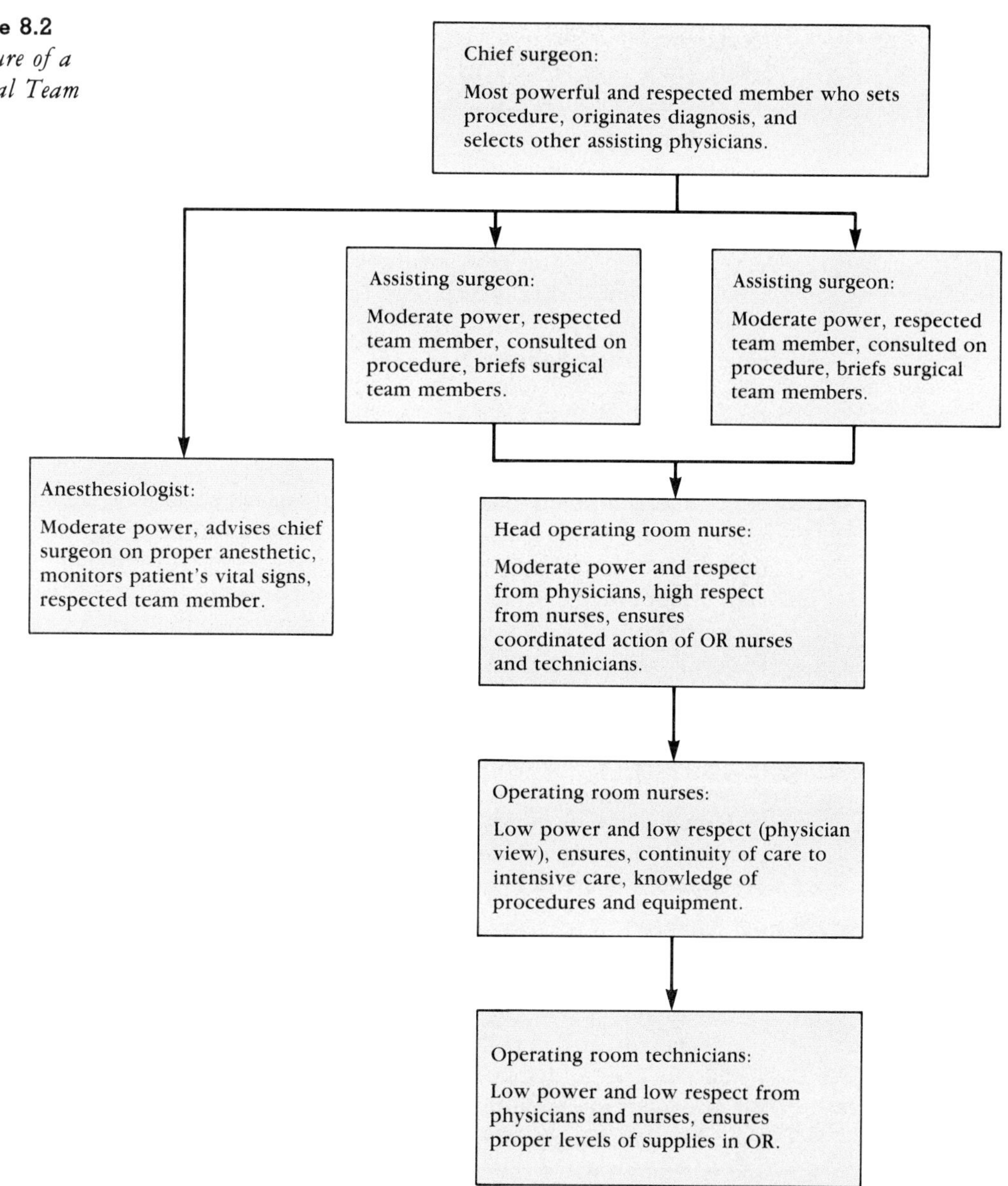

SOURCE: Adapted from G. Steiner, *Group Dynamics*, 2nd ed. New York: McGraw Hill, 1981.

prestige attached. Positions that are higher up in a group's chain of command usually have more role requirements attached as well. For example, the chief surgeon undoubtedly has other important organizational roles that he or she fills besides being a chief surgeon. This is probably not the case for the nurses or technicians.

As is the case in most groups, the highest position in terms of status carries the most responsibilities for group leadership (e.g., setting policies, formally settling disputes, and representing the group in other organizational matters) (28). Positions at the top of a chain of command are also the most critical in terms of setting goals and achieving performance. Loss of the leader often causes productivity to drop. If an OR technician were to quit or be replaced by a substitute, the effects on team performance would be much less noticeable.

The example of the surgical team becomes even more dramatic when we consider the DeVries team that does artificial heart transplants for Humana Hospitals in Louisville, Kentucky. Dr. DeVries is one of a handful of surgeons authorized to perform these delicate operations. He fills an enormous number of roles, which vary from those associated with developing new operating procedures to being a public relations spokesperson for patients and their families.

Importance of Group Status

Status is the rank that attaches to a person or to his position in the group. It is an important determinant of individual behavior and how members react to the group. Status usually has precise meaning in the group or organization. In fact, it can be a powerful motivator for increasing member effort and performance. Organizations have long recognized the motivational properties of status. Status can be conveyed simply through organizational association, (e.g., "He's with the IRS."). It also can be conveyed by organizational level, (e.g., "She's director of marketing."). Organization status provides a basis for individual comparison, and such comparisons are a powerful mechanism for channeling and directing the behavior of organizational members as they attempt to increase their status.

Money is the most powerful form of status. It conveys meaning about a person beyond organizational affiliation. Table 8.3 classifies status under six organization-related categories.

The role of equity theory in status. Much as equity theory applies to the relationship between job satisfaction, rewards, and job performance, it also is important relative to status hierarchy in groups. For example, group members must perceive the distribution of status rewards within the group to be fair and equitable. If operating room nurses believe that the head nurse got her job because of her seniority and advanced training, then they probably will not perceive inequity. If, however, she got her job because she is dating one of the attending surgeons, then rumors will fly and the nurses will perceive her as being unfairly promoted.

Equity theory and fringe benefits. Job dissatisfaction can occur if benefits are not assigned to positions in proportion to demands of the position. If subordinates make more than supervisors, status inequity will occur. The issue of comparable worth discussed in Chapter 5 is an example of this problem.

Leadership and its status effects. When individuals at the top level of a group try to distort the distribution of status rewards or try to prevent forms of status from moving down the hierarchy, serious problems can occur in the group. If group leaders appear to "be living beyond their means," members may attempt to re-establish equity by leaving the group, removing the leader, sabotaging group performance, or forming a disloyal subgroup.

Table 8.3
Common Forms of Personal Status in Organizations

Titles
- Director
- Manager
- Chief Executive Officer
- Senior Engineer
- Partner

Relationships
- Working for an important person in the organization
- Working with high-ranking members of the organization
- Working with a critical group (e.g., new product design)

Pay and Fringe Benefits
- Expense account
- Travel benefits
- Reserved parking spaces
- Executive dining facilities
- Executive perquisites (club memberships, company car, use of company plane)

Work Schedule
- Day shift work versus night work
- Exempt versus nonexempt status
- Personal work schedule versus organizational schedule

Office Amenities
- Large office with large desk and chairs
- Windows overlooking a pleasant view
- Private secretary to screen visitors

SOURCE:
Adapted from S. Robbins, 1983. *Organizational Behavior: Concepts, Controversies, and Applications.* Englewood Cliffs, N.J.: Prentice-Hall.

Status inequities do not occur only within groups. These perceptions can transfer across group and organizational boundaries. If a firm is oriented largely toward a marketing approach and if marketing's share of the budget pie reflects this orientation, other departments and managers will usually express dissatisfaction with the firm's resource allocation. Governmental agencies may leak information to the press to sabotage hearings that could lead to increased funding for other, competing agencies. Of late the Department of Defense has suffered from such tactics. You can expect to read many more news stories about the cost of screwdrivers and coffee pots used by the armed services. These status inequities in funding of government agencies will cause congressional committees to scrutinize defense budgets closely (much to the displeasure of Pentagon officials).

Status and group structure. The surgical team in Figure 8.2 represents a formal group structure. The placement of the group, its roles, and the definition of member positions are made explicit by the larger organization. In effect, the organization makes the group legitimate and delegates activity and task responsibilities to it. The group then can act on behalf of the organization to accomplish these tasks and goals.

In formal groups, group structure is not dependent on any one member. For example, the structure of the surgical team is not dependent on any particular member. In formal groups, hierarchical status is attached to position and not to the position's occupant. The chief executive officer of a corporation is thus expected to set policy, target company goals, act as spokesperson for the company, and ensure the organization's financial success. Performance of these activities is attached to the position of chief executive officer. How the activities are subsequently carried out is much more a function of the individual characteristics of that officer.

What are some other aspects of group structure that are of interest to managers?

Size affects group behavior. This important aspect of group structure has been shown to relate to a number of important individual and group-level outcomes. As groups become larger, the range of abilities, talents, and skills available for task accomplishment increases. In the language of economics, larger groups have "economies of scale," which can lead to increases in output at an increasing rate. Larger groups provide more opportunities to meet interesting others yet also provide more opportunities for anonymity for shy members (29), but larger groups sometimes present problems for their organization because they can create more interpersonal problems among members. As members become less satisfied with membership in the large group, they tend to form subgroups, which may conflict with the larger group. Let's examine some of the specific effects of group size.

Group Size and Member Participation

Large groups present less opportunities for participation in group activities. Larger groups create more threat and anxiety for individual members because the member's sense of intimacy and personalness is lost in the larger group. As groups grow, members have less face-to-face communication, which adversely affects interpersonal attraction (30). Larger groups also have participation patterns that are confined to the higher positions, thus member participation may diminish considerably at the lower levels.

Group size and leadership. As groups grow in size, they become more complex (i.e., more positions and roles are created), and demands on the leadership increase accordingly. This means that the leader's span of control is increasing. **Span of control** refers to the number of subordinates who report to a given leader or manager. As it increases, demands on the leadership grow. One obvious result of increasing group size is the greater chance that a leader will emerge (31).

Group size and member reactions. As groups get larger, positions become more specialized and differentiated. These tendencies can lead in turn to more alienation and separation among members. Members of larger groups are therefore less attracted to the group and often experience greater tensions associated with membership. Maintaining good interpersonal relations is more difficult because less face-to-face contact occurs among members of large groups. The group must rely instead on written policies and codes that are designed to substitute for direct contact between group leaders and members. This can alienate those in the leadership from those at the bottom of the hierarchy. As an organization grows from a small family business to a complexly structured company with hundreds of employees, alienation among employees becomes common. Those who were with the company when it was small commonly voice increasing dissatisfaction with "all that red tape," and speak in nostalgic terms about "the good old days when everyone knew everybody else's first name." These are the sacrifices that must be made as groups and organizations grow larger.

Large groups may have more absenteeism and member turnover. Large groups may not have the social interaction patterns that are so critical to provision of member need satisfaction. The creation of quality circles, semiautonomous work teams, and temporary project teams are attempts to rebuild, within large organizations, smaller groups that have the social characteristics necessary to satisfy individual needs. Even though employees may be members of departments with hundreds of employees, if they belong to a quality circle or semiautonomous work team, their opportunities for obtaining important personal outcomes associated with group membership are greater.

As group size increases, members often exhibit (1) less agreement, (2) more dislike for each other, (3) less tension, and (4) greater release of tension (32). As organizations grow larger, they must find ways to preserve the beneficial effects of small group membership for employees. If they are not successful in this regard, the chances are that employee unrest (i.e., labor grievances) and increased turnover and absenteeism will grow also. Quality circles, semiautonomous work groups, and the Scanlon plan are all ways to satisfy employee needs for small group membership (see Chapter 6).

Group size and performance. Larger groups generally have more potential for solving problems because they have a better distribution of skills among group members. Difficulties associated with group problem solving and consensus can get in the way, however, because as groups become larger, leaders are much more challenged in finding a common ground for consensus. Disagreements flare and deflect the group from its task. These types of disagreements are more likely to occur in larger groups, so although large groups may have potential for greater performance, their actual productivity may be less.

Managing the effects of group size. Some recommendations follow for managers who must achieve high levels of group performance while considering effects of work group size (Hampton, Summer, and Webber 1982).

1. Middle-sized groups (approximately 5 to 11 members) tend to make more accurate decisions than groups outside that size range.
2. Small groups (approximately 2 to 5 members) tend to be able to achieve consensus more effectively than larger groups.
3. Larger groups generate more ideas, but as size increases, number of ideas relative to number of members decreases (i.e., people become more self-conscious in larger groups). A variety of obstacles cause this effect, including formation of subgroups, some of which develop goals inconsistent with those of the larger group.
4. Groups of 4 or 5 persons appear to foster greater member satisfaction than larger or smaller groups. Very small groups (2 to 3 members) can make members more anxious about their high performance visibility and responsibility (33).

Spatial Arrangements in Groups

Managers have realized for some time that the way people are physically arranged in a meeting area can greatly influence (1) the way the group communicates, (2) perceptions of member status, (3) member reactions to the leader, and (4) member feelings of comfort and satisfaction (34). A number of spatial qualities take on important meaning relative to group behavior. Let's consider them one at a time.

Personal space influences our behavior in group settings (35). If someone gets too close physically in an impersonal business setting, we respond with discomfort, which may be sufficiently distracting to cause us to move or to draw negative conclusions about the encroaching individual. In some circumstances, people "suspend" their personal space needs. For example, when we go to a physician or dentist, we willingly shrink our personal space because of the nature of the visit and according to the credentials of the professional.

Personal space is culture-linked. Vietnamese soldiers are often observed walking arm-in-arm. During the war, U.S. soldiers were taught to interpret this behavior as a cultural characteristic. Our tendency would be to judge this behavior as distasteful, because touching between males is unacceptable in our culture.

Status affects personal space. During group meetings, members of higher status choose positions that reflect their status level. In rooms with a long rectangular table, the higher status members usually occupy the positions at the ends of the table and closest to doors. Since these locations provide the most opportunity for direct eye contact, they tend to be preferred by group leaders.

Personal space and proxemics. Members position themselves around a conference table (Figure 8.3) based on their expectations of what will occur during a meeting (36). Opponents sit across from each other, while cooper-

Figure 8.3
The Message in Seating Arrangements

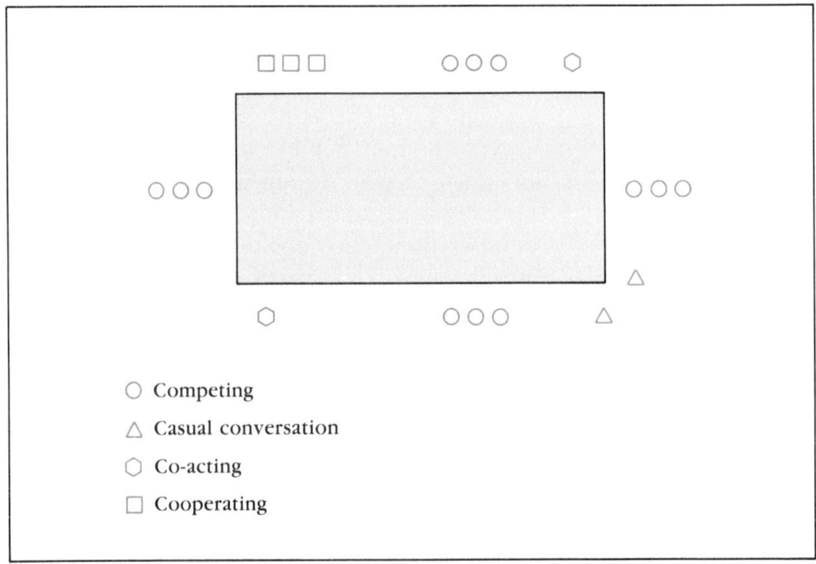

SOURCE: Adapted from R. Sommer, *Personal Space: The Behavioral Basics of Design*. Englewood Cliffs, N.J.: Prentice-Hall. 1969.

during a meeting (36). Opponents sit across from each other, while cooperating members sit next to each other. Those engaged in casual conversation may sit near a corner. Co-acting members often sit at opposite corners (on the diagonal). Study of the effects of group arrangement is called **proxemics,** which is the systematic analysis of how people position themselves in social settings.

Most managers realize the consequences of leaving seating arrangements to chance. As any good hostess knows, if she leaves her seating arrangements to social chance, people will not make new friends and old disagreements may easily flare around the dinner table. As a result, her next dinner party may not be so well attended.

Spatial arrangements and group effectiveness. The positioning of leaders appears to have an effect on group performance (37). Leadership-neutral arrangements (members seated equidistant from each other) and leadership-emergent arrangements (no designated leader, but seating arranged in hierarchical structure) were compared.

Researchers found that the neutrally structured groups (1) produced better decisions, (2) reached decisions more quickly, and (3) achieved greater consensus than leadership-oriented arrangements. In addition, neutral arrangements tended to create more satisfaction among the membership. These results are interesting in terms of the effects of spatial arrangement on member satisfaction and the success of group problem solving (38).

The field of organizational behavior is beginning to recognize the influence of spatial arrangement on a variety of important behavioral outcomes. For instance, in Chapter 7 you learned that the physical characteristics of the work environment (e.g., temperature, noise, humidity, light) influence employee productivity. Management has become more concerned with creating "user friendly" workspaces (39).

What are examples of user friendly work environments?

Workspaces and their effect on employees. Recall from our study of job redesign that the Volvo Corporation revamped the relationship between auto assemblers and their work space in the Kalmar plant. Management is becoming increasingly oriented toward the creation of more compatible work environments for white collar and professional employees. In planning new office buildings, designs reflect an increased concern for the welfare of building occupants. Lighting is being redesigned to remove up to 40 percent of the glare that formerly accompanied fluorescent lighting. People are no longer expected to conform to a "light grid." New designs do the reverse; they conform the lighting to employee needs.

People and computers. Computerization of the white collar work force has necessitated new designs for office social patterns, integration of computer facilities into office space, and office furniture. Successful design that satisfies the requirements in these three areas results increasingly in the following features (39):

1. Increased use of daylight versus artificial light.
2. Use of outdoor views to create less stressful work spaces.
3. Use of atriums and courtyards to encourage more informal face-to-face employee contact.

4. Personalized yet changeable work spaces that recognize the employee need for privacy while ensuring comfort with new colors and furniture design.
5. Noise control that uses "white noise" to mask other unpredictable and distracting noise (see Chapter 7).
6. Flexible power systems that allow low cost design changes because power outlets are portable and not fixed in the walls (40).

Workspace arrangement and organizational performance. Not many studies have been conducted in this area, but managers generally believe that the workspace influences worker productivity. Consider the following comment by Don Korell, a manager with Steelcase Company:

> If a worker makes $14,000 a year for his 30–year career, then retires at half-salary, the worker represents a $3–million cost to the company. If we had a machine that cost that much we would have a host of specialized talents to install it and study and retrain the operators. We'd maintain and polish it and show it off to visitors to the plant. We don't want the people to be regarded as machines, but we do want them regarded as important assets rather than as an expense because you try to reduce expenses and you try to maintain assets (41).

Many executives in Fortune 500 firms agree with Korell's observation. Their collective opinions can be summed up as: "Bad surroundings distract. If environment is bad, people will spend more time complaining than being productive." (42)

You may have recognized an old issue shrouded in new terminology. In Chapter 3, we studied Herzberg's two factor theory of motivation. His theory states that good hygiene factors are a necessity but are not sufficient to produce job motivation. User friendly work environments are simply organizational attempts to create good hygiene—new terms for an old concept. The important focus of management in designing spatial arrangements for the work environment should be the creation of an environment that facilitates rather than lowers productivity. Attention to how spatial arrangements influence group behavior is an important part of environmental design.

Knowledge Check

1. Group structure refers to the size and composition of the group. T or F?
2. Is job satisfaction contingent on perceived status of one's position in a group?
3. Group size affects only the degree of specialization in a group. T or F?
4. If you wanted consensus among group members to occur more quickly, would it help to reduce the size of the group?
5. Is it safe to say that the effects of leadership can be increased by controlling spatial arrangements in groups?

Answers:

1 F, 2 yes, 3 F, 4 yes, 5 yes

Summary Points

- A **group** represents two or more individuals who interact, perceive common interests and goals, and get together to accomplish work.
- Functional groups and project teams are examples of formal groups. A **formal group** has two or more members who have defined interaction patterns, a stated purpose, and members who are aware of and are involved in the group.
- Project teams have specific purposes to be accomplished within a given period of time. The group is disbanded once the goal is accomplished. These groups enhance the flexibility of the organization.
- **Interpersonal attraction** is a primary reason why people join groups. Interpersonal attraction can be based on physical attractiveness, attitude similarity, personal similarity (e.g., race, social status, and economic status), perceived ability, group activities, group goals, and value of membership per se.
- **Group composition** refers to the similarities or differences among group members regarding the group bases for interpersonal attraction. When members share a number of characteristics, the group is said to be **homogeneous.** When members have little in common, the group is **heterogeneous.**
- When **group norms** about performance agree with organizational norms, cohesiveness then contributes to group performance. When this congruency does not exist, cohesiveness does not contribute to performance as defined by the organization.
- **Groupthink** is the suspension of critical thinking by a group. It results from excessive cohesiveness, pressures to achieve consensus, and conformity.
- Groupthink can be remedied by lessening leader influence, creating devil's advocates, and altering decision-making processes. Groupthink does not always cause groups to make bad decisions, especially if the group has all of the information necessary to make the decision.
- **Group structure** represents the arrangement of roles within a group. **Roles** are defined by **status, prestige, and recognition.**
- **Group size** has predictable effects on participation, satisfaction with group membership, levels of conflict, and performance.
- The **spatial arrangement** of work areas influences work group behavior in terms of employee satisfaction, job stress, and performance.

Questions

1. Describe the organizational conditions that would make the use of project teams desirable. When using project teams, what management rules should be followed?
2. Think of a group that is very important to you. List all of the reasons why you value your membership in this group. When you have completed your list, compare it with the factors shown in Table 8.1. How similar are your reasons to the factors that cause group formation?
3. Describe at least three methods that managers can use to influence group composition. Why does management want to influence the composition of work groups?
4. What are the factors that lead to cohesiveness in work groups? Does cohesiveness always lead to high levels of group performance?
5. What are the features of norms in groups? Do norms apply in the same way to all group members? Why or why not?
6. Describe the conditions that lead to groupthink. What are the symptoms of groupthink, and how can they be eliminated?
7. What are the functions of group structure? How does status operate relative to the structure of a group?
8. What do you think of a management strategy that tries to influence group norms by changing group size and group composition exclusively? What will happen to group performance under these conditions? Develop an example of your thinking based on your experience at work or in school.

9. What would happen in a group setting if the following characteristics were in place: (a) you disagree with the leader's "pet solution" to a problem, (b) the leader has a high need for personal power, and (c) your fellow group members perceive you to be an informal leader with a high socialized need for power?
10. Write a two paragraph description of a group that is about to fall apart. Try to base the example on your own experience.

EXPLORING: *P&G Fights Back*

Adapted from P&G Fights Back. *Industry Week* (15 October 1984):64–69.

In Cincinnati, word flashes through the eleventh floor executive suite that the United Steel Workers Local 2028 has been ousted by employees at the P&G soap plant in Kansas City, Kansas. P&G officials consider this a triumph of their efforts to alter work practices radically and to improve efficiency in the company's 50 plants and mills. P&G has 23,000 employees in the United States alone, and 64,000 worldwide. It is the 23rd largest company in the United States. The 147 year-old firm has been hounded by the competition and hobbled by outdated management practices and poor labor relations.

Kimberly Clark Corporation had cut into P&G's market for disposable diapers, and Lever Brothers was attacking its soap and detergent markets. While public attention has focused on P&G's attempts to regain its markets, internal changes have been altering the way P&G operates. At the nonunion P&G plant in Lima, Ohio, employees work under the "open system" concept in which teams of employees make decisions about production goals, ways to achieve those goals, and job rotation. Each team determines by vote who can belong to it. P&G has assigned fast-track managers to work in the Lima plant. They are then reassigned to older and larger plants to help overcome management resistance to the "open system" program. Workers and their immediate supervisors are not always receptive to the new program. They are apprehensive about increasing productivity, declining market share, automation, and layoffs. Managers and white collar workers are not immune from the jitters either. "It's becoming a company where there's no place to hide," says Mr. Thomas, a P&G manager. "In the last year and a half they've asked two divisional managers to leave. This never happened before to anyone there who rose so high. I mean never in the history of the company."

P&G management tries to establish strong ties with its employees. A top corporate officer visits each plant at least once a year. He listens to workers recount grievances, and solicits suggestions for correcting them. Employees receive liberal pay and fringe benefits, and can participate in a profit sharing plan.

Discussion Questions

1. Do you think that the internal changes at P&G will increase or decrease work team cohesiveness under the "open system" plan?
2. How might the new management practices influence employee satisfaction with group membership?
3. Will the "open system" plan influence group attractiveness in predictable ways?

APPLYING: *Correcting Groupthink*

Jim Taylor was head of the production division in the Spandex Company. For some time, Jim had been using the Scanlon plan as a basis for rewarding group performance in his division. He had a number of production committees that did the initial work on suggestions designed to lower production costs. His foremen headed these committees. One committee was evaluating the feasibility of relocating several pieces of machinery to cut the time required for completing several key operations. The committee was composed of a foreman, five operators, and three clerks who oversaw parts movement in the plant.

The clerks viewed their membership on the committee as unusual, because they had never been expected to consider cost savings measures. While they were pleased to be part of the committee, they believed that the production people knew a lot more about problems of parts flow. The foreman had initiated the plan to relocate the machinery, so he was seen by all committee members as being committed to making the plan succeed. All members were attracted to the committee and looked forward to committee meetings.

The committee appraised the potential advantages and disadvantages of machine relocation on the shop floor. It solicited the opinion of other production committees. Two team members even went to a competitor and asked to talk with some production people about machine placement in their shop. After much deliberation, the production committee decided to make a positive recommendation to rearrange the equipment. The committee then moved on to confront the details involved in the relocation.

The committee discussed ways to move materials from one machine to the next. During these meetings, members had little contact with plant management and did not discuss their ideas with other plant personnel (e.g., warehouse and inventory control). Most committee members were now aware of the fact that Mr. Taylor, the foreman and committee head, firmly supported the new layout.

The group members continued to enjoy each other's company, and meetings were frequently punctuated with stories about past decisions that had proved very effective. The members even began to discuss the possible size of their bonuses once the idea was finalized and the department had saved money. During many meetings, members often reinforced Taylor's opinion about the value of the plan. As time passed, details of the plan took shape, yet little consideration was given to warehouse employees or those who operated forklift trucks.

The committee members became very confident about the screening committee's eventual adoption of their idea. They were in fact so confident of the outcome that they failed to invite any members of the screening committee to their meetings.

In general, it was as if a decision had already been made, and all that was needed was to start the plan. One committee member was unwilling to decide about the new plan; she refused consistently to take a stand on the issue. Another member expressed some doubts about the support of the warehouse people, but other committee members quickly pointed out that this was a production issue exclusively. In private conversations, this committee member, who had doubts about the support of warehouse personnel, was much more aggressively negative about the plan. As time passed, she increasingly withheld her strong reservations during committee discussions. To all outward appearances, she seemed to back all of the committee decisions. Two other members were, however, aware of her reservations.

The committee's attention now focused on a discussion of employee job satisfaction. They viewed the new layout as a beneficial design that would give employees more opportunities for social interaction while they worked.

Employees could move around more freely and follow-up on product quality. Under the old system, employees had no face-to-face contact and were unable to see the final machined product. Committee members were pleased with the "social impact" of their plan. They saw this as an excellent side benefit and came to believe that the new layout was right for all employees on the shop floor. For this reason, the committee dropped a plan to survey employee opinions about the machine relocation. A plan to develop an educational program to show employees how the new system would work (using a series of scale models) was also dropped.

Several other production committees had learned of the plan to relocate machinery and their leaders asked if they could attend some of the meetings of Taylor's committee. By now, Taylor felt very good about his committee's work, so he decided that a lot of outside intrusion would simply slow down the process. He assured the other committee heads that they could be part of the actual implementation, rather than bother attending meetings.

Because of Taylor's high level support, approval of the plan by the screening committee was a mere formality. The production committee had one last meeting on the plan. By this time, bringing up any outside objections was taboo. Nevertheless, one member who had missed several meetings asked whether or not the opinions of other foremen had been sought during the final deliberations. The other members almost ran him out of the room. The consensus of opinion was that he had missed so many meeting that he could not be very concerned about the plan's success or failure.

Taylor was a little surprised at the group's strong reaction. He said that there was no need for the committee to get off track, and proposed taking a quick hand vote on the plan (even though it was close to lunch and everyone had agreed earlier). He asked members to raise their hand if they favored implementing the plan as soon as possible. All hands went up in favor of moving ahead. Everyone applauded the unanimous vote, and the committee broke for lunch.

The committee was then charged to work with engineering to finalize the details of machine placement under the plan. Taylor held a brief meeting with his department heads and explained the new configuration. Several department heads (especially warehousing and purchasing) expressed considerable surprise that they had not been consulted on this important procedural change. The implementation process soon began to encounter delays. Forklift operators questioned the new routes from warehouse to machine area. They said that the proposed routes were unsafe for them and for other employees. (They had to drive through areas where employees were required to wear eye and ear protection.)

After many revisions and delays, the plan eventually was implemented. At the end of eight months, it became apparent that the plan was not resulting in cost savings. Instead, labor overhead and scrap rates had risen in Taylor's division. By year-end, Taylor had decided to move the machinery back to the old arrangement. This was expensive, but he knew he had no choice.

Instructions

Now that you have read the case, your instructor will divide the class into teams. A spokesperson should be appointed by each team to present the team analysis to the class. The team goals to be accomplished during the next thirty minutes are:

1. Identify the symptoms of groupthink that are present in this case.
2. How did Taylor contribute to the committee's groupthink?
3. Why did the program fail?

Use the analysis chart to channel team discussion. Working from your team's list of symptoms, fill in the information under columns 2, 3, and 4. When you have finished, the instructor will give your team further instructions.

Analysis

	(1)	(2)	(3)	(4)
	Symptoms of Committee Groupthink	Case Facts that Support the Symptom	Taylor's Effect on the Symptom	How the Symptom Contributed to the Plan's Failure
1				
2				
3				
4				
5				
6				

Suggested Readings

Davis, K. 1978. Low Productivity? Try Improving the Social Environment. *Business Horizons* (27–29 June 1978).

Dyer, W. 1977. *Teambuilding: Issues and Alternatives.* Reading, Mass.: Addison-Wesley.

This is a book for individuals who have regular responsibility for making groups productive. The author suggests ways to build a strong base for teamwork and cohesiveness.

Grove, A. How (and Why) to Run A Meeting. *Fortune* (11 July 1983):132–140.

Janis, I. 1972. *Victims of Groupthink,* Boston: Houghton Mifflin.

This book details the author's original work on the groupthink phenomenon. It is interesting reading because he applies his theory of groupthink to some notable historic fiascos. These analyses help deepen one's understanding of the importance of the groupthink problem.

Jewell, L., and Reitz, H. 1981. *Group Effectiveness in Organizations.* Glenview, Ill.: Scott Foresman.

This practical little book provides an excellent overview of group behavior without overdoing the research results. It also offers some practical guidelines for managing groups.

Malcolm, A. 1976. *The Tyranny of the Group.* Totowa, N.J.: Littlefield, Adams.

Schrank, R. 1978. *How to Relieve Worker Boredom. Psychology Today* 12:79–80.

Tropman, J. 1980. *Effective Meetings.* Beverly Hills, Calif.: Sage Publications.

References

1. Shaw, M. 1981. *Group Dynamics,* 2nd ed. New York: McGraw-Hill.
2. Dunham, R. 1984. *Organizational Behavior.* Homewood, Ill.: Irwin.
3. Leatt, P., and Schneck, R. 1984. Criteria for Grouping Nursing Subunits in Hospitals. *Academy of Management Journal* 27:150–165.
4. Peters, T., and Waterman, R., Jr. 1982. *In Search of Excellence.* New York: Harper & Row.
5. Ibid.
6. Shaw, M., op. cit., 1981.
7. Ibid.
8. Senn, D. 1971. Attraction as a Function of Similarity-Dissimilarity in Task Performance. *Journal of Personality and Social Psychology* 18:120–123.
9. Shaw, M., op. cit., 1981.
10. Schacter, S. 1959. *The Psychology of Affiliation.* Stanford, Calif.: Stanford University Press.
11. Brown, R., and Williams, J. 1984. Group Identification: The Same Thing to All People? *Human Relations* 35:547–560.
12. Wanous, J., and Youtz, M. 1986. Solution Diversity and the Quality of Group Decisions. *Academy of Management Journal* 29:149–159.
13. Collins, E., and Guetzkow, H. 1964. *The Social Psychology of Group Processes in Decision Making.* New York: Wiley.
14. Shaw, M., op. cit., 1981.
15. Ibid.
16. Piper, W., Marrache, M., Lacroix, R., Richardson, A., and Jones, B. 1983. Cohesion as a Basic Bond in Groups. *Human Relations* 34:93–108.
17. Terborg, J., Castore, C., and DeNimmo, J. 1976. A Longitudinal Field Investigation of the Impact of Group Composition on Group Performance and Cohesion. *Journal of Personality and Social Psychology* 34:782–790.
18. Shaw, M., op. cit., 1981.
19. Ibid.
20. Ibid.
21. Hackman, J. Group Influence on Individuals. In Dunnette, M. (ed.) 1976. *Handbook of Individual and Organizational Psychology.* Chicago: Rand McNally.
22. Feldman, D. 1984. The Development and Enforcement of Group Norms. *Academy of Management Review* 9:47–53.
23. Zander, A. 1982. *Making Groups Effective.* San Francisco: Jossey Bass.
24. Janis, I. 1982. *Groupthink,* 2nd ed. New York: Houghton Mifflin.
25. Ibid.
26. Ibid.
27. Schweiger, D., Sandberg, W., and Ragan, J. 1986. Group Approaches for Improving Strategic Decision Making: A Comparative Analysis of Dialectical Inquiry, Devil's Advocacy and Consensus. *Academy of Management Journal* 29:51–71.
28. Shaw, M., op. cit., 1981.
29. Ibid.
30. Indik, B. 1965. Organization Size and Member Participation: Some Empirical Tests of Alternatives. *Human Relations* 18:339–350.
31. Shaw, M., op. cit., 1981.
32. O'Dell, J. 1968. Group Size and Emotional Interaction. *Journal of Personality and Social Psychology* 8:75–78.
33. Hampton, D., Summer, C., and Webber, R. 1982. *Organizational Behavior and the Practice of Management,* 4th ed. Glenview, Ill.: Scott, Foresman.
34. Davis, T. 1984. The Influence of Physical Environment in Offices. *Academy of Management Review* 9:271–283.
35. Sommer, R. 1969. *Personal Space: The Behavioral Aspects of Design.* Englewood Cliffs, N.J.: Prentice Hall.
36. Ibid.
37. Cummings, L., Huber, P., and Arendt, E. 1974. Effects of Size and Spatial Arrangements on Group Decision Making. *Academy of Management Journal* 17:460–475.
38. Ibid.
39. Friedland, L. 1985. When High Tech and Humans Meet. Sky, Halsey Publications, February 1985, 52–57.
40. Ibid.
41. Ibid.
42. Ibid.

Group Decision Making in Organizations

Chapter **9**

Chapter Goals

By the end of this chapter, you will be able to:

1. Describe the meaning and importance of each stage of group development.
2. Predict the nature of group process losses for each stage of group development.
3. Explain the factors that can shift a mature group to an earlier stage of development.
4. Explain why groups can inhibit creativity.
5. Develop the reasoning behind the current view of the "risky shift" phenomenon.
6. Identify the pros and cons of using participation in group decision making.
7. Contrast brainstorming, nominal group technique, and the Delphi technique with interacting group decision making.
8. Suggest practical guidelines for managing task activities and maintenance activities in groups.
9. Diagnose conflict between groups and suggest an approach for handling conflict.
10. Differentiate the advantages and disadvantages of several methods of handling conflict between groups.

Dilemma The Student Marketing Team

Tom Murphy, a marketing instructor, had organized his class into student teams. Each team was responsible for a major project requiring library and field research on a hypothetical product. All project teams seemed to be working effectively, and the second part of each team's assignment was due. Professor Murphy was sitting at his desk going over his grading sheets when his phone rang. Andy Thornton was the caller, and he had this story to tell:

> Dave Reimer is in our project group and he's done nothing! The four of us (Dave, Andy, Ruth, and Phil) divided the work. Dave said that he would write the analysis of our survey results, and he was supposed to have that analysis to me by 4:00 P.M. Friday so I could integrate it into the report.
>
> By 5:30 P.M. on Friday, Dave still had not shown up, and we were all getting nervous. What made things worse was the fact that Ruth saw Dave at the student union with the guys from his intramural basketball team!
>
> Saturday I called everyone, including Dave, and set up a meeting on Sunday at 1:00 P.M. Everybody showed up but Dave! We worked until 9:00 P.M. and were able to slap together an analysis of our survey results. We did Dave's work ourselves.
>
> I wanted to tell you about our decision to leave Dave's name off of our team paper. We all agreed that since he did none of the work, we wouldn't carry his grade. The rest of us have worked hard in your course; we want to do well. That's difficult when you have a freeloader on your team who won't pull his own weight. Since I drew the short straw, I'm the one who had to make this tough phone call. I hope you understand.

Murphy was perplexed; he became still more confused when his phone rang later that afternoon and Dave Reimer was on the line:

Hi, Professor Murphy. Did you get my paper yet? (Murphy grabbed the stack and found Dave's in the middle.) I just wanted to tell you that I had to turn mine in without any team affiliation. To my surprise, I learned that my team had left my name off the report I helped prepare! I was surprised but I guess I had sort of anticipated it at the same time. By the way, I included some extra material on pricing strategies for new products. I worked at the library all day Sunday to prepare it. I hope you understand and that working alone won't hurt my grade.

Murphy did not understand. He had devoted a lot of effort to the student team assignments, which were based on a number of factors. His formula had always worked before. Why the problems this time? At the beginning of each semester, Murphy explained the group projects to the class. He then asked students to fill out cards eliciting the following information: (1) age, (2) work experience, (3) career objective, (4) intended major, (5) gender, (6) address and phone number, and (7) personal interests. He also asked each student to turn in a sheet with the names of three classmates who he or she believed would make good team members. Dave and Andy had each listed the other on his sheet.

Murphy decided to investigate further. He called Dave and Andy and asked them to meet with him in his office on Wednesday. He decided to see them together. He reasoned that seeing the other team members was not necessary, for he had talked only to Andy and Dave. At 4:30 P.M. both students appeared in his doorway. He invited them in, and the following conversation took place:

Dave: Professor Murphy, I'm sorry about this mess, but I had to turn in my report by myself. I hate working in groups. Other people always let you down, and you wind up having to do their work and your own work too!

Andy: That's not true! We had meetings all of the time and Dave never came! He was always too busy with basketball practice—something about winning the league championship.

Dave: Sure we wanted to win the league championship. At least I feel as if I'm part of the basketball team. You guys on the marketing team were always trying to be so cool and spout off your big ideas, just because you had some retail work experience. Since when does that make you all Lee Iacoccas?

Realizing that the argument was getting pretty heated, Murphy broke in. He asked who the group leader was.

Andy: Well, Ruth started off as leader because she said that she'd had some summer work experience in a retail furniture store. One of her jobs was to help the owner set prices for merchandise. That sounded relevant to us, so we made her group leader. But then because of some problems at home, she had to take a part-time job, so I became team leader.

Dave: Yeah, he took over without asking any of us. All of a sudden Andy's giving the orders. Nobody liked it, but because we were getting close to the deadline, we decided to put up with him.

Andy: Put up nothing! You never came to any meetings, so how can you say that?

Dave: Easy, watch my lips.

At this point, Murphy broke off the meeting. He told Dave and Andy that he would arrive at a decision later in the week. As both students stalked out of his office, it was clear to Murphy that they were no longer friends. He wondered what had gone wrong with the group, which had seemed to have so much potential at the beginning of the semester.

Questions

1. How effective was Professor Murphy's method of organizing project teams?
2. What is the best way to handle important individual differences among group members?

3. What techniques could Professor Murphy have used to improve decision making within Andy's project team?

4. Is there a method for Murphy to use to manage the conflict in Andy's project group?

Stages of Group Development

Group behavior is easier to understand if the stages of group development are isolated. Once you are able to recognize these stages, then you can design effective strategies to help work groups to be as productive as possible.

Numerous explanations of the developmental phases of groups have been proposed (1). We cannot describe all of these here. We focus instead on one explanation, which is very useful because it deals with two key aspects of work groups: (1) interpersonal relations, and (2) the group task (2). The group manager must be concerned about these factors because they have a significant impact on group performance. Figure 9.1 shows our chosen model of group development.

General properties of group development. First, groups move through the stages of development at different speeds. Some groups get to stage 4 very quickly because of high cohesiveness and members who are used to working with each other. In contrast, some groups labor through the initial stages and never get to stage 4. (This happened to the marketing team in the opening dilemma.) Second, the boundaries between developmental stages are not always clear. Each stage lasts until the major issues associated with that stage are solved. Major group-based needs are associated with each stage and must be met before the needs of the next stage can be addressed by the group. Third, a group may sometimes find itself moving backwards. In the model (Figure 9.1), a group at stage 4 may drop back to stage 3 or 2 because new members are added or the task is changed. These three general properties emphasize the dynamic nature of group development. Let's look now at each stage of the model, analyze the features of each stage, and identify the major group-based needs that must be met before the group can move on to the next stage.

Stage 1: FORMING. This stage is defined as the phase-in, during which members move from an individual to a group orientation. In stage 1, group members try to identify (1) the behaviors that are most acceptable (and important) to the group, (2) the skills and abilities that each member possesses, (3) the goals and motives of individual members, and (4) the degree of involvement and commitment of each member to the group. During this stage members test each other's assumptions about hard work and cooperation. The formally assigned leader (or the leader who emerges initially to take charge) is very important. This in-

Figure 9.1
Stages of Group Development

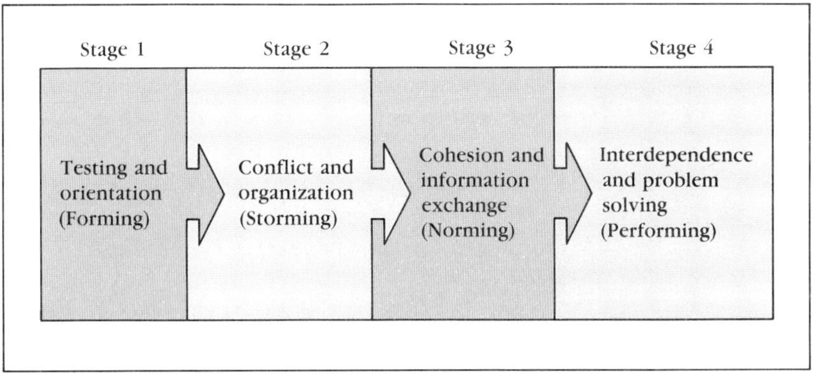

SOURCE: B. W. Tuckman, 1965, Developmental Sequence in Small Groups. *Psychological Bulletin* 63:384–399.

dividual sets the norms concerning the group's task, how work will be divided, and how much effort members will expend (see Chapter 8). In effect, the leader takes over a disorganized collection of new individuals (they really are not a group because a common purpose is not yet established) and provides them with job structure to reduce role ambiguity. In the introductory dilemma, we can assume that Ruth served as the first group leader. Her personal problems caused the role to be passed to Andy. The marketing team realized that they needed a leader to help them progress through the stages of group development.

Stage 1 creates group-based needs that must be satisfied before the requirements of stage 2 can be addressed. For example, in stage 1, members are very concerned with clarification of their group roles and with what is expected of them. They want to know what the group norms are going to be, especially those concerning effort and performance. Second, the group seeks direction in stage 1 by testing a number of ideas. The leader (if one has emerged) and the group members try out ideas about group purpose and direction. These ideas are examined, discussed, and then discarded or kept as deemed appropriate by all members. This process is important because it implies that the leader's position is not solidified in stage 1. Although the leader's formal position may be acknowledged by group members, the individual's credibility may not be firmly established in the minds of members. The dilemma reinforces this point; Dave never felt that Ruth or Andy were legitimate leaders of his marketing team.

Stage 2: STORMING. Conflicts emerge as the group enters stage 2. As members gain experience interacting with each other, they become more definite in their opinions regarding the group's purposes, methods for accomplishing tasks, and the norms that govern member behavior. This stage may topple the first leader. If members doubt the leader's capabilities, he will be replaced. This process may be accelerated if group members have high needs for power and achievement (see Chapter 3). Indeed, conflicts can become so common that members may conclude that no one trusts anyone else and that group membership is pointless.

Conflicts can obscure the importance of getting organized. Stage 2 is concerned with development of trust and collaboration. Roles are changing, and members may consider leaving the group if they judge disagreements to be insurmountable. If the group has a member with a high need for affiliation, she will quickly assume the role of "conflict resolver."

Conflicts resolve slowly. Some individuals may leave the group in stage 2; others may change their role and degree of group involvement. If the group lasts through stage 2, it is on the road to becoming an effective work group.

Stage 2 group-based needs are trust and cooperation. Individuals still believe that their personal needs can be better met through their own actions than through the mechanism of group activity. The group is not yet cohesive, and members perceive the benefits of group affiliation as being outweighed by its costs. These unmet needs of trust and cooperation create process losses in the group. **Process losses** are defined as problems that prevent the group from achieving its performance potential (3). Both stage 1 and 2 have high process losses. As the group struggles to become more organized, members' lower order needs are emphasized (i.e., safety, security, and social needs). Trust and cooperation emerge only as members see each other behaving according to established norms that concern effort, goal direction, and task activities. In stage 2, process losses may include dissatisfied members who leave the group, new members joining the group, members consciously cutting back on their group involvement (some individuals become marginal members who only participate superficially in group activities), and questioning of leadership.

The dilemma indicates that Dave exhibited many of the stage 2 symptoms. His personal involvement diminished as he sought to satisfy his needs elsewhere, that is, through his membership on the basketball team. He further contributed to process losses by avoiding meetings and missing work deadlines. In a word, Dave sabotaged the group activities because he acted as if the group was suspended in stage 2.

Stage 3: NORMING. In stage 3, the group develops an identity of its own. The group's personality is now established. By this stage, members are fully aware of their involvement and commitment to the group. The benefits of group membership now outweigh the costs in the minds of members. They feel good about each other, and the leader position is established. Members understand the group norms and disagreement about norms is minimal. The group members are now "good citizens," and the group is organized and congenial.

Solidification of member roles. The hierarchy of the group is accepted by members, and they are comfortable with their membership. Harmony and agreement are tangible characteristics of a stage 3 group. In fact, harmony and agreement may be so pervasive that the group runs the risk of groupthink (see Chapter 8). In stage 3, members believe that the group effectively meets their personal needs. Because members feel very comfortable with their roles, an external threat may trigger groupthink process losses. Groupthink does not occur in any other stage of group development. In stages 1 and 2, an adequate basis for consensus does not exist.

Process losses need not occur in stage 3. If the group develops healthy information exchange mechanisms and if group members assume appropriate roles (e.g., devil's advocate, leader not pushing pet solutions), then groupthink can be avoided. If a group is to have healthy information exchange mechanisms, it must create numerous formal and informal pathways for gathering information. People outside the group must be invited to participate in meetings as needed.

Stage 3 group-based needs focus on the quality of group-based decision-making processes. Conflicts in stage 3 are less associated with personal feelings than with clashes over ideas and information, which may slow the group decision-making process. By this stage, all members are extremely loyal to the group. Indeed, protecting the group is almost as important to members as protecting themselves. If members perceive external threats to the group, they can unwittingly compromise the quality of group decision making in the interest of preserving harmony and solidarity (cohesiveness). The group, while cohesive, is nonetheless vulnerable to rigid adherence to group norms (i.e., the group does not tolerate deviance from norms that promote harmony).

Stage 4: PERFORMING. Stage 4 is usually not achieved by work groups unless they have managed to escape the pitfalls of conflict and poor leadership, which create insurmountable process losses. If a group succeeds in arriving at stage 4, then **actual productivity is probably close to potential productivity. Potential productivity** is the capacity for excellence in decision making as represented by the combined skills and abilities of group members. **Actual productivity** represents group accomplishment after the process losses associated with stages 1, 2, and 3 have occurred. Andy's marketing team had high potential productivity (excellent skills and abilities among members), but process losses were high (Dave dropped out of the group). The net effect for the team was low actual productivity.

What are the characteristics of a group that is operating in stage 4?

Characteristics of stage 4 groups. Group members exhibit collaboration. **Collaboration** refers to willingness to confront conflict that surfaces both in interpersonal and task-related issues. Trust abounds in the collaborative group, and members willingly take the time to reassess norms, goals, and activities. Collaboration occurs when there is widespread understanding and acceptance of group member roles. In stage 4, members exhibit involvement, motivation to contribute, acceptance of responsibility, and active participation.

Stage 4 groups are mature groups. Mature groups are defined as groups that have members who are confident about their personal abilities and who willingly communicate their confidence in the capabilities of the group. The mature group quickly attacks any evidence of process loss that might compromise actual productivity, and the group knows how to minimize process losses (Figure 9.2). This perception separates the stage 4 from the stage 3 group. The stage 3 group is not capable of recognizing its process losses.

Figure 9.2
Relationship Between Components of Group Performance

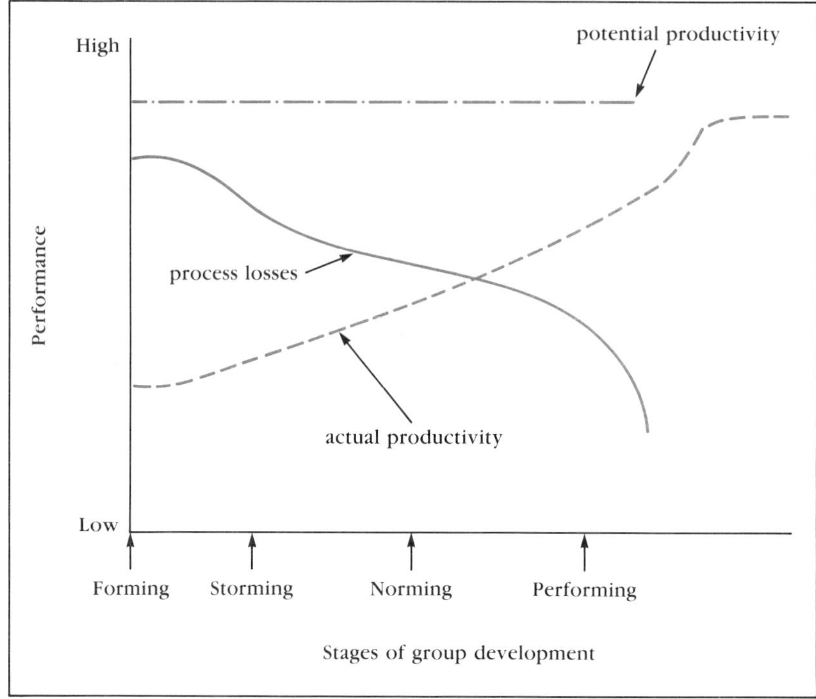

NOW IT'S YOUR TURN . . .

Go back and reread quickly the introductory dilemma and note the process losses experienced by Andy's marketing team. Choose five of the team's process losses and explain how each is related to a specific stage of group development. (Note your selected process losses and the stage to which each applies in the space provided.)

	Process Loss	Stage
1.	______________________	______________________
2.	______________________	______________________
3.	______________________	______________________
4.	______________________	______________________
5.	______________________	______________________

Compare your results with those of a fellow student. How do you account for the differences?

Groups cannot stay in stage 4 indefinitely. Just as individuals cannot self-actualize continuously (see Maslow's hierarchy), so groups cannot occupy stage 4 continuously. Turnover among members, changes in group priorities, and variations in the external environment all conspire to push the group out of stage 4. (In Chapter 12 we will examine how the leadership role helps hold the group in stage 4 longer.)

Dropping out of stage 4. All groups and their organizations are by definition dynamic and developmental. Groups are the changing building blocks of the organization. Through their variability, organizations (and groups) find ways to be flexible and capable of self-renewal. Remaining in stage 4 indefinitely would deny the forces of change. Indeed, organizations become more effective and dynamic by virtue of the stages of group development. Any management system that attempts to suspend the inevitable movement of work groups through the developmental stages is doomed to fail. The trick is instead to manage the development of work groups.

Solving the Dilemma

How effective was Professor Murphy's method for organizing project teams?

Professor Murphy's system was fine, but he was too dependent on it. His system was an acceptable first step toward creating an awareness among the students that they were now members of a marketing group. After that first step, however, Murphy stopped managing the stages of group development. He assumed that similarity of personal background and career interests would propel each group through the four stages of development, but without firm leadership on his part, group movement to stage 4 was left to chance! Professor Murphy's mistake is another version of *not* "managing by walking around." He could and should have ensured that each group's developmental process was on the right track.

Knowledge Check

1. The stages of group development resemble the features of Maslow's hierarchy because the stages are related in a step-wise fashion with respect to each other. T or F?

2. A group in the norming stage is most vulnerable to groupthink. T or F?

3. Stage 3 conflict is most often associated with ideas instead of personalities. T or F?

Answers:

1 T, 2 F, 3 T

Group Performance and Decision Making

Simply recognizing the stages of group development does not make one an effective manager of group activities. Skillful managers must be familiar with the processes and characteristics of group decision making. In this section we focus on developing the tools for effective management of group decision making.

Creativity in Group Decision Making

Group creativity versus individual creativity. In most instances, groups are less creative than individuals. Remember, we said MOST! This indicates that groups somehow inhibit creativity (4, 5). Groups seem to be as creative as their most creative member. The belief that groups somehow make less creative members more creative is not supported by research. Indeed, individuals working alone often generate more ideas than groups, and in many studies, individuals are shown to often generate twice as many ideas as groups (6).

Why do groups inhibit creativity?

Groups generate many process losses when creativity is involved. For instance, groups become preoccupied with a single line of thinking, and ideas then become variations on that theme. Groups generate pressures that suppress deviance, and members often choose to remain silent rather than have their ideas destroyed by higher status members. When group members fear losing their self-esteem, they will either keep silent or lessen the creativeness of their contributions. Finally, the interpersonal dynamics of group decision making often impede creative decision making. Consider the following example:

> Phyllis prided herself on being a skillful leader of group discussions, so she accepted willingly her professor's invitation to chair a panel discussion on corporate ethics. The goal of the panel was to propose "new corporate policies that would help preserve the environment." Two students and two executives from the chemical industry participated on the panel. Phyllis decided to focus the panel's attention on the technology of nuclear waste disposal. The two industrial experts protested, stating that disposal was currently a "technical issue" and that the stated purpose of the panel was the formulation of broader corporate policy addressing the full spectrum of environmental issues. Phyllis responded by replying that the experts were "afraid to touch the issue and were too vague." The two students on the panel agreed with Phyllis, and the discussion then deteriorated into a monologue by Phyllis on trivial technical issues.

This example shows how interpersonal dynamics can sidetrack creativity. The desire of the students on the panel to go along with Phyllis's leadership and Phyllis's personal interest in pursuing the technical issue of nuclear waste disposal redirected the panel and neutralized the creativity of the industry experts. The key issue of corporate policy was submerged in Phyllis's pet issue. Phyllis tried to win support for her issue through sheer stubbornness and competitiveness. Her fellow students were caught up in her fervor, and the panel was reduced to "three against two"!

Group creativity may be poor because of the beliefs of the leader (7). Here's how the logic works: Supervisors are dependent on the work group to produce (i.e., the supervisor's success is measured by the group's productivity). When the group is less creative, the supervisor concludes that the members are the problem (versus the resources available to the group or the way the group's task is designed). The supervisor usually blames the group and its members without doing a thorough analysis of possible external reasons for poor group creativity. If the supervisor tends to use punishment instead of rewards, creativity will deteriorate even further.

Group effectiveness in evaluating idea quality. Groups cannot generate as many creative ideas as individuals working separately, but they are superior when it comes to evaluating quality of ideas. Groups improve the creative process in organizations if they are employed strategically to evaluate the quality of creative ideas generated by individuals. 3M, Texas Instruments, IBM, and Xerox use project groups in this way (8). In many successful organizations, scientists and engineers are expected to become the idea and product champions who generate new ideas for products and services. Before the firms commit resources to idea development, however, the "product and idea champions" must convince work teams of expert evaluators to back their ideas.

Risk Taking in Decision-Making Groups

Individual and group-based risk taking. Are groups or individuals more risk-oriented about making decisions? The evidence concludes that groups are no more inclined to be risk oriented than are individual decision makers (9). Stoner (1961) reports on a series of studies analyzing individual and group orientation to risk taking (10). Under certain conditions, groups were found to be more risk-oriented than individuals trying to solve the same problems. Stoner calls this phenomenon "risky shift" (11). Two explanations for the phenomenon are proposed:

1. **Diffusion of responsibility.** The group is more risk-oriented than the individual because responsibility for the decision is spread across more than one person, so the member's responsibility is diluted. In other words, responsibility is spread across all group members.
2. **Risk-oriented leaders.** Because leaders have a greater influence on group decisions than other members, if the group leader is risk-oriented, then the group will pursue riskier decisions. If the leader is assertive and competent, then members are more likely to follow and to dare to take risks.

These explanations have not fared well. The most accepted viewpoint is that groups take risks or are cautious depending on how members value the risk of a particular decision. For example, if a marketing team is deciding whether to bring out a new product, the chances are that the group will be very risk oriented. Marketing is supposed to support new product introductions, so a "bias toward risk" exists for such decisions. On the other hand, if the issue is the firing of an employee for harassing other employees, then the group may be very cautious and ask for additional data as well as legal advice. The closer an organizational decision is to morale, job satisfaction, and group cohesiveness, the more cautious decision-making groups become. Firing personnel, disbanding cohesive groups, or organizing widespread layoffs are actions that upset the organizational climate. Such actions often are the subject of much deliberation and discussion. Decision-making groups do not like to upset employee harmony and goodwill, so groups will avoid risk and will take longer to make such decisions. Other determinants of group risk taking are shown in Table 9.1.

To summarize, if group members value risk taking, then group decisions will be riskier than individual decisions. If caution is the group norm, then the group will be more conservative than an individual decision maker.

Acceptance of Group Decisions by Members

Commitment to group-based decisions. Managers are interested in the value of participation in group settings. The issue is whether participation increases the likelihood that group members will be more committed to group decisions, and indeed, participation does seem to increase member commitment to group decisions and goals. When people participate in group decisions, they have a personal stake in the outcomes of the decision. Participation helps members understand the goals of the decision and the process that supports the group's decision.

Groups often implement decisions. In organizations, many decisions are made by individuals, but the implementation of those decisions then becomes a matter of group acceptance and support. The broader the participation base for a decision, the more likely the decision is to be smoothly implemented. In broad-based decision making, a larger number of employees share expectations and accept the goals advanced for a particular decision. Let's look at an example.

> Cheryl is in charge of the company Affirmative Action program. Her job is to see that the firm adheres to federal guidelines regarding hiring of minority employees. She is responsible for determining how many minority employees should be hired and also for working with college recruiters to ensure a uniform recruiting of minorities. Cheryl believes that the best way to ensure uniformity of hiring practices among recruiters is to work with the recruiters in small groups and to get their first-hand reactions to company hiring policies. Six months before the beginning of each college recruiting season, she holds group meetings with recruiters and college placement officers. She briefs each group on

Table 9.1
Determinants of Group Risk Taking

The Task Group Is Risk Oriented if:	*The Task Group Is Conservative if:*
1. The group is expected to be risk oriented and members value risk.	1. Members do not value risk.
2. The decision has little to do with the status quo or organizational politics.	2. The issue involves human resource decisions that can influence morale and job satisfaction.
3. The leader is risk oriented.	3. The leader is risk adverse.

the firm's progress regarding Affirmative Action. Cheryl has also established an advisory board composed of current employees and three college placement officers. The function of this board is to evaluate employee suggestions for improving minority hiring practices.

In the example note that Cheryl tries to build as wide a base for Affirmative Action decisions as possible. She works hard to gain the commitment and support of recruiters and college placement officers, for these individuals have an impact on company hiring policy.

Participative decision-making programs in industry. In both the Scanlon plan and the Lincoln Electric program employees are involved actively in solving company production problems. Quality circles also use the same participative mechanism. Note, however, that not all group decision making is improved through participation (see Table 9.2).

Participant Satisfaction in Group Decision Making

Successful participation accommodates individual differences to satisfy individual needs. We have studied individual differences that are related to autonomy: (1) locus of control, (2) need for achievement, (3) need for affiliation, (4) need for power, and (5) growth need strength. All can be influenced by group participation, which creates the conditions for satisfaction of individual needs. For example, the employee with a socialized need for power (see Chapter 3) finds the group to be the best possible mechanism for satisfying personal needs. This member is likely to satisfy her needs for more power if she becomes a group leader. The affiliative group member will be more attracted to a participative group featuring activities that encourage member interactions. The affiliative employee thrives in this situation. In the participative group, the individual with an internal locus of control can demand to be included in decision making, which is important to him because he feels so strongly about controlling his own destiny at work.

Managers can achieve organizational goals and satisfy employee needs through participation in group decision making. When employees possess

Table 9.2
Pros and Cons of Participation for Group Decision Making

Participation Is Better When:	*Participation Is Worse When:*
1. Managers do not possess enough information to solve the problems alone.	1. Managers do not have sufficient time to make a decision.
2. The problem is unclear and the group is needed to outline the problem at hand.	2. Decision outcomes do not affect employees directly.
3. Acceptance of the decision by subordinates is critical to decision success.	3. Acceptance of the decision by subordinates has little to do with decision success.
4. Employees share the goals of the leader.	4. Employees perceive participation as manipulative or of little value.
5. Employees have strong feelings about an issue and want to exercise their judgement.	5. Employees are indifferent to the decision and its outcomes.

the individual differences noted in the previous paragraph, they value the intrinsic rewards created by participation in group decision making. Participation increases the likelihood that employees can gain these rewards.

Solving the Dilemma

What is the best way to handle important individual differences among group members?

Professor Murphy did not develop an understanding of the individual differences of the students on Andy's marketing team. He knew about the students' interests and expectations, but he did not understand their individual needs. He should have spent more time with each group to try to comprehend each student's motivation. Knowing what motivated the various students would have put him in a better position to keep the group moving through the stages of group development.

Knowledge Check

1. Groups are more effective as evaluators of new ideas than they are as generators of new ideas. T or F?
2. The group's values about risk taking are the best predictor of the degree of risk members will take in making group decisions. T or F?
3. Group decision making should not be used when time pressure is excessive and when decision outcomes are of little importance to group members. T or F?
4. Managers should be aware of the relationship between individual differences and group performance. T or F?

Answers:

1 T, 2 T, 3 T, 4 T

Methods for Improving Effectiveness of Group Decision Making

A knowledge of group development and of the principles of group decision making lays the foundation for understanding group behavior in organizations. The next step is to develop solid techniques to ensure that actual group productivity is as close to potential productivity as possible. In this section we look at the problems of and approaches to decision making in three group configurations: (1) interacting groups, (2) nominal groups, and (3) Delphi groups.

Interacting Groups and Decision Making

Interacting groups are the most common type of group in organizations. An interacting group is a group that holds face-to-face meetings, which often are poorly organized. Such groups accomplish most of the group-based work in organizations. The student marketing team in the introductory dilemma is an interacting group. (Table 9.3 summarizes the characteristics of interacting groups.)

Problems with interacting groups. The standard procedure for making decisions in an interacting group is as follows: (1) the problem is identified and discussed, (2) solutions are proposed and evaluated, and (3) a decision choice is made by voting. The interacting group is very susceptible to process losses such as groupthink, conflict, low participation, limited commitment to solutions, and risky shift. Interacting groups may be the easiest to set up, but they can be the most difficult to manage for the reasons noted in Table 9.4. All of the problems listed are process losses. Let's consider some ways to manage interacting groups effectively to minimize process losses.

What are the guidelines for making interacting groups more effective?

Making interacting groups effective. The main theme that pervades the problems noted in Table 9.4 is the group tendency to move toward consensus too quickly. This tendency can be avoided if interacting group members are encouraged to follow these steps (12):

1. Avoid arguing for your own rankings. Present your position as lucidly and logically as possible, but listen to other members' reactions and consider them carefully before pressing your point.
2. Do not assume that someone must win and someone must lose when discussion reaches a stalemate. Look instead for the next-most-acceptable alternative that satisfies all participants.
3. Do not change your mind simply to avoid conflict and to reach agreement and harmony. When agreement seems to come too quickly and easily, be suspicious. Explore the reasons for agreement and be sure that everyone accepts the solution for basically similar or complementary reasons. Yield only to positions that have objectively based and logically sound foundations.
4. Avoid conflict-reducing techniques such as majority vote, averages, coin-flips, or bargaining. When a dissenting member finally agrees, do not feel that he must be rewarded by having his way at some later point.
5. Differences of opinion are natural and to be expected. Seek them out, and try to involve everyone in the decision-making process. Disagreements can help the group's decision making by eliciting a wide range of information and opinions, which increases the chance that the group will hit on more adequate solutions (13).

These guidelines can reduce process losses (see Table 9.4). Problem diagnosis is facilitated by following steps 1 and 5. When group members do not diagnose problems, a tendency exists to jump too quickly to solutions. This often happens because members do not listen carefully when they are

Table 9.3 *Comparison of Qualitative Differences Between Three Decision Processes Based on Evaluations of Leaders and Group Participants*

Dimension	Interacting Groups	Nominal Groups	Delphi Technique
Overall methodology	Unstructured face-to-face group meeting High flexibility High variability in behavior of groups	Structured face-to-face group meeting Low flexibility Low variability in behavior of groups	Structured series of questionnaires and feedback reports Low-variability respondent behavior
Role orientation of groups	Socioemotional Group maintenance focus	Balanced focus on social maintenance and task role	Task-instrumental focus
Relative quantity of ideas	Low, focused "rut" effect	Higher, independent writing and hitchhiking round robin	High, isolated writing of ideas
Search behavior	Reactive search Short problem focus Task-avoidance tendency New social knowledge	Proactive search Extended problem focus High task centeredness New social and task knowledge	Proactive search Controlled problem focus High task centeredness New task knowledge
Normative behavior	Conformity pressures inherent in face-to-face discussions	Tolerance for nonconformity through independent search and choice activity	Freedom not to conform through isolated anonymity
Equality of participation	Member dominance in search, evaluation, and choice phases	Member equality in search and choice phases	Respondent equality in pooling of independent judgments
Method of problem solving	Person centered Smoothing over and withdrawal	Problem centered Confrontation and problem solving	Problem centered Majority rule of pooled independent judgments
Closure decision process	High lack of closure Low felt accomplishment	Low lack of closure High felt accomplishment	Low lack of closure Medium felt accomplishment
Resources utilized	Low administrative time and cost High participant time and cost	Medium administrative time, cost, preparation High participant time and cost	High administrative time, cost, preparation
Time to obtain group ideas	1½ hours	1½ hours	Five calendar months

SOURCE: A.H. Van de Ven and A.L. Delbecq, 1974. The Effectiveness of Nominal and Delphi Techniques in Interacting Group Decision Making Processes. *Academy of Management Journal* 17:618.

Table 9.4
Forms of Process Losses in Interacting Groups

Problem Diagnosis
- Confusing facts with opinions
- Confusing problem symptoms with root causes
- Scapegoating (i.e., looking for people to blame for the issue)
- Proposing solutions before problem is understood
- Biasing problem diagnosis to favor pet solutions

Solution Generation
- Suggesting solutions irrelevant to the problem
- Discussing what should have been done versus what needs to be done
- Discussing strengths and weaknesses of solutions before all solutions are suggested
- Focusing on old solutions used in past versus generating new solutions

Solution Evaluation
- Failing to devote adequate attention to all solution consequences
- Presenting biased judgments to favor pet solution
- Attacking group members to deflect attention from solutions
- Making quick choices before evaluating adequately

Solution Choice
- Confusing silence with agreement and consensus
- Considering minority views minimally if at all
- Putting individual self-interest before the generation of a high quality decision
- Focusing all attention on the first solution presented, which tends to be adopted

SOURCE: Adapted from K. N. Wexley and G. A. Yukl, 1977. *Organizational Behavior and Personnel Psychology,* Homewood, Ill.: Richard D. Irwin, pp. 132–135.

trying to avoid differences of opinion. By using steps 1 and 5, the group avoids the pitfalls of poor problem diagnosis by deliberately developing a full analysis of the problem.

Solution generation can be improved by following recommendation 3. The process loss in solution generation is caused by haste in moving through the group decision-making procedure. Haste is responsible for low objectivity and a tendency to adopt the first solution rather than the best solution. This process loss is increased when individuals change their minds without first requesting an objective reason for doing so. The group decision can be improved if members "stick to their guns" and require the advocate of an alternative solution to present a strong factual argument for her position.

Solution evaluation can be improved in interacting groups if members use steps 1 and 2. The major problems in solution evaluation are haste and personal bias. Avoidance of arguing for one's own biases keeps the evaluation of solutions more open. Do *not* assume that someone in the group must win and that someone else must lose. The win-lose mentality ruins collaboration and trust, and can cause formation within the group of subgroups and factions, which promote pet solutions at the expense of wider discussion and analysis.

Solution choice is improved when group members observe recommendation 4. If any conflict exists, members tend to revert to middle-of-the-road decision-making processes. They may use bargaining, voting, or coin flips as a way to reach agreement. These methods may smooth conflict, but they leave many questions unanswered and increase the chances that self-interest will prevail over group-interest because votes often are cast along the lines of group factions. (**Group factions** are defined as the personal views of subgroup leaders rather than the views of the wider group.)

Making the interacting group effective through brainstorming. **Brainstorming** is a method of interacting group decision making that lessens the group's tendency to be too critical of new ideas; it is a process that clearly separates the generation of ideas from the evaluation of ideas. The objective of brainstorming is to generate as many ideas as possible while delaying the evaluation of those ideas until a later phase of the group decision-making process. The reason for separating these two activities, generating and evaluating, is to prevent unproductive thinking in the group, which might cause ideas to become simply routine and unimaginative. The following guidelines apply to members of a brainstorming group:

1. Always try to say exactly what is on your mind.
2. Be as nonjudgmental as possible when people suggest ideas. (Avoid high pitched laughter and muffled groans!)
3. Do not worry about idea quality, but try simply to generate as many ideas as possible.
4. Try to build your ideas on the suggestions of other group members.
5. Be enthusiastic and innovative in your thinking. Encourage far-out ideas.
6. Worry about idea quality only after many ideas have been generated.

Brainstorming does not eliminate all of the process losses that can occur in interacting groups. Problems with dominant members, member boredom, and falling into the bad habit of rehashing old, tired ideas are not completely eliminated by brainstorming. Brainstorming does, however, tend to get the group back on the creative track.

Alternative approaches to brainstorming. We focus next on two alternative approaches: the nominal group technique and the Delphi technique. Both approaches rely on rigid procedures that are designed to minimize process losses.

The Nominal Group Technique to Improve Group Decision Making

Because of interacting group process losses, the manager may have to choose an alternative way to arrive at group solutions. Transforming an interacting group into a nominal group is fairly easy. The **nominal group** is a special group arrangement that follows a set procedure for decision making. This is a highly objective process aimed at reaching creative group decisions. Participants in a nominal group know each other and meet in a face-to-face situation. Nominal groups improve idea building among members (hitchhiking; see Table 9.3). They also cause members to search for ideas longer (proactive search). Other characteristics of nominal groups are shown in column two of Table 9.3, which presents the dimensions of nominal groups.

The interaction of nominal group members is carefully controlled by the following procedural steps:

1. Seven to ten participants convene around a table in view of one another.
2. After the problem for discussion is presented, members silently list their ideas on a pad of paper.
3. When 5 to 10 minutes have elapsed, the individual charged with recording group activities obtains one idea from each group member and writes each member's idea on a flip chart for everyone to see.
4. Step 3 is repeated until all ideas are written on the flip chart.
5. Each idea is discussed. Participants ask questions and indicate their degree of support or nonsupport for the various ideas.
6. Each participant records anonymously a rank ordering (from best to worst) of all of the recorded ideas.
7. The solution that emerges with the highest average ranking becomes the selection of the group (14).

Advantages of the nominal group technique (see Table 9.3). The procedure creates equality among members. Those individuals who are particularly outspoken or forceful are placed on an equal footing with individuals who are more retiring and shy (but who may nonetheless have excellent ideas). The nominal group technique is, however, a public process, so all members can see how high status individuals in the group respond to the various ideas discussed (step 5).

The nominal group technique is an effective group decision making approach, especially when it is used for fact finding and generation of ideas (15). To the extent that interacting groups do *not* inhibit members in the generation of ideas, the advantages of the nominal group technique begin to subside (16). The nominal group technique does minimize the process loss of groupthink by reducing effects of the leadership role. The strong tendency for concurrence that exists in groupthink situations is avoided by the nominal group technique. Steps 2, 3, and 6 are designed specifically to prevent premature concurrence in group decision making.

The nominal group technique leads to more objective decisions than do interacting group methods. The nominal group technique is problem-centered rather than person-centered. For this reason, nominal groups do not have to go through the stages of group development to become an effective problem-solving unit. Although the approach has many rules and steps, it may still be more efficient than creating a group that must inevitably go through the stages of development. (Critics of the technique claim that it is time consuming and artificial.) The technique takes a group of individuals and quickly manages them to generate ideas while avoiding the process losses associated with the first three stages of interacting group development.

In summary, nominal groups can often outperform interacting groups in creative idea generation, and they need not take more time or consume more resources. Indeed, nominal groups that brainstorm may get on with the job of group decision making fast because they focus more on the problem at hand than on the personalities of group members. For groups that are composed of uninvolved and unmotivated members, the nominal group technique and brainstorming are powerful ways to inject new life into the group. A new sense of group identity can lead to increased participation and more active member involvement. These two procedures, the nominal group technique and brainstorming, can be used to improve lazy and unproductive interacting groups!

The Delphi Technique for Group Decision Making

The Delphi technique attempts to circumvent process losses. This technique was specially formulated for decision making when group members are physically dispersed. It relies on separation to eliminate the process loss problems outlined in Table 9.4. The **Delphi technique** consists of five steps:

1. Each group member independently and anonymously records comments, suggestions, and solutions to the problem facing the group.
2. All the data generated by step 1 are sent to a centrally located individual who is responsible for data compilation and reproduction.
3. Each member receives a copy of all written comments of other members.
4. Members generate feedback on other member comments, and all second-round feedback is written down and sent to the centrally located individual.
5. Steps 3 and 4 are repeated as many times as are necessary to reach consensus (17).

Are Delphi groups effective?

Some evidence indicates that Delphi groups can be more effective than interacting groups. It was found that average performance was higher for Delphi groups than for interacting groups when both groups worked on a comparable problem-solving task (18). Delphi groups eliminate the effects that personality and individual status have on group decision making and this may make them more effective. The Delphi group technique has great promise as a structured method for decision making (19).

Delphi groups differ from nominal groups in the following ways:

1. Delphi participants are unaware of who other group members are, but nominal group members are acquainted with each other.
2. Delphi members never meet; nominal group members meet face-to-face around a table.
3. The decision-making procedure in a Delphi group relies on a central processing mechanism or on a centrally located individual who collates member contributions. In the nominal group, member communication is always direct, although sometimes anonymous.

A final word about interacting groups. In studies on group decision making, interacting groups often outperform nominal and Delphi groups. When group performance is dependent on having a knowledgable expert in the group, interacting groups prove to be the most successful (20). The knowledgable expert can more easily dominate the decision-making process in the interacting group. In other words, messy and undisciplined interacting groups can beat their more organized competition under certain conditions.

The preceding sections provide a foundation for understanding participation in group decision making. We next consider the managerial implications of group decision making in organizations.

Practical Guidelines for Managing Groups

Managers must be concerned with two general categories of group activities: task activities and maintenance activities. **Task activities** are defined as those activities that cause members to contribute directly to the group's purpose. When group members exert effort to define a problem and accomplish a group goal, then task activities are occurring. **Maintenance activities** are defined as functions that nurture and sustain the emotional qualities of the group. When members deal with such issues as group member satisfaction and well-being, then maintenance activities are occurring. Table 9.5 lists the various aspects of task activities and maintenance activities in relation to the group decision-making process.

Effective groups show flexibility in maintenance and task activities. Stage 4 groups have members who willingly address both task and maintenance activities. If a group is in an earlier stage of development, the burden of managing these activities generally falls on the group leader. The fully functioning stage 4 group may have less need for leadership because members willingly perform task and maintenance activities themselves.

A group must be able to vary the emphasis on task and maintenance activities relative to its stage of development (Figure 9.3). The volunteer fire department in a small town must devote effort to maintenance activities

Table 9.5
Task Activities and Maintenance Activities in Group Decision Making

Task Activities	*Maintenance Activities*
Getting the group started by introducing ideas, diagnosing the problem, and creating dissatisfaction with the status quo.	**Nurturing good emotional climate** by encouraging agreement and praising group members.
Requesting objective information to ensure accuracy and proper attention to detail.	**Setting norms for task activities and effort** to ensure common expectations regarding importance of achieving group goals.
Providing timely information about the task and group goals to ensure that logical milestones are set.	**Going along with participant-generated ideas** to ensure continued involvement in group processes and commitment to group goals.
Spelling out relationships between ideas so the broader picture is not lost.	**Resolving interpersonal conflict among group members** to lower process losses.
Summing up group progress on ideas, activities, goals, and implications for solutions.	**Linking the group to the organization** to ensure that group action is always consistent with organization goals.
Coordinating member activities to ensure steady progress toward group goals.	**Managing levels of status among group members** to ensure continued participation and involvement.
Reporting to higher organizational levels regarding group progress toward solutions.	**Assessing periodically the quality of group processes** to ensure effective decision making.

Figure 9.3
Stages of Group Development and Emphasis on Task and Maintenance Activities

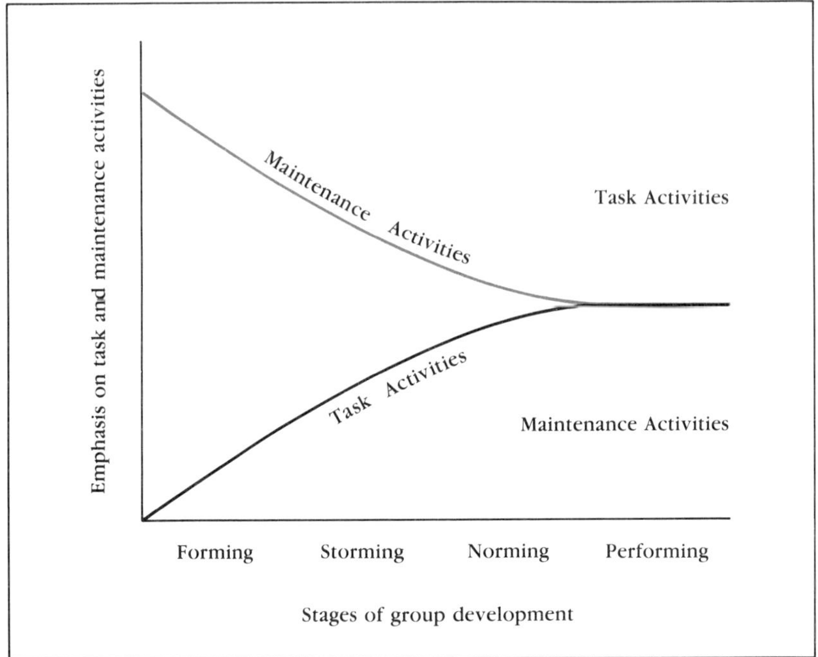

to keep its members interested in the organization. Although the volunteers may be highly trained fire fighters, they must feel cohesive and involved enough in departmental activities to maintain their membership. Social organizations such as fraternities and sororities confront the same problems in balancing task and maintenance activities. Issues related to member satisfaction are just as important as the organization goals.

The skills required to manage both task and maintenance activities in groups can be learned. You already have considerable personal experience with groups, and you have the knowledge gained from Chapter 8 and this chapter. For example, being able to identify the relevant stage of group development helps a manager to judge how much emphasis to place on task versus maintenance activities (see Figure 9.3). Similarly, recognition of a group process loss such as groupthink signals the need for refined task activities like brainstorming or the nominal group technique. The key to successful group management is the realization that you can influence group processes and that you do not have to be buffeted about by unpleasant experiences with groups!

NOW IT'S YOUR TURN . . .

Place a T (for task activity) or an M (for maintenance activity) in the space next to each statement about the marketing team in the introductory dilemma.

Team Activity	Classification
1. Andy writes the analysis of survey results.	________
2. Andy calls team members and sets up meetings to work on the marketing project.	________

3. Team members agree to leave Dave's name off of the group report. ________

4. Dave complains about being more a part of his basketball team than of the marketing team. ________

5. Ruth resigns as team leader because of personal problems. ________

6. Andy complains to Professor Murphy about Dave's poor attendance at team meetings. ________

Answers:

1 T, 2 T, 3 M, 4 M, 5 M, 6 T

Solving the Dilemma

What techniques could Professor Murphy have used to improve decision making within Andy's project team?

Professor Murphy could have applied the nominal group technique to Andy's team to generate a usable list of ideas for accomplishing the group task goals. After leading the group through the nominal technique, he should have explained the importance of task and maintenance activities. After the group understood these two key features, Murphy should then have placed the team on a reporting schedule that required a systematic analysis of group progress. To make reporting effective, Murphy could have required the attendance of group members at the reporting sessions. This agenda creates more work for Murphy, but it would help ensure a good group experience for his students and the generation of higher quality product ideas.

Knowledge Check

1. Interactive groups are those which are the least likely to experience process losses. T or F?
2. Interacting groups are always less efficient in their use of time than other forms of group decision making. T or F?
3. Generally conflict reducing techniques such as majority vote and bargaining are good ways to help an interacting group become more effective. T or F?
4. The nominal group technique is applied to existing interactive groups in organizations. T or F?
5. Nominal groups are always superior to interactive groups in terms of creativity of ideas. T or F?
6. Stage 4 groups have less need for flexibility in task and maintenance activities than groups at earlier stages of development. T or F?

Answers:
1 F, 2 F, 3 F, 4 T, 5 F, 6 F

Groups in Competition and Conflict

Competition and conflict among groups are so pervasive in organizations that no discussion of group behavior would be complete without considering both. In this section we also discuss some effective methods for managing competition and conflict in groups. Let's begin with an example:

Members of the university accounting department were meeting to discuss the addition of a new course to the curriculum. It would require students to work with accounting personnel in small businesses to develop better money control procedures. Many students had expressed an interest in such a course, so the accounting group decided that the time was right to include it in the course offerings.

Members of the finance faculty did not, however, share the accounting group's enthusiasm. The head of finance approached the dean of the business school and requested that the new accounting course be removed from the catalog listing. He said that the finance department had been teaching a course for the past four years that did exactly what the proposed accounting course would do.

The conflict escalated when the dean learned that several finance professors were counseling students to avoid the new accounting course because "it was poorly developed and a rehash of finance."

The dean was puzzled by the open warfare between the two departments. Students were complaining about the behavior of professors in both areas. Conscientious students, who had expressed interest in both courses, were caught in the middle. The dean did not know what to do.

Two Organizational Views of Conflict Between Groups

The dean in the example above probably adheres to the view that conflict is dysfunctional for the organization. This is the traditional view, which sees conflict as unhealthy for the organization because it disrupts organizational processes and goals and upsets existing employee satisfaction. In the example, these three outcomes are certainly occurring. The dean would have difficulty getting the two departments to cooperate on other matters of concern to the school. The accounting and finance faculties are not likely to share important information. In short, the list of negative consequences could be very long indeed.

The traditional view encourages suppression of conflict. In other words, the organization must develop systems that keep conflict under tight control. Job descriptions and defined areas of responsibility prevent disputes between individuals. Similarly, the authority hierarchy is designed to eliminate conflict between subordinate groups and individuals. This view holds that the manager should develop personal skills to prevent conflict between groups (21). Most management performance appraisal forms have an item that rates the manager's effectiveness at preserving group harmony. In the traditional view, managers must therefore learn to influence conflict and competition between groups (22).

The traditional view preserves the old way of doing things. It encourages an organizational norm that requires tranquility in group relations. Deviation from this norm leads to the application of more control by the organization. To make conflict disappear, offenders are transferred or fired. This view implies that conflict is untidy and not in the best interests of either the organization or its employees. It is to be avoided at all costs because careers are on the line if too much conflict surfaces!

The contemporary view takes the position that conflict has two sides. This view recognizes the negative consequences of conflict as real and significant, but asserts that the effects of avoiding all conflict can be even more costly to the organization. According to the contemporary view, if no conflict exists, the manager should be suspicious that work groups are becoming complacent and that problems are impending! No conflict means that organizational issues (i.e., goals, activities, policies) are not being sufficiently re-examined.

When the organization does not recognize conflict, danger exists. This view implies that conflict is an inevitable aspect of organizational life and that attempts to design conflict-free organizations are foolish and wasteful. A proponent of the contemporary view would recommend that the dean in our example jump right in, confront the conflict, and try to find an appropriate solution. He must first find the cause of the conflict, establish rules that facilitate constructive (versus destructive) conflict, and resolve the conflict to minimize hostility and to achieve the school goals.

Methods for Addressing Conflict Between Organizational Groups

Conflict management strategies are of four types: (1) avoidance, (2) defusion, (3) containment, and (4) confrontation (23). Each category has several strategies, so we start by describing the category and then outlining the features of each strategy.

Conflict avoidance refers to preventing the conflict from coming into the open. (In the conflict episode described, the dean has no choice; he cannot avoid the conflict because it is in the open and disrupting school processes.) Two strategies surface if conflict avoidance is followed. A manager can choose to **ignore the conflict.** This "do nothing" strategy means that the managing individual simply refuses to deal with any information or behavior associated with conflict between groups. More often than not when this strategy is used, the conflict gets worse. (The dean's continued inattention to departmental conflict will cause the conflict to escalate further.) Yet avoiding conflict is not always as short-sighted a strategy as it might at first seem. For example, if the conflict is extremely trivial, then it makes sense to ignore it. Ignoring conflict over one issue may be necessary to resolve a related conflict effectively. This means that one source of intergroup conflict may be an indicator of a deeper, more important source of conflict. (The accounting and finance faculties might also dispute the way in which student assistants are assigned to their department. This conflict, although not trivial, would most likely be a symptom of the larger conflict over the courses.)

Imposing a solution on conflicting groups is a second avoidance strategy. This strategy works through its "appeal to the organizational hierarchy." The conflict rises to an authority level with sufficient power to resolve the conflict. When a manager states what the conflict solution is to be "and that's that," he is using the legitimate authority of his position to resolve conflict. In the example, the dean could tell the accounting group to remove its course from the curriculum, thus imposing a solution. In short order the course probably would disappear, but the conflict would deepen and resurface later with even more symptoms than before!

When to impose a solution. If time is critical or if the decision maker believes that the two fighting groups will never be able to cooperate, then imposing a solution can be a functional response. Time is generally required for authority-imposed solutions to be accepted. Indeed, a complete change in the composition of the competing groups may have to occur before the imposed solution is accepted.

Conflict defusion strategies attempt to contain the conflict at a certain level while cooling down the emotions of hostile group members (24). A common defusion technique is **smoothing.** A manager who plays down the significance of a conflict and suggests that the hostile groups are really closer to agreement than they realize is practicing this technique. If the dean followed this strategy he would:

1. Circulate among the faculty and say that it's easy to lose perspective on the school's mission.
2. Go to students and calm their concerns about course issues.
3. Approach the department heads separately and say that problems can be worked out after everyone calms down.
4. Tell the department heads that keeping the conflict under control and not damaging the school's reputation are extremely important concerns.

Usefulness of smoothing. This strategy helps dampen the tendency for conflict to be blown out of proportion. It soothes hurt feelings and encourages a return to rationality. You have probably been unhappy with a test grade at one time or another, but experience tells you to "cool off" for a while before asking your professor why you received that grade. Delaying confrontation can lower the intensity of conflict and prevent the situation from deteriorating further. Smoothing at the group level works the same way.

Inserting superordinate goals is a second defusion technique that can deflect warring groups from the immediate conflict. A **superordinate goal** is defined as a goal that neither group can accomplish without the help of the other. For example, the dean might say to the two department faculties that the school's image among potential students is being badly damaged, which has caused enrollment to decline by 10 percent. Correcting the enrollment deficit becomes a superordinate goal that both departments can work to solve. A superordinate goal creates mutual dependence between the conflicted groups. Neglecting the superordinate goal means that both groups go down in flames! Not surprisingly, the most common superordinate goal is the shared fate associated with organizational survival. Falling school enrollment is an example of such a superordinate goal.

Conflict containment is another strategy, which tightly controls the conflict issues that are allowed to surface and controls how those issues are addressed. **Bargaining** is a good example of containment. It is defined as a process of extracting concessions until a compromise is obtained. A negotiator or a neutral third party tries to extract concessions from each group until an agreement is reached (25). Bargaining may be a good strategy for the accounting and finance departments because they are approximately equal in status and power. A compromise might be to team-teach the course under dispute. In addition, the two departments could work out a cosponsored student advisory program for the course. Bargaining works best when the conflicting parties have equal power and when several possible solutions exist. The dean could occupy the negotiator role and work out the details of the compromise solution.

Organizing and structuring the interaction between conflicting groups is another containment strategy. This approach requires that the number of conflict issues be limited and that rules be established for handling those issues. The conflicting groups are taught some rules about "how to fight fair." In the example, the dean might require the departmental faculties to:

1. Refrain from making comments to students about the conflict.
2. Elect three representatives to analyze their department's major grievances.
3. Hold a series of closely managed meetings with the representatives from each faculty to discuss the features of each department's grievances.
4. Set up a meeting with the dean and the two department heads to review the information generated by steps 1, 2, and 3.

This approach controls the conflict and keeps it from getting further out of hand. The steps show that conflict can be handled in an orderly process. Organizing and structuring conflict is another name for the seeking of diplomatic solutions. The diplomacy process is one that all parties recognize as "a fair way to disagree."

Conflict confrontation is the last strategy category. It relies on getting all of the issues out in the open and on the conflicted parties' desire to seek a mutual solution through trust and understanding. The most important method of confrontation is called **problem solving,** and is defined as the integration of the needs of both groups by finding a mutually satisfactory conflict solution. Its steps are summarized as follows:

1. Define the problem by using "shared fact finding" (instead of the biased perceptions of one group or the other).
2. State the problem in specific versus vague terms.
3. In the beginning, elicit facts about the disagreement, and focus on the facts versus the disagreement.
4. Conduct nonjudgmental discussions of the problem (avoid attacking the other group).
5. Collaborate on alternatives that could generate the best mutual solution, *not* on the alternatives that serve the interests of one group.
6. Develop criteria for evaluating the quality and acceptability of the proposed solutions for the different groups. Solutions must be appraised for equity.

7. Make agreements tentative until all facets of the conflict have been addressed. No implementation of solutions should occur until the entire plan has been worked out and both groups have a stake in the outcome (26).

Problem solving is a powerful method for attacking the causes of conflict. The effect of successful problem solving in the school dilemma would be improved relations between the departments. This strategy would help professors from both areas to develop common expectations about their roles in maintaining good departmental relations. The faculties also would acquire an understanding of the constraints and problems faced by the faculty in the other department. The solutions arrived at through problem solving tend to last longer and to have wider benefits for the organization.

Benefits of problem solving. The most important long-term benefit is not the solution of the immediate problem. It is, rather, the formation of a belief that conflict can be healthy and that it is often a starting point for finding better ways to function. Problem solving leads to improvement in the work environment of the organization. Employees come to believe in the capacity of the organization to find constructive solutions that balance individual, group, and organizational needs. It is not coincidence that problem solving requires huge doses of participation. Indeed, it may be the most laborious of the methods of handling conflict, but it pays the biggest dividends. Employees learn that they can address internal organizational problems constructively and intelligently.

Solving the Dilemma

Is there a method for Murphy to use to manage the conflict in Andy's project group?

Although the problem in Andy's group exists on an interpersonal level (no between-group competition or conflict exists), the rules for problem solving apply quite nicely. Professor Murphy could take the time to move Andy's team through the steps in the problem solving strategy. Before doing this, Murphy would have to make two determinations: (1) Is there enough residual trust among group members to enable the process to work, and (2) is there enough time left in the semester to make the hard work of problem solving worthwhile.

Knowledge Check

1. The contemporary view holds that conflict has mostly positive outcomes for the organization and its participants. T or F?
2. Conflict avoidance requires that only certain aspects of the conflict are addressed at a given time. T or F?
3. Imposing a solution on groups in conflict can be effective, especially under severe time constraints. T or F?
4. Problem solving is the least time efficient method for handling conflict, but it may in the long run be the best method for the organization. T or F?

5. Organizing and structuring the interaction between conflicting groups depends on a minimal level of trust between the groups. T or F?

Answers:

1 F, 2 F, 3 T, 4 T, 5 F

Summary Points

- **Group development** proceeds through four stages: (1) **testing and orientation (forming)**, (2) **conflict and organization (storming)**, (3) **cohesion and information exchange (norming)**, and (4) **interdependence and problem solving (performing).**
- Groups are considered to be **immature** when they are **not capable of recognizing and correcting process losses.** This most commonly occurs in groups that have not reached stage 4.
- **Interacting groups generally suppress creativity in the idea generation phase.** They can be highly effective, however in the **idea evaluation phase.** The use of **brainstorming** in interacting groups can make them more effective in the idea-generation phase.
- The **risky shift phenomenon** recognizes the importance of the **group norm about risk taking.** Groups are not necessarily more or less inclined to take risks than are individuals making decisions alone.
- Among interacting groups, process losses generally occur in four areas: (1) **problem diagnosis,** (2) **solution generation,** (3) **solution evaluation,** and (4) **solution choice.**
- The **nominal group technique** and the **Delphi technique** are designed to address process losses in the four areas noted.
- The effective group leader can judge when **task or maintenance activities** are of greatest concern to the group. The skills that facilitate effective group management in these two areas can be learned.
- Depending on the organization's orientation to conflict, it will generally favor one of these four strategies for handling conflict (1) **avoidance,** (2) **defusion,** (3) **containment, or** (4) **confrontation.**
- **Avoidance and defusion** generally result in conflict solutions that are fragile and do not address the underlying causes of conflict.
- **Containment and confrontation** result in solutions that address the causes, and these solutions tend to be more durable. In addition, these approaches tend to build the belief that conflict can have positive consequences for the organization and for individual employees.

Questions

1. Develop your reasoning as to how brainstorming might be used to help move a group through the four stages of development. Do you think it is possible to use a "method" to facilitate group development?
2. Using your knowledge of individual differences (Chapters 2 and 3), develop an explanation for the conflict that existed in Andy's marketing team. Was Professor Murphy effective in the way he formed his groups? What recommendations would you make to him?
3. Why is problem solving a superior method for handling conflict (as compared with avoidance or defusion strategies)? What are the benefits of problem solving for the individual and for the organization?
4. Suppose that you are an expert on group decision making. Your boss is concerned because several quality circles in the plant are not at present very effective (i.e., they are not producing many innova-

tive ideas, and several suggestions as to how they might improve their performance have not been implemented by the groups). Develop a strategy to make these groups more effective.

5. Professional sport players unions often present franchise owners with demands that are seen by the owners (and the fans) as unreasonable. Why do you suppose that these conflicts are most often worked out through bargaining methods versus other forms of conflict resolution?

6. Why will a student team not be effective if it concentrates on maintenance activities only? Be sure to answer this question in terms of group development, types of process losses, and methods for resolving conflict. Lastly, apply this reasoning to the interactions of a social group that you belong to.

Exploring: *Where Teamwork Is More Than Talk*

Based on *Business Week* (16 May 1983). A Plant Where Teamwork is More than Just Talk, p. 48.

Inside the Cadillac engine plant, work life is very different from conditions in the typical automotive factory. Hourly workers and supervisors dress in the same way and cooperate closely in "business teams." The teams organize the work and make decisions usually left to management. General Motors has nine plants that use the "pay-for-knowledge" concept to make factory work less boring and more productive. The approach seems radical when compared with the practices in most union shops where workers perform specialized and narrow functions. At the Cadillac engine plant, production workers can learn all of the jobs in their section, which gives management flexibility in assigning work and filling in for absent employees. Workers are paid according to the skills they acquire, so employees have an incentive to learn new skills. The plant uses less manpower than similar plants, and the scrap rate has fallen by 50 percent. In 1982, worker suggestions saved the plant more than $1.2 million.

The plant produces 1,200 engines each day and is divided into 15 departments, which are in turn subdivided into business teams of 10 to 20 employees. The business teams consist of production workers who assemble the engines and perform unskilled maintenance duties. These teams meet weekly on company time to consider such issues as safety, housekeeping, raises, job rotations, and suggestions for redesigning work flow.

Members of a typical business team rotate among 12 to 13 jobs on the assembly line. The plant has been able to streamline wage levels for experienced workers. The range is $9.63 to $10.08 per hour for a "job setter"—a worker who sets up and changes tooling on the assembly line. A worker reaches the top rate after he has learned all of the skills in the business team.

"In the traditional plant, you might have 90–100 job setters," says Peter Ulbrich. "Here, you have the opportunity for 1,200 to 1,300 people to get there." This system can produce an expensive work force. "It is a neat way to get short-term productivity results," says one teamwork expert, "but you wonder what they will do when everyone reaches the top rate."

Discussion Questions

1. How does this case illustrate the relationship between group performance and job enrichment?
2. Do you think that all of the employees will be motivated to become tool setters for their business team?
3. What suggestions would you make to a business team that wanted to improve the quality of its evaluation of productivity improvement suggestions?

Applying: *Assessing Group Creativity*

After you read this case, which describes the group decision making undertaken by a manufacturer of children's toys, we have an interesting group assignment for you to do. The project requires your team to identify the features of a creative group.

The Exector Company is a medium-sized firm that makes and sells children's toys. Exector has been a major force in the industry for years. Jack Kabot, the company president, believes that the company's only problem is development of new products. Over the last ten years, the market for the firm's products has become more competitive as a result of declining birth rates and increased competition from firms that manufacture small household appliances who are branching out to children's toys.

Kabot was particularly interested in new product development because he started in that area of the firm. He believed that the company should create a new product development group. After much thought, he decided to form a group of eight people with diverse and unorthodox backgrounds to work full time on product development. A chart showing the backgrounds of the new team members follows:

The Product Development Group at Exector

Name	Age	Degree	Background
John Randell	28	Math	Worked for a consulting firm in marketing
Phil Cones	29	History	Worked for a consumer products safety commission
Sally Reider	29	Art history	Assistant curator of a small city museum
Bob Licter	28	No degree	Worked as a product designer for navigation instruments
Sue Schmitt	27	English	Worked as a paralegal in a large law firm
Lynn Thompson	27	Chemistry	Worked for a small firm that specialized in new adhesives
Rob Mills	29	No degree	Owned a firm that made musical instruments

Kabot wanted one group member to report to him, but decided to avoid any further structuring of the group. John Randell was appointed head of the group. When they started work, they did not know each other, nor did they know what they would be doing on a day-to-day basis. Given the differences in their background and training, they all had very different interests. For example, Cones was interested in consumer safety issues and was comfortable with systems analysis. Reider had never worked in a business environment before. Licter had a keen interest in finding new ways to do things, so he tended to approach a procedure by looking first at other ways in which it might be done. The group members even had diverse tastes in work dress—from coat and tie to tee shirt and jeans. Schmitt had worked in a law firm before coming to Exector so she was used to wearing formal business attire. Thompson had taken the Exector job in part because she perceived the environment as informal. She did not want to dress up.

Kabot made it clear to the new product development team that they had a lot of freedom. His only requirement was the biweekly progress report to him, and their only stated goal was to develop ideas for durable and inexpensive children's toys.

The group spent the next few weeks familiarizing themselves with the company. Kabot came to their area once a week, and often brought new information that he believed would be useful to them.

The group divided themselves into functional areas on the basis of interests, training, and expertise. Schmitt took responsibility for coordinating cash flow projections. Reider used her artistic ability to translate ideas into three-dimensional models. Cones provided data synthesis, and Licter became the "conflict resolver" when the group hit snags. Thompson became a coleader because of her general business background and her ability to communicate with the staff in engineering.

The group quickly developed routines at work. Group members began to bring their lunch and to eat around a large table in their work area. Over lunch breaks and coffee they brainstormed. Anyone could start the process. Nobody came to work at the same time (indeed, they came and went as they pleased), but everyone tended to show up on weekends and when an important test was scheduled to be run.

Mills became a source of tension for the group because he preferred to work alone. He seldom joined in when the others wanted to brainstorm. He said that it was more important that he finish his work rather than join in. After a while he had missed so many sessions that he started to get kidded about his "antisocial tendencies." This had no effect, so the other members began to exclude him from their conversations. Eventually the group discussed the importance of regular meeting attendance and decided that attendance should not be mandatory. Everyone then agreed to include Mills, but he still preferred to remain on the edge of the group.

After the product development group had been in existence for six months, Kabot realized that the group had developed a variety of innovative and unique product ideas. Furthermore, group members were enthusiastic about their work. By year-end the group came out with a new product, and within six months, the product had won a 20 percent market share. The product was widely acclaimed by consumers for its durability, safety, and reasonable price. One Friday the group met away from the office to celebrate their success. No one returned to work that afternoon.

Instructions: Working in teams, use the preceding description of the new product development group to answer the following questions:

Discussion Questions

1. What are the primary features of the group's structure? How did Kabot facilitate the development of the group's structure?
2. What key roles emerged in the new product development group? How did each of these roles contribute to the group's creative abilities?
3. How did the group composition foster creativity? Do you agree with Kabot's rationale for selecting team members?
4. Isolate and describe three group processes that facilitated creativity.
5. Does your team perceive the new product development group as having a particular style that contributed to creative success?

Suggested Readings

Archer, E. 1980. How to Make a Business Decision: An Analysis of Theory and Practice. *Management Review* (1980); 56–61.

Feldman, D. 1984. The Development and Enforcement of Group Norms. *Academy of Management Review* 9:47–53.

Ford, D., Jr., and Nemiroff, P. 1975. Applied Group Problem Solving: The Nominal Group Technique. In Pfeffer, J. W. and Jones, J. (Eds.) *The 1975 Handbook for Group Facilitators.* LaJolla, Calif.: University Associates Publishers, pp. 179–182.

This practical guide provides a method for using the nominal group technique to make group decisions. Instructions are easy to follow, and the guidelines should prove helpful in making group decisions involving idea generation.

Herold, D. 1979. The Effectiveness of Work Groups. In Kerr, S. (Ed.) *Organizational Behavior.* Columbus, Ohio: Grid Publishing.

Hill, G. 1982. Group Versus Individual Performance: Are N + 1 Heads Better than One? *Psychological Bulletin* 91:517–539.

Maier, N. 1967. Assets and Liabilities in Group Problem Solving. *Psychological Review* 74:239–249.

Maier, N. 1970. *Problem Solving and Creativity in Individuals and Groups.* Belmont, Calif.: Brooks Cole.

This interesting book does an excellent job of comparing the features of individual and group decision making. The author also deals with individual and group creativity and offers many practical ideas for more effective management of groups.

Tersine, R., and Riggs, W. 1976. The Delphi Technique: A Long Range Planning Tool. *Business Horizons* 17:51–56.

Van De Ven, A. 1974. *Group Decision Making and Effectiveness.* Kent, Ohio: Kent State University Press.

This book deals with a number of important issues concerning group effectiveness. It is readable and contains many excellent suggestions for effective managing of group behavior and group decision making.

References

1. Shaw, M. 1981. *Group Dynamics,* 2nd ed. New York: McGraw-Hill.
2. Tuckman, B. 1965. Developmental Sequence in Small Groups. *Psychological Bulletin* 63:384–399.
3. Shaw, M., op. cit.
4. Borchard, T. 1971. What Ever Happened to Brainstorming? *Journal of Creative Behavior* 5:182–189.
5. Van De Ven, A., and Delbecq, A. 1979. The Effectiveness of Nominal, Delphi, and Interaction Group Decision Making Processes. *Academy of Management Journal* 17:605–632.
6. Taylor, D., Berry, P., and Block, C. 1958. Does Group Participation in Brainstorming Facilitate or Inhibit Creative Thinking? *Administrative Science Quarterly* 3:23–47.
7. Brown, K. 1984. Explaining Poor Group Performance: An Attributional Analysis. *Academy of Management Review* 9:54–63.
8. Peters, T., and Waterman, R., Jr. 1982. *In Search of Excellence.* New York: Harper & Row.
9. Shaw, M., op. cit.
10. Stoner, T. 1961. *A Comparison of Individual and Group Decisions Involving Risk.* Massachusetts Institute of Technology, Cambridge, Mass.: Unpublished masters thesis.
11. Ibid.
12. Shaw, M., op. cit.
13. Hall, J. 1971. Decisions. *Psychology Today* (November 1971):63–69.
14. Van De Ven, A., and Delbecq, A., op. cit.
15. Ibid.
16. Feldman, D., and Arnold, H. 1983. *Managing Individual and Group Behavior in Organizations.* New York: McGraw-Hill.
17. Dalkey, H. 1969. The Delphi Method: An Experimental Study of Group Opinion. Rand Corporation Memorandum, RM 5888–PR, June 1969.
18. Steiner, I. 1972. *Group Process and Productivity.* New York: Academic Press.
19. Ibid.
20. Ibid.
21. Schockley-Zalabak, P. 1984. Current Conflict Management Training: An Examination of Practices in 10 Large Corporations. *Group and Organizational Studies* 9:491–508.
22. Rahim, M. 1983. A Measure of Styles of Handling Interpersonal Conflict. *Academy of Management Journal* 26:368–376.
23. Feldman, D., and Arnold, H., op. cit.
24. Ibid.
25. Blake, R., and Mouton, S. 1984. Overcoming Group Warfare. *Harvard Business Review* (November-December 1984):98–108.
26. Wexley, K., and Yukl, G. 1977. *Organizational Behavior and Personnel Psychology.* Homewood, Ill.: Irwin.

Sales
Chemistry
Computers

Communication in Organizations

Chapter 10

I. Dilemma: Ellery's Message Is Not Well Received
II. Key Concepts of Communication
  A. Communication variables
  B. How the communication process works
III. Creating Understanding
  A. Words in communication
  B. Using pictures
  C. Nonverbal communication
IV. Communication Barriers
  A. Three reasons for barriers
  B. Our individuality causes barriers
  C. Context makes a difference
  D. The communication climate
  E. How to avoid barriers
V. Formal Communication in Organizations
  A. Downward communication
  B. Subordinates communicate upward and horizontally
  C. Electronic communication: Does sanctioned communication occur only with people?
VI. Informal Communication
  A. Hints on gossip and rumors
  B. Managing your boss
VII. Summary Points
VIII. Questions
IX. Exploring: ABC Tries to Control Its Communication
X. Applying: Making a Public Presentation in Class
XI. Suggested Readings
XII. References

Chapter Goals

By the end of this chapter, you will be able to:

1. Define communication and identify the critical steps in the process of sending and receiving information.
2. Identify different channels for sending messages and make decisions about which channel is most effective for a given message.
3. Define communication barriers in a given situation and suggest steps to overcome those barriers.
4. Sense the effect of the verbal and nonverbal communication on your messages.
5. Analyze more effectively how communication works when it "flows" vertically and horizontally in an organization.
6. Use newfound communication skills to manage your manager.
7. Make more effective public presentations and more effectively communicate in organizational settings.

Dilemma Ellery's Message Is Not Well Received

Ellery was working at his first major job. He had wanted to start his career early and do well, so was happy when summer arrived and he could begin work at the machine shop. Although he had had a few short-term jobs during high school, graduation meant to Ellery that the time had come for him to "get serious" and get a "real job." He chose the machine shop position because he liked to make things with his hands, was fascinated with how the different machines worked, and liked the social atmosphere of working closely with a group. During his interviews at Gelding Steel, he liked everyone he met.

As Ellery's boss, Sandy was responsible for Ellery's orientation and for setting up his on-the-job training and daily work schedules. She knew more about the machine shop than anyone else. She could work every machine and was respected by all of the shop employees.

The workers joked with Sandy about her long blonde hair and her stories about her participation in the 60's anti-war protests. Sandy did not exactly fit the mold of a typical manufacturing supervisor, but she was generally perceived as being very effective in her work.

After two weeks in the shop, Ellery began to feel as if Sandy were out to get him. He noticed that she talked more with the other employees than with him and gave them what seemed to Ellery to be preferable work schedules. Ellery also noticed that Sandy spent more time socializing with the other employees than she did with him. One day when Ellery stayed after work to try to finish a particularly difficult machine part, he watched a group, joking and laughing, in the finishing room. He could feel his anger at the others and was also angry at himself for being bothered by such a small thing.

One Saturday, Sandy approached Ellery about some defects in the machine pieces that Ellery had made the day before. The following conversation ensued:

Sandy: Ellery, I need to talk to you about yesterday's work.

Ellery: OK, but I'm right in the middle of some . . .

Sandy: That's all right, let's talk first. I picked up some of the pieces you did yesterday and noticed that the sides were jagged.

Ellery: Yeah, I'm not real sure all the time how to cut the backs of the pieces.

Sandy: Well, you can always ask me. I'll help you.

Ellery: Oh, really? [*sarcastically*]

Sandy: Yeah, sure. I always thought you worked well by yourself and were a fast learner. If you had a problem, I thought you'd ask me.

Ellery: I've tried, but you're always busy.

Sandy: What do you mean *always* ?

Ellery: Every time I want to talk with you, you're over across the room talking to Mort or Alice.

Sandy: They're working on some complicated parts right now. We had a lot of problems at first, and there's been a high turnover in that group. I'm trying to build them up.

Ellery: Well, I'm new, and you don't check on me!

Sandy: I always thought you were in winning shape.

Ellery: Whinin'? You think I complain a lot? I never talk to you. Where did you get that idea? This is ...

Sandy: Wait a minute. I didn't mean that you complain a lot. "Winning" is just an ...

Ellery: A what? I suppose you're going to give me a low rating for this work and for always complaining.

Sandy: Ellery, calm down. You misunderstood me. Besides, the bottom line is simply to be careful about these pieces.

Ellery: What?

By this time, other workers were looking curiously in Sandy and Ellery's direction. Sandy was noticeably upset, and Ellery was still asking her heatedly what she meant by saying that he was "always complaining." Finally Sandy told Ellery to calm down or she would have to reprimand him officially. Ellery walked to the back of the shop and got a drink of water. He was sure that he was going to be fired, and he just couldn't understand why Sandy was being so critical.

Questions

1. Why did Ellery and Sandy get into an argument?
2. What barriers to effective communication are present between Sandy and Ellery?
3. How could Sandy and Ellery have avoided the harsh ending of their confrontation?
4. What can Sandy and Ellery do to keep this type of confrontation from happening again?

Key Concepts of Communication

Without doubt, each of us has attributed an interpersonal problem to failure to communicate. Indeed, we all nod our heads that communication problems exist, but few of us can really explain what we mean by communication or its failure. Let's begin by defining some basic concepts.

Communication Variables

Communication is the sending and receiving of **messages** from one person to another. It is the process by which people reach others with ideas, thoughts, feelings, values, and expressions. In essence, communication is the way that people link with each other to form an understanding that did not exist previously between them.

Communication demands a sender and a receiver. The communication process has several important characteristics. First, communication cannot occur without *both* parties. If the sender sends a message that no one receives, communication has not occurred. Consider the foreman who stands up in a meeting and makes several announcements to the workers present. No matter how often those workers and that foreman are together on a day-to-day basis, communication has not occurred until each message is actually received and understood by the employees. In other words, a communication message is what the receiver understands, which is *not* necessarily the same message that the sender thinks he conveyed.

Communication is exchanged in a variety of ways. A second important characteristic of communication is that messages can be exchanged in a variety of ways. They can be sent with words that carry meaning. They can be sent without words—through our bodies or the physical space that we set up. They can be sent through pictures that we see or create. These various communication **channels,** or ways of sending messages, are very important. In a given circumstance, one channel may be much more effective than another, and at times several channels may conflict. A picture *is* sometimes worth at least a thousand words! What happens, for example, when a person asks your opinion but continues to write while you are talking? Which channel do you "listen" to, the verbal or the nonverbal one? Consider how the channels conflict in the following account:

> A student goes to talk to his professor about an upcoming examination. The student stands erect, with arms folded and a frown on his face. He *says* how comfortable he is with the material and that he knows he is going to do well, but his body actions belie his words. As he speaks, his body becomes more rigid, and he begins to talk louder. The professor comments that the student seems anxious, at which point the student grits his teeth, says "I am not!" and stalks out of the professor's office. The student returns two hours later, apologizes sheepishly for his outburst, and confesses that he is in need of help.

Communication involves two people taking responsibility for the message. The effective sending and receiving of information is accomplished when both parties take responsibility for the information transfer. To say "It was his fault, he didn't communicate with me," is to miss the point about effective communication. Communication is a process involving two or more people who try to understand each other.

Why is communication important?

As social creatures, we rely on communication. Without it, we would not know how to interpret and react to our environments. Without communication, organizations could not tell the public what products are for sale or what the organization does, and members of the organization could not cooperate with each other to reach common goals.

From the employee's viewpoint, communication is vital to knowing what to do. Work-related communication occurs in many ways—written job descriptions, verbal directions, memos about specific tasks or schedule changes. Employees use communication to establish relationships with co-workers, to influence the organization to make their work more satisfying, and to respond to other workers' needs.

From the manager's viewpoint, all management goals must be passed on to other workers in such a way that information is received as the manager intended, and workers proceed as management expects. The best plans are worthless if they are not adequately communicated. Communication is also important for maintaining social contact with others. We like to explore different ideas, meet different people, and try to understand each other. We do all of this relationship building through communication. If communication is effective, employees are stimulated to be better performers and are more satisfied with their jobs. (1) One hotel employee stated it this way: "I like to accomplish things when I know what they [the managers] want. If the managers could be clear and let me ask questions more frequently, I could give them 110% of my effort, and we'd all be happy."

How the Communication Process Works

The statement "communication is a process" has many implications. By viewing communication as a process, we do not assume that the sender can sit back once the message is sent and watch the receiver get the message. Instead, for communication to occur, both sender and receiver must take an active part, make mutual adjustments and clarifications, and help each other understand the thought, idea, or feeling.

Before we explore the intricacies of communication, consider Figure 10.1, which diagrams the communication process. The simplest way to understand the process is to view the **sender** as transmitting a **message (#4)** to the **receiver,** who then responds with **feedback (#8)**. Many variables complicate the process, however, so let's use Figure 10.1 to expand our knowledge.

Figure 10.1
The Process of Communication

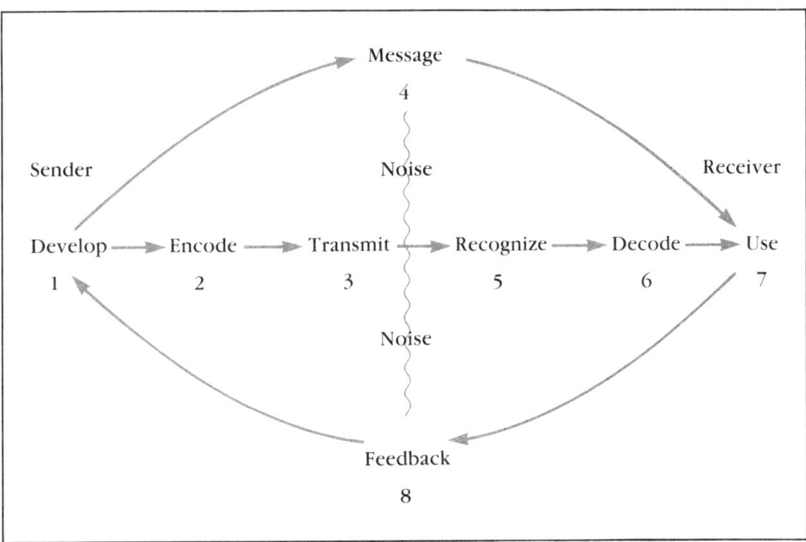

Start with a sender who conceives of a message, finds the best way to deliver it, and actually transmits it. The sender can be an individual, group, or organization.

The sender first thinks and develops ideas to send (#1). These ideas may be thoughts, feelings, or information that the person wants to share or "make common" with the receiver. This thinking and developing of ideas may occur quickly, or may take some time if we cannot find something to say!

The ideas must then be put in a format that can be understood by the receiver. This is called **encoding (#2)**, which involves taking ideas and translating them into language, actions, or pictures that will be meaningful to others. During this phase the sender may choose certain words or phrases to deliver an idea. Some frustration in communication occurs when we cannot find the "right" words to express our feelings. Who of us has not had an idea to communicate, yet we were frustrated because the right words just would not come!

Using various channels (#3), we transmit the message (#4). These channels involve the senses—primarily touch, sight, and sound. We send messages by talking to another person, by using body language, or by presenting symbols (i.e., words or pictures or both). Channel selection is very important, because the message may not mean much to the receiver if the sender uses an inappropriate channel.

The process is not over once the message is sent. The receiver is now responsible for recognizing the message (#5). This recognition often involves heightened attention and active reception of the information. After recognizing that the message is being sent, the receiver tries to internalize the message in his or her own manner. **Decoding (#6)** involves the receiver's unique interpretation as that individual tries to figure out what the sender "really means."

Once the message is decoded, the receiver then uses the information (#7) to obtain new knowledge, to try to understand the sender, and to establish relationships. An important aspect of the communication process is that the receiver then becomes the sender, who gives feedback (#8) to the original sender.

The communication process thus involves sending and receiving messages to make information common to two or more parties. The process may have to go many rounds before a given piece of information is truly shared by all parties concerned. A list of the basic criteria needed to ensure effective communication follows:

1. Each party to the communication has a desire to communicate.
2. The sender is aware of the receiver's interests and needs.
3. Information is transmitted using the proper channels and meanings.
4. The receiver senses a supportive climate.
5. The receiver is receptive to sender's information.
6. Each party tries to maintain the communication process.

Solving the Dilemma

Why did Ellery and Sandy get into an argument?

The primary reason for the communication breakdown was a lack of "process awareness." Ellery thought he heard the word "whinin'," without checking it out with Sandy. Sandy, who was not sensitive to Ellery's feelings, acted from her perspective without asking many questions. If both parties had asked more questions and had an awareness that communication is a process, they could have avoided what became a complicated and negative employee-supervisor interaction.

Creating Understanding

Communication always involves creating a common understanding or **meaning** because senders and receivers use the process to make an idea common to all parties. This "making meaning" is not as easy as we would like it to be. Since we generally represent an idea through language, we often leave ourselves open to misinterpretation by others or we are frustrated by not being able to find the right words. Consider Alice's frustrations in the following excerpt:

> "I don't know what you mean by 'glory,' " Alice said.
>
> Humpty Dumpty smiled contemptuously. "Of course you don't—till I tell you. I meant 'there's a nice knock-down argument for you!' "
>
> "But 'glory' doesn't mean a nice knock-down argument,' " Alice objected.
>
> "When I use a word," Humpty Dumpty said, in rather a scornful tone, "it means just what I choose it to mean—neither more nor less."
>
> "The question is," said Alice, "whether you can make words mean so many different things."
>
> "The question is," said Humpty Dumpty, "which is to be master—that's all" (2).

Words in Communication

Words are very difficult to use, so we often have trouble finding the right ones. Consider an example of why this symbol-using process is so difficult. The word "slip" has many meanings. If you ask the simple question, "Do you have a slip?" the receiver may be in a quandary. Do you mean a sailboat slip? A slip of paper? A slip of the tongue?

These multiple meanings are necessary in language because we use relatively few words to express an amazingly wide range of ideas. Meanings get even more complicated when we use such linguistic devices as metaphors or similes, or expressions that suggest a resemblance by means of an illustration.

Context is important. Fortunately, words and their combinations rarely occur in isolation. When these multiple meanings are possible, we try to get help from the **context** to clarify meaning. Indeed, the context in which the sender delivers a message has a great deal to do with the way others interpret that message. Using our example of "slip," if we are talking about boats with a person who sails, the reference becomes much clearer.

We also use words to indicate our relationship to others. For example, if we call a person by her first name, we are denoting a degree of intimacy. We might say that we know her on a "first name basis." If we call another individual by her title, "Doctor," we are saying that we recognize her professional degree and that the relationship is more formal, or that the context warrants formality, as in a professional meeting.

Using Pictures

Every organization uses pictures extensively in its day-to-day work. These could be maps, blueprints, pictures on the wall, drawings, models, or videos. Pictures are often an extremely effective way to send a message (Figure 10.2). One communication expert claims that most people do not use enough pictures or body language to communicate their messages (3). When making a presentation, for example, we tend to use too many words and not enough pictures to depict what we mean. In the following example, an illustration is used effectively to dramatize a point.

> A consultant from a marketing firm was trying to demonstrate to a client what a serious mistake the client was making by spending $300,000 for a marketing campaign that would not pay off. The consultant said, "Let me show you how I think it will come out. See this large circle? That's the market. This smaller circle inside is your market share. Now, this is how much your market share will grow after you spend the money." The

Figure 10.2
International symbols: Signs for the 1968 Olympic Games. (Reprinted with permission from *"The Visual Image,"* by E. H. Gombrich, *Scientific American*, September 1972, p. 86.)

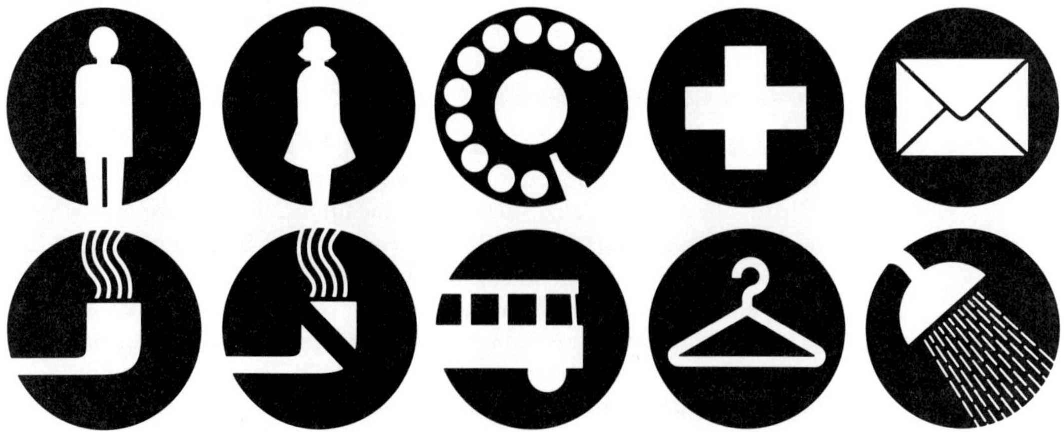

client said, "But it's the same size!" The consultant sat back and grinned. Her point was made—the intended message had been received.

Nonverbal Communication

Nonverbal communication is often a powerful and unconscious way of sending messages. It refers to the gestures, movements, signs, room arrangements, and so forth that we use to substitute for words. We all use nonverbal behavior to send our unique messages and to amplify our verbal messages, as when we use our hand to accentuate a point or move our body to denote emphasis.

Three unique messages sent nonverbally. More important than amplifying a message, we use nonverbal behavior to send unique messages to others. Albert Mehrabian studied this phenomenon and concluded that we tend to send three general types of information through nonverbal behavior.

1. Liking and disliking
2. Dominance and submissiveness
3. Degree of responsiveness to the other person (4)

To send a message such as liking, we make all sorts of gestures to let the other person know our intent. We turn toward the individual, smile at them, exhibit listening behaviors, and try to establish eye contact that is soft and "easy-going."

If we want to show dominance, we often exhibit a certain stiffness of body posture, remain somewhat formal during the exchange, and use our physical space to let the other person know that we "own that space." The character of an office space is an important nonverbal indication to employees of how they should act and the degree of responsiveness expected. Consider the following experience of a college professor who was considering taking a job in industry.

> The professor had an appointment to see the president of a large publishing company for a job interview. The office lobby was plush and expansive, so the candidate expected the president's secretary to come out of a nicely appointed doorway visible from the lobby. Instead, the secretary emerged from what appeared to be an exit door. As the professor followed her to the president's office, he noticed boxes on the floor and the lack of carpeting. When he reached the area outside the president's office, he had to walk around an array of desks. He finally reached the president's office, an extremely large room furnished expensively. During the interview, the president spoke in a gentle tone as he paced *behind* the candidate. At the end of the interview, the president offered the candidate a job, which the professor declined almost simultaneously.

From this example we see that managers can set up their office space to invite people in or to keep them away. The president certainly wanted his privacy! A manager and an employee are in a one-on-one situation in the office. The manager can choose to sit behind his desk or to move away from it and talk face-to-face with the employee. Each choice that he makes denotes a certain relationship with the employee and sends a message about dominance-submissiveness, liking-disliking, and responsiveness.

Effects of appearance. How we look tells others a lot about what we want to say. A woman may choose to wear a dress to work rather than blue jeans. Both men and women comb their hair. Many of us even spend a great deal of money on the right fabrics and colors to decorate the setting in which we work. We strive to send messages through appearance by our matching dress with the situation and by trying to get a receiver to feel a certain way about us. For example, a coat and tie worn at a company picnic might connote arrogance, but in the office the same attire is perceived as totally appropriate. The coat and tie at work is matched correctly with the situation.

Touch makes a difference, too. Touching another person can be a powerful means of communication. We touch others by kissing them, shaking hands, or simply by touching an arm to reinforce a point. Touch can be a more effective means of getting somebody's attention than saying "please listen and pay attention."

In our society, touch can also get us in trouble. Some people are offended if one does not shake hands with a certain degree of force or if someone touches their arm when they are not expecting it. More than any other means of communication, Americans use touch the *least* effectively. In short, we tend not to touch each other, particularly in work settings.

Eye contact. Most studies on eye contact demonstrate our ability to understand another person's communication by watching their eyes. For example, a person who is lying tends to shift the eyes rapidly and to look upward. A person with low self-esteem (see Chapter 3) tends to glance away when speaking to another person, particularly if that person is perceived as higher in status (5).

Consider these major points about the use of nonverbal communication:

1. The physical location in which a message is delivered must be selected carefully.
2. Use face-to-face communication to avoid communication breakdowns.
3. Change voice tone to maintain listener interest.
4. Experiment with the office space to find the most effective set up for communication.
5. Reinforce verbal messages with nonverbal behavior.
6. Use nonverbal behavior to show liking, dominance, and responsiveness to others.
7. Do not hesitate about interpreting what a person means by his nonverbal behavior. Your interpretation will probably be right!

After the Knowledge Check, we turn to some barriers that inhibit effective communication and look at some practical tools for improving communication and avoiding these barriers.

Knowledge Check

1. Communication is something that is sent to a receiver. T or F?
2. A communication message is what the (receiver, sender) understands.
3. When words are ambiguous, the ____________ helps clarify the message.

4. The three unique messages sent by nonverbal behaviors are liking or disliking, dominance or submissiveness, and ________.
5. Decoding a message is what the (receiver, sender) does.
6. A manager who sits behind her desk and gives feedback to a subordinate is probably demonstrating dominance through nonverbal communication. T or F?

Answers:

1 F, 2 receiver, 3 context, 4 degree of responsiveness, 5 receiver, 6 T

Communication Barriers

What makes one communication experience flow easily and with great common understanding while another experience gets bogged down and does not flow at all? This question has puzzled many employees. Let's examine the key reasons for communication difficulties.

Three Reasons for Barriers

Three major reasons for communication barriers have been identified:
1. Reasons having to do with the individuals involved
2. Reasons having to do with context
3. Reasons having to do with the way messages are sent

Our Individuality Causes Barriers

Ineffective communication is to a large extent attributable to the fact that we are all individuals who act autonomously from each other. We each have our own needs (see Chapter 2), our own communication expertise, and our own "filters" through which we view the world.

Frame of reference. One clear barrier to effective communication is that we all have our own **frame of reference,** or view of reality. This view is determined by our values, beliefs, past experiences, and attitudes, and by our individual abilities or inabilities to perceive information. For effective communication to take place, the parties involved must have similar frames of reference. We tend to generalize this perceived similarity to the behaviors we observe in others, as if they also have the same point of view and their behavior means the same as our behavior.

An informal experiment in an organizational behavior class illustrates this point. Two people were brought to the class who had been asked by the professor to deliver exactly the same speech. Each had practiced the speech for many days, and the two individuals were judged by several experts to sound similar, given their individual voice differences. The professor, however, introduced them differently to the class. One person was introduced as "an expert in his field and well-known around the world." The other was introduced as a "local volunteer." After the speeches were delivered, the audience was asked several questions about the speeches, for example, Which person had the best information? Which person had the best support for his or her arguments? What was remembered from each speech? You guessed it! The volunteer did not do too well; she received very poor ratings for the same speech the "expert" had given. The key variable was the introduction on which the audience based their perceptions of each person.

This experiment dramatizes the point that communication can be hampered by our perceptions of others. We tend to judge before they speak, or at least to form an impression during the first few minutes of interaction (6).

Expertise. Another factor that has to do with the individuals participating in the interaction is **expertise** in communication behaviors. Those who have studied communication behavior and are comfortable with communicating probably will not experience as many communication breakdowns. In contrast, some individuals are reticent about speaking and experience all of the symptoms of stress at the thought of having to speak to a group or even to another individual.(7) We are all made somewhat anxious by a public speaking situation, but some people literally lose control, become physically sick and incapacitated, and may even try to escape the speech situation.

Individual differences. Our individual differences (see Chapter 2) create different perceptions for sending and receiving messages. Ideally, all of us would perceive each other accurately, but we know that this is not how the world works. Consider, for example, how the person who is oriented toward achieving personal power ignores others' feelings if those others do not feed his personal power need. The comments of co-workers are viewed simply as information to further personal gain, rather than as a means for understanding others. In the following dialogue, a power-oriented manager, Jim, has an extremely high need for control, which he communicates during this exchange with a partner on a joint project.

Jim: Hey, Sue, I finished the reports we discussed and sent them off to the client.

Sue: But why didn't you let me review them first?

Jim: Well, I wanted to get them off. We can call him if you have any corrections. I also talked with Mat [the client] and went over the report with him. I told him about my ideas for a follow-up study.

Sue: This is the first you've mentioned a follow-up study!

Jim: Well, it will get him thinking.

Sue: What did he say?

Jim: He wants to get together with us next Tuesday. I'll arrange the meeting. You look over the report in the meantime.

Jim's need for power and control has caused him to ignore Sue's role in the relationship.

The psychologist R.D. Laing, believed that individuals tend to get themselves into "knots," or to create communication barriers by playing games with each other and by using misperceptions about others to set up communication. He starts his book, entitled *Knots,* as follows:

They are playing a game. They are playing at not playing a game. If I show them I see they are, I shall break the rules and they will punish me. I must play their game, of not seeing I see the game.

Laing gives many examples of how people get themselves tied in knots through their use of language. Here is a short example (8):

Jill: I'm upset that you are upset.

Jack: I'm not upset.

Jill: I'm upset that you're not upset that I'm upset you're upset.

Jack: I'm upset that you're upset that I'm not upset that you're upset that I'm upset, when I'm not.

Context Makes a Difference

How many times have you thought: "This isn't the time to say that!" Effective communication is indeed a product of *when* and *where* something is said. Some times and places are better than others for sending and receiving messages. When and where we say or do something is referred to as the **context** of the message.

Physical location. The physical location of a communication experience can be a definite barrier. Consider trying to hold an intimate conversation with a friend when the two of you are separated physically by 20 feet. Or visualize yourself trying to explain a key point in a presentation when construction workers are immediately outside jackhammering the street.

One teacher documented the effects of environment when he tried to study two curricula prepared for schoolchildren. His new curriculum was delivered on Tuesday and Thursday of each week. The usual curriculum was delivered on Monday and Wednesday. By coincidence, on Tuesdays and Thursdays the maintenance people had scheduled mowing and tree trimming. When the teacher analyzed the test results, he found that the students who had received the old curriculum got much better grades than those who had the new curriculum. But did the curriculum cause the effect, or was the noise outside the problem?

Some people have an amazing capacity to overcome noise in the communication environment by blocking out extraneous sounds. Children were found to have a much better capacity to do this than adults(9). Could it be that they really can watch television and study at the same time?

When and where we choose to say something affects communication. A classic mistake made by many managers is to chastise a subordinate publicly. Public embarrassment and confrontation do not work positively for anyone. Instead, people are involved who have no business being involved. Because of the manager-employee power relationship, the reprimanded employee is left defenseless and unable to respond to the manager. As a result, the manager probably will get only a dissatisfied employee rather than a change in employee behavior.

The Communication Climate

The climate we create for communication is probably the most important potential barrier. Climate is usually inferred by the receiver from the *way* the sender's messages are stated. In other words, **climate** refers to the receiver's perceptions about how willing we are to engage in effective

Table 10.1 *Creating the Communication Climate*

Creating a Defensive Climate	*Creating a Supportive Climate*
Evaluation: "You're a bad writer."	**Description:** "You made a grammatical error."
Control: "I'm the boss."	**Problem orientation:** "What can we do about it?"
Strategy: "Just let me handle this my way."	**Spontaneity:** "I'm not sure what to do."
Neutrality: "I don't care how you feel, just get the job done."	**Empathy:** "I care about you."
Superiority: "I'm better at this than you are, so let me handle it."	**Equality:** "We each have our strengths on this project."
Certainty: "I know I'm right."	**Provisionalism:** "I think this is the way to do it."

SOURCE: Modified from Gibb, J. 1961. Defensive Communication. *Journal of Communication* 11:143.

communication. The message intent is inferred from factors such as choice of words, message delivery (e.g., written or verbal), and use of nonverbal behavior. To create a positive climate for communication, some general principles should be observed:

The more supportive the climate, the more willing people are to communicate. Table 10.1 above, gives some examples of statements that create a defensive versus a supportive communication climate.

Participation is important. The behaviors critical to creating a supportive communication climate are those that give the other person a chance to participate, as opposed to forcing the person to be merely a "receiver of orders." Participative behaviors usually involve many questions, asking for feedback, asking others to state their ideas, and giving feedback descriptively rather than evaluatively.

Solving the Dilemma

What barriers to effective communication are present in the interchange between Sandy and Ellery?

In the interaction between Ellery and Sandy, all three barriers to effective communication are present. The perceptions of the two people are far apart. Indeed, they are operating from different frames of reference. Second, the timing and place of the discussion could have been better. Supervisors should give performance feedback in private and should try to introduce ideas systematically. Selection of a private location would have avoided the embarrassing situation that occurred when other employees watched the interaction. Finally, Sandy's choice of words only made Ellery more defensive. The two did not communicate effectively.

Organizations that do not facilitate communication are likely to suffer in concrete ways (e.g., decreased revenues, loss of quality long service employees, and prevailing organizational depression). Consider the following example.

> The chief executive officer thought that the work force should "learn its lesson" from a recent layoff and "work harder." The work force was looking for a sign of strength in the CEO's communication. Instead, the CEO simply stated repeatedly that "we've done a bad job—we must do better." The first result of the CEO's message was that workers and top management stopped trusting one another, which resulted in turn in a defensive communication climate. All elements of the defensive climate were present. The workers perceived a secret strategy on the part of the CEO for further layoffs, the CEO appeared neutral to workers, elements of control were perceived by workers as offensive, and lack of participation was continuously present.

In the previous example, the CEO is insensitive in the extreme, but in many situations, communication breaks down even when everyone concerned is trying hard to "make meaning." How can we break through the barriers to effective communication and create a process that works to maximize meaning between people? The next section outlines some strategies for use in the workplace to accomplish these breakthroughs.

How to Avoid Barriers

Picture yourself as consultant to an organization that is experiencing communication problems. The employees argue constantly with each other. Workers feel defensive when they talk with management and are antagonistic toward any proposed changes. Departments will not cooperate with each other, and little formal communication occurs. In general, communication barriers abound! What approach do you take?

First, you make a "communication assessment." An example of such an assessment is featured in the following Now It's Your Turn section.

NOW IT'S YOUR TURN . . .

A major difficulty for managers is diagnosing communication breakdowns. Consider your class as an organization in which the instructor is your manager. Or, you may want to select an organization with which you are familiar and try to complete this diagnostic form on that organization. Apply the following scale to each statement about the organization:

3 = Almost always, 2 = 50% of the time, 1 = Almost never.

Factor 1: Superior-Subordinate Communication

______ Your superior makes you feel free to talk with him/her.

______ Your superior listens to you when you talk.

______ Your superior cares about communicating with subordinates.

Factor 2: Quality of Information

______ People in top management say what they mean and mean what they say.

_____ You are kept informed about what is going on in the organization.

_____ People in the organization exchange information freely.

Factor 3: Credibility

_____ You believe that your superior is frank and candid with you.

_____ Colleagues are open and frank with you.

Factor 4: Channels

_____ Formal communication channels (e.g., memos, group meetings, organization journals) keep you informed effectively.

_____ Formal communication channels are more accurate than informal channels.

_____ You can choose from among a variety of formal and informal ways to communicate with top management.

Add up the scores. A total of 30 or more points suggests excellent communication-awareness in the organization. Any score below 18 represents a serious communication problem. Go back to those items that received a "1" and consider them as places to start your "communication effectiveness program" (10).

To improve communication quality and effectiveness, managers and subordinates have to take responsibility for creating a supportive communication climate. This includes listening and giving feedback according to well-defined guidelines to ensure that the communication process is ongoing (Figure 10.3).

Figure 10.3 *Overcoming Communication Barriers*

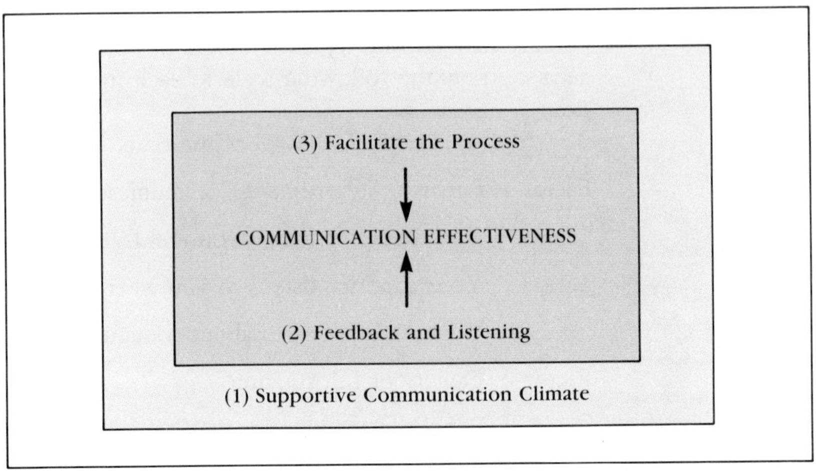

How can people create a supportive communication climate?

Use face-to-face communication. When possible, managers and employees should use face-to-face communication. The primary benefits of such direct interaction come from the use of both verbal and nonverbal cues. When such cues can be both observed and heard, messages are more clearly understood and improved feedback can occur. The face-to-face guideline is also applicable to the relationship between company employees and customers.

> American Airlines had the legal right to fire a flight attendant because he did not smile enough. In 1981, U.S. District Judge David O. Belew, Jr., ruled against an employee who sued the airline because he was fired for not smiling. The judge said that his decision for the airline was "upholding American's policy of requiring a 'friendly facial expression' because it is essential in the competitive airline industry" (11).

Grievances should always be handled in person. The most common grievance-handling procedure is the open door policy adopted by many companies. This procedure usually works because employees are given access to various levels of management to discuss work-related problems. Some organizations even rate managers on their willingness and ability to facilitate face-to-face communication (12).

This communication method is most effective when used for nonroutine procedures or to handle emotionally laden interactions. For more routine work-related activities, face-to-face communication can be inefficient and may even create situations in which managers and employees simply rehash already decided policies and procedures.

Use questions. The manager's primary tool for creating a supportive communication climate is to ask many different types of questions. To practice the question-asking process, study the following summary of question types and examples of each.

Types and Examples of Questions

- **Open-ended:** Has potential to elicit varied responses and can take discussion in various directions. Used in social exchanges, getting to know an employee, when time is not a factor, and when feelings are discussed.
  EXAMPLE: What do you know about the company?
- **Closed:** Opposite of open-ended questions. Used when time is tight, when high precision is required, and when control is important.
  EXAMPLE: Which of these two reports has population data?
- **Primary:** Introduces a topic or suggests new areas for attention within a particular topic area.
- **Secondary:** Follow-ups to primary statements. Secondary questions can be verbal or nonverbal.
  EXAMPLES: "Yes?" "What happened next?" "Uh huh?" "Explain further the point that . . ."
- **Neutral versus leading:** Managers sometimes unwittingly lead employees to answers. Consider the following comparison of neutral and leading questions, which demonstrates how easily a manager can lead an employee to a given response.

Neutral	*Leading*
How do you feel about work? Do you like detail work?	You like detail work, don't you?

Note that different types of questions can be combined. For example, a primary question that is neutral and open-ended is: "How do you feel about the new company insurance plan?"

Available information suggests that effective managers are distinguished from their less effective counterparts by the number and type of questions they ask (13). They use questions to direct attention to a particular idea ("What would happen if we ran the data through a different statistics program?"), to determine if the employee has all of the facts ("Is any other company doing this?"), and as a way to gather information needed to make decisions ("Can you help me determine the market share of that product?").

Use nonverbal behaviors. A third way to create a supportive communication climate is to manage the use of nonverbal behaviors in a positive manner. Body position is probably the most powerful way to let people know whether or not you are approachable and the extent to which you want to talk with them. Figure 10.4 pictures two managers. Evaluate the body position of each. Which one do you think is more receptive to ideas? Which one would be more willing to talk with employees?

Arrange office space to create a supportive climate. The thoughtful arrangement of office space is another powerful communication tool that

Figure 10.4
Body language is a powerful nonverbal means of communication. Which manager would you rather interact with on a day-to-day basis?

can solicit conversation and facilitate interaction (14). Consider the two office arrangements in Figure 10.5. In which office would you feel more comfortable talking to a manager? Which space is more likely to elicit conversation about feelings or innovative ideas? The variety of possible office spaces and arrangements is enormous (15), but you can experiment with the space in your workplace and your position in that space by making some simple changes:

1. Rearrange a few pieces of furniture in your office to try to create a friendlier atmosphere.
2. When talking with people, move from behind your desk and sit next to them.
3. Alter the lighting in your office. Either brighten or lower it, and watch the effect on visitors and on their conversation with you.

The effective use of questions, body position, and work space are all key ways to create a supportive communication climate. Another way to create effective communication is to use certain behaviors and techniques for listening and giving feedback.

What are the suggested techniques for listening and giving feedback?

Listening. Ralph Nichols (16) estimates that managers spend about 45 percent of their day involved in listening, yet when subordinates are asked

Figure 10.5
Office arrangements have a signigicant effect on the communication climate. Which environment would you prefer?

about their manager's communication effectiveness, particularly listening ability, they generally rate the manager as a "poor listener" (17). Since most of us speak at a rate of 130 words per minute, and since the rate of listening is nearly three times the rate of speaking, our attention may wander from listening. We tune in and out and generally get some sense of the message intended by the sender. The redundancy of the average communication helps us get the sense of the message, but we generally tend to operate inefficiently while listening to a conversation. In fact, studies show that most of us operate at less than 25 percent of our listening capability (18).

What can we do to improve our listening skills? We can use effective **listening behaviors.** As you consider a communication encounter, try the following:

1. Anticipate what the other person will say. The more prepared you are, the more likely you are to understand the message. Be careful, however, that you also are receptive to information that you do not anticipate.
2. Keep yourself interested by constantly personalizing the message. For example, consider the relevance of the message to your job and to the organization.
3. Look for meaning in nonverbal behavior.
4. Give the speaker nonverbal cues to designate understanding or lack of understanding.
5. Empathize with the speaker. Try to take the sender's point of view and to understand why she or he is giving you the information.
6. Ask questions.
7. Some people are note takers, others are not. Find out which you are and facilitate your listening with note taking if you are a note taker.
8. You cannot listen when you are talking. Don't forget this!

Feedback. Once the information is received, you may find it necessary to "feed back" information to the speaker. The skillful use of feedback is crucial to effective communication. Some guidelines for giving effective feedback follow (19):

1. Intend to help the recipient of your feedback.
2. Be descriptive rather than evaluative. Say "I observed your behavior," rather than "You're a bad person."
3. Be specific rather than general, and use clear and recent examples. Avoid using phrases such as "You're always late."
4. Choose a time and a place to give feedback that you judge to be good for the recipient.
5. Do not tell the recipient more than he or she can handle at any particular time.
6. Check out the validity of your ideas and perceptions with others.
7. Give feedback on those issues that the receiver might be expected to do something about.
8. Use the following rule: Explain to people what you want them to do, show them how to do it, let them try it, give them feedback, and reward them for progress (20).
9. Expect employees to perform better gradually, *not* all at once.

Ask Yourself Questions to Improve Communication

Ensure that the communication process is considered constantly. This is accomplished by making a "checklist of communication effectiveness" to determine whether or not you can improve any aspect of the communication situation. This checklist should include the following questions:

Questions for Effective Communication

1. Is the physical space set up for effective communication?
2. What are my preconceived ideas about this topic?
3. How can I improve my listening?
4. What words and gestures could I use to be more effective?
5. What is the other person thinking?
6. What channel is most effective for this communication?
7. Who should be involved in this communication?
8. When is the best time to communicate this message?
9. How do I feel about this message? How can I communicate my feelings?
10. How can I make the climate more supportive?

The previous section is probably one of the most important in this chapter because it addresses the ways in which you can communicate more effectively in organizations. Effective managers and employees are those who realize that others' perceptions of their competence are almost totally dependent on one's ability to communicate effectively.

Knowledge Check

1. The three key reasons for communication barriers have to do with __________, __________, and __________.
2. Frame of reference has to do with the words one uses to express ideas. T or F?
3. "Neutrality" and "certainty" describe ways to create a __________ communication climate.
4. Face-to-face communication is least useful when dealing with emotion-laden employee grievances. T or F?
5. When time is tight and high precision is needed, neutral, open-ended questions should be used. T or F?
6. Good feedback behavior is to be as general as possible so the listener can get as much information as possible. T or F?

Answers:

1 individuals, context, and the way messages are sent, 2 F, 3 defensive, 4 T, 5 F, 6 F

Formal Communication in Organizations

A recurring theme in the study of organizational communication is how superiors send messages to subordinates to "get them to do something." In our view, this theme covers only part of the complex workings of communication in organizations. It does not do justice to the importance of subordinate employees or to the dynamic process of how people "make meaning." Our approach, therefore, is to complete the study of organizational communication with discussions of both the *formal, or sanctioned,* communication processes and the *informal, or nonsanctioned* processes.

What are sanctioned communication processes?

Sanctioned communication is defined as the purposefully designed way in which an organization establishes communication both within and outside the firm. This formal process is established to provide organizational members with ways to send and receive messages consequential to getting their business done. In other words, sanctioned communication is the way in which management chooses to send and receive information and the way in which management requests employees to communicate with one another.

Downward Communication

One way in which a sanctioned communication process flows is **downward,** to carry directives from superiors to subordinates. Many different mechanisms are designated for sending this type of communication. Some of the most prevalent are these:

1. **Newsletters** are often published inside the organization and feature items such as employee accomplishments, personal notes about employees, new policies and procedures, and management changes.
2. **Memos** are frequently initiated by management. They are a formal means of communicating a message that must be acted on or kept for future reference.
3. **Policy statements** or procedures are written in a particular format and placed in a policy handbook or maintained in a file.
4. **Operating and financial statements** are formal financial and operating summaries of results such as a profit and loss statement or an exceptions report on manufacturing operations.
5. **Organization charts** are formal diagrams, sanctioned by the firm, of the organization's structure, authority, and coordination of departments.
6. **Meetings** are the most common and dreaded form of communication because they usually waste both the manager and employee's time. Meetings are used most often as decision-making tools, to gather information from various sources, or as a means to facilitate interpersonal interaction. (Many of the pitfalls of ineffective meetings can be avoided by implementing the ideas in Chapter 9.)

What are the purposes of this sanctioned downward communication?

The sanctioned downward communication in organizations has five general purposes (21):

1. To give specific task directives relevant to job instructions
2. To give information about organizational procedures and practices
3. To provide information about the rationale for the job
4. To tell subordinates about their performance
5. To provide information to facilitate goal acceptance

The previous list is arranged in order of decreasing frequency of communication about each of the items (i.e., frequent interaction occurs regarding job instructions and much less frequent communication occurs concerning performance feedback or ideological information involving goals). Note that the effectiveness of communication improves the more the manager communicates about all five items. As Katz and Kahn suggest, "If people know the reasons for their assignment, this will often insure their carrying out the job more effectively; and if they have an understanding of what their job is about in relation to their subsystem, they are more likely to identify with organizational goals" (22).

As the manager moves down the list, face-to-face communication should be used increasingly to exchange information. This channel is preferable because more opportunities for miscommunication exist in the interaction.

> The leading executive of a large television network often violated this last guideline in his communication with subordinates. When he gave instructions about job-related activities, he called his subordinates into his office, provided them with explicit instructions, and gave them an opportunity to ask questions and even to negotiate job tasks. At performance review time, however, he sent each subordinate a memo detailing "some points for improvement." He believed that the memo would have a more lasting effect on each person than other channels of communication. Every year he addressed the company employees about "what it is like to work for this company." The address was, however, written and disseminated in a company newsletter. Employee reactions to this executive in an attitude survey were that he was "cold and ineffective." "You never know," subordinates said, "where you stand with him or why you're doing a particular job."

Downward communication is not the only sanctioned communication process in organizations. Sanctioned communication can flow upward, as well.

Subordinates Communicate Upward and Horizontally

Subordinates use sanctioned communication channels to send information upward to their managers, and horizontally to other employees at their level. We begin with a discussion of upward communication, the most difficult and usually the least successful means of sanctioned organizational communication.

Upward communication takes many forms, some of which follow:

1. **Use of formal reporting relationships** provides management with information.

2. **Attitude surveys** are periodic questionnaires that solicit feedback from employees for management use. They usually include a variety of areas about which employees are asked their opinions. The surveys are usually anonymous.
3. **Grievance procedures** are formal appeal processes, usually written as policy statements, that provide for a free exchange between management and employees about grievances. A less formal procedure is an "open door" policy, that is, a continuous invitation to subordinates to talk with managers.
4. **Formal and well-run meetings** can offer opportunities for employees to tell managers about work-related issues and to ask questions about the organization.

Do these sanctioned forms of upward communication work?

Employee-initiated communication has many problems in most organizations. The major problem is that every employee-initiated communication carries with it the implications of the boss-subordinate power relationship. If a grievance surfaces, the manager has the power to ignore the requests of the subordinate. The opposite is not true.

Another major problem with upward communication is the employees' tendency to communicate what they think the boss wants to hear and to distort information so the boss gets only good news and neutral information. One study showed that wide-spread inaccuracies existed between perceptions of superiors and subordinates about factors such as job duties, performance requirements, future changes, and obstacles to job performance (23).

Many organizations have tried to institute ways to improve communication between superiors and subordinates to avoid the problems mentioned in the preceding paragraphs. Grievance procedures, open door policies, attitude surveys, participation techniques, and liaison roles have all been tried and will continue to be tried. These tend to work only in environments that have very supportive communication climates and managers who are accomplished in using the communication process.

In short, effective upward communication is a product of management attitude and management willingness to allow subordinate participation in decision making.

What occurs when communication flows horizontally?

Communication flows extensively between employees and can be a major force in organizational effectiveness. One observational study found that as much as 41 percent of a production manager's communications were sent horizontally, and that 40 percent of communications received were from horizontal sources (24).

Horizontal communication is communication with persons of relatively equal status who are on the same organizational level. This type of communication avoids many of the problems associated with subordinate to superior communication and provides both needed social support and information for task coordination. (See Table 10.2.)

The major purposes of horizontal communication are (25):

1. Task coordination: coordinating people who should work together

Table 10.2
Pros and Cons of Horizontal Communication

Pros
- Less likely to involve power relationships
- More likely to be comfortable for both parties
- More likely to involve social support
- More likely to produce communication about similar problems
- More likely to create task coordination

Cons
- Can lack information
- Can be inefficient and time consuming
- More likely to create conflict than vertical communication

2. Problem solving: getting people together to make decisions
3. Information sharing: having people tell each other what they do, supply information needed to the jobs done, or just "keeping in touch"
4. Conflict resolution: helping to resolve conflicts between units

W.L. Gore and Associates, Inc., takes horizontal communication very seriously. This Delaware-based company makes a synthetic fiber called Gore-tex, which is used in camping equipment and many other products. Bill Gore, owner and founder, refers to his organization as a lattice that has these attributes.

- No fixed or assigned authority (information sharing)
- Sponsors, not bosses (task coordination)
- Natural leadership defined by followership (task coordination)
- Person-to-person communication (conflict resolution, problem solving, information sharing, task coordination)
- Objectives set by those who must make them happen (task coordination)
- Tasks and functions organized through commitments (task coordination)

Bill Gore uses horizontal communication as the primary means of "defining" his organization. He sums up the governing principles of his organization in these four objectives:

> Everyone will: (1) Try to be fair. Sincerely try to be fair with each other, our suppliers, our customers, and all persons with whom we carry out transactions; (2) allow, help, and encourage his associates to grow in knowledge, skills, scope of responsibility, and range of activities; (3) make his own commitments—and keep them; (4) consult with his associates before taking actions that might be "below the waterline" and cause serious damage to the enterprise (26).

The liaison role. The most innovative and potentially powerful sanctioned horizontal communication is the **liaison role.** This role denotes a connector, a link, and a coordinator. The literature on organizational behavior refers to a "linking pin" notion, which specifies that organizational groups ought to be linked by: "magnetic centers," or "opinion leaders" (Table 10.3). Each of these terms refers to individuals or groups of individuals who function as connectors between other people and groups to facilitate work and interpersonal relationships (27).

Two points should be made about these roles. First, the organization is best served by making this role a formal one. It should be well-known

Table 10.3
Summary of Research on Liaison Roles

Effective liaisons tend to:
1. Have longer service in the organization
2. Have high formal status in the organization

Liaisons perceive themselves to have:
1. Greater numbers of communication contacts
2. Greater amounts of information on content about the organization
3. Greater influence than others
4. A more open communication environment in which to work than non-liaisons have

Others perceive liaisons to have:
1. Greater power
2. More information than others
3. Control over flow of information

Liaisons are effective if they are:
1. Dynamic and sociable
2. Perceived as trustworthy
3. Emotionally stable
4. Competent

to others in the organization and backed by management. In this way the manager's job is made easier because conflicts get resolved by the liaison before they are "kicked upstairs." Second, the person who fulfills the liaison role should be skillful in communication behaviors. A liaison with quality skills can both cause effective communication and teach effective communication behaviors to others.

Solving the Dilemma

What can Sandy and Ellery do to keep this type of confrontation from happening again?

Sandy must consider using sanctioned communications in addition to informal communications. She should have regular meetings with each subordinate, provide specific feedback to each, and use questions to see if the message she sent was received by the employee.

Ellery needs to be more direct with Sandy and ask her what she means by a certain phrase before jumping to conclusions. At this point, he needs to ask Sandy for more meetings on a sanctioned basis, and to try also to relate to her informally.

Electronic Communication: Does sanctioned communication occur only with people?

No! This question refers to electronic transmission and receiving of information. Over the last ten years, the use of electronic communication has increased substantially. Indeed, communication in industry has been transformed. Consider these facts.

1. Computer hardware costs are decreasing on average 7 percent per year.
2. By 1990, three U.S. automakers will be using 21,000 robots (28).
3. Milliken, the privately owned South Carolina textile giant, uses computers to reproduce a color photo of an office. Designers can then refurbish the office electronically with 5,000 different carpets and fabrics to determine how the office will look redecorated.
4. Shelternet works like a financial blind-dating service. It matches borrowers, whose financial qualifications and needs are typed into the system, with lenders, such as large banks and savings and loans, which post the terms of mortgages they will accept. Once a match is made, the system speeds up paperwork—automatically printing out letters requesting credit reports, for example. For each loan closed through the system, First Boston collects $200 (29).
5. Work stations and minicomputers in the price range of $25,000 to $100,000 have increased from a $3 billion industry in 1981 to a $6 billion industry in 1985 (30).
6. Sales of small mainframe computers (price range $700,000 to $1.75 million) have steadily decreased since 1981 to reach an all-time low five years later of $2.7 billion (31).

One conclusion we can draw from this information is that personal computers are very available for individual use to perform many tasks in our everyday lives. Indeed, computers have become an important vehicle of communication. The implications of this are summarized in Table 10.4.

A new company executive was given a computer linked to a phone. She was told that "this is the way memos and important notices are sent." For example, her phone was capable of receiving an electronic message from another executive. The personal computer would then show her the message on a screen, and a printer would produce a hard copy of the message. This technology virtually eliminated the need for secretaries to type memos and routine correspondence. The phone-computer system

Table 10.4
Implications of Computer Technology on Communication in Organizations

Organization Design

1. Entire organizational layers may disappear
2. Role of liaison will increase
3. Integration problems may arise

Organizational Power

1. Will reside with those who have data
2. Will create problems if data are not integrated

Individual Satisfaction

1. Individuals may have more control over their job
2. Individuals may have less face-to-face contact with co-workers
3. Executives may prefer not to type and may therefore not use computers

Individual and Organizational Performance

1. Increased performance on routine procedures
2. Greater standardization of information may lead to less individual flexibility
3. Cost problems related to rapid changes in technology

could also maintain the executive's calendar, make routine phone calls with the push of one button, and do routine computer tasks such as financial analyses and word processing.

In sum, sanctioned organizational communication can flow vertically and horizontally. The most effective of these is downward communication, followed by horizontal communication, and then, a distant third, upward communication. Each type serves specific organizational purposes and can be useful if implemented according to the principles cited earlier in this chapter.

Knowledge Check

1. The ways in which management requests employees to communicate are called __________.

2. Examples of sanctioned communication include all *except* which of the following?
   a. memos
   b. policy statements
   c. rumors
   d. organizational charts

3. One reason for downward communication is to provide information about job expectations. T or F?

4. Upward communication is easier than downward communication because managers are trained to listen to employees. T or F?

5. A liaison role is important in __________ communication.

6. Which of the following is an implication of computer technology on organizational design?
   a. power resides with those who have the data
   b. individual control will increase
   c. some organizational layers may disappear
   d. less personal contact will occur

Answers:

1 sanctioned communication, 2 c, 3 T, 4 F, 5 horizontal, 6 c

Although sanctioned communication is the recognized form of communication in organizations, nonsanctioned communication is equally if not more powerful in its influence on behavior. In the next section we explore the little understood area of informal communication.

Informal Communication

During the 1950s and 1960s, applied organizational research concentrated largely on the nonsanctioned types of communication found in organizations, in particular, the "grapevine" and rumor networks. This research shows that informal networks are (32):

1. Used extensively
2. Highly accurate
3. Initiated anywhere in the organization
4. Clustered (i.e., people who work near one another are likely to be on the same grapevine)
5. Focused on recent news, factors that affect work, and people known to the participants in the network.

Table 10.5 compares sanctioned and nonsanctioned organizational communication.

Hints on Gossip and Rumors

Why do people gossip and tell rumors in organizations? In general, employees use informal channels because the formal or sanctioned channels do not satisfy their communication and information needs. They come to believe that the grapevine uncovers the "real" information about organizational issues. Informal communication is also more flexible and faster than formal channels.

Many researchers believe that informal communication actually benefits the organization. Company managers sometimes encourage people to attend parties and coffee breaks so employees can exchange ideas and information. John Kotter, in his recent book *Power and Influence,* notes that the most effective managers are those who use the informal grapevine selectively (33). The informal communication network seems to complement the formal organization in ways impossible to achieve through sanctioned communication channels. For example, a sales department trying to expedite an order is helped significantly by a particular salesperson who is on a first name basis with the shipping clerk.

Informal communication keeps formal communication in check. The formal communication channel cannot tell the whole story because the formal

Table 10.5
Differences Between Sanctioned and Nonsanctioned Communication

Sanctioned	*Nonsanctioned*
1. Official	1. Unofficial
2. Position-specific	2. Person-specific
3. Communication through channels	3. Uses grapevine, rumors, and informal discussions
4. Authority and responsibility important	4. Playing politics and influencing others important
5. Easily controlled	5. Difficult to control

channel is often rigid, full of power relationships, and sometimes very out of touch with the way the organization is operating. Some organizations try to "go public" with the grapevine so valuable information can be used to increase productivity and satisfy employees. One manager describes the public strategy this way (34):

> In our company, we have campaigned, and believe effectively, to make the grapevine public. We have a "Heard from the Grapevine" section of our employee newsletter. We have a "Grapevine Square" on our bulletin boards, upon which any employee can place and/or correct grapevine information. And all managers are encouraged to incorporate and discuss grapevine information in their regular department meetings. Our president, in fact, sets the example by including grapevine items, if there are any, on the agenda of his weekly planning meetings.

Most new employees worry about informal communication channels because they may not be included immediately, or they may be the rumor subject. In this situation, the new manager can act to manage the perceptions of others. For example, employees tend to take on labels through the informal networks (Table 10.6). Managers who want to be known as "a hard worker" or as "task-oriented," must therefore act accordingly. Co-workers gather clues about our roles from the way we behave and what we say. Manage these perceptions to your advantage, and remember, even if you are the topic of discussion, you are quite

Table 10.6
Informal Roles of Employees

Roles Played in Relationship to the Task at Hand:

1. Task-oriented: play the role of getting the job done, known to be performers
2. Technique-oriented: masters of procedure and methods

Roles Played in Relationship to the Organization:

1. Rule enforcers: play it by the book
2. Rule evaders or deviants: do it their own way
3. Isolates: aloof
4. Newcomers: need to be socialized
5. Detached: "along for the ride"
6. Old-timers: been there forever
7. Stickers: those comfortable with their job and with the organization
8. Associates: new term used by some organizations instead of the more formal "employees"

Roles Played in Relationship to Others in the Organization:

1. People-oriented: patron saints or good Samaritans
2. Nay-sayers: always the devil's advocate
3. Yea-sayers: always agreeing with others

Roles Played in Relationship to the Boss:

1. Apple polishers: always trying to get in good with the boss
2. Mentorees: favorites of the boss
3. Pass-on-ers: certified-reliable gossips used by managers to pass rumors to others

SOURCE: Adapted from Gross, B.M. 1968. *Organizations and Their Managing.* New York: The Free Press, pp. 242–248.

probably being paid a compliment. As Oscar Wilde said, "There is only one thing in the world worse than being talked about, and that is not being talked about."

Managing Your Boss

Informal communication is probably the most effective way to manage a boss. As stated earlier, sanctioned upward communication mechanisms are generally ineffective, so employees are left with the informal network as the channel to use to influence managers.

Employees often resent the fact that on top of their other duties they also have to "manage their boss." Consider, however, that managing the boss greatly simplifies your job and even makes you more effective in the eyes of your boss and the organization.

How does one get started managing the boss?

The critical part of managing the boss is to know the boss's goals and objectives and the pressures the boss is under, as well as his or her strengths, weaknesses, blind spots, and preferred work style (35).

> One employee never took this advice and assumed that the formal channels gave him all of the needed information. His new boss of two weeks said that she wanted the employee to develop a research plan for a new cosmetic product line. The product was of particular interest to the company because, for the first time, the organization would be selling a generic item with little brand recognition.
>
> The employee was excited about the opportunity and never thought to examine his manager's goals. He just assumed that the manager meant that he should "go for it." In fact, his manager gave many clues that other tasks were important to her, but the employee chose to stick to the formal communication of "develop a research plan." After two months work, the manager told the employee that she was very dissatisfied with his performance because he had not participated in any meetings concerning other marketing activities. The employee was also told that he had not kept the boss adequately informed of his activities.

The moral of the story is to keep in constant contact with the boss until the boss's objectives, goals, style, strengths, weaknesses, and pressures are well understood. Assess what you are like and how you work best with the boss. What can you offer this boss?

Finally, develop and maintain a relationship that fits both your needs and style and those of the boss. Keep the boss informed through informal channels that involve short exchanges. Use the boss's time effectively to get maximum benefit from those exchanges. Be sensitive to the boss's desires for information, and remember that the most productive exchanges probably take place *outside* sanctioned communication channels.

Solving the Dilemma

How could Sandy and Ellery have avoided the harsh ending of their confrontation?

Sandy, as the supervisor, could have asked Ellery to talk in private rather than on the shop floor. She also needed to be more sensitive to Ellery's feelings behind the words he was using and acknowledge those feelings to him.

Ellery should have asked for help and feedback long before he got so angry. He could have avoided the harsh ending of the confrontation by expressing his feelings to Sandy.

Knowledge Check

1. Communication research has shown that informal communication can be highly (accurate, inaccurate).
2. Informal communication almost always starts at the bottom levels of an organization. T or F?
3. Which one of the following descriptive phrases does *not* apply to non-sanctioned or informal communication?
   a. unofficial
   b. person-specific
   c. uses grapevine
   d. easily controlled
4. People get clues about your role in the organization from the way you behave and what you ___________.
5. Matching your style to the boss's is a poor technique for managing the boss because managers want to employ unique individuals. T or F?

Answers:

1 accurate, 2 F, 3 d, 4 say, 5 F

Summary Points

■ **Communication** is the sending and receiving of messages from one person to another; it is the process of creating understanding.

■ A **communication message** is what the receiver understands, *not* what the sender sends.

■ **Communication** is a **process,** not a product.

■ The primary elements of the process are the **sender, channels, receiver, message, and feedback.**

■ **Meaning** can be made through **words, pictures, and nonverbal means** such as body posture and use of space.

■ **Communication barriers** arise because of individual differences, problems of context in which communication is delivered, and the way messages are sent.

■ **Key ways to overcome communication barriers** are to set up communication encounters in a purposeful manner, create a supportive communication climate, observe guidelines for effective listening and feedback, and never forget that communication is a process.

■ Organization-wide communication occurs both as a **sanctioned** and a **nonsanctioned** activity.

■ The critical mechanisms for successful **upward communication** are open door policies, regular superior-subordinate meetings, focused groups, attitude questionnaires, ombudsmen, and communication training for employees and managers.

■ **Computer technology** continues to alter the ways we communicate in organizations. Organizational design, power, performance, and individual satisfaction are affected by electronic communication.

■ **Informal communication networks** can be powerful mechanisms for employee satisfaction and for innovation. The same results are not likely to occur through sanctioned networks.

Questions

1. Explain the communication process as it would occur in a lecture versus a discussion with a friend.
2. What are some techniques for improving organizational communication?
3. Suggest three ways to "manage the boss" through communication behavior.
4. An executive in a large conglomerate sent a one sentence mandate to all employees stating: "From this date forward no memo is to be longer than one page." What do you think about this rule? Suggest the positive and negative aspects of such a rule.
5. Some managers believe that employees cannot be taught to communicate effectively (i.e., they either have the ability or they don't). Can communication skills be taught, and can employees learn to be skillful communicators? Does desire to communicate affect the learning process?
6. Organizations with an excellent public relations department can create an image that is not verified by the company's actions. For example, one organization was pictured as "socially responsible," yet two years later the company was found to be extremely negligent about polluting the environment. To what extent should a government agency monitor corporate communications to make sure that the projected image is accurate and indicative of the company?

EXPLORING: *ABC Tries to Control Its Communication*

[Adapted from "Culture Shock Rattles the TV Networks," *Fortune* (April 14, 1986): 22–27.]

ABC is best known for its television communication, but recently the organization has had to face some internal communication challenges. During 1985, ABC sold its company to Capital Cities Communications, a company one-fourth the size of ABC. From a financial perspective, the sale made sense. From an internal management point of view, the problems were massive.

After some battles for top management position, Capital Cities Chairman Thomas Murphy named John Sias as president of ABC. Sias, who headed a Capital Cities subsidiary, had never worked for ABC. Other executives from Capital Cities were also appointed to key positions within ABC.

Sias's main goal was to maintain quality programming while cutting costs. Some problems he faced in achieving these goals related to the organizational communication within ABC. Rumors were rampant that 1,500 people (more than 10 percent of the work force) would get "pink slips" (i.e., be fired)! Capital Cities did not help this rumor by appointing a "sunset committee" to track paper flow throughout ABC. Many qualified executives were demoted, and others who were not demoted expected to get a pink slip imminently. Not surprisingly, employees were finding it hard to work in such a climate, filled with rumors and gossip rich with all sorts of stories.

To complicate matters more, ABC and Capital Cities management had very different styles of running a company. ABC was used to "high rolling," that is, taking big risks. Capital Cities was used to very calculated risks accompanied by little fanfare.

If you were the new ABC president, John Sias, what would you do about the massive amount of informal (and often erroneous) communication? After all, management cannot afford to have communication problems stifle the company. CBS and NBC are not going to sit idly by until ABC solves its problems. They are going to maintain their organizations and further their position in the marketplace in relation to ABC.

Develop a strategy for the president to use to control the internal communication at ABC. Be specific about the following factors:

1. Vertical communication
2. Horizontal communication
3. What the president should say to ABC employees
4. What you would want to hear from the President if you were an employee at ABC

APPLYING: *Making A Public Presentation*

For most of us, giving a public presentation in front of a large audience causes extreme apprehension. We get butterflies in our stomach, have sweaty palms, and do what we can to avoid this type of situation. Yet almost all of us will, at one time or another, have to give such a presentation. The following steps will help you deal with this type of speech situation.

Step One: All speech is meant to persuade. We are always trying to persuade others to believe us or to alter their ideas based on the information we give. For example, a speech on improving classroom learning may have the following intent:

I want to try to persuade other students to take responsibility for their own learning and not to be greatly influenced by the personality of the instructor.

Step Two: Determine the main message. This is the one idea that you want the audience to remember, even if they cannot recall anything else you said. Formulate and write down this main idea in a precise manner such as: The main message is that we, as students, are responsible for our learning.

Step Three: Analyze the audience. Determine what you think your audience is expecting to hear. What do they like or dislike? If you are not sure about who your audience is, question someone who will be there or who has been with that audience before. For example, "My classmates probably want me to suggest how instructors should improve. They are interested in improving instruction. They each could give examples of effective and ineffective teaching."

Step Four: Determine how to get the attention of the audience. Several methods are effective. Use activity or movement, refer directly to people in the audience, use humor if you can do so comfortably. (Nothing is worse than a good joke told by someone who can't tell jokes.) Use of novelty (e.g., unique visuals or an unusual method of dress to accentuate a point) almost always engages audience interest.

Step Five: Determine how you will support your key ideas. Forms of support include explanation, analogy or comparison, illustration, use of specific examples, statistics, and expert testimony. For example, if you are telling the audience that they should stop nuclear weapon development, provide them with statistics to demonstrate the inherent dangers of nuclear weapons, and give them a specific example of what could happen if a nuclear weapon were unintentionally set off.

Step Six: Put your presentation together. The easiest way to organize a speech is to follow the age-old wisdom of Plato: "Tell them what you're going to say, tell them, then tell them what you told them."

The introduction should grab audience attention and establish the need to listen. Tell them your main idea and make sure that they are set to listen. Write the introduction *last,* after you have written the body and conclusion of the speech.

The body of the talk is where you deliver the critical information. The material can probably be arranged in many different ways, but try to keep the order logical. Stress the main point repeatedly. Use internal transitions or summaries periodically to sum up your ideas and information for the audience. This use of internal summaries constantly reinforces your main ideas and helps your audience keep up with you.

The conclusion should summarize again your main ideas and should also leave the audience with a positive feeling. If possible, give them something to do with your material, rather than simply being informed.

Step Seven: Practice your presentation. Ideally, you should not need to use a written transcript of the speech. Work on making your delivery smooth and spontaneous. Talk in front of a mirror and in front of friends. If possible, go to the actual location of the talk to see how it feels to speak there. Remember: Audience attention is never captured by watching someone read a speech.

Step Eight: While giving the speech, observe these pointers: (1) Do not move around a lot if you have a tendency to get very nervous. Plant your feet firmly on the ground and *do not move.* (2) Establish eye contact with the audience. Choose a person on either side of the room and look at each individual periodically for five seconds. (3) Whenever possible, use visualizations. Pictures seem to have a greater impact than words.

You may want to consult two excellent sources, *Principles and Types of Speech Communication,* by Ehninger, Monroe, and Gronbeck, and *Speech Communication and Human Interaction* by Schiedel. Both books are among the suggested readings for this chapter.

Our purpose here is to help you design a public presentation so you can practice a situation that is a common occurrence for most people who work in organizations. We suggest that you choose one of the following three topics for a presentation to your class:

1. Make a presentation on how to manage the boss. What are some techniques that new workers might use to gain control over their work and to influence the boss?
2. Make a presentation on how to determine worker needs. Assume that you are talking to a group of supervisors in a factory and that they have asked you to speak on this subject. They know that you have taken a course in organizational behavior and that you have some expertise on the subject.
3. Make a presentation on avoiding communication breakdowns. Your goal is to help students in the class avoid the ill effects of communication problems.

Your instructor may want everyone to write a speech but only a few people to give them. In this way, you can see and hear others present ideas and learn from their delivery. The talks should last only 5 to 6 minutes each. This is enough time to try some of the ideas suggested without overburdening the class or yourself with preparation and presentation.

Suggested Readings

Ehninger, D., Monroe, A., and Gronbeck, B. 1978. *Principles and Types of Speech Communication,* 8th edition. Glenview, Ill.: Scott, Foresman.

Farb, P. 1975. *Word Play.* New York: Bantam Books.

This book is an interesting treatment of communication as a general topic. Chapters are divided into sections entitled "The Game," "The Strategies," "Is the Game Rigged?," "Born to Speak" and "The Changing Game." Of particular interest are Farb's examples.

Fisher, D. 1981. *Communication in Organizations.* St. Paul, Minn.: West Publishing.

Gibson, J., and Hodgetts, R.M. 1985. *Organizational Communication.* New York: Academic Press.

Goldhaber, G., Dennis, H.S., Richetto, G., and Wiio, O.A. 1979. *Information Strategies: New Pathways to Corporate Power.* Englewood Cliffs, N.J.: Prentice-Hall.

The unique feature of this book is its focus on diagnostics. The major premise is that information is power and that power is enhanced through communication. Thus the better an employee can diagnose communication, the more information (i.e., power) that individual can gain. Of particular note is the Chapter 8 discussion of the Organizational Communication Development Audit.

Littlejohn, S.W. 1978. *Theories of Human Communication.* Columbus, Ohio: Charles E. Merrill.

This book explains many of the theories that underlie modern thinking about communication in organizations. Chapters 8 through 10 are particularly useful for understanding organizational communication.

Rosenfield, L., Hayes, L., and Frentz, T. 1976. *The Communicative Experience.* Boston: Allyn and Bacon.

Schiedel, T. 1976. *Speech Communication and Human Interaction.* Glenview, Ill.: Scott, Foresman.

This book takes an excellent and practical look at communication in the contexts of interpersonal and group interactions. Of particular interest are Schiedel's comments on speech making and how to be effective when making presentations.

References

1. Werther, W., Ruch, W., and McClure, L. 1986. *Productivity Through People.* St. Paul, Minn.: West, p. 487.
2. Caroll, L. *Through the Looking Glass.* 1960. New York: Signet Books, p. 186.
3. Roberts, K.H. 1984. *Communicating in Organizations.* Chicago: SRA.
4. Mehrabian, A. 1971. *Silent Messages.* Belmont, Calif.: Wadsworth.
5. Ibid.
6. Brown, R. 1965. *Social Psychology.* New York: The Free Press, Ch. 11.
7. Phillips, G.M., Butt, D., and Metzger, N. 1974. *Communication in Education: A Rhetoric of Schooling and Learning.* New York: Holt, Reinhart & Winston.
8. Laing, R.D. *Knots.* 1971. New York: Pantheon Books, pp. 1, 21.
9. Bjork, R.A. 1985. *Memory.* Presentation to the Institute for Management Studies, New Orleans, La.
10. This diagnostic is designed to give you an overview of the organization. If you desire a more in-depth analysis, see Goldhaber, G.M., Dennis, H.S., Richetto, G.M., and Wiio, O.A. 1979. *Information Strategies: New Pathways to Corporate Power.* Englewood Cliffs, New Jersey: Prentice-Hall.
11. *Fortune* 1985. Now We Know Why They're so Friendly. 112:120.
12. Clausen, A.W. Listening and Responding to Employees' Concerns. *Harvard Business Review* (Jan.–Feb.1980):104.
13. Kotter, J.P. 1982. *The General Managers.* New York: The Free Press.
14. Sommer, R. 1972. *Design Awareness.* San Francisco: Holt, Reinhart & Winston.

15. Hall, E.T. 1959. *The Silent Language.* New York: Doubleday; Hall, E.T. 1966. *The Hidden Dimension.* Garden City, N.J.: Doubleday.
16. Nichols, R. 1957. *Are You Listening?* New York: McGraw-Hill.
17. Goldhaber, G.M., et al., op. cit.
18. Nichols, R., op. cit.
19. Anderson, J. Giving and Receiving Feedback. In Athos, A., and Gabarro, J.J. (Eds.) 1978. *Interpersonal Behavior Communication Understanding in Relationships.* Englewood Cliffs, N.J.: Prentice-Hall, p. 87.
20. Leavitt, H., and Mueller, R. 1951. Some Effects of Feedback on Communication. *Human Relations* 4:401–410.
21. Katz, D., and Kahn, R.L. 1978. *The Social Psychology of Organizations,* 2nd ed. New York: Wiley, p. 440.
22. Ibid., p. 443.
23. Meir, N., Hoffman, L.R., Hooven, J., and Read, W. 1961. *Superior-Subordinate Communication in Management.* New York: AMA, p. 9; Gaines, J. 1980. Upward Communication in Industry: An Experiment. *Human Relations* (Dec.1980):929–942.
24. Simpson, R.L. 1959. Vertical and Horizontal Communication in Formal Organizations. *Administrative Quarterly* (Sept.1959):195.
25. Goldhaber, G.M., et al., op. cit.
26. Levering, R., Moskowitz, M., and Kiltz, M. 1984. *The 100 Best Companies to Work For in America.* Reading, Mass.: Addison-Wesley.
27. Farace, R.V., Monge, P.R., and Russell, H.M. 1977. *Communicating and Organizing.* Reading, Mass.: Addison-Wesley.
28. *WSJ* (13 April 1985):1.
29. *Fortune* (2 August 1985):46.
30. Kiechell, W., III. 1985. Managing a Downsized Operation. *Fortune* (22 July 1985):155–160.
31. *Business Week* (24 June 1985):28.
32. Goldhaber, G.M., et al., op. cit., p. 160.
33. Kotter, J.P. 1984. *Power and Influence: Beyond Formal Authority.* New York: Free Press.
34. Adapted from Gross, B. M. 1968. *Organizations and Their Managing.* New York: The Free Press, pp. 242–248.
35. Gabarro, J., and J. Kotter. 1980. Managing Your Boss. *Harvard Business Review* (Jan.–Feb. 1980):92–100.

Power and Politics

Chapter 11

Chapter Goals By the end of this chapter, you will be able to:

1. Define power as distinct from political activity.
2. Identify sources of position and personal power.
3. Define major instances of legitimate and illegitimate use of power in organizations.
4. Suggest at least three ways to gain power in the vertical hierarchy.
5. Suggest at least three ways to gain power in the horizontal network in organizations.
6. Identify at least three organizational areas in which political activity is most likely to be found.
7. Describe the environmental factors for empowerment of employees.

Dilemma The Boss's Son

Jim Davis was the perfect employee according to Ellen Blair, the resort owner. Jim had been with the resort for over 15 years, and as head of the kitchen and restaurant facility, he was precise about what he wanted from his employees. The employees respected him and were proud to be associated with the resort facility that got the most compliments.

Jim's health was a problem for him. He tended to tire easily, and he was in and out of the hospital for tests because he had frequent headaches. He also had a flair for bumping into things. He had recently spilled the entire coffee machine on two waiters, and last year he broke his leg while walking backwards down the stairs as he talked to two employees about the need for excellence in service.

Jim was very dogmatic about how things should be run. Employees who wanted to survive learned one rule: agree with Jim and you *will* survive.

Jim's son, Virgil, was in his first year of college and was home on summer break. Jim thought that by working with him at the resort that Virgil could learn a lot. Virgil was exactly like his father in his attitudes toward the world. He was self-assured and often commented that although he was young, he already knew a great deal about people and the way they worked best. Unfortunately, however, Virgil lacked his father's work ethic.

The Kitchen and Restaurant Group

The kitchen and restaurant group at the resort was composed of 15 employees, 5 of whom worked in the kitchen and the other 10 in the restaurant. Most of the employees were in their early twenties, except for the cook and maitre d', who were 45 and 38, respectively.

The group worked well together and often pitched in to help each other at peak times. The head cook, June Alexander, often did some of the more menial chores when the other kitchen people needed help, and the maitre d' stayed after hours frequently to help clean up.

When Jim was ill or away from the resort, June assumed the leadership role. All of the complaints about everything seemed to go to June because she was a good listener and showed that she liked her coworkers. June was a very hard worker herself and was viewed by the staff as Jim's natural successor.

Jim Gets Sick

In July, Jim got sick and had to take a three-week leave of absence. June took over as facility manager while maintaining her role as chief cook. She was careful to let the other employees know that she was simply filling in for Jim until he got better. June did not want to cause any problems for Jim or for herself when Jim returned.

June knew that Virgil was not a good employee. She had observed that he was more interested in girls and golf than in work. His dad often let him leave early or gave him assignments that accommodated the young man's social schedule. In fact, Virgil pretty much set his own work schedule, yet Jim paid Virgil more than he did any of the other summer help. Word of this spread quickly and continued to cause problems when June took over.

June Makes Some Changes

After two days, however, June saw a need to make some changes in the work load. She hired another college student to help in the kitchen. She also reassigned some people to different tasks so the jobs that were less pleasant were divided among more employees. For example, two of the worst jobs were the garbage detail and night cleanup. Instead of having only two people do this work, as Jim had, June decided to give everyone a share of these assignments.

Virgil's social activities were soon interrupted, and so was his golf playing. He began by complaining bitterly and soon tried to get other workers to complain about June's actions. No one was fond of Virgil, so the work group really did not want to back him, yet they were apprehensive about how to act since Jim would probably return soon. Virgil complained that things were running smoothly until June took over and that his dad "should be told how things are going." The crew agreed that the operation certainly was not running as smoothly as before. Virgil was probably the major cause of this, but the others agreed that they wanted things to be the way they were. At this point, management started to get some complaints about the restaurant, and Ellen Blair asked June what was going on.

June was thoroughly frustrated. She didn't know what to do.

Questions

1. What positional and personal power bases did June have?
2. What legitimate and illegitimate power did Virgil use?
3. What power techniques could June use to solve the situation?
4. Where could June use politics, and what should she do politically?

The Meaning of Power

Several recent books have demonstrated a renewed interest in the concept of power in organizations. The titles of these books are *Power and Influence, Power Talk* and *Corporate Power and Social Responsibility* (1). "Power and Influence" is also the title of some college courses. These books and courses have helped increase the general information base about power-oriented behavior and demonstrate the importance of studying power in organizations. They also attest to the fact that "power" is not a dirty word!

A theme common to most definitions of power is that power is used to influence others with the goal of attaining desired outcomes for the powerholders. Three frequently used definitions of power are:

1. Power is the ability of a person (or group) to induce another person (or group) to behave in the way that one desires.
2. Power is a personal or positional attribute that is the base of one's influence.
3. Power is the ability to get someone else to do something we want done, or the ability to make things happen in the way that we want (2).

For our purposes, we define **power** as "the capacity to modify the conduct of other employees in a desired manner, together with the capacity to avoid having one's own behavior modified in undesired ways by other employees" (3). In short, a person, department, or organization has the capacity to control others and to avoid being controlled. Power is both a function of what we potentially can do to others, and the reaction of others when we actually try to use power. The definition states that power is *not* an action, that is, one person cannot "power" another. A person can, however, use power on others. Power is thus a capacity that is used. Some authors call this use of power **influence.**

For example, if a manager tells an employee to come to work on Saturday to complete a work assignment and if the employee does not show up, we would question the capacity of the manager to influence that employee. We would question the manager's power, especially if the manager does not take action against the employee for not complying with the initial request to come to work.

In a practical sense, power and influence are used interchangeably. We therefore refer to **power** throughout our discussion.

Isn't power simply a "bag of tricks" to manipulate others?

"Power" is not a dirty word! It is the capacity to exert influence on others. It is in the broadest sense the ability to make things happen, *not* a sneaky set of tactics for pushing others into the ground. Indeed, power is a necessary and exciting part of organizational life. We all know that it can be used irresponsibly with selfish and cunning motives, but keep in mind that power is in fact necessary and can be used responsibly. In this chapter you will learn about ways to use power responsibly and ways to recognize when others are not being responsible. (The ethical considerations of using power are discussed in Chapter 15.)

Power for Individuals

Former President of the United States Harry Truman often remarked that **leadership** is the ability to get people to do what they don't want to do and like it. As most people who are in leadership positions discover, this is easier said than done. Leaders do not usually "get people to do" anything. The key is persuasion through the use of power.

Power cannot happen in isolation from others. The person who wants to use power must find someone to receive it. Furthermore, it's a rare situation in which only one person has all of the power. An example will clarify this idea.

Early one morning, Walter found out that his boss was about to give him a huge assignment and to ask that Walter not go on vacation. Walter had heard that this assignment was coming. He knew that his boss, Frank, had a report to get out and needed Walter's help. About 9:00 A.M., as predicted, Frank arrived and the following discussion ensued:

Walter: Hey Frank, how are you?

Frank: Great, couldn't be better. Listen, do you have a minute to talk about something?

Walter: Sure.

Frank: You remember that sales campaign we were going to do and never got around to. Well, guess what? They want us to go ahead with it by next month. Harry [Frank's boss] wants me to give him a report by the end of next week. He's so unreasonable at times!

Walter: Yeah, I know what you mean, but without you, he couldn't get started. You know the stuff.

Frank: Well, I guess you're right.

Walter: Besides, didn't you put together all that data we gave you?

Frank: Yeah, I did.

Walter: I'm sure glad you have all that stuff. As you know, I'm going on vacation next week, and I'd hate to work all weekend getting those figures. It looks as if you're all set.

Frank: I guess so, but . . .

Walter: If you need any help, just let me know. I can work on it until I leave, which should give you everything you need. O.K.?

Frank: O.K., let's talk once I've had a chance to return some phone calls.

Walter: Good.

When you analyze this situation, Frank may be the boss, but who had the most power here? If you answer "Walter," does this mean that Frank is a weak boss or ineffective? We don't know, do we, but we agree that the balance of power went to Walter.

Positional and Personal Power

An important distinction suggested by the Frank and Walter interaction is to determine whether power is **positional** or **personal**. **Positional power** is given to the holder of an office or key position. An example is the manager or the team coach. These positions carry a title (i.e., "manager" or "coach") and the individual who holds the position has certain rights as a result. The individual can call meetings, award jobs, give out rewards, and even punish others.

The acquisition of **formal power** is usually a product of an individual's being assigned a given position in a company. This assignment conveys **authority,** which has two distinct aspects:

1. The person in authority has power because he or she holds a certain position, *not* because of personal characteristics;

2. Employees initially comply with individuals in authority because they assume that people in formal leadership positions have a legitimate right to exercise the position's authority.

In contrast to positional power, **personal power** is not given to an individual, but it nevertheless affects others. Walter has no formal position, but we see how influential he is. Personal power is more a matter of personality or persuasive ability than of formal authority.

SOLVING THE DILEMMA

What positional and personal power bases did June have?

June had the formal position of acting manager and the formal position of head chef. Her formal position as acting manager is somewhat weak and needs to be supplemented by personal power to be effective. Her personal power bases come from her compelling personality and her cordial relationships with the staff. Ultimately, June will have to rely on her personal power if she wants to get things done at the resort.

Legitimate Versus Illegitimate Influence

In addition to the distinction between positional and personal power, two other concepts must be explored: legitimate versus illegitimate influence. **Legitimate influence** is exerted by a person who is perceived as having the right to influence others in a given area. **Illegitimate influence,** on the other hand, is exerted when someone does *not* have the right to influence others in a given area.

Consider a manager who holds a formal position, as Jim does at the restaurant. Jim would be exercising legitimate power if he gave orders about how to set up the dining room, buy food, or organize the days-off schedule. He would be exercising illegitimate influence if he tried to tell June how to handle her money or what type of social activities were right for her children.

Another interesting example concerns military procedure. In the army, soldiers are taught to salute the uniform, not the man, which suggests that rank guarantees legitimacy. Situations can arise, however, in which soldiers consider the influence attempts of rank to be illegitimate. If an officer were to show extreme favoritism or were excessively abusive to a particular person, the soldiers might not comply with orders. At times, this noncompliance might be somewhat concealed. For example, they might drag their heels about getting jobs done, or they might literally follow all of the rules in the rule book.

Combining the categories of power. Having positional power does not ensure legitimate influence. If we combine these two categories, we get some ideas about how power is used in organizations. Table 11.1 shows how this combining process works.

Table 11.1
Examples of Types of Power and Influence

	Positional (Assigned)	*Personal (Not Assigned)*
Legitimate (Accepted as Proper)	Boss gives work related orders.	Classmate is knowledgeable, so you ask her questions before asking the instructor.
Illegitimate (Not Accepted as Proper)	Teacher shows extreme favoritism to a student.	Boss's son, to the irritation of other employees, gets workers to do work even though he has no supervisory responsibility.

As you study the combinations in the table, you will see the different ways in which power is used. **Position-legitimate** influence is what we usually mean when we say that a person has "the authority to act." This is the exercise of power that is both assumed with a position and seen as the right to exert influence. The right to hire, fire, pay people, assign them to work schedules, and represent work groups are all viewed as legitimate managerial activities.

Effective leaders try to take legitimate actions. One goal of an effective leader or employee is to try to ensure that one's actions are perceived by others as legitimate for the position. The more that one's behavior comes under this designation of "legitimate," the easier it will be to influence others.

New managers often confront the problem of trying to gain legitimacy for making decisions. A student who becomes head of an activities group may have the same problem. The individual may hold the office of "president," but other students usually challenge this authority until the person becomes established in the position. This process changes perceptions of the leader from position-illegitimate to position-legitimate. Later we examine techniques that accomplish this movement.

The **position-illegitimate** influence is usually exercised when individuals try to extend their formal legitimate power beyond the intended areas. Those in management positions tend to enter this domain because subordinates often give them the benefit of a doubt. For example, a unit manager has considerable say over what happens during an employee's day, so employees often have a difficult time separating what is legitimate influence from what is not.

A clearcut example of illegitimate use of influence is the male manager who makes advances to females in the workplace and who trades their attentions to him for promotions or financial gain. From the perspective of the organization, society, the victims, and other employees, this use of power is totally illegitimate. The legal system has attempted, in such cases, to hold the manager directly responsible for his actions, rather than hold the company responsible for the manager's actions. In other words, although the manager might be considered a representative of the organization in some situations, this type of abuse of a formal position is considered so heinous that the courts hold the managers *themselves* responsible.

Personal-illegitimate influence. The most common way a person could gain this power is by personal access to valued rewards or threats of punishment. The department hothead who threatens coworkers is an example of this type of influence. One worker tells of being threatened physically by a co-worker because he was "working too hard" and "making the rest of us look bad." The organization operated an incentive system, and the employee was out-performing his coworkers. Management was delighted, but they were also pressuring other employees to match the worker's performance.

Personal-legitimate influence. This type of influence is usually based on a person's expertise, knowledge, personal charm, or charisma. Individuals who have personal-legitimate influence are respected and sought for their advice and information. These persons cannot be identified by looking at an organization's formal positions chart or by asking "Who is the manager of administration?" Just because a person holds a formal position does not mean that he or she is the most influential person in the organization.

Solving the Dilemma

What legitimate and illegitimate power did Virgil use?

As an employee, Virgil has opportunities to talk with his manager, make decisions within the limits of his job, and influence his job design to the extent that job design changes would make him more effective.

Virgil, however, exercised many illegitimate uses of power. He tried to act as if he were the manager, and tried to reverse June's formal power as if it were his. Virgil also took it upon himself to set his own schedule (or at least to try to set it) without checking with June. He thus used illegitimate power to make decisions not within his job scope.

How do people gain power?

The remainder of the chapter addresses this question, for the essence of effectiveness in an organization is gaining and using power. The goal of any organization member is to gain as much power as possible, either by positional or personal means.

Table 11.2 identifies the six major bases for gaining power in an organization.

TABLE 11.2
Ways to Gain Power

	Action	*Name of Power*
1.	Giving rewards	Reward
2.	Administering punishment	Coercive
3.	Authority—having a position	Legitimate
4.	Referent—having ability to appeal to or charm others	Referent
5.	Expertise—having knowledge, or being an expert	Expert
6.	Problem-solving power—solving critical problems for the organization	Problem solving

Gaining power means that a person who is perceived in a certain way will be able to exert influence over others. As you will see, some of these power bases are easier to obtain and to use than others.

Giving rewards or administering punishment, the first two ways of gaining power, are accomplished when others perceive that you can give them rewards or punish them if they comply or do not comply with you, respectively. These power bases are why employees may follow orders and do something, even when they are convinced privately that the boss is wrong or may even be exercising illegitimate authority. Employees want to keep their jobs, get good raises, and be perceived as "supportive of the boss." In short, they want to gain the **rewards** given by the boss and to avoid **punishments** that can be inflicted.

The expectancy model, discussed in Chapter 3, shows how managers can gain reward power. Employees are told that if they work hard they will receive certain rewards. Once the employees decide that the work is worth it, they can anticipate certain rewards when they comply. They also know that the manager is the one who administers the rewards. The manager has thus gained reward power because employees are willing to work in a way prescribed by the manager.

Managers should understand the distinction between reward power and punishment power. First, as a practical matter, lower level managers may not have any formal reward power, although they may be given limited punishment power. Second, as you will recall from the discussion of reinforcement theory (see Chapter 4), the two have different applications: punishment is appropriate to suppress undesirable behaviors, while reward can be used to increase desirable behaviors.

Authority, a third way to gain power, is the designation by others that one has power. This is the positional power that we discussed earlier. The way that one gets authority is by being employed by an organization to fill a managerial position or by owning a company. These means of gaining power are the most common and the most immediately recognized by others. Followers respond to one's position. A student who assumes the presidency of a campus association automatically receives questions about the association, its direction, and various operating procedures. Unless this person had great informal power, she would not be asked one question about these matters if she did not have the title of "president." Power of authority is impersonal, because it comes with position and does not really have much to do with individual behavior in the position. Authority is also highly predictable. In fact, most organizations have job descriptions that define this type of power base.

Referent power, a fourth way to gain influence, is the quality that we call "charisma"—that intangible something that some people seem to have. Sometimes these individuals have personality traits (e.g., being extroverted or having high self-esteem) that make them appealing. Others typically follow a person with referent power because that individual is likable or very dynamic.

An example of behavior that elicits referent power is "dressing for success." Others seem to respond to certain clothing in a way that attributes power to the wearer. Wearing soiled uniforms or mismatched colors are all ways to lose power according to the experts on dress (4). Gaining power through dress includes pin-striped suits, appropriate use of uniforms, and certain hair styles. Giving the appearance of power is almost as important as having a legitimate power position. In fact, one can lead to the other. Note, however, that the problem with this type of power base is that it is very performance-dependent. When the individual does not perform as expected, the power base is destroyed.

Expertise is also based on performance (i.e., the observation of others that a person's behavior shows special knowledge or skill). A typical way to gain power through expertise is to use information not possessed by others. By being connected to the grapevine, a person can gain power in the organization. As with charismatic leadership, however, this type of power base also depends on performance. If, for example, a rumor does not pan out, influence may be withdrawn from the person.

Problem-solving power comes from a person's ability to solve critical issues innovatively for the organization. The primary power source is ability to enhance the organization positively in relation to its key problem areas. Those who can help the organization achieve its goals by overcoming the most difficult, pressing, and dangerous problems are likely to wield great power. Consider a timely example:

> The health care industry is currently going through enormous change because of competition, government regulation, and consumer awareness. As a result, two primary activities are important: (1) sophisticated management techniques, and (2) marketing. People who engage successfully in activities related to either area will, in all likelihood, gain great power in the organization. Nurses and physicians have the most difficulty with this change in the industry because they believe that the quality of care may be compromised when so much attention is devoted to management, budgets, and cost control. They also have not been trained in management; their professional focus is in how to care for patients. Interestingly, a major shift in nursing education is the introduction of nursing management courses. Today's nurses are being trained both as providers of health care and as those responsible for managing the organization.

These six bases of influence—coercive (administering punishment), reward, authority, referent, expert, and problem-solving—are the major ways in which people gain power in organizations. The more bases of power an individual has, the more capable that person is of influencing others. This also means that the powerful person receives more communication and response from others. Table 11.3 summarizes other findings concerning these power bases (5).

Is power something that keeps changing?

Yes, definitely! A primary example of power bases that are changing for a group of positions are the power bases in the U.S. health care industry. Traditionally, physicians have been considered as close to omnipotent as one can get. They have formal authority to practice medicine, the expertise to pass judgment, and in a sense, they also have the coercive and reward power to give us health. An individual physician who has charisma could

Table 11.3 *Research Findings on Bases of Power*

Giving rewards and administering punishment

1. Can be inconsistent or unrelated to performance.
2. Can affect frequency of employee performance.
3. Can produce undesirable side effects of frustration, fear, and alienation.
4. Requires considerable surveillance of employees.

Authority

1. Is important for compliance with manager's wishes.
2. Is an inconsistent factor in organizational effectiveness.
3. Is good for initial employee contacts.
4. Can enhance feelings of frustration and powerlessness among employees.
5. May lead to minimal compliance only and an increase in resistance.

Referent

1. Is of only moderate importance to formal power gain within the organization.
2. Is related to organizational effectiveness.
3. Can lead to enthusiastic and unquestioning trust, loyalty, and compliance of subordinates or co-workers.
4. May lead to highly personal and selfish gains and to manipulation of subordinates.

Expertise

1. Is most strongly and consistently related to satisfaction of followers and performance of person with expertise.
2. Is closely related to climate of trust, which can influence employee motivation.
3. Is very effective under conditions of structured tasks, and may eliminate or diminish need for close supervision.

Problem-Solving

1. Is most effective combined with expert power.
2. Is closely related to climate of trust.
3. Is effective in ambiguous conditions.

SOURCE: Adapted from French, J.R., Jr., and Raven, B. The Basis of Social Power. In Cartwright, D. (Ed.) 1959. *Studies in Social Power.* Ann Arbor, Mich.: Institute for Social Research, University of Michigan, pp. 150–167.

cover all of the power bases! For these reasons, physicians have commanded sustained public attention and money, as well.

For a variety of reasons, the power bases of physicians are being questioned more and more. The public has discovered that we can do many things on our own to make ourselves healthy. Other health models, besides physician care, can be used (e.g., prevention and controlling one's environment). Physicians will probably always maintain their power by authority, but they seem to be losing some expert power as the public realizes that no one physician can have the entire picture concerning an individual's health and well-being.

What are the signs of power in an organization?

In many organizations, there are visible signs of the distribution of power. The following ten visible signs of power are indicators for recognizing people who have more power than others in an organization. Those who

Table 11.4
Major Points About Power

Basis of Power	*How Obtained*	*How Maintained*
Coercive and reward	Being able to give rewards or administer punishment; followers must want rewards or fear punishment	Keep giving rewards or punishment
Authority	Holding a formal position; relatively easy power to get	Keep the job
Referent	Charisma; personality; knowing the right people; difficult to get	Performance must not conflict with image; get a press agent
Expertise	Special knowledge; difficult to get	Maintain skill or knowledge
Problem-solving	Able to solve important problems	Solve problems critical to organization

have more power also have many of these rights, privileges, and characteristics.

1. Maintain a larger staff than other departments.
2. Meet with top management on a frequent basis.
3. Put items on the agenda of key decision-making meetings.
4. Get preferred schedules.
5. Sign checks for the organization.
6. Are approached for information about top management.
7. Have an office located near the boss.
8. Are deferred to in meetings.
9. Are talked about by employees in terms of "What does this person want from a particular task?"
10. Run a department that is unique in the organization (i.e., nobody else is able to perform the department's work).

An interesting exercise is to consider why we tend to respond to some people as if they have power and not to others. Consider your classroom environment. Why are some teachers more influential than others? Could it be that the more influential have a more solid power base than do the others? Table 11.4 above, summarizes the major points that we have made about how one gains power in an organization:

Knowledge Check

1. Power is the use of influence to get others to act in a specific way. T or F?
2. A manager who tells a subordinate to rewrite a report is using:
   a. formal-illegitimate power
   b. formal-legitimate power
   c. informal-illegitimate power
   d. informal-legitimate power
3. Dressing for success is an example of reward power. T or F?
4. The most predictable means of gaining power is by __________.

5. Abuse of power in an office refers to people who are exercising formal-__________ influence.
6. Power, once obtained, will not change hands. T or F?

Answers:

1 F, 2 b, 3 F, 4 authority, 5 illegitimate, 6 F

Power of Organizational Units

Power is often described as a personal characteristic of how one person can influence or dominate another (6). Power in organizations is the result of the complex relationships of roles, tasks, goals, and design of how people work together. For example, some people may have more power because they are working on a new invention or report to top managers in the hierarchy. These organization-wide power sources are best described as either vertical power or horizontal power.

Vertical Power

Vertical power is the use of power bases to influence various levels of the organization. The formal hierarchy of authority gives power and authority to managers. People at the top of the hierarchy have greater influence than lower level participants. They can set goals that are used by the entire organization and can cause people to alter their actions. The authority granted to management is reflected in the structure and design of the organization. This power allocation can be described as follows:

> The design of an organization, its structure, is first and foremost the system of control and authority by which the organization is governed. In the organizational structure, decision discretion is allocated to various positions and the distribution of formal authority is established. Furthermore, by establishing the pattern of prescribed communication and reporting requirements, the structure provides some participants with more and better information and more central locations in the communication network (7).

As a result of the vertical relationships in an organization, the power of managers in the hierarchy comes from five sources: formal position, resource distribution, experience, control of decisions, and access to information (8).

Managers have certain rights, responsibilities, and opportunities that are given to them because of their *formal position*. The higher a manager moves up the organizational hierarchy, the more he or she gains power because of position. Based solely on position, a president, chief executive officer, or chairman of the board has the most power. We referred to this power basis earlier as *authority.*

Managers have a substantial say about the *distribution of resources* to employees. As noted earlier, resource allocation can be used to reward or punish. It also creates a relationship in which employees depend on managers for the physical and financial resources necessary to do tasks.

Managers often have power because of their *experience.* For example, many managers have experienced upsurges and downswings in business, so they know what to expect in terms of budgeting, personnel, and customer response. Lower level employees often lack both the experience and the broad perspective to cope effectively with these changes.

Vertical power is enhanced because managers *control decision making.* The primary control comes from the type of decisions made. Top managers usually make decisions about the entire organization. Lower level managers are concerned with specific operating procedures and budget expenditures. The more defined the decision is, the less power is gained by the manager.

Managers have more *access to information* than other organizational members. Information is power, as we saw in Chapter 10. The higher up in the organization a manager is, the more information that individual has. Higher level managers are "allowed access" to unique information sources not available to other employees. For example, the higher the level of the manager, the more she can access financial data and be privileged to the ongoing negotiations involving an acquisition or merger.

These five factors (i.e., formal position, resource distribution, experience, control of decisions, and access to information) are all sources of power in the vertical hierarchy of an organization.

Can a lower level employee participate in vertical power?

The answer is *yes.* If an employee can observe a few key principles of vertical power, she is more likely to gain power. These principles, their implications, and examples of each are summarized in Table 11.5.

How can one gain power in the vertical hierarchy?

Table 11.5 answers that question. The first column shows the design factors, or characteristics, of the vertical hierarchy of an organization. The second column suggests a way to generate power in terms of each design factor. For example, if a job has only a few rules associated with it, the job holder is more likely to have power than the person whose job has many restrictions. The final column contains an example of each factor. For instance, to maximize an employee's power in terms of the job rules factor, the manager would remove as many rules as possible that pertained to the employee's work role (9).

Power can be controlled. Indeed, one can have a great deal of control over one's power in an organization, more than most employees realize. The power base starts as soon as the employee takes a job (i.e., a routine, highly mechanized job offers fewer power opportunities than a job that is less rigid and newer to the organization).

Refer again to Table 11.5, which gives many examples of how lower level employees can gain power. This list should be helpful to the new

Table 11.5
Ways to Gain Power in the Vertical Hierarchy

Design Factors	*Maximum Power Increase*	*Example of Increasing Power*
Rules in the job	Fewer rules	Manager removes rules from employee job.
Job design	Take a new job	Introduction of a new type of job for which the organization has no experience.
Number of tasks	Take on many tasks	Assigned tasks are much more varied.
Rewards for innovation and unusual performance	Get a job with these	Organization rewards innovation rather than compliance with routine or rules.
Approvals needed to act	Few	Be your own boss as much as possible.
Type of task	Central to organization	Focus on concerns of top management.
Physical location	Central	Locate your office near the boss.
Contact with others	Frequent	Combine work and social opportunities when mixing with employees
Participation in extra work	High	Join task forces and volunteer for central jobs of interest to management.
Expertise	High	Learn as much as possible about the company and about your job; seek opportunities to tell others what you know.

SOURCE: Modified from Kanter, R.B. 1983. *Change Masters: Innovation for Productivity in the American Corporation.* New York: Simon & Schuster, pp. 65–77.

employee, for hard work is not the only way to become effective. Indeed, many employees find that hard work is only part of the story.

Some organizations actually try to distribute power to lower organizational levels because management realizes that everyone becomes more productive when this occurs. McCormick and Company, Inc., is the largest spice maker in the United States. Charles P. McCormick, whose uncle founded the company, wrote a book entitled *The Power of People,* which is still the key management guide for the organization (10). At McCormick and Company, power is distributed throughout the organization by means of "multiple management" boards. Thirteen boards serve as junior-level boards of directors, which attack specific problems of each of the major operating divisions. The boards address questions as far ranging and diverse as what computer to buy, whether the company should enter a new business, and how to orient new employees. The boards also bring employees and management much closer to one another than they are in most organization structures. As a result, the company remains largely nonunion. It is profitable, and it also has a rule that all employees will be called by their first name, including the president "Hilly" (Hillsman Wilson).

Horizontal Power

People who have worked in organizations for some time will tell you that the vertical power hierarchy is only one way to define who has power. Employees and departments at the same formal level have different amounts of power. Horizontal power is the capacity to influence individuals or units at the same organizational level as the influencer.

This discussion focuses on some specific studies (11), which identified factors that accounted for certain organizational departments being rated more powerful than others by employees. Five factors consistently influenced the horizontal power relationships among departments:

1. Ensuring that others must contact or depend on the department
2. Controlling financial resources
3. Ensuring that all information goes through the department
4. Maintaining lack of substitute ability
5. Developing ability to cope with uncertainty

Ensuring contact with a department is a necessary by-product of dividing work among organizational units. Some units are more critical than others, and therefore have more power. The oil industry frequently shifts power among various departments depending on the prevalent economic conditions. When times are good, the geological, geophysical, and technical departments gain prominence. In hard times, the financial departments have more power. The powerful departments can initiate strategic plans, control resources, and generally run the company.

The strength of dependency can be established by the *number* of dependencies. When eight to ten departments must go to the strategic planning department before initiating a new marketing idea, the strategic planning department gains power.

Control over financial resources is another important source of power. These resources are primarily money and people. Departments that generate money for the organization create power for themselves. Departments that have the most people tend also to have power. One interesting process of resource allocation is the budgeting process. "Power accrues to those departments that bring in or provide resources that are highly valued by the organization. The power enables these departments to obtain more of the scarce resources allocated within the organization" (12).

Ensuring information, or centrality, refers to a department's role in the primary activity of the organization. Several measures reflect the centrality of the department, but the most important is how closely the work of the department affects the final output of the organization. In most organizations, those departments that deliver direct service to customers or produce a product have more power than other departments. Typically, the personnel department struggles to gain recognition while the engineering department of an engineering consulting firm has great power (13).

Maintaining a lack of substitute-ability is the degree to which other departments, outside agencies, or other people can not perform the same work as a particular department. An interesting example of increasing high substitute ability is occurring in information services departments. One study shows that when computers were first introduced, programming was a rare and specialized profession. Programmers were difficult to hire and demanded a great deal of power within organizations (14). At present, programmers are much more plentiful, and other company departments commonly have computer experts too. Therefore programmers can be substituted easily.

Coping with uncertainty refers to the ways in which departments handle the inevitable uncertainty of busy schedules, crises, and lack of necessary information to complete tasks. Powerful departments use three techniques to cope with uncertainty: obtain prior information, absorption, and prevention (15). **Obtaining prior information** enables a department to anticipate events and thus prepare for them. **Absorption** means reacting effectively to a negative event to ward off adverse consequences. **Prevention** means building a strong department.

> One department used these techniques of coping to gain power. The training and development department of a real estate company was a five-person group. Their budget was low, few other departments used their services, and others in the company believed that they could get adequate training outside the organization. The training and development department reacted by bringing in some consultants who taught courses on how to analyze the market, how to deal with customers, and how to identify the financial impact of an investment. When agents were confused about how to proceed with a customer, the department became an excellent source for "coping with uncertainty." It also became very influential with top management.

Horizontal power is thus a product of these five factors—dependency, financial resources, centrality, substitute ability, and ability to cope with uncertainty. These factors, when combined, can indeed be a powerful force. As Lucy says in a "Peanuts" cartoon when she looks at her fingers separately, "They ain't much; but when they get together, they can be real powerful."

Solving the Dilemma

What power techniques could June use to solve the situation?

June should not use her formal position, because she is only acting manager and her role as chief cook does not offer her enough power to make changes or to confront Virgil. Her best hope is to use her expertise to keep things moving smoothly. She also needs to separate Virgil from the other employees. She clearly should enforce company policy with Virgil.

June needs to make herself the person on whom the other workers depend for information. Before she makes more changes, she may want to re-establish her relationships with coworkers, which is best accomplished one-on-one. June should work to communicate to her subordinates that she is the manager and is able to make all of the necessary decisions that go with the job.

Knowledge Check

1. Which of the following is *not* a source of vertical power:
   a. formal position
   b. experience
   c. access to information
   d. resource distribution
   e. dependency
2. When a job requires many approvals to act, the job holder tends to have greater power than others. T or F?
3. The more defined the type of decision to be made, the (less, more) power is gained by the manager.
4. The power of a department is influenced by these factors: dependency, coping with uncertainty, centrality, __________ and __________.
5. Three ways departments cope with uncertainty are __________, __________, and __________.

Answers:

1 e, 2 F, 3 less, 4 substitute ability, and financial resources, 5 obtain prior information, absorption, and prevention

Politics: Tactics for Success

Politics relates to the ways in which organizational members earn and gain power, especially during times of uncertainty. **Organizational politics** is defined as any action taken to gain power or to prevent others from influencing individuals or groups in undesired ways.

In this section we examine what it takes to be perceived as an expert, how to gain referent power, how to establish an informal yet legitimate power base, and generally how to be influential in an organization.

Studies of managerial attitudes toward politics in organizations yield consistent findings. Managers have a negative view toward politics and believe that politics hurt rather than help the organization. They also believe that political behavior occurs more frequently at upper management levels than at lower levels, but they also perceive that politics is common to all organizations at all levels. Finally, political behavior seems to arise in certain types of decisions, such as those concerned with structural change, but seems to be relatively absent from other decisions, such as handling of employee grievances (16).

As with the term "power," *politics* often has a negative connotation. Some employees would say, "Oh, she's always playing politics." If they mean that she is effectively using and gaining power, then good for her. If they mean, however, that she is pursuing her own goals rather than those of the organization, then management has cause for concern.

When Political Activity Is Most Likely to Occur

The three situations in which employees most noticeably engage in political activity are (1) when the organization is reorganized, (2) when interdepartmental coordination is attempted, and (3) when decisions are being made about resource allocation. All involve considerable uncertainty.

When an organization changes its structure, we can expect enormous political activity, because when the structure is changed, people's power positions are also changed. At the same time, designation of formal authority is not always clear in a new structure, so alert employees see many opportunities to gain power. They engage in a "jockeying for power" that is noticeable in the many interchanges with management about "what I can do." One way to gain power is simply to perform as if you have it. If others in the organization do not respond negatively, you assume that you can keep the power.

Playing politics escalates when departments try to coordinate their activities. A small high-technology company found this out the hard way. The marketing department had just completed an extensive survey of the company's primary markets. The marketing people wanted to tell the design engineers what they had found so the engineers could build component parts to respond to the market. The engineers were invited to a meeting to discuss the new component parts. As a result, however, of extremely poor interdepartmental relationships, the engineers who showed up at the meeting refused to evaluate the information honestly. This passive resistance frustrated the marketing department's attempts to influence the engineers. An interesting result of this behavior was that top management decided to fire the entire design engineering department and to hire a new department with the mandate that "you get your information about the market from the marketing department, and we expect you to respond." This mandate redefined the organizational politics and firmly established the power base for decisions with marketing.

The allocation of scarce resources causes political activity. The resources most frequently at the root of politics are money and staffing. A local beer distributorship bought a brewery that had about 200 employees. The new owner was convinced that costs could be cut by employing fewer people. Soon after he announced his views to key managers, he noticed an active political environment. Managers furiously wrote reports to justify their personnel. There were many "it was his fault" type of comments and many departmental attempts to hire new people, presumably so the new workers could then be the ones "trimmed" from the work force, rather than the present personnel. He also noticed that top managers were more often in their office—talking about the needs of their people. The owner had difficulty stopping the politics until he remembered that political activity increases with uncertainty. His solution was to bring in a consultant to establish staffing guidelines, including productivity figures for each department. Once this was done, the managers made their own recommendations, and political activity decreased dramatically.

The effective use of power during such situations can result in power shifts. Let's see what happens when employees "engage in politics."

Engaging in Politics

Many specific behaviors are used when people play politics in organizations. These behaviors, or tactics, can be *overt* or *covert.* We can summarize the various tactics used to gain power.

1. **Image building** encompasses those activities designed to create and maintain a good image. These include having confidence about work activities, drawing attention to one's successes, dressing in certain ways, being enthusiastic about the organization, and maintaining status symbols.
2. **Gaining support** involves those activities that gain endorsement, backing, a mentor relationship, or legitimacy to perform.
3. **Selective use of information** includes withholding information or giving only selected parts to others (i.e., compiling reports that state what one wants and that interpret information in a favorable way).
4. **Managing responsibility,** that is, blaming others for failure and taking credit for success.
5. **Networking and alliances** ensure that one has friends and coworkers who are favorably disposed to oneself. This includes doing favors for others, letting others win when one could win, and making others believe that one is going to do well by the organization.
6. **Compromise** is giving in on contested issues.
7. **Rule manipulation** involves sticking closely to the rule book when it is to one's advantage, and trying to change rules and procedures when the need arises.
8. **Gaining resources** means getting bigger budgets, more physical space in the organization, and more rights to make time management decisions.
9. **Delegation** refers to gaining work, information, or responsibility given by a manager.

Not only is using political tactics important, but pursuing new and innovative ideas for organizational development is critical to increasing an individual's power. (Recall our earlier discussion of the different types of power.) This means that individuals will gain power to the extent that they are perceived as trying to improve things by solving key organizational problems.

Some companies try to encourage problem solving in a variety of ways. In other words, they enable individuals who perform effectively to gain as much power as they want. These organizations believe that an infinite amount of power exists and that individuals can have as much as they want, as long as that power works for attainment of organizational goals.

NOW IT'S YOUR TURN

To illustrate these political tactics, let's see what you would do in the following situation. Analysis of this case will give you some personal experience with playing politics in an organization.

Harry was about 55 years old and had been with the Texas Exploration Company for about three years. He was manager of human resources for the entire organization. Previously he had been with another oil company and had served as special assistant to the president.

Harry hired two managers from another oil company, one in the employee relations area to hire and train employees, and one to assume responsibility for employee benefits and pay. Each individual was given the formal title of "Manager," so the organizational structure of the human resources department looked like this:

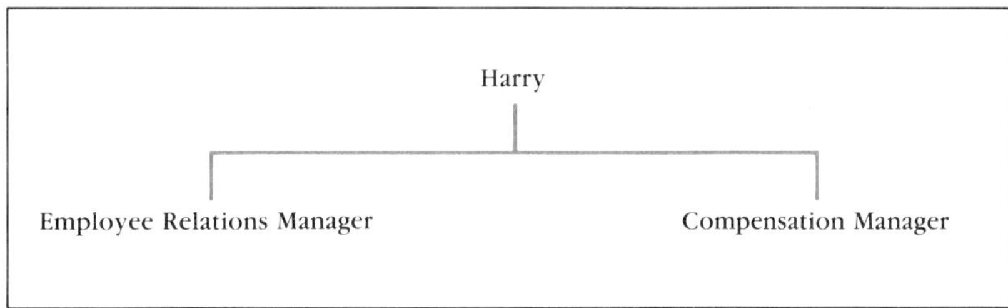

Harry's incompetence was exceeded only by his arrogance. He would give assignments to his staff, dictate the way assignments should be performed, and if things did not work out, he would chastise his subordinates. Harry's department had been spending money foolishly on poorly conceived training programs, consultants, Harry's lavish travels, and in numerous other areas that were useless to the organization. Harry was liked by some of the company managers only because they did not know or care how the work got done in his department and because Harry did favors for them. Harry was skillful at making himself look good to those outside the department.

Assume that you are the employee relations manager in Harry's department. Be careful, for if you blow the whistle on Harry and the organization does not act, you get fired. If you make a big deal about departmental incompetency and Harry does get fired, management may still resent your actions. You want to stay with the organization only if Harry leaves. Consider the tactics for engaging in politics and outline how you would proceed.

1. Image building—build your image and try to destroy Harry's.
2. Selective use of information—do not give Harry essential information. Begin to leak information to the organization about Harry's incompetence.
3. Managing responsibility—blame Harry for everything that goes wrong.
4. Forming alliances and networks—make friends in high places and tell them about what is going on.

5. Compromise—trade favors for support of Harry's removal.

6. Rule manipulation—call Harry on the rules and get others to notice his violations.

The following are the political actions taken by the manager of employee relations in a similar real-life situation.

Harry had legitimate power, that is, he held the position of department manager, and by virtue of his position, he had access to higher level managers in the organization. The employee relations manager therefore had to be careful *not* to appear self-serving by trying to get Harry out of the organization.

The first strategy used was to feed information selectively to Harry, so he could not act as effectively. The chief danger in doing this was that the organization might get hurt, but the employee relations manager rationalized that ultimately the organization would benefit by getting rid of Harry. He also gave Harry an enormous amount of irrelevant information.

Second, the employee relations manager used his networks to feed information into the organization. He commented frequently on how much more effectively "things could be if the department had enough money."

Third, the employee relations manager spent a great deal of time building his own image as a competent, supportive member of the organization. He discussed ways that the department could be used to improve employee relations, and he worked hard to produce quality reports on new programs. (He was trying to contrast his behavior with Harry's.)

The organization finally did respond. Management began to realize what was going on. Key people in the organization began to ask questions, which put Harry on the defensive and occupied his time trying to talk to others in the organization. Top managers began to get involved in the department, and after one year, they asked Harry to leave the company.

Knowledge Check

1. Politics is the activities of power. T or F?

2. The goal of an effective manager is to remove politics from the organization. T or F?

3. Structural change frequently results in political activity in organizations? T or F?

4. Politics is most likely to occur as a result of these three organizational activities: structural change, resource allocation, and ________.

Answers:

1 T, 2 F, 3 T, 4 Interdepartmental coordination

Solving the Dilemma

How could June use politics, and what should she do politically?

June's first line of attack should be to rebuild her networks with employees. These networks will enable her to get information on how to improve the work force and the operations. June has a formal position, and she may want to use it to go to her boss to explain the problem and ask for advice. She could also give Virgil jobs that would isolate him from the other workers so the informal networks are broken. Politically, June must make sure that she does not become isolated from others in the organization.

Empowerment

Doesn't engaging in politics cause more harm than good? Not really. Many organizations are designed to help individuals search for power. The organization lets them have information, money, and support of key people, and may even allow time off from their regular duties to "tinker around with new ideas."

Rosabeth Kanter, who has studied the flow of power in organizations, has developed the idea of **empowerment** (17). She asked the question: What is unique about organizations that makes power more widely accessible? She wanted to know what organizational conditions actually help members play politics! She considers this political "game" to be healthy. Indeed, she views it as the major way in which organizations can innovate.

Her answer to the question about accessibility to power led to some unique tactics and to some pertinent conclusions concerning organizational climate. To make power readily available to people in the organization, three major factors have to be present: open communication systems, network-forming arrangements, and decentralization of resources. These factors create a greater power base for all employees and make the organization as a whole more powerful.

Open communication systems refers to open meetings and to the free exchange of information and results. For example, the organization announces every meeting openly to all employees, and employees can attend meetings of other departments. In these ways, information is exchanged freely.

Network forming arrangements refers to the ways in which employees are linked so they can share ideas. In companies that facilitate a climate of sharing, employees have a great deal of mobility and are given job security so they can explore new ideas without threat of reprimand, and can make extensive use of formal and informal teams. People are expected to spend some work time meeting with others and exchanging ideas.

Decentralization of resources is the final way in which some companies create a climate of power for employees. Decisions are pushed to the lowest level possible, and groups of employees, rather than top management, are given decisions to make. The Hewlett-Packard Company, an electronics firm that makes computers, calculators, and various other precision instruments, believes in empowerment. Units are kept small. There are no time clocks, and offices are arranged in clusters to facilitate communication. Bill Hewlett is quoted in company manuals as saying, "Men and women want to do a good job, a creative job, and if they are provided the proper environment, they will do so" (18).

When an organization uses these three means of distributing power, it is trying to distribute power in such a way that power becomes less necessary, and that all employees can be as effective as they want to be. The degree to which power is granted or withheld from individuals is one operative difference between those companies that stagnate and those that innovate (19). Change-oriented organizations have a large number of integrative mechanisms that encourage fluidity of boundaries, free flow of ideas, and empowerment of employees to act on new information.

Summary Points

- **Power** is the capacity to modify the conduct of other employees in a desired manner together with the capacity to avoid having one's own behavior modified in undesired ways by other employees.
- **Positional power** is given to the holder of an office or other formal position.
- **Personal power** is a matter of personality, charisma, or persuasive abilities.
- Employees and managers can use power in **legitimate** or **illegitimate** ways.
- **Power bases** are formed by ability to give rewards or administer punishment, by having formal authority, by having charisma, through expertise, and through effective problem solving.
- **Expert power** is most strongly and consistently correlated with satisfaction and performance.
- **Formal position** is the least useful means of gaining power in the organization.
- **Politics** refers to the ways in which individuals earn and gain power.
- Politics is most likely to occur during **structural change, interdepartmental coordination,** or **resource allocation.**
- **Empowerment** is a means of distributing power. Three key ways to do this in the organization are through **open communication systems, network-forming arrangements,** and **decentralized operations.**

Questions

1. In your own words, describe the difference between positional and personal power sources. Give an example of each.
2. What are the most visible signs of a person's power in an organization? Couch your discussion in terms of a new employee who is trying to figure out who has or does not have power. What should this employee look for?
3. Should colleges offer courses on "power and influence"? Some professors and students believe that such a course can be invaluable to one's success in organizations, while others believe that the course is simply a lesson in backstabbing and how to manipulate others for personal gain and goal accomplishment. How do you feel? What are the major benefits and drawbacks of such a course?
4. Some top executives have suggested that their organizations would do much better if they could get rid of politics. Based on the discussions in this chapter, do you think that the complete elimination of political behavior is possible? Is politics in fact desirable? If you believe that politics cannot be eliminated, how would you suggest that these executives make political behavior more profitable for the organization?

5. Some managers believe that empowerment of employees would create chaos. Develop an argument for putting Rosabeth Kanter's ideas in use within organizations. Include comments on how empowerment affects employee performance and satisfaction.

EXPLORING: *Intel and Petrie Stores Have Executive Secretary Power.*

[Adapted from "Executive Secretary: A New Rung on the Corporation Ladder," *Business Week* (April 21, 1986):75.]

At Intel Corporation, Jean Jones is an executive secretary to Chairman Gordon E. Moore. She is officially titled "curator of the museum," but most of her power derives from the duties she performs as executive secretary. She screens her boss's telephone calls, goes through his mail and decides what he should see, and schedules his calendar. This power is similar to that of a colleague of Jean Jones who works at Petrie Stores. Hilda Gerstein, now age 75, started out at age 16 as secretary to Chairman Milton J. Petrie of Petrie Stores Corporation. She is now vice-chairman and earns approximately $350,000 per year.

These women are examples of how the executive secretary of an organization can gain more power than the managers and employees who are responsible for profits, growth, and overall company affairs. The secretaries claim that their job is risky because they are tied to the boss's success. Managers in these organizations claim that the executive secretary position has too much power.

Similarly, Nanette Buckhout, executive secretary of John Scully at Apple Computer, is encouraged by Scully to submit her own proposals to improve internal company operations.

Discussion Questions

1. Using the information gained from this chapter, how do you think the executive secretaries got their power?
2. What are the positive and negative aspects of the power gained by executive secretaries?
3. If you were a manager who wanted to see the boss, and if the secretary were not putting you on his calendar, what could you do?

APPLYING: *Gaining Power by Empowerment*

The purposes of this exercise are to increase your awareness of the meaning of power and to enable you to experience giving, receiving, and not receiving power. You will need a small group of classmates to complete this exercise. Eight to ten members works best.

Each person must have two slips of paper and a pencil. The group should be seated in a circle. Complete the following steps:

1. Each participant writes his or her name on two slips of paper.
2. Each participant next imagines that he or she is very powerful in the group, that is, each member imagines having great influence over other group members.
3. Imagine also that your group comprises an organization, the members of which must work closely together.

4. Participants then define their concept of power and write these thoughts on the two slips of paper.
5. Now, participants give the slips of paper to another person in the group—a person whom they feel comfortable "empowering." Participants should give papers to members who they think will use the power effectively or should therefore have more power.
6. Prior to receiving the slips of paper, each member of the group must predict how many slips of paper he or she will receive and why they think they will receive that number.
7. Recipients of the slips of paper should read the comments on the papers to the group. This is a useful exercise, which stimulates much discussion.

Discussion Questions

1. For those people who received no papers, why do you think this occurred?
2. For those who received papers, why do you think this occurred?
3. As the descriptions of power are read, what do you notice about people's definitions of and ideas about power?

Suggested Readings

Greiner, L. E. 1967. Patterns of Organization Change. *Harvard Business Review* 45(3):119–130.

Greiner approaches organizational change from the perspective of the use of various power distributions. The continuum goes from unilateral power (decree, replacement, and structural change) to shared power (group decisions and group problem solving) to delegated power (data discussion and sensitivity training).

Halberstam, D. 1979. *The Powers That Be.* New York: Dell.

Kanter, R. M. 1983. *The Change Masters: Innovation for Productivity in the American Corporation.* New York: Simon & Schuster.

Kotter, J. 1985. *Power and Influence.* New York: The Free Press.

Kram, K. E. 1985. *Mentoring at Work: Developing Relationships in Organizational Life.* Glenview, Ill.: Scott, Foresman.

A comprehensive review of the nature of mentors at work, this book is indispensable to anyone interested in how to become more powerful in an organization. Most important are the discussions of power in Chapters 1, 2, and 7.

McCormack, M. H. 1984. *What They Don't Teach You at Harvard Business School.* New York: Bantam Books.

This book about power in organizations is not a research treatment of the subject, but it gives interesting and valuable insights from the perspective of a successful manager. In the preface, McCormack makes the following statement, which sets the climate for the rest of the book: "As an introduction to business, an M.B.A.—or an LL.B.—is a worthwhile endeavor. But as an education, as part of an on-going learning process, it is at best a foundation and at worst a naive form of arrogance."

Pfeffer, J. 1981. *Power in Organizations.* Marshfield, Mass.: Pitman.

References

1. Kotter, J. 1985. *Power and Influence: Beyond Formal Authority.* New York: Free Press; Flacks, N., and Rasberry, R. 1983. *Power Talk.* New York: Free Press; Jacoby, N. 1977. *Corporate Power and Social Responsibility.* New York: The Free Press.
2. Pfeffer, J. 1981. *Power in Organizations.* Marshfield, Mass.: Pitman; Cobb, A. T. 1984. An Episodic Model of Power: Toward an Integration of Theory and Research. *Academy of Management Review* 9:482–493.
3. Cobb, A. T., op. cit.
4. Malloy, J. T. 1976. *Dress for Success.* New York: Warner Books.
5. Mintzberg, H. 1983. *Power In and Around Organizations.* Englewood Cliffs, N.J.: Prentice-Hall; Shultz, Y. K. 1978. Managerial Power and Organizational Effectiveness: A Contingency Analysis. *Journal of Management Studies* (May 1978):178–181.
6. Korda, M. 1977. *Power: How to Get It and How to Use It.* New York: Simon & Schuster; Ringer, R., 1974. *Winning Through Intimidation.* Los Angeles, Calif.: LA Publishing.
7. Pfeffer, J., op cit.
8. Daft, R. 1983. *Organizations Theory and Design.* St. Paul, Minn.: West, p. 384.
9. Kanter, R. B. 1983. *Change Masters: Innovation for Productivity in the American Corporation.* New York: Simon & Schuster, pp. 65–77.
10. McCormick, C. P. *The Power of People.* The McCormick Corporation.
11. Pfeffer, J., op. cit.; Hinings, C. R., Hickson, D. J., Pennings, J. M., and Schneck, R. E. 1974. Structural Conditions of Intraorganizational Power. *Administrative Science Quarterly* (1974):22–44.
12. Daft, R., op. cit., p. 396.
13. Ibid.
14. Kanter, R. B., op. cit.
15. Hickson, D. J., Lee, C. A., Schneck, R. E., and Pennings, J. M. A Strategic Contingencies' Theory of Intraorganizational Power. *Administrative Science Quarterly* (1971):216–229.
16. Pfeffer, J., op. cit.; Bacharach, S. B., and Lawler, E. J. 1980. *Power and Politics in Organizations.* San Francisco: Jossey-Bass.
17. Kanter, R. B., op. cit.
18. Ibid.
19. Ibid.

Effective Managers: One Key to Work Group Success

Chapter **12**

I. Dilemma: Mac Has Trouble With His New Job
II. The Nature of the Manager's Job
  A. Leadership defined
  B. The roles of the manager
  C. Kinds of managers: the horizontal and the vertical perspectives
  D. Changing roles of the manager
III. Understanding Effective Management
IV. Universalists—May the Best Person Win
  A. The great man and trait approaches
  B. Universalist approach—the answer to the right way
V. Situational Approaches to Managerial Effectiveness
  A. The situational leadership model—leader meets follower
  B. The path-goal model
  C. Other contingency approaches
VI. Substitutes for Leadership
VII. Entrepreneurs and Small Business Owners
  A. The entrepreneur
  B. The small business owner
VIII. Summary Points
IX. Questions
X. Exploring: The Small Business Administration's New Boss
XI. Applying: Talking to Managers in the Workplace
XII. Suggested Readings
XIII. References

Chapter Goals

By the end of this chapter, you will be able to:

1. Define the difference between leaders and managers.
2. Define the manager's job in terms of its functions, roles, and relationships to the organization.
3. Describe effective managers in terms of two different groups of theories.
4. Use universalist approaches to describe effective managers according to their personalities or traits.
5. Use situational approaches to choose effective management behaviors.
6. Understand the special situation of higher level managers.

Dilemma Mac Has Trouble With His New Job

Mac sat behind his desk thinking how nice it would be to go home, even if it was only 11:30 A.M. He had just emerged from three successive appointments with subordinates, and each one seemed to involve a major problem at work. Each of the subordinates had started the conversation with "Mac, I need your help," and each conversation had ended with a statement such as "Well, Mac, I'll wait to hear from you before I go further."

Mac had been made manager of the sales department five months ago, in part because of his proven ability "to define what people are supposed to do." He also had a history of controlling expenses better than anyone else in the company. Before taking over sales, Mac had worked for six years in the production department of PACK–EM. (The company made boxes for pizza, cakes, and other food items.) During those six years as production manager, he was seen as a fair but hard-nosed manager who knew operations and wanted to do well. He was also known as a loyal company man who would rather work for less money than see the company get into financial trouble.

Edna Donovan picked Mac for the sales department managership because the department was not performing well, and as Edna put it, she needed "a strong boss to straighten the place out." For example, Edna found out that last year the sales department had promised several customers that the company could make custom-designed boxes on the same schedule as the standard boxes. The salespeople had not checked with production to see if such a schedule were possible. In fact, it was not, and customers were furious.

During his first few weeks on the job, Mac wanted to establish his authority, so he changed much of the paperwork routine and forced employees to check with him on every matter. For example, Mac told sales department employees that he wanted them to discuss every purchase order with him, regardless of amount. He also maintained strict rules about when employees arrived at work and when they left at day's end.

Mac spent long hours alone, drawing up plans to try to figure out the best way to run the department. He called in a local consultant who interviewed several key people to develop a strategy. Most of the consultant's interviews pointed to the fact that Mac tended to approach every problem the same way. Regardless of the nature of the problem or person with whom Mac was dealing, he followed a three-step process: First, he drew up a plan of action *on his own.* He next asked another manager (who knew nothing about sales) to review the plan to evaluate whether it made sense and seemed feasible. Third, he communicated the new plan to his subordinates. Mac had found this process to be successful when he worked in production. Now he intended to duplicate his success in sales.

Another point that emerged from the consultant's interviews was that sales employees had different skill levels and tended to have varied backgrounds in terms of sales experience. Several were very ambitious and seemed to have excellent ideas about how to make sales profitable. Two of the department employees were very inexperienced and were, according to the consultant, "confused, yet worth keeping."

Mac reviewed the consultant's findings and decided to add an assistant to his staff. This individual would work with the inexperienced people and help Mac keep records on various matters. The assistant's major responsibility, according to Mac, was "to keep close tabs on everyone so the department runs more efficiently."

After doing all of this work, Mac was still stymied. Every time he confronted a sales problem that required the use of his managerial skills, things just didn't seem to work. Either his subordinates were upset, or Mac got more work to do!

Edna, meanwhile, wanted to see some results. She was getting concerned that Mac was not doing an adequate job. She had imagined Mac acting more like an entrepreneur and instilling an innovative spirit in the department. Edna also wanted Mac to achieve more sales by creating a drive toward excellence.

For their part, the salespeople wanted Mac to support them and to listen to them. They wanted him to lighten up—to become one of them. After all, wasn't he a member of the department too? If Mac would only take the time to learn their business, he could help them accomplish some of the goals set by Mac and Edna. The salespeople all wanted their department to thrive; they believed that their potential for success was unlimited.

Mac was frankly confused about what to do next. What would it take for him to be effective in his present job?

Questions

1. What is Mac's job as a manager?
2. What special skills or traits does Mac have for managing the sales department?
3. To what extent has Mac adapted his behavior to the needs of the subordinates and the work situation?
4. What could Mac do to be more effective?

The Nature of the Manager's Job

The study of managerial behavior in groups is in some ways the study of leadership. Before examining what makes managers effective, we first define "leadership" and distinguish it from management.

Leadership Defined

In the most basic sense, **leadership** is the power of one individual to guide the actions of another. Leaders are those who guide others toward the accomplishment of goals in such a way that the followers want to follow. Successful leaders convince others to follow the direction they set. They seem to know how to get things done when others are not even able to get started.

Leadership is also a **product,** or **set of behaviors.** In other words, leaders not only act so others want to follow, but they are also perceived by followers as possessing certain characteristics that cause them to stand out. Typical leadership characteristics are a strong self-concept, logical thinking, stamina, adaptability, and concern for making things better in the organization.

Are leaders different from managers?

Yes! A **manager** is one who performs the specific functions of management; someone who holds a formal title or plays a formal role in the organization. For example, a production manager is the individual who plans production schedules, structures production operations, is responsible for motivating production department employees, and controls the production process. In most cases, a manager is the person responsible for the performance of one or more subordinates in an organizational work unit. A **leader,** on the other hand, is *anyone* who is able to influence others to pursue goals. The execution and study of leadership is thus much broader than the study of management.

As Mac views his job, he is responsible for planning, organizing, leading, and controlling the sales unit. He makes decisions about future activities in the sales area (**planning**), and he makes sure that the right people are doing the right tasks and coordinating with others (**organizing**). He also keeps people motivated to work hard and intelligently (**leading**), and he makes sure that the planned activities are completed on schedule (**controlling**). He performs these functions because they are his job—that's what the organization wants him to do (1).

One researcher believes that the manager's job is more complicated than simply describing these four management functions. Mintzberg perceives managerial jobs as calling for very specific behaviors. He has accordingly developed the "roles perspective" (2).

The Roles of the Manager

Mintzberg studied managers as they performed the functions of management. He kept detailed records of his observations of managerial behavior and concluded that the manager's job can be described in terms of ten **roles** that occur at work. These roles are what managers do to perform their job. Mintzberg categorized the roles as belonging in one of three areas: interpersonal, informational, or decisional (see Table 12.1).

Interpersonal roles relate to all managerial behaviors used to establish relationships with others. The **informational roles** designation encompasses those roles involved in collecting and distributing information. **Decisional roles** includes those that are used to set, implement, and monitor progress toward goals. The manager's job is seen as relating to others, setting direction, and collecting necessary information, as in the following example.

Table 12.1 *Interpersonal, Informational, and Decisional Roles of the Manager*

The Roles		*What the Manager Does*
	Interpersonal	
Figurehead—performs ceremonial duties		Goes to parties Greets new people
Leader—acts as motivator of unit		Cheers people on Recognizes achievements Hires and fires
Liaison—makes contacts		Meets other managers Makes friends Answers department mail
	Informational	
Monitor—scans for information		Reads industry information Goes to conferences Listens to gossip
Disseminator—shares information with other organization members		Holds meetings Writes memos Forwards mail to others
Spokesperson—shares information with outsiders		Makes speeches Keeps owner informed
	Decisional	
Entrepreneur—seeks to change		Looks for new ideas Initiates new projects
Disturbance handler—responds to pressures and crises		Acts quickly in crises Faces problems willingly
Resource allocator—gives resources to others		Manages the budget Authorizes people to do things Makes up schedules
Negotiator—reaches agreements		Solves contract disputes Solves employee arguments

Source: Adapted from Mintzberg, H.1973. *The Nature of Managerial Work.* New York: Harper & Row.

Cathy, a clerk at a furniture store, observed her manager in these roles. She had worked only four days at the store when her manager asked her how things were going. She recalls that they spent almost fifteen minutes chit-chatting about her family, her horse (which she loved dearly), and school. The next day, Cathy noticed that the manager "seemed like a different person" as he walked around the shop floor "as if he were looking for something." He was cordial to employees but was not interested in stopping to talk. A week later, Cathy observed that some changes had been made in the floor design of the sofa area. She also overheard the manager telling an employee that the floor was too dirty, and that customers were complaining that service was slow.

What Cathy observed is a perfect illustration of Mintzberg's roles (3). The manager used interpersonal roles to establish a relationship with her. She observed him in the informational role, collecting information about the environment and keeping tabs on the sales people. Finally, she saw him use the decisional roles to change the floor layout and to respond to problems related to him by customers.

Notice that these roles are sequenced in a way that helps managers decide which roles aid in the development of other roles. Consider a new manager on the job, such as Mac. The roles perspective may have implications not only for describing what Mac's job entails but in prescribing what he should do first. Consider that the broad role categories outlined by Mintzberg should be used in order (i.e., managers first should use the interpersonal role, then the informational, and lastly the decisional). Following this sequence, Mac would first get to know his subordinates and become involved with other departments (interpersonal roles). This networking would enable him to collect pertinent information from all areas of the organization, which in turn would enable him to make intelligent decisions and to initiate needed changes. (According to Mintzberg's role perspective, Mac started at the wrong place! He started by using his decisional roles to make changes and implement new ideas *before* he even established relationships with others or gathered information about what needed to be changed.)

These role descriptions present a reasonably accurate picture of the manager's job. We all know, however, that organizations have different managerial **levels** ranging from president or owner to supervisors who are more closely involved in the production operations of the firm. Although managers at all levels perform management work, they do more or less of it in relation to their technical work as their level changes.

In summary, leadership is the power of one person to guide the actions of another. Managers are leaders who perform specific functions and roles within the organization.

Is technical work different from managerial work?

Consider an employee in the accounting department who is trained in accounting principles and procedures to perform assigned technical tasks. This work might be keeping track of payments, running analyses, or checking on departmental expenditures. As soon as this person becomes a manager, he or she is expected to perform some management work as well as some technical work. Although running analyses may still be part of the person's job, as a manager that individual must also establish relationships with employees, act as a spokesperson for department personnel, monitor progress toward plans, and solve day-to-day employee problems. **As a rule, the higher the manager's level in the organization, the more that person does managerial work only.** Consider Figure 12.1 as an illustration of this principle.

The relationship between technical and managerial work presents problems for managers. The higher a manager goes in the organization, the less she is called on to use the skills for which she was originally hired. The accounting manager may spend half of the day checking subordinate's work schedules, talking about morale issues, and helping subordinates—rather than running analyses or checking the accounting books. In other words, managerial work and technical work are fundamentally different from each other.

To this point we have said that managers must perform certain functions, play important roles, and perform different mixes of technical and managerial work according to their job level. These functions, roles, and the mix of

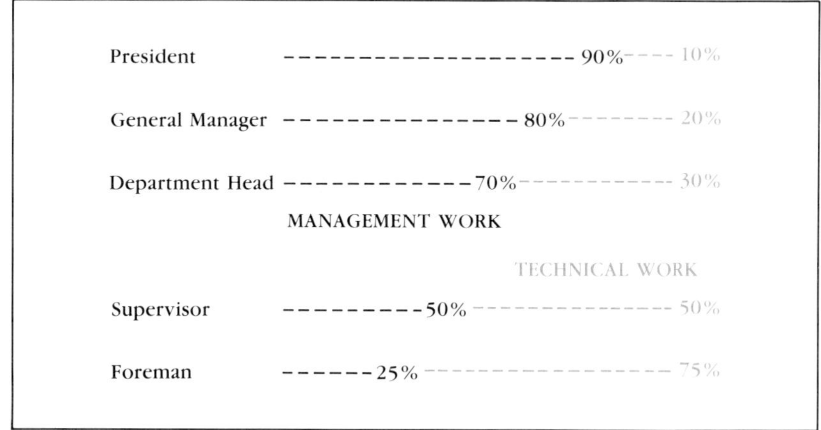

Figure 12.1 *Relationship of Managerial and Technical Work to Level of Manager*

work can be used to describe any given management job accurately. But is that all that's involved?

Do managers relate differently to different people in the organization?

Absolutely! As stated in earlier chapters, all employees relate differently to various types of positions in the organization. The manager is no exception. Managers perform their job in the context of a set of important relationships with other people. These relationships are illustrated in Figure 12.2. Each relationship demands something from the manager, either in terms of performance or the satisfaction of a personal need.

For example, consider your class as a work unit. The **subordinates** are the students, because they are the ones being managed by the instructor, that is, the **manager.** This relationship is labeled as "1" in Figure 12.2.

Who are the **superiors?** From the instructor's perspective, the department heads and deans fulfill these roles. This relationship is shown as "2." **Outsiders** are a combination of people in other departments at the university

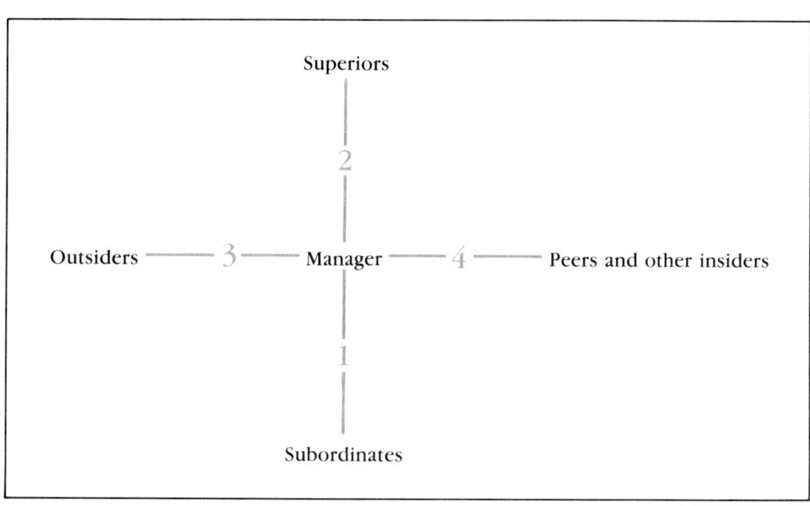

Figure 12.2 *Relationships in the Organization*

and in the community. Sometimes these outsiders include parents and even other universities. For the instructor as a manager, this relationship is labeled "3." Finally, the **peers and other insiders** are those at the school or college who teach in a similar academic area. This is relationship "4."

Peers and the department head (superior) are concerned with academic credibility and integrity. They want to be sure that the instructor teaches appropriate information to students and that, as a colleague, the instructor offers help and support. All managers, including the instructor, are faced with the responsibility of understanding these relationships and satisfying their requirements. You might say that effective managers are good at getting others what they need to accomplish goals.

One of the authors learned this lesson when he held a managerial position in a large oil company. Being somewhat naive about the ways of organizations, he had difficulty distinguishing the different levels of management and the relationships that existed between various levels. During an interdepartmental meeting, he began to give managers from other departments a long speech about the internal workings of his department and some of the key problems he was having with particular individuals. After 30 minutes of this, another manager remarked, "Why am I listening to all this? All we need from you is an idea of when the project will be completed and what we need to do to help you get it completed. Spare us the details." Lesson learned!

How do managers spend their time?

Studies have been conducted on how managers spend their time with others. Although the allocation of time varies with managerial level, approximately 48 percent of managerial time is spent with subordinates, 7 percent with superiors, and 44 percent with peers and outsiders (4). Other studies show that managers spend most of their time with others and spend very little time alone (5). Any manager's daily routine consists of frequent interruptions by many different people who want to talk about varied topics that involve considerable nonwork-related information. The point for managers to remember is that these interruptions are precisely what keep them involved in the organization and able to fulfill their roles and functions. Unfortunately, many managers report that they view these "interruptions" as taking them away from their "real job." One perceptive manager described his job as follows:

> Being a manager is the most frustrating, infuriating, and demanding job anyone could ask for. You don't get time to yourself, and you're constantly "on call." You always have to watch out for everyone else. For these reasons, I wouldn't do anything else.

Kinds of Managers: The Horizontal and Vertical Perspectives

Different types of managers can be identified by horizontal and vertical lines drawn through the organizational structure (Figure 12.3).

The **horizontal perspective** is for identifying different kinds of managers (i.e., managers in marketing or finance). The **vertical perspective** focuses on managerial levels within the organization.

The vertical perspective. Most people envision three **levels** of management: **top, middle,** and **first-line.** These levels tend to differ in several ways.

Figure 12.3
The Horizontal and Vertical Perspective on Management

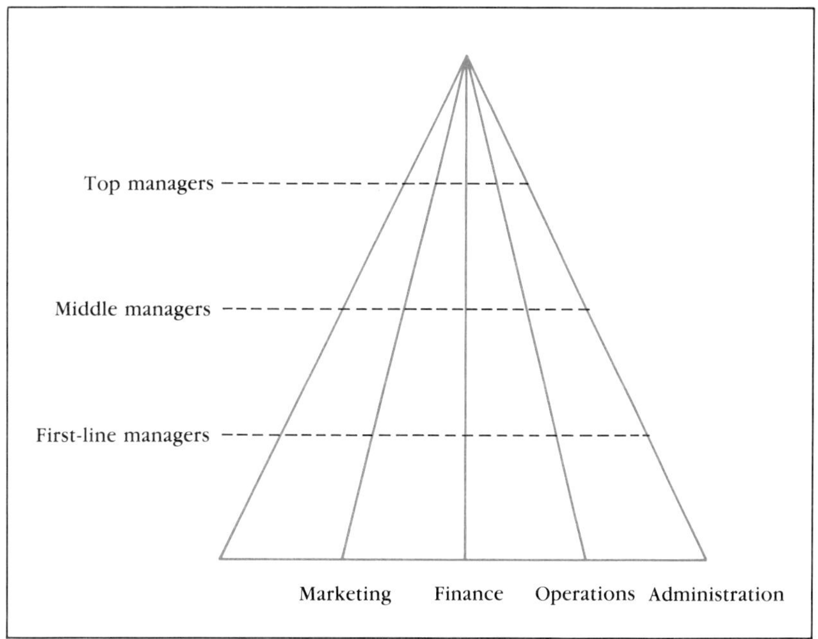

Top managers comprise a relatively small group of executives who control the organization. The titles found in this group are "president," "chief executive officer," and "chief operating officer." Top management is faced with responsibilities such as setting organization goals, establishing company policies, and conceiving general strategies. Top management also represents the organization officially to external organizations and major customers. The salaries at this level are often high, and the decision-making powers vast. (So also are job responsibility and pressure.) Top managers typically work long hours and spend even their spare time preoccupied with company affairs. Recent studies show that their role is one of value carrier, that is, they set the tone for how the organization will function (6).

The 3M Company provides an interesting example of a firm whose chief executive officer performs the role of value carrier and has been promoted from within the organization. The company makes over 45,000 different products, from Scotch tape to orthopedic casts, and employs about 50,000 people. 3M rarely hires managers from outside the organization and demands that the CEO be someone who has spent considerable time in the organization and has been successful at developing new products.

The next managerial level are the **middle managers,** who comprise the largest group of managers in most organizations. Common middle management titles include "plant manager," "division head," and "administrator." These managers are responsible for implementing policies and procedures, strategies, and ideas established by top management. They also supervise and coordinate the activities of first-line managers (7). For example, the administrator of patient services in a hospital must ensure that all of the nursing departments are fully staffed and are carrying out the patient care policies established by top management. The plant manager in a company that prints financial forms must ensure that materials are ordered properly, that customer orders are communicated accurately to operations personnel, that presses are set up properly, and that expenses are controlled. Recall from Figure 12.1 the amount of management and technical work performed at different managerial levels. About 60 to 75 percent of the middle manager's job is management work.

First-line managers, the third management level, supervise and coordinate activities of operating employees. Common titles for managers at this level are "foreman," "supervisor," and "coordinator." Such positions are often the first management job held by employees when they stop doing 100 percent technical work. The major responsibilities of first-line management are to communicate operations procedures to workers and to keep records on data such as attendance, work schedules, and staffing.

These three levels of management comprise the vertical perspective. The managerial levels are arranged in a hierarchy, and the amount of managerial work performed depends to a great extent on the level of the position in the vertical hierarchy.

The horizontal perspective. We now shift to the horizontal perspective, which focuses on the managerial function independent of level. For example, in the financial area an organization may have a supervisor of accounts receivable (first-line manager), a department head of treasury (middle management), and a vice president of financial affairs (top management). Although the positions are at different levels, the function is the same for all, that is, financial management.

Changing Roles of the Manager

Managers will always be important to organizations, but the roles of the manager are changing rapidly (8). In one report about the changing role of the foreman (a first-line manager), the following statements (9) make the point about this changing role:

- "They (foremen) aren't going to control people anymore. They have to coach them, help do the planning, approve organizational direction, and make sure the directions are clear. It will be an enabling function rather than a control function."
- "The use of self-management work teams reduces the need for production supervisors."
- "The participatory style allows a foreman to concentrate on improving production and quality rather than always looking over my shoulder." (10)

Solving the Dilemma

What is Mac's job as manager?

Mac's position in the vertical hierarchy of the organization is at the top managerial level. His functional role is in sales. Given his vertical level, he probably spends about 80 percent of his time doing management work and 20 percent doing technical work. He is responsible for all four management areas (planning, organizing, leading, and controlling), and is expected to fulfill all of the managerial roles. At this point, he is emphasizing the decisional role, and this emphasis may cause him some problems because he did not spend much time initially using interpersonal or informational roles. As sales manager, his primary responsibility is managing others to develop the customer base that the company needs to sell its products profitably. He probably is not responsible for advertising or market research; Edna has a marketing manager to handle those areas. Mac needs to focus on his functional responsibility and to begin using the roles perspective as a guide to what he should do. His primary task at this point is to take one step back and to begin establishing relationships with his subordinates.

Knowledge Check

1. Leadership is only a process of human interaction. T or F?
2. What are the four functions of management?
3. Technical work is different from managerial work. What is the approximate percentage mix of each type of work for a middle manager?
4. A foreman and a general manager probably do about the same amount of managerial work. T or F?
5. Middle managers are expected to spend about 85 percent of their time with bankers, stockholders, and key customers. T or F?
6. The vertical perspective focuses on a manager's function within the organization. T or F?

Answers:

1 F, 2 planning, organizing, leading, and controlling, 3 30% technical and 70% managerial, 4 F, 5 F, 6 F

Understanding Effective Management

Our discussion, so far, has centered on what a manager does. Ultimately, those who work in organizations must know not only what to do but how to do it effectively so they are considered excellent performers. This section provides some insight into effective management and leadership and gives examples of effective managers and leaders in organizations.

In general, two groups of approaches have been used to describe effective leaders. The first group, called **universalist theories,** prescribe that a particular style of behavior is the best way to manage every situation. The second group, called **contingency theories,** prescribe that different situations demand different leadership behaviors. These two groups of theories lead to very different conclusions about how managers should act to be effective. In the following sections, we favor the contingency approach because it is tied more directly to development of managerial skills, it has been shown to lead to better prescriptions for managerial behavior, and it builds on the best parts of universalist theories.

Universalists—May the Best Person Win

By all accounts, the universalist approach to understanding effective leadership has lasted for a long time. In fact, many managers still subscribe to this view of effective management. In short, this group of theories suggests that an effective manager is one who has certain traits or uses the same style of behavior consistently in every situation. Table 12.2 summarizes these theories.

The Great Man and Trait Approaches

Many people believe strongly that some are born to lead and that others are not. This idea is behind the legacy of kings, that is, the royal family supposedly possessed some innate ability to lead. For those of us who are trying to understand management and how to be effective, being born into the right family is probably not very relevant. Besides, little verification of this idea exists.

Large systematic studies have reviewed over 120 empirical studies of the personal factors associated with leadership (11). These studies were of

Table 12.2 *Universalist Theories*

Theory	*Components*
Great Man Theory	1. Certain people become leaders because they have outstanding character or abilities.
	2. The qualities of the leader are the critical determinants of leader success.
	3. Employees follow because the leader reaches goals and controls and motivates them.
Trait Theory	1. Effective leaders possess certain personality traits necessary for success.
	2. Individual qualities determine success of leaders.
	3. Employees will follow a manager if he or she has these traits.
Leader Behavior	1. Two effective behaviors are initiating structure and consideration.
	2. The leader influences others by using these behaviors.
	3. Employees prefer consideration behavior although they will respond to the initiating of structure behaviors.
Theory X and Theory Y	1. Theory Y assumptions should replace Theory X assumptions.
	2. Managers fall into one of these categories. Theory Y is more effective.
	3. Employees want managers to use Theory Y assumptions in how they treat them.

various types of groups (e.g., children's play groups, athletic teams, and famous people). The results suggest some trait categories and individual differences that distinguish leaders from those who do not lead. Table 12.3 summarizes the key findings of this research (12).

It is interesting to consider those traits that are indicative of effective managers and then to try to match ourselves against those traits. Indeed, some traits do tend to correlate with individual promotability. For example, managers who have significant positions in organizations tend to be more intelligent, taller, and to have greater self-confidence than those who do not achieve such positions. Do these traits cause success? Probably not, but they may help, given two otherwise equally qualified candidates applying for the same position. The person with some of these desirable traits will probably get promoted over the person who does not possess these traits. As we will see, however, managerial effectiveness involves more than traits.

Universalist Approach—the Answer to the Right Way

A universalist approach that remains useful today originated in the 1950's. Researchers at the Ohio State University and the University of Michigan, two institutions known for their work on leadership effectiveness, analyzed leaders in a wide variety of situations and isolated important types of behaviors used by the most effective leaders (13). A typical approach was for researchers to ask managers to comment on the behaviors that they use and find particularly effective. The researchers also asked managers to think of another person, also an effective manager, and to say why that person was effective. Finally, the researchers followed up with interviews of employees about their managers.

Through these studies, two basic types of behaviors were identified consistently with effective management: initiating structure and consideration behaviors. **Initiating structure** refers to those leader behaviors that are highly directive, such as giving orders, checking on people, and setting schedules. **Consideration behaviors** are the ways in which leaders create

Table 12.3
Sample Traits of Effective Managers and How They Appear in Action

Traits	*What to Look For in a Manager*
Logical thinking	Tries to put ideas into a simple model or diagram
	Is able to persuade others
	Can explain things in a unique way
Persistence	Calls setbacks "only a little mistake"
	Works long hours
	Keeps trying to succeed even when the cause looks hopeless
Empowerment	Gets people excited about working on his or her goals
	Is exciting to be around
	Makes employees feel as if they can accomplish a great deal
Self-control	Can keep working under extreme pressure
	Does not yell constantly when things do not go well
	Is not threatened easily by powerful people

SOURCE: Adapted from Bennis, W., and Nanus, B. 1985. *Leaders: The Strategies for Taking Charge.* New York: Harper & Row.

good feelings among subordinates, such as joking with employees, saying "you're doing a good job," and listening to employee problems.

Initiating structure behaviors tend to focus on performance. They are important for making sure that employees do what they are supposed to do and for helping employees perform well. Consideration behaviors are important for making everyone feel that he or she is a part of the team and for creating a satisfying work climate.

NOW IT'S YOUR TURN . . .

How do you rate on the two dimensions?

These items were selected from a longer instrument that assesses leadership behavior (14). Respond to each item according to the way you would be most likely to act if you were the leader of a work group. Circle whether you would behave in the described way: always (A), frequently (F), occasionally (O), seldom (S), or never (N).

A F O S N 1. I would permit the members to use their own judgment in solving problems.

A F O S N 2. I would let some members have authority which I could keep.

A F O S N 3. I would consult the group before taking action.

A F O S N 4. I would explain my actions to the group.

A F O S N 5. I would go as fast as the group indicated they could go.

A F O S N 6. I would act as the spokesperson for the group.

A F O S N 7. I would stress being ahead of competing groups.

A F O S N 8. I would push for increased production.

A F O S N 9. I would keep the work moving at a rapid pace.

A F O S N 10. I would assign group members to particular tasks.

Scoring instructions:

1. Check the numbers for which you circled A (always) or F (frequently).
2. For questions 1 through 5, give yourself 5 points for each A and 4 points for each F. The total is your consideration score.
3. Add up items checked A or F for questions 6 through 10, using A = 5 and F = 4. This is your initiating structure score.
4. Now add the scores for steps 2 and 3, and record your total score on the chart. Note that your score could vary from 0 to 25.

If you tended to be high on consideration, you would probably contribute greatly to the satisfaction of subordinates (assuming you were a manager).

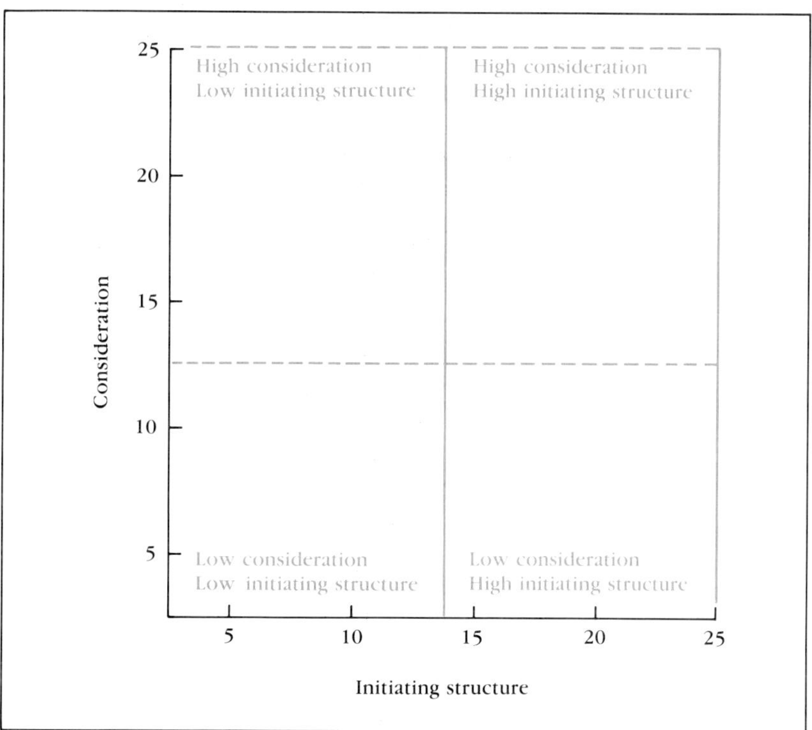

Less turnover and fewer grievances would occur in your workplace than in those of other managers (15). If you were high on initiating structure, you would probably have greater than average turnover in your unit and more grievances (16).

Notice that we have talked only about employee satisfaction. The relationship of these dimensions to worker performance is not as easily summarized. Studies have shown that group performance cannot be predicted accurately from measures of leader consideration and initiating structure.

Solving the Dilemma

What special skills or traits does Mac have for managing the sales department?

Mac seems to have persistence and a general feel for the business. He is an owner's dream inasmuch as he believes in doing a good job and gets satisfaction from task accomplishment. He probably has a high need for achievement and a healthy self-concept, and he probably tends to emphasize the initiating structure dimension of leadership. (Note that other people in the company describe him as "hard-nosed.") He also seems to have an internal locus of control, because he's more than willing to take charge of situations. He probably likes being a manager.

As more and more information is accumulated on these two dimensions, we can draw several basic conclusions. First, the two dimensions can be used to summarize a variety of attitudes and behaviors exhibited by leaders. Second, no consistent research findings link these two dimensions to subordinate performance, and the two dimensions are only weakly linked to subordinate satisfaction. The biggest problem with these behavioral-style approaches is that more and more research is accumulating in support of the contention that leadership behavior, to be effective, must adapt to the situation. So although the two dimensions outlined seem to describe leadership behaviors, we cannot assume that they should be used extensively or all of the time. We must learn more about the given "situation" to decide what behaviors are most likely to be effective.

Knowledge Check

1. Universalist theories tend to emphasize one best way to manage. T or F?
2. The two basic dimensions of leader behavior that have been cited in many studies are ___________ and ___________.
3. Managers who show a high degree of concern for their employees tend to have employees who perform more effectively. T or F?
4. Situational approaches to leadership contend that a manager's behavior is learned from doing, not from studying about leadership. T or F?
5. Given a choice between the two dimensions of leadership behavior, Mac's best approach would probably be to emphasize ___________ managerial behaviors.

Answers.

1 T, 2 initiating structure and consideration, 3 F, 4 F, 5 initiating structure

What do we mean by the "situation"?

Beginning in the 1960's, many managers became interested in how their behavior changed depending on such factors as the work to be done, the type of organization, and the expertise of subordinates. In other words, effectiveness was becoming viewed as a fit between what the situation required and the behaviors of the manager.

Situational Approaches to Managerial Effectiveness

The analysis of four variables helps to determine what the best or most effective managerial approach would be. These variables are as follows:

1. **The manager**—including the individual's personality, needs, past performance, and view of the way the work ought to get done.
2. **The subordinates**—including their abilities and desires, and their views on the way work ought to get done.
3. **The work**—including the tasks to be done and the demands of others to get the work done.
4. **The organization**—including the rules, goals, and environment of the workplace.

To explain how these four variables work, we use two popular approaches that build on universalist ideas. Each is relevant to an understanding of the situational approach to leadership effectiveness.

The first approach is called **situational leadership,** and focuses on the desires and abilities of subordinates as the major determinant of effective leadership behaviors (17). The second approach is called the **path-goal theory,** and builds on our earlier explanation of expectancy theory (see Chapter 3) (18).

The Situational Leadership Model—Leader Meets Follower

This leadership model is based on the amount of direction (task behavior) and the amount of socio-emotional support (relationship behavior) that a leader must provide given the situation and the maturity level of the follower or group.

The **situational leadership model** is the best attempt so far to provide managers with decisional rules for behaviors. It assumes that no single, all-purpose leadership style exists, and that successful leaders are those who can adapt their behavior to meet the demands of the followers.

The situational leadership model expects the manager to change his behavior as the employee demonstrates more maturity on the job. The manager uses combinations of initiating structure and consideration behaviors that are adjusted to the maturity level of subordinates.

What is maturity?

Maturity is the capability and willingness of individuals to assume responsibility for directing their own behavior. The manager asks herself, "At what point can this employee perform these tasks without me having to show support or give constant directions?"

Ability is measured by past experience, job knowledge, and understanding of job requirements. **Willingness** is measured by the extent to which the employee agrees to take responsibility and to achieve goals and by the employee's sense of commitment to the task.

The model makes it easy for managers to choose their behavior according to employee maturity level because of a concise pictorial representation (Figure 12.4). First, the model borrows the two dimensions explained previously: consideration and initiating structure. The only difference is that consideration is referred to as **relationship behaviors** and initiating structure as **task behaviors** in the model.

Second, maturity levels are categorized as being of four types: low ability, low willingness (**M1**); low ability, high willingness (**M2**); high ability, low willingness (**M3**); and high ability, high willingness (**M4**) (19).

As shown in Figure 12.4, maturity levels are at the base of the situational leadership graph, and the two managerial dimensions are at the top. If, therefore, we want to know what behaviors a manager should use, we need to match employee maturity levels with the top part of the graph. In figure 12.4, a curved line is drawn, which matches the four managerial styles with the four maturity levels.

How the model works. Let's say that you, the manager, decide that a new employee has low ability and low willingness (M1). You take out your situational leadership graph and draw a line straight up from the M1 employee level, whereupon you hit the curved line at the high task-low relationship section. Originators of this approach call this style **telling.** Thus, given an M1 employee, you now know that you should adopt a telling style, or one that is very directive.

Let's say that you change your mind after a period of time and decide that the employee is now more able, but you are still not sure of her willingness to work, especially her commitment to the task. This combination is identified as an M3 level, so you draw a line upward from M3 on the graph and find that you should adopt a participative style, or one that is high-relationship oriented. In other words, your managerial behaviors are calculated to maintain motivation and to build commitment.

Figure 12.4
The Situational Leadership Graph (17)

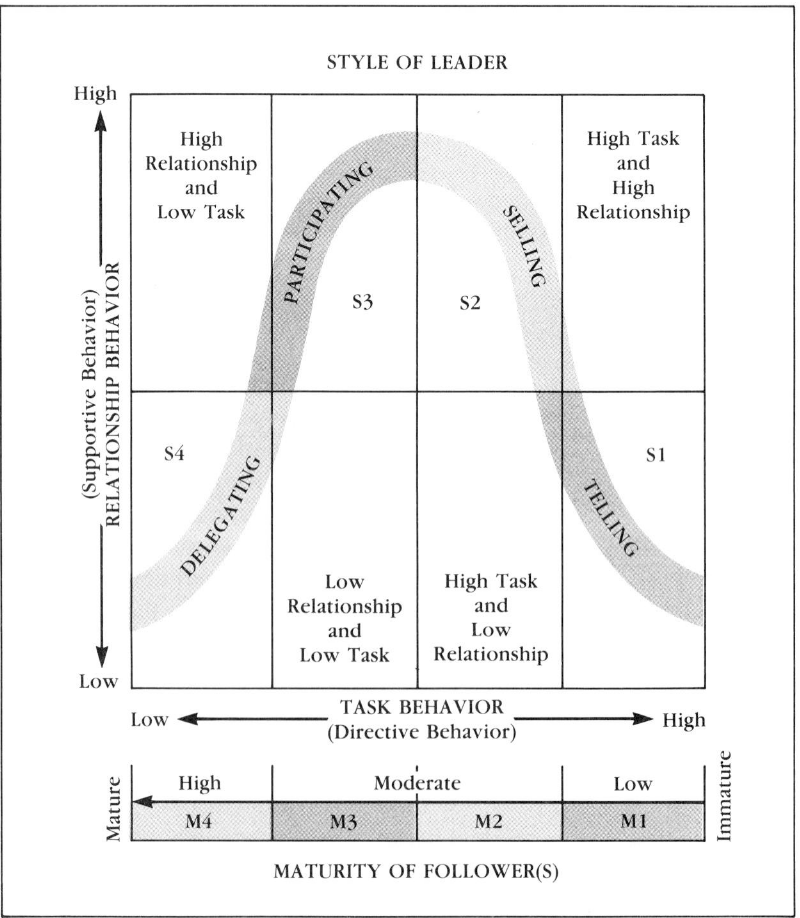

As employee maturity level increases, the manager's need to manage closely decreases. The model helps managers decide what behaviors are most useful with a given employee. As manager, you take an employee at her level and adapt your behaviors accordingly, and the model tells you how to change your behaviors as the employee's maturity level changes. What a switch from earlier theories that the most desirable management style was high initiating structure and high consideration. This style (called **selling** in the situational leadership model) is only one of four approaches. In fact, your goal as manager is to move as many employees as you can to M4 level so you can use the **delegating** style. In this way, subordinates become their own managers, capable of carrying out organizational goals but in a way that does not demand your constant supervision.

In summary, the key to effectiveness in the situational leadership model is the relationship between leader and follower. The leader must choose appropriate behaviors based on indications of the follower's maturity and ability levels. The model then provides certain decision rules that the manager can use to match employee maturity level with appropriate leader behaviors (20).

Doesn't the situational leadership model demand great flexibility from the manager?

Absolutely! The model suggests that managers should manage everyone differently and should be constantly aware of employee maturity levels. While this model probably describes accurately many situations that occur in management, it also emphasizes the difficulty of managing others. Managers must be versatile. Those managers who attempt to use the model, follow these steps:

1. Determine what needs to be accomplished through follower(s). Ask: "What is the task or goal?"
2. Determine maturity level of the follower or group that is relevant to the task. Do not go beyond the task, and do not try to use a style that will work "all of the time" with the employee or group. Consider:
   a. Achievement motivation—"Is the individual or group able to set high but realistic goals?"
   b. Responsibility—"How willing is the individual or group to assume responsibility? How able is the individual or group to assume responsibility?"
   c. Education and experience—"Does the individual or group have the education or experience necessary to accomplish the task?"

   At this point, the manager can mark the relevant maturity level on the graph (Figure 12.4), that is, make an educated guess about where the employee or group stands on the maturity continuum.
3. A line can then be drawn from the maturity level up to the leadership-style curve. The point where the line and curve intersect is the most appropriate leadership style given the follower (or group) and the particular situation. The manager then uses the appropriate combination of task and relationship behavior (i.e., S1, S2, S3, or S4) to deal with the employee or group.

Can managers really change?

Some managers suggest that changing the situation is much easier than changing their leadership style. In fact, one researcher suggests that the organization should choose situations that will best fit the manager's behavioral style.

Fiedler analyzed situations in terms of three variables: leader-member relationships, extent to which tasks are structured, and how much position power the leader had. After analyzing these variables and the leader's dominant style, Fiedler suggested that he could predict which leaders would be successful and those who would not (21).

We can do this by using the Hersey-Blanchard situational leadership model depicted in Figure 12.4. If, as a manager, you believe that you cannot accommodate your behavior to different employees, then you may want to choose the employees according to your preferred style. For example, if you tend to accentuate relationship behaviors, you would do best with employees who are at the M2 or M3 level. If you accentuate task behaviors, you would do best with employees at the M1 level. While adapting the situation to fit our needs or to choosing employees according to our managerial style might be optimal, the manager is in reality the one who usually needs to change to be effective.

Solving the Dilemma

To what extent has Mac adapted his behavior to subordinates' needs and to the work situation?

How well has he assessed the new situation?

Mac has not assessed the situation much or adapted his behavior to the new situation. Instead, he is using the managerial behaviors that were effective in production. He seems to have jumped into the sales department by "doing things," rather than setting up interpersonal relationships and trying to get some sense of what the key problems are. Why did Mac bring in a consultant? Mac himself needs to get out and meet his people. Long hours in the office only isolate a manager from what is going on. If Mac had to choose two factors to analyze to help him understand the situation in sales, they should probably be maturity level of his subordinates and the nature of the work.

In many cases, the situational leadership model may be too simplistic to enable the manager to understand fully the leader-follower behaviors. For example, the model does not tell us anything about the effect of leader behavior on employee satisfaction. The manager may be able to stimulate performance by using this model, but the employee satisfaction may be slighted.

To explain more behaviors in a given situation and to address employee satisfaction more fully as a product of managerial behavior, House has developed a model that applies to managers and is based on expectancy theory (see Chapter 3). This model is the focus of our next section.

The Path-Goal Model

The **path-goal theory** (22) tries to integrate previous studies to explain more of the managerial behavior observed in day-to-day interactions. The path-goal approach uses these perspectives: the two universalist dimensions of leadership—initiating structure and consideration, the expectancy theory of motivation, and relationships between employee satisfaction and performance.

The first important idea borrowed from earlier studies is that leadership behavior contains at least two dimensions—initiating structure and consideration. House uses these dimensions to develop four behavioral styles: directive, achievement-oriented, participating, and supportive. Second, path-goal approaches borrow heavily from expectancy theory. Expectancy theory demonstrates that a person is motivated to perform because he or she expects that performance will lead to desired payoffs or avoidance of unpleasant outcomes.

In Chapter 3, we learned that two kinds of payoffs exist, first level outcomes and second level outcomes. First level outcomes lead to attainment of second level outcomes, such as money to buy necessities. In path-goal theory, those second level outcomes and the way in which they relate to first level outcomes are the paths to the broader goal of need-fulfillment. We also learned that employees make decisions about what they will and will not do based on their assessment of the relationships between performance, effort, and outcomes.

A final concept borrowed from earlier studies is that managers who initiate structure for their groups are rated higher by their superiors and tend to have higher producing groups (23). The relationship between initiating structure and employee satisfaction is not, however, clear.

What is the role of the manager in this approach?

House suggests that the manager's job is to increase worker payoffs for achieving work goals. The manager facilitates goal achievement by:

1. clarifying the path to goals
2. reducing blockages that prevent workers from reaching goals
3. behaving in a way that increases worker satisfaction on the way to goal achievement

The path-goal approach assumes that the leader's behaviors influence subordinate performance and satisfaction, and that the characteristics of the subordinate and of the task influence leader behavior. The following example shows how this model can be useful to a manager.

At the 3M corporation, the reward system supports both worker teams and the individual. Edward Roberts, a professor from MIT, describes the 3M system this way:

> The individual involved in a new venture will have automatic changes in his employment and compensation categories as a function of sales growth of his product. He starts out, for instance, as a first-line engineer at the top or bottom of the salary range for that job. As his product enters the market he becomes a "product engineer." When annual sales volume hits $1 million, it will automatically become a full-fledged product, and his job title changes. His salary ranges change too, because he now has something at $1 million a year in sales. When a product hits the $5

> million mark, he passes the next threshold. He is now a "product line engineering manager." If the product reaches $20 million, it suddenly becomes an independent product department, and if he is the key technical person associated with it, he now becomes "manager of engineering or R & D" for that department (24).

If you were the manager of individuals involved in a new venture, how would you be most effective? At first, you would have to consider the employees and their characteristics. You might ask yourself: Do these persons have the ability to work by themselves, or do they need help? Do they have the willingness?

You also would have to consider the work environment. In this instance, you are familiar with the 3M culture and know that it is supportive of product innovators. You must consider also the benefits of product development to the organization and the benefits to the employee.

Once you make this assessment, you can choose behaviors that make you and the employees most effective. Remember, your job is to show employees how to reach goals and to clear the paths to these goals. In the example given, would you choose a task-oriented managerial behavior? Or would you choose a supportive behavior (i.e., consideration)? In path-goal theory, two other choices are offered. The manager can choose a **participative style,** that is, a style that emphasizes sharing information, working closely with subordinates, and using their ideas to make decisions. Finally, the manager can elect to use an **achievement-oriented behavior** by setting challenging goals, expecting high performance, and seeking continually to improve. In the 3M example, you might choose the participative style, because your job as manager is to facilitate employees who have their own ideas and are motivated to achieve.

Path-goal theory suggests that the manager's first task is to assess the situation for factors related to the subordinate and the work environment. Once this assessment is made, then the leader considers the possible outcomes of any behaviors chosen. The manager tries to gauge whether the particular behaviors will lead to positive outcomes for the organization and for the employee. Finally, the leader chooses one of the four behavioral styles: directive, supportive, participative, or achievement-oriented.

If we compare the path-goal model with the situational leadership model discussed earlier, we see that the path-goal model emphasizes the relationship dimension of the leader's behavior. The manager's major role is to set the climate and to make clear what is expected so employees can perform to their maximum and achieve valued second level outcomes.

This model has many exciting implications for the study of management. For example, one implication is that the manager must learn how to listen and adapt to employees. The CEO of a large hospital gave testimonial support to this trend (and to the path-goal model) in the following statement made at a convention:

> My job has changed and so have the attitudes of employees. We no longer can mandate change or policies. We can no longer cause things to happen with the wave of a hand. We are obligated to show the direction, be charismatic enough to entice people to follow along and be partners in an exciting industry. We not only must show employees how to succeed

but must provide them with the rewards once they actively support our goals. We, as hospital administrators, have a challenge before us.

What do researchers say about the path-goal model?

Subordinates who tend to be close-minded and to respond to authority generally want to be managed by a highly directive leader. Directive behavior is especially important when the task to be completed is ambiguous and needs constant clarification. Tasks that are highly repetitive, unpleasant, stressful, or frustrating are best handled with supportive leader behaviors. If the leader tries to be highly directive in this latter situation, subordinates resist the leader and tend to perform at a much lower level. Open-minded employees with a high degree of self-control (i.e., internal locus of control) prefer the manager to use participative leadership behaviors. They want the leader to consult with them, to use their suggestions, and to involve them in decisions. When dealing with this type of employee, the finding holds true for all types of tasks, repetitive to nonrepetitive (25).

Other Contingency Approaches

The models of Fiedler, Hersey, Blanchard, and House are called "contingency models" because they present leadership style as contingent on the situation. These models have paved the way for more complex models that view the leader or manager in a richer, broader, more dynamic manner than previous models. Two contingency approaches are of particular interest.

The **Vroom-Yetton model** concentrates on leader behavior in several specifically defined decision-making situations (26). The chosen leadership style ranges from the leader's making a decision by himself or herself to the leader's sharing problems with subordinates as a group. Among the contingencies used by the leader in selecting a style are such attributes as identifying who has the information to make the decision, deciding whether subordinates will accept a decision made by the leader, and determining whether the problem is well defined and the importance of employee involvement.

For example, picture yourself as the manager of an insurance agency. You would like to introduce a new report form for use by employees. You are in a hurry to start using the form because you believe that it will tell you whether or not the agency is making money on a new type of policy. You suspect, however, that the other employees will not like using the new form. You apply the Vroom-Yetton model, which leads you through a series of steps that help you decide on the type of approach to take to introduce the new report form.

Another contingency model, the multiple-influence model of leadership (MIML) (27), assumes that the organization's environment, size, technology, structure, and work units all influence the leadership role. The entire model is too complicated to present here, but the core prediction can be summarized as follows: As the organization's environment, work, and structure become more complex, the leader is called on to narrow the gap between expected conditions and actual conditions. To narrow that gap, the authors of the model suggest careful management of rewards, providing direction, and strengthening networks throughout the organization (28).

For example, if a department faces a sudden shift in priorities, the leader's job is to make sure that everyone understands what is going on and works to meet the new conditions. Leaders may also contact trusted colleagues in the organization to gather more information about this "new environment."

These two theories (i.e., the Vroom-Yetton model and the multiple-influence model of leadership) and the models of Hersey, Blanchard, Fiedler, and House all emphasize that effective leadership is contingent on a number of important variables: the leader, the subordinates, the work, and the organization. A leader's analysis of these variables helps him to determine the best or most effective approach to take.

Knowledge Check

1. Which of the following define maturity level?
   a. Achievement motivation
   b. Responsibility
   c. Task behavior
   d. Education and experience
   e. Delegation

2. As employee maturity level increases, the need to manage closely also increases. T or F?

3. Fiedler believes that managers should choose those situations in which they will be effective, rather than adjust their behavior to the situation. T or F?

4. Match the descriptions on the right with the leadership styles on the left:

_____	High task, high relationship	a. Delegating
_____	Showing concern for subordinate status and well being	b. Selling
_____	Low task, low relationship	c. Achievement-oriented
_____	Constantly emphasizing excellence in performance	d. Supportive

5. Supervising tasks that are highly repetitive, unpleasant, stressful, or frustrating usually requires which of the following managerial styles:
   a. directive
   b. supportive
   c. achievement-oriented
   d. participative

Answers:

1 a, b, d, 2 F, 3 T, 4 b, d, a, c, 5 b

Solving the Dilemma

What could Mac do to be more effective?

Mac certainly can be more effective. He should have started with relationship and network-building activities, but it's not too late!

Mac must first acknowledge that his expertise is management—not sales. He should encourage more participative behavior among the salespeople. He needs to get rid of the consultant and to encourage the sales staff to set their own goals. Mac also needs to get out of his office—to talk to other managers in the organization and to solicit their support. At the same time, he can try out some of his ideas to see if others in the organization think they are worth accomplishing. Finally, Mac needs to make a more thorough assessment of the situation. He has M2 employees, which calls for a "selling" behavior style (instead of the "telling" style he is now using). When subordinates come to his office to discuss problems, Mac must make sure that they leave with the problems (and solution suggestions), instead of depositing their problems with him. He may even want to try to complement the "selling" behavior with "achievement-oriented" behavior, as outlined in the path-goal theory.

Mac does not seem to have the symptoms of a manager doomed to fail. He is not preoccupied with salary, status symbols, or himself. He is currently isolating himself from others and tends to withhold his feelings and ideas from others. If he will step back and work to establish relationships before trying to get his agendas in place, he can probably be successful.

Substitutes for Leadership

Some researchers and practitioners propose that leadership behavior may be unnecessary or redundant in certain situations (29). Substitutes for leadership can exist in the nature of the task, in the employee, or in the organization (Table 12.5).

For example, craftspeople or professionals, such as engineers, may have so much experience and ability that they do not need managerial direction to be successful or to feel satisfied. Similarly, employee indifference to organizational rewards may neutralize leadership attempts. An example would be the dedicated musician who plays, not for money, but because he loves the music.

In general, if employees are unskilled or inexperienced, if tasks are unstructured, and if the administrative climate is unfavorable in any of several ways, managers are extremely important. If workers are accomplished, however, and if tasks are structured and the climate is favorable, managers may not be necessary, at least according to the employees.

The notion that certain tasks and certain employee or organizational characteristics can take the place of leadership may explain why certain leadership behaviors do not seem effective. Some employee behaviors are beyond the manager's control and may even be hampered by manager

Table 12.5
Examples of Substitutes for and Neutralizers of Leadership

If:	*Then:*
Subordinates have experience, ability, and training,	The manager does not need to use task oriented behaviors.
The task is very structured,	The manager does not need to use task oriented behaviors.
The task is intrinsically satisfying,	The manager does not need to use consideration oriented behaviors.
The organization has very cohesive groups,	Leadership may not be needed.
The organization is very formal and has many rules,	The manager does not need to use task oriented behaviors.

intervention. In these situations, excellent management may be occurring when the manager is *not* at the workplace. Indeed, if employees can achieve goals and maintain motivation without constant presence of their manager, the leader has probably done an excellent job of managing.

Entrepreneurs and Small Business Owners

This section introduces you to small business management. We first demonstrate the uniqueness of the entrepreneur, then we define small business management and outline the unique skills and styles best suited to the small business owner. You may be inspired to investigate this exciting area further and even to act on one of your ideas and form your own company!

To succeed in small business, men and women must generally exhibit managerial skills and styles that differ sharply from those of their counterparts in big business. Some of these differences can be explained in the context of **entrepreneurship,** that is, the skill of having an idea and forming an organization to support that idea. As one who conceives of both an idea and an organization, the entrepreneur, also assumes the role of small business owner, which calls for many more diverse skills than the conceptualization of a new idea.

In the last few years, the focus has been on those who made it big in small businesses. "Small is Beautiful," "Power to the Entrepreneur" and "Smart People Think Small" are all phrases that have found their way into the popular press and business courses. At colleges and universities, courses now carry such titles as Entrepreneurship, Small Business Management, and The Family-Owned Business. Some universities even have degree programs in entrepreneurship (30).

What is an entrepreneur? Would the managerial concepts discussed thus far have to be changed to be useful to small business owners? Are these people really different from other managers?

The Entrepreneur

George Jenkins' story is an impressive example of entrepreneurial behavior. Jenkins, founder and chairman of Publix Super Markets, Inc., owns a chain of over 260 stores located in Florida. At age 17, Jenkins went to Florida from Georgia with $9 in his pocket. Within five years he began operating the first Publix Food Store (31).

Indicative of his entrepreneurial spirit is George's insistence that the basics of the business are what is important. At the opening of a new store, Jenkins could be found bagging groceries and wheeling customers' purchases to their cars.

Jenkins lives and breathes his business. While on vacation, he can probably be found eyeing grocery stores to see if he could pick up any ideas for Publix. He demands a great deal of employees and expects them to be entrepreneurial as well.

Frederick Smith, founder of Federal Express, wrote an economics paper about an airline that carried small packages overnight from city to city. The airline had its own aircraft and truck fleet, operated independently of commercial schedules and routes, and delivered its cargo anywhere in the United States. His paper received a grade of "C."

To be an entrepreneur is among the most durable of American dreams. The young man or woman with a new product or service concept decides to form his or her own company. He takes his money, and perhaps that of his family or a friend, and starts the new venture. The entrepreneur typically works eighteen hours a day and loves it. Sales start slowly but eventually take off, and profits boom. He makes it big, but the road was full of enough mistakes to fill five or six textbooks. The entrepreneur becomes richer than he ever expected.

To understand these entrepreneurial successes would take a book not only on leadership but on finance and marketing, as well. The people involved do seem, however, to have some common characteristics that make them stand out as leaders.

Their skills tend to be unique, and they often start with a special expertise in a technical area. This technical skill seems to be the reason why they went into business and accounts for their ability to design a unique product.

Another characteristic of entrepreneurs is their persistence and vision. They believe in what they are doing and are willing to risk all they have to make their ideas work. Warren Bennis (32) refers to the **Wallenda factor,** which describes this persistence and unending belief in an idea. Karl Wallenda was the most famous tightrope aerialist in the world. He often commented that the only time he felt truly alive was when he walked the tightrope. Bennis points out that successful leaders, most notably entrepreneurs, simply do not think about failure, and in fact, do not even use the word. They refer instead to "glitches," "false starts," or "errors."

Wallenda fell to his death in 1978 while traversing a 75-foot-high tightrope in downtown San Juan, Puerto Rico. His wife commented after the fall that all Karl had thought about for the previous three months was falling. She stated that this was the first time that he had ever thought about falling, and that he seemed to have put all of his energy into *not* falling rather than into walking on the tightrope. Bennis observes that when Karl Wallenda poured his energies into not falling rather than into tightrope walking, he was virtually destined to fall.

Another characteristic of entrepreneurs is that they tend to be able to empower others with their vision. Others believe in them, want to follow them, and are inspired to work toward the entrepreneur's goals.

From these descriptions, one might conclude that entrepreneurs are simply skillful people who have enormous energy. They possess the skills and the vision to attain excellence. To distinguish them from managers, one would have to examine their ability to perform the functions and roles of management. Being a manager only happens to the entrepreneur by circumstance, because others are involved with him or her. (The key characteristics and behaviors of entrepreneurs are summarized in Table 12.6.)

We can thus conclude that entrepreneurs are leaders and that they tend to introduce ideas and concepts rather than to begin as managers of these ideas. Entrepreneurs do at times evolve into professional managers who perform all of the functions necessary to get things done through others. Bringing in management people from the outside is not an uncommon practice, for entrepreneurs often realize that their real skill is either technical or in turning an idea into a product. They wisely perceive that professional management is best done by others. Many entrepreneurs sell their company before it grows too large, and thus avoid having to manage large numbers of people.

Table 12.6
Important Characteristics and Behaviors of an Entrepreneur

Characteristics	*Entrepreneurial Behaviors*
High need for achievement	Constantly wants to do something unique
	Restless and innovative
	Likes to take personal responsibility for solving problems
	Takes calculated risks
Special technical skill	High interest in one problem
	Talks to other experts about their knowledge
	Reads and collects information about the skill area
Persistence	Looks at setbacks as temporary, and only as minor "blips"
	Does not give up easily
	Ignores gloomy statements about the business
Vision	Can inspire others about what he or she wants to do
	Expresses own ideas as being better than others
High opinion of self	Others observe the entrepreneur's self-confidence
	Expresses self as one who will be successful
Empowerment to others	Can excite others to work on his or her ideas
	Gives others resources to help them accomplish goals.

The Small Business Owner

The majority of self-started companies stay small and do not make fortunes for their owners. Although the owners may do very well financially, they do not become millionaires overnight. Small business owners are thus unique, and are successful as a result of skills that differ from those of big business managers.

What is a small business?

The definition of "smallness" varies. Even agencies within the federal government differ widely as to what they consider a "small business." Indeed, definitions vary depending on number of employees, industry, and level of sales. For example, to be considered a small grocery business by the Small Business Association (a federal agency created to help small businesses), sales must be less than $14.5 million per year. Aircraft manufacturers must have less than 1,500 employees to qualify as a small business. This means that the aircraft company could have sales exceeding $100 million and still be considered a small business.

In the most general terms, a **small business** is one that does not dominate its market, has less than 500 employees, and has sales less than or equal to 1 percent of the total market.

Small business starts have been on the upswing in the last few years. The increase in the number of new businesses has averaged approximately 10 percent per year from 1976 to 1987. The risks are great, too. Approximately 45 percent of new businesses fail within the first 18 months, and only one in five lasts as long as 10 years (33).

Given the risks, why do people start small businesses?

The reasons tend to vary just as the entrepreneurs vary. Some people get fired and have no alternative. Some people, like the entrepreneur, have a vision. Still others buy existing companies because they think they can manage them more efficiently.

Some people go into small business because they want to be their own boss. A poll showed that well over 50 percent of all men and women in the United States prefer to work for themselves rather than for someone else (34).

Small businesses offer many rewards and do tend to out-perform large businesses. In other words, they tend to earn higher profits and to yield a higher return on owner equity. They also present many opportunities to invent and innovate. This may be why some large organizations, such as 3M and IBM, have tried to build small business management ideas into their large organizations. In this way, they foster a climate conducive to innovation. Small businesses are also the largest creators of jobs in the economy. In 1984, small businesses with fewer than twenty employees each created 66 percent of all new jobs.

Why do small businesses fail?

Many reasons for small business failure are relevant to the content of this chapter. Over 90 percent of the failures have to do with incompetence, lack of managerial experience, or inexperience in that product or service area (35). In other words, management plays an enormous role in small business success.

Given their limited resources, small business owners must define their organization in terms of skills rather than in terms of people. They usually cannot afford to hire a marketing manager, accountant, and other specialized individuals.

Instead, they find themselves performing a variety of functions and handling a variety of problems and situations. For example, they are probably responsible for handling both technical and management problems. The technical issues may revolve around product design or service and how to get others in the organization to adhere to the necessary guidelines for production or delivery. The managerial job is as we described it earlier in this chapter. The key difference, then, between the small business person and the manager in a larger organization is that the small business person is *top management* yet he or she must do at least 50 percent technical work and 50 percent managerial work.

This is why running a small business successfully requires a special type of person who is willing to learn managerial skills yet has the persistence to put up with a great deal of day-to-day work. To bring home these points, let's consider a typical afternoon and evening in the life of a small business owner who makes containers used primarily by the army and navy. The company has annual sales of about $10 million and less than 75 employees.

12:20 P.M.	Leaves office for luncheon meeting and visit to plant.
1:30	Returns from lunch. Five messages on desk.
1:40	Tours the plant—stopping several times to talk to people.
2:15	Returns phone calls.
3:00	Accounting is having problems with daughter's car insurance. Needs her current license number and wants to know what happened about her speeding ticket.
3:10	Goes to the bank to establish credit line for new warehouse.
4:45	Returns to find that the bank in Dallas is still not satisfied with customer's credit line. Calls Dallas bank, but the vice president has gone home for the day.
5:15	Works on bid for new customer.
6:00	Calls customer to meet for a drink and to discuss new designs.
7:30	Arrives home with three bids to check.
10:50	Falls asleep in front of T.V. with only two bids reviewed.
2:45 A.M.	Wakes up thinking about the third bid.

Summary Points

- **Managers** hold formal positions in organizations.
- **Management jobs** can be described in terms of the functions performed (planning, organizing, leading, and controlling), the roles played (interpersonal, informational, and decisional), amount of managerial versus technical work performed, organizational level, and functional responsibilities.
- Two basic groups of theories explain why managers are or are not effective: **the universalist approach and the contingency or situational approach.**
- The **universalist approach** to managerial effectiveness emphasizes one best way to manage or one best person to be manager.
- Universalist theorists have identified two key dimensions of leadership behavior: **initiating structure and consideration.**
- The **situational approach** emphasizes that effective managerial behaviors are those behaviors that match the requirements of the particular situation. This approach is more useful for learning managerial effectiveness than the universalist approach.
- Four major variables are used frequently to describe the situational requirements of managerial behavior: **the leader, the follower, the work, and the organization.**
- The two major theories that emphasize the situational leadership approach are **the situational leadership model and the path-goal model.**
- **Small business owners** differ from other types of managers in two basic ways: their need to be their own boss and their willingness to be top manager and still do at least 50 percent technical work.

Questions

1. What is meant by "adapting managerial behavior to the situation"? Discuss the major variables used to define the situation. Consider both the situational leadership model and the path-goal model in your answer.
2. If you were to list three management principles for small business success, what would they be? List the principles in order of importance for a manager starting a business. How might you change the list for a small business owner who has been successful for over ten years.
3. A major disagreement exists among managers and theorists as to whether or not people can be taught to be effective managers. Some managers say that experience is not only the best teacher but the *only* teacher. Others say that without some education about management, people have a difficult time being effective managers and are less likely to succeed. What do you think? Can managers be taught to be effective?
4. Some authors suggest that organizational behavior researchers have made too much of leadership. These authors point out that over 75 percent of employee performance is a product of how the task is arranged, the organizational climate, and the employee's internal motivation. The major effect the manager can have is to screw things up—not make employees more productive. Could it be that the managerial leadership role in organizations is overrated? Discuss your views.
5. Psychologist Robert Rosenthal reported that 100 airmen at the U.S. Air Force Academy Preparatory School were assigned randomly to one of five math classes. Their teachers were unaware of this random assignment. Instead, the teachers were told that their students were selected either on the basis of high or low ability. Students in the supposedly "high-ability" classes improved their math scores substantially more than those in "low-ability" classes, yet at the start, the classes were of equal ability. This phenomenon is known as **self-fulfilling prophecy,** or the Pygmalion effect (named after the sculptor in Greek mythology whose story *My Fair Lady* is based). Many studies have replicated this effect, even when experimenters were observing the behavior of rats. Consider this phenomenon in the organizational setting. Could it be that employee performance is directly related to managerial expectations (36)?

EXPLORING: *The Small Business Administration's New Boss*

[Adapted from the *Wall Street Journal* (September 12, 1986):1.]

Charles Heatherly, age 43, has been acting administrator of the Small Business Administration since 1 April 1986. Without doubt, his leadership style has made him one of President Reagan's most controversial appointments.

Heatherly's main goal is to end the SBA's existence as an independent agency. Here are a few of the actions that he has or has not taken to achieve that goal:

1. On 2 April 1986, he fired six of the SBA's ten regional administrators.
2. On 3 April 1986, he sent a memo to all employees emphasizing his eagerness to prepare the agency for an orderly transition to a new configuration as a part of the Department of Commerce.
3. Heatherly next fired James H. Carrington, chairman of the SBA's National Advisory Council, and dismissed several members of its executive committee.
4. He is delaying key decisions concerning loan guarantees and ways to increase agency effectiveness.

As you might guess, morale at the Small Business Administration is very low.

Heatherly has had a lot of experience working in government agencies. He seems to be a strong leader who is not afraid to take a stand on an issue. He is mild-mannered in person, yet some critics describe him as "a fanatic with no connection to reality."

Discussion Questions

1. If Heatherly's goals are to dismantle the organization, what type of management style does he need to adopt?
2. Can Heatherly maintain morale at the SBA and still get employees to dismantle the organization?
3. What specific traits must Heatherly have to be able to manage the organization during this transition, and to manage such outside forces as the U.S. Congress and the small business community of the country?
4. How might SBA employees "manage up" to ensure that they keep their jobs, and possibly to change Heatherly's mind or to demonstrate to him the best aspects of the SBA?

APPLYING: *Talking With Managers in the Workplace*

This exercise gives you a chance to use what you have learned in this chapter to interview practicing managers, supervisors, or group leaders.

Goal: To obtain information about effective management from practicing managers.

Procedure: Interview someone who has been a manager or a leader for at least one year. Choose a manager who works in a relatively large organization and who you believe is effective in her or his job. If you have difficulty making contact with a manager, consider interviewing one of the following people who would probably be more accessible to you: the dean of your school, a parent who is a manager, the manager of a local organization near your home, or a manager for whom you have worked or are currently working.

After you have interviewed the individual, write a short summary that includes the following:

1. Brief background sketch of the manager and her or his major job responsibilities. If possible, obtain an organization chart that shows the manager's formal position in the organizational structure and a copy of her or his job description.
2. List of questions you asked in the interview.
3. Summary of your findings based on the answers to your questions.
4. Two areas in which you think the manager could improve to make her or him more effective.

You can ask any questions that you judge to be appropriate. As a starting point, here are some that should help you get in-depth information. These questions are arranged in the suggested order to use when talking with the manager.

1. What are some of your major responsibilities?
2. How do you know when you are being effective as a manager?
3. What are the critical characteristics of an effective manager?
4. Do you tend to manage your subordinates differently? If so, how do you change your behavior?
5. Does your boss manage you differently from other people? If so, what does he or she do differently with each person?
6. Did you have or do you now have a mentor who showed you the ropes and how to be effective?
7. How do you encourage your subordinates to be innovative?
8. What advice would you give me as the best way to become an effective manager?

Suggested Readings

Allen, R. W., and Porter, L. W. 1983. *Organizational Influence Processes.* Glenview, Ill.; Scott Foresman.

Bennis, W. 1983. *More Power to You.* Garden City, N.Y.: Doubleday.

Child, J., and Partridge, B. 1982. *Lost Managers: Supervisors in Industry and Society.* Cambridge, Mass.: Cambridge University Press.

Caplow, T. 1976. *How to Run Any Organization.* Hinsdale, Ill.: The Dryden Press.

Despite the somewhat pretentious title, this books contains some interesting material for the practitioner. (Although the book has been retitled and updated since 1976, the material in the 1976 edition is best presented.) Five chapters cover authority, communication, productivity, morale, and change. At the end of each, the author gives his prescriptions for effectiveness.

Hersey, P., and Blanchard, K. 1982. *Management of Organizational Behavior,* 4th ed. Englewood Cliffs, N.J.: Prentice-Hall.

This book presents a clear, straightforward review of earlier theories of leadership and then presents the situational leadership model. Ken Blanchard is also one of the authors of *The One Minute Manager.* You will find this book worthwhile.

Lee, J. 1980. *The Gold and the Garbage in Management Theories and Prescriptions.* Athens, Ohio: Ohio University Press.

This book reviews some of the major management theories and provides insight into the research supporting (or not supporting) each approach. While the presentation is detailed, it is very readable and provides insights not obtainable elsewhere. The material is, however, somewhat dated, so some important new ideas and research are not included.

Levering, R., Moskowitz, M., and Katz, M. 1984. *The 100 Best Companies to Work for in America.* Reading, Mass.: Addison-Wesley.

Mantz, C. 1983. Improving performance through self-leadership. *National Productivity Review* (Summer):288–297.

Mintzberg, H. 1983. *Power In and Around Organizations.* Englewood Cliffs, N.J.: Prentice-Hall.

O'Toole, P. 1984. *Corporate Messiah.* New York: William Morrow.

This book reviews recent examples of corporate leaders who were hired from outside to save failing companies. Different examples are given of these "messiahs," and the conclusion is that most corporate leaders fail at their task for a variety of reasons.

Vance, S. C. 1983. *Corporate Leadership: Boards, Directors and Strategy.* New York: McGraw-Hill.

References

1. Fayol, H. 1949. *General and Industrial Management.* (Translated by C. Storrs) London: Pitman.
2. Mintzberg, H. 1973. *The Nature of Managerial Work.* New York: Harper & Row.
3. Ibid.
4. Ibid.
5. Kotter, J. 1982. What Effective General Managers Really Do. *Harvard Business Review* pp. 156–167.
6. Kotter, J., Peters, T., and Waterman, R. 1982. *In Search of Excellence.* New York: Harper & Row.
7. *Business Week Special Report.* 1983. A New Era for Management. (25 April 1983):49–86.
8. Boone, L.E., and Johnson, J.C. The 801 Men (and 1 Woman) at the Top: A Profile of the CEOs of the Largest U.S. Corporations. *Business Horizons* (February 1980):47–52.
9. *Business Week,* op. cit., pp. 74–75.
10. Ibid.
11. Stogdill, R.M., and Coons, A.E. (Eds.) 1957. *Leader Behavior: Its Description and Measurement.* Ohio State University, Bureau of Business Research, Columbus, Ohio.
12. Boyatzis, R. E. 1982. *The Competent Manager.* New York: John Wiley; Bennis, W., and Nanus, B. 1985. *Leaders: The Strategies for Taking Charge.* New York: Harper & Row; McGregor, D. 1967. *The Human Side of Enterprise.* New York: McGraw Hill; Fox, S. 1984. Leadership: It Can Make a Difference. *Academy of Management Journal* 27:765–776.
13. Stogdill, R.M., and Coons, A.E., op. cit.; Likert, R. 1961. *New Patterns of Management.* New York: McGraw Hill; Katz, C., Maccoby, N., and Morse, N. 1950. *Productivity, Supervision and Morale in an Office Situation.* U. of Michigan Survey Research Center, Ann Arbor, Mich.
14. Pfeiffer, J.W., and Jones, J. 1974. *A Handbook of Structural Experience for Human Relations Training,* vol. 1. LaJolla, Calif.: University Associates, pp. 10–11.
15. Korman, A. 1977. *Organizational Behavior.* Englewoods Cliffs, N.J.: Prentice-Hall.
16. Nystrom, P. C., and Starbuck, W. 1981. *Handbook of Organizational Design,* vol. 2. Remodeling Organizations and Their Environments. New York: Oxford University Press.
17. Hersey, P., and Blanchard, K. 1982. *Management of Organizational Behavior,* 4th ed. Englewood Cliffs, N.J.: Prentice-Hall.
18. Greene, C. Questions of Causation in the Path-Goal Theory of Leadership. *Academy of Management Journal.* March 1979:22–41; House, R. A. 1971. Path-Goal Theory of Leadership. *Administrative Science Quarterly* 16:321–338.
19. Hersey, P., and Blanchard, K., op. cit.
20. Fiedler, F. 1967. *Theory of Leadership Effectiveness.* New York: McGraw Hill; Fiedler, F., and Chemers, M. 1974. *Leadership and Effective Management.* Glenview, Ill.: Scott, Foresman; Fiedler, F. 1972. How Do You Make Leaders More Effective? New Answers to an Old Puzzle. *Organizational Dynamics,* pp. 3–18.
21. Hersey, P., and Blanchard, K., op. cit.
22. House, R.A., op. cit.
23. Ferralt, T. and Storks, F. Satisfaction, Motivation and Productivity: The Complex Connection. In J. Gray and F. Starke (Eds.) 1977. *Readings in Organization Behavior.* Columbus, Ohio: Charles E. Merrill, pp. 74–86.
24. Peters, T., and Waterman, R. 1982. *In Search of Excellence.* New York: Harper, p. 227; Isen, A. M., Clark, M., and Schwartz, M. F. 1976. Duration of the Affect of Good Mood on Helping: Footprints on the Sands of Time. *Journal of Personality and Social Psychology* 34:385–393.
25. Greene, C. N. 1979. The Reciprocal Nature of Influence Between Leader and Subordinate. *Journal of Applied Psychology* 60:187–193.
26. Vroom, V.H. A New look at managerial decision-making. *Organizational Dynamics* (Spring 1973):66–80.
27. Hunt, J.G., and Osborn, R.N. 1981. Toward a macro-oriented model of leadership. In Hunt, J.G., Sekran, U., and Schreisheim, C. (Eds.) *Leadership:*

Beyond Establishment Views. Carbondale, Ill.: Southern Illinois University Press, pp. 196–221.
28. Ibid.
29. Ken, S. and Mermier, J. 1978. Substitutes for Leadership: Their Meaning and Measurement. *Organization Behavior and Human Performance.* December 1978:375–403; Howell, J., and Dorfman, P. 1981. Substitutes for Leadership: Test of a Construct. *Academy of Management Journal* (December 1981):714–728.
30. Babson College, for example.
31. Watters, P. 1980. *Fifty Years of Pleasure.* Lakeland, Fla.: Publix Supermarkets, Inc.
32. Bennis, W., and Nanus, B., op. cit.
33. WSI, 1982; Hot Growth Companies. 1987. *Business Week* (May 25, 1987):82–97.
34. Ibid.
35. Siropolis, N. 1982. *Small Business Management,* 2nd ed. New York: Houghton Mifflin.
36. Rosenthal, R. 1973. The Pygmalion Effect Lives. *Psychology Today* (September 1973):56–63.

The Details of Form and Function: Organizational Design

Chapter 13

I. Dilemma: Two Bosses for One Employee
II. Organizational Design: The Bricks and Mortar of Managing
III. Structure: The Framework for Work
    A. The linking pin concept
    B. Functionalization leads to specialization—A balancing act
    C. Line, staff, assistant, and assistant to positions
    D. The structure of units: fitting people together
IV. Authority in Organizations: The Cement of Working Together
    A. Delegation—giving authority away
    B. Principles of delegation
    C. Centralize or decentralize—two sides of the same coin
V. Coordination—The Details of the House
    A. Vertical coordination
    B. Lateral coordination
    C. Using coordination to build innovation into the organization
VI. Summary Points
VII. Questions
VIII. Exploring: The New Yorker Gets a Kick in the Print
IX. Applying: Analyzing a Change in Design
X. Suggested Readings
XI. References

Chapter Goals

By the end of this chapter, you will be able to:

1. Identify the three major considerations in the design of an organization: structure, authority, and coordination.
2. List the ways in which organization design affects individual behavior.
3. Describe how managers divide work among employees, and describe the difference between functional and scalar relationships of positions.
4. Compare and contrast different organizational structures according to their effects on behavior.
5. Define delegation, and suggest major principles for effective delegation.
6. Specify the effects on behavior of centralizing or decentralizing operations.
7. Provide several strategies for coordinating units within an organization.

Dilemma Two Bosses for One Employee

Anita sat behind her desk and listened to the consultant's analysis. She was ambivalent about the progress made by the Information Systems Department.

The company that Anita works for is an engineering firm, which specializes in school buildings and public facilities. The organization has a total of 350 employees, including Anita's department. Half of the engineers work on school buildings and half work on public facilities. In addition to the engineering and information systems departments, the company also has an accounting and an administration department. All departments report to the company president. The chart diagramming this structure is shown in Figure 13.1.

Anita had decreased turnover among the programmers, and morale and productivity were currently high. She was even pleased about the managers who reported to her. Everything was going well with one exception: all of those who used the department services were complaining that they could *not* get their work done on time. Two or three complaints had filtered back to Anita's boss, who was now getting on her back!

The Information Systems Department had 15 people arranged in three subdepartments. The first subdepartment was the systems people. Their job was to define broadly the needs of those who used the department services. Employees in the second subdepartment, programming, wrote all of the programs for the computers. Employees in the third subdepartment, operations, ran the computer equipment.

If Anita were to diagram the structure of her department, it would look like the chart in Figure 13.2.

Anita was naturally concerned about satisfying the other departments that used her department's services. These were "user departments," as the computer people called them.

Anita knew that her primary job was to serve the engineers, because they were the ones who made all of the money for the company. The administration and accounting departments were important, but they existed to serve the public facilities and schools departments also.

When the consultant went to the user departments (i.e., public facilities and schools) he gathered some interesting data. The engineers who worked on the school projects had problems that were quite different from those of the public facilities engineers. The school projects always had a predictable time frame, whereas the public facilities projects did not. The designs for public facilities posed a constant problem of meeting unrealistic deadlines imposed by civic groups, city councils, and citizens who wanted everything to be large, beautiful, and cheap. Requests for information were enormous when a public facility was in the planning stage. The profits, however, were also large.

The consultant produced a report that was not met with approval by Anita. In short, he recommended that Anita reorganize her department to meet user demands more effectively. He recommended a design that included two project managers in information systems.

Anita was baffled. She did not want her department overloaded with unnecessary employees. Besides, hadn't she always been able to keep up with all of the projects? She also did not know much about project management and was worried that she would not be able to handle the new way of operating. The consultant told Anita: "What I am proposing is a matrix structure, in which employees have two bosses."

Anita couldn't believe what she was hearing. "Two bosses?" she thought. "Is this guy crazy? Here we are getting complaints all over the place, and he thinks two bosses will solve our problems!"

Questions

1. What caused Anita's problems in the first place?
2. Should Anita use a two boss design?
3. Can Anita use better means of coordinating?
4. How can Anita make sure that her department will continue to innovate?

Figure 13.1
Organizational Structure of Anita's Company

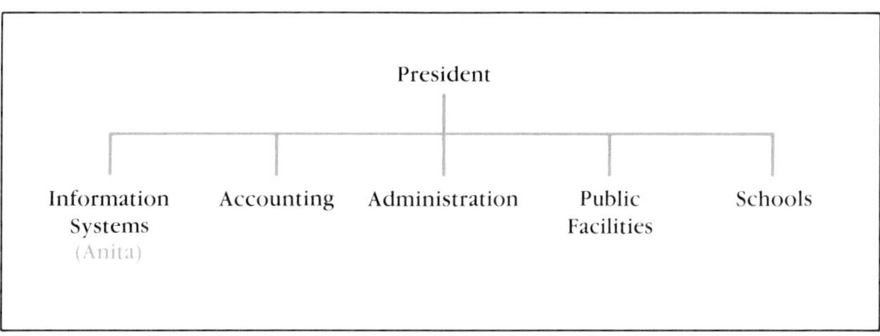

Figure 13.2
Organizational Structure of Anita's Department

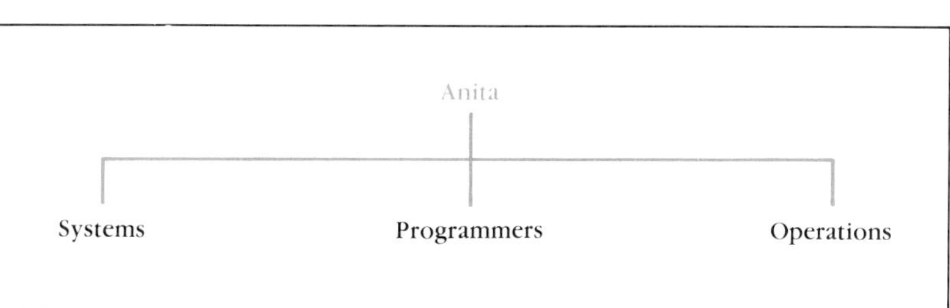

Organizational Design: The Bricks and Mortar of Managing

In this section we discuss three basic concepts necessary to the understanding of any organization design: structure, authority, and coordination. First we define these three concepts, then we use them to explain how you can analyze and purposefully manage organization design. **Organization design** is defined as the way in which organizational managers arrange people in the organization to give employees authority and to ensure that organizational members coordinate their activities.

What is an organization?

In chapter one, we referred to people as the foundation of the organization. This is the key to our present discussion as well. Organizations are made up of people. In fact, an organization is defined by the set of relationships that exists among the people in the company. Ideally, these relationships are put together, or designed, in a way that enables the organization to achieve its goals.

Consider the example of a frustrated small business owner who had a shoe store. He employed only five people, yet he was puzzled as to why he had so much difficulty getting those people to carry out some suggested changes in sales technique and store design. One day, over a cup of coffee, he remarked to a friend, "I think the problem is not what I want to do but the way I go about giving employees work, the way they work together, and the way we try to pass along information." This manager was expressing concern about his organizational design.

Does organizational design affect behavior?

Without doubt, organizational design has a profound effect on behavior. The organizational design forms employee expectations. The design tells employees who to go to when they have a problem to discuss, or when they want to find out what to do next. The design also tells them who the boss is. (An exasperated baseball player, age 8, on a Little League team expressed the problem of not knowing what to do or what was expected of her when she boldly stated: "If nobody wants to be boss, I'm going to tell them what to do!")

The design of the organization can help or hinder individual performance. When employees cannot get the needed information to do their job or when they have to check with too many people before doing anything, they become paper pushers, instead of effective performers. Well designed organizations help individuals in their efforts to meet organizational goals.

The design of an organization may or may not facilitate company goals. For example, the design of Anita's department may not be optimal for meeting user needs. We will analyze the structure of Anita's department and suggest a new design that may help her.

The design of an organization lets outsiders know how to interact with the company. It lets others know who really makes decisions, who is manager in charge of purchasing, who does the work, and who is responsible for hiring and firing.

In sum, organizational design

1. Sets expectations
2. Helps or hinders individual performance
3. Facilitates or does not facilitate organizational goals
4. Lets outsiders work better with the organization.

Organizational design can affect employee behavior in many ways. We look next at the various structural alternatives that managers can use to give authority and to coordinate employee activity. We discuss first the structure of organizations.

Structure: The Framework for Work

Organizational structure is the arrangement of roles and reporting relationships that govern employee behavior. When one is trying to understand a firm's structure, one must take the individual elements and build them into a whole picture. The place to start is with the basic element, the job.

How do managers divide work among employees?

All organizations—no matter how small—use the concept of **division of work.** This is the manner in which work is divided into jobs or groups of jobs. Consider Anita's department. She has divided the work into her job, the jobs of three managers who report to her, and the jobs of twelve other people who report to the managers. The picture of the entire department is shaped like a triangle (Figure 13.3). Employees 1–4 report to the manager

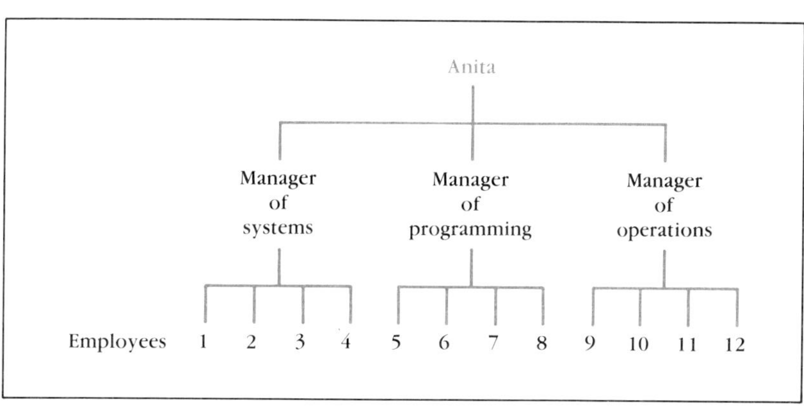

Figure 13.3 *Anita's Departmental Organization Structure Showing Employees*

of systems, employees 5–8 report to the manager of programming, and employees 9–12 report to the manager of operations.

Note that the department is organized into different levels and that functions are then assigned to people at various job levels. Division into a hierarchy of levels is called the **scalar process,** because it provides a scale or grading of duties according to level of authority and responsibility.

In Anita's department, the work is also divided into different kinds of duties. Anita decided that she wanted her department separated into subdepartments that handle three kinds of **functions:** systems, programming, and operations. The difference between Anita and her subdepartment managers is therefore **scalar,** whereas the difference between the three subdepartment managers is **functional.** Using these two distinctions, we can map any organizational structure by drawing an **organization chart,** or diagramming positions and reporting relationships in the organization.

Consider Figure 13.4, which charts a university center organization: If you were to detail the scalar and functional relationships in this structure, what would they be? (See Table 13.1.)

On the chart, the representation of cafeteria personnel is a combination of scalar relationship and functional title. People outside the organization can thus get an accurate idea of the person's place and function in the organization just by the title. We know that a person with the title of General Manager, University Center, is probably the individual in charge of the entire center. We know also that a person with the title of Supervisor, Hot Foods, probably concentrates on hot foods and reports to a manager.

The Linking Pin Concept

When scalar and functional processes are in place, the result is a set of relationships that link the people in a working organization. Rensis Likert, a management theorist, describes this as the **linking pin concept** (1). This concept refers to the interrelationships of positions, whereby a change in one position affects all others.

The scalar and functional relationships are held together by having each manager serve as a linking pin to other groups in the organization. If all linkages are working and effective, then we can expect the organization to be effective. For example, if you want to get some information from your boss's boss, in most organizations you are required to use the linking pin,

Figure 13.4
Organizational Structure of a University Center

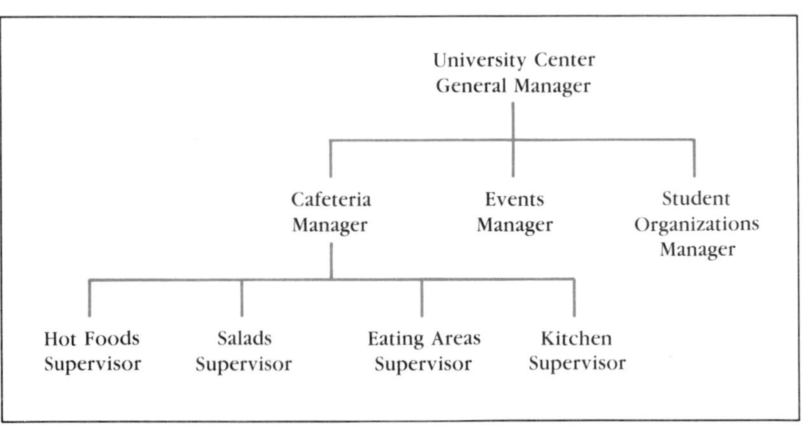

Table 13.1
Scalar and Functional Relationships in a University Center

Scalar	*Functional*
General Manager	University Center
Managers	Cafeteria, Events, Student Organizations
Supervisors	Hot Food, Salads, Eating Areas, Kitchen

that is, your boss, who in turn asks his or her boss for the information. This process may seem slow and inefficient, but in many organizations, this procedure ensures that the participants know what is happening and that the "chain of command" is preserved.

"Weak links" can occur if a manager is not skillful or is not motivated to perform the job. We have discussed political activity in the organization (see Chapter 11). Managers who view themselves as "separate" from the rest of the organization or those who see themselves as "the center of attention" cause weak linkages. They tend to make or break links to promote their personal needs rather than the goals of the organization.

> A head football coach, who was new in his job, inherited an assistant who was not pleased about being second in command. The assistant told the other coaches that if they had a problem, they should come to him, *not* to the head coach, because the head coach was "too busy to handle day-to-day problems." The head coach caught on quickly, and after much counseling was forced to remove the unyielding assistant. The tragedy was that the assistant was an excellent technical person who could have benefitted the team, yet he was not helping anyone and was undermining the organization.

Functionalization Leads to Specialization—A Balancing Act

When managers let people specialize in tasks, they can develop expertise that benefits the company. For example, one organization hired a tax accountant to review all of its records and to advise managers on capital purchases. The accountant's salary was $45,000, but by the end of the first year, he had saved the company $250,000. Did the organization make a wise decision to specialize the task?

If people become too specialized, however, they may lose money for the company. As a particular organization grew, so did the number of jobs and departments. Some of the jobs got absurd! For example, in one department, the manager created a job entitled "Manager, Planning," but when the job description was reviewed, the person's sole apparent responsibility was coordinating the locations of company meetings. The salary was $34,000 per year, plus a bonus.

The major benefits of specialization are economic and technical; the disadvantages are often human. If a manager can justify specializing a job or a series of jobs by showing how specialization will save the company money or bring in *critical* expertise, then the specialization is probably a good idea (2). If, however, neither of these justifications exists, then the job or group of jobs is probably best left alone.

The creation of more organizational levels (i.e., increasing specialization) often results in the following:

1. Awareness of the existence of a higher level increases the tendency to "pass the buck".
2. Communications and misunderstandings increase as more levels are added.
3. Unwanted time lags occur with more levels.
4. Organizational members experience a loss of control when too many levels exist.
5. Employees have a greater tendency to get stuck in a job because they become over-specialized.
6. More support staff is needed.
7. More written communication, documentation, and rules of behavior are required.

Consider the following attempt to create levels in an organization responsible for a nursery school. The owner was an excellent teacher who loved working with children. He had also helped many parents get through difficult times. As his school grew, he added classrooms for grades one through five, and he then began to worry that he was "not being organized." After attending a seminar entitled "Small Business Growth and You," he created several reporting levels within the organization. After two months, his employees and the children's parents complained so much that he returned to the old organization. He had put in levels because he thought he should have them, *not* because he needed them.

Keep in mind this general principle: **the fewer the levels of supervision, the smaller the number of people required to achieve organizational objectives, and the more satisfied and productive the employees** (3).

Be careful if you are the one creating jobs or for whom a job is created. We have already discussed job design and how people can be motivated by a design change. In essence, a change in job design often trades specialization for motivational impact, that is, a job becomes more interesting and challenging the *less* it is specialized.

Specialization can also determine employee levels, span of control, and job grouping. These topics are our next focus.

How many people should report to a manager?

This age-old question relates to **span of control,** or the number of people who report to a manager.

Sir Ian Hamilton, a general in World War I, offered a simple solution to the problem of span of control: "no more than six subordinates." This principle, although clear, does not always work. A Japanese manager told one of the authors that in his country supervisors commonly have as many as 50 to 75 employees reporting directly to them, and this number, in the manager's opinion, was not high enough. Rather than endorse a particular number, we offer some rules to help managers arrive at the optimal number in any given situation. When considering span of control, therefore, consider these rules:

1. The lower the scalar position in the organization, the larger the span of control can be. This is because lower level jobs tend to have more in common than upper level jobs.

2. The more the manager must control employee activities, the less the span of control should be. More supervisors may be needed if a manager has to supervise different locations.
3. In terms of number of employees per unit, extensive research shows that large unit size correlates with lower job satisfaction, lower performance, and higher turnover (4). For this reason, companies such as 3M have ruled that when a division grows beyond a certain limit, the division is split into smaller units (5).

As a general rule, tall structures (i.e., those with many levels) lead to less employee satisfaction and lower individual output. These effects are countered by greater managerial control and increased opportunity for individuals to progress up the organization ladder. Many companies insist that having so many levels provides opportunity for people to move up in the organization.

Not only large organizations have problems with tall structures. A small junior college asked students to form an organization that would arrange social events for the student body. The students held elections and formed an executive committee. In an attempt to get organized, the executive committee appointed several committees to solicit other workers. A committee coordinator was appointed, then another coordinator was appointed. Finally, a senior coordinator was appointed to manage the two coordinators. You get the picture!

The following principles apply to the creation of any organizational structure.

- **Easy to do:** Create the boxes on the organization chart.
- **Difficult to do:** Ensure coordination among people.
- **Important to reinforce:** Try to get everyone to use the linking pins in the organization.
- **Don't do this:** Create unnecessary levels of supervision or put in people who are not necessary.
- **Try to do this:** The lower the position in the organization, the larger you can make the span of control.
- **Remember:** Tall structures tend to lead to lowered satisfaction and lowered output.
- **Your goal, as always:** Keep it simple!

Line, Staff, Assistant, and Assistant to Positions

As organizations grow larger, one finds that new positions are created. These are often advisory in nature or are created to help managers accomplish special studies that have to be done. Such positions are referred to as **staff positions.** The advantage of adding staff positions to the organization is that managers are then freed to concentrate on the primary work of the business. All positions that are not advisory are referred to as **line positions.** For example, an individual in a staff position to an operations manager might do a special study on a new way to motivate employees. The operations manager and everyone in the operations department (i.e., those in line positions) would then be responsible for carrying out the recommendations if they so desired.

In short, staff positions are those that advise others but do not have direct decision-making capability. Line positions are those that are directly responsible for running the business; they make the final decisions. These distinctions are summarized in Table 13.2.

Some organizations allow this line and staff relationship to vary depending on the decision. Indeed, an effective way to view line and staff distinctions is in terms of the given situation. Whenever one person in an organization relates to another as an advisor, the advising person becomes staff. If an employee can make decisions or exercise authority, then that person is in a line position.

Too often managers create unnecessary staff positions by creating either assistant positions or assistant to positions. An **assistant** position usually carries a functional title similar to the manager's. For example, if the manager is titled "Manager, Purchasing," she may have an "Assistant Manager, Purchasing." The distinction is scalar; the functional area is the same. Responsibilities of the assistant manager are to help the manager run the department, to take over in the manager's absence, and to do more of the operational tasks, which frees the manager to walk around the organization and observe what is going on. Managers sometimes create this relationship as a way to train their successor. Indeed, this relationship can be found at the very top of the organization (e.g., the chief executive officer has a chief operating officer). The chief executive officer relates to the board of directors and to key outside people, sets policies and procedures, and tends to have only the chief operating officer reporting to him. The chief operating officer is the one who oversees the organization's day-to-day operations and is responsible for making routine decisions.

Another way to set up a staff assistant is alongside the manager. This is called an **assistant to.** The assistant to position often handles special projects and helps out when the manager gets overloaded. The person who occupies the assistant to position usually has a special skill that the manager needs. This position is like a consulting relationship.

Both the assistant and assistant to positions can be dangerous, for individuals in these positions can destroy the organization linkages. The assistant manager may alienate the manager from the department. Employees may get confused about who really runs the department, and some may become jealous of the assistant manager, who, because he works closely with the manager, may be perceived as being next in line for the manager's position.

Table 13.2
Differences Between Line and Staff Positions

	Line	*Staff*
Basic difference	Makes decisions that directly affect key product or service	Advises others; affects product or service indirectly
Example	Director of marketing	Assistant to the president
Possible benefits	Focus on production, direct decision making, develops generalists	Focus on one problem, develops and uses special skills
Possible drawbacks	Too much involvement in day-to-day work	Can become too powerful; makes more work for others

In summary, the three major components of organizational design are structure, authority, and coordination. An organization is defined as the set of relationships that exist among the employees. Organizational design affects employee behaviors by setting expectations, helping or hindering individual performance, by facilitating organizational goals, and by enabling outsiders to work with the organization. Important considerations in understanding organizational structure are the division of work, how positions are linked, and the relationship between scalar and functional specializations. Line and staff relationships refer to whether a particular position is advisory or directly responsible for the organization's product or service.

Solving the Dilemma

What caused Anita's problems in the first place?

Anita has not adapted her departmental structure to the needs either of the department or the organization. She probably has perceived the scalar and functional aspects correctly. The problem seems to reside in the structuring of the departmental work units. In other words, the subdepartments of systems, programming, and operations seem to be a logical arrangement, yet this structuring is not able to respond adequately to user needs. Anita's problem is *not* the individual whom she selected to be systems manager. The problem is that the systems manager is hindered by the structure. So, although Anita's departmental structure seems to be set up logically, she needs to change it to meet her users' needs.

Knowledge Check

1. Organizational design refers only to the structure of how jobs are placed together. T or F?
2. Which of the following is *not* the effect of organizational design?
   a. Sets expectations
   b. Helps or hinders individual performance
   c. Lets outsiders work better with the organization
   d. Lets stockholders make a profit
   e. Facilitates or does not facilitate organizational goals
3. The scalar process refers to:
   a. Division of work into tasks
   b. Division of work into levels
   c. Division of work into kinds of duties
   d. Division of work by deciding who gets to be a linking pin
4. The linking pin concept refers to the location of employees at key communication points in the organizational structure. T or F?
5. Tall structures tend to enhance the job satisfaction and productivity of individual employees. T or F?

Answers:

1 F, 2 d, 3 b, 4 T, 5 F

The Structure of Units: Fitting People Together

An important issue remains to be addressed in our discussion of structure, that is, how to place all of the units together. This placement is a matter of how much emphasis is put on the functions performed by different departments. An example will help set the scene.

Consider a small wholesale plumbing supply company that sells parts to plumbers and contractors. The supply company has ten different locations, each of which has the same employee configuration:

- 2 salespeople who go to job sites to sell supplies
- 1 salesperson who sells supplies at the place of business
- 1 purchasing agent
- 1 clerk
- 1 warehouse person
- 1 truck driver
- 1 manager

The president's job is to structure the company "to get as many sales as possible." Hank, the president, has a number of options. He can have each location manager report to him, which would create a span of control of ten. Hank decided that was too large a span. He also considered appointing two "regional managers." If he used that structure, one regional manager would supervise the five branches in the west, and another manager would supervise the five branches in the east. Hank next thought about categorizing the branches according to sales volume. He could have all of the larger branches managed by one manager and all of the smaller branches by another. Yet another way to categorize the branches was according to type of customer. Some branches were patronized mostly by commercial plumbers; others were used mainly by residential plumbers. Lastly, Hank could create functional managers of areas such as purchasing or sales. The purchasing manager would supervise all of the branch purchasing people, the sales manager would supervise sales personnel from each branch, and so forth.

As you can see, Hank has many options. The following discussion will help you decide which structure is best for him. Hank should consider four basic designs (6) as follows: functional, product, territory, and matrix. These design alternatives are diagrammed in Figure 13.5.

How is the functional design arranged?

Hank could structure his organization according to job **functions.** If he used this design, he would create a series of jobs at his location that would assume responsibility for watching over each function at the various branches. For example, he might have a manager of purchasing, a manager of sales, a manager of finance, and a manager of administration. The manager of purchasing would purchase materials for *all* of the branches; the manager of sales would set sales policies for *all* of the branches; and so forth. (See Figure 13.5, option 1, for a chart of this structure.

The functional structure has many advantages:

1. The structure is a logical reflection of the organization's functions.
2. It follows the concept of specialization (i.e., the purchasing manager is an expert in purchasing and can help each branch achieve maximum performance in this area.

3. It helps train people. An employee in the purchasing department will probably learn everything there is to know about purchasing plumbing supplies.
4. Hank can keep tight controls of the organization.

Figure 13.5
Hank's Options for Organizational Structure

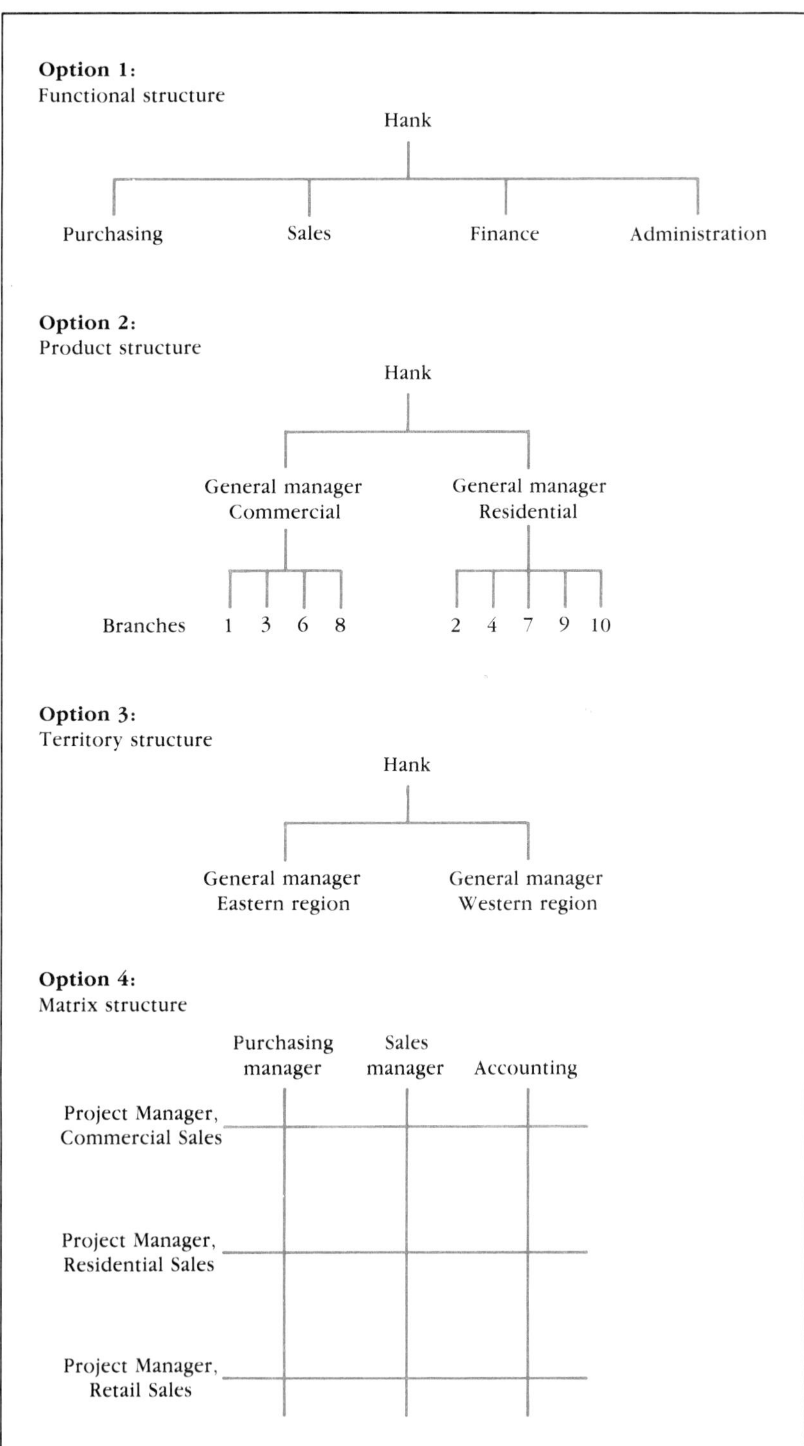

Several disadvantages of a functional structure are:

1. Responsibility for profits is at the top only. Branch managers and functional managers never have direct control of profits. The salespeople can always say that profits were low because the purchasing agent did not get good prices from the manufacturers.
2. It can create over-specialization and narrow the business viewpoint of personnel.
3. It limits the development of branch managers. How can a branch manager come from the purchasing department? Department employees are trained in one functional area only.
4. It reduces coordination between departments. Unless the President forces some coordination among units, purchasing personnel could go for an entire year without talking to the salespeople.

Considering the pros and cons of the functional design, Hank might consider another alternative. Perhaps a product structure would be best for his organization.

How are product designs different from other structural designs?

Product structures emphasize the **products sold,** or the **types of customers** that the organization has. Hank could organize the branches according to the type of business that they have. Since he has already ruled out the option of all branch managers reporting to him, he might hire two general managers. One general manager would be responsible for all of the branches that handle primarily commercial plumbing business. The other general manager would be responsible for the remaining branches, which handle primarily residential plumbing business. The chart for this design looks like option 2 in Figure 13.5.

A product structure has many advantages:

1. It focuses attention and effort on the customer type. The "general manager, commercial," would be expected to know everything there is to know about commercial plumbing work.
2. It also places responsibility for profits at the division level. If the five branches run by the general manager, commercial, do not make much money, then Hank can hold that manager accountable. He knows right where to go!
3. It improves coordination of functional activities. In essence, the general manager is the focal point for purchasing, administration, sales, and everything else. He may choose to hire assistants to help him in these functional areas, but these assistants (for the general manager, commercial) would handle issues related to commercial sales only.
4. It helps train general managers. Employees learn all facets of the business.
5. It permits growth and diversification of products.

The product structure is not without its disadvantages:

1. It requires more people. Each general manager is likely to hire assistants, and each would need a specialist in accounting, purchasing, and so forth. The organization, by doing this hiring, may be duplicating services that would have been centralized in the functional structure. To make matters worse, what usually happens with this type of structure is that the president also hires a few assistants!

2. The president tends to have less control of operations. If each general manager is doing his or her own purchasing, Hank will have difficulty centralizing policies and procedures for buying supplies.
3. This structure creates another kind of specialist—the product specialist.

These points have left Hank a bit unsure about what he wants. Let's explore another alternative that he has heard about, the territory structure.

What is the territory design?

Hank could arrange his organization according to geographic **territory,** or region. A general manager would be assigned to oversee the five branches in the eastern region and another manager would be assigned to the five branches in the western region. The chart would look like the one in option 3, Figure 13.5.

This structure has many of the same advantages and disadvantages of the product design structure, but in this case the emphasis is on **uniqueness of the region.**

This type of design is most effective when each geographic region does have unique characteristics that affect the business. For example, Saga Corporation feeds people in colleges, hospitals, corporate dining rooms, and public restaurants. The organization has over 1,000 locations across the United States. Saga could be structured according to type of client (e.g., hospitals, campus locations, and corporate offices). Each of the regions of the country, however, has unique food tastes. The territory structure helps Saga respond to these unique tastes, otherwise the company might lose business. If the corporation had a product structure, Saga would be obligated not only to have a hospital division, but a regional division within each product division to focus on local food preferences.

Structures can be combined. The Saga example points out that structures can be combined. An organization might have a product structure (e.g., hospitals, college campuses, and businesses) and within each of these divisions have a territorial breakdown. As you can see, the options are limitless.

At this point, Hank is baffled. He wants all of the designs because each has advantages. Moreover, he realizes that his industry is very competitive and that he needs to respond quickly to his customer's needs. He also wants a more dynamic and "fluid" organization, an environment in which people can work on several tasks at the same time.

We offer Hank one more choice. (This is, by the way, the same choice we offer Anita for restructuring the Information Systems Department.)

Can a design include two bosses for one employee?

Yes, it's called a **matrix structure.** This structure is defined as an overlay of a project design on a functional design with two chains of command to direct employees. The effect of this structure is to create two work emphases. Let's apply this structure to the example of the plumbing supply business.

Hank would create one structure according to the functions he needed done. He would have a purchasing agent, a sales manager, a finance specialist, and a manager of administration. Hank would also create several project teams that would be responsible for the types of products being sold to customers. Hank could have three project managers. one for commercial sales, one for residential sales, and one for retail sales.

Option 4 in Figure 13.5 shows this structure. Hank would create specialists not only in the functional areas but also in the various product lines. In this way, if a new product were to come on the market, the project manager would be aware of it and could easily inform the purchasing agent. The project manager would also coordinate with the sales manager to design a marketing campaign for the new product. The project manager's expertise with a new product would be supplemented with experts in purchasing and sales.

The effect of the matrix structure is to separate some of the organization's activities into project areas. Resources and people are then focused on these areas. In this way, the organization maintains centralized functions such as purchasing and finance, but is also able to respond quickly to market changes and customer needs. For the branch manager, this may mean that she has several bosses. One boss might be the regional manager who directs commercial sales. Another boss might be the production manager who directs the branch manager on how to purchase items.

In a matrix structure, a project manager is established to direct all work toward completion of a major project, such as development of a new type of business. Employees assigned to that project are supervised by the project manager. Once the project goal is achieved, the employees return to their functional department or are assigned to a new project. In Hank's case, he would reassign the three general managers once the competition subsided or when he judged that he was firmly entrenched in the business and that the branch managers could work on their own. (Table 13.3 compares Hank's structural alternatives.)

The matrix design has definite advantages. As you can see, this type of structure has the advantage of being adaptable and responsive to change.

Table 13.3
Comparison of Different Organizational Structures[7]

	Functional	*Product*	*Territory*	*Matrix*
Focus of attention	Basic functions of work	Products	Customer location; regional divisions	Projects and functions
Who is responsible for profits?	Top manager	Product managers	Territory managers	Various managers; primarily project managers
Good for developing management skills?	No	Yes	Yes	Maybe
Good for developing technical expertise?	Yes	Maybe	Maybe	Yes
Good for central operations?	Yes	No	No	Maybe

SOURCE: Adapted from Daft, R. 1986. Organization Theory and Design, 2nd ed., St. Paul, Minn.: West Publishing.

1. A great deal of information can flow through the organization because more information is available to more people.
2. This type of design is often referred to as the structure that is most democratic, because it forces people to problem solve together and to discuss issues (rather than simply doing something "because the boss said to do it.") (7).

The matrix design also has some disadvantages.

1. The design is confusing. Employees may not know who their "real boss" is. The project manager is worried constantly about his project, and the functional manager is worried constantly about her function. Consider a two parent family. Isn't this a matrix design? Both parents are responsible for planning, organizing, leading, and controlling the family unit. The children, having two bosses, can easily play one against the other: "But Mommy said it was OK!" They may also withhold key information from one parent because of an anticipated response. In the absence of frequent and high quality communication between parents, children can play the organization for all it's worth (8)! The matrix design in a business organization has similar problems. With multiple bosses, game playing occurs frequently and questions often arise.
2. The design requires an enormous amount of planning and problem solving.
3. It also demands that managers have high quality communication skills, including both ability and willingness to communicate.

In summary, the matrix design is most effective under the following conditions:

1. Special projects need to be done.
2. Complex issues of coordination exist in the organization.
3. Markets are changing rapidly, and the company needs to focus attention on special issues.
4. The organization needs to be energized.

In this section, we outlined four types of organization structure: functional, product (or customer), territory, and matrix. By far the most complex is the matrix design. These structures differ mainly in the effect that each has on individual employee behavior and in the emphasis that each places on certain aspects of the business.

Not all companies adhere strictly to organization structures like those we have described. In fact, the more innovative companies come up with their own variation.

> One example of this type of innovation is CRS Sirrine, Inc., a large architecture and construction management firm that also owns an interior design company and a construction firm. It employs around 3,500 people.
>
> CRS has used the team concept for years. Today, architects work in groups of six to eight, with each group working on three to six different projects at one time. Members of a CRS team usually see a project through to the end. In this way they learn various facets of the business—from dealing with clients to handling on-site problems.
>
> A few years ago, the teams were organized by function, so each project had a design team, a production team, and a construction team. The company changed its structure design primarily to stimulate its employees. With the project team design, people at the firm's lower levels often are given a great deal of responsibility. The company has been very

successful with the new structure. One wall of the firm's headquarters displays more than 300 different awards won by the company for buildings designs. The employees call this the "ego wall."

Solving the Dilemma

Should Anita use a two boss design?

The matrix structure should work for Anita. She needs to create project teams, which would overlay a project structure on the functional design. The organization structure would then look like Figure 13.6.

In this structure, Anita has the technical expertise established with her systems, programming, and operations units, but she also has managers who can focus on the special needs of users. A side benefit of the design is that Anita can offer new recruits many work options. In the past, she typically started new people on an easy project in operations, so they could get a feel for completed systems with little pressure placed on them. She next moved the recruits to a new project in the operations area or to the design department.

This structure solves many problems. It gives users someone to talk to about their specific projects, decreases response time because it concentrates effort, and provides exciting opportunities for new recruits.

Knowledge Check

1. Design structures can be divided into two types, centralized or decentralized. T or F?
2. One major advantage of a functional structure is:
   a. Quick response time to market changes
   b. Development of general managers
   c. Ease with which a chart can be drawn
   d. Logical breakdown into functional units
3. In a territorial structure, units of the organization are grouped according to geographic areas in which the company does business. T or F?
4. A matrix organizational structure is usually designed so that:
   a. A project team is overlaid on a functional design
   b. Some employees are outside the usual structure
   c. Two bosses occupy the same position
   d. Two positions are given to one person
5. The design that calls for highly developed skills in communications and planning is:
   a. Functional
   b. Territory
   c. Tall
   d. Matrix

Answers:

1 F, 2 d, 3 T, 4 a, 5 d

Figure 13.6
Anita's department with a matrix design

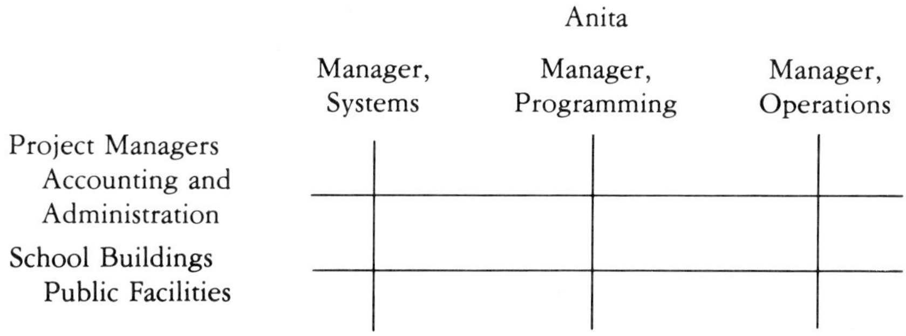

	Anita		
	Manager, Systems	Manager, Programming	Manager, Operations
Project Managers			
Accounting and Administration			
School Buildings			
Public Facilities			

Authority in Organizations: The Cement of Working Together

When you take a job in any organization, you are usually given a title and some idea about what you are supposed to do. The organization not only tells you what your major responsibilities are but how much authority you have to spend funds, to make decisions, and to coordinate the activities of others. **Authority** is defined as the legitimate right to influence employee behaviors and expectations. If you are a manager, one type of authority that you are given is the authority to manage others in their work. Oddly enough, one key issue that managers must resolve is how much of this authority to give to others to ensure that their own time is productively spent doing management work instead of technical work. In other words, to work effectively as a manager, you must learn how to give others the authority to make decisions and carry out work. These considerations all involve delegation.

Delegation—Giving Authority Away

The process by which authority is distributed downward to employees is called **delegation.** We explore how this process works, because many managers express great frustration over trying to give authority to employees only to find that it is not accepted. The process of delegation is very important to management. Consider an example.

> An executive was concerned that Victor Reid, an accountant in the tax department, might make costly mistakes if he were given more authority. When the executive reviewed the types of errors that could be made and the costs involved, she found that the costliest mistake that Victor could make was \$35,000; yet it could cost the organization as much as \$125,000 in executive time, forms, and other stopgaps to prevent the loss. She decided, after considering the difference in costs, to give Victor more authority.

Why delegate?

From the manager's perspective, delegation is critical to success. Because the manager cannot do all of the work alone, people must be found to help, even with the most important tasks. In this way, the manager can take advantage of employee expertise and develop employees to take on increasingly complicated tasks (9).

From the employee's standpoint, receiving authority is one of the only ways to grow. Authority increases employee motivation and capability to perform technical and management work.

Principles of Delegation

To be effective at delegating work, the manager cannot simply give away the shop. He must plan carefully who will be responsible for what. By keeping in mind the following rules, a manager can become an effective delegator:

Rule 1: For every responsibility delegated to a subordinate, an equal amount of authority must be given. This means that if you are going to make someone do the work, you must give that person the authority to use the necessary resources to get the job done.

Rule 2: All decisions should be delegated to the lowest organizational level possible (i.e., the level at which people who know what to do can act promptly and wisely). Herman Miller makes office furniture better than anyone else because the company tries to help create a participative environment for the workers who make the furniture. Herman Miller adopted a Scanlon plan, named after the originator of a productivity sharing idea (Chapters 5 and 6). Company employees participate in a "Scanlon Information Meeting" once a month to discuss ways to improve their performance. Bonuses are paid to everyone involved when an idea results in savings for the company. The company is willing to trust employees to come up with ideas that are good for the organization and is willing to pay for results!

Rule 3: Manage by exception. This means that the manager should become involved personally in the operation only when an exception to the routine occurs. When managers leave people alone to carry out their responsibilities and to exercise their delegated authority, the managers then have time to do what they should be doing. They do not lose touch, but they don't meddle, either. As a result, people grow and managers manage.

Rule 4: When you delegate, tell subordinates not only what to do but how to do it. Managers should consider telling subordinates not only what they should accomplish, but how they might go about doing it. In this way, you do not leave employees wondering exactly what to do. If you are the employee receiving the delegation, remind the manager that to do a good job you must not only know what is expected as an end product, but you also must have some concept of preferred ways to achieve the needed results. By understanding the principles of delegation, an employee can manage up as well as manage down.

Rule 5: The responsibility of subordinates to their superiors is absolute, and superiors cannot escape responsibility for the performance of their subordinates. This means simply that the boss cannot hide by saying "Well, my subordinate didn't do his job." Ultimately, all managers are responsible for the work of subordinates. The owner of a pharmacy in a small rural town in Pennsylvania has a sign on his counter that exemplifies this principle. "Everyone here has the authority to help you in any way, but I have the responsibility to help them help you."

In summary, the five rules of delegation are as follows:

Rule 1: Authority should match the level of responsibility.
Rule 2: Delegate to the lowest level possible.
Rule 3: Manage by exception.
Rule 4: Tell subordinates what and how to do something.
Rule 5: The boss is always responsible.

Centralize or Decentralize—Two Sides of the Same Coin

Centralization refers to the retention of authority to make decisions by top management. The final consideration for understanding authority in the organization is how much the manager should centralize operations. Recall the plumbing supply business referred to earlier. If Hank's operations were centralized, he would have everybody report to headquarters and employees would use uniform procedures, policies, and ways of operating that were dictated by Hank. If operations were decentralized, each branch would operate as it saw fit.

Rarely do companies consider this choice as an either/or decision. In reality, the choice is to emphasize one over the other (10). To make this choice requires some concept of the consequences that will occur once the choice is made. Table 13.4 summarizes the consequences of decentralization.

We now turn to the final aspect of organizational design, that is, the coordination of people and units. Coordination refers to those processes and devices that help individuals gain clarity about their jobs and the necessary relationships needed to get work completed.

Table 13.4 *Behavioral Consequences of Decentralization*

1. Spreads management load; lower levels make on-the-scene decisions.
2. Best training for managers.
3. Managers more able to cope with change.
4. Managers and employees are challenged when they make decisions on their own.
5. Coordination between employees may be difficult.
6. Some employees may find that they duplicate the work of other employees.
7. An employee may overlook expertise of others if the employee is expected to make decisions on his or her own.

The Now It's Your Turn exercise that follows will help you clarify your preferences for working in various organizational designs.

NOW IT'S YOUR TURN . . .

Individuals experienced in the working world often find that they prefer to work in certain organizational designs more than others. The purpose here is to assess your preferences and to offer some advice based on the results.

Address the following issues as honestly as you can by using this scale:

1 = Yes, very much

2 = Not always, but usually

3 = Not much

4 = Never

_____ 1. I like to have clear directions when I work.

_____ 2. I rarely like discussing things with others before we all get to work.

_____ 3. I want to be a boss. I like to lead others and to show them how to work.

_____ 4. When I work, I like to be left alone to get the task done.

_____ 5. When decisions are made, I think they should be made by one person who runs the organization.

_____ 6. I don't need to feel part of the organization by having a say in the way things get done.

_____ 7. For me, job satisfaction comes from doing good work, not by getting constant recognition for work.

_____ 8. I don't like to have a lot of people around me during the day when I'm working.

_____ 9. People like to have me around because I am very task-oriented and get a lot of things done.

_____ 10. The chain of command is very important to getting things done at work.

Add up your score. If you have a score near 35–40, then you would probably enjoy working in an organization that is highly centralized with clear chains of command and a functional structure. You may also be able to adapt to a tall organization structure and to be productive in it. You would probably be able to work effectively even though you would not get a lot of feedback. You would also tend to observe the chain of command.

If your score was in the lower range, such as 20–25, you might prefer an organization that is more loosely configured, such as a matrix design or even a mixed organization that has many different orientations. You like to be included in decision making and you want to have feedback. From the analysis in Chapter 3, you probably discovered that you have a high need for achievement and a low need for power. You should find an organization that has a relatively flat structure and that tends to include many people in the decision-making process.

Coordination—the Details of the House

The coordination of structures and authority is like a running brook. You can try to focus on a specific section, but the changes are so rapid that you're never quite sure if you're looking at the same section. In fact, you are probably *not* looking at the same section of water, so to understand the flow of the water, you try to get a feel for it. You abstract from your experience by taking a picture of a section of water.

Coordination in organizations is as difficult to grasp as that section of flowing water. Because organizations are changing constantly and relationships are changing, the specifications of the structure and of the authority never do justice to the complexity of an organizational design. One way to more accurately represent how organizations are put together is to outline how events are coordinated.

How much coordination is needed?

Lawrence and Lorsch are two researchers interested in the ways in which organizations coordinate activities. After reviewing many different research studies and performing their research, they believe that the critical basis of an organizational design is the amount of information that must be processed during actual task execution (11).

If an employee knew what was to be done and exactly how to coordinate her activities with others, then minimal information would have to be processed or exchanged to get the job done. On the other hand, when tasks are unclear and when people are unsure about how to proceed, a great deal of information processing has to occur.

Turbulent environments require a great many ways to coordinate. The researchers found that organizational environments that were changeable and dynamic forced organizations to find varied and unique ways to coordinate. Organizational departments, sections, and jobs had to be unique and very specialized. Because of this diversity, a great deal of integration between departments and among various members of the organization was required to get a job done.

Stable environments require fewer ways to coordinate. Organizations with more stable environments did not need as much coordination and were able to use standard rules and procedures to integrate units. These "stable environment" firms tended to be more centralized and to have taller structures. The researchers also found, however, that these more centralized firms tended to be more successful in stable environments and less successful in turbulent environments. The more dynamic and differentiated structures tended to be more successful in turbulent environments and less successful in stable environments.

What makes organizations effective? Research on this topic suggests that the organization must fit its environment and must be organized according to what is demanded of it by the stability or lack of stability in the environment. The message is that effective organizations have at their disposal many different coordination mechanisms to help achieve goals.

This adaptability through coordination was exemplified by the response of Johnson and Johnson to the problems with Tylenol. In short, someone had put poison in bottles of Tylenol, and a few people died as a result. This sent shock waves across the country, and Johnson and Johnson found itself in a turbulent business environment. The organization had to make some very quick decisions. Instead of using the normal channels of communication and chain of command, the company implemented task forces to react quickly to the situation. Through this rapid coordination and through other efforts, Johnson and Johnson responded quickly to the problem and also set industry standards for the safe packaging of drugs. They used a coordinating mechanism to pull together key parts of their organization to make quick decisions.

The major job of any coordination mechanism is to reduce uncertainty about what everyone is supposed to do. In a sense, structures and specifications of authority are such mechanisms, but these mechanisms are effective only if everything goes perfectly. The coordination mechanisms we discuss next handle most of the other times. First, let's examine the different mechanisms used to handle uncertainty (12).

Can information needs be reduced?

Yes! One way to coordinate more effectively is to reduce the need to coordinate by using the strategies noted below. This may seem paradoxical, but many organizations do choose this strategy.

Lower expectations. Some organizations reduce the required level of performance and allow mistakes to occur because someone either did not coordinate effectively or because not as much pressure was put on employees to perform. In this environment, the organization's tolerance of mistakes is a way *not* to need to coordinate. This creation of "slack resources," as it is called, gives employees more time to find things out by chance or to learn from their mistakes. As you might imagine, this solution can be costly! Organizations that make a great deal of money tend to use this strategy because they can afford mistakes that cost them profits.

Very specialized jobs. Another way to reduce coordination needs is to define jobs and groups of jobs very specifically. This technique of increased specialization is called "creation of self-contained tasks." For example, if a small aerospace company were putting together a plane, it might create assembly units for each major section of the aircraft (e.g., wing, cabin, body, and tail). Each assembly group would have its own engineers, assembly personnel, and testing procedures and facilities. The personnel duplication means that each unit has an expert and that very little need exists to acquire information from other units.

Both of these strategies are costly and are usually ineffective when people need to work together in a dynamic organization. The creation of slack resources and self-contained tasks tends to pull the organization apart rather than to coordinate. We mention these strategies mainly to contrast them with a more useful approach—that of increasing employee abilities to process information through effective coordination.

What devices can be used to increase the capacity to process information?

We emphasize these alternatives because in our experience they are more useful and tend to be more effective than other strategies for most people.

The two devices of importance here are ways to increase the vertical flow of information in the organization, and ways to increase the lateral flow of information across an organizational level.

Vertical Coordination

Effective vertical coordination increases the linkages between organization levels. To be effective, the coordination must *decrease* uncertainty in the minds of employees. The major question to ask when setting up a vertical coordination mechanism is: Does it clear things up?

Use groups. One way to increase coordination up and down the organization is to create more group decision making. This method includes the calling together of various people at all organizational levels to help solve problems.

> For example, the top management of a relatively small company that printed business forms wanted to put in a new machine. By all estimates, this should be simple, yet every time something of this sort happened in the company, employees thought that their jobs were being threatened by technology and weeks of upheaval ensued. The owner therefore decided to increase coordination by creating a group of employees from every organizational level to select the type of machine to purchase and to research how to install it most effectively. Not only was the machine well accepted by employees, but those not in the group asked to be included in the next task force.

One word of caution, however. Recall the possible problems with groups that were discussed in Chapter 9. If you are a group member, keep in mind ways to avoid the problems with group decision making.

Use planning. Another effective coordination mechanism is to implement extensive planning. For example, managers frequently use the management by objective process referred to in earlier chapters. In this way, information flows up and down the organization in response to some well-defined goals. All employees are clearly informed about *when* work needs to be completed and *what* needs to be done.

Use performance appraisal. A tool not often perceived as an information system but indispensable for coordinating tasks is the performance appraisal system. Assuming that the organization has such a system, it can be used both to control individual performance and to inform managers at various levels about the people in the organization. Consider how this might work. At specific times during the year, a manager and subordinate would discuss the subordinate's performance. After assessments were made about the person's performance, these assessments would be communicated to the next level of management. If the linking pin concept is working, then all of the vertical linking pins would have information about the employee. In this way, managers in other parts of the company are able to make more effective judgments about each employee. For example, a new position may come up in another part of the organization. The manager doing the hiring recalls a relevant performance appraisal. Based on that appraisal, she is able to make judgments about whether or not to hire the employee from outside her department. In addition to vertical coordination, the organization also must create ways to transport information across similar employee levels. We discuss ways to accomplish lateral coordination next.

Solving the Dilemma

Can Anita use better means of coordinating?

Besides adopting a new organizational structure, Anita has other means of getting the performance she wants from her people so the department satisfies user needs. She should consider seriously the use of task forces to gain information and to solve problems quickly.

Finally, Anita could use her performance appraisal system to communicate more actively her desires to meet user demands. This system would help her to identify those people who need more training in this area and those who deserve special rewards for giving excellent service.

Lateral Coordination

Lateral coordination is integration that occurs between workers at a similar level to ensure that work gets done. The major purpose is to reduce the number of decisions that must be referred upward, thus increasing discretion at lower levels of the organization and helping managers delegate authority.

Use the informal organization. One form of lateral coordination is the **informal organization** (see Chapter 11), a network of personal and social relationships not established or required by formal authority but arising spontaneously as workers associate with one another. Most effective managers use the informal network to a great extent. They might put it this way. "If we had to go through channels, we'd never get anything done."

Scott Sorter reported directly to the executive director of a book publishing company who in turn reported to the board of directors. Scott was responsible for the administrative duties related to educational materials and for various new products such as computer software and a program for consumers in South America.

One day Scott found out during a conversation with the executive director that it was "going around" that Scott did not get along with some of the people in other departments. He was "too aggressive" in demanding deadlines and requiring people to deliver on time. While it was "good" to be aggressive, "we must watch out for people's feelings," said the executive director.

Scott was puzzled as to how the director had found this out. When he checked, he discovered that another manager, who had worked with the director for over 20 years, sought information constantly from a group of women in the organization. This group met often to discuss their "common plight of being female in a male-dominated organization," and how they could become more effective. The group had no official sanction or title, yet it was a powerful force in the organization and was quite capable of making trouble for Scott.

Use direct contact. Another option for lateral coordination strategies is often the easiest: direct contact with another person. If two managers know that they share a common problem, then they meet to solve it.

Use liaison roles. Another possibility is for managers to establish liaison roles, or formal positions to link two departments. In an oil company, the marketing people often had trouble with the refinery people. The marketing staff understood which products were selling at high prices and which were not. The refinery people, however, were simply supplying those products that were easiest to produce. The solution chosen by top company management was to appoint a liaison person. The job title was "Oil Products Coordinator," and the sole responsibility was to make sure that marketing knew what the refinery was doing.

Use task forces. When direct contact or liaison roles are not powerful enough, a third option is to create a temporary group called a task force. A task force usually is made up of representatives of several departments and lasts only as long as a particular problem exists. For one large manufacturer, task forces are a way of life. When a problem arises on the assembly floor, the foreman calls the process engineer and representatives from the company laboratory, quality control, and purchasing. The group works on the problem until it is solved, then all members return to their normal duties.

Create a matrix structure. A final lateral coordination process is creation of matrix structure. The interesting attribute of the matrix is that it serves not only as a structure, but seems also to facilitate coordination. It is such a dynamic system that it can house both the formal and informal configurations that exist in every company. (It can also, as we pointed out earlier, be very confusing.)

Only your imagination limits the devices and strategies available. As you consider what will work in a given organization, keep in mind that the best approach is to pick a strategy or device that is as temporary as possible yet still gets the job done. You may want to consider how a sense of innovation and excitement can be built into an organization. Indeed, innovation is of so much concern to employees and managers that we have devoted a special section to it.

Using Coordination to Build Innovation Into the Organization

Our discussion focuses on three basic ways to coordinate to ensure innovativeness.

1. Designing roles that coordinate
2. Creating greenhouses and reservations
3. Blending people together.

These designations may sound odd, but read on. At the end of this section, you will have an opportunity to determine whether or not you could work in an environment that calls for high innovation. (As you will see, highly innovative environments are difficult places to work.)

Do organizations typically have people who play special innovative roles?

Like other organizational activities, innovation is brought about through the efforts of people who interact in a combination of roles. Innovation is not an individual attribute—it demands interaction. Some organizations have formalized this interaction through creation of specific roles.

Every innovation starts with someone generating an idea. The person in this role is called an "**idea champion**" (13). This is an employee who generates an idea and retains responsibility for that idea in the organization. This individual is usually a lower level person who experiences a problem and develops a new response. As Galbraith says, "The lesson here is that many ideas originate down where the rubber meets the road" (14).

Every idea must have not only a generator but a **sponsor.** This is the person who discovers the new concept and funds the increasingly disruptive and expensive development and testing efforts that shape the new product or service. The sponsor, who may be someone in a completely different department, lends authority and resources to the idea. The best sponsors have been found to be those who were once idea generators themselves. They are usually middle managers who like to innovate and who can tolerate the pressure of being innovative.

For a new idea to work, however, organizations must have people who play a third role, sometimes called the **orchestrator,** or **godfather**. The godfather handles all of the political implications of the new product or service. This individual is usually the president or general manager who has the authority to say to the organization "we're going to develop this product." The godfather makes resources available, gets various parts of the organization to work on the product, and helps to soothe hurt feelings or cajoles nonbelievers. The best godfathers are those who were themselves idea generators, who have sponsored other people, and who have a significant position in the organization.

Most of us would like to be idea generators when we first enter an organization. If we are lucky enough to join a firm that allows innovating roles, we may find ourselves spending 75 percent of our time doing the job for which we were hired and 25 percent of our time innovating. Once we conceive of a new product or service, we begin to get others together to coordinate how the concept can become a reality in the organization. We need to form a team with a sponsor, and we need a godfather.

How are the teams formed?

Just as plants sometimes need greenhouses, so new ideas need unique places to grow. Another coordinating mechanism used by innovative organizations is to create a special place for people to develop their ideas. Galbraith calls these places **reservations** and **greenhouses.** Both terms refer to a place that nurtures fertile thought. Both are housed in physical locations separate from the main organization.

The greenhouse is physically different from other parts of the organization. It may be located in a warehouse or in a separate building wing. One small organization allowed two employees to rent an apartment where they set up models of new products and worked on them after hours.

As you can imagine, greenhouses take on unique characteristics. One manager described the difficulty of tolerating a greenhouse occupied by five computer "whiz kids."

> The floor was cluttered with all sorts of magazines, a stereo blasted away, and photos of scenes from various science fiction movies decorated one corner. These employees did not come to work until 10:00 A.M., but they did not leave until 11:00 P.M. This went on for four months. At the end of that period, the manager asked one employee what they had accomplished. The employee responded, "We've finally found the key problem that users are having with our software. They don't like the way the screens present information." When asked why it took four months to make this discovery, the employee responded, "Why not? We now know the key to what makes the product sell or not sell." Within two months, the group presented a highly innovative software package that contributed significantly to the firm's sales.

Innovation occurs outside the usual organization structure. The lesson here is that innovation is best facilitated when initial efforts are separated from normal organization operations and controls. Innovating and operating activities have fundamentally opposing logic (15). Once the new idea is generated, however, it must be slowly integrated back into the operating organization. This is when the sponsor and the godfather are so important.

In addition to greenhouses and reservations, the organization can generate and blend ideas more directly by introducing an idea looking for a sponsor, or by formalizing ways that ideas can be shown to others.

Solving the Dilemma

How can Anita make sure that her department will continue to innovate?

By now Anita understands how to restructure her department to meet user needs. Another problem she faces is how to ensure that her department does not stagnate by not keeping up with the newest technology and the latest ideas in the field. How can she build in innovation?

A key way for Anita to accomplish this innovation is to allow a few of her people to work in a special location where they have the freedom to progress at their own pace and to invent new ideas. This "greenhouse" could be set up at the beginning of a new project and could include members from other departments as well. Anita may find that some employees benefit by getting away from the workplace every once in a while.

Anita also could use education as a way to maintain innovation. She should allocate a sizable portion of her budget to education for her people. She may want to send both her personnel and some employees from other departments to seminars. This would facilitate interdepartmental discussion of problems and would encourage personnel from different departments to have a mutual respect for one another.

A final option is for Anita to arrange a brainstorming session with other managers so she can get ideas from other departments. She may want to sponsor a lunch for the purpose of brainstorming ways to increase responsiveness of the Information Systems Department to users. Without doubt, users would appreciate the opportunity to share their insights with Anita.

How can organizations design for innovation?

In most accounts of innovation, getting the idea occurs by happenstance. You are brushing your teeth one morning, and the idea hits you.

Getting the idea to the right sponsor is another problem altogether. Without a sponsor, an innovative idea will not survive, so getting ideas to sponsors is an important coordination problem (16).

Some organizations set up events at which sponsors can "shop around" for ideas. Sponsors attend annual fairs where booths are set up by idea generators. One organization has a "shake the tree event" during which idea people throw out ideas, which they hope will be pursued by attending sponsors. Organizations that believe in innovation devote both time and energy to linking ideas with sponsors, and all of this is accomplished outside the usual structure and authority of the operating organization (17).

Blend people together. Blending ideas is important to combining the various types of expertise that exist in an organization. Innovation must be fed by blending different types of people who interact in unique ways. An example of one way to do this is to choose a few departmental positions that will be rotating positions through which various people flow. These positions could be occupied for three to six months by one individual. The rotation gives people an opportunity to network and to gain some understanding of the problems and processes of different units. This method has been suggested as a way for school administrators to better understand teachers' problems, by being required to teach at least a few days each year.

For you, the most important determination is whether or not you would like working for an organization that actively encourages innovation. Now It's Your Turn presents a way for you to find out.

NOW IT'S YOUR TURN . . .

Could you be an idea generator?

The following instrument will help you determine whether or not you could be an idea generator in an innovating company. The instrument does *not* determine whether or not you are indeed innovative, but only whether you are suited to play the role of idea generator.

Rate each statement honestly by using the following scale:

1 = Always describes me

2 = Often describes me

3 = Sometimes describes me

4 = Never describes me

_____ 1. I don't worry about getting poor grades or getting a bad job performance rating.

_____ 2. I more often attempt difficult tasks that I am not sure I can do than easier tasks that I know I can do.

______ 3. I would rather do something that I feel is challenging and difficult than something that is easier and relaxed.

______ 4. I would prefer to have a job in which my role is defined by me, rather than by the job description.

______ 5. It is very important for me to do my work as well as I can, even if it means not getting along well with my co-workers.

______ 6. I rarely ask for directions from my manager or teacher even when instructions are not clear to me.

______ 7. My idea of how my success in organizations should be measured is not by my ability to get promoted or to get good grades.

______ 8. When I work, I like situations in which I can't get everything done.

______ 9. I make things happen when I work. I can accomplish things no matter what the work climate is like.

______ 10. I don't expect to succeed all of the time. The important idea is to have more attempts at trying new ways of doing work.

Add up your score. If the total is over "32," then you are probably a good bet for an organization that puts pressure on employees to innovate. You tend to tolerate ambiguity, to feel as if you can control your own work, not to be concerned with position or legitimate power, to be stimulated by work overloads, to be a risk taker and to be persistent about accomplishing things even at difficult times.

You also are somewhat hard to get along with and would not be afraid to break company policies. You tend to have a strong ego and could work well only in organizations that have many innovating mechanisms. You have an irreverence for the status quo. You get your kicks from doing things that others have never tried.

If you scored below "20," you would probably favor an organization that rewards adherence to rules and procedures and has very specific goals for performance. You are probably easy to get along with and would be a good corporate citizen.

So, where do you stand? You can see that life as an idea generator is not all roses. You will have to confront many doubters and people may even try to stand in your way. Other organizational members will block your coordinating attempts and may regard you as an outcast. The positive side to all this is the excitement and the ultimate rewards.

Knowledge Check

1. Delegation is the process of assigning relationships, duties, and authority to others. T or F?
2. Which of the following is *not* a rule of delegation?
   a. authority matches level of responsibility
   b. delegate to the lowest level possible
   c. manage by exception
   d. tell subordinates *what* to do, not *how*
   e. superiors are always responsible for subordinate performance
3. The amount of coordination needed is best determined by the number of people in the organization. T or F?
4. Two types of devices or strategies are used to reduce uncertainty, thus enhancing coordination: those that reduce the need for information and those that increase the capacity to process information. T or F?
5. An example of vertical coordination is:
   a. performance appraisal
   b. matrix structure
   c. job descriptions
   d. quality circles

Answers:

1 T, 2 d, 3 F, 4 T, 5 a

Summary Points

- This chapter focused on (1) how managers organize people into jobs, departments, and groups of departments, (2) how managers give authority to others to make decisions, and (3) how managers coordinate people, departments, special interests, and unique happenings.
- The purpose of organizational design is to facilitate the organization's accomplishment of goals.
- Structure is represented by an **organization chart,** which shows the arrangement of people and departments in terms of **scalar** and **functional** relationships.
- Important considerations in choosing a structure are **effects of structure on behavior, span of control, line and staff positions, and arrangement of departments** (i.e., functional, product, territory, or matrix configuration).
- The different structures vary primarily in the extent to which they (1) facilitate development of general managers, (2) focus on responsibility for work, and (3) require interpersonal versus impersonal behavior to make the structure work.
- **Authority,** the next component of design, helps managers decide who is responsible for what.
- The two major considerations in shaping authority are **delegation** and whether or not operations should be **centralized.**
- The key to successful organizational design is the **coordination** of people. **Coordinating mechanisms** exist to handle exceptions that occur when things are not proceeding as planned or when uncertainty arises.
- By using **vertical** and **lateral coordination** devices, organizations become more versatile and can facilitate innovation.
- Innovation usually occurs outside the routine organization structure. Mechanisms such as "greenhouses" and "reservations" help facilitate new ideas in work settings.

Questions

1. Consider the points made about using coordination to ensure innovation. What types of people, in terms of personality attributes, would work best in a highly innovative organization? Consider the information learned in the chapters on personality as well as the information in this chapter.
2. What effect does a change in organization design have on individuals in the organization? List at least four major effects that you might expect if you were the manager changing your organization's design.
3. When a person is first hired by an organization, do you think that the new employee should be told about the formal and informal organizations that exist? What is the danger of having a manager tell a new recruit about the informal organization? What are the benefits?
4. Innovative companies will not be all that productive if the individuals in the organization are not suited to the environment. How would you fit in, in an innovative organization as described in this chapter? What problems would you have? What real benefits might such an environment provide?

EXPLORING: *The New Yorker* Gets a Kick in the Print

[Adapted from "Change at the New Yorker Is the Talk of the Town," *Business Week* (March 10, 1986):122.]

In May 1985, Steven Florio and business partner bought the 60–year–old magazine *The New Yorker*. In Florio's view, the magazine's circulation and ad-sales departments had grown inbred, clubby, and complacent (18). Florio has made a number of changes since 1985, including firing many senior managers, vigorous circulation promotions, and an aggressive courtship of Madison Avenue. At this point, however, competitors and supporters alike believe that the thoughtful, often difficult copy is outdated. *The New Yorker* is the only magazine of letters that has ever been commercially successful—it could be that it has run its course.

Florio has identified problems still to be addressed: (1) editorial changes will probably have to be made; (2) managers must get out and see ad agencies and find out what the agencies want; (3) the magazine needs to find ways to increase circulation; (4) Florio wants to keep the best of the "old," yet change with the times; (5) a controversey exists concerning "acceptable" advertising, because the magazine is now considering ads (e.g., those of L.L. Bean) previously rejected by the old guard as not in keeping with the magazine's image.

At this point, Florio calls you in to help him with his problems. He does not expect you to be a magazine expert, but rather, an expert in organizational design and innovation.

Discussion Questions

1. Could Florio redesign his organization to cause a change in ideas?
2. What innovation strategies could you recommend?
3. If he wants more responsiveness to advertisers, can you suggest an organization structure that would help him achieve this?

APPLYING: *Analyzing a Change in Design*

Read the case and then answer the questions at the end of the case study.

The Case

Paul Warren had recently received word of his appointment as plant manager of Tobric Company, Inc. Paul was to be completely responsible for management of all functions and personnel except purchasing and sales.

The Organization

Tobric, Inc., does business throughout the southern United States. The organization was started in 1955 by an entrepreneur who was convinced that he could produce electronic equipment cheaper than others in the industry.

Production operations and certain other departments were under the supervision and control of a senior vice president. The company structure is shown in Figure 13.7. For many years, Tobric, Inc., had operated a highly centralized, functional type of manufacturing organization. The plant in Shreveport, Louisiana, had no general manager position. Each of the managers and supervisors reported on a line basis to their functional counterpart at the corporate office. For example, the manufacturing department manager reported

Figure 13.7
Tobric Company organization chart (old design)

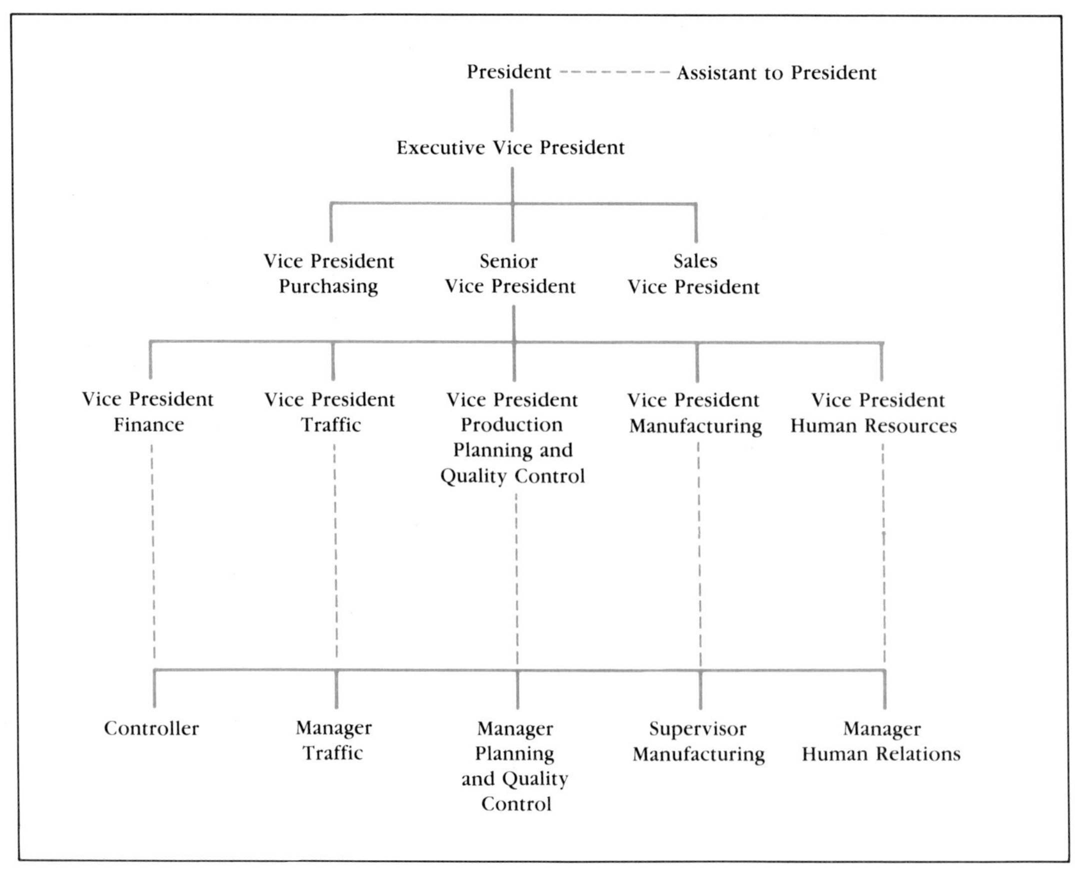

to the vice president in charge of manufacturing at the corporate office. This was the arrangement for all four Tobric plants.

The president was disappointed in the company's overall performance. In an attempt to improve the situation, he decided to try a new way of manufacturing, and to use the Shreveport plant as a test situation. A consultant's report to the president stated that "two requirements for improved operations are to lower costs and reduce manpower." To accomplish these goals and to maintain a competitive position in the market, a new way of manufacturing and scheduling jobs was proposed for Shreveport. Since some of these features of plant operations would be new to both employees and management, the report suggested that a pilot project be implemented before making these changes at all locations.

New Operations Mean a New Structure

The president also decided to use this opportunity to change the organizational design of the Shreveport plant. He wanted to test a decentralized operation and to create a general manager position (Paul's new job). Figure 13.8 shows the new organizational structure.

Paul described the situation as follows:

> I am going into a situation involving a large number of changes. This will be a new operation with new methods. Most of all I will be trying to manage a new set of relationships. Before this, the managers and supervisors reported to their functional counterparts in the corporate office. Now they will report to me, and I am a complete stranger to them.

When Paul talked with the senior vice president at headquarters about his new assign-

Figure 13.8
Tobric Company Organization Chart (New design, Shreveport pilot project)

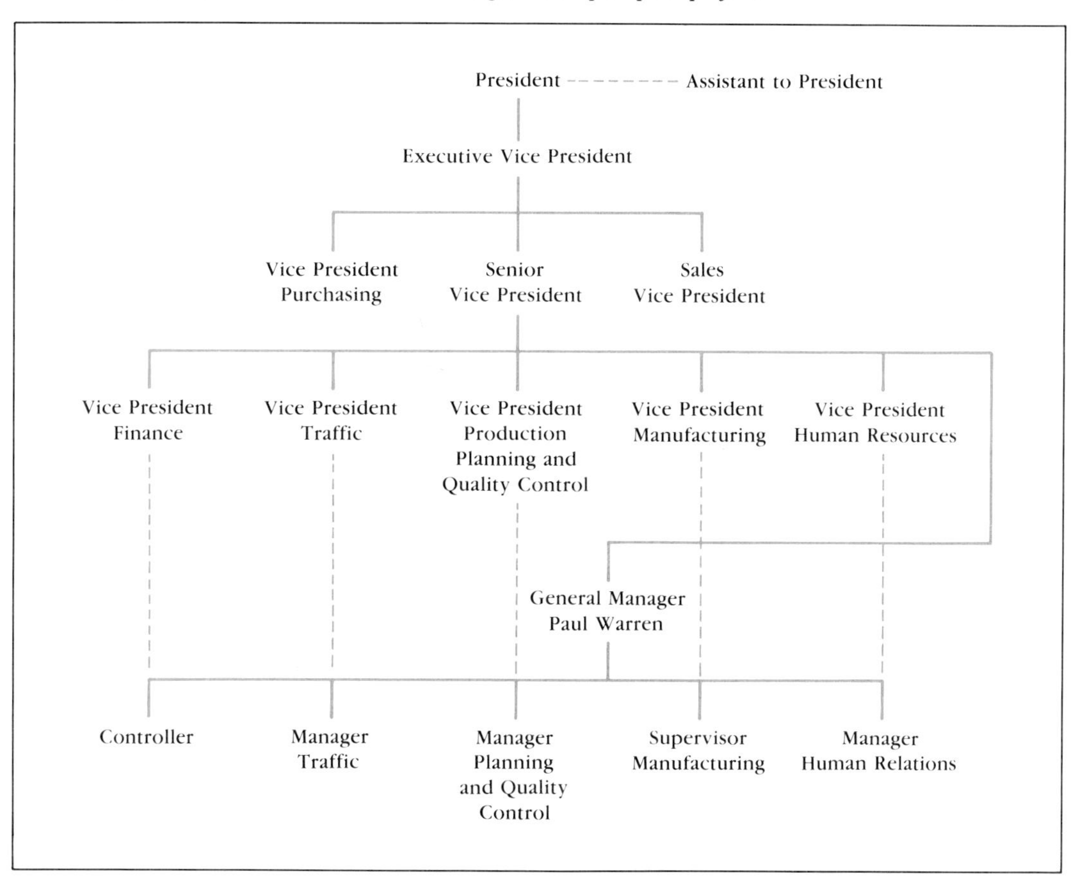

ment, that executive asked Paul to meet with each of the vice presidents. When Paul did this, he learned that some of the vice presidents, in planning how best to deal with the new Shreveport plant structure, had decided to issue all instructions from headquarters to Paul as plant manager. These executives were cutting off their connections with their counterpart in the plant. Others of the vice presidents were, however, more interested in maintaining their direct contact with plant personnel informally. Paul quickly realized that these two different intentions on the part of the headquarters staff would create problems for him. He worried about how he would manage both the plant and the vice presidents effectively.

Questions

1. What are the present goals of the organization?
2. How would you describe the structure of the organization?
3. What is the scalar process at Tobric?
4. How are departments linked?
5. What is the span of control of the president?
6. What is the span of control of the executive vice president?
7. What is the span of control of the vice president of sales? of the vice president of purchasing? of the senior vice president?
8. What coordination mechanisms exist?

Debriefing the Case

1. What are the present goals of the organization?
   a. Increase production efficiency
   b. Lower costs of processing
   c. Improve product quality
   d. Maintain a competitive leadership
2. How would you describe the structure of the organization?
   a. Before the change—functional and centralized
   b. After the change—territorial and decentralized

Suggested Readings

Daft, R. 1986. *Organization Theory and Design,* 2nd ed. St. Paul, Minn.: West Publishing.

This focuses exclusively on macro organizational behavior issues. The writing is clear, and the information will be useful to those who are working and to those interested in following up on many points made in this chapter.

Davis, S., and Lawrence, P.R. 1977. *Matrix.* Reading. Mass.: Addision-Wesley.

This book about matrix designs presents a clear, concise picture of the many issues surrounding the use of this complex design. Pay particular attention to Chapters 5 and 6, for the issues presented are often overlooked when using this type of design.

Mintzberg, H. 1979. *The Structuring of Organizations.* Englewood Cliffs, N.J.: Prentice-Hall.

Mintzberg presents more information about the organization configurations mentioned in the Exploring section of this chapter. He provides many examples and practical hints for working with each type of design.

Neiman-Marcus. *Harvard Business Review Case.* # 9–475–077.

This is an interesting example of an organization faced with having to change its design. The business has many personalities and conditions that make the choice difficult.

Perrow, C. 1986. *Complex Organizations*, 3rd ed. New York: Random House.

Tosi, H. 1984. *Theories of Organization,* 2nd ed. New York: John Wiley and Sons.

Warren, D.I. 1968. Power, Visibility and Conformity in Formal Organizations. *American Sociological Review* (December 1968):951–960.

References

1. Likert, R., 1961. *New Patterns of Management.* New York: McGraw-Hill; Likert, R. 1967. *The Human Organization.* New York: McGraw-Hill.
2. Daft, R. 1986. *Organization Theory and Design,* 2nd ed. St. Paul, Minn.: West.
3. Thompson, V. 1965. Bureaucracy and Innovation. *Administration Science Quarterly,* 10:1–20; Blau, P. 1970. A Formal Theory of Differentiation in Organizations. *American Sociological Review* 35:201–218.
4. Blau, P.M. 1955. *The Dynamics of Bureaucracy.* Chicago: University of Chicago Press; Blau, P., and Meyer, M.W. 1971. *Bureacuracy in Modern Society,* 2nd ed. New York: Random House; Child, J. 1975. Managerial and Organizational Factors Associated With Company Performance—Part II, A Contingency Analysis. *Journal of Management Studies;* Lawrence, P.R., and Lorsch, J.W. 1969. *Developing Organizations: Diagnosis and Action.* Reading, Mass.: Addison-Wesley.
5. Kennedy, T., and Deal, A. 1982. *Corporate Culture.* Reading, Mass.: Addison-Wesley; Child, J. 1982. Professionals in the Corporate World: Values, Interests and Control. In Dunkerley, W., and Salaman, D. (Eds.) 1982. *The International Yearbook of Organization Studies 1981;* Routledge and Kegan, P. 1983. In K.S. Cameron and D.A. Whetten (Eds.). *Organizational Effectiveness.* Academic Press.
6. Child, J. 1984. *Organization,* 2nd ed. London: Harper & Row.
7. Duncan, R.B. 1973. Multiple Decision-Making Structures in Adapting to Environmental Uncertainty: The Impact on Organizational Effectiveness. *Human Relations* 26:30–36.
8. Davis, S., and Lawrence, P. 1977. (Eds.). *Matrix.* Reading, Mass.: Addison-Wesley.
9. Meyer, M.W. 1973. A Note on Expertness and the Supervisory Components in Organizations. *Human Organization* 32 (4):379–384.
10. Hage, J., and Aiken, M. 1969. Routine Technology, Social Structure and Organizational Goals. *Administrative Science Quarterly* 14:368–379.
11. Lawrence, P.R., and Lorsch, J.W. 1967. *Organization and Environment.* Cambridge, Mass.: Harvard Business School.
12. Galbraith, J.R. 1973. *Designing Complex Organizations.* Reading, Mass.: Addison-Wesley; Galbraith, J.R. 1977. *Organization Design.* Reading, Mass.: Addison-Wesley.
13. Galbraith, J. 1982. Designing the Innovating Organization. *Organizational Dynamics* (Winter 1982):5–25.
14. Ibid.
15. Ibid., p. 10.
16. Galbraith, 1982, op. cit.
17. Galbraith, 1977, op. cit.
18. *Business Week* 1986. Change at "The New Yorker Is the Talk of the Town." (10 March 1986:122.

Climat
Feedbac
Input

Organizational Culture, Climate, and the Basics of Organizational Development

Chapter 14

Chapter Goals

By the end of this chapter, you will be able to:

1. Understand the components of organizational culture and how culture relates to organizational climate.
2. Develop a rationale for why managers must be concerned about organizational climate.
3. Explain the differences between organizational culture and organizational climate to a fellow student or employee.
4. Link organizational culture, climate, and Likert's systems 1 and 4 organizations.
5. Explain the importance of organizational development as a process for improving organizational effectiveness.
6. Develop the features of an action research process for organizational development interventions.
7. Discuss the pitfalls of action research with managers.
8. Classify organizational development methods by their characteristics.
9. Suggest organizational development methods for different types of organizational problems.

Dilemma A Turnaround in the Sales Division at Tentex

Susan Ramsey, an expert in management systems, works for Tentex Corporation, a manufacturer of computer software and peripheral computer equipment. Recently, the company had been experiencing low growth in sales, continued high turnover among salespeople, and quality control problems with software. Susan was told that her goals were to improve sales by 8 percent, to cut turnover by 20 percent, and to design a plan to process customer complaints about quality of products manufactured in the San Jose facility.

Susan first investigated each of the problems that she had to solve. She consulted the sales managers to get their view of the sales and turnover problems. She learned that the salespeople often complained about having little control over pricing and about "too much red tape between them and customer complaints." In short, sales personnel believed that going through a customer complaint department to get action on sales problems (which they felt should be under their individual control) was an inefficient system. Sales managers also noted that the company sales commission system seemed unfair in terms of the manager's job. The salespeople worked under a liberal commission system, but sales managers had to work on a straight salary basis. Several managers had recently returned to sales to raise their compensation level!

During her three-week investigation, Susan had a number of opportunities to interview salespeople who were quitting their jobs at Tentex. She conducted five of these "exit interviews," and found that the major reason given for quitting was frustration over the inability of sales personnel to deal personally with customer complaints. Susan learned that Tentex was the only firm in the industry that operated a customer complaint department. She learned also that customer complaints often took five weeks to process—even for a simple request to replace defective software!

Susan decided to visit the San Jose plant to get more information about product quality problems. There she learned that raw materials were scarce and that the plant was often forced to purchase inferior supplies, which arrived late. Employees had grown tired of complaining about poor supply quality, and a general "who cares?" attitude had developed at the plant. Of even more immediate concern was the plant manager's belief that a layoff was imminent because of sluggish demand for Tentex products. The layoff rumor had spread quickly through the plant, and as a result, employees were distrustful and suspicious.

After Susan had studied the situation in depth, she decided on a systematic course of action designed to change the organization in three problem areas. First, she set up a series of "change committees" composed of individuals who were especially interested in getting the various problems solved. In the sales division, she selected several salespeople and two sales managers to serve on the sales change committee. She also invited representatives who worked for five valued customer firms to provide the committee with customer input. The committee that was to focus on the salespersonnel turnover problem was composed of three sales managers and six salespeople whose Tentex work experience varied from 1 to 20 years. Product quality problems were addressed by a committee composed of salespeople, plant personnel, and two valued Tentex suppliers.

Susan then set up a planning committee composed of top management. The role of this committee was to study all of the ideas and proposals submitted by the three task force committees. The work of the planning committee was separated specifically into two phases: assessment of ideas in terms of corporate impact, and organization of company resources to back change programs.

Susan had each committee meet during the same two-day period at a local resort. The group spent the first day brainstorming about their individual problems. That evening, Susan and her assistants compiled all of the ideas generated by the brainstorming sessions and produced an overall summary, which she then distributed to each group. During the morning of the second day, each group re-evaluated their ideas in light of the work done by the other groups. During the afternoon of the second day, Susan facilitated a problem-solving session with all team participants present.

Two weeks after the retreat, Susan issued a report detailing an action plan for correcting the three problem areas. Her program retained the management committee as a way of keeping corporate perspective and to give Susan a means of controlling the change process in sales and production.

Susan was pleased about how well the process of organizational change was working. The various change committees were highly cohesive and several major changes had been suggested by each one. In fact, many of the improvement suggestions had come from employees—an indication that word of the programs was spreading throughout the organization.

Even the company president, Tom Philson, became involved in the program and showed up frequently at change committee meetings. He frequently presented awards for outstanding achievement. In addition, he made a point of following up on the change committee programs to gauge how employees were responding. The success of the change program coupled with Philson's meetings raised employee morale. Customers noted the change in the attitudes of the Tentex salespeople toward their work. (The sales change committee had instituted a system that allowed salespeople to do their own follow-up on customer complaints up to a value of $500). In addition, the committee had worked out a plan that tied the compensation of sales managers to the performance of the sales personnel reporting to them. Implementation of this idea had the effect of reducing turnover at the managerial level.

Employee work attitudes at the San Jose plant also had improved. The plant change committee had discovered that employees were improperly trained in the use of supplies and machine setup. Suppliers' representatives had worked with Tentex employees to design purchasing and assembly training programs for plant personnel. The effects of these programs were a 12 percent drop in scrap rates. The San Jose plant manager was particularly pleased because the tentative layoff had been cancelled in light of improved plant productivity.

Employee commitment to the company grew at all levels. A new commitment to excellence began to take shape at Tentex. Managers reported that employees were now interested in organizing quality circles to identify other ways to cut costs and improve product quality. Tom Philson became a minor industry celebrity, and was asked frequently to speak at industry meetings. Several professors from the Harvard University Business School were writing a case report about the Tentex program successes. As for Susan, she went on to establish a successful consulting practice that specializes in turning around distressed companies.

Questions

1. How is the organizational culture at Tentex impeding progress in sales and production?
2. What problems exist in the Tentex organizational climate?
3. What action research steps did Susan follow in her intervention at Tentex?
4. What are the major features of Susan's company change program?

Organizational Culture: The New Symbol of Corporate Excellence

Each organization has a different set of customs and traditions. These attributes may be hard to describe, but the organization employees know that their company is different from other firms. Just as each family has its own traditions and stories about various members and branches, so each company has legends and stories about unusual successes and major breakthroughs in products or markets. Likewise, firms have various operational procedures and systems that make them different from their competitors and from other organizations. These differences are often referred to as "variations in organizational culture and climate." Although the two concepts are related, culture is a much broader and more encompassing property of the organization than climate.

The concepts of culture and climate are natural progressions in the study of organizational behavior. Early in the text we studied individual personality traits and how these traits energize motivated behavior and performance. In the middle portion of the book we addressed the important property of group cohesiveness and problem-solving style. Now we look at the overall organization and its features. We thus have shifted from the individual to the group and finally to an analysis of organizational characteristics. By developing a thorough understanding of organizational culture and climate, we will be in a position to address the important issues of how organizations deal with change and uncertainty. This application of organizational behavior is called **organization development (OD).** The latter half of this chapter introduces you to an important set of tools that can be used to influence organization development.

Recognizing Organizational Culture

Experts define **organizational culture** as a system of shared values and beliefs that produce norms for behavior (1, 2). Organizations transmit values (i.e., what is important about the company and what the company does) to employees through training programs, work experiences, and communications. Beliefs (how organizational processes and practices work) are also transmitted through these mechanisms. Together, communicated values and beliefs crystallize as shared employee expectations. If these shared expectations are widespread and are accepted by employees, then performance-oriented norms develop in the organization. Peters and Waterman believe that organizational culture can have a profound effect on organizational success (3). Here are a few examples of corporate culture:

1. Conant designs interior work spaces for major corporations. The firm uses architectural, marketing, and graphics experts to generate a total design for the client. Conant's success has been attributed often to its culture, which is based on four values: (a) problem-solving orientation, (b) intensity of effort, (c) mutual trust and respect among employees at all levels, and (d) commitment to solving employees' personal problems (4).
2. The most dominant aspect of IBM's culture is the importance of customer service. The company keeps this value in front of all employees from the chief executive officer to the worker on the factory floor. At sales meetings, stories of excellent customer service are exchanged regularly (5).
3. At Hewlett-Packard, all employees know that they are supposed to be innovative. The company accordingly places extraordinary emphasis on employee communication. In the Palo Alto facility, meeting rooms are regularly full of groups of people who are all working on various problems. These groups include personnel from research, marketing, manufacturing, sales, and engineering. The company has developed the "technology of keeping in touch" (6).
4. Procter and Gamble has a deep commitment to all aspects of product quality. All product complaints are sent back to the relevant brand manager, who works with engineering or product design to improve the product without compromising quality (7).

Poor cultures (i.e., those with counterproductive norms) can be huge obstacles to performance excellence (8). For example, many publicly regulated utilities have developed cultures that are out of step with business practices. Today, many large utilities continue to push for construction of more nuclear facilities, yet public opinion has turned around completely on the issue of nuclear power. Consumer groups and public utility commissions are no longer willing to support higher utility rates to pay for reactors that are over budget. Utilities have grown accustomed to operating in a manner that disregards social interests and simply passes the operations costs on to consumers. Management of these utilities has not been required to account to consumer groups or to regulatory agencies. As the pressure increases for efficient generation of nonnuclear energy, the cultures of these public utilities will change (i.e., become more streamlined, more effective, and more responsive to public opinion).

What are the components of organizational culture?

In general, an organization's culture has its origins in management's assumptions about what motivates people to work and how the organization can best facilitate performance and commitment. Experts have developed a **culture awareness checklist.** Components of such a device are: commitment to a common purpose, competence to deliver superior performance, and consistency in perpetuating commitment and competence (9). Table 14.1 shows some of the items for assessing each component. The measuring scale indicates how the components are assessed.

The questionnaire in Table 14.1 makes several important points about organizational culture. First, **culture** can be perceived by employees, and they are quite capable of describing its characteristics. It can thus be measured and evaluated, and since culture is subject to evaluation, all individuals probably do *not* have the same understanding of the dimensions of their company's culture. Second, the organizational culture can be changed and perfected. It is therefore a *changeable* concept that can be influenced by systematic management activity. This concept is very important, for organizations frequently make the mistake of not generating a high employee awareness of the organizational culture. If a thorough understanding of organizational values and beliefs is *not* instilled in employees, then development of the organizational culture is left to chance. When the culture is based on chance and on uncontrolled evolution, the organization is taking a passive approach to the development of culture. It is foregoing the opportunity to develop a set of enduring and dependable standards that could be meaningful to employees. In the absence of conscious culture development, the organization "forgets what it does well," or never learns what it can do well.

When organizations have a poor culture, problems arise. The organization becomes ineffective and prominent indicators of cultural decline surface. These include accelerated turnover rates, widespread employee dissatisfaction evidenced by lower organizational commitment and lessening job involvement, performance declines and dissatisfaction with reward systems, increasing rates of customer dissatisfaction, increased emphasis on avoidance or suppression of conflict, and loss of innovative flair among employees. Several of these problems were evident in the Tentex Corporation in the introductory dilemma. Indeed, the three problem areas that Susan had to confront were employee discontent, customer dissatisfaction, and declines in product quality.

When organizational culture begins to deteriorate, managers should ask several key questions. The first key question is: Who has responsibility for corporate culture? When a company has a healthy culture that generates a strong interest in performance excellence in the work force, then the answer to this question is "all employees." When the culture is in disarray, however, or is deteriorating, then the answer is "the boss." In most cases, the boss (i.e., the president, chief executive officer, or owner) is the single most important person in any organization relative to culture. Lee Iacocca is an American folk hero because he successfully turned around Chrysler Corpo-

Table 14.1
Culture Awareness Checklist

Commitment to Common Purpose	Always	Often	Seldom	Never
1. Can you state your organization's purpose, philosophy, or central theme in one clear sentence?	4	3	2	1
2. Do 90 percent or more of your people display commitment to the common purpose?	4	3	2	1
3. Do individual employees perceive personal benefits from committing themselves to the common purpose?	4	3	2	1
4. Are you genuinely committed to the common purpose yourself?	4	3	2	1
Competence to Deliver Superior Performance				
5. Can every employee recognize the organization's areas of distinctive competence?	4	3	2	1
6. Are people committed to maintaining distinctive competencies at all costs?	4	3	2	1
7. Do your organization's areas of distinctive competence produce superior performance?	4	3	2	1
8. Do customers, competitors, and observers value your organization's superior performance?	4	3	2	1
Consistency in Perpetuating Commitment and Competence				
9. Will the current degree of commitment and competence remain at a high level?	4	3	2	1
10. Do you thoroughly screen candidates for employment to ensure a match with the organization's commitment and competence?	4	3	2	1
11. Do you deal swiftly with a new employee's lack of commitment by providing additional development or by terminating the employee?	4	3	2	1

ration's headlong plunge into cultural decline. Here are some observations about Lee Iacocca (10).

> . . . his life embodies just the kind of happy ending that Americans like to celebrate: he had reverses, he fought back, he came out on top . . . Iacocca's nip-and-tuck struggle to save Chrysler was something of a pop spectacle: the stakes were so high, and the auto company's decline and fall so conspicuous, that from 1979 to 1982 the cliff hanger drama of corporate survival unfolded in the press almost like a weekly serial. Throughout the crisis, this big, not quite familiar guy named Iacocca was attracting bursts of public notice standing his ground before congressional committees and giving snappy, sometimes scathing, answers at press conferences. He seemed sincere. More important, he seemed absolutely resolute and tough.

Iacocca's biggest successes may have been tied to his ability to become a highly visible salesperson for Chrysler's new corporate culture, which quickly took shape under his leadership. Consider the following:

> Down the hall he puts in 9½ hour days running the company. "Some guys in this business slow down, retire and take it easy," he says. "A couple of months later they're dead." Not Iacocca. He has spent almost 39 years in America's pivotal industry, and he still glories in the hurly burly of his factory floors. . . . Iacocca likes it best when he can make managing a car company seem like a martial task, urgent and vast and possibly heroic. . . . Iacocca's definition of management by consensus is revealing. "Consensus," he says, "is when we have a discussion. They tell me what they think. Then I decide" (11).

Iacocca grasped the extent of Chrysler's cultural decline and decided that the only way to right the floundering company was to become its strongest public advocate. He succeeded remarkably well at this task. Although the company needed a congressional loan to avoid bankruptcy, Iacocca nevertheless charged ahead with his claims of product quality and craftsmanship. When this message was combined with several new product offerings (principally vans and turbo-charged, upscale autos) and with improved productivity, the company quickly turned around under Iacocca's leadership. The final proof was Iacocca's well publicized last installment repayment of the $1.5 billion government loan, repaid seven years early.

Unquestionably Iacocca's personality and managerial style had a major impact on the Chrysler organization. The company was in such a precarious position that quite possibly only someone with Iacocca's personal force and drive was capable of saving the company.

Solving the Dilemma

How is the organizational culture at Tentex impeding progress in sales and promotion?

Commitment to a common purpose is not evident in the sales or production departments. Sales people are not able to act directly on customer complaints, and the compensation system for sales managers is poorly designed. Sales personnel are quitting in record numbers. The production employees have not worked out a solution for maintaining raw materials quality. Competence to deliver superior performance has declined as well, and workers are expressing their frustration in their "who cares" attitude. Tentex has been negligent about developing a companywide value of consistent excellence. The firm's policy of no commissions for sales managers has had the effect of removing the motivation for managers to monitor sales work closely. Poor corporate response to the problems in the San Jose facility attests to a lack of commitment to excellence.

Organizational Culture in Japanese Firms

Organizational culture has become a prominent issue in the United States because of the success of Japanese firms in our markets (12). Matsushita Electric is a firm that defines its values and culture very explicitly. The cornerstone of the firm's cultural system is the belief that people are the company's most valuable resource. To underscore this belief, the firm tries to practice lifetime employment. Rather than fire an employee, the company asks a dissatisfied worker how he could better contribute to the company. (This occurs only after job coaching and training have failed to produce the desired results.) Instead of terminating the employee, the individual is moved through a series of planned job transfers.

Employee participation is widespread at Matsushita, and employee suggestions concerning production and quality are considered vital to product improvement. The company uses quality circles in all of its operating divisions, and has a well-developed ability to replicate its culture in new divisions and locations. Management believes strongly in recognition and employee praise, and managers are trained to motivate employees with these tools.

The company emphasizes training and indoctrination in company values. Cooperation, fairness, harmony, and "struggle for betterment" are all company values that employees understand in personal terms. These values are reflected in the behavior of Matsushita executives. Top managers demonstrate high involvement and commitment to recruiting, hiring, and promoting the company's values both with customers and employees. All top managers are expected to reflect the company's values in their personal life as well as in their work life.

The company maintains tight planning and fiscal control while providing divisional managers with considerable entreprenurial latitude. Division managers share their performance data with each other on a quarterly basis. During these meetings, managers present their results in order of divisional success with the best performing divisions presenting results first. Other than this public assessment of performance by order of presentation, no forms of embarrassment or pressure for higher performance are used. All company decisions have a built-in acceptance time, so that enough time is allowed for conflict and disagreement to occur. Virtually all employee experiences are described as "training and development exercises."

Problem solving, troubleshooting, production stoppages, new product development, and marketing problems are also employee development exercises. This idea is extremely important, for it welds the employee's experience with the company's experience. When all of the company's hundreds of thousand of decisions are viewed in this way, the boundary between company and individual employee blurrs rapidly. The net effect is a fusion of company values with personal employee values.

A central component of many corporate cultures in Japanese firms is the high value placed on employees and the importance of human resource systems. In addition, many Japanese firms develop sophisticated systems for "agreeing on how to disagree." Consensus-based decision making is the rule rather than the exception. The decision-making process may take a little longer in Japanese firms, but once the decision is made, commitment is companywide. When these processes are joined with state-of-the-art production systems (e.g., computer-controlled robots), aggressive marketing in foreign markets, and government cooperation, the competitive power of Japanese companies is formidable indeed. If you don't believe us, look down the street and count the Toyotas!

The Concept of Organizational Climate

Organizational culture is a much broader concept than organizational climate. The culture of the organization is represented by the values and beliefs that are shared by employees at all levels. **Organizational climate,** on the other hand, represents employee perceptions of relatively stable organizational characteristics and processes. The relationship between these two organizational properties, culture and climate, is defined in Table 14.2.

Organizational climate is related to organizational performance, employee work attitudes, and organizational survival (13). Most researchers define organizational climate as "a relatively enduring quality of the internal environment of an organization that: (1) is experienced by its members; (2) influences their behavior; and (3) can be described in terms of the values of a particular set of characteristics of the organization" (14).

Table 14.2.
The Relationship of Organizational Culture and Climate

Organizational Culture (Values and Beliefs) as Defined by.	*Organizational Climate (Perceptions of the Organization) as Defined by.*
The existing normative system in the organization.	Durable employee perceptions of organizational systems and processes (performance appraisal).
Expressed through common language, stories, traditions, and organizational history.	Measurable with questionnaires, interviews, and study of organizational records.
Translated into action through management philosophy and the company mission.	Separated into distinct measurable components that can vary from one subunit to another.
Often extolled in company reports, public relations activities, and sales promotions.	Usually more apparent to employees than to outsiders.
May be well understood and copied by competitors.	

The importance of organizational climate has to do with the link between perceptions, attitude formation, and behavior. Organizational climate determines employee perceptions of organizational features and systems. These systems in turn generate rewards and penalties that shape employee attitudes through behavior modification and social learning. These countless encounters with the various aspects of organizational climate eventually shape and harden employee attitudes. The features of organizational climate emerge when these attitudes are measured.

Assessing Organizational Climate

Researchers do not agree on the dimensions of organizational climate (15, 16). For our purposes, we use the following dimensions to represent the concept (17).

1. **Structure:** the feeling that employees have about the constraints in the organization—the number of rules, regulations, and procedures.
2. **Responsibility:** the feeling of autonomy and being your own boss.
3. **Reward:** being rewarded for a job well done with reward being defined by an emphasis on positive reinforcement versus punishment.
4. **Risk:** the sense of challenge and risk in work, with the relative emphasis on taking calculated risks versus playing it safe.
5. **Warmth:** the extent to which good fellowship prevails and work groups emphasize friendliness.
6. **Support:** the perceived helpfulness of employees in the organization.

To deepen your understanding of organizational climate, complete the Now It's Your Turn.

NOW IT'S YOUR TURN ...

Directions: The following statements represent the various aspects of organizational climate just described. Recall your most recent organizational work experience, then use the scale to assign a number to each statement.

1 ---------- 2 ---------- 3 ---------- 4 ---------- 5

Always true Mostly true I'm not sure Mostly false Always false

______ 1. The organization has many rules and procedures that regulate how employees do their jobs.

______ 2. In this organization, each employee would say that he is pretty much his own boss.

______ 3. Supervisors are fond of criticizing how employees do their job in this organization.

______ 4. Employees in this organization regularly go out on a limb to test new ideas.

______ 5. The work groups in this organization are really friendly and open to new members.

______ 6. Supervisors go out of their way to help subordinates handle job-related problems.

______ 7. This organization does not rely on red tape or complicated procedures to control employees' work.

______ 8. You always have someone looking over your shoulder in this organization.

______ 9. The organization uses liberal amounts of praise and recognition to reward employees for a job well done.

______ 10. When new projects come up, employees avoid volunteering and generally try to play it safe.

______ 11. It takes a long time to be accepted in a work group in this organization.

______ 12. Employees do not go out of their way to help newcomers in this organization.

Scoring: The first step is to correct several reverse-scored items. For questions 1, 3, 8, 10, 11, and 12, your score must be changed by using the following table:

Your Score	Corrected Score
1	5
2	4
3	3
4	2
5	1

Now add the scores as indicated below:

1. Structure: question 1 + 7	______	range 2–10
2. Responsibility: question 2 + 8	______	range 2–10
3. Reward: question 3 + 9	______	range 2–10
4. Risk: question 4 + 10	______	range 2–10
5. Warmth: question 5 + 11	______	range 2–10
6. Support: question 6 + 12	______	range 2–10
TOTAL ORGANIZATIONAL CLIMATE SCORE	______	range 10–50

A low score (12–29) represents a supportive climate; a high score (30–60) indicates a tense, hostile climate.

Solving the Dilemma

What problems exist in the Tentex organizational climate?

A number of problems existed in the Tentex organizational climate. Salespeople complained about having little control over pricing and about too much red tape hindering the solving of customer complaints. Perceptions of the sales commission system also were not good among sales managers. In the San Jose assembly facility, the employee frustration level was high because of inferior supplies, which were also scarce. Risk taking to solve problems was low because workers feared that a layoff was imminent. These problems combined to create unfavorable employee perceptions of climate.

The change program undertaken by Susan did much to improve the Tentex climate, and as the climate improved, employee work attitudes and performance also improved. This is the interdependent nature of the relationship between organizational climate and organizational effectiveness. As organizational climate deteriorates, so also do indicators of organizational effectiveness.

Likert's System of Organizations and Climate

In Chapter 6, we studied the effects of participation in organizations. While discussing this important topic, we presented Likert's system 1 and system 4 organizations (18) (see Table 6.1). With your new understanding of organizational climate, we can now integrate these two concepts. You will recall that system 1 organizations were described as being very traditional and oriented toward the principles of scientific management. In contrast, system 4 organizations were oriented to problem solving and active involvement of employees in a variety of organizational decisions.

System 1 and system 4 organizations each have a particular organizational climate. In the system 1 organization, control, power, authority, and decision making are concentrated at the top. Subordinate input is not sought for decision making. Employees are viewed as followers who are paid wages and salaries to take orders. Control of employee behavior is achieved through coercion and threats (e.g., demotion, transfer, termination). Communication in the system 1 organization is always from the top down. Many informal groups form with goals that do not integrate with the goals of the organization. The level of work involvement is generally low, and employees have little commitment.

The system 1 organization has a poorly developed climate relative to the six dimensions listed in the previous section. If lower and middle level employees of a system 1 organization filled out the questionnaire in the Now It's Your Turn, their scores would be in the 40–50 range. Only top management might score in the supportive climate range (12–29). A discrepancy between top management and lower level employee perceptions of climate is a common feature of system 1 organizations.

The system 4 organization is highly participative and oriented to providing opportunities for individual autonomy and job control. Involvement in decision making occurs at all levels. Leadership is based on trust and support, and employees feel generally comfortable discussing problems in the system 4 organization. Communication flows in all directions with little distortion, and coercion or fear are not used to motivate behavior. Informal and formal group goals are much more likely to parallel organizational goals. Work groups are more likely to be stage 4 groups (see Chapter 9) and to demonstrate a problem-solving orientation toward conflict. Process losses are generally lower for groups in system 4 organizations.

The system 4 organization has lower and middle level employees who would score in the 10–20 range on our organizational climate quiz. They would perceive the climate as supportive and risk oriented. Top management in the system 4 organization would also generate scores in the 10–20 range. In contrast to the system 1 organization, perceptions of the organizational climate as high quality are much more likely to occur at all levels of the system 4 organization.

What does it mean if perceptions of organizational climate are uniformly favorable and similar in the system 4 organization?

It means that the organization is more flexible and capable of adapting to change. Employees tend to believe in the organizational goals (i.e., little sabotage of goals occurs) and effort is channeled to achieve them. Furthermore, work groups tend to confront and resolve conflict versus avoiding it or smoothing it over. In short, the system 4 organization is less resistant to change because its climate reinforces risk taking and provides the emotional support for employees to become more entreprenurial. Employees consequently develop higher needs for achievement (see Chapter 3).

Managerial Implications for Organizational Culture and Climate

Culture and climate are overlapping concepts. Culture is broader, and refers to shared beliefs and values; climate reflects employee perceptions of specific organizational characteristics. The writing and research on these two concepts conclude that they are important and relevant managerial issues. A useful way to highlight the implications of culture and climate is to look at the roles played by employees and managers relative to the two concepts.

Culture, climate, and employees. Employees need to recognize that culture and climate cannot be changed by one person alone. Both organizational features have tremendous inertia, that is, they resist alteration. It is precisely this inertia that buffers and protects employees from uncertainty and turmoil in understanding their job expectations. Employees must not think that culture and climate issues are irrelevant. If problems become apparent, they should point them out to superiors in an attempt to change management practices to improve culture or climate factors. Employees should also recognize the fundamental relationship between individual differences, group atmosphere, and organizational culture and climate. These three analytical levels contribute to culture. If, therefore, you are a job candidate, be sure that the organization's culture is consistent with your personal values.

Culture, climate, and managers. Our presentation of the characteristics of culture and climate included measuring devices to assess these organizational qualities. Both culture and climate can be assessed as a part of ongoing diagnosis of the quality of organizational functioning. Managers should be concerned with monitoring all relevant aspects of culture and climate. Consistent attention to these two qualities signals management's interest in "being the best organization we can be both for our employees and customers." Although culture and climate may be perceived as complex features, they are in fact quite readily apparent to employees and customers. In many respects, the firm's "goodwill" is tied closely to these organizational qualities. Wise managers make sure that both aspects of the organization are synchronized with organizational goodwill.

Moving the organization's climate and culture from system 1 to system 4 requires more than a management policy change. Alteration in leadership styles and changes in organizational structure and processes must be included to effect such drastic changes. Leaders must learn to recognize more than task-related employee problems. Indeed, they must learn to match their leadership style successfully with the maturity level of employees (see Chapter 10). Leaders will need improved training and development programs to accomplish this. Organizational design also must be altered to match the decentralized approach represented by the system 4 climate and culture. This also requires alteration of the organization's reward system (19). Authority and responsibility must be pushed down the hierarchy to work units. As you can see, the managerial responsibilities involved in shifting culture and climate to a system 4 configuration are a major undertaking. To ensure that such a change is executed properly, managers should receive training in the important area of organizational development. The next two sections deal with this important topic.

Knowledge Check

1. Organizational culture is composed of shared values, norms, and work systems. T or F?

2. Organizational culture does not include which one of the following properties:
   a. commitment to common purpose
   b. consistency in perpetuating commitment and competence
   c. satisfaction with leadership styles

3. Organizational culture and climate are properties that are largely beyond the employee control. T or F?

4. The example of Lee Iacocca and the Chrysler Corporation turn-around illustrates the key role played by leadership in changing corporate culture. T or F?

5. Organizational climate is generally considered to be a broader concept than organizational culture. T or F?

6. In the system 4 organization, you would expect to find great differences between management and labor's perceptions of organizational climate. T or F?

7. Management can safely ignore leadership training in attempts to alter organizational climate. T or F?

Answers:

1 F, 2 c, 3 F, 4 T, 5 F, 6 F, 7 F

Organizational Development

In Chapter 13, we discussed how to improve the way the organization functions through alterations in its design and structure. While this is an important method for improving organizational effectiveness, it is somewhat limited in scope, that is, it does not deal directly with attitudes and behavior. The activities that focus specifically on changing behavior and attitudes are referred to as **organizational development (OD).** Organizational design is a structural approach to change, while organizational development is a social process approach to organizational change.

Organizational development is relevant to organizational culture and climate. These organizational properties are frequently the targets of organizational development efforts. In the introductory dilemma, Susan attempts to alter certain aspects of the Tentex culture and climate. Her program of planned organizational change would be classified as an organizational development program. Before we can analyze her program, however, we must do the following: (1) discuss the meaning of organizational development, (2) describe the role of the change agent, and (3) develop a classification system for organizational development methods.

The Meaning of Organizational Development

As Huse and Cummings point out, "a number of conceptions of organizational development exist, with considerable overlap among them." They advance the following definition of **organizational development:** "A systemwide application of behavioral science knowledge to the planned development and reinforcement of organizational strategies, structures, and processes for improving an organization's effectiveness" (20). These experts also note that organizational development has a number of qualities that differentiate it from other approaches to organizational change and improvement (21). These qualities are shown in Table 14.3.

Table 14.3 details the characteristics of organizational development, which represent certain attitudes toward human nature and how organizations should function. Organizational development rests on a belief in the application of humanistic principles to organizational behavior so the organization functions in a participative way. It focuses also on the growth-seeking tendencies of individuals. In other words, organizational development programs typically increase the intrinsic rewards available to employees. Most programs therefore try to increase the opportunities for employees to satisfy their higher order needs. In many respects, organizational development takes an optimistic view of human nature in the work setting. In essence, the field tends to promote the contemporary view that all employees are capable of assuming more responsibility, and to promote the belief that under the proper conditions all employees can make lasting contributions to the organization.

Table 14.3 *Major Qualities of Organizational Development*

Organizational Development Qualities	*Implications*
1. Organizational development focuses on an entire organizational unit (work group, department, division, or the entire organization).	▪ Changing the management information system does not constitute organizational development. ▪ Individual employee counseling programs are not organizational development. ▪ Organizational development focuses on the social and behavioral aspects of organizations.
2. Organizational development is based on behavioral science knowledge at both the micro and macro levels.	▪ Organizational development does not emphasize the technological or engineering aspects of the organization. ▪ Leadership, group dynamics, organizational design, and organizational strategy are components of organizational development.
3. Although organizational development is concerned with planned change, it is not associated with business planning or forecasting.	▪ Organizational development plans are flexible and can be altered as circumstances require. ▪ Organizational development programs always begin with diagnosis of the organization's problems.
4. Organizational development involves the creation and reinforcement of organizational change.	▪ Organizational development goes through the phases of diagnosis, change, and stabilization of the organization in a new mode of functioning.
5. Organizational development involves strategy, structure, and process changes in the organization.	▪ Organizational development programs can focus on individual behavior, on the way in which work is designed, or on how the organization is set up and coordinated (i.e., organizational design).
6. Organizational development has as its primary goal improving organizational effectiveness.	▪ Effective organizations are better able to solve problems. ▪ Effective organizations are better able to attract and hold effective employees.

SOURCE: Huse, E., and Cummings, T. 1985. *Organization Development and Change*, 3rd ed. St. Paul, Minn.: West Publishing.

Organizational Development Terminology and the Role of the Change Agent

When a practitioner of organizational development alters an organization, an intervention is underway. An **intervention** is the application of a method or approach designed to solve an internal organizational problem. Practitioners of organizational development are called "change agents." A **change agent** is someone who precipitates change in the organization; the individual usually has had training in the methods of organizational development. If the change agent is an employee of the organization seeking change, then she is referred to as an **internal change agent.** If an **external change agent** is hired, then the organization pays him a fee for services rendered. **Client organizations** (i.e., users of the change agent's services) frequently require internal change agents to work with external change agents on organizational development intervention.

In addition to competence, the most important skill that the change agent has is **ability to generate trust.** If trust does not exist between the client organization and the change agent, the organization is not likely to follow through on the change agent's recommendations. Trust thus becomes an important prerequisite to successful intervention.

Why is trust so important in the relationship between client organization and change agent?

Interventions occur in less than ideal organizational circumstances. For example, many organizations undertake interventions only after top management perceives a serious threat to the internal health of the organization. Many of these programs are therefore started during periods of considerable employee uncertainty and confused expectations. Change agents first conduct an organizational diagnosis to identify the true causes of poor organizational functioning. An **organizational diagnosis** is a fullscale audit of all behavioral, attitudinal, and performance information inherent in the organizational environment. The two primary diagnostic tools are interviews and questionnaires. Employees often fear these tools and are concerned that their questionnaire responses may be used to make termination decisions. To address these concerns, Nadler recommends that the change agent deal with eight major issues, which build a bridge of trust between the agent and organization members (22). These trust issues are summarized in Table 14.4.

Another important quality of the change agent is ability to act as a catalyst for change. This ability is defined as the change agent's using himself as an instrument for change in the organization. When a change agent functions in this way, he does not have his personal values or beliefs changed; rather, he triggers change in those who are in the client organization. In the opening dilemma, Susan Ramsey functioned as a catalyst for change at Tentex when she implemented her intervention.

A major problem associated with the change agent role involves the catalyst function. Strict adherence to this role means that the change agent does *not* function as an outside expert who suggests solutions to the problems of the client organization. The change agent instead facilitates the development of an internally generated solution that has been suggested and refined by employees. Many change agents find this a difficult position to occupy, for they are often pressed to take the role of expert advisor (i.e., the typical consultant role), which involves recommending specific solutions to the client organization.

Action Research in Organizations

If an intervention is to be effective, some of the diagnosis must be based on employee perceptions of organizational problems and on employee recommendations for improving effectiveness of the organization. In the dilemma, Susan interviewed sales managers and conducted "exit interviews" of employees who were quitting. She also conducted numerous interviews of employees at the San Jose facility. These activities were the first stages of her action research. **Action research** is defined as a process for the systematic collection of data related to a client organization's problems, the feeding back of data to facilitate solution planning, and the evaluation of results

Table 14.4
Building Trust Between Client Organization and Change Agent

Question the Change Agent Should Answer	*Answer the Change Agent Should Give*
1. Who am I?	▪ The change agent has a professional responsibility to get to know those employees who will be asked to provide diagnostic data.
2. Why am I here and what am I doing?	▪ The change agent should define the goals of the diagnosis and data-gathering activities.
3. Who do I work for?	▪ This answer addresses the questions of who hired the consultant and who does the change agent report to in the organization. This relationship should be clearly explained and well understood by all parties.
4. What do I want from you and why?	▪ This answer should specify how much time and effort employees are expected to contribute to generate meaningful and valid data. The fact that participation is voluntary also should be specified.
5. How will I protect your confidentiality?	▪ This question is key to reducing employee concerns about data use. Employees should be confident that they will not be punished for giving honest answers.
6. Who will have access to the data?	▪ Employees should be told who will see the data, and they should be shown their own results.
7. What's in it for you?	▪ This answer should explain the benefits of the program in terms that employees fully understand.
8. Can I be trusted?	▪ This is the ultimate question that must be answered to the satisfaction of participants. The best way to answer this question is through the consultant's actions. The change agent must be available to address employee concerns.

SOURCE: Nadler, D. 1977. *Feedback and Organization Development: Using Data-Based Methods.* Reading, Mass.: Addison-Wesley.

in terms of collecting and analyzing more data (23). The foregoing is actually a simplified definition of a very complicated process. Take a look at Figure 14.1, which illustrates the process flow.

The appeal of action research is that the process is objective. Since the process uses actual company data, the diagnosis tends to be both systematic and pertinent, and the change agent and participants in the intervention get a much clearer picture of current organizational conditions. The action research model shown in Figure 14.1 is both incremental and gradual. Indeed, these properties are critical to allowing participants in the client organization time to adjust to the various program phases. In short, action research adjusts employee expectations so personnel become more comfortable with the intervention.

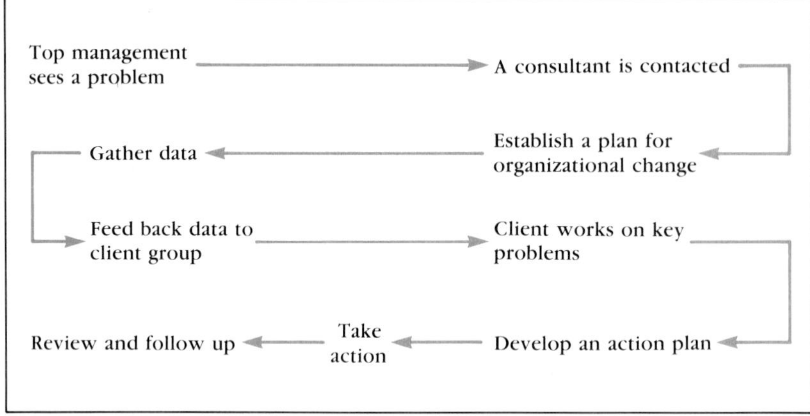

Figure 14.1
The Action Research Process

Solving the Dilemma

What action research steps did Susan follow in her intervention at Tentex?

Susan's intervention conforms closely to the action research model in Figure 14.1. We can assume that Tom Philson triggered the process by recognizing the problems and authorizing Susan to begin a study of sales, turnover, and product quality. Susan, as change agent, developed a data-gathering plan and enlisted the assistance of the management change committees to help her construct the plan. Once the plan was completed, she interviewed employees (data gathering). The first four phases of the action research process helped her establish the trust of those employees who would be affected by the outcomes of her intervention. During these phases, she was able to communicate the goals and processes involved in the intervention.

Once the data was gathered and analyzed, Susan fed back the data to the change committees, and used them to develop solutions at the management retreat. After the data gathered at the retreat was integrated with the suggested solutions, she issued an action plan for each change committee. She employed the general management committee as a steering committee to evaluate all intervention strategies from the corporate perspective.

At this point, new behaviors begin to emerge in the action research cycle. The company president became personally involved in the intervention (the Philson success meetings). Employee behaviors began to change as a result of alterations in production and sales jobs. Sales managers became more committed to excellence through the new compensation system. Suppliers were even induced to become committed to Tentex excellence, and to help the production facility design a training program for production personnel. This last point is notable, for systematic action research interventions frequently change the behavior and attitudes of people *outside* the client organization. The benefits of such changes can be significant. Better relationships with suppliers and customers were two major benefits reaped by Tentex. Given this promising beginning, the action research cycle may continue at Tentex as the firm finds new ways to modify its structure and processes.

Action research is an especially powerful procedure for installing planned changes in the organization. The procedure does, however, have some pitfalls, which are as follows:

1. Top management gives permission to make changes in the organization but does not get personally involved in the process. This leads to the employee perception that top management is not committed to the intervention.
2. The change agent does not gain employees' trust, so the intervention is shallow and superficial. Employee satisfaction deteriorates even further as a result.
3. The key client groups do not do a good job of managing the expectations of employees who will be affected by the intervention. Uncertainty about intervention goals thus leads to tension and anxiety among employee groups.
4. The change agent has a favorite technique for improving the organization, so the diagnostic phase of action research is not done properly. For example, the change agent might advocate job redesign as a solution to any type of organizational problem.
5. The organization may not be willing to commit the time or money necessary to make a thorough problem diagnosis, or the organization may not want to reveal the data generated in diagnosis to employee groups. These organization responses can create further tension and anxiety in employee groups.
6. Management may think that they already understand what the problems are, so they conclude that diagnosis is not necessary.

The problems confronting action research have some key features. First, they cluster in the early phases of the research. This is the time when any intervention is the most vulnerable, because commitment to the process and its goals are not widely distributed in the organization. Second, all of the problems are related to diagnosis. The diagnostic portion of the research is always most vulnerable for several reasons. Diagnosis is expensive and time consuming, and it is supposed to occur *before* any action is taken to solve organizational problems. These diagnostic properties run counter to traditional management values, which promote decisive action and prompt problem resolution. In other words, managers and owners tend to be so action oriented that they want to leap directly to the solutions once the decision has been made to attack the organizational problems. Haste and impatience are thus the two major enemies of methodical diagnosis. Lastly, the change agent also may prefer to de-emphasize diagnosis because he is getting direct pressure from the client or because he favors particular techniques for handling all organizational problems (e.g., job redesign or leadership training).

In summary, the action research model is an important process aimed at improving organizational effectiveness and developing new knowledge that can be relevant in other organizational settings. The use of sequential activities (i.e., general problem identification, consultation with a behavioral expert, data gathering, and so forth) helps ensure that the process for changing employee behaviors and expectations is methodical. Although problems can occur in the action research cycle, if the change agent develops employee trust and uses employee participation effectively, the organization should benefit from the action research process.

Knowledge Check

1. Organizational development is a process for changing organizations by altering the technology used to produce goods and services. T or F?
2. Organizational development generally is thought of as a method that uses both behavioral science and engineering knowledge to improve the way organizations function. T or F?
3. Which of the following is *not* a part of organizational development?
   a. program focuses on an entire organizational unit.
   b. business planning and forecasting
   c. strategy, structure, and process
4. Susan's work at Tentex would be classified as an organizational development intervention. T or F?
5. A change agent is someone who functions as a catalyst for organizational change. T or F?
6. One of the client groups in Susan's Tentex intervention was the company's customers. T or F?
7. One of the reasons for the successful intervention at Tentex was that top management not only gave permission to change how the company functioned, but top managers also became personally involved in the intervention. T or F?
8. Action research is a problem-solving process that conforms well to the way in which most managers approach and solve problems. T or F?

Answers:

1 F, 2 F, 3 b, 4 T, 5 T, 6 T, 7 T, 8 F.

Intervention Methods in Organizational Development

The field of organizational development has grown rapidly in the last 20 years. An explosion in the number of different applications and techniques has led to efforts to classify strategies used by change agents to alter organizational functioning. The full exploration of these classification schemes is beyond the scope of this book. Our goal here is to discuss intervention strategies in the major areas of organizational development. Experts generally agree that interventions can be classified as: (1) interpersonal and group, (2) systemwide process changes, (3) organization structure and design changes, (4) quality of work life changes, and (5) goal setting, or the management by objectives process (24).

Interpersonal and Group-Based Organizational Development

Interpersonal and group based techniques represent the traditional origins of the field of organizational development. These two areas emerged from the laboratory training approach developed in 1946 at the National Training Laboratories in Bethel, Maine. Under the sponsorship of several organizations (NEA, Office of Naval Research, MIT, and others), Kurt Lewin and his colleagues from MIT developed group interaction procedures that became known as the T-group procedure (25).

T-groups, or sensitivity training groups, are designed to provide members with realistic experiences, in the areas of group dynamics, leadership, and interpersonal relations (26). If the group's purpose is to help members gain deeper personal knowledge and development, then the group is referred to as an **encounter group.** While pure encounter groups are not as common today as they used to be, their legacy is the wide array of support groups currently available in the United States. **Support groups** are typically problem-focused groups. Examples of support groups are Alcoholics Anonymous, groups composed of divorced parents, and groups of parents with handicapped children. Such groups continue to provide important forms of support and encouragement to their members.

T-groups focus on a blend of improved personal understanding of group processes and enhanced personal awareness. They are generally composed of 10 to 15 members who may or may not be strangers. Individuals from the same firm may be organized as "cousin" or "family" T-groups. **Cousin groups** are composed of people from different functional areas and from different hierarchical levels in an organization. A **family group** represents a superior and his immediate subordinates.

A facilitator works with the T-group. A **facilitator** is defined as a resource person for the group to use who does not take a leadership role. Accordingly, group members define the processes and agenda for the group. This usually confuses members who typically try various roles and interpersonal styles as ways to create structure for the group. Some members often resist attempts by other members to take over the group. Eventually, the focus of the group becomes "the here and now" versus discussion of problems in members' work organizations. From time to time, the facilitator makes interventions that deepen personal understanding or encourage analysis of group processes.

The T-group's emphasis on the here-and-now coupled with candor and support encourage participants to develop improved work relationships through caring about and understanding the feelings of others. These new skills and understanding are supposed to have considerable "carry-over" to the organizational setting.

The T-group process sounds good in theory, but what are the actual outcomes of the approach?

T-groups and their organizational effects. The results of the T-group approach are mixed. Research indicates that T-groups have little impact on decision-making processes, productivity, efficiency, and absenteeism (27, 28). Bowers notes that T-groups can improve group processes but that they have minimal impact on the organizational culture (29). The lack of cultural impact is probably owing to the reluctance of managers to support widespread use of T-groups.

Huse and Cummings suggest that the effectiveness of T-groups in organizations depends on three factors: (1) The T-group must be structured (i.e., problem focused) so learning can be explicitly transferred back to the organizational setting. (2) The use of T-groups should be tied to an ongoing organizational development intervention. (3) The culture of the organization must support the use of T-groups (30). The third factor means that employees must believe that conflict can be managed (versus avoided or suppressed), that information is readily shared, and that openness is supported.

A second method of interpersonal and group-based organizational development is called team building. **Team building** is defined as a task-oriented method of group process improvement. It is a method accepted much more readily by organizations than the T-group method, because team building emphasizes the solving of real organizational problems. Some typical objectives of team building are summarized in Table 14.5.

While considerable variation occurs in the use of team building, it is useful to consider a typical program in a large industrial organization (31). (As you study these steps, note how closely they parallel the action research steps in Figure 14.1.)

1. **Team skills workshop.** Structured group exercises help unfreeze attitudes and get the groups ready to accept change.
2. **Data collection.** Team members fill out a questionnaire that measures organizational climate, leadership patterns, and job satisfaction.
3. **Data confrontation.** Consultants present the teams with the results of step 2. Using group problem solving, consultants help the teams develop recommendations for change.
4. **Action planning.** The teams develop specific plans to bring about the changes isolated in step 3.
5. **Team building.** Barriers to team effectiveness are isolated and methods for removing them are developed.
6. **Intergroup team building.** Teams with interdependent goals meet to establish collaborative methods for handling joint activities.

Team building is a process widely accepted by organizations. Much of this acceptance occurs because people are comfortable with the values and

Table 14.5.
Problems Targeted by Team Building

Team Building Targets for Formal Work Groups (Supervisor and His or Her Subordinates)	*Team Building Targets for Special Groups (Task Forces, Project Teams)*
1. Developing a method to make decisions and set goals	1. Developing a plan for handling conflict between departments
2. Improving the relationships between group members and the group's manager	2. Developing solutions for problems which affect all employees (noise, safety, etc.)
3. Solving product or service quality problems (quality circles)	3. Developing job design changes (job focus group)
4. Clarifying job requirements and work expectations	4. Attacking departmental or organizational problems

procedures associated with teamwork. Most organizations possess cultural values that promote these goals. Team building does not generate anxiety or tension among managers and employees to the same extent as T-groups.

Research on team building generally supports the more favorable responses of organizations to this method. In the study that outlined the steps previously noted, researchers found that the organization's performance improved and that employee attitudes and perceptions were favorably affected by team building (32). Other researchers have documented similar effects (33). The research tends to indicate that group effectiveness, member influence, and job involvement are all improved by systematic team-building efforts.

The main problem with team building seems to be the "fade-out effect" (34). The **fade-out effect** is defined as the tendency for team-building outcomes to disappear in the work setting when team building is not done at the work-site (most team building takes place off site). Experts maintain that the problem can be minimized if the team leader holds weekly or biweekly meetings after the team building is completed (35). The objective of these meetings is to clarify member roles, thus ensuring continued personal accountability for the results of the team building.

In summary, techniques aimed at interpersonal and group relations represent the starting point for the field of organizational development. T-groups are not generally used in organizations because employees are uncomfortable with the unstructured approach. These groups have evolved into encounter and sensitivity groups, which serve as support groups in our society. Organizations tend to favor team building, which focuses on problems that have their origins in group relations. Team building programs have been shown to improve both performance and employee attitude.

Systemwide Process Change

The most common systemwide organizational development method is **survey feedback.** The survey feedback approach is based on the action research model. The process consists of collecting questionnaire data from organization members, summarizing the data, feeding it back to employee groups, and then using the groups to diagnose problems and develop action plans to solve them. The basic steps in the survey feedback method are as follows.

1. Top management assists an external consultant in setting up a steering committee (temporary project team) composed of highly respected employees. This group helps the consultant compile an acceptable organizational survey.
2. The organizational questionnaire is pilot tested, modified by the consultant and the steering committee, and then given to all employees.
3. The change agent analyzes the data away from the organization (to protect confidentiality of employees who participated voluntarily in the survey).
4. Survey results are fed back to top management, the steering committee, and all department heads and employees who participated in the survey.
5. Department heads, top management, and other relevant employee groups are brought together to develop action plans that address problems identified by the survey. For example, survey results might have

revealed a need to focus on improved productivity, job satisfaction, *reward* system design, or performance appraisal system design.

6. The change agent develops a list or organizational priorities for change and presents them to top management and the steering committee. Target areas for change are identified and relevant action plans implemented.

The sheer volume of information about survey feedback programs used in organizations is overwhelming. Virtually all Fortune 500 firms, as well as major government agencies (military and administrative departments), have used survey feedback. The process has been adopted in European firms also. As widespread as such programs are, little documented evidence exists testifying to their effectiveness.

Bowers claims that survey feedback was the most successful procedure for improving organizational climate in 23 organizations (36). His research study involved 14,000 blue and white collar employees who participated in such programs over a five-year period. The consensus seems to be growing that survey feedback is best used as an intermediate step between data gathering and developing the action plan (see Figure 14.1). This point of view argues that the simple gathering and feeding back of data to groups of employees is not sufficient in and of itself to alter attitudes or behavior. Survey feedback is thus seen as a step in the action research process. This view advocates that survey feedback be characterized as a diagnostic and communication tool.

Survey feedback is a key tool in organizational development programs. The usefulness of the approach for quick diagnosis of organizational problem areas is unchallenged. Knowledgeable users of the survey feedback technique avoid many of the pitfalls of using generalized approaches by modifying questionnaires and interview formats to fit the needs of the client organization. The same basic rule that should govern all organizational development applies to survey feedback. The primary mission of the change agent is establishment of trust and support among employees.

Solving the Dilemma

What are the major features of Susan's company change program?

Susan's program consisted of survey feedback and team building embedded in the action research model. She established project teams called change committees, and she used off-site team building to deal with the information that she generated through survey feedback. The change committees were her tools for installing solutions to the three problems noted in the dilemma. She used the survey feedback process between the action planning step for gathering data and the development of problem solutions at the management retreat. Recommendations from team building research indicate that she should also hold follow-up meetings with members of her change committees to ensure that everyone understands his or her role in the change process.

Organizational Structure and Design Changes

Organizational structure and design interventions attempt to develop an organizational structure that fits the needs of the organization. The needs of the organization are determined by external environmental factors and by internal task requirements (see Chapters 13 and 15). The structural features of the organization can be adjusted to balance the opposing needs of specialization (division of work) and coordination (integrating various task specializations into a unified system).

Organizational designs come in three basic varieties: functional, product, and matrix. In Chapter 13 you learned that functional organizations represent the standard pyramid and chain of command structure depicted by the organizational chart in Figure 14.2. In the **functional form,** the organization is divided into different departments created according to function, such as accounting, manufacturing, engineering, marketing, and purchasing. The functional design was based on early management theories that proposed a design universally applicable to any organization. The functional configuration stresses specialization, span of control, lines of authority and responsibility, and line and staff relations.

In the functional organization, the major divisions are staffed by specialists. Tentex is set up as a functional organization. The heads of the various Tentex divisions (e.g., production, sales, and so forth) are managers who have worked their way up the technical specialties in their division. Staff functions in Figure 14.2 have similar promotion patterns for managers. The difference for staff departments is that they do not directly make decisions

Figure 14.2
Functional Organization Design With Staff Departments

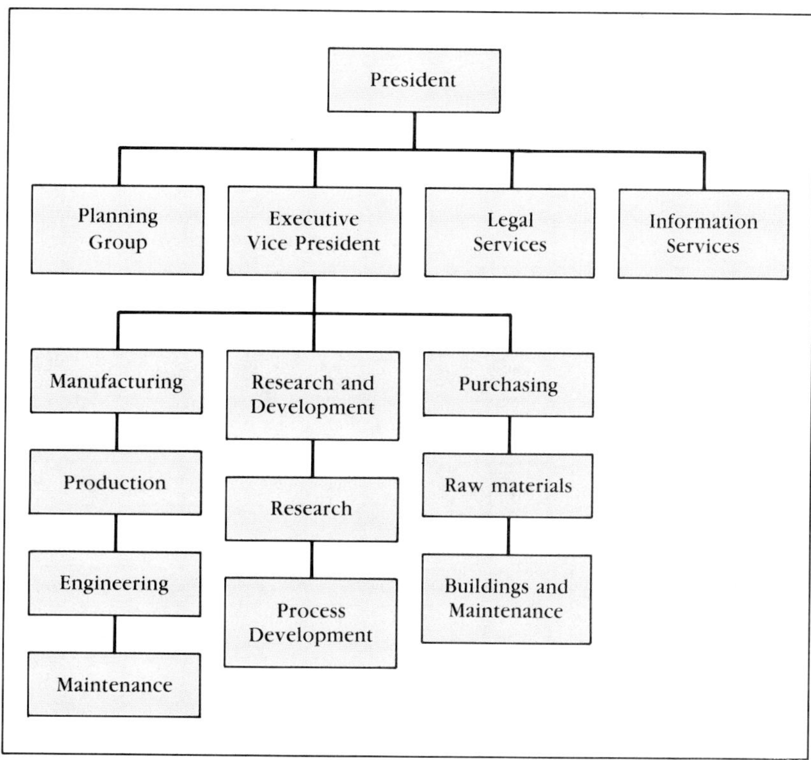

about operations and how resources should be allocated (these are decisions made by managers in line positions).

If the environment confronting the organization is more turbulent and unstable, the organization may choose a **product structure.** With this design, the organization duplicates managerial and technical positions within each division manufacturing related products. For example, General Motors has divisions that make Buicks, Chevrolets, Cadillacs, Pontiacs, and so on. The divisional managers have autonomy to design their own sales campaigns, to deal directly with their dealers, and to set production levels. Within each product division, the basic design structure is the functional organization. Increased autonomy is a direct organizational response to greater environmental uncertainty.

The last structural alternative is the **matrix design.** This configuration is the most flexible and adaptable of the three discussed. It relies on project teams to accomplish the main work of the organization, and team members may be drawn from any of the various functional divisions. Project leaders act as coordinators linking functional divisions and the technical specialists who are working on the project. Figure 14.3 shows a simplified matrix design.

The experts drawn from different functional areas remain on the project teams for as long as the project lasts. In the matrix organization, each expert has at least two superiors: the superior in the functional division, and the project leader. Experts may find themselves serving on more than one project team at a time in the matrix organization, which means they may have more than two direct bosses.

Figure 14.3
Simplified Matrix Design

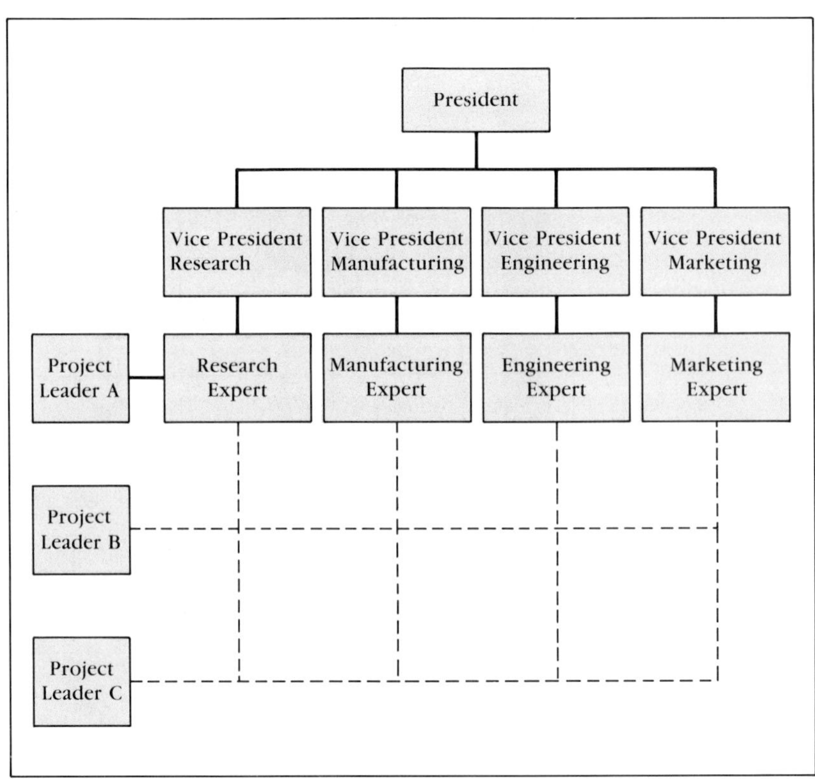

The advantages and disadvantages of the three organizational designs are summarized in Chapter 13. As the organization moves from functional to product to matrix design, the environment becomes increasingly uncertain and dynamic. In addition, the technologies used by the organizations become more complicated in the matrix designs. The organizational development expert must do a thorough diagnosis of the organization's environment and the firm's strategic goals before recommending a particular structure. New structures usually are hybrids of the three configurations discussed.

Quality of Work Life Approaches

Job redesign is such an important concept that it reappears in organizational development. Recall from Chapter 6 that job redesign is the key method for improving quality of work life in the organization. The main principles that govern successful job redesign are:

1. Participation by employees in the redesign process
2. Pushing the planning and doing portions of the job down the hierarchy to the lowest level possible (i.e., vertical job loading)
3. Deciding if job design should be done at the individual or work team level (i.e., semiautonomous work groups

When job redesign is incorporated into organizational development, it is usually broadened. For example, Huse and Cummings state that organizational development job redesign programs typically include the following elements (37):

1. **Participative problem solving.** If this is not possible at first, the organization's culture and climate can be adjusted through team building to establish a basis for effective participation by employee groups.
2. **Work design.** Jobs are changed to better match employee needs and task requirements.
3. **Innovative reward systems.** New compensation systems may be installed along with job redesign. Group based rewards (e.g., Scanlon plan, profit sharing, forms of employee ownership) can complement the quality of work life program.
4. **Work environment improvements.** Environmental engineering might accompany the program. For example, at Volvo's Kalmar assembly facility, the company radically altered the work spaces of assembly teams (see Chapter 6).

As quality of work life programs become more common, the participative base of these programs will expand, and the net effect will be a gradual change across the spectrum of corporate cultures. Quality of work life programs are now well understood in terms of their effects on productivity and employee attitudes. In some instances, these programs are even spreading into new areas of application. For example, quality of work life programs are emerging as a part of negotiated labor contracts (38). Union leaders are recognizing that the needs of union members can be met through a variety of cooperative projects that build better labor-management relations.

Quality of work life experts are realizing that improvements must be made in reward systems to sustain the gains achieved through job redesign. Accordingly, organizations are "rediscovering" incentive systems that mesh with job redesign both at the individual and group level. These new incentive systems are anchored to the work design systems. Employees are also encouraged to suggest ways to cut costs and to improve productivity. When the organization rewards successful employee productivity suggestions, a powerful pathway is created to achievement of both intrinsic and extrinsic rewards. Every employee group has an incentive to become entreprenurial, for employees know that the organization will reward them for their innovative efforts. This basic motivational connection forges new connections between organizational systems and job redesign.

Goal Setting: The Management by Objectives Process

Goal setting has long been recognized as a key organizational activity. The new emphasis on employee participation in goal setting is believed to be a powerful device for increasing employee commitment, job involvement, and performance. **Management by objectives (MBO)** is the method most widely used for establishing goal-setting systems in organizations. Management by objectives is a system designed to improve the goal-setting process. Superiors and subordinates hold meetings (1) to establish goals, (2) to review periodically goal activities and results, and (3) to resolve conflicts or to modify goals as needed. These systems are highly cyclical in nature. MBO experts believe that the following three properties are critical to the success of any management by objectives system (39).

1. **Knowledge of what is expected.** MBO can reduce role conflict and ambiguity for both superiors and subordinates. Reduction of these performance inhibitors is accomplished by formation of common work expectations.
2. **Knowledge of results.** MBO systems place a high priority on performance feedback. In general, the feedback, to be effective, should be supportive, immediate, and focused.
3. **The superior functions as a coach.** The superior works to provide feedback that is task-oriented rather than personality-oriented.

The qualities of MBO systems look a lot like the features of a job redesign program. Are these two approaches to work similar?

The qualities of the successful management by objectives system resemble closely the type of superior-subordinate relationship established in job redesign programs. Compare the three properties of the MBO system with the critical psychological states in the job characteristic model (see Figure 6.1). Both job redesign and MBO systems require improved, open relationships between superiors and subordinates. The key feature of these relationships is the formation and maintenance of trust.

The focus of job redesign and management by objectives varies. Job redesign highlights the features of the job and how the employee feels when he works to fulfill task requirements. Management by objectives focuses on the results of task activities and the provision of regular feedback on performance. Both management by objectives and job redesign rely on autonomy, and in both systems, considerable authority and responsibility are delegated to subordinates. Both systems also have considerable potential for increasing availability of intrinsic rewards. Improving the quality of the superior-subordinate relationship is another key ingredient of both approaches.

Steps in the MBO process. Much information exists on the characteristics and methods of management by objectives. Besides focusing attention on results, an MBO system can be a major feature of the organizational culture and of management philosophy. The common steps in the process are detailed in the following list. Note the emphasis on participation and regularized feedback, and note the prominence of goal refinement and flexibility.

Steps in the MBO Process

1. Members of the department or work unit establish goals and action plans for achieving those goals.
2. Discussion of departmental work goals ensures that everybody understands the goals.
3. Employees in the work unit develop their own action plans for achieving their individual goals. The supervisor participates in one-on-one meetings. The goals are specified clearly and quantified if possible. If they cannot be quantified, time lines should be set.
4. The superior and the subordinate establish performance criteria for assessing success. This is done through mutual discussion.
5. The supervisor conducts formal and informal feedback sessions on a regular basis. These sessions can address both individual and departmental level goals. The supervisor must be aware of every aspect of the employee's progress toward reaching specified goals.
6. The objective-setting system must be documented. All goals should be set down on paper, and both supervisor and subordinates should have their own copy of the agreed upon goals.

MBO systems are frequently installed following insufficient diagnosis of organizational problems. In these cases, the system only addresses the symptoms, not the causes, of organizational problems, and failure of the MBO program will soon follow. Other common reasons for MBO program failure are as follows:

1. Employees develop tunnel vision about results and do not give adequate attention to how task activities should be done.
2. The system degenerates into a "paper chase," with the emphasis on red tape and completing forms in triplicate.
3. Superiors fall into an "either punish or reward" mentality regarding results achieved by subordinates.
4. The participative aspects of the system are soon lost as everyone gets increasingly worried about accomplishing her particular goals (40).

Management by objectives is an important way for organizations to direct systematic effort to achievement of important organizational goals. Programs tend to be more effective when certain aspects of the organizational culture and climate are in place. For example, in the introductory dilemma Susan successfully rebuilt the Tentex culture by using a survey feedback approach coupled with team building. As a result, Tentex became a more open and flexible organization. Once the new work expectations were established for employees, installation of an MBO system to ensure continued accountability would be reasonable.

The Tentex example contains an important message. Organizations should always devote some of their resources to staying in the action research cycle. An ongoing orientation to action research means that the organization looks continually for better ways to accomplish its goals and to meet the needs of its work force. In addition, by adopting an action research management philosophy, the organization is more likely to view organizational development interventions as logical refinements that can be installed at different phases of the organization's existence. When the organization adopts this perspective, it increases its capacity for renewal and for adjusting to new circumstances.

Organizational Development Interventions and Creativity

We have discussed several organizational development intervention categories, but we do not want to give the impression that these methods are unrelated or entirely distinct from one another. An integrated perspective of organizational development demands the reverse point of view. The action research model is based on problem diagnosis and joint action planning by client and change agent. Effective problem diagnosis brings difficulties out in the open, and effective action planning uses solutions from more than one intervention category.

The change agent must guard against the tendency to use only one approach to solve all organizational problems. Indeed, change agents often specialize in a particular intervention. When this is the case, the change agent may tend to avoid systematic problem diagnosis. Even experienced change agents find it difficult to resist the temptation to jump right to the "solution" after top management has identified the "problem." The creative organizational development process is best preserved by sticking to the action research model. As change agent and client organization move through the action research process, they pick and choose aspects of various interventions to solve the organization's unique problems. When organizational development specialists try to become experts in using certain techniques, their client organizations often suffer in the long run.

Knowledge Check

1. Most experts in organizational development would agree that T-groups are the same as team building. T or F?
2. Team building typically concerns itself with the personal development and self-awareness of group members who are strangers to one another. T or F?
3. The fade-out effect refers to erosion of team building improvements in the work setting. T or F?
4. The ___________ organization design uses project groups.
5. Management by objectives is a participative process aimed at improving the organizational climate. T or F?
6. Regular feedback on achievement of performance goals is generally the least important component of a management by objectives program. T or F?

7. The problems associated with management by objectives can generally be avoided if the programs are nonparticipative. T or F?

Answers:

1 F, 2 F, 3 T, 4 matrix, 5 F, 6 F, 7 F

Summary Points

- **Organizational culture** is the organization's system of shared values and beliefs that create a set of norms for employee behavior. When organizational culture is well formed and well communicated, employees have uniformly high expectations about excellence in job performance.
- A healthy organizational culture has these characteristics: (1) **commitment to a common purpose,** (2) **competence to deliver superior performance, and** (3) **consistency in perpetuating commitment and competence.**
- **Organizational climate** consists of stable dimensions that can be measured by questionnaires. The most common dimensions of climate are: **structure, responsibility, reward, risk, warmth, and support.**
- Both culture and climate protect employees and organizational systems from uncertainty and random change. Both organizational features should be periodically assessed to see if they are conforming to the organization's mission and goals.
- **Organizational development** is the systemwide application of behavioral science knowledge to the planned development and reinforcement of strategies, structures, and processes to improve organization effectiveness.
- **Action research** is the organizational development process that generalizes to any behavioral problem in the organization. It is different from traditional business planning in that it relies on data-based change. Action research gradually changes the organization's behavior over time.
- Organizational development interventions can be classified as (1) **interpersonal and group-based change,** (2) **systemwide process change,** (3) **organizational structure and design change,** (4) **quality of work life changes, and** (5) **goal-setting systems changes.**
- **Survey feedback** is a data-based change process that uses **questionnaires** and **interviews** to compile information on current organizational problems. This information is then addressed by employees, and action plans are implemented to correct the problems.
- **Management by objectives** (MBO) has some principles in common with **job redesign.** Both systems are designed to improve the relationship between employees and their job. Management by objectives clarifies work expectations by specifying results to be achieved. The process works best if (1) it is highly participative, (2) it focuses on employee needs and skill development, and (3) paperwork and red tape are minimized.

Questions

1. Using the model of the action research process, develop and describe six of Susan's action research steps in the opening dilemma. What are three organizational development change methods that she used at Tentex?

2. Explain the components of organizational climate, then use those components to analyze the climate in one of your current classes. Choose two dimensions of the class climate that are below par and describe how you would improve them.

3. What are four problems that can surface in MBO systems? What are the major issues that organizations must keep in mind to ensure that management by objectives will be successful?
4. Suppose that an organization hires you to do an intervention similar to the one Susan implemented at Tentex. The company president says that he knows what the problem areas are in his company, so he recommends that you not bother with a diagnosis. He gives you a list of problems and tells you to get on with the solutions. How would you respond to his point of view?
5. Your friend says: "Organizational culture is really just a lot of academic mumbo jumbo. Why don't you business students forget about that kind of stuff?" What would you say to your friend to convince him of the importance of organizational culture?
6. Do you think that the action research model could be applied to make constructive changes in one's personal life? If you believe that the model could be used in this way, develop a change that you would like to make in your own life from the action research perspective.
7. A midlevel manager in a marketing firm made the following statement: "Management by objectives is the best thing that ever happened to this company. Supervisors have found that it's an excellent way to tell employees what their goals should be. Employees resented the MBO approach at first, but now they're falling into line." Please comment on what you think will happen in this company relative to the following:
   a. Employee participation in goal setting.
   b. Emerging management philosophy behind the MBO system.
   c. Impact of the MBO system on aspects of organizational climate and culture.

EXPLORING: *Starting Over*

[Based on: "Starting Over: Business Slump Spurs a Rejuvenation," *Industry Week* (February 4, 1985):29–30.]

Over a two-year period, Mr. Gorcyca, the division manager, implemented a human relations manufacturing plant overhaul. Now machines are arranged in "a family of products cluster." (The serial assembly line concept was scrapped.) A program of "enterprise manufacturing" was installed, and worker's pay increases were pegged to learning to operate several machines in their family products cluster. Workers could receive up to a 7 percent increase for each new machine they mastered. Now employees sit in on management staff meetings as well.

The division's management structure was flattened, so each manager now has a span of control of ten employees. Quality circles were installed, and a new corporate culture was encouraged. Status symbols were eliminated, including the reserved parking spaces for managers.

The effects have been astounding. Production time for valves has been cut by 20 percent. Productivity per employee has jumped nearly 80 percent, and the scrap rate has dropped from 15 to 5 percent. The "family of products" clusters are much more responsive than the old assembly line to orders with short delivery time. Employees have reacted well to the program, and their suggestions have cut retooling time from 1.5 days to just 3 hours on some processes!

Employees are also optimistic that a new era of improved labor-management relations is at hand. For example, Tom Karr, a manager, says that he now takes his turn—one week every few months—pitching in to help clean the lunchroom. He also has difficulty finding a parking place on occasion. He used to have a reserved parking space right next to his office entrance. That was before Mr. Gorcyca launched his "cultural revolution"!

Discussion Questions:

1. What dimensions of the organizational culture did Mr. Gorcyca's program influence?
2. Why do teamwork and quality circles seem to play an important role in programs designed to change organizational culture?
3. What might be some of the fears of management when confronted with a program like Mr. Gorcyca's?

APPLYING: *The On-Site Visit*

Jeremy was visiting with Andrew Wells, Director of Personnel at Basic Products, Inc. Jeremy had been invited for a job interview. He and five other university seniors had been selected to visit the company's headquarters. Jeremy was interested in the company and had done considerable research on their products and sales performance. The financial characteristics of Basic Products looked good. Furthermore, the firm had come out with four new products last year, and all of them were doing well in the marketplace. As Jeremy waited for his flight, he thought about several aspects of the interview that had troubled him.

He wondered why everyone seemed so harried at company headquarters. Andrew's secretary had hardly responded to Jeremy's light conversation while Jeremy waited in the outer office for Andrew to begin the company tour at 8:00 A.M. He had tried to start a conversation about company success, but she seemed indifferent. Later in the morning, Jeremy met with a group of new employees who were being rotated through various work divisions as part of their on-the-job training. Several of the trainees complained about lack of supervisory interest in new ideas. This had clearly frustrated the trainees who had been told by recruiters that Basic really valued innovative employee ideas. Jeremy had asked the group about the quality of Basic's incentive system, but none of the trainees was able to explain the system to him.

During the afternoon, Jeremy met with his potential boss (if Jeremy got the job offer). His name was Sam. During this meeting, Sam's assistant entered the room and handed Sam a schedule of proposed production runs. After a quick glance, Sam threw the schedule back at the subordinate, told him the report was "lousy," and that he'd "better check those figures with Phil in assembly." The flustered assistant left the office immediately. Later, Jeremy overheard Sam's assistant describing the incident in very negative terms to a friend. The assistant's friend simply shook her head and said "So what else is new?"

The last part of Jeremy's visit was spent in the production area. He noticed that many employees were standing around talking while maintenance engineers worked on assembly line equipment. Several employees seemed to be engaged in some horseplay with unpainted parts. Jeremy asked his guide if employees were required to keep their own work area clean. His guide replied that most of the workers on the day shift left clean-up to the night shift workers. In response to this treatment, the night shift workers often left the parts bins by the machines empty for the day shift workers.

Jeremy's final observation about Basic Inc. concerned the parking lot. Company executives had reserved parking spaces under the large shade trees near the main entrance. Clerical workers and plant employees had to park in a larger lot on the other side of a busy road. As he waited for his plane, Jeremy tried to picture what it would be like to work at Basic.

Discussion Questions

1. What features of Basic's organizational climate can you identify?
2. Based on the information presented in this chapter, would you say that different climates exist at Basic? Be sure to comment on climate as perceived by new employees, climate in administration versus production, and climate as perceived by department heads and midlevel managers.
3. Should Jeremy take a job with Basic? Use your knowledge of organizational climate and culture to explain why you think he should or should not take the job if it is offered.

Suggested Readings

Barnes, L. 1981. Managing the Paradox of Organizational Trust. *Harvard Business Review,* (March–April 1981):107–116.

This article has direct bearing on the important issue of how change agents and consultants acquire the trust and support of client organizations in interventions.

Bluestsone, I. 1980. How Quality of Worklife Projects Work for the United Auto Workers. *Monthly Labor Review* 103:39–41.

Fordyce, J., and Weil, R. 1979. *Managing With People: A Manager's Handbook of Organizational Development Methods.* Reading, Mass.: Addison-Wesley.

French, W., and Bell, C., Jr. 1984. *Organization Development: Behavioral Science Interventions for Organization Improvement,* 3rd ed. 1984. Englewood Cliffs, N.J.: Prentice Hall.

This excellent book describes clearly and in detail the "territory of OD." The authors do a good job of illustrating OD concepts with examples of organizational experiences.

Galbraith, J. 1982. Designing the Innovating Organization. *Organizational Dynamics* 5–25.

Jackson, J. 1981. Using Management by Objectives: Case Studies of Four Attempts. *Personnel Administrator* (1981):78–81.

Mares, W., and Simmons, J. 1983. *Working Together: From Shopfloor to Corporate Boardroom.* New York: Knopf.

Miles, R., and Rosenberg, H. 1982. The Human-Resource Approach to Management: Second-Generation Issues. *Organizational Dynamics* (Winter 1982):26–41.

Nadler, D. 1976. The Use of Feedback for Organizational Change. *Group and Organizational Studies* 177–186.

Swartz, H., and Davis, S. 1981. Matching Corporate Culture and Business Strategy. *Organizational Dynamics* (Summer 1981):30–48.

References

1. Smircich, L. 1983. Concepts of Culture and Organizational Analysis. *Administrative Science Quarterly* 28:339–358.
2. Porras, J., and Berg, P. 1978. The Impact of Organizational Development. *Academy of Management Review* 3:249–266.
3. Peters, T., and Waterman, R., Jr. 1982. *In Search of Excellence.* New York: Harper & Row.
4. Hickman, C., and Silva, M. 1984. *Creating Excellence: Managing Corporate Culture, Strategy, and Change in the New Age.* New York: NAC Books.
5. *Wall Street Journal,* 17 April 1986.
6. Peters, T., and Waterman, R., Jr., op. cit.
7. Ibid.
8. Porras, J., and Berg, P., op cit.
9. Hickman, C., and Silva, M., op. cit.

10. A Straight Talking Tycoon Becomes a Superstar. *Time* (1 April 1985).
11. *Time,* Ibid.
12. Pascale, R., and Athos, A. 1981. *The Art of Japanese Management: Applications for American Executives.* New York: Simon & Schuster.
13. Litwin, G., and Stringer, R. 1968. *Motivation and Organizational Climate.* Boston, Mass.: Graduate School of Business Administration, Harvard University.
14. Taguiri, R., and Litwin, G., eds. 1968. *Organizational Climate: Explorations of a Concept.* Boston, Mass.: Graduate School of Business Administration, Harvard University.
15. Field, R., and Abelson, M. 1982. Climate: A Reconceptualization and Proposed Model. *Human Relations* 35:181–201.
16. Schneider, B., and Reichers, A. 1983. On the Etiology of Climates. *Personnel Psychology* 36:19–40.
17. Litwin, G., Humphrey, J., and Wilson, T. 1978. Organizational Climate: A Proven Tool for Improving Performance. In W. Burke, ed. *The Cutting Edge: Current Theory and Practice in Organization Development.* La Jolla, Calif.: University Associates, pp. 187–205.
18. Likert, R. 1967. *New Patterns of Management,* 2nd ed. New York: McGraw-Hill.
19 Sethia, N., and Von Glinow, M. 1985. Managing Organizational Culture by Managing the Reward System. In R. Kilman, M. Saxton, and R. Serpa, eds. *Managing Corporate Culture.* San Francisco: Jossey Bass.
20. Huse, E., and Cummings, T. 1985. *Organization Development and Change,* 3rd ed. St. Paul, Minn.: West Publishing.
21. Ibid.
22. Nadler, D. 1977. *Feedback and Organizational Development: Using Data-Based Methods.* Reading, Mass.: Addison-Wesley.
23. French, W., and Bell, C. 1978. *Organizational Development: Behavioral Science Interventions for Organizational Improvement,* 2nd ed. Englewood Cliffs, N.J.: Prentice-Hall.
24. Huse, E., and Cummings, T., op. cit.
25. Marrow, A. 1967. Events Leading to the Establishment of the National Training Laboratories. *Journal of Applied Behavioral Science* 3:145–150.
26. Huse, E., and Cummings, T., op. cit.
27. Ibid.
28. Ibid.
29. Bowers, D. 1973. OD Techniques and Their Results in 23 Organizations: The Michigan IGL Study. *Journal of Applied Behavioral Science* 9:21–43.
30. Huse, E., and Cummings, T., op. cit.
31. Kimberly, J., and Nielsen, W. 1975. Organizational Development and Change in Organizational Performance. *Administrative Science Quarterly* 20:191–206.
32. Ibid.
33. Friedlander, F., and Brown, L. 1974. Organizational Development. In M. Rosenzweig and L. Porter, eds. *Annual Review of Psychology.* Palo Alto, Calif.: Annual Reviews.
34. Boss, W. 1985. *Journal of Applied Behavioral Science* 18:15–23.
35. Ibid.
36. Bowers, D., op. cit.
37. Huse, E., and Cummings, T., op. cit.
38. Drexler, J., Jr. 1977. A Union Management Cooperative Project to Improve the Quality of Work Life. *Journal of Applied Behavioral Science* 13:373–386.
39. Huse, E. 1966. Putting in a Management Development Plan That Works. *California Managment Review* 9:73–80.
40. Levinson, H. 1970. Management by Whose Objectives? *Harvard Business Review* 48:125–143.

The External Environment

Chapter **15**

I. Dilemma: Management in the Next Century
II. Factors in the Macroenvironment
III. Social Responsibility
  A. Considerations that guide socially responsible behavior
  B. Successful ethical inquiries
IV. Unions and Employee Rights
  A. Union membership
  B. Management's response to changes
V. Emerging Trends in the Environment
  A. Megatrends
  B. Four specific trends
VI. Summary Points
VII. Questions
VIII. Exploring: Stater Brothers Fired Chief Finds Power in the Union
IX. Applying: You're the Judge
X. Suggested Readings
XI. References

Chapter Goals

By the end of this chapter, you will be able to:

1. Identify the factors present in the organization's environment that affect organizational and employee behavior.
2. Identify two dimensions that define the impact of the environment on the organization.
3. Give examples of two coping strategies that organizations can use to adapt to change in the environment.
4. List the areas of social responsibility for organizations.
5. List questions to ask to guide corporate decisionmaking to ensure that outcomes are socially responsible.
6. Analyze the implications of the decrease in union membership and power in terms of employee rights through legal action.
7. List at least three management actions to accommodate changes in the legal environment.
8. List at least five emerging trends in the environment that affect organizations and managers.

Dilemma Management in the Next Century

Imagine that it's the year 2000. You have just finished college and are interviewing with several companies for a job as a manager. Today you had an interview with the SBH Hospital, which employs about 2,000 people and runs a hospital, nursing home, and several ancillary clinics. The interview consisted of talking with the personnel manager and taking a tour of the facilities.

During your interview with the personnel manager, Joanna Reid, she described the hospital's operating philosophy: "We consider ourselves to be very 'people oriented.' Everything we do here is based on the kind of people we employ and what their needs are. If we have a problem, we involve our employees in the solution, get their ideas, and try to find a way to overcome it. Anyone who works here has to have the same philosophy. It's the way things are now."

At the end of the day, you collect your thoughts and try to put together a mental picture of the hospital. The following facts come to mind:

1. All employees are organized in work groups, which function autonomously. A group may have many workers with different jobs. There is considerable trading of jobs among employees, since each person is usually able to do several tasks.
2. The groups have no formal manager, but there is a team leader who serves as a resource when needed.
3. Although each team has some "good jobs" and some "bad jobs," no one is assigned permanently to any one job. For example, there are no nurses' aides; everyone takes a turn at doing the more menial tasks.
4. Screening of job applicants is done primarily by the team.
5. The pay system is geared to the number of different jobs a person can perform, not to seniority or job type. Team members teach one another their jobs and sometimes teach members of other teams as well, so the majority of employees in the hospital earn the highest wage level.
6. Employees are in charge of their own quality control, and occasionally they are sent to see patients.

7. There are no set working hours except for a narrow range of core hours during the day and a requirement that employees work a minimum number of hours during each three-month period. Each team decides its own work schedule, which is constructed around the core hours.
8. All employees share the same parking lot and eating facilities. Ample space is reserved for group activities and meetings.
9. A joint policy-making board governs the entire hospital operation. Employees elect representatives to sit on this board. Although only three employee representatives sit on the twelve-person board, it is understood that any board member has the right to veto any proposal or decision.
10. The hospital does not have a performance appraisal system. Group members do a peer evaluation of other members, and these evaluations are then discussed in group sessions. Each group designs its own evaluation process with input from personnel.
11. The hospital policy on fringe benefits allows employees a choice of benefits packages. Each year many employees trade their paid sick leave for an extra week's vacation provided, of course, that the team agrees to carry their load during the extra week off.
12. Once a year, a representative from each team attends a two-day retreat with other team representatives to discuss the year's performance and to set goals for the coming year.
13. The hospital business is experiencing enormous turmoil, so employees are often asked to try new jobs with little notice.

After considering these points, you begin to realize that this organization is very different from the ones you studied in school. You are now trying to understand the organization from a macro perspective, and you are also wondering whether you have the skills necessary to work in this hospital (1).

Questions

1. What are the critical environmental elements that will guide your decisions if you go to work for this organization?
2. What skills are most needed by employees to perform well in the type of organization used by SBH Hospital?
3. What are the key social responsibility issues of SBH Hospital?
4. How will managers and employees solve problems concerning employee rights?

Factors in the Macroenvironment

All organizations operate within a larger context, which is generally referred to as the **macroenvironment.** This environment is composed of several factors that directly affect the behavior of individuals within a particular organization. Our purpose in this chapter is to develop a framework for analyzing the more important components of the macroenvironment and to show how those components affect human behavior within the organization.

Figure 15.1 is a graphic illustration of the key macroenvironmental factors (2). While all of the factors are important in terms of the organization and its behavior, we focus here on two major areas that have influenced employee and managerial behavior repeatedly in organizations. The first area, **culture,** has been the focus of renewed interest from various sectors of the business community. Of particular note in environmental culture is the **social responsibility** of an organization, that is, the responsibility of an organization to make decisions and choices which are morally and legally in the best interests of society. In the last 20 years, the second area, **human resources,** has undergone major changes that have had an enormous impact on organizations. Of particular note are the changes in labor unions.

These two areas are our major focus in this chapter. Lastly, a third section explores some of the future environmental trends that we predict will affect organizations, especially as those trends represent megatrends in our society.

How do these factors affect the organization?

The impact of environmental factors is primarily on the amount of uncertainty created for the organization (3). Organizations, to be effective, must cope with and manage uncertainty. Decision makers have more or less information about environmental factors, which allows them to feel more or less certain about the decisions they make. The amount of uncertainty affects the risk of failure surrounding organizational actions and affects the ability of organization members to act in a consistent manner.

The computer industry is a prime example of how a change in environment can create great uncertainty within organizations. Computer

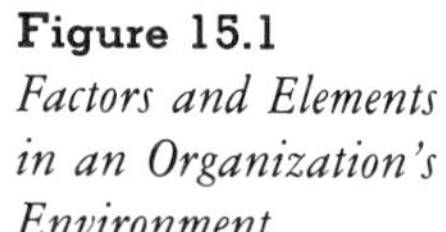

Figure 15.1
Factors and Elements in an Organization's Environment

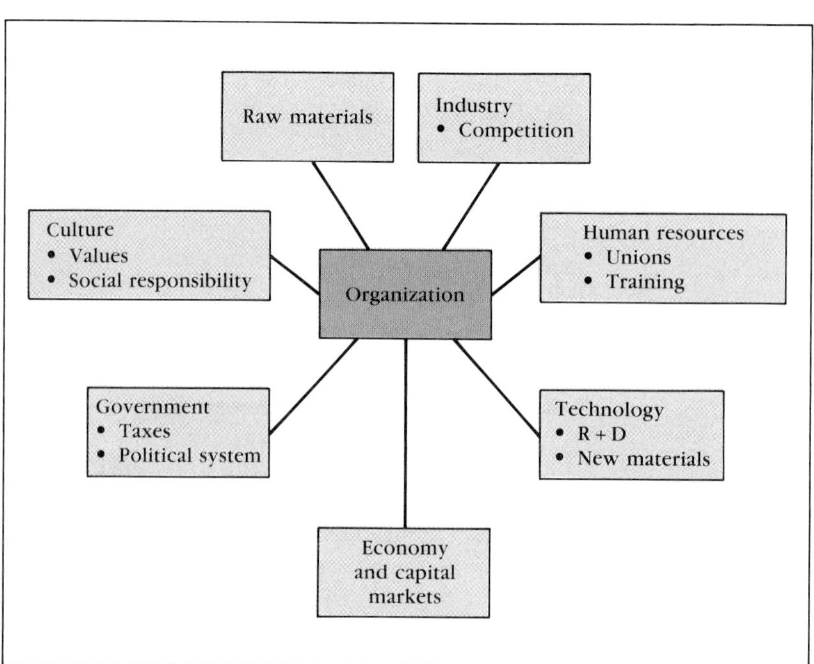

buyers have not purchased as many computers as predicted (4). Manufacturers usually buy one third of all computers, but because manufacturing has been in a slump, these businesses did not purchase as predicted. Still other companies are waiting to examine new models, instead of purchasing present inventory. Many individuals are shying away from the purchase of a personal computer because the machines are perceived as hard to use. Most businesses want networking of all computers, but the technology is not present. Finally, confused by too many choices, buyers are sitting still (5).

In a more systematic vein, the impact of the environment on the organization can be analyzed along two dimensions: first, the extent to which external domains are stable or unstable, and second, the extent to which external domains are simple or complex (see Figure 15.2) (6).

Environmental complexity. The number of external factors and their elements that are relevant to an organization's operations define the **environmental complexity.** In a simple environment, only one or two external factors may have a significant influence on the organization. A complex environment may involve nearly all of the observable factors.

In the late 1970s and early 1980s, Chrysler Corporation faced a complex environment. The market for automobiles was changing. Customers wanted smaller cars that were built with quality. The economy was experiencing a recession, and the automobile industry was experiencing a lot of competition from the Japanese. Few financial institutions were willing to lend money to Chrysler, suppliers were not as willing to extend credit to the company, and unions were worried about job security. All of these factors seemed to affect Chrysler at once, causing the organization to pursue its only hope, a federally guaranteed loan.

Figure 15.2
Impact of the Environment on the Organization

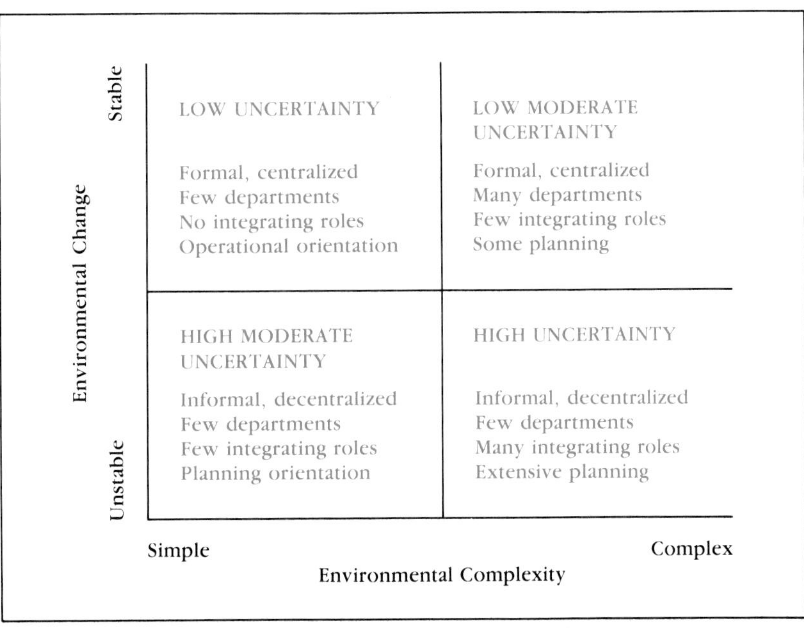

Environmental change. The impact of the environment on the organization can be analyzed along a second dimension labeled **environmental change.** This dimension refers to the stability of the elements in the environment. A stable environment will not present an organization with many unpredictable events; an unstable environment will.

Public utility companies and other highly regulated organizations generally face stable environments because they can predict how the various factors in the environment would respond to rate changes, for example. AT&T found out what happens when this stability is upset by deregulation and divestiture. The company was required by the courts to break up its monopoly and to compete in the marketplace like any other organization. The new AT&T found itself responding to an entirely new environment, which was much less stable than the old one. As a result, many changes were made in the company, including a reduction of the work force by more than 20 percent.

Solving the Dilemma

What are the critical environmental elements that will guide your decisions if you go to work for this organization?

The critical environmental factors are the culture and the human resources (see Figure 15.1). The culture offers a unique set of elements that are influencing the company. It is a variable that probably meshes with the internal environment to create a climate that is highly responsive to employees. The human resource element is a factor for nonunion activity and contains a labor force able and willing to accept the culture.

Figure 15.2 shows how to assess the impact of environment on the organization. The two dimensions, environmental change and environmental complexity, are placed at right angles to form a grid. Four conditions result:

1. Low uncertainty—small number of external elements that remain the same or change slowly.
2. Low moderate uncertainty—large number of external elements that remain the same or change slowly.
3. High moderate uncertainty—small number of external elements that are changing continuously.
4. High uncertainty—large number of external elements that are changing continuously.

Organizations placed in one of these four environmental conditions tend to have certain characteristics. These characteristics are listed in Figure 15.2.

Companies can be categorized according to the type of environment they face. For example, the airlines have found that deregulation has brought an increased chance of profits, but increased competition and a complex environment as well, which is undergoing change (i.e., high uncertainty). On the other hand, legal services have enjoyed a relatively smooth, stable, and uncomplex environment, which has allowed these organizations to predict environmental changes and to structure the organization to survive (i.e., low uncertainty). Figure 15.3 illustrates this line of discussion by providing additional examples of industries categorized by environment conditions. One of the major challenges facing business organizations is how to cope with the macroenvironment.

What can organizations do to cope with the environment?

Organizations generally follow two coping techniques (7). First, the organization can change internally by altering the design, internal work patterns, policies, and planning systems. Second, the organization can try to change the external environmental conditions. In short, one technique is reactive, and the other is proactive.

Table 15.1 analyzes these two coping techniques in terms of environmental effects on the organization. The techniques are divided into the two areas mentioned, that is, **internal reactive responses** and **external proactive responses** (8). The techniques suggest that there is a meshing of the environment and how the organization's response to the environment. For example, a good fit occurs when an organization that is structured informally and decentralized with few departments is operating in an unstable yet relatively simple environment, such as an emerging computer company in the microcomputer industry. A bad fit would be to have a company that is lobbying hard for changes in government regulation when the environment is stable and simple. This is like rocking the boat for excitement when the lake is calm.

Figure 15.3
Examples of Industries According to Impact of Environment on the Organization

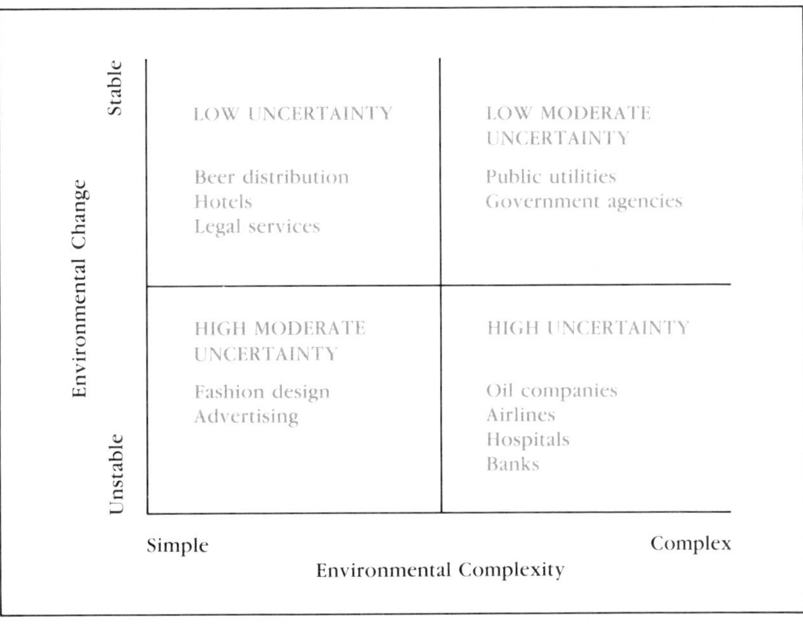

Table 15.1
Two Coping Techniques to Respond to Environmental Factors

If	*An Internal Response May Be:*	*A Response to the Environment May Be:*
Changes are infrequent and in single elements (i.e., simple, stable)	▪ Take an operational orientation ▪ Keep the structure formal and centralized ▪ Have few departments	▪ Grow within areas of operations ▪ Find cheaper suppliers and advertise ▪ Appoint influential customers and suppliers to the board
Changes are infrequent but occur in clusters (i.e., complex, stable)	▪ Do some planning ▪ Have many departments ▪ Keep structure formal and centralized ▪ Require few integrating roles	▪ Advertise ▪ Diversify operations and use mergers ▪ Acquire a company that can offset environmental uncertainty
Changes are frequent but occur in single elements (i.e., unstable, simple)	▪ Take a planning orientation ▪ Keep the structure informed and decentralized ▪ Have few departments and few integrating roles	▪ Advertise ▪ Engage in a political lobby to erect barriers against foreign competition ▪ Pool resources through association
Changes are frequent and occur in clusters (i.e., unstable, complex)	▪ Keep structure informal and decentralized ▪ Have many departments and many integrating roles ▪ Use extensive planning and forecasting	▪ Establish favorable linkages through mergers and joint ventures ▪ Hire new executives ▪ Seek new environmental relationships that are less volatile ▪ Diversify

SOURCE: Adapted from Pfeffer, J., and Salancik, G.R. 1978. *The External Control of Organizations: A Resource Dependent Perspective.* New York: Harper & Row, p. 138.

Knowledge Check

1. The major impact of environmental factors on the organization is the amount of uncertainty faced by decision makers. T or F?
2. Environmental factors can best be understood in terms of change and complexity. T or F?
3. When the environment is more complex, the organization is more likely to have a simple, centralized structure. T or F?
4. A stable yet highly complex environment leads to:
   a. low uncertainty
   b. low moderate uncertainty

c. high moderate uncertainty
d. high uncertainty

5. An effective proactive response to an unstable, complex environment would be to:
   a. do nothing; wait it out
   b. change areas of business operation
   c. restructure the company
   d. establish a planning department

6. An example of a fit between environment and organization structure would be:
   a. few departments in a simple environment
   b. no integrating roles in a complex environment
   c. planning orientation in a simple, stable environment
   d. many integrating roles and a merger strategy in a simple environment

Answers:
1 T, 2 T, 3 F, 4 b, 5 b, 6 a

Solving the Dilemma

What skills are most needed by employees to perform well in the type of organization used by SBH Hospital?

Interpersonal skills and planning are paramount. Interpersonal skills will help employees to solve conflicts on their own, to participate more effectively in autonomous work groups, and to create a general network of productive relationships. Planning skills will help employees anticipate developments in the complex, changing business environment of the health care industry. While technical skills will always be important, the new environment presented in the dilemma calls for more human relations skills than have been required in other organizational settings.

Social Responsibility

Many recent events have increased the demands that organizations act with more social responsibility. In short, many observers of business believe that organizations should be responsible for more than their legal obligations. They insist that the decisions and behavior of organizations should also be ethical and should contribute to the good of society. In this context, **social responsibility** is defined as the organization's willingness and ability to participate in solving society's critical problems and to act ethically while conducting business.

Some of the events that have raised questions about the social responsibility of companies include the following:

1. Union Carbide India, Ltd., a subsidiary of the U.S. Union Carbide Corporation, operated a plant in Bhopal, India. The plant produced methyl isocyanate, a colorless chemical compound that affects humans and animals like a lethal form of tear gas. A chemical leak at the Bhopal plant caused over 2,500 deaths in one week, and an estimated 150,000 injuries. Union Carbide management had not informed the Bhopal plant of a report (dated three months prior to the disaster) that warned of a possible problem in the production of the chemical. The Bhopal plant personnel did not receive the same training as their U.S. counterparts (9).
2. Three corporate officials of Film Recovery Systems, Inc., each faced a minimum 20–year prison term for an employee death that resulted from unsafe plant conditions. President Steven J. O'Neil admitted that he was aware of the dangers of working with cyanide, the cause of at least one worker's death. After some time, he also conceded that he knew that plant workers were becoming ill (10).
3. For years corporate directors were protected from liability for faulty decisions by the so-called business judgment rule. This rule says, in effect, that the courts will not second-guess decisions made by a board, provided that the board has taken "prudent steps to make an informed judgment." In 1985, however, a Delaware court found the directors of The Trans Union Corporation, a diversified holding company, to be in breach of their fiduciary responsibility by selling the company on an irresponsible basis. If found guilty, the ten directors will have to pay stockholders their fair share (11).
4. T. Boone Pickens buys Phillips Petroleum stock, and Phillips worries about a takeover. Pickens says that he'll sell back the stock at a premium, and he does. Carl Icahn tries to take over Phillips. Most observers say that Icahn is bluffing and won't come up with the needed cash. (Even Icahn's backers confess that Icahn doesn't really want the company; he just wants to make money on the situation by selling the stock at a higher price). Icahn and Pickens have done this before to other companies. The public cries "foul"!

These are only a few of the many recent examples of how companies and individuals can act irresponsibly toward society. Not every case of social irresponsibility is illegal either, as evidenced by investors who take over companies for no reason other than personal gain. At present, extending the discussion of organizational social responsibility to encompass public concerns is mostly a voluntary response on the part of organizational members. Legal sanctions usually come only after many problems have been created by socially irresponsible companies.

NOW IT'S YOUR TURN . . .

One way to explore opinion about a subject is to examine the extreme views of the topic. The following exercise is best done with a group of people to better understand your views and their views concerning the social responsibility of organizations.

1. Rate your response to each statement by yourself.
2. Join a group with others who have completed the questionnaire.

3. For each statement, arrive at a concensus on the answer. Observe the following guidelines:
   a. You cannot vote. You must discuss the statements to reach a concensus.
   b. If you cannot decide on an answer, you may reword the sentence slightly.
   c. Try to avoid using the "U" option.

Exercise on Social Responsibility

Answer each question with TA (Thoroughly Agree), A (Agree), U (Undecided), D (Disagree), or TD (Thoroughly Disagree)

1. ______ All discussions of business strategy *must* include considerations of ethical issues.
2. ______ Businesses should be *required* only to live up to their legal obligations for ethical conduct.
3. ______ Ethical conduct of organizations must vary according to the country in which the firm does business.
4. ______ Ultimately, the chief executive officer is the only one responsible for a company's ethical behavior.
5. ______ The range of corporate involvement for *social* responsibility is limited to the local community.
6. ______ All boards of directors should be required to have a public responsibility committee.
7. ______ Organizations must *demonstrate* the extent to which they have met their social responsibility goals.
8. ______ The concept of social responsibility of companies is too vague to warrant serious attention.
9. ______ The government should enact specific laws that address corporate social responsibility.

What is a company's range of involvement for being socially responsible?

Table 15.2 lists different ranges of involvement and gives an example of a socially responsible and socially irresponsible organization action in each range. (12)

Notice how far-reaching a particular company decision can be. One manager in an organization may decide to allow slippage in safety standards of equipment used in foreign operations. The result may be widespread accidents that affect many people in various parts of the world.

Everyone in the company must take responsibility. Table 15.2 underscores the importance of everyone in the organization acting in a socially responsible manner and the importance of the organization's implementing a means of control to ensure ethical behavior. These control mechanisms are the focus of our next discussion.

Table 15.2
Areas for Social Responsibility of a Company

Range of Involvement	*Example of Socially Responsible Behavior*	*Example of Socially Irresponsible Behavior*
The World	▪ French company undertaking joint venture in an African country to develop local management rather than insisting on full ownership	▪ U.S. company helping a revolutionary group because "it's good for business"
	▪ Training nationals to perform skilled jobs rather than import labor	▪ Using lower safety standards for foreign operation
The Nation	▪ Upholding affirmative action for hiring various groups of employees	▪ Leaving a product on the market after reports indicate that the product has been tampered with
	▪ Participating actively in United Way campaigns	
The Local Community	▪ Contributing profits to socially needed programs, to education, and the arts	▪ Polluting the environment because the fine costs less than installing pollution-preventing equipment
	▪ Hiring local people	▪ Not providing support during a local disaster
Industry	▪ Enforcing product standards beyond those legally required for the industry	▪ Knowingly introducing a drug not fully tested for side effects
		▪ Cheating customers because others in the industry are doing it
The Company	▪ Not complying with the boss's request to falsify safety reports on a new product	▪ Firing employees who do not comply with sexual advances made by executives
	▪ Firing subcontractors because they do not adhere to the company's ethical standards	▪ Not warning workers of health risks associated with their work

SOURCE: Adapted from Andrews, K.R. 1980. *The Concept of Corporate Strategy,* revised ed. Homewood, Ill.: Richard D. Irwin.

Considerations that Guide Socially Responsible Behavior

A socially responsible management must consider and agree on three basic attitudes. First, management must have an awareness of the firm's obligations to solve some of the problems facing society. This awareness of social problems must take into account the firm's customers, owners, employees, suppliers, creditors, management, government, and community. Second, there must be a willingness on the part of the firm to help solve some social problems. Not all of the problems of society can be solved by business organizations, but the firm must be willing to tackle some of them. Third, and more specifically, the firm must attempt to make decisions and to actually commit various resources to solving those problems.

Solving the Dilemma

What are the key social responsibility issues of SBH Hospital?

The most important issues will probably involve employee rights and the local community. One emerging trend is a renewed emphasis on local politics and local control of social issues (see the last section of this chapter). Organizations will have to assume more responsibility for worker satisfaction and for making sure that employees receive fair treatment in the workplace. SBH Hospital could have employee groups set up to monitor whether the hospital is being socially responsible and responsive.

To be socially responsible, an organization must be active, not passive. To be active is to search continually for better solutions both to problems that may be the pressing issues of the day and to problems that are as yet unperceived by the unsuspecting public. Social responsibility is not simply conforming to the rules and regulations. It demands that one go far beyond legal expectations, to explore the ethical features of business decisions.

Successful Ethical Inquiries

To examine the ethics of a manager's business decision, we suggest that the following series of questions be asked (13). These questions can be used when a major decision may have implications for acting socially responsible. Note that questions 7 through 10 deal directly with open disclosure. These questions are usually most effective in disclosing socially irresponsible acts inherent in a business decision.

Twelve Questions for Examining the Ethics of a Business Decision

1. Have you defined the problem accurately?
2. How would you define the problem if you stood on the other side of the fence?
3. How did this situation occur in the first place?
4. To whom and to what do you give your loyalty as a person and as a member of the corporation?
5. What is your intention in making this decision?
6. How does this intention compare with the probable results?
7. Whom could your decision or action injure?
8. Can you discuss the problem with the affected parties before you make your decision?
9. Are you confident that your position will be as valid over a long period of time as it seems now?
10. Could you disclose without qualm your decision or action to your boss, your CEO, the board of directors, your family, and society as a whole?
11. What is the symbolic potential of your action if understood? If misunderstood?
12. Under what conditions would you allow exceptions to your stand?

Table 15.3 provides some indications of how an organization can encourage socially responsible behavior. Like the list of questions for examining one's ethics, Table 15.3 has three major themes:

1. Organization managers must set an example of ethical conduct if the rest of the organization is to support the firm's goals of social responsibility.
2. The process of problem solving in a socially responsible way must be active, not reactive (i.e., a response to unforeseen events).
3. Socially responsible behavior is *not* a luxury in today's business environment. It is, rather, an extremely important area of business activity that is the responsibility of everyone in the organization.

In short, one major goal is for organizations to ensure that they are being socially responsible. A second area of environmental activity that affects the organization significantly is unions. This environmental factor is the focus of the next section.

Unions and Employee Rights

The study of unions and the changes they are experiencing is an interesting example of how environments influence organizations. Unions are declining in American business. With this decline, however, has come an increase in strength of the legal environment. As one factor (unions) has decreased in importance and influence on the organization this loss of power has strengthened another factor (the legal environment), which has gained in prominence.

Table 15.3
Conditions of Successful Ethical Inquiries

Condition	*Possible Action*
Fixed time frame	Take specific time to ponder the problem.
Unconventional location	Hold important discussions away from the office.
Resource	Use an outsider to help stimulate discussion.
Participation of CEO	Discussions need the perspective and legitimization of the key authority in the organization.
Credo	Articulating the corporation's values and objectives provides a reference point for group inquiry and implementation. The *process* of articulation is as useful as the values agreed on.
Homegrown topics	The inquiry should draw on the company's experience.
Resolution	There should be some resolution: either a vote on the issue, adoption of a new policy, a timetable for implementation, or formulation of a specific statement of values.

SOURCE: Nash, L. 1981. Ethics without the sermon. *Harvard Business Review* (Nov.–Dec. 1981):81.

The purpose of this section is to explain the change from employee reliance on union strength to reliance on the legal system to uphold employee rights. This change has many implications in terms of management and employee behavior, particularly in environments that are traditionally dominated by union influence.

What are unions?

A **labor union** is an association of employees, which has as its main purpose the influencing of employee decisions about conditions of employment. From the employee's perspective, it is an external component that can influence greatly the company's activities. For example, a unionized employee is responsible to a company supervisor for work output and to a union representative or **steward** for union activities.

Unions originated in Great Britain and the United States in the late 18th and early 19th centuries as associations of workers who had the same skill. At first, unions were formed in part as social clubs, but they soon became increasingly concerned with improving wages and working conditions through collective bargaining. With growing industrialization, the local associations banded together to form national unions. The focus changed quickly, too, to an economic one.

Why unions began. Labor unions arose out of the combined protest of workers and intellectuals against a social and political system based on discrimination (e.g., discrimination surrounding ancestry, social status, and income). Because of the discrimination against workers, both personal and collective in nature, employees had few avenues for their advancement. During the early years of unionization, the labor unions thus became the instruments for improving working conditions, wages, and other desired outcomes.

Union Membership

Between 1950 and 1985, union membership has dropped from about one third of the non-farm work force to less than 18 percent. Membership may be stronger in some industries than in others (e.g., construction and shipping versus high technology), but most commentators suggest that unions are slowly eroding as a force in American business (14).

The weakening of unions is one force stimulating the growth of an employee rights movement that will quite possibly forge revolutionary changes in the workplace and in the way companies manage people. At the same time, the courts and the state legislatures are becoming effective champions of employee rights. Managers who think they are obtaining a union-free environment, may in fact be obtaining a legalized environment instead.

What are the implications of this change?

The implications of this change from unionization to an employee rights environment are important for both employees and management to understand. Collective bargaining will yield increasingly to public law (15). When a problem evolves in the workplace, an employee will be more likely to look to a lawyer rather than to a shop steward.

One recent and interesting legal change involves the boss's right to fire. The following case illustrates the varied factual situations and the variety of claims that may accompany an allegation of unlawful discharge and a subsequent judicial exception to the "termination at will" rule (16).

Debra Agis was employed as a waitress by the Howard Johnson Company at a restaurant known as the Ground Round. Defendant Dionne notified all waitresses at a meeting that there was "some stealing going on" at the restaurant, but the identity of the culprit(s) was not known. He also said that until it was determined who was responsible, he would begin firing all waitresses in alphabetical order, starting with the letter "A." Dionne then fired Debra Agis.

Agis sought to recover damages from the owner and manager of the restaurant for mental anguish and emotional distress allegedly caused by her summary dismissal. Her husband sought to recover damages for loss of services, love, affection, and companionship of his wife. The Supreme Judicial Court of Massachusetts held that the complaint stated a cause of action for intentional or reckless infliction of severe emotional distress, without resulting bodily injury, and that her husband had a cause of action arising out of that distress.

Federal and state courts have long held to a "termination at will" rule under which an employer in a private institution may terminate an employee, with or without specific cause, in the absence of a written employment agreement. The rule is based on the assumption of mutuality, that is, that the employee may quit at any time, without notice and for any reason, and therefore the employer may likewise discharge the employee at any time without notice and for any reason. Employment relationships that are not covered by a contract or a collective bargaining agreement are therefore considered to be "at will" in that they continue to exist only at the pleasure of either party, and either party may terminate that relationship for any reason. This rule of termination at will, also called "absolute right to discharge," is being modified gradually and challenged by various courts and legislative bodies (17).

Solving the Dilemma

How will management and employees solve problems concerning employee rights?

This organization would be unique in the present-day business world in this respect, for SBH Hospital employees probably would not have to resort to outside legal action to handle grievances. At least three different mechanisms would exist to solve employee problems. First, the hospital would have a board composed of employees and managers to hear cases involving alleged unfairness to employees. Second, both managers and employees would be trained extensively in fair labor practices. Third, the hospital and the work groups would have policies and procedures to guide decision making, and these policies and procedures would be designed to be detailed, explicit, and useful. Employees would have many opportunities to set policies and to suggest ways in which management could improve employee relations.

Management's Response to Changes

The managerial response to these legal rulings should be to ensure that the organization's human resource systems are effective and responsive to employees. Four critical considerations for managers are as follows:

1. Rewards must be distributed on job-related bases rather than on seniority union or union bargaining contracts.
2. Corrective justice systems, such as discipline or demotion, must be formal and operational. A system not used but described in a policy manual will be highly susceptible to legal action.
3. Managers must develop skills, data, and procedures to support the distribution of rewards and corrective justice. For example, managers must know what constitutes lawful and unlawful behavior. In some cases, managers may have to be selected and rewarded based on their ability and willingness to support employee rights.
4. Decisions must be based on the highest level of moral reasoning possible, that is, on an orientation to an ethical principle (18).

Peter Drucker suggests that unions are in trouble and that to survive, they must adapt. He concludes a *Wall Street Journal* article as follows:

> Management, no matter who "owns" and no matter whether the institution is a business, a government agency or a hospital, has to have considerable power and authority—power and authority grounded in the needs of the enterprise and based on competence. And power, as the drafters of the American Constitution knew, needs to be limited by countervailing power. Modern society, a society of organizations each requiring strong management, needs an organ such as the labor union—events in Poland are showing this again. The alternative is an uncontrolled and uncontrollable government bureaucracy. But to become again a dynamic, effective, legitimate organ, the labor union will have to transform itself drastically. Otherwise my union friends will be proved right: The union will become irrelevant (19).

How will these changes affect employee behavior?

The unions loss of strength and the corresponding increase in protective employee legislation will affect employees, managers, and executives who run organizations.

Employees will realize quickly that they have increased power to influence organizational decisions. If an employee is protected from being fired without cause, she will feel freer to challenge management. For example, at least 21 states now have laws protecting employees who "blow the whistle" on company actions that are illegal or unethical.

Employees also will be increasingly ensured of a safe environment in which to work, for legislation addressing employee safety and health will force companies to put in place new safeguards at work.

Managers will find that they have yet another authority over their actions in the form of the legislative bodies that monitor and enforce these laws. These authorities are not always known to or understood by managers. Indeed, a common fear among managers is that even if they want to act in accordance with new laws, they may not always be able to define exactly how to act or to which standards to adhere. They will find themselves in the position of being responsible for monitoring legally mandated changes. "An executive of a large company remarked recently that ten years ago his principal legal worries centered on antitrust matters; everything else was lumped together as a poor second. But not today, he commented" (20). The urgency of various legal requirements, especially employee rights, is a high priority for management, and the nature of the executive's job has been changed as a result of this environmental influence.

We have examined two powerful forces in the environment that affect organizational member behavior. The first force is a trend requiring companies to act in a socially responsible manner. Responding to this trend means that internal decision making must involve social responsibility considerations.

The second trend is the shift from union representation of employees to protection of employee rights by increased legislation. As a result of this environmental force, companies must monitor carefully their human resource practices and policies. This trend also will redistribute some of management's power to employees.

In the next section we consider briefly other trends that will influence organizational behavior in the future.

Knowledge Check

1. Social responsibility considerations are not as important as legal considerations. T or F?
2. A company's areas of social responsibility could include all of the following *except:*
   a. the world
   b. the local community
   c. the local laws
   d. the company
   e. the industry
3. One condition for a successful ethical inquiry is never to vote or reach a distinct resolution; you should simply hold discussions. T or F?
4. Union membership has (increased, decreased) over the last 20 years by about (15%, 20%, 40%, 60%).
5. "Termination at will" is an example of:
   a. a new law reinforcing union rights
   b. employee legal protection
   c. an old law, giving managers power to fire, which is now being challenged
   d. punishment technique

Answers:

1 F, 2 c, 3 F, 4 decreased, 15%, 5 c.

Emerging Trends in the Environment

Some exciting literature has been written in the last few years concerning the trends and changes confronting managers. The work of one writer, John Naisbitt, is particularly noteworthy concerning organizational behavior (21).

Megatrends

John Naisbitt has written two significant books that identify some major trends, or **megatrends,** in the world today. The following lists of trends were compiled from these works:

Some Megatrends for the Next Twenty Years

1. Unemployment will give way to labor shortages.
2. Hispanics will become the number one minority group.
3. The challenge of industry will become retraining of managers.
4. Education technology will go on-line with computers.
5. Food problems will erupt as the major environmental issue.
6. International trading will be a major business force.
7. Computers and telephones will merge as an information network.
8. If you want to stay in business, convenience will count.

By 1984, two years later, Naisbitt was hard at work revising the list. His updated megatrends list is as follows:

1. Move from an industrial society to an information society.
2. When new technology is introduced, it will be accompanied by interpersonal and human responses.
3. We will move from a national economy to a world economy.
4. American business will focus increasingly on long-term planning.
5. Decentralized business and politics will be a way of life.
6. Self-help groups will replace institutional help.
7. Networking will be the critical way of doing business.
8. People will move to the South from the North.

Two purposes here are to carry these speculations a step farther and to relate them to many of the concepts discussed in this text.

Four specific trends

The effect of these trends is a matter of speculation, but we can make a guess about the effects of specific trends. We judge four trends to be particularly important.

Trend 1: The challenge for most organizations will be to retrain managers to become teachers, mentors, and partners in growth.

This trend will call for many changes in the way decisions get made in organizations. Chapter 5 described quality circles as a way in which workers could improve productivity without the direct involvement of management.

As organizations gain expertise in this type of decision making, top management will rely more on workers for information.

Middle managers will probably decrease in number and will become generalists, especially in translating vertical communication to and from workers (22). This role change means that middle managers will have to learn new ways of managing other than the use of legitimate power (see Chapter 11). Emphasis will be placed increasingly on managerial people skills. The technical parts of the job will be managed by the workers themselves. The manager will be expected to provide a supportive climate that encourages worker performance and job satisfaction.

Trend 2: Entrepreneurship will be expected by large companies.

A relatively recent trend is the emphasis on innovation and creativity in the workplace. Although this emphasis has always been prevalent in excellent organizations, many other organizations are "getting on the bandwagon" (23). An expectation is growing that workers should innovate on the job and be responsible for contributing new ideas that lead to increased corporate productivity. As a result of this trend, we predict that compensation systems will be changed to reward innovation. We also envision an entirely new organizational structure that allows people to move more freely throughout the organization to establish networks to facilitate creative behavior.

We also note a trend toward smaller business structures, that result from the formation of efforts to break up companies that are perceived as "too large." The break-up of AT & T is only one recent example.

Trend 3: The organization will be effective only if it is networked with other organizations in its market.

Trends continue to emerge suggesting that increased cooperation will occur among companies, and this increased cooperation has several implications. First, all employees may be judged by their ability to create networks with people *outside* the organization. For example, a skilled worker on the assembly line floor will get training from a central training center *outside* the organization. She may take orders from a fellow employee about a project, and she may even be traded to another company unit to increase her opportunity to use her skills.

Second, companies may decide to disassemble some departments and to use more contract labor in the network. Clothing manufacturers are finding it more cost effective to have clothes sewn by workers in Southeast Asia rather than develop new factories in the United States. This networking means that organizations as we know them today will shrink in size. This smaller size has the potential in turn of creating more satisfied workers and of giving management greater control over the environment.

Third, purchasing and capital formation will be accomplished through these networks, because that is how the smaller organizations can survive. Sun Alliance is a good example of this. The organization was formed by several hospitals in the South, which joined together to compete more effectively with many of the for-profit chains of hospitals such as Hospital Corporation of America and National Medical Enterprises. The alliance performs purchasing functions and gets discounts from vendors that would otherwise be impossible for a single small hospital to get.

Trend 4: Service, service, service!

The increase in service industries is by now well known (24). What is not well known is the impact of this trend on workers in organizations.

One prediction is that workers will be asked to have more customer contact, regardless of their function. They may also be urged to take direct responsibility for product quality. This could mean, for example, that workers in the accounting department will be asked to meet with customers to maintain an appreciation for the business and to determine what customers want. Companies will increase their competitive edge to the extent that they can provide quality through service.

These four trends will confront every worker in the near future: change in role of middle managers, increased emphasis on entrepreneurship, networking of organizations, and an increase in service industries. The critical question facing any individual in an organization is how to cope with these changes. Employees who find effective answers for themselves and their companies will be valued highly.

Summary Points

- Seven major factors account for the macroenvironment of the organization: culture, government, economy and capital markets, technology, human resources, industry, and raw materials.
- The impact of the environment on the organization is best analyzed in terms of two dimensions—**environmental change and environmental complexity.**
- To cope with the environment, organizations either change their internal operations or they try to change their environment.
- The social responsibility of organizations ranges from world concerns to issues involving individual employees.
- A socially responsible management must consider ethics in decision making.
- Unions are undergoing major changes, and the percentage of workers who belong to unions is significantly lower.
- The legal environment is replacing unions, especially in the area of employee rights.
- Several trends are emerging in the macroenvironment, including changes in organization design, changes in the role of the middle manager, and increasing impact of environmental issues on corporate social responsibility.

Questions

1. Describe the major environmental factors affecting the modern organization, and give an example of a particular element in each factor. For example, technology is a major factor, and a particular element would be research and development centers.
2. Assume that you have ten minutes to address a group of top executives at a computer company about social responsibility. What major points would you make in your presentation?
3. If you had the attention of several top union organizers, how would you advise them to avoid the "impending doom" of shrinking union membership? Be sure to address ways in which the unions could be relevant to today's work force.

4. The last section of this chapter listed a number of emerging trends in the business environment. Relate at least five of these trends to the dimensions of environmental change and environmental complexity and describe their effect on a firm's uncertainty.
5. Bribery, in some countries, is considered merely a means of doing business. Why should or shouldn't an American company be subject to penalties if it uses bribery in a country in which bribery is a common business practice? Consider the ethical and legal standards by which we should judge American companies doing business in foreign nations.
6. Consider the decline in union membership and the change to reliance on legal sanctions. Some managers say that the change will be "worse than having the unions around." What do you think? Could American business eventually find itself in trouble and unable to control its workers if so much government intervention is allowed?

EXPLORING: *Stater Brothers Fired Chief Finds Power in the Union*

Adapted from "Man Bites Dog: Unions Back Boss," *Fortune* (May 26, 1986):40.

An unusual event is when the union goes out of its way to show solidarity with the boss. This is exactly what happened, however, at a 94-store California supermarket chain. Chairman Bernard Garrett suspended the president and chief executive, Jack Brown. Garrett claimed that Brown had deliberately understated inventories by $600,000 to reduce the price of the stock and to make it easier for him and his associates to buy the stock.

Members of the Teamsters and United Food and Commercial Workers unions have staged demonstrations supporting Brown in his fight to regain his job. The unions even gave Brown money to buy Stater stock, so Brown could try to take control of the company.

The unions favor Brown because he worked his way up from the bottom to top jobs in two organizations (Pantry Food Markets and Hinky Dinky Supermarkets). He also refused to lock out the Teamsters when the union struck against other supermarkets for eight weeks in 1985.

In short, organized labor is playing a crucial role in a management battle for control of this California supermarket chain.

Discussion Questions

1. To what extent should the union become involved in this management struggle?
2. If Brown wins his battle, he may lose the war. If he takes control of the company, will the unions take control of Brown? Do you think this progression of events is possible?
3. If you were Garrett, what would you say to the unions to try to win them over to your side?

APPLYING: *You're the Judge*

In this chapter, we tried to make you aware of the various factors in the environment that are affecting organizations. The goal of this section is to let you play judge in three cases that exemplify an organization's response to the environment.

Read each case and then answer the questions that follow. Use the material in this and other chapters to arrive at the most satisfactory answer possible.

Case 1: Randy is a highly talented professional who worked as a planner in an oil company's marketing department. His major job was to take information from the production plant and to match it against market demand. If a product looked as if it were going to sell at a loss, then he recommended production alterations or worked to change sales decisions. Randy also served as a team member in an active department.

Randy's employment interview and background check had been extensive. Copious notes were still available that detailed his shortcomings, assets, and abilities in the planning areas. His major asset was his ability to do the technical work that was needed by the company. He performed well in that area and did what he was told to do. His major shortcoming was his inability to innovate or initiate activities.

Randy was hired just before a major downturn occurred in business. Top company management soon decided to trim some jobs from the work force of 500 employees. This was the first time in the company's 60–year history that such action had been taken. The process was therefore slow and involved a great deal of time and education on the part of all managers.

Randy's boss, Sam, was puzzled by the process but participated as best he could. His superior asked for a candidate for termination. Sam wanted to do what he could to please his boss, so he offered Randy. To terminate Randy was definitely the most comfortable situation for Sam, who did not want to face other, more serious problems with longer term employees. One individual, with ten years of service, was at present performing so marginally that he was virtually doing clerical tasks at a manager's salary. Sam, however, saw an opportunity to take the path of least resistance.

The personnel manager challenged Sam on his decision. She argued that the company could suffer legal action against it as a result. The rules of equal employment opportunity and affirmative action would dictate that not enough evidence had been accumulated to justify the decision to terminate Randy (Randy was over age 40 and of Asian origin). Sam's colleagues suggested that Randy was a nice person, had a good background in the field, and should be given an opportunity to perform. The personnel manager was pressured to find Randy another slot in the company. "Law and order" arguments abounded, as did the moral judgment that "It just isn't nice to do that to a person you just relocated from the North."

An initially uninvolved person heard all of the testimony associated with the case. This person asked several questions, such as "Have you told Randy of your dissatisfaction?" "Did you know about these shortcomings before you employed him?" "Do you have anybody else who is performing at a lower level?"

This person also questioned the basic values being used to terminate employees. Given the company history and its past dedication to employees and employee rights, the person asked the most basic question: "Should we be firing people?" The savings arguments used to justify the layoff were shown to be in error. Only a handful of employees would ultimately be let go, and the organization unrest caused by the potential layoffs could hamper productivity for months. Many worthy long-service employees might leave prior to the layoff, not out of fear, but out of protest against the new methods of operation.

The ultimate decision was to terminate Randy. No ramifications occurred on the legal front, everyone ultimately got back to business and forgot the incident.

Did Sam act in an ethical manner? Why or why not?

How could the organization have made the decision in a more socially acceptable manner?

Case 2: Lex Motor Company, a subsidiary of Lex Service Group, Ltd., had been losing market share at a 20 percent rate per year in a declining market, and Depot B's performance was the worst of all. Two nearby Lex depots could absorb B's business easily, so closing Depot B seemed the only sound financial decision. Lex's chairman, Trevor Chinn, hesitated to approve the closure, however, on the grounds that putting 100 people out of work was not right when the well being of the corporation itself really was not jeopardized by B's existence. Moreover, seven department managers, who were all within five years of retirement and had had 25 or more years of service at Lex, were scheduled to be made redundant.

The company values statement provided no automatic solution, for it placed value on both employee security and shareholder interest. Should they close Depot B? At first Chinn thought not: Why should the little guys suffer disproportionately when the company was not performing well? Why not close a more recently acquired business where employee service was not so large a factor? Or why not wait out the short-term situation and reduce the head count through natural attrition?

Lex's emphasis on short-term financial performance had led to a series of acquisitions and subsequent divestitures when the company had failed to meet its financial objectives. After each acquisition or divestiture, the people who had served the longest had been retained and assigned to Depot B. As a result, by 1980 the Depot B facility had more managers than it needed and a high proportion of long-service employees.

The very factors that had created the performance problems were now making the closure decision difficult, and the very solution that Chinn was inclined to favor again would worsen the situation!

How would you advise Trevor Chinn to make the decision?

What options are available to the company?

Case 3: Top executives are receiving, on average, 70 percent of their annual salary in the form of bonuses, benefits, and perks. Average yearly compensation to chief executives today is almost $750,000.

Perks are those special benefits limited generally to the corporation's top executives. Not too long ago, perks were considered to be typically British. Executives in England, faced with a punishing income tax rate of over 80 percent, pioneered the managerial philosophy whereby their company provided them, in place of salary, Rolls-Royces, expensive apartments, and custom-made suits.

A sampling of the variety of perks at the highest levels follow:

Transportation—A supply of expensive cars for executives to use for business purposes, as well as airplanes and helicopters to shuttle top executives.

Low interest loans—Executives can borrow large amounts of money at rates 50 percent lower than those offered by conventional financial institutions. Sometimes the executives pay no interest at all.

Housing allowance—Allowances of thousands of dollars are given to the executive to pay for housing.

Other, more common perks are executive physical exams, luncheon club and country club memberships, executive vacations, excess personal liability insurance, various stock plans, and group life insurance.

For perks to be nontaxable, they must meet certain prerequisites. Health insurance, for example, must be available to all employees, so also must pension plans. Housing allowances must be for the employer's job-related convenience, memberships in eating and country clubs must be used for business purposes, automobile titles must be kept in the companies' name and company cars must be used for company business. Cash rewards must be on a onetime basis for some unusual accomplishment.

When considering the issue of whether to tax perks, three important areas of consideration come to mind. The government stand, the social issues, and the corporate viewpoint.

The government takes a firm stand on perks as an income-producing benefit, which at present represent a loss of tax revenues. Indeed, recipients often pay taxes on some of the perks they receive, but this tax is almost always less than the tax that the recipient would have had to pay on the extra income necessary to actually buy the perk's equivalent.

The predominant social issue is that employees and lower level management receive none of these benefits. In some cases employees are even taking pay cuts for the benefit of the company, while top executives are still being awarded top dollar perks. This has caused an uproar among union officials. Do CEO's need any more incentives to do their job than their half million dollar salaries?

Companies and top executives greatly favor nontaxable perks for a variety of reasons. The companies believe that these incentives are necessary to retain valuable executives and as legitimate rewards for superior performance. The corporate view is that without perks, valuable executives would leave the organization, that is, the perks are needed to remain competitive. The companies also claim that perks contribute to the corporate image and are beneficial in corporate recruiting and furthering business development.

In battling the avalanche of perks in the corporate world, the government has enacted various tax laws to enable the taxation of corporate perks. Companies must disclose an executive's perks if they are above $15,000 or are equal to 10 percent of the executive's salary, whichever is higher. Companies must keep logs on their cars, and a $12,000 cap is placed on depreciation over a 3-year period. Following in the wake of these rulings is a total tax reform involving perks.

Should the government tax executive perks as ordinary income?

If perks are taxed, will executive motivation suffer?

Suggested Readings

Ackoff, R. 1981. *Creating the Corporate Future: Plan or Be Planned For.* New York: John Wiley and Sons.

Ackoff, R., Broholm, P., and Snow, R. 1984. *Revitalizing Western Economies: A new Agenda for Business and Government.* San Francisco: Jossey-Bass.

Hawken, P. 1983. *The Next Economy.* New York: Holt, Rinehart & Winston.

Kelley, R.E. 1985. *The Gold-Collar Worker.* Reading, Mass.: Addison-Wesley.

Naisbitt, J., and the Naisbitt Group. 1984. *The Year Ahead.* New York: AMACOM.

This update of the previous works of Naisbitt and his group proves to be better in many ways than the original works.

Roszak, T. 1986. *The Cult of Information.* New York: Pantheon.

By the author of *The Making of a Counter Culture,* this book claims that "technical mumbo jumbo and promotional gimmickry" are exaggerating the computer's role in changing society. Roszak is a social scientist and addresses the role of the computer in our lives. The relevance to organizational behavior is his ultimate conclusion that computers are not the way to organizational excellence.

Silk, L., and Vogel, D. 1976. *Ethics and Profit: The Crisis of Confidence in American Business.* New York: Simon & Schuster.

References

1. Gray, J.L., and Starke, F.A. 1984. *Organization Behavior: Concepts and Applications,* 3rd ed. Columbus, Ohio: Charles E. Merrill, p. 623.
2. Vancil, R.F. 1976. Strategy Formulation in Complex Organizations. *Sloan Management Review* (Winter 1976):4.
3. Aldrich, H. 1979. Organizations and Environments. Englewood Cliffs, N.J.: Prentice-Hall.
4. *Business Week.* The computer slump. (June 24, 1985):74.
5. *Business Week* (September 2, 1985):70.

6. Duncan, R. 1972. Characteristics of Organizational Environment and Perceived Environmental Uncertainty. *Administrative Science Quarterly* 17:313–327; Dess, G.G., and Beard, D.W. 1984. Dimensions of Organizational Task Environments. *Administrative Science Quarterly* 29:52–73; Jurkovich, R. 1974. A Core Typology of Organizational Environments. *Administrative Science Quarterly* 19:380–394; Emery, F.E., and Trist, E.L. 1965. The Causal Texture of Organizational Environments. *Human Relations* 18:21–32.

7. Pfeffer, J., and Salancik, G.R. 1978. *The External Control of Organizations: A Resource Dependent Perspective.* New York: Harper & Row, p. 138.

8. Ibid.

9. *Time* 1984. All the World Gasped. 124:20–38.

10. *Business Week.* A murder verdict jolts business. (July 1, 1985):25.

11. *The Business Month* (March 1985):19.

12. Andrews, K.R., 1980. *The Concept of Corporate Strategy.* Homewood, Ill.: Richard D. Irwin, revised edition.

13. Nash, L. 1981. Ethics without the sermon. *Harvard Business Review* (Nov.–Dec. 1981):78–89.

14. Drucker, P. 1982. Are Unions Becoming Irrelevant? *The Wall Street Journal* (September 22, 1982).

15. *Business Week* 1975. Beyond unions. (July 8, 1975):72; *The Economist* 1983. The de-unionization of America. (October 29, 1983):71; *The Futurist* 1983. The Future of the American Labor Movement. :70.

16. Agis v. Howard Johnson Company, 355 N.E. (Mass.1976).

17. Fogel, D.S., and Tidwell, G.L. 1985. *Termination at Will: A Challenge in Human Resource Management.* Tulane University.

18. Fogel, D.S., and Tidwell, G.L., op. cit.

19. Drucker, op. cit.

20. Steiner, G. 1983. *The New CEO.* New York: MacMillan, p. 15.

21. Naisbitt, J. 1982. *Megatrends.* New York: Warner Books; Naisbitt, J., and Aburdene, P. 1984. *Re-inventing the Corporation.* New York: Warner Books.

22. *Business Week.* Special report: A new era for management. (April 25, 1983).

23. Peters, T., and Austin, T. 1985. *A Passion for Excellence.* New York: Harper & Row.

24. *Business Week* (April 25, 1983), op. cit.

Cases

Kodak Develops Employee Problems

Eastman Kodak is the largest employer in Rochester, New York. The firm, with 53,400 employees, is considered to be a central, stabilizing force in the metropolitan area of slightly more than one million people. In December 1985, the unemployment rate for the area was 5 percent, which was well below the state average. On 17 January 1986, 500 Kodak employees received pink slips. Shock and anger rippled through the company and the community.

A Change in Feelings About Kodak

The company's image was badly tarnished by the unexpected terminations. A company spokesperson said that the myth of "cradle to grave" employment with Kodak was no longer valid. The company had been experiencing intense competition; guaranteed employment was a dinosaur that had outlived its existence.

This message clashed strongly with the impressions of many Kodak employees, however. For over a century, the "Great Yellow Father" had cared for its employees, and layoffs were unheard of. Employee sentiment was so pro-Kodak that no labor union had ever succeeded in organizing the Kodak work force.

Kodak's Competitive Environment

The Kodak Company had been operating in an increasingly unstable market with more and more foreign competitors producing quality products at lower cost. The Kodak organizational structure had become inefficient and top heavy with too many administrators and middle managers. To a great extent, the firm had dealt with its high labor costs in 1983 and 1984. In January 1983, the company laid off 1,100 temporary employees assigned to the division responsible for making the disc camera. In May of the same year, 1,600 full-time employees were cut and several thousand employees over age 55 were offered early retirement. The total reduction in the Kodak work force came to 7,000 employees, 5,000 of whom left voluntarily. In addition, the company decided not to fill 2,000 part-time summer jobs usually held by local college students. By 1985, Kodak was streamlining again, and the Rochester headquarters cut 480 more jobs.

This history indicates that Kodak had had ample practice at downsizing its work force. The 1983 and 1984 layoffs were handled by informing employees in advance and by providing them with a letter of explanation. The company also conducted small-group sessions to help employees adjust to their new situation. The latest cuts were handled differently. Those who lost their job were not given any adjustment period; those who remained felt anxious and threatened.

Some Features of Kodak's Layoff Policy

Since Kodak is a nonunion company, it does not have to observe the reverse seniority rule. Employees with a long Kodak work experience were therefore as likely to be terminated as less senior employees. Fired employees received their notice on Friday afternoon and were told not to come to work on the next Monday. Kodak officials, pressed by the media to explain the new company layoff policy, stated that termination decisions were based on employee performance, but that was not the only criteria. The officials declined to comment on how other factors such as absenteeism, maternity leave, and tardiness, figured in the layoff decisions. In effect, Kodak officials were saying that layoff policy was an internal personnel matter not to be subjected to public scrutiny.

The company retained Drake Beam Morin, Inc., a human resources consulting firm, to handle outplacement activities. The fired employees were invited to attend presentations and workshops on career development and counseling, which were held at a local hotel. Kodak also gave severance pay based on number of years of service, and terminated employees will be retained on Kodak life insurance and medical insurance in the near future.

The employees who were fired in January 1986 have gone on record as being deeply troubled by Kodak's actions. Newspaper accounts of interviews with these employees show the depth of employee dissatisfaction. One employee stated, "We were told that it was a workforce reduction. How can they tell the media we're bad apples?" Another employee acknowledged that he "was sick one day in three years." Yet another noted, "I had 'highly proficient' ratings." One woman pointed out that she still had two weeks left of her maternity leave when she was informed that she was fired. When she complained, a company official told her that the leave was over since she was no longer employed by Kodak.

The termination process has left deep scars. Those employees who were fired believe that their employment record is unfairly tainted. They also are concerned about their future job prospects, for they have been unable to obtain letters of recommendation because they were terminated.

The layoffs have left their mark on employees who remain at Kodak. While reluctant to express their opinions openly, many admitted that they fear they will be the next to go. Some noted that very capable employees are looking actively for jobs elsewhere, and many expressed concern over Kodak's lack of clarity about layoff and termination policies. Many employees are unwilling to state that they find Kodak's policies fairly applied in matters of layoff and dismissal.

Adapted from William A. Nowlin, Employment Woes Develop at Kodak, *Business and Society Review,* Summer 1986, no. 58, pp. 13–16.

Discussion Questions

1. What kinds of long-term stressors is Kodak creating for employees who are not terminated?
2. Apply the expectancy theory to explain how Kodak employees might connect performance with reward under the company's current job conditions.
3. How can you use Herzberg's model to explain levels of job satisfaction and motivation for employees who continue to work for Kodak in Rochester?

How Humana Hospital-University Cares for Indigent Patients

Humana Inc. owns and manages hospitals for profit. Humana runs the university hospital in Louisville, Kentucky, under an affiliation agreement with the University of Louisville. The company has a reputation of catering to the better paying patients while putting the squeeze on labor and operating costs. The university hospital, on the other hand, had the reputation of being a teaching hospital, which often supported unprofitable medical research and education programs. The hospital also was viewed as the medical institution that treated a large share of Louisville's poor and indigent.

The key question that emerges is this: Can a company noted for its profitability and finely tuned operating margins provide a good management system for a university hospital with its varied missions as a training center for new doctors and medical students?

Trends in Health Care

Humana is not the only for-profit hospital corporation getting a toe-hold in academic medicine. The Hospital Corporation of America owns a teaching hospital of the University of Kansas and manages teaching hospitals in other cities. American Medical International, Inc. owns the principal teaching hospital of Creighton University in Omaha, Nebraska, and has proposed to lease and manage the George Washington University Hospital in Washington, D.C.

These new links between corporations and the world of academic medicine have all been forged since 1984 and have their origin in the turbulence and uncertainty surrounding the health-care industry.

A profile of the costs and benefits of these new alliances is emerging. For the companies, the teaching hospitals become showplaces and referral centers that can shore up deteriorating hospital occupancy rates at other facilities owned by the firm. For the teaching institutions, the company may represent a source of capital and cost-efficient management at a time when the hospital, as a revenue-producing business, faces sharp competition.

Louisville, Kentucky, is Humana's headquarters city. The citizens of Louisville are especially sensitive to the fact that Humana now runs 4 of the 12 hospitals in Louisville. Opinion about Humana is clearly divided. Rival hospitals have tried to isolate Humana and have characterized the firm as being too profit driven. A rival Catholic hospital once ran an advertisement that contrasted the image of St. Anthony with a businessman in a three piece suit to dramatize the difference between "saints and profits." The chief executive officer of Humana replied, "You can't claim the moral high ground by assertion. You only claim that by performance."

Humana Comes to University Hospital

The university-owned hospital was clearly in trouble; the facility was showing its age. It was several decades old and had limped from one fiscal crisis to another. As problems unfolded, the top management team was reshuffled, and middle management was virtually nonexistent. Employee morale was low and staff turnover was at unacceptably high levels. The prescription was a new 404-bed hospital and a new clinic building that cost $73 million. As the opening date neared, hospital management feared that the new facility would operate at a deficit, so proposals were sought from private firms that owned or managed hospitals for profit. Humana won the contract because it promised a quick infusion of capital.

The newly struck agreement required Humana to lease and operate the hospital and to turn over 20 percent of pretax profit to the university for support of its medical programs. Seventy-five percent of the medical school faculty voted in favor of the agreement.

Humana Builds a Business Focus at the University Hospital

Changes came quickly. Humana replaced all top hospital management with its own managers. Gary Shelock, the hospital's new executive director, says that the Humana newcomers were wary initially of physician-academics but soon concluded that they were "very rational, given data." The data given often concerned profitability. For instance, one report showed categories of disease, number of admissions per category, and percentage breakdown of patients by zip code and type of insurance. This information is now being used to help determine annual return on equipment purchased.

This report has had an effect on physician-academics. Joseph Allegra, Chairman of the Department of Internal Medicine, says that he no longer argues for the purchase of new equipment by saying, "I want it to help a new assistant professor to study a disease." He now puts in a plug for the business merits of the decision. Shelock has been applauded for his willingness to make quick purchasing decisions when new equipment makes both financial and clinical sense.

Equipment purchasing decisions can take on political and social overtones quickly. When the company resisted development of a special burn unit, local firefighters claimed that Humana was reneging on a commitment. Shelock points out that Humana simply wanted more time to study the commitment, especially since the company had just taken over the hospital management contract. Several months later, the company caved in and dedicated $5.7 million to a state-of-the-art burn unit that would be fully operational by early 1987.

Physicians and managers are not the only ones affected by the Humana management contract. Some segments of the hospital's work force have experienced deep cuts. Computer-managed systems have reduced the hospital's central supply unit from 90 to 50 employees. On the other hand, the nursing unit has grown from 480 RNs to nearly 600 during the same time interval. Overall, the employment rate has remained about the same, but the room-occupancy rate has climbed from 55 to 75 percent.

Productivity monitoring has entered the picture as well. A portable device, which resembles a time clock, produces daily printouts of number of employees in each job category on each nursing floor. These devices, located near patient rooms, facilitate the tracking of employee time devoted to various types of disease and patient needs.

New Directions for Humana Hospital-University

Humana's management system has precipitated an impressive financial turnaround. In 1985, Humana received after-tax profits from the hospital of $3.7 million on revenues of $95 million. The university received $1.5 million as its share of the profits. Mr. Jones, a university official, believes that Humana saved the hospital, indeed, pulled it back from the brink of collapse.

Donald Swain, President of the University of Louisville, takes friendly exception to the brink-of-collapse view. He does, however, deem the arrangement successful because infusion of Humana capital has allowed the hospital to offer new services more quickly.

Humana also acknowledges the advantages of the management arrangement. The indigent patient care system is a good example of this. The hospital's care of indigent patients is cushioned financially by a system of local and state subsidies. A fund was created from county and state contributions to subsidize care of Louisville-area residents who cannot pay their bills. By 1985, the fund totaled $20.6 million. Humana estimates that the fund enables the hospital to break even on indigent-care cases. Shelock notes, however, that the hospital may still incur losses if an indigent patient requires expensive long-term care. (The arrangement has generated resentment among other local hospitals that do not benefit from it.)

The university hospital's revived strength is also attributable to an infusion of patients with private insurance. These patients are a must if a hospital is to make a profit because private insurance pays more for health care than either Medicare or Medicaid. In the new hospital, privately insured patients now represent 22 percent (double the percentage of the old hospital) of the growing number of total patients. The increased number of patients with private insurance is attributable largely to the much improved physical appeal of the facility. The hospital now has a floor of private rooms, which doctors have dubbed the "Gold Coast."

The Transition Creates Some Tensions

The transition is still unfolding, and tensions have flared on occasion. Humana recently decided to install a high-tech diagnostic device called a magnetic resonance imager. The device was installed at a corporate hospital instead of at the university hospital. This decision irked university physicians, and the company has sought regulatory approval for another device to be installed at the university hospital. The incident was repeated when Humana decided to install a kidney stone blaster, called a "lithotripter," in its Suburban Hospital instead of at the university hospital. University urologists were stunned and hostile. Humana has since worked out an arrangement whereby university urologists can practice at Suburban when they need the lithotripter.

The question that most concerns university physicians and officials seems to be the extent to which Humana will make the university hospital a flagship in the corporation structure. There is no doubt that the University of Louisville Hospital and Humana Incorporated have met their mutual needs successfully.

Adapted from the *Wall Street Journal* (21 January 1986).

Discussion Questions

1. How has the new arrangement between the university hospital and Humana helped the hospital to survive?
2. What are the likely reactions of nurses, technicians, and other hospital employees to the new management arrangement? Do you think that the new system could affect adversely some quality of worklife issues for employees?
3. Do you think that the best interests of society are served in the long run by corporate acquisition of teaching hospitals? What might be some of the dangers inherent in this trend?

Ma Bell Gets Competition

On 1 January 1984, American Telephone and Telegraph Company carried out their agreement with the United States Justice Department to split the company into a "new" Ma Bell and seven regional telephone holding companies. The stated reason for the breakup was "to foster competition in the communications business."

The names of the new regional telephone companies generally reflected their geographic focus (e.g., Pacific Telesis or Pacetel for phone services in the western coastal region, Nynex for New York and New England, and Bell South for service in Florida and Alabama). AT&T had to surrender its use of the Bell name and all use of the Bell logo. The logo was replaced by the now familiar white globe symbol.

AT&T estimated that the breakup cost would reach $1.9 billion by the end of 1987 and that the bulk of the expense would involve changing the nationwide system of transmission lines, switching equipment into separate networks for the divested units, and improving local access equipment for long-distance telephone services.

What Were the Pros and Cons of the Breakup?

Opinion about the wisdom of the AT&T breakup can be categorized as follows: complete confusion, support for the breakup, and complete disagreement with the breakup. The confused group were mainly customers who were not sure whether the breakup would mean either better service or lower rates. Those in favor of the breakup cited five major benefits: new competition would (1) lower equipment prices and long distance rates, (2) hasten the introduction of new technologies and services, (3) ensure more equitable pricing of phone service, (4) provide easier access to discount long-distance carriers, and (5) enable the new "baby bells" to compete in other businesses. Those opposed cited five reasons against the breakup: (1) loss of one-stop telephone service, (2) higher residential phone rates, (3) lower overall quality of service, (4) higher cost of equipment installation and services, and (5) more customer confusion over telephone bills.

Debate over the advantages and disadvantages of the breakup continued. After a brief period of decline in services during early 1984, phone service has been generally adequate, and rates continue to drop as competition increases. Indeed, the one company that has not done very well as a result of the breakup is AT&T.

AT&T Searches for Its Niche

When the Bell companies broke up in 1984, AT&T quickly announced its entrance into the computer business. The venture has not been successful, and AT&T lost millions of dollars in a very competitive marketplace.

In early February 1984, the Justice Department recommended that the regional companies be allowed to compete with AT&T's two core businesses, long distance service and the manufacture of telecommunications equipment.

As of 1987, the company was still in the process of reorganizing, and tens of thousands of employees were being laid off. Since the breakup, the company has cut its work force in half, revenues are back to 1984 levels, and profits have declined severely. Indeed, analysts have raised questions about the future of what was once one of America's most smoothly run corporations, and industry analysts claim that AT&T is now for the first time realizing the implications of the breakup. The following tables reflect AT&T operating data:

Dollar Amounts in Thousands (Except for Earnings per Share)

	1985	1986
Revenues	$34,417,000	$34,087,000
Net income	1,556,800	139,000
Earnings/share	1.37	.05

Main Lines of Business

Long-distance	56%
Product sales	30%
Rentals	14%

Number of Employees

As of 12/31/86	317,000
As of 12/31/83	375,000

The decline in income resulted from a number of factors: consumers purchasing rather than renting their telephone equipment, competitive forces in the computer business, and the company's inability to enter foreign markets. (Telephone systems in foreign markets are run mainly by government agencies that strongly favor domestic suppliers.) AT&T is a smaller company than it once was and its marketplace power is no longer guaranteed.

The Fate of Bell Labs

One of the expected benefits of the breakup was the ability of AT&T to focus on the accomplishments of Bell Labs, winner of seven Nobel prizes

The lab is so successful that an average of one patent per day is received. The major change for the lab has been its loss of national regard as a "treasure of research." Instead, it has become simply a huge corporate research and development laboratory subject to all of the vagaries of the bottomline.

This change in status means that Bell Labs no longer produces the technology for complete communications systems. Until the breakup, the lab had one clear mission: to build the world's best phone network. As a result, its annual budget grew to over $2 billion. Now the labs are simply servicing AT&T, and lab personnel have to work on computer technology for consumers. Some of the labs best people are being reassigned to other company divisions to do research and develop specialized product lines. The central laboratory mission is lost.

In 1985 the lab was asked to cut its budget by 25 percent and to deliver more and more commercial products. By the end of the first year of the breakup, 150 administrative jobs had been eliminated. By early 1987, technical employees were leaving in droves, and recruiting had become difficult compared with former times. This trend of cutting budgets and personnel seems likely to continue for at least another two to three years, through 1989 or 1990.

AT&T Management Must Make Some Choices

Are AT&T's problems the result of the breakup or are they the result of an inability to compete in a competitive market? AT&T was always sheltered by an umbrella of regulation and government aid. As long as the company produced services for the public at a fair rate, as determined by agreement between government and company, AT&T could operate its phone systems profitably. Some argue that this sheltered existence made the company incapable of running an efficient and effective business. Others support this argument by pointing out that no company should get so big that it dominates an industry. These critics believe that the government's role is to keep companies small enough so that the marketplace can foster competition among many organizations.

Adapted from AT&T Tries to Unsnarl its Future, *New York Times* (15 February 1987, section 3, pp. 1, 29), and Special Report (on AT&T), *Business Week* (3 December 1984, pp. 86–124).

Discussion Questions

1. When a company grows as large as the old AT&T, should the government step in and break it up? Why or why not?
2. Should the government help AT&T to make the transition from a totally regulated company to one that must compete in the marketplace? For example, should the government have "eased in" the breakup so AT&T could have prepared better for the competitive market?
3. Given the conditions described, what recommendations would you make to senior management at AT&T and Bell Labs?

McDonald's Goes McWorld

Robert Kwan, the 36-year-old managing director of McDonald's Restaurants, Singapore Pte., Ltd., was impressed with the McDonald's Corporation from the start. He attended one of the four Hamburger Universities, a college-like environment where management techniques are taught to new managers of McDonald's franchises. He met often with company consultants who advised on topics ranging from promotional campaigns to employee training. Kwan says that the company attitude is "What can we do for the franchise owner?" rather than "What can the franchise owner do for us?"

Kwan was more than well trained; he was able to produce more than $5 million in annual sales, thus setting a new McDonald's franchise record. Many owners of McDonald's franchises outside the United States are in a situation similar to that of Kwan and his company. What makes McDonald's so successful?

Exporting Skills, Not Just Hamburgers

The biggest success factor is McDonald's ability to communicate management skills to each McDonald's restaurant manager. McDonald's also joins the advantages of bigness (centralized purchasing and marketing) with an entrepreneurial style exemplified by its franchisees and suppliers. These "partners," as they are called, are energetic and innovative people who put their own money into the business. A franchise in the United States can cost as much as $250,000 before the cost of the building, land, equipment, and furniture.

McDonald's supports four universities where executives and store owners are trained. The company is intent on maintaining those skills and values that have made it great. McDonald's accordingly employs an executive, James S. Kuhn, who carries the title "Vice-President for Individuality." His job is to think of ways to make the company feel small. Kuhn develops award systems, meeting plans, and conventions that support the major tenets of the "McDonald's way." The company also helps spread the word about McDonald's by showing a videotape about Ray Kroc, the founder.

Within this organizational culture, McDonald's does not compromise on its detailed operational procedures. Indeed, one expert commented that such detailed and rigid procedures make McDonald's a breeding ground for the robots who worked on yesterday's assembly lines. Others disagree and say that this level of control has led to McDonald's successful expansion in other countries.

The Rules

The operations rules for a particular store are meticulously detailed in a manual that resembles a phone book. The manual covers everything, from how often the bathrooms must be cleaned to the exact temperature of the skillet and grease. McDonald's demands product and service quality, and strict procedures ensure consistency.

The rules are an interesting contrast to the "feel-small" entrepreneurial spirit of the company. Some management consultants call this the "loose-tight" property: operating procedures are tight but the company's culture permits a loose approach to individual creativity.

An example of the loose approach is the ability of franchises to adapt the menu to local tastes. Brazilian franchises offer guaraná, a drink made from berries found in the Amazon region. Patrons in Singapore can order milkshakes flavored with an aphrodisiac.

Another example of the loose-tight property is that franchise design is set rigidly by McDonald's home office in Chicago. Store location, however, is a matter of understanding the local environment. Suburban locations, typical of U.S. franchises, do not work in Japan because of the differences in Japanese life-style.

Every job in a franchise is broken down into very small steps, which automates the whole process. The french fries videotape, for example, starts with boxes of frozen fries rolling off a delivery truck. The viewer is shown how to stack the boxes in the freezer, how much room to leave between stacks (1 inch), and how to retrieve a bag from the boxes for cooking. In all, 19 steps are demonstrated for the preparation of french fries.

McDonald's holds a mini-Olympics in which all franchise owners demonstrate their skills at following the rules. Crews compete against each other to make a burger in exactly the prescribed manner, including order of preparation, taste, and temperature when the burger is delivered to the judges. A slight variation by even a second could disqualify a crew.

Other Management Techniques

A company strength is McDonald's ability to foster interaction between people from different locations. This encourages sharing of information about what does and does not work. Franchise owners have frequent meetings and travel to other locations to observe and to talk with other employees and owners.

Hiring techniques also support McDonald's management style. The company and its franchise owners seek individuals who truly believe in the rules and the company. Hiring officials are not looking for restaurateurs but for people who have an entrepreneurial flair, share the company values, and want to be part of the McDonald's family. This hiring philosophy is the single most important reason why McDonald's is so successful at exporting its management systems.

One story in particular illustrates the McDonald's hiring process. Norman Sinclair lives in Perth, Australia, where he owns a franchise. In 1978, he quit his former job, sold his home, and made an offer to McDonald's to buy a franchise. Sinclair then discovered that McDonald's was interested in more than money. After being approved by the interview panel, Sinclair was required to work in a local McDonald's for five days. He was next required to give 1,800 hours of unpaid service, which included mopping floors, cleaning toilets, and carrying boxes of french fries. The company figures that this is all part of building awareness of the culture and gaining commitment to the management system that has worked for over 7,000 stores.

Germany, Britain, and Japan already have their own Hamburger Universities—sophisticated settings where one can learn the McDonald's way.

The universities even brag about having a professor's exchange program. Note, however, that formal education counts for little at McDonald's. Fewer than half of its corporate officers have graduated from college, and the company does not employ a single Harvard MBA. Fred Turner, Chairman and Chief Executive, is now in his fifties and has been with the company since he was 23. President Michael Quinlan started with the company as a mail clerk when he was 18.

All of these management techniques seem to have paid off, for McDonald's profits have grown steadily and the company boasts that it opens one new store per day.

Potential Problem Areas

Major problems do exist, however. First, Wendy's and Burger King pose fierce competition and are becoming more sophisticated about duplicating their own success.

Another problem is the difficulty of duplicating McDonald's impressive supply system, which ensures timely delivery and quality and consistency of products. Strict standards are applied to the raw products used at McDonald's.

Foreign franchises tend to be slower to mature as investments. Canadian operations opened in 1967 are only now, in the mid-1980s, showing the profits that McDonald's expects from a successful franchise.

McDonald's future growth depends on its ability to attract new customers in far-off locales. No one expects problems with this since the management style and detailed operating procedures will almost ensure success. Analysts are concerned, however, that some of the novelty of the new stores located outside the United States may soon wear off and affect business adversely.

Finally, management experts wonder how such a large company can maintain its family spirit. Given all of these cultures and diverse locations and the need for constant communication and consistency of operation, the coordination task is immense.

Adapted from: McWorld? *Business Week* (13 October 1986) pp. 78–82, 86.

Discussion Questions

1. Use your knowledge of organizational behavior to identify and list the major McDonald's success factors operating at the individual, franchise, and company levels.
2. Review the coordinating mechanisms outlined in Chapter 13. Which of these mechanisms could be used by McDonald's to ensure that its family atmosphere is retained.
3. To what extent could the McDonald's success factors be applied to the following industries: personal computer sales, public schools, and hotels.

Texas Air Demands Deep Cuts at Eastern

Texas Air Corporation acquired Eastern Airlines for over $600 million in December 1986. At that time, Eastern Airlines had had several back-to-back years of poor performance. The once successful company suffered from the effects of deregulation of air travel, extremely high labor costs, a shabby aircraft maintenance record, and inadequate documentation of aircraft maintenance work. Texas Air finally agreed to pay a record fine of $9.5 million for Eastern's aircraft maintenance infractions. Given this situation, Texas Air is trying to refurbish Eastern's image while containing costs.

The Pressure Builds at Eastern

Texas Air's continuing effort to cut costs triggered a series of labor-management disputes that could threaten the existence of the airline. Texas Air, by seeking deep wage cuts, indicated willingness to engage in a long battle with organized labor to lower Eastern's high operating costs. Early in 1987, the parent company tried to renegotiate several labor contracts that would not expire until the end of the year. The cuts are uneven across the contracts, but the average concession sought by the company is a 29 percent reduction in wages and benefits.

This proposal is an extension of the confrontational strategy adopted by Frank Lorenzo, Texas Air's chief executive officer, toward labor unions. By a series of careful acquisitions, Lorenzo transformed Texas Air from a small regional carrier to the nation's biggest airline. In each case, he sought wage concessions from unions and reduced operating costs by other stringent measures.

"Our labor-cost structure is a cancer," said Philip Bakes, President of Eastern, at a Houston news conference. "The employees don't like the medicine, but they know it has to be taken."

Union leaders representing a large number of Eastern's 38,000 employees vowed to resist the demand for wage cuts. "The issue of opening our contract is a non-issue," declared Charles Bryan, head of the Eastern machinists union. (Texas Air's top management had removed Mr. Bryan from Eastern's corporate board. Bryan was named to the board by Eastern's former president, Frank Borman.) At a news conference Mr. Bryan rejected Texas Air's demand for wage concessions by saying, "We negotiated an agreement and we don't go back and ask for more. But they come back and ask for less. That's not what an agreement is for . . . Somewhere along the line, someone is going to tell Frank Lorenzo he has to live within the law."

Wage reductions cannot be imposed while current contracts are in force, but Texas Air clearly has leverage. For example, the parent company can take Eastern assets and move them to the nonunion Texas Air side of the business. Sweeping layoffs could also be announced to pressure union leadership. As of early 1987, Texas Air had kept Eastern employees guessing.

Texas Air Shapes Its Proposal

Outlines of the Texas Air proposal, developed by Bakes, called for $490 million in wage concessions, or a 29 percent reduction in Eastern's former annual labor cost of $1.7 billion. Allocations for mechanics and related maintenance workers would be cut 47 percent, pilot costs would be cut 27 percent, and flight attendant costs cut 31 percent. About $40 million of the proposed cost reductions would occur through an incentive plan for early retirement and resignation. Incentives for eligible employees would consist of severance pay, lump-sum pay spread over several years, and early retirement benefits.

Texas Air bolsters its claims that wages must be cut by pointing to the wage rate of Eastern baggage handlers. The handlers, who are members of the machinists union, have an average wage of $43,000 per year. Mr. Bakes noted: "The marketplace for people loading and unloading bags is not $43,000 on average."

Texas Air claims that Eastern's survival is at stake. The parent company points out that annual labor costs of Continental employees average $28,200 per employee, while the average cost at Eastern is $43,400. Eastern employs 38,000 people to operate 286 planes; 30,000 Continental employees operate 312 planes. "The unions are living in a dream world," said Lorenzo in a fall 1986 interview.

Union Resentment Builds at Eastern

Many Eastern union leaders believe that these announcements are moves designed by Texas Air to support the get-tough campaign of Eastern's new management team. Robert Callahan, President of Eastern's flight attendant union, stated: "This whole thing is being orchestrated to create fear and anxiety among employees." Some union members believed that fears of company failure were raised on purpose so some employees would "take the hint" and look for work with other major airlines. Union officials speculated that Eastern would then turn around and hire inexpensive, entry-level employees to replace those who left.

Eastern's new management has drawn the battle lines willingly with union officials. In January 1987, Eastern union members gathered for an informal session with Bryan, head of the machinists union. Management responded by banning Bryan from company property unless he had "official permission" to be on the property.

Texas Air is also firing flight attendants for work-rule infractions at six times the rate of pre-Texas Air days. At the same time, labor grievances that were handled formerly in two to three weeks take up to 20 times as long to process.

Eastern's Employees Are Worried

By early 1987, managerial and pilot morale at Eastern were at low ebb. The pilots union had hired a full-time psychologist to help employees deal with the increased job stress that accompanied the Texas Air takeover. "It's like working in a war zone," Bryan says. Employees at Eastern headquarters report that working for the company has never been as difficult.

Texas Air has shown its resolve to cut costs by switching Eastern planes and routes to Continental, a nonunion carrier. (In terms of total traffic, Continental is about the same size as Eastern.) Union leaders perceive this as an ominous move, which will create conditions that justify the layoff of Eastern employees. In effect, Texas Air won't lose any business, but the conditions created could idle several thousand Eastern employees (baggage handlers included).

Union leaders also believed that management was trying to provoke a skirmish that would lead to a strike or work slowdown. According to union leaders, either situation would give the new Eastern management a legitimate excuse to fire highly paid employees. The Eastern labor unions thus have many reasons to avoid a strike. In 1983, Lorenzo kept a downsized Continental Airlines flying during a pilots' strike. He unburdened Continental of its expensive pilot contract by pushing the airline into Chapter 11 bankruptcy-law protection. These tactics earned him the contempt of airline unions, but Continental resurfaced from reorganization as a highly profitable company.

The same procedures cannot be used at Eastern, however. In 1986, Congress enacted legislation that prevents companies from using bankruptcy laws to shed union contracts. In addition, several Eastern unions have already accepted salary cuts and tighter work rules. These union members point to their more highly paid counterparts at Delta, United Airlines, and American Airlines. "We've gone as far as we are going," says Jack Bavis, head of the Eastern pilots' union. In 1986, the pilots' union accepted a 20 percent pay cut in its current contract.

As of early 1987, Texas Air continued to wage the cost-cutting war at the operational level. When Eastern was taken over, Texas Air immediately fired 1,500 employees; another 240 were let go in January 1987. Three hundred outside machinist jobs (i.e., subcontracted employees not in Eastern's machinist union) were terminated. This action prompted a labor grievance by machinist union members who claimed to be overworked as a result of the firings.

Texas Air is using the 1986 Eastern performance figures to drive its campaign forward. In the first nine months of 1986, before the Texas Air takeover, Eastern had a $136.7 million loss on revenues of $3.07 billion. (Compare this with a profit of $73.7 million on revenues of $3.69 billion for the same period in 1985.)

The unions have tried to undo Texas Air's acquisition of Eastern in the federal courts. The company has countersued the unions in an action citing the unions' abortive attempt to take over Eastern through an employee ownership plan.

The conflict sharpened some ugly personal vendettas as well. Bryan's machinist union membership recently presented him with a plaque featuring a laminated newspaper photo of Bryan shouting down an Eastern board member. Bryan accepted the plaque at lunchtime in front of several hundred Eastern employees gathered on a ramp at the Miami Airport. The company responded by revoking Bryan's free travel pass and further restricting his access to company property.

Lorenzo has refused to communicate by telephone with any union officials, nor would he respond to a telegram from union officials seeking a meeting to discuss the future of the airline.

Eastern passengers are caught in the crossfire! Flight attendants complain that they are being forced to fly on filthy planes because Texas Air has cut back on cleanup crews. The attendants are also fuming over a violation of their contract, for they are now expected to pick up trash from the floor of the plane. Some attendants believe that they shouldn't have to do this, especially at the start of a shift. This new work rule for flight attendants could provoke more firings, because attendants can now be fired for insubordination. In addition to the trash battle, management recently tightened the policy on absences, and 600 Eastern flight attendants discovered that they were in immediate jeopardy of being fired. All of these changes have led to charges and countercharges, and labor grievances are being pursued in record numbers.

Adapted from the *Wall Street Journal* (22 January 1987).

Discussion Questions

1. In terms of conflict resolution strategy, what do you think is the strategy of choice for the Eastern labor unions? What is your opinion of the strategies adopted by management?
2. How would you describe the organizational culture at Eastern? What sorts of challenges does the Eastern president face in this area?
3. Do you think that Texas Air is behaving in a socially responsible way in its efforts to cut costs and expand business?

A CEO Resigns: Diamond Shamrock's Bricker Falls to Pressures

On 2 February 1987 William Bricker resigned as Diamond Shamrock's chief executive officer. Immediately before his resignation, Bricker was confronted with many questions: How had a once profitable chemical company become so debt-ridden with continuous losses? Why did Diamond Shamrock's board reject three very attractive offers to sell the company (although each offer was lower than the last)? Why had Bricker himself changed his management style from participatory to autocratic? Why had the board been so compliant during all of those years when the company was dwindling in value. Why did Bricker use company resources to maintain his personal life-style?

Many approaches were taken in attempts to analyze the company's actions and to get Bricker to answer these and other questions. One approach seemed particularly productive—the analysis of Bricker's management style and behaviors as he rose in the organization.

Bill Bricker's Background

William Bricker grew up in western Michigan and studied agriculture and horticulture at Michigan State University. His initial job experience was in the international arena working for the Bayer Chemical Company.

In the mid–1960s he joined Velsicol Chemical Corporation to head the international sales division. By 1969, Bricker had been noticed for his management ability and was given a chance to work in Diamond Shamrock's Cleveland office. In 1976, at age 44, Bricker was given the opportunity to be chief executive officer. He accepted and took immediate action to make the company more efficient. He sold unrelated businesses and bought new technology for the organization's operations.

Diamond's Last Ten Years of Performance

The milestones of the last years show a steady decline in both Diamond's shareholder wealth and Bricker's effectiveness:

1976: Diamond earned $140 million on sales of $1.4 billion; the stock was $34 per share.
1979: Bricker bought Falcon Seaboard, a coal producer, for $250 million and moved the corporate headquarters to Dallas. The purchase of Falcon Seaboard was justified by Bricker's stated goal of making Diamond a major energy company.
1981: Bricker bought Amherst Coal Company for $220 million; Diamond had record earnings of $230 million on $3.4 billion sales. During the year, the stock climbed as high as $40 per share.
1982: Diamond Shamrock bought Alaska's Beaufort Sea drilling rights for $161 million. Company earnings fell 35 percent and the stock dropped to $17 per share.
1983: $1.5 billion was paid for Natomas Oil Company. Diamond wrote off a major part of the Beaufort Sea project. The company had $6 million losses for the year.
1985: Diamond wrote off $891 million because of the energy situation and the failure of Natomas. $605 million in losses were reported, and the stock price was $14.
1986: Bricker refused to sell the company to T. Boone Pickens. This was the second time that another company had offered to buy Diamond Shamrock.
1987: Another offer was made by T. Boone Pickens; Bricker resigned as CEO.

These various events show the steady decline in both earnings and value of the company coupled with constant pressure from investors interested in buying Shamrock. Faced with falling oil prices and high debt, the company needed to act quickly to save itself.

Bricker's Management Style

Before he became CEO, Bricker was always described as an executive who believed in participatory management and the value of teamwork. Unanimous approval of his appointment as chief executive officer was based on this style of management and Bricker's seeming desire to include others in the decision-making process.

Once he was appointed CEO, however, his style was described as very autocratic. This change and many of Bricker's business decisions alienated his supporters. One decision in particular illustrates Bricker's new style. He decided to move the company headquarters from Cleveland to Dallas to be closer to the center of the oil patch. Raymond Evans, the previous CEO and Bricker's main fan and mentor, resigned over this decision. Evans believed that Bricker was not listening to anyone when he made decisions on this or any other major issue. Other board members eventually followed Evans and also resigned because they did not agree with Bricker's decisions and were unwilling to comply with his wishes. Many senior executives concluded that they must either quit their jobs or go along with Bricker, because Bricker was making all of the decisions alone. Indicative of this attitude is the lack of questioning on the part of the remaining board members. Input from others was not sought by Bricker, who did not listen to others and seemed to have his own vision of the future of Diamond Shamrock—a vision that he felt would make the company financially stronger.

Allegations were made that Bricker was favoring certain people and certain deals that were not good for the company. One such "favored" individual was Vittoria de Nora, a 75-year-old Italian businessman. de Nora, an investor, owned 4 percent of the company stock by 1973 and sat on the board. Fellow board members did not want de Nora, who was trying to do business with competitors, on the board. de Nora did leave eventually but maintained his contacts with Diamond Shamrock, and unusual deals followed. For example, a Diamond Shamrock subsidiary was sold to de Nora at an "attractive price," and Diamond helped de Nora to sell another business.

Other allegations concerning personal benefits received were levied against Diamond Shamrock executives. Riverside Farms, a company ranch outside Hamilton, Texas, was valued at about $9 million and was *not* a typical hunting camp. As company earnings fell, executives nevertheless continued to use this ranch for personal and business trips. Company planes were sold, but executive travel was supported by charter jets. Some former managers also claim that Bricker used charter planes for personal use on several occasions.

Bricker defends his decisions and actions by pointing to the fact that plenty of oil company executives missed the mark on the price of oil and that their companies also suffered. His supporters claim that if Diamond Shamrock were doing well, Bricker's executive style would be praised as an effective way to manage. The key to whether an executive is judged effective has nothing to do with his style, they say, but everything to do with whether the company prospers. Other successful companies have executives who are autocratic and constantly make deals without senior management input.

Bricker's Resignation

Bricker resigned following a difficult few years during which corporate raiders tried to buy the company stock, criticism of his decisions and lack of support for his management style grew, and employees felt increasingly defeated. The one particular battle that led finally to Bricker's resignation was his failure to effectively manage T. Boone Pickens's attempted takeover of Diamond Shamrock. Bricker was quoted as saying "My staying makes it easy for Boone to turn a proxy fight into a personal fight, and on that basis he could possibly win ... I'm an easy target for him." On 2 February 1987, Bricker resigned.

Adapted from The Downfall of a CEO, *Business Week* (16 February 1987, pp. 76–80, 84).

Discussion Questions

1. Using the situational leadership model, can you defend Bricker's behavior? Was his change in style probably a function of the situation or of his natural push to be autocratic?
2. Do you think that Bricker was the scapegoat for a company that would have had financial troubles regardless of leadership?
3. Why did the board let Bricker take this situation so far?

Glossary

Absolute standards A method whereby employee performance is judged against a fixed standard.

Action research A systematic and cyclical process for accomplishing organizational change.

Adaptation stage The body's use of coping systems to deal with stressors.

Affective component The feeling or emotional component of an attitude.

Association The transfer of part or all of an attitude to another person or event.

Attitude A learned predisposition to respond in a positive or negative way to certain stimuli.

Attribution theory The study of how people assign causes for behavior.

Authority The legitimate right to influence employee behavior and expectations. Authority resides in the relationship between organizational positions.

Autonomy The amount of personal control that an employee has over his or her job.

Baseline audit Determination of the existing rate of employee behavior before reinforcement is instituted.

Behavior anchored rating scale (BARS) Rating scales developed by raters and ratees that use critical behavioral incidents on each scale. The system usually has 6 to 10 scales.

Behavior modification An approach to motivation that uses operant conditioning principles.

Behavioral component The tendency to act toward the focus of an attitude in a given way.

Behavioral shaping Requiring closer approximations to a desired behavior to initiate reinforcement.

Brainstorming A group decision-making process that manages creativity to generate information.

Cafeteria-style fringe benefits A system that allows employees to choose fringe benefits within organizational guidelines.

Central tendency error The giving of all employees about the same rating.

Centralization The dimension of organizational structure that retains authority to make key decisions with top management.

Change agent An expert who precipitates change in an organization.

Classical conditioning Association of positive or negative feelings with an object or event. Learning that occurs at the reflexive level.

Cognitive component The opinion or idea component of an attitude.

Cohesiveness That quality of a group defined by level of group attractiveness, member desire to sustain membership, and group morale.

Communication The sending and receiving of messages from one person to another.

Comparable worth Determining compensation level for various jobs by using compensable factors instead of the market pricing mechanism.

Compensable factors Those factors that are used to determine wage level for a job.

Composition Degree of similarity or difference among group members.

Conceptual work Devising of new ways to operate an organization.

Conflict avoidance A strategy that ignores disagreements in a group.

Conflict confrontation Use of problem solving to surface and resolve conflict in a group.

Conflict containment Use of bargaining to manage conflict between two parties of equal power.

Conflict defusion Containment of conflict to reduce hostilities in a group.

Consideration Those leader behaviors that emphasize good relationships with subordinates.

Content theory of motivation A theory that emphasizes the importance of internal needs to an understanding of human behavior.

Contingency theory A theory that emphasizes the role of both internal and external factors in the shaping of behavior.

Core job dimensions The job factors that can be changed to influence performance and motivation.

Critical incidents A method of performance appraisal that uses recorded examples of employee success and failure to determine performance level.

Critical psychological states The mental conditions that are important to job design.

Decentralization The pushing down of decision-making processes to the lowest possible level in the organization.

Decisional roles Those managerial behaviors that set, implement and monitor progress toward goals.

Delegation The process that distributes authority downward in an organization.

Delphi technique A group decision-making method that emphasizes member anonymity.

Depression Chronic low self-esteem and feelings of not being in control of one's life.

Direct compensation Money or near-money equivalents.

Diseases of adaptation Chronic mental and physical ailments associated with persistent stress overload.

Displaced aggression Aggressive behavior that is redirected at nonthreatening people or targets.

Ego need The external and internal aspects of experienced adequacy.

Employee assistance program An organizational program that helps employees cope with emotional, financial, family, and drug-related problems affecting their performance.

Employee growth need strength A cluster of higher order needs that indicate receptiveness to an enriched job.

Employee hardiness A state of mind characterized by psychological and physical resistance to diseases of adaptation.

Emotionality A set of traits that predisposes the individual to internal emotional distress.

Empowerment The process by which power flows to individuals in the organization.

Eustressor A stressor with a positive psychological interpretation.

Executive emotionality Neurotic executive behavior.

Exhaustion phase Depletion of the body's ability to adapt to stress.

Expectancy A subjective probability that effort will result in performance.

Expectancy theory A cognitive process theory of motivation.

Experiential theory A theory based on personal experience only.

Expertise power Power based on knowledge or skill.

External consistency The relationships in a theory are consistent with the phenomena being studied.

Extinction The weakening of a behavior by removing a pleasant consequence or by presenting a neutral reinforcer.

Extrinsic rewards Rewards provided by the organization.

Extroversion A personality trait characterized by outgoing and gregarious behavior.

Fade out effect Loss of the training effects of teambuilding in the work setting owing to lack of support for newly acquired team skills.

Fight or flight response Activation of the body's stress defense mechanisms.

First-level outcome The result of expending effort in a directed way (e.g., performance, problem solving, and so forth).

First-line manager The lowest level manager who coordinates activities of operating employees.

Formal group A group created by the organization to accomplish a task.

Forming First stage of group development, which highlights awareness of the group by its members.

Four-day work week A work system of 10-hour days, four days per week.

Frame of reference The individual's personal view of reality.

Frustration The human reaction that occurs when an obstacle exists between a behavior and its goal.

Functional group A group of individuals with like specialization in an organization (e.g., an accounting group).

General adaptation syndrome The body's adjustment to stress.

Generalizability A quality of a theory that enables the theory to be used to explain many similar situations.

Graphic rating scales A method of performance appraisal that uses scales to record degree of performance characteristics of employees.

Grievance procedure A formal organizational process used to handle employee problems.

Group A collection of individuals who interact, have common interests, and accomplish a task.

Group structure The arrangement of roles in a group.

Groupthink Suspension of critical thinking by a group.

Halo effect The drawing by a rater of a general performance conclusion based on one employee characteristic.

Heterogeneity Diversity among members of a group.

Home employment Gainful work done at home, which has occurred largely with development of personal computers.

Homogeneity Similarity of characteristics among group members.

Hoopla Nonfinancial rewards used by organizations to motivate employee behavior.

Horizontal job loading The giving of more tasks to an employee without increasing authority or responsibility.

Hot stove rules An effective system of use of punishment by managers.

Human work Managerial actions that influence employee welfare.

Hygiene In Herzberg's two-factor theory, the factors in the context of work.

Hypothesis A specified relationship between two components of a theory.

Idea champion An employee who generates a creative idea and retains responsibility for that idea in the organization.

Indirect compensation Rewards that are not performance-related. These rewards are most often related to an individual's job level.

Individual differences Those key aspects of personality that affect employee behavior in the workplace.

Industrial psychologist A behavioral scientist who examines the behavior of employees at work.

Informal group A group that develops because of friendship instead of organizational assignment.

Informational roles Those managerial behaviors designed to collect and distribute information.

Initiating structure Those leader behaviors that emphasize completion of task activities by work group members.

Instrumentality In expectancy theory, the employee belief that first-level outcomes will lead to second-level outcomes.

Internal consistency In reference to components of a theory, the quality of being logical and free of contradictions.

Interpersonal attraction The extent to which individuals are attracted to others in a group.

Interpersonal roles Those managerial behaviors used to establish relationships with others.

Intrinsic rewards Those personal rewards that occur inside the individual as his or her work unfolds.

Intropunitive aggression Aggression that is channeled inward and suppressed by the individual.

Introversion The quality of being less oriented than many others to external social stimulation.

Job analysis A process whereby job descriptions are updated and elements that make up a task are isolated.

Job involvement The degree to which an employee identifies with the job and participates in it, and the extent to which the job influences the employee's perception of self-worth.

Job redesign Application of motivation theory to how jobs are set up and arranged.

Job rotation The cycling of employees through different jobs on a planned basis.

Job satisfaction A work attitude influenced by such components as coworkers, supervision, pay, promotion, and working conditions.

Job sharing A work situation in which two people fill one job for a given work period.

Lateral coordination The creation of organizational positions to facilitate horizontal coordination in the organization.

Law of effect The behavior modification relationship which states that behavior followed by pleasant consequences tends to be repeated.

Leadership The power of one individual to guide another and to have others follow.

Legitimate power Having the right to influence the behavior of others by virtue of job position in the organizational hierarchy.

Liaison role A position designed to manage vertical or horizontal communication in the organization.

Line position A position with formal authority to commit resources and responsibility to implement actions.

Locus of control A person's beliefs about the relationship between his or her behavior and its outcomes.

Lump-sum pay Paying an employee a given sum for periods of up to one year in advance.

Machiavellian personality A personality characterized by traits of interpersonal coolness, amorality, rationality, and desire to manipulate others.

Maintenance activities Those group activities that focus on the needs of group members.

Management by objectives (MBO) A control system that focuses employee activities on meeting organizational goals by establishing goals jointly with supervisors.

Manager An individual who achieves results by motivating and supervising other people in the organization.

Matrix structure An organizational design that superimposes a project design on a functional design.

Middle managers Managers who implement policies, procedures, strategies, and ideas established by top managers.

Motivational potential score A job's ability to activate employee involvement, job satisfaction, and performance.

Motivator A factor in the content of work, e.g., responsibility, challenge, and so forth.

Motive A condition that pulls behavior in a predictable direction.

Need An experienced state of deficiency that affects behavior.

Need for achievement Task-oriented need for risk-taking and feedback on performance.

Need for affiliation Need for belongingness and giving and receiving of social support.

Need for power Need to gain control of situations to influence others.

Need hierarchy A system of interdependent human needs.

Negative reinforcement Strengthening behavior by removing an unfavorable consequence.

Negative reinforcer An unpleasant consequence of behavior.

Neutral reinforcer An unpleasant consequence that follows behavior.

Nominal group technique A structured group decision-making process for generating information and minimizing impact of outspoken members.

Nonverbal behavior Human gestures, signs, expressions, and other symbols that substitute for words in communication.

Norm A rule that governs the behavior of group members.

Norming The stage of group development in which members become comfortable with their role and the level of effort that must be expended.

Open salary information An organizational system designed to avoid secrecy about pay.

Operant conditioning A process for modifying behavior through its consequences.

Organization chart A pictorial representation of the positions and reporting relationships in an organization.

Organizational behavior The study of attitudes and behaviors of people in organizations.

Organizational behavior modification A system based on behavior modification that is used to change employee behavior.

Organizational climate A set of employee perceptions of organizational characteristics and processes.

Organizational commitment The strength of an employee's identification with the organization.

Organizational culture A system of shared values and beliefs that produces norms for employee behavior in the organization.

Organizational design The arrangement of people and their levels of authority to ensure coordination in the organization.

Organizational development A set of methods that use the behavorial sciences to change organizational strategies, structures, and processes.

Organizational productivity Production of goods and services with the least expenditure of resources.

Organizational structure The arrangement of roles and reporting relationships that govern employee behavior.

Participation A behavioral inclination to be psychologically involved, motivated, and responsible at work.

Participative pay plans A strategy that involves employees in design of the pay system.

Path-goal theory of leadership A theory of leadership that integrates expectancy theory, job satisfaction, performance, and leader behavior.

Perceived equity A social comparison of personal inputs and outputs with the inputs and outputs of others.

Performing The last stage of group development in which process losses are minimized and the group becomes mature.

Personal bias Those personal feelings of a supervisor that can influence his or her ratings of subordinates in performance appraisal.

Personality The relatively permanent psychological structure of traits and characteristics that govern a person's situational interactions.

Physiological needs The lower-order needs for food, water, shelter, and sex.

Political science The study of power and its distribution in organizations and other social systems.

Positional power The power that is assigned to an organizational role irrespective of the role holder.

Positive reinforcement The strengthening of behavior by occurrence of pleasant consequences following the behavior.

Positive reinforcer A pleasant consequence of behavior.

Power The capacity to influence the behavior of others or to avoid having one's own behavior modified.

Process theory of motivation A theory that explains how motivation occurs.

Profit-sharing plan A system of direct compensation based on organizational performance for a one-year period or less.

Project team A work group that is intact only as long as the project lasts.

Proxemics The study of how people position themselves in social settings.

Psychology The study of the control, measurement, and prediction of animal and human behavior.

Punishment The weakening of behavior with an unpleasant consequence.

Quality circle A group of employees given the task of solving product or service quality problems.

Quality of work life The meaningfulness of work in the life of employees.

Recency error The type of evaluation error that occurs when a supervisor ignores performance appraisal information until the last minute.

Referent power That influence based on the personal characteristics of an individual.

Risk-taking The extent to which individuals or groups set ambitious goals or plan activities that could fail.

Risky-shift A phenomenon of groups being more risk-oriented than individuals.

Role ambiguity Absence of clarity in work demands.

Role conflict Inconsistent work expectations or work demands that are incompatible.

Sanctioned communication Authorized ways to communicate inside and outside the organization.

Scalar process Division of the organization into vertical levels.

Scanlon plan A bonus system based on a method of employee participation to achieve cost savings.

Schedule of reinforcement The frequency with which a given reinforcement accompanies a given behavior.

Scientific management The breaking down of work into simplified tasks with time and motion studies.

Scientific theory A set of beliefs based on objective analysis and observation.

Second-level outcomes Those outcomes with personal meaning or valence that are associated with first-level outcomes.

Self-actualization The need to grow personally and professionally.

Semiautonomous work groups A self-contained work group that makes many of its own work decisions.

Similarity error Mapping of the supervisor's personal qualities onto employees.

Situational leadership model A theory that integrates the leader's task behavior, relationship behavior, and maturity level of subordinates.

Skill variety The extent to which a job requires various talents and abilities.

Skill-based evaluation A process of evaluating employees based on their ability to master new job-related skills.

Smoothing A conflict defusion strategy that emphasizes a cooling off period.

Social learning theory A theory that integrates personality, behavior, and the role of the person's environment to achieve an understanding of behavior.

Social need The desire to give and to receive affection and love.

Social psychology The study of group behavior and its effects on individuals.

Social responsibility The organization's willingness and ability to help solve social problems and to behave in an ethical manner.

Socially acquired need A need that is learned through interaction with people in social settings.

Sociology The study of social systems and organizations.

Span of control The number of subordinates who report to a manager.

Staff position Those advisory positions without hierarchical authority in the organization.

Status In a group, a person's achieved rank, which is perceived and acknowledged by others.

Storming The second stage of group development in which conflict over roles emerges.

Stress response threshold The point at which performance starts to deteriorate owing to excessive stress.

Stretching the ratio A process for shifting the reinforcement schedule from one rate to another.

Strictness Harsh employee ratings given by supervisors.

Superordinate goal A group goal that requires member cooperation to achieve.

System 4 organization A people-oriented organization that emphasizes teamwork and participation.

Task activities Those group behaviors that focus on getting the job done.

Task identity The degree to which a job is done from beginning to end.

Task significance The degree to which a job has substantial and lasting effects on the job holder and others.

Technical work Managerial use of equipment and technology to improve productivity.

T–group A group that stresses personal learning and emotional development of members.

Thematic Apperception Test A semi-projective test for measuring socially acquired needs.

Theory A set of statements that defines relationships among facts or events.

Trait theory of leadership The view that leaders possess certain qualities necessary for leadership effectiveness.

Two-factor theory Herzberg's theory that two different sets of factors lead to job dissatisfaction and to job satisfaction and motivation.

Type A personality Individuals who exhibit qualities such as hurry sickness, competitive hostility, denial of stress, and impatience.

Type B personality Individuals who are able to match effectively their reactions to the experienced level of stress.

Universalist theory The view that one best set of leader behaviors exists for every similar situation or event.

Valence The personal value assigned to outcomes in expectancy theory.

Vertical power The power that reflects a person's position in the organizational hierarchy.

Wellness program An organizational program designed to help employees manage stress, smoking, drug usage, nutrition, and exercise.

Work overload A job stressor that refers (1) to too much to do in too little time (quantitative overload) or (2) to a poor match between an employee's abilities and job demands (qualitative work overload).

INDEX